21st Pacific Asia Conference on Language, Information and Computation 2007 (PACLIC 21)

Seoul, South Korea
1 – 3 November 2007

ISBN: 978-1-5108-4020-1

Scalable Deep Linguistic Processing: Mind the Lexical Gap[*]

Timothy Baldwin

Department of Computer Science and Software Engineering and
NICTA Victoria Laboratories, University of Melbourne,
VIC 3010, Australia, `tim@csse.unimelb.edu.au`

Abstract. Coverage has been a constant thorn in the side of deployed deep linguistic processing applications, largely because of the difficulty in constructing, maintaining and domain-tuning the complex lexicons that they rely on. This paper reviews various strands of research on deep lexical acquisition (DLA), i.e. the (semi-)automatic creation of linguistically-rich language resources, particularly from the viewpoint of DLA for precision grammars.

1. Introduction

Over recent years, computational linguistics has benefitted considerably from advances in statistical modelling and machine learning, culminating in methods capable of deeper, more accurate automatic analysis, over a wider range of languages. Implicit in much of this work, however, has been the existence of **deep language resources** (DLR hereafter), that is resources which encode precise symbolic linguistic knowledge. DLRs aim either to capture a particular feature of a language, such as verb argument structure (e.g. COMLEX (Grishman et al., 1994) or PropBank (Palmer et al., 2005)) or lexical semantics (e.g. WordNet (Fellbaum, 1998) or FrameNet (Baker et al., 1998)), or alternatively to model a language in its entirety, in the form of a precision grammar (e.g. the English Resource Grammar (Flickinger, 2002), various ParGram grammars (Butt et al., 2002) or CCGBank (Hockenmaier and Steedman, 2007)).

In line with Baldwin (2005a), we consider the development of DLRs to be made up of two basic tasks: (1) design of a data representation to systematically capture the generalisations and idiosyncracies of the dataset of interest (**system design**); and (2) classification of data items according to the predefined data representation (**data classification**). In the case of a deep grammar, for example, system design encompasses the construction of the system of lexical types, templates, and/or phrase structure rules, and data classification corresponds to the determination of the lexical type(s) each individual lexeme conforms to. Naturally, the two tasks are tightly integrated, and actual DLR construction involves successive iterations over the design of analyses (with the data classification informing the system design), and the application of those analyses over data (with the system design informing the data classification).

One common problem pervading all DLRs is that of coverage, which we define as the proportion of relevant data points in a representative text that are adequately described in a given DLR. Based on our bifurcation of the DLR development process, lack of coverage is caused by either: (a) deficiencies in the system design, e.g. a precision grammar not containing an analysis of a given construction, or a lexical semantic DLR not capturing a particular verb frame type; or (b) deficiencies in data classification, that is certain words simply not having been classified,

---

or being only partially described in the DLR. This arises through simple resource constraints on DLR development, domain effects, or the DLR not capturing generalisations effectively (e.g. not supporting conversion between noun countabilities).

While system design is a highly specialised, manually-intensive task with little scope for automation to battle the effects of coverage,[1] the data classification lends itself readily to automation, particularly once the system design is relatively mature and the DLR in question has been populated with seed instances. The focus of this paper is the task of automated data classification, or **deep lexical acquisition** (DLA), in the context of maximising the lexical coverage of a given DLR.

The purpose of this paper is to give a brief introduction into the current state of DLA, centring around precision grammars. As part of this, we present a classification of DLA research along three axes: general-purpose vs. targeted, *in vitro* vs. *in vivo*, and token- vs. type-based. Note that while the bulk of our examples and references relate to English, all claims about the nature of DLA are intended to be language-inspecific.

DLA research falls into two broad categories: general-purpose DLA and targeted DLA. **General-purpose DLA** is a generic approach to DLA which is applicable to any DLR, e.g. in learning the senses for a given word in a wordnet, or the lexical types (or equivalent) for a given lexical entry in a precision grammar. **Targeted DLA**, on the other hand, takes the form of a dedicated expert system or classifier for a specific lexical feature.

DLA methods generally use preprocessing or feature extraction to model lexical items, providing another basis for classification according to the relationship between the preprocessing/feature extraction method and the target DLR: ***in vitro*** methods use secondary lexical resource(s) to model lexical items, whereas ***in vivo*** methods are embedded within the target DLR and extract features directly from it.

Finally, DLA methods can be classified as either type- or token-based. **Type-based** methods make predictions about lexical items out of context, e.g. about whether a given verb can participate in various subcategorisation frames, while **token-based** methods make predictions about a lexical item in a given context, e.g. about the precise subcategorisation associated with a given lexical item in a given context.

In the remainder of this paper, we first describe the recent confluence of DLR development and statistical natural language processing (Section 2.). We then briefly outline and review each of general-purpose and targeted DLA (Section 3.), *in vitro* and *in vivo* DLA (Section 4.), and type- and token-based DLA (Section 5.).

2.   DLR Development and Statistical NLP

This paper is certainly not novel in proposing that machine learning and statistical natural language processing (NLP) enter the fray of DLR development. While the conventional view is that there exists an unbridgable gulf between DLR development and statistical NLP, in practice an increasingly symbiotic relationship has developed between the two (Baldwin et al., 2007). Indeed, statistical NLP has provided a strong consumer base for DLRs, as illustrated by the "core" English language technologies of:

- POS tagging (developed primarily using the Penn Treebank (Marcus et al., 1993))

- treebank parsing (based almost exclusively on the Penn Treebank (Marcus et al., 1993))

- word sense disambiguation (based on SemCor (Landes et al., 1998) and the Senseval tasks)

---

[1]Although there have been notable successes in porting system designs across languages for a given resource type, e.g. in ontology induction (Maedche, 2002; Nichols et al., 2005).

- semantic role labelling (based on PropBank (Palmer et al., 2005) and FrameNet (Baker et al., 1998))

That is not to say that it has been a one-way street, however, and modern-day DLR developers are calling upon statistical NLP techniques in more and more of their day to day work. In this paper, we focus specifically on the import of (largely) statistical DLA in the context of DLR expansion, to help scale DLRs to greater coverage.

3. Applicability

DLA methods differ in their relative portability to different DLRs, with general-purpose DLA being applicable to any arbitrary DLA task, and targeted DLA being tailored to a specific sub-task.

3.1. General-purpose DLA

General-purpose DLA methods are designed to be applicable to any DLR, and generally employ a combination of type- and token-level features. For example, Baldwin (2005a) uses a set of character-level n-grams based on the lexeme and derivational features from a derivational lexicon, in addition to token-level contextual features from the simple word context, a POS tagger, a chunk tagger and a full parser. Pantel and Pennacchiotti (2006) and Snow et al. (2006) independently proposed methods of automatically inducing templates for use in learning semantic relations, but in a manner which could equally be applied to any other DLA task. In this same vein, Joanis and Stevenson (2003) propose a general-purpose verb feature set which they show to be applicable in a range of DLA tasks relating to English verbs.

For token-level DLA tasks, general-purpose DLA can take the form of supertagging over a sufficiently general feature set. **Supertagging** can be defined as the process of applying a sequential tagger to the task of predicting the lexical categorie(s) associated with each word in an input string, relative to a given DLR. It was first introduced as a means of reducing parser ambiguity by Bangalore and Joshi (1999) in the context of the LTAG formalism, and has since been applied in a similar context within the CCG formalism (Clark and Curran, 2004). Baldwin (2005c) used supertagging to learn token-level lexical types for the ERG, based on the full template set of the FNTBL 1.0 English tagger (Ngai and Florian, 2001). Blunsom and Baldwin (2006) revisited these experiments with a generalised feature set, and performed the lexical type prediction task relative to both the ERG and the JACY grammar of Japanese (Siegel and Bender, 2002).

A third form of general-purpose DLA is resource alignment, which can be as general as simply assuming that the two DLRs (i.e. system designs) correspond to a common tree or graph data structure. One common example of resource alignment is mining lexical items directly from a DLR (e.g. a machine-readable dictionary (Sanfilippo and Poznański, 1992) or WordNet (Daudé et al., 2000)).

3.2. Targeted DLA

With targeted DLA, a specialised methodology is proposed to (automatically) learn a particular linguistic property. The outputs from a suite of targeted DLA methods are then combined to form fully-specified lexical items. For example, in the following lexical entry for the noun *admission* in the English Resource Grammar (Copestake and Flickinger, 2000; Flickinger, 2002):

```
admission_n1 := n_pp_mc-of_le &
  [ STEM < "admission" >,
    SYNSEM [ LKEYS.KEYREL.PRED
```

```
              "_admission_n_of_rel",
    PHON.ONSET voc ] ].
```

the key values are the lexical type (n_pp_mc-of_le) and the onset (voc).[2] The lexical type
states that the word is a noun (n) which optionally subcategorises for a PP (pp), is either countable
or uncountable (mc), and that the selected PP is headed by *of* (of). The onset value states that
the word has a vowel (rather than consonant) onset. Given separate targeted DLA classifiers for
subcategorisation frames and countability, we could construct the fully-specified lexical type for
the lexical item, and combine this with the onset prediction to complete the lexical entry.

Subcategorisation frame learning is one of the most widely-researched areas of targeted DLA
(Brent (1993), Manning (1993), Briscoe and Carroll (1997), Korhonen (2002), Schulte im Walde
(2003), inter alia). Systems generally employ tagging and/or parsing to form token-level subcategorisation frame hypotheses, based on manually-constructed templates. Various statistical filters
are applied to these hypotheses to form type-level predictions.

Corpus-based noun countability learning operates in a similar fashion, in tagging and/or parsing sentences containing a noun of interest, and running extraction templates over the output of the
preprocessors. These are then pooled together as inputs to a classifier which returns a type-level
prediction (Baldwin and Bond, 2003; Nagata et al., 2006). Similarly to subcategorisation learning,
the filtering of the tagger/parser output analysis is highly tuned to countability classification, and
not immediately reusable for any other DLA task.

This same general approach can also be used to learn the lexemes themselves in the case of
multiword expressions. For example, Baldwin (2005b) learns which verbs combine with intransitive prepositions to form verb particle constructions in English, and at the same time predicts the
lexical type(s) of each such verb particle.

Other examples of targeted DLA include ontology alignment (Knight and Luk, 1994; Atserias et al., 1997; Daudé et al., 2000; Klein, 2001), grammatical gender prediction (Cucerzan and
Yarowsky, 2003; Nicholson et al., 2006), classifying the semantics of derivational affixes (Light,
1996), and verb aspect learning (Siegel and McKeown, 2000).

Note that it is possible to hybridise targeted and general-purpose DLA, e.g. in building or
reusing a targeted DLA system to learn lexical properties in one format and then mapping this
onto the DLR of choice via a general-purpose alignment method (e.g. Carroll and Fang (2004) for
verb subcategorisation learning).

4.   Reliance on Secondary DLRs

DLA systems tend to be made up of a variety of preprocessors, feature extractors and machine
learners. To spell out the reliance of a given method on external resources, and its relative separation from the target DLR, we differentiate between *in vitro* and *in vivo* DLA.

4.1.   In Vitro DLA

As the name suggests, *in vitro* DLA is based on analysis of lexemes in a context independent of
the DLR we are looking to learn lexical items for. That is, we make use of a secondary LR or
independent preprocessor to model lexical similarity, and use the target DLR only in classifying
training instances.

In vitro DLA can be the only means available of performing DLA if we do not have access to
annotated data for a given DLR. This would be the case if we were wanting to carry out DLA over

---

[2]Note that the third value in the lexical entry, other than the lexeme itself, i.e. ("a_admission_n_of_rel"), is a
unique string identifier for the predicate associated with the lexical entry, which can be set to an arbitrary value.

a WordNet-style lexical ontology for which sense-annotated data did not exist,[3] or over a precision grammar which did not have sufficient coverage to parse significant amounts of corpus data.

The most widely-practised method of *in vitro* DLA extrapolates away from a DLR to corpus or web data, in analysing occurrences of words in template-based contexts which are predicted to correspond to particular lexical types, e.g. as seen above for targeted DLA (Section 3.2.).

In vitro DLA can also take the form of resource translation, as seen above for general-purpose DLA (Section 3.1.).

4.2.   In Vivo DLA

In vivo DLA directly leverages the target DLR to learn new lexical items. This is most commonly performed via an annotated corpus, e.g. a sense-annotated corpus in the case of a lexical ontology, or parsed data of some description (e.g. a treebank) in the case of a precision grammar. Note that we do not consider raw corpus data to be a secondary LR as long as any filtering/analysis of the data is performed based on techniques derived directly from the target DLR (e.g. using the tokeniser built in to a precision grammar), independent of any external pre-processor. That is, DLA which aligns templates from raw corpus data directly with classes in the target DLR is considered to be *in vivo* DLA.

A particularly poignant example of *in vivo* DLA is the research of Fouvry (2003) on token-based DLA for unification-based precision grammars. Here, partially-specified lexical features are generated for an unknown word in a given sentence context via the constraints of syntactically-interacting words, and combined to form a consolidated lexical entry for that word. That is, rather than relying on indirect feature signatures to perform lexical acquisition, the DLR itself drives the incremental learning process.

Supertagging is also a classic instance of *in vivo* DLA, as all of its feature extraction and op-timisation over label sequences is based on the target DLR, with the qualification that we classify a precision grammar and its associated treebank, e.g., as a single DLR due to the tight linkage between the two (Oepen et al., 2002; Hockenmaier and Steedman, 2007).

In an intriguing piece of research, Zhang and Kordoni (2005) combine these two in a two-stage *in vivo* token-level DLA system for unknown words in precision grammars. First, a targeted DLA system is run over each unknown word in a given sentence to predict an N-best list of lexical type hypotheses (similarly to a supertagger, but without the sequential learning element). These are passed onto the target precision grammar, which generates a parse forest for the given sentence. The final selection of lexical type is then made by the grammar proper in unpacking the preferred parse from the parse tree, based on the parse selection module.

Once again, it is theoretically possible to hybridise between *in vitro* and *in vivo* DLA, e.g. in modifying the Zhang and Kordoni (2005) method to have the first-stage classifier incorporate features from a POS tagger and/or chunker, making the first step *in vitro*. If these predictions are passed onto the grammar and parse selection module as before, the second step would remain *in vivo*.

5.   Data Point Granularity

Finally, DLA methods can either be applied to token-level instances of a given lexical item, or alternatively perform type-level classification.

It is important to note that DLRs can similarly be type-based, such as wordnets or precision grammars, or token-based, such as treebanks or sensebanks. That is not to say, however, that type-based DLRs are exclusively associated with type-based DLA methods, or token-based DLRs with

---

[3]Noting the possibility of learning from monosemous relatives, c.f. Leacock et al. (1998) and Martinez et al. (2006).

token-based DLA methods. For example, subcategorisation lexicons are type-level, but subcategorisation learning is conventionally performed by performing token-level analysis of the subcategorisation properties of individual token instances of a given lexical item, and combining this into a type-level prediction (see Section 3.2.). Equivalently for (token-level) sensebanking—that is, the annotation of lexical items with word sense information in a given context—it is possible to have type-level sense induction inform the sensebanking (Agirre and Soroa, 2007).

5.1. Token-level Classification

We have seen a number of token-level classification tasks in our discussion above, namely: supertagging and token-level unknown word lexical type prediction for precision grammars. Another example is multiword expression identification (Lapata and Lascarides, 2003; Kim and Baldwin, 2006),

5.2. Type-level Classification

Once again, we have discussed a number of type-level DLA tasks above, including: subcategorisation learning, countability learning, type-level unknown word lexical type prediction for precision grammars, grammatical gender prediction, and ontology induction and alignment. Other examples include word sense discrimination (Schütze, 1998; Agirre and Soroa, 2007), semantic relation harvesting (Hearst, 1992; Pantel and Pennacchiotti, 2006; Snow et al., 2006), learning qualia structure (Bouillon et al., 2002; Yamada and Baldwin, 2004), and extraction of multiword expressions (Baldwin, 2005b; Baldwin, 2005d; Villada Moirón, 2005).

6. Conclusion

This paper has presented a broad survey of research on deep lexical acquisition, particularly in the context of precision grammars. We developed a classification of DLA methods along three broad axes: general-purpose vs. targeted, *in vitro* vs. *in vivo*, and token- vs. type-level classification. We hope this will provide a framework for continued cross-fertilisation across tasks and methodologies in the area.

Acknowledgements

This paper builds off research with a number of collaborators, including Phil Blunsom, Francis Bond, Ann Copestake, Dan Flickinger, Valia Kordoni, Jeremy Nicholson, Stephan Oepen and Yi Zhang. I would like to thank the PACLIC-21 organisers for giving me the opportunity to present this research.

References

Eneko Agirre and Aitor Soroa. 2007. SemEval-2007 task 02: Evaluating word sense induction and discrimination systems. In *Proc. of the 4th International Workshop on Semantic Evaluations*, pages 7–12, Prague, Czech Republic.

Jordi Atserias, Salvador Climent, Xavier Farreres, German Rigau, and Horacio Rodríguez. 1997. Combining multiple methods for the automatic construction of multilingual wordnets. In *Proc. of RANLP 1997 (Recent Advances in Natural Language Processing)*, Tzigov Chark, Bulgaria.

Collin F. Baker, Charles J. Fillmore, and John B. Lowe. 1998. The Berkeley FrameNet project. In *Proc. of the 36th Annual Meeting of the ACL and 17th International Conference on Computational Linguistics: COLING/ACL-98*, pages 86–90, Montreal, Canada.

Timothy Baldwin and Francis Bond. 2003. Learning the countability of English nouns from corpus data. In *Proc. of the 41st Annual Meeting of the ACL*, pages 463–70, Sapporo, Japan.

Timothy Baldwin, Mark Dras, Julia Hockenmaier, Tracy Holloway King, and Gertjan van Noord. 2007. The impact of deep linguistic processing on parsing technology. In *Proc. of the 10th International Workshop on Parsing Technologies (IWPT-2007)*, pages 36–8, Prague, Czech Republic.

Timothy Baldwin. 2005a. Bootstrapping deep lexical resources: Resources for courses. In *Proc. of the ACL-SIGLEX 2005 Workshop on Deep Lexical Acquisition*, pages 67–76, Ann Arbor, USA.

Timothy Baldwin. 2005b. The deep lexical acquisition of English verb-particle constructions. *Computer Speech and Language, Special Issue on Multiword Expressions*, 19(4):398–414.

Timothy Baldwin. 2005c. General-purpose lexical acquisition: Procedures, questions and results. In *Proc. of the 6th Meeting of the Pacific Association for Computational Linguistics (PACLING 2005)*, pages 23–32, Tokyo, Japan. (Invited Paper).

Timothy Baldwin. 2005d. Looking for prepositional verbs in corpus data. In *Proc. of the Second ACL-SIGSEM Workshop on the Linguistic Dimensions of Prepositions and their Use in Computational Linguistics Formalisms and Applications*, pages 180–9, Colchester, UK.

Srinivas Bangalore and Aravind K. Joshi. 1999. Supertagging: An approach to almost parsing. *Computational Linguistics*, 25(2):237–65.

Phil Blunsom and Timothy Baldwin. 2006. Multilingual deep lexical acquisition for HPSGs via supertagging. In *Proc. of the 2006 Conference on Empirical Methods in Natural Language Processing (EMNLP 2006)*, pages 164–71, Sydney, Australia.

Pierrette Bouillon, Vincent Claveau, Cécile Fabre, and Pascale Sébillot. 2002. Acquisition of qualia elements from corpora – evaluation of a symbolic learning method. In *Proc. of the 3rd International Conference on Language Resources and Evaluation (LREC 2002)*, Las Palmas, Canary Islands.

Michael R. Brent. 1993. From grammar to lexicon: Unsupervised learning of lexical syntax. *Computational Linguistics*, 19(2):243–62.

Ted Briscoe and John Carroll. 1997. Automatic extraction of subcategorization from corpora. In *Proc. of the 5th Conference on Applied Natural Language Processing (ANLP)*, pages 356–63, Washington DC, USA.

Miriam Butt, Helge Dyvik, Tracy Holloway King, Hiroshi Masuichi, and Christian Rohrer. 2002. The Parallel Grammar project. In *Proc. of the COLING-2002 Workshop on Grammar Engineering and Evaluation*, pages 1–7, Taipei, Taiwan.

John Carroll and Alex Fang. 2004. The automatic acquisition of verb subcategorisations and their impact on the performance of an HPSG parser. In *Proc. of the First International Joint Conference on Natural Language Processing (IJCNLP-04)*, pages 107–14, Sanya City, China.

Stephen Clark and James R. Curran. 2004. The importance of supertagging for wide-coverage CCG parsing. In *Proc. of the 20th International Conference on Computational Linguistics (COLING 2004)*, pages 282–8, Geneva, Switzerland.

Ann Copestake and Dan Flickinger. 2000. An open-source grammar development environment and broad-coverage English grammar using HPSG. In *Proc. of the 2nd International Conference on Language Resources and Evaluation (LREC 2000)*, Athens, Greece.

Silviu Cucerzan and David Yarowsky. 2003. Minimally supervised induction of grammatical gender. In *Proc. of the 3rd International Conference on Human Language Technology Research and 4th Annual Meeting of the NAACL (HLT-NAACL 2003)*, pages 40–7, Edmonton, Canada.

Jordi Daudé, Lluis Padró, and German Rigau. 2000. Mapping WordNets using structural information. In *Proc. of the 38th Annual Meeting of the ACL*, Hong Kong, China.

Christiane Fellbaum, editor. 1998. *WordNet: An Electronic Lexical Database*. MIT Press, Cambridge, USA.

Dan Flickinger. 2002. On building a more efficient grammar by exploiting types. In Stephan Oepen, Dan Flickinger, Jun'ichi Tsujii, and Hans Uszkoreit, editors, *Collaborative Language Engineering*. CSLI Publications, Stanford, USA.

Frederik Fouvry. 2003. *Robust Processing for Constraint-based Grammar Formalisms*. Ph.D. thesis, University of Essex.

Ralph Grishman, Catherine Macleod, and Adam Myers. 1994. COMLEX syntax: Building a computational lexicon. In *Proc. of the 15th International Conference on Computational Linguistics (COLING '94)*, pages 268–272, Kyoto, Japan.

Marti Hearst. 1992. Automatic acquisition of hyponyms from large text corpora. In *Proc. of the 14th International Conference on Computational Linguistics (COLING '92)*, Nantes, France.

Julia Hockenmaier and Mark Steedman. 2007. CCGbank: a corpus of CCG derivations and dependency structures extracted from the Penn Treebank. *Computational Linguistics*, 33(3):355–96.

Eric Joanis and Suzanne Stevenson. 2003. A general feature space for automatic verb classification. In *Proc. of the 10th Conference of the EACL (EACL 2003)*, pages 163–70, Budapest, Hungary.

Su Nam Kim and Timothy Baldwin. 2006. Automatic identification of English verb particle constructions using linguistic features. In *Proc. of the Third ACL-SIGSEM Workshop on Prepositions*, pages 65–72, Trento, Italy.

Michel Klein. 2001. Combining and relating ontologies: An analysis of problems and solutions. In *Proc. of the IJCAI-2001 Workshop on Ontologies and Information Sharing*, Seattle, USA.

Kevin Knight and Steve K. Luk. 1994. Building a large-scale knowledge base for machine translation. In *Proc. of the 12th Annual Conference on Artificial Intelligence (AAAI-94)*, pages 773–8, Seattle, USA.

Anna Korhonen. 2002. *Subcategorization Acquisition*. Ph.D. thesis, University of Cambridge.

Shari Landes, Claudia Leacock, and Randee I. Tengi. 1998. Building semantic concordances. In Christiane Fellbaum, editor, *WordNet: An Electronic Lexical Database*. MIT Press, Cambridge, USA.

Mirella Lapata and Alex Lascarides. 2003. Detecting novel compounds: The role of distributional evidence. In *Proc. of the 10th Conference of the EACL (EACL 2003)*, Budapest, Hungary.

Claudia Leacock, Martin Chodorow, and George A. Miller. 1998. Using corpus statistics and WordNet relations for sense identification. *Computational Linguistics*, 24(1):147–65.

Marc Light. 1996. Morphological cues for lexical semantics. In *Proc. of the 34th Annual Meeting of the ACL*, pages 25–31, Santa Cruz, USA.

Alexander D. Maedche. 2002. *Ontology Learning for the Semantic Web*. Springer.

Christopher D. Manning. 1993. Automatic acquisition of a large subcategorization dictionary from corpora. In *Proc. of the 31st Annual Meeting of the ACL*, pages 235–42.

Mitchell P. Marcus, Beatrice Santorini, and Mary Ann Marcinkiewicz. 1993. Building a large annotated corpus of English: the Penn treebank. *Computational Linguistics*, 19(2):313–30.

David Martinez, Eneko Agirre, and Xinglong Wang. 2006. Word relatives in context for word sense disambiguation. In *Proc. of the Australasian Language Technology Workshop 2006*, pages 42–50, Sydney, Australia.

Ryo Nagata, Atsuo Kawai, Koichiro Morihiro, and Naoki Isu. 2006. Reinforcing English countability prediction with one countability per discourse property. In *Proc. of COLING/ACL 2006*, pages 595–602, Sydney, Australia.

Grace Ngai and Radu Florian. 2001. Transformation-based learning in the fast lane. In *Proc. of the 2nd Annual Meeting of the North American Chapter of Association for Computational Linguistics (NAACL2001)*, pages 40–7, Pittsburgh, USA.

Eric Nichols, Francis Bond, and Daniel Flickinger. 2005. Robust ontology acquisition from machine-readable dictionaries. In *Proc. of the 19th International Joint Conference on Artificial Intelligence (IJCAI-2005)*, pages 1111–6, Edinburgh, UK.

Jeremy Nicholson, Timothy Baldwin, and Phil Blunsom. 2006. Die morphologie (f): Targeted lexical acquisition for languages other than English. In *Proc. of the Australasian Language Technology Workshop 2006*, pages 67–74, Sydney, Australia.

Stephan Oepen, Kristina Toutanova, Stuart Shieber, Christopher Manning, Dan Flickinger, and Thorsten Brants. 2002. The LinGO Redwoods Treebank: Motivation and preliminary applications. In *Proc. of the 19th International Conference on Computational Linguistics (COLING 2002)*, pages 1253–7, Taipei, Taiwan.

Martha Palmer, Paul Kingsbury, and Dan Gildea. 2005. The proposition bank: An annotated corpus of semantic roles. *Computational Linguistics*, 31(1):71–106.

Patrick Pantel and Marco Pennacchiotti. 2006. Espresso: Leveraging generic patterns for automatically harvesting semantic relations. In *Proc. of COLING/ACL 2006*, pages 113–20, Sydney, Australia.

Antonio Sanfilippo and Victor Poznański. 1992. The acquisition of lexical knowledge from combined machine-readable dictionary sources. In *Proc. of the 3rd Conference on Applied Natural Language Processing (ANLP)*, pages 80–7, Trento, Italy.

Sabine Schulte im Walde. 2003. *Experiments on the Automatic Induction of German Semantic Verb Classes*. Ph.D. thesis, Institut für Maschinelle Sprachverarbeitung, Universität Stuttgart. Published as AIMS Report 9(2).

Hinrich Schütze. 1998. Automatic word sense discrimination. *Computational Linguistics*, 24(1):97–123.

Melanie Siegel and Emily M. Bender. 2002. Efficient deep processing of Japanese. In *Proc. of the 3rd Workshop on Asian Language Resources and International Standardization*, Taipei, Taiwan.

Eric V. Siegel and Kathleen McKeown. 2000. Learning methods to combine linguistic indicators: Improving aspectual classification and revealing linguistic insights. *Computational Linguistics*, 26(4):595–627.

Rion Snow, Daniel Jurafsky, and Andrew Y. Ng. 2006. Semantic taxonomy induction from heterogenous evidence. In *Proc. of COLING/ACL 2006*, pages 801–8, Sydney, Australia.

Begoña Villada Moirón. 2005. *Data-driven identification of fixed expressions and their modifiability*. Ph.D. thesis, Alfa-Informatica, University of Groningen.

Ichiro Yamada and Timothy Baldwin. 2004. Automatic discovery of telic and agentive roles from corpus data. In *Proc. of the 18th Pacific Asia Conference on Language, Information and Computation (PACLIC 18)*, pages 115–26, Tokyo, Japan.

Yi Zhang and Valia Kordoni. 2005. A statistical approach towards unknown word type prediction for deep grammars. In *Proc. of the Australasian Language Technology Workshop 2005*, pages 24–31, Sydney, Australia.

The Semantics of Semantic Annotation[*]

Harry Bunt

Department of Communication and Information Sciences,
Tilburg University
P.O.Box 90153, 5000 LE Tilburg, The Netherlands
harry.bunt@uvt.nl

Abstract. This is a speculative paper, describing a recently started effort to give a formal semantics to semantic annotation schemes. Semantic annotations are intended to capture certain semantic information in a text, which means that it only makes sense to use semantic annotations if these have a well-defined semantics. In practice, however, semantic annotation schemes are used that lack any formal semantics. In this paper we outline how existing approaches to the annotation of temporal information, semantic roles, and reference relations can be integrated in a single XML-based format and can be given a formal semantics by translating them into second-order logic. This is argued to offer an incremental aproach to the incorporation of semantic information in natural language processing that does not suffer from the problems of ambiguity and lack of robustness that are common to traditional approaches to computational semantics.

Keywords: semantic annotation, semantic interpretation, temporal annotation, reference annotation, semantic roles, underspecified semantic representation.

1. Introduction

The most interesting and challenging computer applications of natural language require the exploitation of semantic information. This is for example the case for intelligent spoken or multimodal dialogue systems, and for interactive question answering given a data base of natural language texts. Efforts to make computers exploit the semantics of utterances and texts have so far met with very limited success, however. This has two fundamental reasons: the *ambiguity problem* and the *robustness problem*.

1. The ambiguity problem: Computing the meaning conveyed by natural language expressions requires the availabilty of a vast amount and wide range of context information, such as knowledge of the domain of discourse, knowledge of the interactive (or other) setting in which language is used, knowledge of what occurred earlier in the discourse, knowledge of what nonlinguistic sources of information are available (e.g. shared visual context), and so on. In the absence of such information, natural language expressions are massively ambiguous; it has been estimated, for example, that a printed sentence of average length in Dutch or English has more than half a million possible readings when considered in isolation (Bunt and Muskens, 1999). Well-established methods of formal semantics, such as Montague-style or DRT-style semantics, capitalize on the context-*independent* interpretation of syntactic structure and function words, and have hardly any devices for taking context information into account. It may be noted that

---

[*] Thanks to Kiyong Lee for comments on an earlier version.

the ambiguity problem that arises in context-independent interpretation of natural language is to some extent artificial: it is in part caused by the aim to derive 'disambiguated interpretations' within the framework of a formal logical system, which brings a level of granularity which forces one to deal with issues that are often irrelevant in practical situations.

2. The robustness problem: The methods of formal semantics tend not to be robust enough when applied to practical uses of natural language, such as spoken dialogue, on-line chatting, sms messages, or dynamic web pages. This is because linguistic semantic theories have been developed as components of grammatical theories, and have been informed primarily by the analysis of carefully constructed, grammatically perfect sentences rather than by the informal, elastic way in which language is used in spoken and multimodal interaction, which commonly involves nonsentential and grammatically irregular utterances that work semantically and pragmatically quite well.

In this paper I explore a novel approach to the computation of semantic information, namely through semantic *annotation*. I will argue and illustrate that this approach may make it possible to address both the amibguity problem and the robustness problem successfully. I will argue that the approach offers the exciting perspective of a practial, incremental approach to the automatic use of semantic information from natural language; a use which may become more and more powerful as more sophisticated semantic annotation tools and methods are developed.

2. Semantic Interpretation and Semantic Annotation

Attempts to address the ambiguity problem include relaxing the aim of deriving fully disambiguated interpretations to the more modest aim of constructing *underspecified semantic representations*. These are partial representations of the meaning of an utterance, which leave open certain aspects of the meaning for which no or incomplete information is available. Underspecified semantic representations can be viewed as quasi-formal representations of partially disambiguated sentences; *'quasi*-formal' in the sense of being cast in a formal syntax but not having a formal semantics. In computational work, underspecified semantic representations are treated as an intermediate stage of semantic interpretation, and can be used in computations (such as inferencing) only after being disambiguated – which takes the form of replacing the underspecified bits by fully specified parts (see e.g. van Deemter, 1996; Bunt, 2007). Underspecified semantic representations are a computationally attractive idea, but if they always have to be disambiguated before anything can be done with them, then they may help to postpone having to deal with ambiguity explosions in natural language processing systems, but they don't really present a solution to the ambiguity problem.

Robustness problems in natural language processing, especially in syntactic processing, are often addressed by replacing the aim of producing a full syntactic disambiguation (i.e., producing a set of full parses) by that of identifying important *chunks*, such as noun phrases and preposition phrases; this is often pursued in combination with statistical or machine learning techniques. Only identifying syntactic and semantic chunks, without information about their semantic role in the sentence, can be useful for certain applications (such as spoken dialogue systems based on semantic slot filling), but is semantically primitive. Corpus-based, statistical and machine learning approaches to language processing have proved to be more robust than traditional approaches based on predefined grammars; however, while successful for syntactic processing, these approaches have so far not been applied with much success in the area of computational semantics.

The approach that is outlined in this paper is based on the observation that semantic annotations are intended to capture some of the meaning of the annotated text. Annotations have traditionally been viewed as a kind of *labels*, potentially useful for identifying linguistic patterns in corpora. But since semantic annotations capture semantic characteristics of linguistic material, it ought to be possible to interpret them as partial descriptions of the meaning of that material. In other words, it should be possible to view semantic annotations as expressions in a language which has a well-defined semantics. In fact, the use of a semantic annotation language *without* a semantics would make little sense, since there is no reason to think that semantically undefined annotations would describe the meanings of natural language expressions any better than the expressions themselves (cf. Bunt and Romary, 2002; 2004). Still, existing work in this area, for instance on semantic role annotation (as in the FrameNet and PropBank initiatives) or on the annotation of temporal information (as in the TimeML effort) make use of uninterpreted annotation languages. (It is only recently, as part of an ISO initiative to develop annotation standards, that an effort has begun to define an annotation language for temporal information which has a formal semantics.)

While the semantic annotation schemes that have been applied so far do not have a formal semantics, I believe that it is possible to define annotation languages for such schemes which do have a well-defined semantics. In fact, defining a formal semantics for an existing annotation scheme may be helpful for improving the scheme's design.

3. Semantic Annotation Schemas

The inspiration of this paper comes mostly from participating in two recent and ongoing efforts in the area of semantic annotation, namely in the International Organisation for Standards ISO, in particular in its expert group on semantic content (http://iso-tdg3.uvt.nl), and in the European eContent project LIRICS (Linguistic Infrastructure for Interoperable Resources and Systems, http://lirics.loria.fr). One of the most important activities in the ISO expert group concerns the development of an international standard for the annotation of temporal information in documents, provisionally known as ISO-TimeML. Other activities, performed in concert with the LIRICS project, concern the design of sets of well-defined and well-documented (following ISO standard 12620) concepts for semantic annotation in an on-line registry. The focus of the latter activities is in three areas of semantic annotation: semantic roles, referential relations, and communicative functions of utterances in interactive discourse ('dialogue acts'). In this paper we focus on the interpretation of annotations concerned with temporal information, referential relations, and semantic roles.

The combination of semantic annotations for different areas requires a common, integrated format. The ISO and LIRICS activities, while aiming at the use of standardized annotation concepts, do not provide standardized *formats*. XML is a de facto standard in many NLP applications, however, and we believe that an XML-based in-line format as used in ISO-TimeML documents is slightly more readable than a stand-off format. (Stand-off representations are more expressive than in-line representations, since the latter have a problem in marking up discontinuous markables; moreover, stand-off annotations keep the annotated material unaffected, and also have the benefit of allowing multiple annotations to be linked with the same source material. Stand-off representations are therefore recommended by ISO.) We will call the XML-based semantic annotation language that we will develop in the course of this paper "SemML", and define its semantics following the familiar 'interpretation-by-translation' approach, translating SemML expressions into a well-known formal logical language.

3.1 Temporal Information

For temporal information, our point of departure is the ISO-TimeML standard under development. ISO-TimeML is a further development of the TimeML annotation language

(Pustejovsky et al. 2003; 2007) within ISO, taking other studies of temporal information into account and a wide range of natural languages (see ISO, 2007).

The following types of temporal information can be expressed in ISO-TimeML annotations:

- Times (12:25), days (Tuesday) dates (29 February), years (2007), and so on;
- Periods, such as *last week, next year, yesterday, the 20th century,…*
- Durations (*5 minutes, 2.5 hours, seven days,…*)
- The temporal anchoring of events and states: *John drove to Boston last Monday; Harry will meet Sally tomorrow at noon, Mary is pregnant since August,,…*
- Temporal relations between events: *After his talk with Mary, John drove to Boston*

As an example, consider the (slightly simplified) ISO-TimeML annotation of sentence (1a), illustrating both the annotation of temporal event *anchoring* and temporal ordering of events:

(1a) After his talk with Mary, John drove to Boston

```
(1b) <TIME_STRUC>
<SIGNAL sid="s1">
After </SIGNAL>
his
<EVENT eid="e01" eiid="e1" eventclass="OCCURRENCE" pos="NOUN"
    tense="NONE" aspect="NONE">
talk </EVENT>
<SIGNAL sid="s2">
with </SIGNAL>
Mary, John
<EVENT eid="e02" eiid="e2" eventclass="OCCURRENCE" pos="VERB"
    tense="PAST" aspect="NONE">
drove </EVENT>
<SIGNAL sid="s3">
to </SIGNAL>
Boston
<TLINK eventInstance="e2" signalID="s1" relatedToEventInstance="e1"
  tempRelType="AFTER"/>
</TIME_STRUC >
```

The ISO-TimeML draft proposal (ISO, 2007) specifies a formal semantic interpretation of the temporal markup using Interval Temporal Logic (ITL), a first-order approach to reasoning about time (see Pratt-Hartman, 2007 and http://www.cse.dmu.ac.uk/STRL/ITL/) . On this approach, the annotation structure (1b) is interpreted as a statement about the time intervals associated with the two events mentioned in the sentence. This interpretation is represented as in (1c), where P_1 and P_2 stand for unary predicates that characterize those sets of intervals during which John talked with Mary and John drove to Boston, respectively. The interval variables should be understood to be existentially quantified.

(1c) $P_1(I_1) \wedge P_2(I_2) \wedge AFTER\,(I_2, I_1)$

Note that only the temporal markup is interpreted here. Temporal relations between events are interpreted as relations between temporal intervals. Other information about the events, such as who did what, is not represented (but is hidden in the predicate constants P_1 and P_2). A sentence such as (2a), stating a temporal relation between an event and a temporal interval is treated as shown in (2b) and (2c), where the predicate $P_{2004\text{-}01\text{-}31}$ should be interpreted as characterizing the (singleton) set of time-intervals coinciding with the 31st of January, 2004.

(2a) John drove to Boston on Saturday, January 31, 2004.


```
<2b)<TIME_STRUC>
John
<EVENT eid="e01" eiid="e1" eventclass="OCCURRENCE" pos="VERB"
    tense="PAST" aspect="NONE">
drove
</EVENT>
<SIGNAL sid="s1">
to
</SIGNAL>
Boston
<SIGNAL sid="s2">
on
</SIGNAL>
<TEMP_ENTITY tid="t1" value="2004-01-31">
Saturday, January 31
</TEMP_ENTITY>
<TLINK eventInstance="e2" signalID="s1" relatedToTime="t1"
  tempRelType="DURING"/>
</TEMP_STRUC >
```

(2c) $P_{2004\text{-}01\text{-}31}(I_1) \wedge P_2(I_2) \wedge \text{DURING}(I_2, I_1)$

Of interest is also the treatment of negation in this approach. A sentence like *John did not drive to Boston* is interpreted as "within some contextually determined interval no event of John's driving to Boston took place. If we represent our contextually determined interval using the variable I_{ei1} (corresponding to the eiid value of the relevant EVENT tag), then we can express these truth conditions using the formula

$$\neg \exists I_1 \; \text{DURING}(I_1, I_{ei1}) \wedge P_{e1}(I_1)\text{"}$$

(ISO 2007, p. 35). Note that on this approach events do not have to be represented explicitly. A predicate such as P_{e1}, expressing that John drove to Boston during a certain interval of time, can for instance be expanded as $P_{e1} = \lambda I. \text{ DRIVE(john, boston, I)}$. The inclusion of a temporal argument in event predicates suffices for representing temporal information.

3.2 Coreference Information

Representing only the temporal information in a sentence is not very useful. Knowing that an event of a certain type occurred at a certain time is only useful when we have information about that event, such as who was involved, and in what way. As a first step towards representing the latter type of information we now turn to annotation structures for referential entities and coreference relations. We will subsequently turn to the annotation and representation of the involvement of referential entities in events, in subsection 3.3.

We will take the LIRICS annotation scheme for reference annotation as our point of departure, which is based on the reference annotation framework proposed by Salmon-Alt and Romary (2005). This scheme (see Bunt and Schiffrin, 2007), allows annotations to capture information about referential entities, coreference and anaphoric relations. Using elements from the LIRICS scheme, we can represent the referential information in sentence (1a) in SemML as shown in (4a).[1]

```
(4a) <REF_STRUC>
After
<REFENT rid="x1" animacy="ANIMATE" naturalGender="MALE" pos="PRON"
    case="GEN" cardinality="1">
his </REFENT>
talk with
<REFENT rid="x2" animacy="ANIMATE" naturalGender="FEMALE" pos="PN"
    cardinality="1">
Mary </REFENT>
<REFENT rid="x3" animacy="ANIMATE" naturalGender="MALE" pos="PN"
    cardinality="1">
John </REFENT>
drove to
<REFENT rid="x4" animacy="INANIMATE" naturalGender="NONE" pos="PN"
    cardinality="1">
Boston </REFENT>
<REFLINK referent="x1" antecedent="x3" refRelType="OBJECTAL_IDENTITY" />
</REF_STRUC>
```

A formal semantic representation of the information in this annotation structure calls for the introduction of variables ranging over individual objects other than temporal intervals, to allow the expression of the anaphoric relation through the equality of the variables corresponding to "John" and "his". This could be done in first-order logic as follows:

(4b) $\exists x_1, x_2, x_3, x_4$: $MALE(x_1) \wedge FEMALE(x_2) \wedge MARY(x_2) \wedge MALE(x_3) \wedge JOHN(x_3) \wedge BOSTON(x_4) \wedge INANIMATE(x_4) \wedge x_1 = x_3$

(Stipulating that John is male, that Mary is female, and that Boston is inanimate may seem redundant but really isn't, as can be seen by replacing "John" or "Mary" in the sentence by "Chris", and similarly by replacing "Boston" by "Nancy", which may refer to a female person or to a town in France.)

While the interpretation of temporal information in ISO-TimeML is accomplished in first-order logic, for information about reference this is in general not possible, since coreference relations may exist not just between individuals but also between sets of individuals. The following example illustrates this.

(5a) After they washed their hands, the men lifted the piano.

Assuming that the men washed their hands individually but lifted the piano collectively, there is no coreference relation between the entities that perform the wash-events and the lift-event, but we do have a coreference relation between the two sets of men involved in the events. As sentence (5a) is structurally identical to (1a), it could be represented by the ITL-formula (1c) $P_1(I_1) \wedge P_2(I_2) \wedge AFTER\,(I_2, I_1)$, with appropriate re-interpretation of the predicate terms, but to represent the identity of the two sets of men we need to expand these predicates. A naïve way to that could be as follows:

(5b) $\forall x$: $MAN(x) \rightarrow [WASHANDS(x, I_1)] \wedge [\forall y$: $MAN(y) \rightarrow LIFT(y, thepiano, I_2)] \wedge PAST(I_2) \wedge AFTER\,(I_2, I_1)$

---

[1] The LIRICS annotation scheme supports a much richer annotation of referential entities with syntactic features that may play a role in identifying coreference relations. Here we only use a few of these features for the purpose of illustration.

As in (1c) above, we have left the existential quantification over the time intervals implicit in (5b). This is not correct, however, since that quantification has to be scoped relative to the quantification over men. Representation (5b) is moreover 'naive' in the sense that it quantifies universally of the set of *all* men, where the expression "the men" should rather be taken to refer to a certain *set of contextually determined men*; the quantification should range over that set rather than over the set of all men; "they" refers to that same set. The interpretation of noun phrases, in particular (but not only) of definite plural ones, in general requires quantification over contextually determined sets of individuals. We will use predicates with subscript '0', like MAN_0 to designate such contextually determined sets. Using this notion and scoping the existential quantification over time intervals correctly gives the following representation:

(5c) $\forall x$: $[MAN_0(x) \rightarrow \exists I_1, I_2$: $[WASHANDS(x, I_1) \wedge LIFT(MAN_0, thepiano, I_2) \wedge PAST(I_2) \wedge AFTER(I_2, I_1)]]$

Note the use of the set-denoting expression MAN_0 as an argument of the LIFT predicate, which makes LIFT a second-order predicate.

Besides identity of referents ("OBJECTAL_IDENTITY" in the annotation structure), the LIRICS annotation scheme also supports the representation of other coreference relations such as SUBSET_OF (for dealing with *"…some of them…"*) and MEMBER_OF (for *"…one of them…"*).

3.3 Semantic Role Information

For annotating semantic roles we need to mark up (1) the elements in a sentence that denote events,[2] in which there are participants; (2) the entities that play a role as participants in these situations; and (3) the semantic roles linking the participants to the situations that they are involved in. Using the SemML notation for marking up events, we can represent the semantic role annotation in example sentence (1a) as in (6a):

```
(6a) <SEMROLE_STRUC>
After
<REFENT rid="x1" animacy="ANIMATE" naturalGender="MALE" pos="PRON"
    case="GEN" cardinality="1">
his </REFENT>
<EVENT eid="e01" eiid="e1" eventclass="OCCURRENCE" pos="NOUN"
    tense="NONE" aspect="NONE">
talk </EVENT>
with
<REFENT rid="x2" animacy="ANIMATE" naturalGender="FEMALE" pos="PN"
    cardinality="1">
Mary </REFENT>
<REFENT rid="x3" animacy="ANIMATE" naturalGender="MALE" pos="PN"
    cardinality="1">
John </REFENT>
<EVENT eid="e02" eiid="e2" eventclass="OCCURRENCE" pos="VERB"
    tense="PAST" aspect="NONE">
drove </EVENT>
to
<REFENT rid="x4" animacy="INANIMATE" naturalGender="NONE" pos="PN"
    cardinality="1">
Boston </REFENT>
<SEMROLES anchor="e1">
  <SEMROLE participant="x1" roleType="AGENT" />
```

---

[2] Throughout this paper we use the term "event" in a very broad sense, including punctual as well as temporally extended events and states. We occasionally use "situation" as a synonym.

```
<SEMROLE participant="x2" roleType="PARTNER" />
</SEMROLES>
<SEMROLES anchor="e2">
  <SEMROLE participant="x3" roleType="AGENT" />
  <SEMROLE participant="x4" roleType="FINAL_LOC" />
</SEMROLES>
</SEMROLE_STRUC>
```

To formally represent the content of the semantic role annotation we cannot again use the ITL-based framework that we used so far, since semantic roles are not relations between referential entities and intervals, but between referential entities and events, since a referential entity may very well participate in several events that occur over the same interval, and play different roles in these events. We therefore introduce event variables in the semantic representations, and instead of using n-ary predicates as in $TALK(john, mary, I_1)$ we use unary event predicates and conjunctions to represent semantic roles, as in $TALK(e_1) \wedge AGENT(e_1, john) \wedge PARTNER(e_1, mary) \wedge DURATION(e_1, I_1)$.

The use of event variables makes temporal interval variables superfluous if we express temporal relations between events directly, rather than between the intervals during which they hold. (This has the additional advantage of staying close to the ISO-TimeML annotation, which employs temporal relations between event instances.) Time-intervals then turn up only when a sentence refers explicitly to a time, as in (2) above.

The information expressed by the SEMROLE annotation structures in (6a) can be captured in first-order event logic as in (6b):

(6b) $\exists e_1, e_2, x_1, x_2, x_3, x_4$: $TALK(e_1) \wedge AGENT(e_1, x_1) \wedge PARTNER(e_1, x_2) \wedge DRIVE(e_2) \wedge AGENT(e_2, x_3) \wedge FINAL\_LOC(e_2, x_4)$

Like the representation of coreference relations, that of semantic roles in general requires the use of variables ranging over sets of individuals. For example, the representation of the sentence *The men lifted the piano* requires, in the collective reading, the expression of the information that the set of contextually determined men designated by "the men" plays the AGENT role in the LIFT event:

(7) $\exists e$: $LIFT(e) \wedge AGENT(e, MAN_0) \wedge PAST(e) \wedge PATIENT(e, thepiano)$

Allowing sets of individuals to act as participants in semantic roles in events is not limited to cases of collective quantification, but is the rule rather than the exception. For consider an sentence such as:

(8a) The men moved some of the boxes.

There is no reason to assume that the men acted purely collectively or purely individually. They may have acted partly collectively, when moving some heavy boxes, and partly individually, when moving boxes that were not heavy. Also, there is no reason to assume that the boxes were involved collectively (moved all in one go), nor that they were involved individually (moved one by one). They may have varied a lot in size or weight, and some of them may have been moved individually, others in piles. So the formal representation should allow sets of men as well as individual men in agent roles, and individual boxes as well as sets of boxes in patient roles. Moreover, the men will in all likelihood have been involved not just in one move-event, but in *a set* of such events. So we need to represent that contextually determined sets of men and boxes were involved in a set of move-events, such that some of the boxes were somehow moved and all the men were somehow involved. The agent and patient roles in these events are played by sets or individual men and boxes. To represent this correctly, we need predicates like AGENT and THEME which are applicable to events and to *sets* of referential entities. We will continue to use AGENT, THEME, and so on as first-order predicates, applicable only to individual entities, and use AGENT*, THEME*, etc. for their second-order counterparts. For a singleton set {a} we have the obvious correspondence: SR'({a}) = SR(a) for every semantic role predicate SR. Using these second-order predicates and, for the sake of compactness, notations of restricted quantification: $\forall x \in X$: P(x) to abbreviate: $\forall x$: [X(x) → P(x)]), and $\exists X \subseteq Y$: P(X) to abbreviate $\exists X$: $X \subseteq Y \wedge$ P(X), we can represent (8a) as:

(8b) $\forall x \in MAN_0$: $\exists X \subseteq MAN_0$: $\exists e \in MOVE$: [X(x) $\wedge$ AGENT*(e,X) $\wedge$ $\exists Y \subseteq BOX_0$: THEME*($e_1$, Y)]] $\wedge$
$\forall z \in BOX_0$: $\exists Z \subseteq BOX_0$: $\exists e' \in MOVE$: [Z(y) $\wedge$ THEME*(e',Z) $\wedge$ $\exists X' \subseteq MAN_0$: AGENT*($e_1$, X')]

A very compact representation of this may be obtained by introducing a second-order predicate expressing involvement in a set of events in a certain semantic role, defined as follows:

$INVOLV^{(2)}$(x, E, X_1, R_1, X_2, R_2) $=_D$ $\exists X \subseteq X_1$, e$\in$E, $Y \subseteq X_2$: [X(x) $\wedge$ R_1'(e,X) $\wedge$ R_2'(e_1, Y)]]

With the help of this predicate, we can rephrase (8a) as follows:

(8b) $\forall x \in MAN_0$: $INVOLV^{(2)}$(x, MOVE, MAN_0, AGENT, BOX_0, THEME) $\wedge$
$\exists x \in BOX_0$: $INVOLV^{(2)}$(x, MOVE, BOX_0, THEME, MAN_0, AGENT)

It may be worth noting that the representations (8a) and (8b) are completely underspecified w.r.t. the relative scopes of the quantifications or their distribution (collective or otherwise). Yet, the representations are not underspecified from a logical point of view: they are well-formed formulas of second-order logic and can as such be used in formal reasoning.

4. Integrated Semantic Annotation and its Interpretation

4.1 General considerations

While the annotation and formal representation of temporal information seem rather well-delineated subtasks, dealing with referential information is more open-ended because it raises issues of quantification, distributivity, and scoping, and of how to deal with such issues in underspecified representations. (See Bunt, 2007) for an overview of underspecified representation techniques.) Rather than going into these issues here, in this paper we focus on the representation of just that semantic information that is captured by semantic annotations.

We also have to address the overlaps beteen semantic role annotation, temporal annotation and reference annotation. Besides temporal relations like AFTER and WHILE, ISO-TimeML also considers subordination links (SLINK relations). For example, in the sentence *John wants to drive to Boston* the annotation of time and events would relate the WANT and the DRIVE event as follows:

```
(9) <TIME_STRUC>
John
<EVENT eid="e01" eiid="e1" eventclass="OCCURRENCE" pos="VERB"
    tense="PRESENT" aspect="NONE">
wants </EVENT>
to
<EVENT eid="e02" eiid="e2" eventclass="OCCURRENCE" pos="VERB"
    tense="NONE" aspect="NONE">
drive </EVENT>
to Boston
<SLINK eventInstance="e1" subordinateEventInstance="e2" relType="INTENSIONAL" />
</TIME_STRUC >
```

Saying that a subordination relation exists between the WANT event and the DRIVE event is more a syntactic than a semantic observation. Semantically, the DRIVE event is a participant in the WANT event: it is what John wants, which corresponds to having the THEME role in the WANT event. Subordination links in ISO-TimeML always come with a relType value, with the possible values INTENSIONAL, FACTIVE, COUNTER-FACTIVE, EVIDENTIAL, NEGATIVE-EVIDENTIAL and CONDITIONAL. In all cases except when relType="CONDITIONAL", the subordinated event has a THEME role in the subordinating one. (The CONDITIONAL case does not correspond to any semantic role relation between the two events, but to an if-then relation.) Should integrated semantic annotation specify both the SLINK relation and the THEME relation between these events? We believe that the relation between SLINKed events is not really a temporal one, but that their THEME relation has temporal consequences which are specific for the embedding event type. Hence we propose not to annotate SLINK relations in the presence of semantic role annotations.

A related issue is the annotation of aspectual relations in ISO-TimeML using ALINK, as in *Mary started (stopped, continued,..) to laugh*. Again, there is a THEME relation with temporal consequences between the events, which are different for each aspectual verb/event.

4.2 Translating semantic annotations into formal representations

An annotation structure in SemML is a list of structures that annotate referential entities, events, (temporal) signals, temporal objects, relations that anchor events in time, temporal relations between events, semantic roles relating referential entities (or events) to events, and coreferential links between referential entities. The identifiers introduced in the various structures can be regarded as variables that have the entire annotation structure as their scope. An identifier has a unique point where it is introduced in an annotation structure. In SemML such a substructure describes either a referential entity, a temporal entity, an event, or a temporal signal.

The translation of SemML structures into the language of Second-Order Logic (SOL) requires a number of components:

1. Semantically significant SemML tags (like attributes and values) need to be translated into SOL.
2. Natural language content words (verbs, nouns, adjectives,..) have to be translated into SOL expressions (typically first-order predicates).
3. Substructures like REF_ENTITY and SEMROLES structures have to be translated into SOL.
4. Combinations of substructures have to be translated into SOL.

Components 1 and 2 naturally take the form of a SemML-SOL lexicon, while 3 and 4 require rule schemata that define a compositional translation.

For the lexical translation of SemML constants and natural language content words we will mostly use the same constants in both languages, translating for instance the SemML attribute values PAST and AGENT to the SOL predicates PAST and AGENT. Some SemML terms have other more obvious translations, for instance OBJECTAL_IDENTIY as '='. Some SemML terms do not translate to SOL as such, for instance, the feature distr="COLL" saying that a quantification is collective, corresponds in SOL to applying a second-order predicate to a argument denoting a set of individuals (a first-order predicate). Spelling out the translations of all SemML terms would require a lot of space and is, we hope, in most cases rather obvious, so we will not make that part of the translation explicit here.

For component 3, the translation of substructures, we will indicate schematic rules for a few important cases, to give a good idea of where this is going. For the substructures for temporal entities and relations, ISO-TimeML already has a partial formal semantics including a small set of translation rules into ITL, which can be reused adapting them to the use of events rather than temporal intervals (except when temporal entities are to be interpreted). For the interpretation of referential links, the translation of the annotation structures is quite straightforward. When we translate the SemML semantic roles simply to SOL predicates, things are simple as long as only first-order individuals are considered as participants in events. Complications arise mainly in relation to non-individual quantification.

For component 4, finally, we will specify a few combination rules for compositionally translating SemML combinations of substructures into SOL.

4.2.1 Translation rules for SemML substructures

The rules listed here are rule schemata, in that they contain variables in their arguments (indicated in *italics*) which can have any of their possible values. Whenever v is such a variable, v' designates its translation into SOL.

A. Rules for events, referential entities, and temporal entities

Rule EV1 (for EVENT structures)
<EVENT eid=*E01* eiid=*e1* eventclass=*C* pos=*PS* tense=*TE* aspect=*AS*>
word </EVENT>
=: λP. ∃e: *word'*(e) ∧ *TE'*(e) ∧ P(e)

where *word* indicates the nominal or verbal markable that is annotated, and *T'* represents the translation of the tense value of the verbal markable; if the *word* is nominal (denoting an event) the tense attribute will have the value NONE, which obviously does not translate to anything in the semantic representation.

Rule RE1 (for REF_ENTITY structures)
<REF_ENTITY rid=*r1* refType="INDIV" pos="PROPER_NAME" >
NP </REF_ENTITY>
=: λP. ∃x: *NP'*(x) ∧ P(x)

Rule RE2 (for REF_ENTITY structures)
<REF_ENTITY rid=*r1* num="PLUR" refType="SET" >
[PRENOM] NOM </REF_ENTITY>
=: λP. ∃X⊆*NOM'*(e) ∧ P'(X)

Rule RE3 (for REF_ENTITY structures corresponding to pronouns)
<REF_ENTITY rid=*r1* refType="INDIV" pos="PERS_PRON" naturalGender=*G*>
word </REF_ENTITY>
=: λP. ∃x: *G'*(x) ∧ P(x)

Rule TE1 (for TEMP_ENTITY structures)
<TEMP_ENTITY tid=*t1* tempType="DATE" value="2007-10-31" >
expression </TEMP_ENTITY>
=: λP. ∃t: YEAR(t,2007) ∧ MONTH(t,10) ∧ MONTHDAY(t,31) ∧ P(t)

Notice that the rules for translating substructures for events, referential entities and temporal entities all introduce an existentially quantified variable. This is important for the combination rules mentioned below.

B. Rules for semantic roles, referential relations, and temporal relations

Rule SR (for SEMROLES structures)
```
<SEMROLES anchor=a>
  <SEMROLE participant=p1 roleType=SR1>
  <SEMROLE participant=p2 roleType=SR2>

  ...
  <SEMROLE participant=pk roleType=SRk>
</SEMROLES>
```
$=: \lambda x_1, x_2, ..., x_k, e. \ SR1'(e,x_1) \wedge SR2'(e,x_1) \wedge ... \wedge SRk'(e,x_1)$

Rule RR (for REFLINK structures)
```
<REFLINK referent=r1 antecedent=r2 refRelType=R>
```
$=: \lambda x_1, x_2. \ R'(x_1, x_2)$

Rule TR (for TLINK structures annotating temporal relations between events)
```
<TLINK eventInstance=e1 relatedToEvent=e2 tempRelType=R>
```
$=: \lambda e_1, e_2. \ R'(e_2, e_1)$

4.2.2 Combination rules
For convenience in formulating combination rules, we introduce a particular type of function application, where a one-argument function is applied to an argument expression of the form $\lambda x_1, x_2, ..., x_k. E(x_1, x_2, ..., x_k)$. We define so-called "late unary application" (notation: F□a) of a unary function F to such an argument as follows.

$$F□\lambda x_1, x_2, ..., x_k. E(x_1, x_2, ..., x_k) =_D \lambda x_1, x_2, ..., x_{k-1}. F(\lambda x_k. E(x_1, x_2, ..., x_k))$$

For instance, if F is the function $(\lambda Q. \exists z: [WOMAN(z) \wedge Q(z)])$ (a function applicable to unary predicates) and the argument is the two-place predicate $(\lambda x_1, x_2. \exists e: TALK(e) \wedge AGENT(e, x_1) \wedge PARTNER(e, x_2))$, then late unary application of that function to this argument goes as follows, resulting in a unary predicate:

$$(\lambda Q. \exists z: [WOMAN(z) \wedge Q(z)])□(\lambda x_1, x_2. \exists e: TALK(e) \wedge AGENT(e, x_1) \wedge PARTNER(e, x_2))$$
$$= \lambda x_1. \exists z: [WOMAN(z) \wedge \exists e: TALK(e) \wedge AGENT(e, x_1) \wedge PARTNER(e, z)]$$

We will also use two other operations. The first one, that we call "lambda insertion-application" combines a lambda abstraction $\lambda a.F$ with an expression of the form $\lambda x_1, x_2, ..., x_k. E_1 \exists z: E_2$ into $\lambda x_1, x_2, ..., x_k, a. E_1 \exists z: F(z) \wedge E_2$. We designate this operation by $\oplus$.

The second operation, that we call "cross-application" and designate by $\otimes$, takes two expressions of the form: $\lambda v. \exists x: E_1(v,x) \wedge E_2$ and $\lambda w. \exists y: E_1(y,w) \wedge E_3$ and merges the two into $\exists x,y: E_1(y,x) \wedge E_2 \wedge E_3$.

Rule C1. Combines an event representation (E') with a semantic roles representation (SR').
$E' + SR' =: E'□SR'$

Rule C2. Combines a referent representation (R') with the representation of an event plus semantic roles (ER').
$R' + ER' =: R'□ER'$

Rule C3. Combines the translation of a TLINK or REFLINK structure with that of the translation of an event structure or a referential entity structure.
T′ + E′ =: T′ ⊕ E′

Rule C4. Combines the translations of two event structures with their participants and referential and temporal relations by means of cross-applications.
E1′ + E2′ =: E1′ ⊗ E2′

4.2.3 Worked example
The rules in the previous subsection are only a small subset of a larger set that will be needed to translate any meaningful SemML annotation structure into SOL. These rules are sufficient to show how the annotations of temporal information, semantic roles, and referential information in the example sentence (1a) *After he talked with Mary, John drove to Boston*, might be formally interpreted by translating it into second-order logic. For ease of reference we have labelled the relevant substructures in the example in **boldface**.

(10a) <SEM_STRUCT>
<SIGNAL sid="s1">
After
</SIGNAL>
R1 <REFENT rid="x1" pos="PRON" refType="INDIV" naturalGender="MALE" num="SING">
he
</REFENT>
E1 <EVENT eid="e01" eiid="e1" eventclass="OCCURRENCE" pos="VERB"
    tense="PAST" aspect="NONE">
talked
</EVENT>
<SIGNAL sid="s2">
with
</SIGNAL>
R2 <REFENT rid="x2" naturalGender="FEMALE" pos="PN">
Mary
</REFENT>
R3 <REFENT rid="x3" naturalGender="MALE" pos="NP" refType="INDIV">
John
</REFENT>
E2 <EVENT eid="e02" eiid="e2" eventclass="OCCURRENCE" pos="VERB"
    tense="PAST" aspect="NONE">
drove
</EVENT>
<SIGNAL sid="s2">
to
</SIGNAL>
R4 <REFENT rid="x4" animacy="INANIMATE" pos="PN" refType="INDIV">
Boston
</REFENT>
<SEMROLES anchor="e1">
  <SEMROLE participant="x1" roleType="AGENT" />
  <SEMROLE participant="x2" roleType="PARTNER" />
</SEMROLES>
SR1 <SEMROLES anchor="e2">
  <SEMROLE participant="x3" roleType="AGENT" />
  <SEMROLE participant="x4" roleType="GOAL" />
SR2 </SEMROLES>
TR1 <TLINK eventInstance="e2" signalID="s1" relatedToEventInstance="e2"
  tempRelType="AFTER"/>
RR1 <REFLINK referent="x1" antecedent="x3" refRelType="OBJECTAL_IDENTITY" />

</SEM_STRUC>

The referential entity substructures **R1-R4** are translated into SOL by rules **RE1** and **RE3**; the event substructures **E1** and **E2** by rule **EV1**, and the relational substructures **SR1**, **SR2**, **TR1** and **RR1** by rules **SR**, **TR**, and **RR**, respectively. By late unary function application, Combination rule **C1** constructs SOL representations from the translations of **E1** and **SR1** and of those of **E2** and **SR2**. The TLINK substructure for the temporal relation between the two events gives rise to an additional conjunct in the representation of each of the events, through application of rule **C3**, because the two identifiers occurring in the temporal relation are introduced in the substructures of these events. Similarly, the REFLINK substructure introduces an additional conjunct in the translations of the substructures in which the identifiers are introduced that occur in the coreference relation. Repeated late unary function application (rule **C2**) adds the referential information of the four noun phrases. Finally, cross-application of the translations corresponding to the two events with their participants and their referntial and temporal relations (rule **C4**), yields the final result (10b):

(10b) $\exists x_1, x_2, x_3, x_4, e_1, e_2$: $MALE(x_1) \wedge TALK(e_1) \wedge FEMALE(x_2) \wedge MARY(x_2) \wedge AGENT(e_1, x_1) \wedge PARTNER(e_1, x_2) \wedge MALE(x_3) \wedge JOHN(x_3) \wedge MOVE(e_2) \wedge PAST(e_2) \wedge INANIMATE(x_4) \wedge BOSTON(x_4) \wedge AGENT(e_2, x_3) \wedge FINAL\_LOC(e_2, x_4) \wedge AFTER(e_2, e_1) \wedge x_1 = x_3$

5. Reflection, Unresolved Issues, and Perspectives

In the above we have sketched an approach to the interpretation of semantic annotations, in particular for three important areas where major annotation efforts have recently been getting under way: temporal information, as treated in the project "Semantic Annotation Framework, Part 1: Time and Events" ("ISO-TimeML") for short, carried out by an expert group within the Internal Organisation for Standards ISO, and semantic roles and reference information, pursued in the European project LIRICS in concert with the ISO expert group TC 37/SC 4/TDG 3 ("Semantic Content").

We have indicated how the annotation of temporal information, semantic roles, and reference information can be integrated in an XML-based annotation language ("SemML"), and how the annotation structures in that language can be interpreted by translating them in a compositional fashion to Second-Order Logic. In passing, we changed the semantic interpretation of ISO-TimeML from being based on Interval Temporal Logic to being event-based, and we noted that the temporal relations between events encoded in ISO-TimeML by means of SLINK and ALINK structures are better encoded as semantic role relations.

Whereas the interpretation of temporal information seems to be possible in first-order logic, the interpretation of coreference relations and quantified semantic roles requires considering relations between sets of individuals, hence it needs the expressive power of second-order logic. Using second-order logic, we proposed a way of interpreting semantic annotations as a kind of underspecified semantic representations; these representations are however underspecified only in the sense of allowing finer-grained interpretations, but these representations are not underspecified in the sense that they would require further specification before being suitable for use in inferential processing. In passing, we proposed a way to represent quantifications with underspecified distribution (collective, individual, or mixed) and underspecified relative scopes in second-order logic in such a manner that they are not underspecified from a logical point of view and can be used in formal reasoning.

The approach that we have outlined is naturally extensible to other areas of semantic annotation than the ones we considered, such as non-temporal ('rhetorical') relations between events. This all seems quite promising and exciting, but there are still many issues to be considered in more detail. ISO-TimeML has a semantics defined only for a fragment of the annotation language, and this limitation is inherited by our reformulation of the interval-based semantics by a semantics which is mostly event-based (and which uses temporal intervals only for interpretating expressions denoting temporal objects). We have explored only parts of what can be expressed in terms of annotations of the style discussed as 'SemML'.

The interpretation that we have suggested of semantic roles is rather laconic in the sense that it takes a certain set of semantic roles as given, without questioning their validity and without asking how semantic annotations with these roles can be produced: Can human annotators use these roles consistently and reliably? Is automatic annotation with these roles feasible? The only evidence that we have which gives a certain confidence regarding these issues is that the set of semantic roles proposed in the LIRICS project (see Bunt and Schiffrin, 2007) and considered further in the ISO organization, has been applied successfully by untrained annotators for English and Dutch (see Bunt, Petukhova and Schiffrin, 2007).

The treatment of annotation structures for semantic roles in connection with plural NPs brings all the issues relating to quantification. In particular, the distributivity and relative scopes of quantified NPs in a sentence is nearly always only partially specified by the sentence and even not even fully by information from the context in which the sentence is used. Underspecified semantic representation of quantification is therefore very important (and the same goes for the representation of modification). Although the approach that we have indicated in this paper seems promising as a way to cast underspecified representations in a form that allows their use in reasoning without requiring further specification, this approach is currently still speculative in the sense that it has not yet been tested for its applicability to the many forms of underspecified quantification that may occur in natural language.

References

Bunt, H. 2007. 'Semantic underspecification: Which technique for what purpose?' In: H. Bunt and R. Muskens eds., *Computing Meaning, Vol. 3*. Berlin: Springer, 55 – 85.

Bunt, H. and R. Muskens 1999. 'Computational Semantics'. In: H. Bunt and R. Muskens eds., *Computing Meaning, Vol. 1*. Dordrecht: Kluwer, 1 – 32.

Bunt, H. and L. Romary 2002. 'Towards multimodal content representation'. In: K.S. Choi ed., *Proc. of LREC 2002 Workshop on International Standards of Terminology and Language Resources Management*, Las Palmas, Spain, May 2002. Paris: ELRA, pp. 54 - 60.

Bunt, H. and L. Romary 2004. 'Standardization in multimodal content representation: Some methodological issues'. *Proc. 4th International Conference on Language Resources and Evaluation (LREC 2004)*, Lisbon, May 2004. Paris: ELRA, pp. 2219 - 2222.

Bunt, H. and A. Schiffrin .2007. 'Documented compilation of semantic data categories'. LIRICS Deliverable 4.3, revised edition, September 2007.

Bunt, H., A. Schiffrin and V. Petukhova 2007. 'Multilingual test suites for semantically annotated data'. LIRICS Deliverable 4.4, August 2007.

Deemter, van, K. 1996. 'Towards a logic of ambiguous expressions'. In: Peters, S. and K. van Deemter eds., *Semantic Ambiguity and Underspecification*. Stanford: CSLI Press, pp. 203 – 237.

ISO 2007. *Language resource management – Semantic annotation framework Part 1: Time and events*. ISO CD 24617-1:2007 iso_tc37_sc4_N412, Geneva: ISO.

Pratt-Hartman, I. 2007. 'From TimeML to Interval Temporal Logic'. In *Proceedings of the 7th International Workshop on Computational Semantics (IWCS-7)*, Tilburg, pp. 166 – 180.

Pustejovsky, J., J. Castano, R. Ingria, R. Gaizauskas, G. Katz, R. Sauri and A. Setzer. 2003. 'TimeML: Robust specification of event and temporal expressions in text.' In *Proceedings 5th Int. Workshop on Computational Semantics (IWCS-5)*, Tilburg, 337 – 353.

Pustejovsky, J., R. Knippen, J. Litman and R. Sauri. 2007. 'Temporal and event information in natural language text.' In H. Bunt and R. Muskens eds.. *Computing Meaning, Vol. 3* , 301 – 346. Studies in Linguistics and Philosophy 83, Berlin: Springer.

Salmon-Alt, S. and L. Romary. 2005. 'The Reference Annotation Framework: A case for semantic content representation.' *Proceedings of the 6th International Workshop on Computational Semantics (IWCS-6)*, pp. 259 -284.

Deep Lexical Semantics: The Ontological Ascent[*]

Jerry R. Hobbs

Information Sciences Institute, University of Southern California
Marina del Rey, California, USA, hobbs@isi.edu

Abstract. Concepts of greater and greater complexity can be constructed by building systems of entities, by relating other entities to that system with a figure-ground relation, by embedding concepts of figure-ground in the concept of change, by embedding that in causality, and by coarsening the granularity and beginning the process over again. This process can be called the Ontological Ascent. It pervades natural language discourse, and suggests that to do lexical semantics properly, we must carefully axiomatize abstract theories of systems of entities, the figure-ground relation, change, causality, and granularity. In this paper, I outline what these theories should look like.

1. Introduction

If we are going to have programs that understand language, we will have to encode what words mean. Since words refer to the world, their definitions will have to be in terms of some underlying theory of the world. We will therefore have to construct that theory, and do so in a way that reflects the ontology that is implicit in natural language.

There are wrong ways to go about this enterprise. For example, we could take our underlying theory to be quantum mechanics and attempt to define, say, verbs of motion in terms of the primitives provided by that theory. A less obviously wrong approach, and one that has sometimes been tried, is to adopt Euclidean 3-space as the underlying model of space and attempt to define, say, spatial prepostions in terms of that.

In this paper, I propose a general structure for a different underlying conceptualization of the world—one that should be particularly well suited to language. It consists of a set of *core theories* of a very abstract character. These theories are too abstract to impose many constraints on the entities and situations they are applied to. In fact, the reader may complain that they apply to anything. But the main purpose of the core theories is to provide the basis for a rich vocabulary for talking about entities and situations. The fact that the core theories apply so widely means that they provide a great many domains of discourse with a rich vocabulary.

These will not be just any core theories, but theories that find their place in a schema I call the "Ontological Ascent". They include a theory of systems or composite entities and the figure-ground relation, which subsumes a theory of scales; a theory of change of state; a theory of causality, which provides support for a theory of goal-directed behavior; and very importantly a theory of shifts in granularity. The Ontological Ascent is described in Section 2. Then in the subsequent sections I sketch the outlines of each of the above theories.

The enterprise is therefore to axiomatize these core theories in as clean a fashion as possible, and then to define, or at least characterize, various words in terms of predicates supplied by these core theories. For example, a core theory of scales will provide axioms involving predicates such

---

as *scale*, $<$, *subscale*, *top*, *bottom*, and *at*. Then, at the "lexical periphery" we will be able to define the rather complex word "range" by an axiom such as the following:

$$(\forall x, y, z) range(x, y, z) \equiv$$
$$(\exists s, s_1, u_1, u_2) scale(s) \wedge subscale(s_1, s) \wedge bottom(y, s_1)$$
$$\wedge top(z, s_1) \wedge u_1 \in x \wedge at(u_1, y) \wedge u_2 \in x \wedge at(u_2, z)$$
$$\wedge (\forall u \in x)(\exists v \in s_1) at(u, v)$$

That is, x ranges from y to z if and only if there is a scale s with a subscale s_1 whose bottom is y and whose top is z, such that some member u_1 of x is at y, some member u_2 of x is at z, and every member u of x is at some point v in s_1. Many things can be conceptualized as scales, and when this is done, a large vocabulary, including the word "range", becomes available.

Two methodological principles should be mentioned first. Above, I said "define, or at least characterize, various words". In general, we cannot hope to find definitions for words. That is, for very few words p will we find necessary and sufficient conditions, giving us axioms of the sort

$$(\forall x) p(x) \equiv \ldots$$

Rather, we will find many necessary conditions and many sufficient conditions.

$$(\forall x) p(x) \supset \ldots$$
$$(\forall x) \ldots \supset p(x)$$

However, the accumulation of enough such axioms will tightly constrain the possible interpretations of the predicate, and hence the meaning of the word.

The second methodological point is that we need to be careful how we use an argument from the "naturalness" of an expression. Not all expressions that will be allowed by our core theories will sound natural. Our knowledge of language consists of thousands of very specific conventions, each of which has a rationale in terms of core theories. But not everything that has a rationale has been conventionalized. Conventional expressions sound natural. Other expressions with a rationale are interpretable, but may not sound natural. For example, it is conventional to say "at work" and "in progress", and recently in corporate America, the expression "on travel" has become conventional. There is no particular reason that these expressions are better than "on work", "on progress", and "at travel". It just happens that the latter did not become conventional. The account of lexical meaning given here is intended to provide a rationale for expressions, but not to explain why one version rather than another has been conventionalized.

2.   The Ontological Ascent

A general pattern in natural language, illustrated in Figure 1, consists of the following five steps:

1. A collection of entities and relations among them can be viewed as a single *system* of entities.

2. An element external to a system can be located *at* an element in a system.

3. There can be a *change* of state from that element's being at one point to its being at another point in the system.

4. An agent can *cause* such a change.

5. At any point in this ascent, we can coarsen the granularity and view the complex entity that has been constructed as an indecomposable entity, itself ready to become the basis for another ascent.

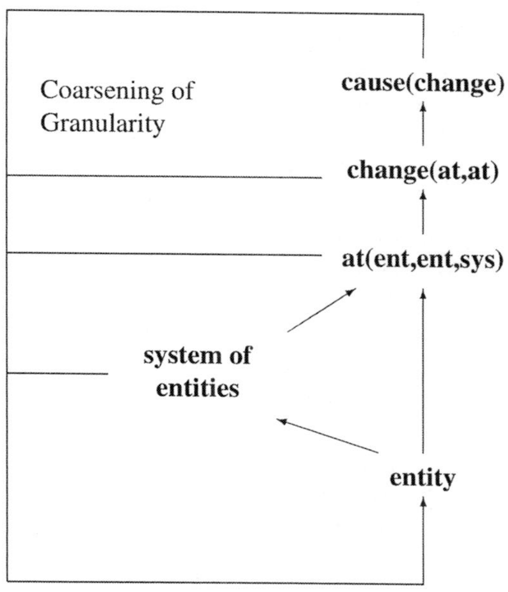

Figure 1: The Ontological Ascent

This ascent is reflected in the common pattern or decomposition for verbs, which we can represent, not quite formally, as

$$cause(a, change(at(b, c), at(b, d)))$$

That is, a causes there to be a change of state from b being at c to b being at d. This schema, or something similar to it, has been central in much work on lexical semantics, including Gruber (1965), Jackendoff (1976), Hobbs (1974), Talmy (1983), and Croft (1991).

The transitive verb "move" illustrates this pattern. If A moves B from C to D, then A causes a change from B being at C to B being at D.

To illustrate just how pervasive this pattern is in natural language discourse, let us consider a random sentence taken from the business news section of a newspaper.

> In a stunning reversal for one of Silicon Valley's fastest-growing companies, Media Vision Technology Inc. said Thursday it will report a sharp decline in sales and "a substantial loss" in the quarter ending March 31 – a jolt that cut its stock price in half. (San Jose *Mercury News*, March 25, 1994, p. 12E)

We will work from the inside out.

Consider the word "sales". Possession can be conceived of as an "at" relation, an entity being at a person within the social network of people, the figure-ground relation. A sale is a change of state from an entity being at one person to the entity being at another person, and a corresponding change in the location of money. When we form the plural "sales", we are first coarsening the granularity to view a sale as an indecomposable entity, and then we are forming the simplest sort of system, a set, out of a collection of them.

"Decline in sales": We first coarsen the granularity on the set of sales, to view it as an indecomposable entity. This entity can be measured in amounts of money. To measure something is to locate it at a point on a particular kind of scale. Here the scale is amount of money. A decline then is a change of state from the set of sales (in a particular time period) being at one point on this scale to the sales (in a more current time period) being at a lower point on the scale.

"Sharp decline in sales": Now the decline itself is viewed as an entity and located at the high end of a scale that encodes the rate of change on a quantitative scale with respect to time.

"A substantial loss": A loss is also a change of state in a downward direction on a scale for amounts of money. Like "sharp", "substantial" is a measure of that change.

"A sharp decline in sales and a substantial loss": The conjunction takes two events, viewed as indecomposable entities, and forms the aggregate consisting of the two of them.

"In the quarter ending March 31": This adverbial applied to the conjoined NP locates the aggregate on the time scale within a particular interval.

"Report": Cognition can be viewed in terms of a figure-ground, or location "at", metaphor. We have ideas in mind, events in memory, and so on. Communication, on this metaphor, is a change of state from a proposition being in one mind to the proposition being in another mind. Of course, this sort of change of location differs from change of phyiscal location, in that the proposition is still in mind of the originator of the message. A report involves just such a communication event. The eventuality described as "a sharp decline in sales and 'a substantial loss' in the quarter ending March 31" moves from being located in the minds of the company officials to the minds of the public. Moreover, this change is caused by the entity issuing the report.

"Will report": "Will" places the reporting action on the time line at some time in the future.

"Media Vision Technology Inc. said ... it will report": Saying is another communication event, and it is caused by the sayer. The future occurrence of the reporting event moves from the minds of the corporate officials to the minds of the public, and Media Vision Technology causes this to occur.

"Media Vision Technology Inc. said Thursday it will report": The adverbial "Thursday" locates the saying action on the time scale.

"Growing": Companies can be located on a scale of sizes. The growth of a company is a upward change of state on that scale.

"Fastest-growing companies": This change is viewed as indecomposable, and it is located on a scale of "fast-ness", its rate of change with respect to time. The set of growing companies is constructed, and their rates of change are located on this scale. A subset of these companies located highest on this scale is selected.

"Silicon Valley's fastest-growing companies": The possessive indicates a kind of "at" relation between each company and Silicon Valley.

"Reversal": A reversal is a change of state from motion on a scale in one direction to motion in the opposite direction. "Growing" gives the initial state, "decline" the final state.

"Stunning": A person's cognitive state can be characterized by the complexity of the thought processes that are possible. This complexity constitutes a scale on which the person can be located. To be stunned is first of all a downward change of state on this scale. Moreover, the size of that change is large, i.e., can be located in the high region of a scale of such changes, and it is rapid, i.e., can be located in the high region of a scale measuring the rate of such changes.

"Stock price": This phrase locates stocks on a scale of prices.

"Cut its stock price in half": A cut is, at least, a downward change of state on a scale, in this case, of prices; this is the aspect of "cut" that is accessed in the metaphor. Because the scale of prices supports arithmetic, "in half" makes sense.

"Jolt": A jolt is a large and sudden change of state in velocity and/or direction. Again, the change is viewed as indecomposable, and located on scales of size and rapidity.

"A jolt that cut its stock price in half": This change in velocity and direction caused the change of state in stock

Nearly every morpheme in this sentence introduces one or more scales or other kind of system, the location of an entity on a scale or in a system, a change in this location, or a causal relation in which a change is a cause or an effect.

Beyond single sentences as well, we see the influence of the Ontological Ascent. The structure of discourse arises out of coherence relations that obtain between successive segments of discourse. These coherence relations can be broadly classified into four principal groups. There are relations, such as parallelism, based on similarity, the sort of similarity that is the basis for forming sets of entities, the simplest sort of system. There are figure-ground relations, such as cases where the first segment provides a backdrop and the second segment describes the action that plays out against that backdrop. There are relations based on change of state, such as the relation that I have called the Occasion relation (Hobbs, 1985a). And there are relations based on causality, such as explanation.

All of this strongly suggests that theories of these concepts must be at the very foundation of any knowledge base adequate for natural language understanding. In this paper, I outline the structure of such theories.

3.   Granularity

A road can be viewed as a line, a surface, or a volume. When we are planning a trip, we view it as a line. When we are driving on it, we have to worry about our placement on it to the right or left, so we think of it as a surface. When we hit a pothole, it becomes a volume to us.

This shifting of granularity is a general property of cognition. We are very good at adopting small, on-the-spot theories of situations that include just the aspects relevant to our current concerns. Notions of granularity must pervade the core theories we build. Many concepts are inherently granularity-dependent, and many other concepts provide us with means for imposing granularities on situations.

A granularity is defined by an indistinguishability relation $\sim$, or equivalently, a set covering. If the set covering is a partition, the indistinguishability relation is transitive. An example is when we are concerned only with the country a location is in and not any finer discrimination. Any two locations in, say, South Korea would be indistinguishable under this relation. If the set covering is comprised of overlapping sets, the indistinguishability relation is not transitive. An example is when we do not distinguish any two points lying within 1 cm of each other. When we view a road as a line, we are not distinguishing between two points that are at the same place along its length, even though they are, for example, in different lanes.

Shifts in granularity are a way of turning complex reasoning problems into simpler problems, with fewer entities and more regular properties.

Granularities are often determined by functionality. A topographical map of the Sierras will show a hiking trail that is one foot wide, and not show a boulder that is twenty feet in diameter.

4.   Systems and the Figure-Ground Relation

A *system*, or composite entity, is a set of entities, their properties, and the relations among them. The concept of system captures the minimal complexity something must have in order for it to have *structure*. It is hard to imagine something that cannot be conceptualized as a system. For this reason, a vocabulary for talking about systems will be broadly applicable.

The elements of a system can themselves be viewed as systems, and this gives us a very common example of shifting granularities. It allows us to distinguish between the *structure* and the *function* of an entity. The function of an entity in a system is its relations to the other elements of the system, its environment, while the entity itself is viewed as indecomposable. The structure of the entity is revealed when we decompose it and view it as a system itself. We look at it at a finer granularity.

An important question any time we can view an entity both functionally and structurally is how the functions of the entity are implemented in its structure. We need to spell out the structure-function articulations.

For example, a librarian might view a book as an indecomposable entity and be interested in its location in the library, its relationship to other books, to the bookshelves, and to the people who check the book out. This is a functional view of the book with respect to the library. We can also view it structurally by inquiring as to its parts, its content, and so on. In spelling out the structure-function articulations, we might say something about how its content determines its place in the library.

A system can serve as the *ground* against which some external *figure* can be located or can move. A primitive predicate at expresses this relation. In

$$at(x, y, s)$$

s is a system, y is an element in the system, and x is an entity not in the system. It says that the figure x is at a point y in the system s which is the ground.

The at relation plays primarily two roles in the knowledge base. First, it is involved in the "decompositions" of many lexical items. We saw this above in the definition of "range". There is a very rich vocabulary of terms for talking about the figure-ground relation. This means that whenever a relation in some domain can be viewed as an instance of the figure-ground relation, we acquire at a stroke a rich vocabulary for talking about that domain.

This gives rise to the second role the at predicate plays in the knowledge base. A great many specific domains have relations that can be stipulated to be instances of the at relation. There must be a large number of axioms of the form

$$(\forall x, y, s)r(x, y) \wedge y \in s \supset at(x, y, s)$$

Such axioms constitute the source of spatial terminology and spatial metaphors. Some examples of at relations are

A person at an object in a system of objects:
>John is at his desk.

An object at a location in a coordinate system:
>The post office is at the corner of 34th Street and Eighth Avenue.

In computer science, a variable at a value in a range of values:
>I goes from 1 to 100.

A person's salary at a particular point on the money scale:
>John's salary reached $75,000 this year.

A particularly important example of an at relation is predication itself. We can view a set of predicates as constituting a system, where the relations among the elements are the implication and mutual exclusivity relations. Axioms of the form

$$(\forall p, x, s)p \in s \wedge p(x) \supset at(x, p, s)$$

say that for a predicate in a system of predicates to be true of an entity is for the entity to be at that predicate in the system. This makes the rich vocabulary of spatial relationships available for predication.

The following expressions, for example, tap into a system of predicates about human activities and states of consciousness:

>at work, at play, on travel, on drugs, . . .

5. Scales

A very common and very useful kind of system is one in which the relations among the entities are an indistinguishability relation $\sim$ and a partial ordering $<$. We can call this a *scale*.

A core theory of scales will provide definitions for such concepts as a subscale, a total ordering, a scale being dense, the top and bottom of a scale, and the reverse of a scale. Allen's relations among time intervals (Allen and Kautz, 1985) are in fact relations among subscales and are straightforward to define. If we have a primitive notion of points on a scale being adjacent, we can define connectedness in terms of it. A scale is a system, so the figure-ground relation applies to it. We can talk about an external entity being *at* a point on a scale.

The integers and the real numbers are scales, and many useful scales have structures isomorphic to these. At the other extreme, a scale might have only its two endpoints, as for the scale consisting of a predicate and its negation, $\{\neg p, p\}$. But various intermediate levels of structure are often useful. In qualitative physics (de Kleer and Brown, 1985; Forbus, 1988), many scales are reduced to negative, zero, and postive regions. It is often necessary to know not the precise value of a quantity but only its order of magnitude or half order of magnitude.

One important example of intermediate structure involves isolating the high and low regions of a scale. We can do this with operators we can call Hi and Lo. The Hi region of a scale includes its top; the Lo region includes its bottom. The points in the Hi region are all greater than any of the points in the Lo region. Otherwise, there are no general constraints on the Hi and Lo regions. In particular, the bottom of the Hi region and the top of the Lo region may be indeterminate with respect to the elements of the scale. The Hi and Lo operators provide us with a fairly coarse-grained structure on scales, useful when greater precision is not necessary or not possible.

The absolute form of adjectives frequently isolate Hi and Lo regions of scales. A totally ordered Height Scale can be defined precisely, but frequently we are only interested in qualitative judgments of height. The word "tall" isolates the Hi region of the Height Scale; the word "short" isolates the Lo region. A Happiness Scale cannot be defined precisely. We cannot get much more structure for a Happiness Scale than what is given to us by the Hi and Lo operators. The Hi and Lo operators can be iterated, to give us the concepts "happy", "very happy", and so on.

In any given context, the Hi and Lo operators will identify different regions of the scale. That is, the inferences we can draw from the fact that something is in the Hi region of a scale are context-dependent; indeed, inferences are always context-dependent. The Hi and Lo regions must be related to common distributions of objects on the scale, so that if something is significantly above average for the relevant set, then it is in the Hi region. They must also be related to goal-directed behavior; often something is in the Hi region of a scale precisely because that property aids or defeats the achievement of some goal in a plan. For example, saying that a talk is long often means that it is longer than the audience's attention span, and thus the goal of conveying information is defeated.

It is possible to define composite scales. If a scale s is a composite of scales s_1 and s_2, then its elements are the ordered pairs $< x, y >$ where x is in s_1 and y is in s_2. An external entity is *at* a point $< x, y >$ in the composite scale s if and only if it is at x in component scale s_1 and at y in component scale s_2. The ordering in s has to be consistent with the orderings in s_1 and s_2; if x_1 is less than x_2 in s_1, and y_1 is less than y_2 in s_2, then $< x_1, y_1 >$ is less than $< x_2, y_2 >$ in s. The converse is not necessarily true; the composite scale may have more structure than that inherited from its component scales.

We need composite scales to deal with complex scalar predicates, such as *damage*. When something is damaged, it no longer fulfills its function in a goal-directed system. It needs to be repaired, and repairs cost. Thus, there are (at least) two ways in which damage can be serious, first in the degradation of its function, second in the cost of its repair. These are independent scales. Damage that causes a car not to run may cost next to nothing to fix, and damage that only causes the car to run a little unevenly may be very expensive.

6. Change

The next primitive concept of central importance in the Ontological Ascent can be represented by the predicate *change*. This is a relation between situations, or conditions, or predications, or eventualities, and indicates a change of state. In this paper, to avoid an overgrowth of notation, I will write

$$change(p(x), q(x))$$

where, strictly speaking, I should, in the ontologically promiscuous notation of Hobbs (1985a), write

$$change(e_1, e_2) \land p'(e_1, x) \land q'(e_2, x)$$

This says that there is a change from the situation of p being true of x to the situation of q being true of x. A very common pattern involves a change of location:

$$change(at(x, y, s), at(x, z, s))$$

That is, there is a change from the situation of x being at y in s to x being at z in s. Here, at is the abstract figure-ground relation, so any domain conceptualized in terms of that automatically inherits the vocabulary provided by a theory of change.

When there is a change, generally there is some entity involved in both the start and end states; there is something that is changing—x in the above formulas. This suggests a view of the world as consisting of a large number of more or less independent, occasionally interacting processes, or histories, or sequences of events. x goes through a series of changes, and y goes through a series of changes, and occasionally there is a state that involves a relation between the two.

The predicate *change* possesses a limited transitivity. There was a change from Reagan being an actor to Reagan being President, because they are two parts of the same ongoing process, even though he was governor in between. But we probably do not want to say there was a change from Reagan being an actor to Margaret Thatcher being Prime Minister. They are not part of the same process.

Any given process, that is, any sequence of events linked by *change* relations, is a scale whose partial ordering is induced by the predicate *change*.

The Time Line could be taken as primitive, with the *before* relation as its ordering and an *at-time* relation relating states and events to points and intervals on the Time Line. The *at-time* relation would be an *at* relation, giving us the common spatial metaphors for time. Such an ontology seems to be justified by the clock and calendar terms in modern languages. In this ontology, we could define the predicate *change* to be true when different properties are true of an entity at different times.

It seems to me, however, that the notion of *change* is more basic. It is built into the more "primitive" parts of language, such as the event verbs. Even the words "before" and "after", which might seem to relate directly to the Time Line, carry a whiff of causality. The sentence,

The French Revolution broke out after George Washington was elected president.

seems to convey some causality or suggest that somehow the two events are part of the same process.

7. Causality

The next primitive predicate of central importance is *cause*. As with *at* and *change*, it has no definition. There is no axiom of the form

$$(\forall\, e_1, e_2)\, cause(e_1, e_2) \equiv \ldots$$

but the knowledge base is rife with axioms of the form

$$cause(p(x), q(x))$$

expressing causal connections among states and events. We don't know precisely what causality is, but we know lots and lots of examples of things that cause other things.

There is a question as to what the arguments of *cause* can be. Some would urge that they can only be events, but it seems to me that we want to allow states as well, since in

> The slipperiness of the ice caused John to fall.

the cause (the first argument) is a state. Moreover, intentional agents are sometimes taken to be the unanalyzed causes of events. In

> John lifted his arm.

John is the cause of the change of position of his arm, and we probably don't want to have to coerce this argument into some imagined event taking place inside John. Physical forces may also act as causes, as in

> Gravity causes the moon to circle the earth.

I have spoken loosely of states and events. We are now in a position to characterize more precisely the intuitive notions of state, event, action, and process. A state is an *at* relationship, $at(x, y, s)$, or more generally, a predication. To be up, for example, is a state. An event is a change of state, a common variety of which is a change of location:

$$change(at(x, y, s), at(x, z, s))$$

For example, the verb "rise" denotes a change of location of something to a higher point. An action is the causing of an event by an intentional agent:

$$cause(a, change(at(x, y, s), at(x, z, s)))$$

The verb "raise" denotes an action by someone of effecting a change of location of something to a higher point. A process is a sequence of events or actions; in terms of the Ontological Ascent, we view particular events and actions as indecomposable and construct a system of them. For example, to fluctuate is to undergo a sequence of risings and fallings, and to pump is to engage in a sequence of raisings and lowerings. We can coarsen the granularity on processes so that the individual changes of state become invisible, and the result is a state. This is a transformation of perspective that is effected by the progressive aspect in English. Thus, fluctuating can be viewed as a state. State, event, action, and process label stages in the Ontological Ascent.

The world is laced with threads of causal connection, and therefore our core theories must be rife with axioms encoding causal connections. In general, if two entities x and y are causally connected with respect to some behavior p of x, then whenever p happens to x, there is some corresponding behavior q that happens to y. Attachment of physical objects is one variety of causal connection. In this case, p and q are both *move*. If x and y are attached, moving x causes y to move. Containment is similar.

A particularly common variety of causal connection between two entities is one mediated by the motion of a third entity from one to the other.

$$cause(p(x), move(z, x, y)) \land cause(move(z, x, y), q(y)) \supset cause(p(x), q(y))$$

This might be called, somewhat facetiously, a "vector boson" connection. In particle physics, a vector boson is an elementary particle that transfers energy from one point to another. Photons, which really are vector bosons, mediate the causal connection between the sun and our eyes. Other examples of such causal connections are rain drops connecting a state of the clouds with the wetness of our skin and clothes, a virus transmitting disease from one person to another, and utterances passing information between people.

Containment, barriers, openings, and penetration are all with respect to paths of causal connection.

The event structure underlying many verbs exhibits causal chains. Instruments, for example, are usually vector bosons. In the sentence,

John pounded the nail with a hammer for Bill.

the underlying causal structure is that the Agent John causes a change in location of the Instrument, the hammer, which causes a change in location of the Object, the nail, which causes or should cause a change in the mental or emotional state of the Beneficiary, Bill.

$$Agent\ -cause->\ change(at(Instrument, x), at(Instrument, Object))$$
$$-cause->\ change(at(Object, y_1), at(Object, y_2))$$
$$-cause->\ change(p_1(Beneficiary), p_2(Beneficiary))$$

Much of case grammar and work on thematic roles can be seen as a matter of identifying where the arguments of verbs fit into this kind of causal chain when we view the verbs as instantiating this abstract frame.

An important role for causality is in linking two scales. It often effects a monotonic, scale-to-scale function. The general pattern is this:

$$cause(change(at(x, y, s_1), at(x, z, s_1)), change(at(w, u, s_2), at(w, v, s_2)))$$

where if $y < z$ on s_1, then $u < v$ on s_2. That is, if there is a change from x being at y on s_1 to x being at a higher point z on s_1, then this causes there to be a change from w being at u on s_2 to w being at a higher point v on s_2. This is the basis of our many "The more ..., the more ..." rules, such as

The more you press on the accellerator, the faster you go.

The longer you leave the toast in, the browner it gets.

We often conceive of graded causality in terms of the concept of "force". Talmy (1985) has shown how this concept pervades language.

A concept closely related to causality is enablement. It can be defined as follows:

$$(\forall e_1, e_2) enable(e_1, e_2) \equiv cause(not(e_1), not(e_2))$$

That is, e_1 enables e_2 if e_1 not happening will cause e_2 not to happen. Enablement is crucial in the core theory of goal-directed behavior.

8.   Goals-Directed Behavior

A core theory of goal-directed behavior is central in human cognition and discourse and rests crucially on a core theory of causality. Its key primitive is the concept of a *goal*. This again will not be defined, but axioms will link it in the right way with axiomatizations of belief and action,

to make available intentional interpretations of human and other behavior. In particular, these core
theories should insure that people's actions can be seen as attempts to achieve their goals, given
their beliefs.

Among the most important facts about goals are those linking them with causality and enablement, for it is by manipulating the causal structure of the world that agents achieve their goals.
The two primary axioms are as follows:

$$(\forall a, q, r) goal(a, q) \wedge enable(r, q) \supset goal(a, r)$$

$$(\forall a, p, q) goal(a, q) \wedge cause(p, q) \wedge choose(a, p, q) \supset goal(a, p)$$

The first axiom says that if an agent a has a goal q and r enables q, then a will have the goal r.
This captures the prerequisites of the STRIPS operators of Fikes and Nilsson (1971).

The second axiom says that if an agent a has a goal q, where p causes q, and a chooses p as
a way of achieving q, then a will have the goal p. I will not attempt to explicate *choose* here, but
something like this is necessary to accomodate nondeterminism. There may be many things that
will cause q, and the agent need pick only one of them. This axiom encodes the "body" of the
STRIPS operators of Fikes and Nilsson (1971).

Thus, to achieve a goal, an agent must satisfy all the prerequisites, removing all the barriers
to the goal, and then choose something that will cause the goal to come about. These two axioms
allow us to construct hierarchical plans, decomposing goals into their subgoals. In the above
axioms, q is the goal, r and p the subgoals. These subgoals can in turn be decomposed into further
subgoals

The depth of decomposition in these plans is one of the prinicpal ways we impose a granularity
on our view of behavior. It may be sufficient for our purposes to know that John drove his car to
the airport, or it may be necessary to view it under a finer granularity that makes visible his actions
of shifting the gears and turning the steering wheel.

A plan is essentially a representation of causal structure. It is therefore useful for explaining not just human behavior, but other phenomena as well. Artifacts and organizations can, for
example, be viewed as plans made concrete.

Much of the knowledge we have about an artifact is best represented by the plan that it implements. Consider a very simple example. The function of a coffee cup is to move coffee. We
decompose this goal into two subgoals—containing the coffee in the cup and moving the cup. The
subgoal of moving the cup is further decomposed into the subgoals of attaching the cup to the handle and moving the handle. It is a very common schema for artifacts that in order to do something
to an object, we set up a causal connection, such as containment or attachment, to another object,
and do something to that other object. We can continue to decompose in this fashion until we have
specified the role or function of all the components of the artifact.

Similarly, organizations can be seen as having a goal and implementing a plan to achieve that
goal, where the structure of the organization reflects the structure of the plan. Thus, the goal of an
organization might be to provide people with cars. This decomposes into the subgoals of having
one division of the organization manufacture cars and another division sell them to people. Each
of these would decompose further. Eventually the plan would bottom out in sets of actions by
single individuals. These sets of actions constitute the members' *roles* in the organization.

Any system that can be viewed as exhibiting functionality can be represented in terms of a
plan that expresses the system's underlying causal structure. A tree, for example, can be viewed
as a goal-directed system whose goal is to grow and reproduce.

9. Summary

A common way to encode knowledge for natural language and other AI programs is to proceed domain by domain. Many of the most common words in language, however, apply across many domains. What I have tried to do in this paper is to suggest some very abstract domains—systems and the figure-ground relation, scales, change of state, causality, and goal-directed systems—that seem to underlie more specific domains.

Moreover, concepts of greater and greater complexity can be constructed by building systems of entities, by relating other entities to that system with a figure-ground relation, by embedding concepts of figure-ground in the concept of change, by embedding that in causality, and by coarsening the granularity and beginning the process over again—a process I have called the Ontological Ascent.

More specific domains can be seen as instantiations of these abstract ones. Language provides us with a rich vocabulary for talking about the abstract domains. When we construct core theories of these domains, then we have a hope of being able to define, or at least characterize, the words in this vocabulary in terms provided by the core theories. When the core theory of an abstract domain is instantiated as a specific domain, then the vocabulary associated with the abstract domain is also instantiated, giving us a rich vocabulary for talking about the specific domain. Conversely, when we encounter general words in the contexts of specific domains, understanding how the specific domains instantiate the abstract domains allows us to determine the specific meanings of the general words in their current context.

Acknowledgments

This paper is based in part on work that was done with William Croft, Todd Davies, Douglas Edwards, and Kenneth Laws. I have also profited from discussions with Annelise Bech, Andrew Gordon, Bente Maegaard, and Costanza Navarretta.

References

Allen, James F. and Henry A. Kautz. 1985. A model of naive temporal reasoning. In Jerry R. Hobbs and Robert C. Moore, editors, *Formal Theories of the Commonsense World*. Ablex Publishing Corp., pages 251–268.

Croft, William. 1991. *Syntactic Categories and Grammatical Relations: The Cognitive Organization of Information*. University of Chicago Press, Chicago, Illinois.

de Kleer, Johann and John Seely Brown. 1985. A qualitative physics based on confluences. In Jerry R. Hobbs and Robert C. Moore, editors, *Formal Theories of the Commonsense World*. Ablex Publishing Corp., pages 109–184.

Fikes, Richard and Nils J. Nilsson. 1971. Strips: A new approach to the application of theorem proving to problem solving. *Artificial Intelligence*, 2:189–208.

Forbus, Kenneth D. 1988. Qualitative physics: Past, present, and future. In Howard Shrobe, editor, *Exploring Artificial Intelligence*. Morgan Kaufmann Publishers, Inc., pages 239–296. Republished in Daniel S. Weld and Johan de Kleer (eds.), *Readings in Qualitative Reasoning about Physical Systems*, Morgan Kaufmann Publishers, Inc., San Mateo, California, 11–39, 1989.

Gruber, Jeffrey C. 1965. *Studies in Lexical Relations*. Ph.D. thesis, Massachusetts Institute of Technology, Cambridge, Massachusetts. unpublished.

Hobbs, Jerry R. 1974. A model for natural language semantics, part i: The model. Technical Report 36, Department of Computer Science, Yale University, October. Research Report.

Hobbs, Jerry R. 1985a. On the coherence and structure of discourse. Technical Report CSLI-85-37, Center for the Study of Language and Information, Stanford University.

Hobbs, Jerry R. 1985b. Ontological promiscuity. In *Proceedings, 23rd Annual Meeting of the Association for Computational Linguistics*, pages 61–69, Chicago, Illinois, July.

Hobbs, Jerry R., William Croft, Todd Davies, Douglas Edwards, and Kenneth Laws. 1987. Commonsense metaphysics and lexical semantics. *Computational Linguistics*, 13(3-4):241–250, July-December.

Jackendoff, Ray. 1976. Toward an explanatory semantic representation. *Linguistic Inquiry*, 7(1):89–150.

Talmy, Leonard. 1983. How language structures space. In Herbert Pick and Linda Acredolo, editors, *Spatial Orientation: Theory, Research, and Application*. Plenum Press.

Talmy, Leonard. 1985. Force dynamics in language and thought. In William H. Eilfort, Paul D. Kroeber, and Karen L. Peterson, editors, *Proceedings from the Parasession on Causatives and Agentivity, 21st Regional Meeting, Chicago Linguistic Society*.

How has belief modality contributed to formal semantics?[*]

Satoshi Tojo

JAIST

Abstract. Looking back the history of formal treatment of linguistics, we cannot disregard the contribution of possible world semantics. Intensional logic of Montague semantics, DRT (Discourse Representation Theory), mental space, and situation theory are closely related to or compared with the notion of possible world. All these theories have commonly clarified the structure of belief context or uncertain knowledge, employing hypothesized worlds. In this talk, I firstly brief the pedigree of these theories. Next, I will introduce the recent development of modal logic for the representation of (i) knowledge and belief and (ii) time, in which belief modality is precisely discussed together with the accessibility among possible worlds. I will refer to BDI (belief-desire-intention) logic, CTL (computational tree logic), and sphere-based model in belief revision. Finally, I will discuss how these theories could be applied to the further development of analyses of natural language.

1. Introduction

Let me introduce two examples how modality is used in natural language semantics.

Firstly, when non-native English learners first learn two meanings of each of 'must' and 'may', that is epistemic/deontic readings, they are baffled: what the two meanings have in common?

	must	may
epistemic	have firm knowledge	have vague knowledge
deontic	force obligation	permit tolerantly

The possible world semantics may (or must?) convince some of them, that is,

must	for all possible worlds, denoted by $\Box$
may	some possible worlds exist, denoted by $\Diamond$

Remember in First-Order Logic, $\forall$ (for all) and $\exists$ (some $\cdots$ exist) are interchangeable each other; i. e., $\forall x\, p(x)$ is equal to $\neg\exists\neg p(x)$ (there exists no x such that $\neg p(x)$). In the similar way, '$\Box$' can be replaced by '$\neg\Diamond\neg$' in modal logic. In Japanese, the deontic reading of 'must' is translated as

–nakere–ba–naranai.

Here, the first '*–nakere–*' is the negation, and the second '*–ba–*' suggests a case, and the third '*–naranai*' is again the negation. Thus, Japanese represent deontic '$\Box$' by '$\neg\Diamond\neg$'.

Secondly, we can introduce a hypothetical belief situation either in the past tense or in the *conjunctive* mood in Indo-European languages, and also we may mention an imaginary current situation in the *conditional* mood,[1] as

„Wenn ich mehr Zeit hätte, so würde ich Ihnen einen längeren Brief
schreiben.“
《S'il venait demain, tu le verrais.》
"Se facesse bel tempo domani, che faresti?"

In English both the conjunctive and the conditional moods have been reduced to the *subjunctive* mood.

"If I were a bird, I would fly to you."

---

[*]Copyright 2007 by Satoshi Tojo
[1]*Konjunctive* in German.

Why do we employ the past tense when we introduce a counterfactual situation? One explanation is that we consider retreating once to a past (by the conjunctive mood) to annihilate the current situation, and restarting from the past to the different 'now' (by the conditional mood) as in the following figure.

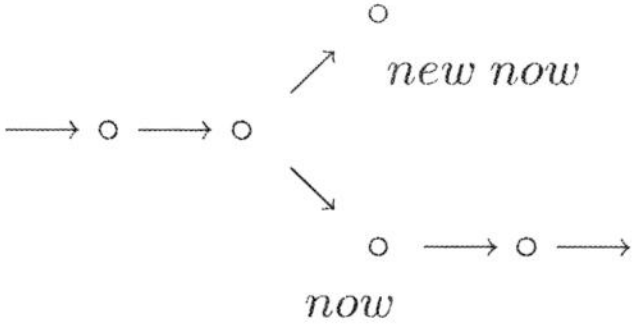

Actually, in English and German which do not possess the conditional mood, 'would' and 'würden' are called *past-future* (future seen from the past). Later, we will explain such a branching time in terms of modal logic.

2. Looking back $\cdots$

2.1. Intensional Logic

One of the outstanding achievements of Montague semantics (Dowty, 1979; Dowty, Wall, and Peters, 1981; Gamut, 1991) is the analysis of oblique sentences (or opaqueness), besides proper treatment of quantification, as in

Electra does not know that the man in front of her is her brother. (1)

Electra knows that Orestes is her brother.
The man in front of her is Orestes.
____
Electra knows that the man in front of her is her brother.

language expression
$\downarrow$
$\langle$intension$\rangle$
$\langle$possible world$\rangle$ $\longrightarrow$ $\langle$extension$\rangle$

de re $=$ extensional $=$ reference (Bedeutung)
de dicto $=$ intensional $=$ sense (Sinn)

To include intensional logic, we need to revise the syntax of formal language. If α is a language expression, then so is $\hat{}\alpha$. For any w_1 and w_2,

$$\llbracket \hat{}\alpha \rrbracket^{w_1} = \llbracket \hat{}\alpha \rrbracket^{w_2}$$

which implies that $\llbracket \hat{}\alpha \rrbracket^{w}$ does not depend upon w. s is an index of a possible world, and the meaning of α depends upon w.

$$\alpha\colon a \leftrightarrow \hat{}\alpha\colon \langle s, a\rangle \leftrightarrow \check{}\alpha\colon a$$
$$\gamma\{x\} \equiv \check{}\gamma(x) \text{ (Brace convention)}$$

However, do we need to suppose that every lexical item depends on a possible world? In the following lexical items, each s represents an index of a possible world W.

John runs fast. (2)

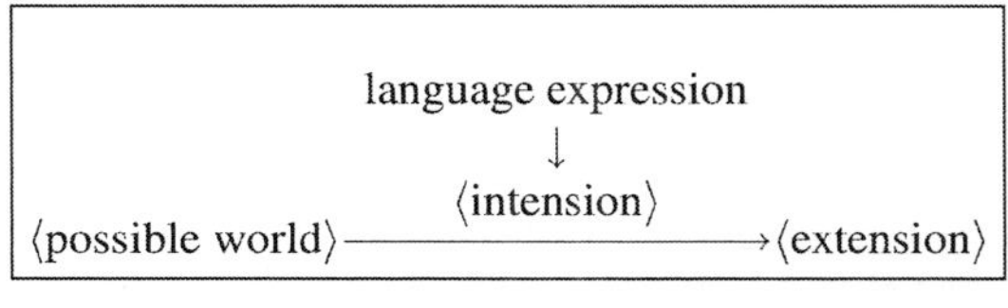

$$john'\colon \langle s, e\rangle$$
$$run'\colon \langle s, \langle\langle s, e\rangle, t\rangle\rangle$$
$$fast'\colon \langle\langle s, \langle\langle s, e\rangle, t\rangle\rangle, \langle\langle s, e\rangle, t\rangle\rangle$$

Here, the number of s is obviously excessive. In order to avoid needless proliferation of Bennet had suggested the following categories.

(individual)		e
sentence	S	t
common noun	N	$\langle e,t\rangle$
verb phrase / intransitive verb	IV	$\langle e,t\rangle$
transitive verb		
(find, love, eat)	IV/(t/IV)	$\langle\langle s,\langle\langle s,\langle e,t\rangle\rangle,t\rangle\rangle,\langle e,t\rangle\rangle$
transitive verb (believe, assert)	IV/t	$\langle\langle s,t\rangle,\langle e,t\rangle\rangle$
noun phrase / proper noun	t/IV	$\langle\langle s,\langle e,t\rangle\rangle,t\rangle$
determiner	Det	$\langle\langle s,\langle e,t\rangle\rangle,\langle\langle s,\langle e,t\rangle\rangle,t\rangle\rangle$

$$\text{John believes a penguin flies.} \tag{3}$$

$$
\begin{aligned}
\text{John} : t/(t/e) &\Rightarrow \lambda P[P\{john'\}]: \langle\langle s,\langle e,t\rangle\rangle,t\rangle \\
\text{believes} : (t/e)/t &\Rightarrow believe': \langle\langle s,t\rangle,\langle e,t\rangle\rangle \\
\text{a} : (t/(t/e))/(t/e) &\Rightarrow \lambda P\lambda Q\exists x[P\{x\}\wedge Q\{x\}]: \langle\langle s,\langle e,t\rangle\rangle,\langle\langle s,\langle e,t\rangle\rangle,t\rangle\rangle \\
\text{penguin} : t/e &\Rightarrow penguin': \langle e,t\rangle \\
\text{flies} : t/e &\Rightarrow fly': \langle e,t\rangle
\end{aligned}
$$

can be interpreted in the following two ways.

(i) There must be a penguin that flies somewhere.

$$
\cfrac{\lambda P[P\{john'\}] \quad \langle\langle s,\langle e,t\rangle\rangle,t\rangle}{}
\cfrac{
  \cfrac{believe' \quad \langle\langle s,t\rangle,\langle e,t\rangle\rangle}{}
  \cfrac{
    \cfrac{\lambda P\lambda Q\exists x[P\{x\}\wedge Q\{x\}] \quad \langle\langle s,\langle e,t\rangle\rangle,\langle\langle s,\langle e,t\rangle\rangle,t\rangle\rangle \qquad penguin' \quad \langle e,t\rangle}{\lambda Q\exists x[penguin'(x)\wedge Q\{x\}] \quad \langle\langle s,\langle e,t\rangle\rangle,t\rangle} \qquad fly' \quad \langle e,t\rangle
  }{\exists x[penguin'(x)\wedge fly'(x)] \quad t}
}{believe'(\,{}^\wedge\exists x[penguin'(x)\wedge fly'(x)]) \quad \langle e,t\rangle}
$$

$$
believe'(\,{}^\wedge\exists x[penguin'(x)\wedge fly'(x)])(john') \quad t
$$

(ii) The penguin overthere flies.

$$
\cfrac{
  \cfrac{\lambda P\lambda Q\exists x[P\{x\}\wedge Q\{x\}] \quad \langle\langle s,\langle e,t\rangle\rangle,\langle\langle s,\langle e,t\rangle\rangle,t\rangle\rangle \qquad penguin' \quad \langle e,t\rangle}{\lambda Q\exists x[penguin'(x)\wedge Q\{x\}] \quad \langle\langle s,\langle e,t\rangle\rangle,t\rangle}
}{}
\cfrac{
  \cfrac{\lambda P[P\{john'\}] \quad \langle\langle s,\langle e,t\rangle\rangle,t\rangle}{}
  \cfrac{
    \cfrac{\lambda P[P\{x_5\}] \quad \langle\langle s,\langle e,t\rangle\rangle,t\rangle \qquad fly' \quad \langle e,t\rangle}{fly'(x_5) \quad t} \qquad believe' \quad \langle\langle s,t\rangle,\langle e,t\rangle\rangle
  }{believe'(\,{}^\wedge fly'(x_5)) \quad \langle e,t\rangle}
}{believe'(\,{}^\wedge fly'(x_5))(john') \quad t}
$$

$$
\lambda z[believe'(\,{}^\wedge fly'(z))(john')] \quad \langle e,t\rangle
$$

$$
\exists x[penguin'(x)\wedge believe'(\,{}^\wedge fly'(x))(john')] \quad t
$$

In the similar way, 'a Democrat' in

$$\text{Anna believes that a Democrat would win.} \tag{4}$$

can be either within or outside of Anna's belief.

(i) But the man she mentions may not actually be a Democrat.

$$believe'(\,{}^\wedge\exists x[democrat'(x) \wedge win'(x)])(anna')$$

(ii) But she does not know the man's face.

$$\exists x[democrat'(x) \wedge believe'(\,{}^\wedge win'(x))(anna')]$$

2.2. Discourse Representation Theory

Discourse Representation Theory (Kamp and Reyle, 1993) has implemented the partiality and the dynamics of information, i. e., the preceding sentence affects on the succeeding one.

Jones owns Ulysses. It fascinates him. (5)

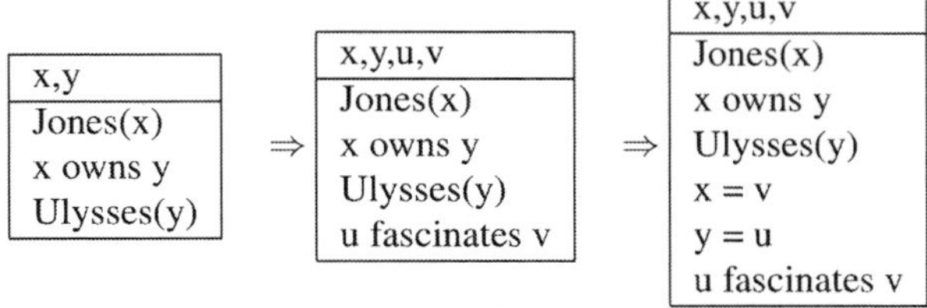

Also, DRT has clarified the process of anaphora resolution.

Bill owns a Porsche or Fred owns it. (6)

- deictic reading: refers what exists in the world.

- anaphoric reading: refers the preceding word, not necessarily an object in the world.

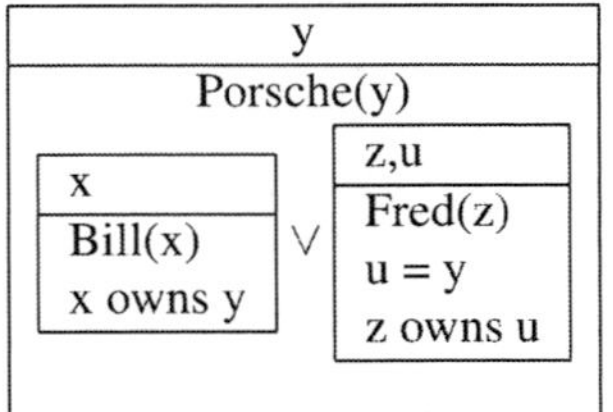

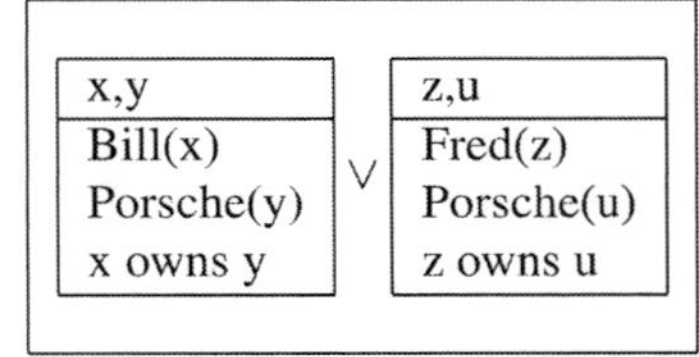

Either Jones doesn't own a car or else he hides it. (7)

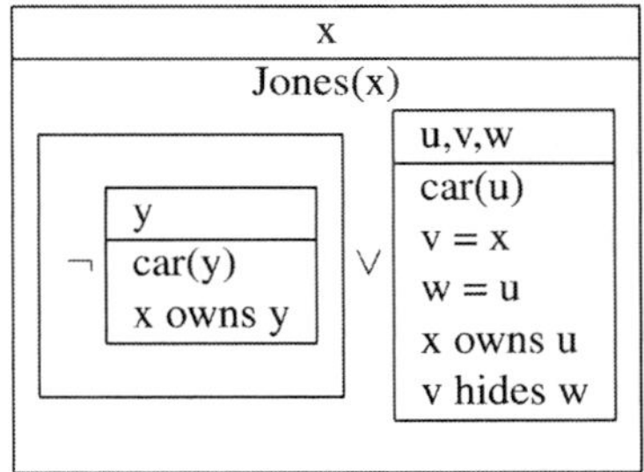

A problem about the environment preoccupies every serious politician. (8)

$$\exists y[problem(y) \wedge \forall x[politician(x) \rightarrow preoccupies(y, x)]]$$
$$\forall x[politician(x) \rightarrow \exists y[problem(y) \wedge preoccupies(y, x)]]$$

2.3. Mental Space

Principle of ID: we can refer one by the other name if they are mapped by *connector* between mental spaces (Fauconnier, 1994; Fauconnier, 1997). In "Plato is on the top shelf" and "The mushroom omelet left without paying the bill," a book of Plato and the person who ate the mushroom omelet are referred to as metonymy, respectively, in the speaker's mental spaces.

When we consider the distinction of *individual* and *role* (viz. deictic/anaphoric), we develop the theory in the following way.

George thinks the winner will go to Hong Kong. (9)

Introduction of a mental space	'George thinks'
attribute P	'will go to Hong Kong.'
role (r)	the winner

- the attribute of the role itself $\cdots$ P(r)

- the attribute of the value of the role $\cdots$ P(r(m))

$$\text{In 1929, the president was a baby.} \tag{10}$$

space introduction	'In 1929'
attribute (P)	'was a baby'
role (r)	the president

(i) In 1929, a certain baby was the president. P(r(M))

(ii) The current president was a baby in 1929. P(F(r(R)))

(iii) In 1929, a president was elected from babies. P(r)

Mental space can be a belief situation, and various beliefs produce multiple interpretations.

$$\text{Hob thinks}_{M_1} \text{ a witch has blighted Bob's mare, and Nob believes}_{M_2} \text{ that she} \tag{11}$$
killed Cob's sow. (Geach 1972)

(i) transparent reading: a certain person in R killed the sow and the mare.

(ii) there exists a certain person in M_1, and the correspondent person exists in M_2.

(iii) a person whose role is 'witch' exists in M_1, and a person of the same role exists also in M_2.

$$\text{Everybody believes that a witch blighted the mare. (Ioup 1977)} \tag{12}$$

- whether *witch* is in 'believe' or not.

- whether is 'every' collective or distributive.

- whether is *witch* a role or a person, while the role is common in every mental space.

(i) A woman exists, and everyone believes that she is a witch. The person who killed the mare is she.

(ii) Everyone believes that there exists a witch, whose image and features are common among them. The witch killed mares.

(iii) Hob believes that a witch is a cute girl with short hair. He believes that the girl killed the mare. Nob believes that a witch is an ugly old woman. She did the crime.

(iv) Everyone believes in witch; but none has seen her, and it is an abstract existence. Everyone just regards that the ominous incident is caused by a witch.

(v) There are two women called Hilda and Brünhilde. Hob believes that Hilda killed the mare, and Nob believes that Brünhilde did it.

3. Belief and Credibility

In this section, we summarize the usage of belief from the viewpoint of artificial intelligence, to consider the agent communication beyond sentential semantics.

3.1. Belief Revision

P. Gärdenfors (Gärdenfors, 1992)

α All European swans are white.

β The bird caught in the trap is a swan.

γ The bird caught in the trap comes from Sweden.

δ Sweden is part of Europe.

From γ and δ, 'the swan in the trap comes from Europe.' With α and β, 'the bird in the trap is white.' What happens if the bird in the trap is black?

Constraints

(i) K, a belief set, should be consistent; i. e., K does not include both of φ and $\neg\varphi$.

(ii) If K logically entails φ $(K \vdash \varphi)$, $\varphi \in K$.

$$K = Cn(K) = \{\varphi | K \vdash \varphi\}$$

We regard $K_\perp$ (a set of all the propositions including inconsistency) as a special belief set. ex. $\{\varphi, \varphi \to \psi\}$ is not a belief set.

(iii) The revision should be minimal. A maximal subset K' that does not entail φ is such that

- $K' \subseteq K$
- $\varphi \notin Cn(K')$
- For any K'' such that $K' \subset K'' \subseteq K$, $\varphi \in Cn(K'')$.

(iv) Sentences with a lower grade of entrenchment should be revised first. Suppose that, by $\varphi \leq \psi$, ψ is more important than, or equal to, φ.
ex. For $\alpha \leq (\alpha \to \beta) \leq (\beta \to \gamma)$,

$$\{\alpha,\ \alpha \to \beta,\ \beta \to \gamma\} * (\neg\gamma) = \{\alpha \to \beta,\ \beta \to \gamma,\ \neg\gamma\}.$$

Revision and Contraction   Belief revision $K * \varphi$: in order to maintain consistency, some of the old sentences in K are deleted.

When φ is logically inconsistent,
$K * \varphi = K + \varphi$ $(\equiv K_\perp)$ where '+' is a simple expansion.
When φ is not inconsistent,
if $\neg\varphi \in K$, $K * \varphi \subset K + \varphi$.
if $\neg\varphi \notin K$, $K * \varphi = K + \varphi$.

Contraction $K \div \varphi$: some sentences in K is retracted without adding any new facts. In order for the resulting set to be closed under logical consequences some sentences from K must be given up.

3.2. Sphere of Possible Worlds

Suppose that a set of possible worlds $\mathcal{W} = \{w_0, w_2, w_2, \cdots\}$ is partitioned by a credibility function κ; i.e., $\kappa(w_i)$ returns a non-negative integer, and 0 implies that the world is most credible. A subset of possible worlds partitioned by κ is called a *sphere* (Hansson, 1999). Given a proposition φ, we can define the credibility of the proposition by

$$\kappa(\varphi) \equiv \min\{\kappa(w) | w \Vdash \varphi\}.$$

We assume that either $\kappa(\varphi) = 0$ or $\kappa(\neg\varphi) = 0$ for any given φ, and

$$\kappa(\varphi \vee \psi) = \min\{\kappa(\varphi), \kappa(\psi)\}.$$

Suppose K is a belief state, which is modelled by a set of possible worlds $Mod(K)$ where all the propositions in K is true.

$$Mod(K) = \{w | \forall \varphi \in K, \ w \Vdash \varphi\}.$$

If the belief state of a person is K, then (s)he believes that $w \in Mod(K)$ is most credible. Thus,

$$\kappa(w) = 0 \iff w \in Mod(K).$$

In any w, either $\varphi \in w$ or $\neg\varphi \in w$.[2] If (s)he believes ψ, then such w that $w \Vdash \psi$ is in $Mod(K)$. Thus, $\kappa(\neg\psi) > 0$ implies that $Mod(K) \cap Mod(\neg\psi) = \emptyset$ and $Mod(K) \subseteq Mod(\psi)$.

When $w \Vdash \varphi$, let

$$\kappa(w|\varphi) = \kappa(w) - \kappa(\varphi).$$

Because $\kappa(w) \geq \kappa(\varphi)$, $\kappa(w|\varphi) \geq 0$. Let

$$\kappa * (\varphi, \alpha)(w) = \kappa(w|\varphi) \text{ when } w \Vdash \varphi,$$
$$\kappa * (\varphi, \alpha)(w) = \alpha + \kappa(w|\neg\varphi) \text{ when } w \Vdash \neg\varphi.$$

Then, $\kappa * (\varphi, \alpha)(\varphi) = 0$ and $\kappa * (\varphi, \alpha)(\neg\varphi) = \alpha$. α is the firmness of φ; the higher the value, the more firmly φ is believed. When $\alpha > 0$ and $\kappa(\neg\varphi) = 0$, then $\kappa * (\varphi, \alpha)$ is a belief revision.

4. Logic of Belief and Time

In this section, we collect such materials that would contribute to the further development of natural language semantics, regarding belief situation and possible worlds.

4.1. Modal logic

We summarize the fundamentals of modal logic with $\square$ and $\Diamond$, which represent K (knowledge) and B (belief), and P (past) and F (future).

Axioms If φ is a formula, so is $\square\varphi$. The following axioms are often employed in modal logic.

K	$\square(\varphi \rightarrow \psi) \rightarrow (\square\varphi \rightarrow \square\psi)$
$Df\Diamond$	$\Diamond\varphi \leftrightarrow \neg\square\neg\varphi$
PL	φ, where φ is a tautology.
T	$\square\varphi \rightarrow \varphi$
5	$\Diamond\varphi \rightarrow \square\Diamond\varphi$
4	$\square\varphi \rightarrow \square\square\varphi$
B	$\varphi \rightarrow \square\Diamond\varphi$
D	$\square\varphi \rightarrow \Diamond\varphi$

All the above axioms are not independent each other. We can find the following dependency.

$$\{\mathbf{K}, \mathbf{T}\} \vdash \mathbf{D}, \ \{\mathbf{K}, \mathbf{T}, \mathbf{5}\} \vdash \mathbf{B}, \ \{\mathbf{K}, \mathbf{T}, \mathbf{5}\} \vdash \mathbf{4}, \ \{\mathbf{K}, \mathbf{4}, \mathbf{B}\} \vdash \mathbf{5}.$$

Choosing different sets of axioms from the above, we can construct different logic systems, among which there is the following hierarchy of strength.

$$
\begin{array}{ccc}
 & KT4 & \\
 \nearrow & & \searrow \\
K \leftarrow KT & & KT5 \\
 \searrow & & \nearrow \\
 & KTB & \\
\end{array}
$$

$$S4 = KT4 = KDT4$$
$$S5 = KT5 = KT45 = KDT5 = KDT45 = KT4B$$

---

[2] Each world is called to be *maximal*.

Kripke frame Given a set of possible worlds $W = \{w_1, w_2, w_3, \cdots\}$ and the accessibility in them $\mathcal{R} = \{w_1 R w_2, w_1 R w_3, \cdots\}$, $\langle W, \mathcal{R} \rangle$ is called a Kripke frame, which gives a semantics to modal logic.

$$w \models \Box\varphi \iff \forall w'(wRw')\, w' \models \varphi.$$
$$w \models \Diamond\varphi \iff \exists w'(wRw')\, w' \models \varphi.$$

axiom	accessibility	
T	reflective	wRw
5	Euclidean	If wRw' and wRw'', then $w'Rw''$
4	transitive	If wRw' and $w'Rw''$, wRw''
B	symmetric	If wRw' then $w'Rw$
D	serial	$\forall w \exists w'[wRw']$

Ex. Given $\{w_1, w_2, w_3\}$: possible worlds, with:

$$\{w_1 R w_1, w_1 R w_2, w_2 R w_2, w_2 R w_3, w_3 R w_3\}.$$

- $\Box\varphi \to \varphi$ is true.

- $\Box\varphi \to \Box\Box\varphi$ is not always true.

4.2. Knowledge and Belief

Operator K and B The most important notion to model a person's knowledge is the partiality. Suppose that (s)he knows only $\{\varphi, \psi, \chi\}$ are true and are ignorant of others. Because each possible world assigns true/false to every propositions (*maximal*), we can model his/her knowledge state by a collection of possible worlds which assigns 'true' to $\{\varphi, \psi, \chi\}$; other propositions may or may not be true. Thus, the knowledge modality K must be accessible to the all the worlds ($\Box$) which satisfies this condition (Fagin et al., 1995).

$K_i\varphi \cdots$ agent i knows φ.
$B_i\varphi \cdots$ agent i believes φ.

B_i represents an uncertain knowledge which may not be true in the real world, while K_i satisfies

T $\quad K_i\varphi \to \varphi$.
If i knows φ, φ.

Besides this condition, both of K_i and B_i should satisfy the following axioms.

D $\quad B_i\varphi \to \neg B_i\neg\varphi$.
If i believes φ, (s)he does not believe $\neg\varphi$.
4 $\quad B_i\varphi \to B_i B_i\varphi$.
If i believes φ (s)he believes what (s)he believes.
5 $\quad \neg B_i\varphi \to B_i\neg B_i\varphi$.
If i does not believe φ, (s)he believes that (s)he does not believe φ.

BDI Logic In addition to K_i and B_i, we are arbitrarily add other mental modalities. D_i (desire) and I_i (intention) are often employed, and together with B_i, the logic is called BDI-logic (Bratman, 1987; Cohen, Morgan, and Pollack, 1990). With this, the following expressions are available.

- $B_i\forall x[bordeaux(x) \to mellow(x)]$
  i believes that any Bordeaux wine is mellow.

- $B_i B_j bordeaux(a)$
  i believes that j believes that a is a Bordeaux wine.

- $B_i\forall j[snob(j) \to B_j\forall y[bordeaux(y) \to mellow(y)]]$
  i believes that all the snob guys believes that any Bordeaux wine is mellow.

- $B_i\forall j D_j \neg I_i\, president(i)$
  i believes that everyone desires that i does not intend to be president.

- $B_j \exists x[mellow(x)]$
  j believes that there exists a mellow x (in his/her mind).

- $\exists x[B_j mellow(x)]$
  There exists some x and i believes it is mellow.

4.3. Temporal logic

Priorian temporal logic   We had better beginning from Priorian temporal logic (van Benthem, 1991; Goldblatt, 1992). For a formula φ,

- $P\varphi$ is true. $\equiv$ At some point in the past, φ is true.

- $F\varphi$ is true. $\equiv$ At some point in the future, φ is true.

- $\star$ $G\varphi \equiv \neg F \neg \varphi$ is true.

- $\star$ $H\varphi \equiv \neg P \neg \varphi$ is true.

Branching Time and CTL   As we have mentioned in Introduction, we need not to stick to the linear time. The branching time is far versatile to represent various linguistic information. We employ the following principles.

- Time is discrete.

- Time steps are called states; among which, there is a state called 'now'.

- The past is a straight chaining of states.

- There is the beginning state in the past.

- Time branches to the future.

- The future persists forever.

A sequence of states from the beginning state to a future, following a branch, is called a path. Together with temporal operators, we can define Computational Tree Logic (CTL) (Rao and Georgeff, 1991).

A	For any path,
E	For some path,
$X\varphi$	In the next state, φ.
$\varphi U \psi$	φ until ψ.
$F\varphi$	φ in some future states. ($\equiv \top U \varphi$)
$G\varphi$	φ in all the future states. ($\equiv \neg F \neg \varphi$)

Now the followings are the sentences of CTL.

$$EX\varphi, \ EF\varphi, \ EG\varphi, \ E(\varphi U \psi), \ AX\varphi, \ AF\varphi, \ AG\varphi, \ A(\varphi U \psi).$$

According to the introduction of CTL, the accessibility of belief modality must be redressed as follows. Suppose that branching time is embedded in each possible world. The accessibility relation $\mathcal{B}_i$ is given between possible worlds with regard to a common time, for each agent (Wooldridge, 2000).

$$(w,t)R(w',t) \in \mathcal{B}_i.$$

We simply write $\langle w, t, w' \rangle$ for $(w,t)R(w',t)$.

$$(w,t) \models B_i \varphi \iff \forall w' \langle w, t, w' \rangle \in \mathcal{B}_i, \ (w',t) \models \varphi.$$

5. Toward Communicative Agent

Departing from intra-sentence analysis of belief situation, we can develop a theory of communication, discussing what an agent comes to believe after an informing act of the other agent. First, we introduce the communication channel between agents to implement the notion of uncertainty. In actual mobile agents, the communication eventually might fail by unexpected causes.

The definition of the original *inform* of FIPA (FIPA, 2002) is as follows.

$$\text{feasibility pre-condition} \quad : \quad B_i\varphi \wedge \neg B_i(Bif_j\varphi \vee Uif_j\varphi)$$
$$\text{rational effect} \quad : \quad B_j\varphi$$

A formula $B_j\varphi$ means that agent j believes φ. Also, $Bif_j\varphi$ and $Uif_j\varphi$ are the abbreviations of $B_j\varphi \vee \neg B_j\varphi$ and $U_j\varphi \vee \neg U_j\varphi$, respectively, where $U_j\varphi$ means that agent j is uncertain about φ but the agent supposes that φ is more likely than $\neg\varphi$. However, is the rational effect enough to represent our linguistic communication? There had been two questions:

- The recipient truly comes to know the information if only the sender informs it?

- The recipient should know more besides the information.

We have introduced *channel variables* (Hagiwara, Kobayashi, and Tojo, 2006; de Saeger, Kobayashi, and Tojo, 2007) and added an extra-condition to FIPA's communicability, as follows.

$$\text{feasibility pre-condition (revised)} \quad : \quad B_i\varphi \wedge \neg B_i(Bif_j\varphi \vee Uif_j\varphi) \wedge c_{ij}$$

where c_{ij} is the channel variable between agent i and j. There had been many ways to embed the notion of channel to the logic, e. g., modality, Cartesian product, proposition, and so on. We adopted to employ proposition since we could inform the channel itself as a payload of channel. According to this, in the rational result, agent j should know that i already had known φ, and i would know that j came to know φ. That is,

$$\text{rational effect (revised)} \quad : \quad (B_iB_j\varphi) \vee (B_iB_j\varphi \wedge B_j\varphi \wedge B_jB_i\varphi).$$

This formalization implies that the future states bifurcates into future dependent on whether the communication has been successful or not. This inevitably requires us to incorporate CTL (Section 4.3.) in each possible world. In addition, we need to employ dynamic logic (Wooldridge, 2000) that formalize the state change by inform actions. The knowledge state of each agent in each possible world changes by the inform action, and thus, the accessibility of belief modality also changes, that is the model updating.

Still, there are other possible ways to include the notion of channel. Suppose that the situation s supports the information φ, and φ implies φ' if some extra-condition s' is supplied. Namely,

$$s \circ s' \models \varphi' \quad \Longleftrightarrow \quad s \models \varphi \,\&\, \forall s' \sim s, s' \models \varphi \triangleright \varphi'$$

where $\circ$ is the connection of situation. This statement can be interpreted in various ways.

- This is a formalization of encryption: if a key s' is supplied, then the received sentence φ is decrypted to a meaningful sentence φ'.

But, in our case,

- If a channel s' is secured in the original environment s, then we can transmit the contents φ' by the form of φ.

Suppose that an agent comes to believe information, based on *history* of communication which is a sequence of inform actions: $H = e_1 \circ e_2 \circ e_3 \cdots$. Then, all the prefixes (initial finite number of sequences) of each history are also regarded as reliable source of knowledge. We call such a collection of prefixes $\mathcal{H}$ *protocol* (Pacuit and Parikh, 2004).

$$(w, H) \models K_i\varphi \quad \Longleftrightarrow \quad \forall(w', H') \sim_i (w, H) \, (H' \in \mathcal{H}), \, (w', H') \models \varphi$$

where '$\sim_i$' is the equivalent accessibility relation of agent i. Furthermore, we can define $B_i\varphi$, restricting the accessible worlds by spheres (Section 3.2.). Then, we can avoid the reflectivity **T** (Section 4.1.) to meet the condition of B_i (Section 4.2.).

How can we formalize the inform action of '*witch*' sentences of Geach and Ioup (Section 2.3.), that is, if an agent tells his community that "a witch killed a horse" each member of the community comes to have a different belief state from person to person? The further objective of our study is belief propagation and group revision, where each belief state is elucidated by DRT/mental space.

Finally, notice that we could have rich byproduct in other linguistic phenomena. In the analysis of tense/aspect and event structure, multi-modal logic of precedence and inclusion would reformulate the preceding theory in a more sophisticated way (Tojo, 2006; Koga and Tojo, 2007). Also, if we assume a long history of communication, the protocol may emerge, evolve, and change. Thus, the study may contribute to the study of language evolution (Nakamura, Hashimoto, and Tojo, 2006; Matoba, Nakamura, and Tojo, 2006).

References

Bratman, M. E. 1987. *Intention, Plan, and Practical Reason*. Harvard University Press.

Cohen, P. R., J. Morgan, and M. E. Pollack, editors. 1990. *Intentions in Communication*. The MIT Press.

de Saeger, S., M. Kobayashi, and S. Tojo. 2007. History based belief updates for communicative agents. *FAMAS*.

Dowty, D. 1979. *Word Meaning and Montague Grammar*. D. Reidel.

Dowty, D., R. Wall, and S. Peters. 1981. *Introduction to Montague Semantics*. D. Reidel.

Fagin, R., J. Y. Halpern, Y. Moses, and M. Y. Vardi. 1995. *Reasoning about Knowledge*. The MIT Press.

Fauconnier, G. 1994. *Mental Spaces*. Cambridge University Press.

Fauconnier, G. 1997. *Mappings in Thought And Language*. Cambridge University Press.

FIPA. 2002. Foundation for intelligent physical agents: Communicative act library specification. `http://www.fipa.org`.

Gamut, L. T. F. 1991. *Logic, Language and Meaning*, volume I and II. The University of Chicago Press.

Gärdenfors, P., editor. 1992. *Belief Revision*. Cambridge University Press.

Goldblatt, R. 1992. Logics of time and computation. second edition, CSLI lecture note, Stanford University.

Hagiwara, S., M. Kobayashi, and S. Tojo. 2006. Belief updating by communication channel. In K. Inoue, K. Satoh, and F. Toni, editors, *Computational Logic in Multi-Agent Systems*, volume LNAI4371. Springer, pages 211–225.

Hansson, S. O. 1999. *A Textbook of Belief Dynamics*. Kluwer Academic Press.

Kamp, H. and U. Reyle. 1993. *From Discourse to Logic*. Kluwer Academic Publisher's.

Koga, T. and S. Tojo. 2007. Tense and aspect in polymodal interval temporal logic. *IWCS-07*.

Matoba, R., M. Nakamura, and S. Tojo. 2006. Utility for communicability by profit and cost of agreement, in symbol grounding and beyond. In P. Vogt et al., editors, *LNAI 4211*. Springer.

Nakamura, M., T. Hashimoto, and S. Tojo. 2006. Language change in modified language dynamics equation by memoryless learners. In C. Lyon, A. Cangelosi, and C. L. Nehaniv, editors, *Emergence of Communication and Language*. Springer.

Pacuit, E. and R. Parikh. 2004. The logic of communication graphs. In J. A. Leite et al., editors, *DALT, LNCS, vol.3476*. Springer.

Rao, A. S. and M. P. Georgeff. 1991. Modelling rational agents within a BDI–architecture. In *Proc. of International Conference on Principles of Knowledge Representation and Reasoning*.

Tojo, S. 2006. Multi-dimensional temporal logic for events and states. *Inference in Computational Semantics (ICoS)*.

van Benthem, J. 1991. *The Logic of Time*. Kluwer Academic Press, 2nd edition.

Wooldridge, M. 2000. *Reasoning about Rational Agent*. The MIT Press.

A Syntactic Account of the Properties of Bare Nominals in Discourse[*]

Hee-Don Ahn [a] and Sungeun Cho [b]

[a] Department of English, Konkuk University,
Seoul 143-701, Korea, hdahn@konkuk.ac.kr
[b] Department of English, Sungkyunkwan University,
Seoul 110-745, Korea, scho1007@skku.edu

Abstract. Case markers in Korean are omissible in colloquial speech. Previous discourse studies of Caseless bare NPs in Korean show that the information structure of zero Nominative not only differs from that of overt Nominative but it also differs from that of zero Accusative in many respects. This paper aims to provide a basis for these semantic/pragmatic properties of Caseless NPs through the syntactic difference between bare subjects and bare objects: namely, the former are left-dislocated NPs, whereas the latter form complex predicates with the subcategorizing verbs. Our analysis will account for the facts that (i) the distribution of bare subject NPs are more restricted than that of bare object NPs; (ii) bare subject NPs must be specific or topical; (iii) Acc-marked NPs in canonical position tend to be focalized.

Keywords: Case markers, bare nominals, left-dislocated NPs, focalization

1. Introduction

Case markers in Korean are omissible in colloquial speech. Many previous studies of Caseless bare NPs in Korean show that subject-object asymmetries are observed in various respects. For example, as observed in the wide range of conversational data (H. Lee 2006b-c), occurrence rate of bare NPs in complement position is higher than that of bare NPs in subject positions. The grammatical contrast in (1) further shows that the distribution of bare NP subject in (1b) is not only less common but also severely restricted in canonical subject position, namely, Spec-T, in contrast to the bare NP object in (1a) in canonical object position.

(1) a. Mary-ka   **Chelswu-(lul)**   manna-ss-e.
       Mary-Nom Chelswu-Acc   meet-Past-Dec 'Mary met Chelswu.'
    b. Chelswu-lul   **Mary-*(ka)** manna-ss-e.
       Chelswu-Acc Mary-Nom meet-Past-Dec 'Chelswu, Mary met.'

It is plausible to assume that the subject *Mary-ka* in (1b) is "frozen" in the subject position, Spec-T, due to the scrambled object *John-ul*. Thus, (1b) sharply contrasts with (1a) in that Nominative Case must be marked unlike Accusative.

---

[*] An earlier extended version of this study appeared in Ahn & Cho (2007a). This work was supported by the Konkuk University (the first author), and by the Brain Korea 21 Project (the corresponding author).

Another subject-object asymmetry is D-linking restriction some non-Case-marked *wh*-phrases show. As initially noted by Ahn & Cho (2006), non-Case-marked subject *wh*-phrase *nwukwu* 'who' has only D(iscourse)-linked interpretation in the sense of Pesetsky (1987), as shown in (2).

(2) a. Nwukwu-∅ Yenghi-lul   manna-ss-ni?
        who   Yenghi-Acc meet-Past-Q
       'Who is such that he/she met Yenghi?'   (only D-linked reading is possible)
    b. Nwu(kwu)-ka Yenghi-lul   manna-ss-ni?
        who-Nom   Yenghi-Acc meet-Past-Q
       'Who met Yenghi?'   (non-D-linked reading is also possible)

However, such restriction isn't observed in the case of bare object *wh*-phrases in (3).

(3) a. Yenghi-ka   nwukwu-∅ manna-ss-ni?
        Yenghi-Nom who   meet-Past-Q   (non-D-linked reading is also possible)
    b. Yenghi-ka   nwukwu-lul manna-ss-ni?
        Yenghi-Nom who-Acc   meet-Past-Q
       'Who did Yenghi meet?'   (non-D-linked reading is also possible)

Interestingly, if the Case marker is absent in the scrambled object *wh*-phrase, only D-linked interpretation is possible, as shown in (4).

(4) Nwukwu-∅ Yenghi-ka   manna-ss-ni?
     Who   Yenghi-Nom meet-Past-Q
    'Who is such that Yenghi meet (him/her)?'   (only D-linked reading is possible)

The third interesting asymmetry is found with specific/non-specific contexts. In (5a), the bare subject NP is not permitted with the non-specific modifier *han/etten*. Note, however, that this restriction does not apply to bare NP objects. Thus, in (5b), Acc Case on the object can be freely absent with non-specific modifier.

(5) a. (Yeysnal-ey) **han/etten namca-*(ka)** sal-ass-ta.
        long.time-at a/a.certain man-(Nom)   live-Past-Dec
       '(Long time ago) there was a man lived.'
    b. (Yeysnal-ey) Mary-ka **han/etten namca-(lul)** manna-ss-ta.
        long.time-at M.-Nom a/a.certain man-(Acc)   meet-Past-Dec
       '(Long time ago) Mary met a man.'

Note further that overt realization of Acc Case in (5b) tends to induce a "focalized/emphatic" reading, as observed in the previous discourse studies (Jun 2005, E. Ko 2000, H. Lee 2006b, Matsuda 1995). By contrast, overt realization of Nom Case in (5a) does not necessarily give rise to a focalized interpretation, which is another instance of subject-object asymmetry of Case realization.

In sum, the subject-object asymmetries, D-linking asymmetries, non-specific adjective modification with regard to non-Case-marking mentioned so far are listed in Table 1, 2 & 3.

Table 1: Subject-object asymmetries on non-Case-marking

Canonical	Subjects	Objects
Non-Case-Marking	Impossible	Possible

Table 2: Asymmetries on non-Case-marking and D-linking restriction

Non-Case-Marked WH	Subjects	Fronted Objects	In-Situ Objects
D-linked Reading	Possible	Possible	Possible
Non-D-linked Reading	Impossible	Impossible	Possible

Table 3: Asymmetries on non-specific adjective modification

Non-Case-Marked	Subjects	Objects
Non-Specific Adjective Modification	Impossible	Possible

This paper aims to correctly predict various kinds of subject-object asymmetries of morphological Case realization under the formal syntactic treatment.

2. Bare NP Object vs. Bare Subject /Dislocated NPs

We suggest that bare NPs can occur in the complement position of V since it can be part of a syntactic complex predicate. In other words, the bare NP object has dual function: namely, it fulfills as an argument of the subcategorizing verb, and it also forms a predicate with the selecting verb in syntax. We claim that this option is only available with bare NPs in Korean (but not Case-marked DPs, for example). Note that this option is excluded if a bare NP occurs outside of V domain. Thus, we can account for the grammatical contrast between (6a) and (6b).

(6) a. Mary-ka   **Chelswu-**∅ manna-ss-e.
       Mary-Nom Chelswu   meet-Past-Dec
       'Mary met Chelswu.'
   b. *Chelswu-lul **Mary-**∅ manna-ss-e.
       Chelswu-Acc Mary   meet-Past-Dec
       'Chelswu, Mary met.'

The nominal *Chelswu* in a VP-internal position in (6a) can be part of a syntactic complex predicate, so a bare NP object is allowed there. This option, by contrast, is not possible in the case of the nominal *Mary* in Spec-T, a VP–external position in (6b).

Regarding the appearance of bare subject NPs in noncanonical subject positions, we adopt a proposal in Ahn (1999) that these bare subjects can be analyzed as Left-Dislocated (LDed) NPs:

(7) Mary$_i$-∅ *pro*$_i$ ku chayk ilk-ess-ni?
    Mary   the book   read-Past-Q
    'Did Mary read that book?'

In (7), although *Mary* is not in a complement position of V, a nominative Case marker can be absent. *Mary* in (7) is analyzed as an LDed NP in a left peripheral position with a null resumptive *pro* in its base-generated position.

Note that LD option is not available for the analysis of the bare subject NP in (6b) since LDed phrases cannot be embedded by other scrambled/moved elements cross-linguistically (see Grohmann 2003).

The next task is how to derive D-linked property of LDed nominals. Boeckx (2003; 2004) and Boeckx & Grohmann (2004) put forward that the peculiar property of LD hinges on the special type of movement.

(8) NP$_i$....[$_{TP}$...[$_{DP}$ RP [<NP$_i$>]]...]

In (8), a resumptive pronoun, RP and its antecedent, NP form a constituent and the resumptive chain is a result of sub-extraction of the NP. We assume with Boeckx (2003) that the resumptive chain results in the D-linked interpretation. The particular derivational step is called SubMove (Boeckx & Grohmann 2004:11). In line with this reasoning, we assume (10) for (9).

(9) Nwukwu Yenghi-lul   manna-ss-ni?
    Who   Yenghi-Acc meet-Past-Q
    'Who is such that he/she met Yenghi?'

(10)

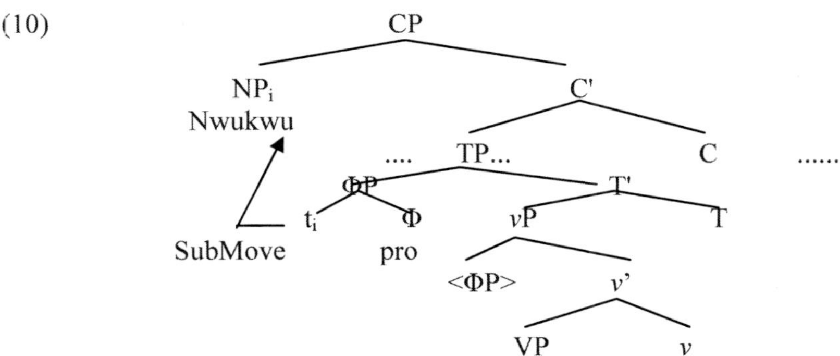

Movement of the bare NP to Spec-C is triggered by the theta-theoretic requirement because the NP cannot obtain a theta role in Φ P since the head of Φ P, namely *pro*, absorbs the theta-role assigned by *v*. Note that *pro* and its antecedent are distinct syntactic entities and they form a constituent upon First Merge. The movement of ΦP to Spec-T is triggered by Φ-features on T (Agree). Note further that the NP undergoes SubMove to Spec-C where it gets a theta-role "aboutness," so it fulfills the Full Interpretation. Consequently, the chain <*nwukwu, pro*> induces only D-linked reading like many other *wh*-resumption or *wh*-clitic doubling constructions (Boeckx 2003, Boeckx & Grohmann 2004, Jaeger 2003 and others).

  A similar explanation is possible for (11). In (11), a non-Case-marked object *wh*-phrase occurs in a left periphery position, and only D-linked interpretation is induced.

(11) Nwukwu Yenghi-ka   manna-ss-ni?
     Who   Yenghi-Nom meet-Past-Q
     'Who is such that Yenghi meet (him/her)?'

Under our analysis, the object *wh*-phrase *nwukwu* in (11) is LDed. Then *nwukwu* undergoes SubMove, leaving *pro* in its base-generated position shown in (12), and the D-linked property of dislocated *wh*-object results.

(12) [$_{CP}$ [$_{NP}$ Nwukwu]$_i$ [$_{TP}$ Yenghi-ka$_j$ [$_{vP}$ t$_j$ [t$_i$ pro]..]T]C]
                                              SubMove

Note further that the parallel behavior between scrambled bare objects and bare subjects cannot be captured under the functional analyses. Put another way, the functional analyses focus basically on functional roles (i.e. subject/object), so the semantic properties of dislocated bare NPs cannot be captured under this proposal. Our formal analysis, on the other hand, is concerned with structural positions of bare NPs (i.e. VP-internal vs. VP-external), and can provide a uniform account for the previously observed semantic restriction of the subject WH and scrambled WH based on syntactic principles since they are all LDed.

3. Semantic/Pragmatic Implications

The structural difference between bare NP subjects and bare NP objects correctly predicts the high occurrence rate of bare NPs in complement positions. Given that the bare NP in a complement position can freely occur as part of a syntactic predicate, restrictions on the bare NP are predicted to be relatively weak. Put differently, the presence of bare objects in canonical positions is grammatically unmarked, and is not regulated by any semantic/pragmatic constraints. By contrast, the dislocated bare NPs in non-complement positions are grammatically designed as such to exhibit extra discourse semantics. Therefore, unlike bare NPs in complement position, those in VP-external positions are expected to be distributionally more marked and semantically more restricted (see D. Lee 2002, Ohara 2001, Shimojo 2006 for similar facts in Japanese).

Given that 1st and 2nd person subjects are given information in the discourse, they are more likely to function as LDed nominals that trigger D-linked reading or topical reading, compared with 3rd person subjects. The relevant examples that may support this argument are given in (13). ('!' indicates a marked use in discourse.)

(13) a. Ne-(!ka)   etiey ka-ss-ni?
     You-Nom where go-Past-Q   'Where did you go?'
   b. Ne-(!ka) kwail-ul elmana sa-ss-ni?
     you-Nom fruit-Acc how many buy-Past-Q 'How many fruits did you buy?'
   c. Wuli-(!ka) etilo   ka-l-kka?
     We-Nom where go-Fut-Q   'Where will we go?'
   d. Wuli-(!ka) mwusun yenghwa bo-l-kka?
     We-Nom   what   movie   watch-Fut-Q 'What movie will we watch?'

S.Ko (2002: 237) notes that the bare NP forms are strongly preferred in (13). Since the referents of 1st and 2nd person subjects are pragmatically assumed in their context, bare NP subjects, which are LDed nominals, are more coherent in these contexts. The unnaturalness of subjects with Nominative Case marker -ka is accounted for parallel to *ga*-marked subjects in Japanese, as discussed in Kuno (1972). According to Kuno (1972: 273), -*ga* as a subject marker in the matrix sentence always signals that the subject conveys new, unpredictable information. Note that the speaker's or hearer's existence or coming into existence is presupposed in a regular conversational discourse. Therefore, it is implausible for the speaker to talk about his or addressee's existence or appearance at the place of his speaking as if it were an entirely new event. This seems to be why all the first/second person nominals with -*ka* marker make the relevant sentences much more unnatural.

We can also account for the contrast that S.Ko (2002: 237) observes for the third person subject which can occur with or without a nominative Case marker, as shown in (14).

(14) a. Chelswu-(ka) etilo ka-ss-ni?
     Chelswu-Nom where go-Past-Q   'Where did Chelswu go?'
   b. Chelswu-(ka) mwusun yenghwa-lul po-ni?
     Chelswu-Nom what movie watch-Q   'What movie does Chelswu watch?'

Since referents of third person subjects are not pragmatically assumed in the discourse, the occurrence of -*ka* marker doesn't make the sentences unnatural unless the subject is mentioned in the previous discourse or presupposed.

Our analysis can further be confirmed by the following examples, which are Korean counterparts of Japanese examples discussed in Kuno (1972).

(15) a. Na-nun i   hoysa-uy pwuhoycang-i-ta.

I-Top   this company vice-president-Cop-Dec
     'I am a vice-president in the company.'
  b. Nay-ka i   hoysa-uy pwuhoycang-i-ta.
     I-Nom this company vice-president-Cop-Dec
     'I am the only vice-president in the company.'
  c. Na-∅ i   hoysa-uy pwu-hoycang-i-ta.
     I   this company vice-president-Cop-Dec
     'I am a vice-president in the company.'

Kuno (1972: 283) observes the subject with the overt Nominative -*ga* marker implies that there are no other vice-presidents in the company. This is, according to him, due to the force of exhaustive listing of -*ga*. He observes that such a connotation does not exist with a topic maker, or with no markers. The same contrasts are found in Korean, as in (15). This contrast is correctly predicted under the LD/sentence-topic analysis of bare NP subjects. LDed NPs share some discourse properties with topics such as specificity or D-Linkedness, so the paradigm naturally follows.

   The following examples further confirm the fact that presence of -*ka* marker is enforced by exhaustive listing meaning the referent has (cf. Ono et al 2000: 70).

(16) Wuli cip-un yecha-*(ka) motwu khu-ta
     our family woman-Nom all big-Dec   'As for my family, women are all big.'
(17) A: Etten tongali-ey kaipha-yess-ni?
        which club join-Past-Q   'Which club did you join?'
     B: Yengehoyhwa-*(ka) cohtako sayngkakhapni-ta
        English conversation-Nom good think-Dec
        'I think that English conversation club may be good.'

In this case, a speaker uses *ka*-marked nominal X in order to convey the following meaning: the meaning of 'X (and only X) ...' or 'It is X that ...' Therefore, the nominal with -*ka* is generally a discourse-new information. Given the fact that Bare NPs in subject positions are either LDed nominals or sentence topics, they are predicted to be ruled out in (16-17).

   The analysis advanced here further explains the fact that definite subjects such as pronouns and names show the higher rate of Case deletion than low definite ones (see H.Lee 2006a,c, K.Lee 2002, Masunaga 1988, Ono et al. 2000, Yatabe 1999).

(18) a. Ce-∅ hyuka-lul   daum tal-lo   milwu-ess-e-yo.
        I   vacation-Acc next month-lo postpone-Past-Dec
        'I (humble) postponed my vacation to next month.'
     b. Ahn Sungbae haksayng-∅   sihem-ul an machiko   nays-e-yo.
        Ahn Sungbae student exam-Acc   not complete submit-Past-Dec.
        'Ahn Sungbae student submitted the exam without completing it.' (cf. H.Lee 2006a: 77)

Definite expressions referring to individuals already known to the hearer are more likely to function as sentence topics or as LDed nominals, and hence definite subjects are expected to occur more frequently without Nom Case than low definite ones.

   Our analysis also makes a correct prediction about bare NP subjects in specific/non-specific contexts in (5), repeated here as in (19).

(19) a. (Yeysnal-ey) **han/etten namca-*(ka)** sal-ass-ta.
        long.time-at a/a.certain man-(Nom)   live-Past-Dec
        '(Long time ago) there was a man lived.'
     b. (Yeysnal-ey) Mary-ka **han/etten namca-(lul)** manna-ss-ta.

long.time-at M.-Nom a/a.certain man-(Acc)   meet-Past-Dec
'(Long time ago) Mary met a man.'

In (19a), the bare NP is not allowed because the modifier *han/etten* can license only nonspecific nominals. Since the bare NP subject is inherently specific or D-linked, it cannot co-occur with nonspecific marker semantically. Note, however, that this restriction doesn't apply to bare NP objects. Thus, in (19b), under our analysis, a bare NP object is a purely optional counterpart of the Accusative Case-marked NP, which can be generated as part of a complex predicate. An Accusative Case marker on the object can be freely unpronounced with non-specific modifier.

Note further that as observed in the previous discourse studies, overt realization of Acc Case in (19b) may induce a "focal" reading (Jun 2005, E.Ko2000, S.Lee2006, Matsuda 1995). By contrast, overt realization of Nom Case in (19a) does not necessarily give rise to a focal interpretation.

This minimal difference implies that our syntactic treatment of Nom/Acc asymmetry is on the right track. In other words, the presence of Nom Case is compulsory in canonical subject position, viz., in non-dislocated position. Thus, overt Nom Case should cover wider range of discourse information in contrast to overt Acc Case considering pragmatic division of labor. Note further that Acc Case in dislocated position, namely, in scrambled position cannot be absent. Thus, it is predicted that the appearance of Acc Case on scrambled NPs does not necessarily give rise to focalization effects on a par with that of Nom Case in canonical subject position. Hence the scrambled NP in (20a) is not necessarily focalized unless it receives extra focal strategy such as special prosody and the like.

(20) a. Way ecey   **Chelswu-lul** Mary-ka   manna-ss-ni?
        why yesterday Chelswu-Acc Mary-Nom meet-Past-Q   (neutral reading is unmarked)
     b. Way ecey   Mary-ka   **Chelswu-lul** manna-ss-ni?
        why yesterday Mary-Nom Chelswu-Acc meet-Past-Q   (focal reading is unmarked)
      'Why did Mary meet Chelswu yesterday?'

Although the judgment is subtle, (20b) contrasts with (20a) in that only the Acc Case-marked object in-situ is more likely to be focalized as in (20b).

Note that the focalization in (20b) is contrastive, which crucially differs from completive focus/information, informational focus, or presentational focus. With this in mind, consider the following examples:

(21) (Over the phone)
     Nay-ka cikum ne-(!lul) pole ka-l-kkey
     I-Nom now you-Acc see go-Fut-Dec   'I'll go to see you now.'
(22) isang   iss-umyen i mwulken-(!ul) pakkwule olkkey-yo
     problem be-found-if this item-Acc exchange go-Dec
     'If a problem is found, I will return this item.'   (S. Ko 2004: 228)

In (21), *ne* 'you' cannot indicate new information and doesn't perform identification function. Thus, unless you intend to emphasize/focalize who you are going to see, the bare NP is preferred in neutral context. A similar explanation can be given in (22). In normal context, it is not necessary to focalize the item you are going to return if it has a problem. In other words, it is naturally expected that malfunctioning items will be returned to the store within a warranty period. Thus, the appearance of Acc marker on the object in (22) is predicted to be unnatural in the usual context under our conception of the functional role of overt Acc Case.

S. Lee (2006) proposes that bare NPs without Acc markers are more restricted or "marked" from the perspective of neo-Gricean pragmatics, utilizing Levinson's (2000) pragmatic inferences. His argument is based on the contrast between Case-marked object and bare NP object in (23).

(23) a. Yengho-nun   Seoul Yek   tayhapsil-eyse   kwutwu-lul tak-ass-ta
        Yengho-Top Seoul Station waiting-room-at shoes-Acc shine-Past-Dec
        'Yengho had his shoes shined at Seoul Station waiting room.'
     b. Yengho-nun   Seoul Yek   tayhapsil-eyse kwutwu-Ø tak-ass-ta.
        Yengho-Top Seoul Station waiting room-at shoes   shine-Past-Dec
        'Yengho was a shoeshine boy at Seoul Station waiting room.'

Unlike the Case-marked form *kwutwu-lul* 'shoes-Acc' in (23a), the Caseless form *kwutwu-Ø* 'shoes' in (23b) is more likely to induce idiomatic reading with its predicate *takassta* 'shined'. Hence, *kwutwu-Ø tak-ass-ta* tends to be interpreted as 'he was a shoe-shine boy'. A similar contrast is given in (24).

(24) a. Nehi apeci-nun   tayhakkyo tanil-cekey Shin Sung-Il ppyam-ul   chi-ess-ta
        Your father-Top college go-when   Shin Sung-Il cheek-Acc hit-Past-Dec
        'When your father was a college student, he hit Shin Seung-Il's cheek.'
     b. Nehi apeci-nun   tayhakkyo tanil-cekey Shin Sung-Il ppyam-Ø chi-ess-ta
        Your father-Top college go-when   Shin Sung-Il cheek   hit-Past-Dec
        'When your father was a college student, he was more handsome than the handsome actor Shin Sung-Il'

Unlike (24b), the Caseless form *ppyam* 'cheek' in (24b) only induces idiomatic reading 'outdo' with its predicate *chi-* 'hit'. (24a), in contrast, induces only literal reading. Thus, it seems that "*ppyam + chi-*" in (24b) is conventionalized as an idiom unlike "*kwutwu ttakk-*" in (24b).
  The complex predicate formation approach to the bare object NPs advanced here correlates directly with this consequence, dispensing with additional (meta)-pragmatic functions since idioms in general can be analyzed as extended complex predicate formations (Marantz 1984; Larson 1988).

(25) 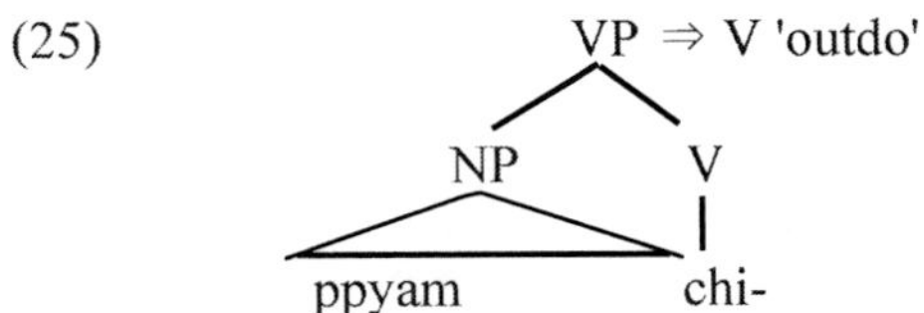

If the preferred or obligatory idiomatic readings with bare objects can be explained by complex predicate formation as in (25), our general claim is still sustained: namely, bare NPs in complement positions are unmarked forms and Acc-marked forms are marked ones containing special information since idioms are usually derived from unmarked formation across languages.
  Crosslinguistly, contrasts similar to (20) are detected in Accusative Case variation in Kannada. Lidz (2006) observes that Acc Case-marked objects receive a specific interpretation only when this morphological marking is optional (this is the case within animate direct objects). When the Accusative Case morpheme is obligatory, specificity effects are positional and are not due to the presence of the morpheme (this is the case with animate direct objects, for instance). In this case, additional morphology is required in order to achieve the specific interpretation. In Korean, the morphological marker *-nun* (often called Topic marker) is widely employed in subject positions to make semantic/pragmatic distinction from Nom Case, instead of overt/covert Nom distinction. The marker *-nun*, however, occurs only in certain very limited contexts in object positions since we can exploit overt/covert Acc distinction here quite freely for "soft" pragmatic distinctions including focalzation/emphasis or implicature (S. Lee 2006). The presence or absence of Nom

Case, on the other hand, gives rise to "hard" semantic/pragmatic effects such as specificity, definiteness, D-Linking, and the like. Thus, extra uses of the marker *-nun* with subjects (and perhaps with the dislocated NPs in general) are relatively more frequent and significant than the one with the objects in situ on pragmatic considerations.

4. Conclusion

In this paper, we have explored subject-object asymmetries of morphological Case realization and semantic/pragmatic implications under the formal analysis proposed by Ahn & Cho (2006; 2007b). According to Ahn & Cho (2006; 2007b), bare NP objects and subjects have different structural sources: bare NP objects form a "syntactic" complex predicate with subcategorizing verb, whereas bare NP subjects are LDed nominals. Hence, the distribution of bare NP subjects is closely related to discourse properties. Specifically, we have shown that such structural difference between bare NP subjects and bare NP objects results in various kind of asymmetries: high occurrence rate of bare NP objects, person/definiteness effects in bare NP subjects, and presence or absence of D-linked interpretation for bare WHs. We also discussed the contexts where overt morphological Case marking is strongly preferred. When the speaker wants to convey the meaning of 'X (and only X) ...' or 'It is X that ...', the subject nominal generally occurs with *-ka* marker. The object nominal, by contrast, occurs with *-lul* marker mostly when contrastive focalization/emphasis is given to it. Our formal account of subject-object asymmetries concerning non-pronunciation of Case markers in Korean sharply contrasts with the functional approaches such as H. Lee (2006a-c) which might basically exploit the idea that subjects and objects prototypically differ with respect to the hierarchies of person, animacy and definiteness. Our analysis can present a firm basis for these hierarchies that underlie the functional flavor of Case marking variations.

References

Ahn, H-D. 1999. Notes on case deletion. In Y-W. Kim, Il-Kon Kim, and J-W. Park, eds.,*Linguistic Investigation: In honor of In-Seok Yang*, 1-16. Seoul: Hankuk Publishing Co.

Ahn, H-D and S. Cho. 2006. *Wh*-topics and unpronounced case markers. *Studies in Generative Grammar* 16: 61-90.

Ahn, H-D and S. Cho. 2007a. Subject-object asymmetries of morphological case realization. *Language and Information* 11, 53-76.

Ahn, H-D and S. Cho. 2007b. Non-Case-Marked *Wh*-Phrases and Left-Dislocation. *University of Maryland Working Papers in Linguistics* 16, ed. A. Omaki, I. Ortega-Santos, J. Sprouse and M. Wagers, 111-141. College Park, MD: UMWPiL.

Boeckx, C. 2003. *Islands and chains*. Amsterdam: John Benjamins.

Boeckx, C and K. Grohmann. 2004. SubMove: Towards a unified account of scrambling and D-linking. In *Peripheries*, eds. D. Adger, Cécil de cat and G. Tsoulas, 241-257. Dordrecht: Kluwer.

Hong, S. 1985. *A and A' binding in Korean and English: Government-Binding parameters*. Doctoral dissertation, University of Connecticut, Storrs.

Jaeger, T. F. 2003. Topics first! In- and outside of Bulgarian *wh*-interrogatives. *Proceedings of the 10th International Conference on HPSG*: 181-202.

Jun, Y. 2005. On the so-called specificity markers in Korean. *Korean Journal of Linguistics* 30: 715-743.

Ko, E-S. 2000. A discourse analysis of the realization of objects in Korean. *Japanese/Korean Linguistics* 9: 195–208. CSLI Publications, Stanford.

Ko, S-j. 2002. On the meaning of *ka* [in Korean]. *Korean Linguistics* 40: 221-246.

Ko, S-j. 2004. *A study of modern Korean particles* I [in Korean]. Hankuk Publishing Company.

Kuno, S. 1972. Functional sentence perspective: A case study from Japanese and English.

Linguistic Inquiry 3: 269-320.

Larson, R. 1988. On the double object construction. *Linguistic Inquiry* 19: 335-392.

Lee, D-Y. 2002. The function of the zero particle with special reference to spoken Japanese. *Journal of Pragmatics* 34: 645–682.

Lee, H. 2006a. Effects of focus and markedness hierarchies on object case ellipsis in Korean. *Discourse and Cognition* 13: 205-231.

Lee, H. 2006b. Iconicity and variation in the choice of object forms in Korean. *Language Research* 42: 323-355.

Lee, H. 2006c. Parallel optimization in case systems: Evidence from case ellipsis in Korean. *Journal of East Asian Linguistics* 15: 69–96.

Lee, K. 2002. Nominative case marker deletion in spoken Japanese: An analysis from the perspective of information structure. *Journal of Pragmatics* 34: 683–709.

Lee, S. 2006. A pragmatic analysis of accusative case-marker deletion. *Discourse and Cognition* 13: 69-89.

Lidz, J. 2006. The grammar of accusative case in Kannada. *Language* 82: 10-32.

Marantz, A. *On the nature of grammatical relations.* Cambridge, Mass.: MIT Press.

Masunaga, K. 1988. Case deletion and discourse context. In W. J. Poser, ed., *Papers from the Second International Workshop on Japanese Syntax*, 145–156. Stanford: CSLI.

Matsuda, K. 1995. Variable zero-marking of (*o*) in Tokyo Japanese. PhD Thesis, University of Pensylvania.

Montabetti, M. 1984. *After binding: On the interpretation of pronouns.* Doctoral dissertation. MIT, Cambridge, MA.

Ohara, M. 2001. Configurationality in Japanese: How grammatical functions are determined. Ms. Shimane University.

Ono, T, S. A. Thompson, and R. Suzuki. 2000. The pragmatic nature of the so-called subject marker ga in Japanese: evidence from conversation. *Discourse studies* 2: 55–84.

Pesetsky, D. 1987. *Wh* in situ: movement and unselective binding. In E. Reuland and A. Ter Meulen, ed., *The representation of (in)definiteness*, 98-129, Cambridge, Mass.: MIT press.

Lidz, J. 2006. The grammar of accusative case in Kannada. *Language* 82: 10-32.

Shimojo, M. 2006. Properties of particle "omission" revisited. *Toronto Working Papers in Linguistics* 26: 123–140.

Yatabe, S. 1999. Particle ellipsis and focus projection in Japanese. *Language, Information, Text* 6: 79–10.

Analyzer to Identify Phrases and the Functional Roles in Sentences: Its Architectural Aspects[*]

Yukiko Sasaki Alam

Department of Digital Media, Hosei University
3-7-2 Kajino-cho, Koganei, Tokyo 184-8584, Japan
sasaki@hosei.ac.jp

Abstract. This paper presents the architectural aspects of the phrase analyzer that attempts to recognize phrases and identify the functional roles in the sentences in formal Japanese documents. Since the object of interest is a phrase, the current system, designed in an object-oriented architecture, contains the *Phrase* class, and makes use of the linguistic generalization about languages with Case markers that a phrase, whether a noun phrase, a verb phrase, a postposition (or preposition) phrase or a clause phrase, can be separated into the content and the function components. Without a dictionary, and drawing on the orthographic information on the words to parse, it also contains a class that identifies the types of characters, a class representing grammar, and a class playing the role of a controller. The system has a simple and intuitive structure, externally and internally, and therefore is easy to modify and extend.

Keywords: Phrase analyzer, Morphological analyzer, Functional roles of phrases, Japanese

1. Introduction

This paper describes the architecture of the small-scale phrase analyzer that attempts to parse into phrases texts transcribed wherever applicable in *Joyo Kanji* (frequently used Chinese characters), and to identify the functional roles of the phrases in the sentences. Such texts are found in articles in newspapers, professional magazines and journals, and government documents. Because there are no spaces between words in Japanese texts, word-breaking is not a straight-forward task. In the past there have been several morphological analyzers: notably, *Juman* (Kurohashi and Nagao, 2003) and *Chasen* (Matsumoto et al., 2000). The two large-scale analyzers parse Japanese texts into morphemes such as prefixes, suffixes, inflections, Case markers, particles and the components of compound words. The main task of the proposed system, however, is to parse sentences into phrases (not morphemes), and identify the functional roles of the phrases, because the objective is to understand sentences in terms of the functional roles of the phrases.

The second difference of the current system is that it is not intended to parse into phrases per se, but to identify the functional roles of the phrases. To recognize phrases, it resorts to a general characteristic of phrases in sentences found in formal documents. The general feature is that the component representing the content of a phrase is transcribed in *Kanji* (Chinese characters) or/and *Katakana* (phonetic characters used for transcribing words of foreign origin), and that the component expressing the function in *Hiragana* (phonetic characters used for transcribing words or morphemes of Japanese origin). There have been developed such morphological analyzers that exploit the orthographic difference between the content and

---

functional components of phrases: to name a few, Asahara (2003), Kazama (2001), Kashioka et al (1998), and Kameda (1996). All of them, unlike the current system, focus on the parsing into morphemes or phrases, but not on the identification of the functional roles of the phrases.

The third feature different from other systems is that it is purely rule-based, unlike Kudo (2002), Sekine (2001), Uchimoto (2002), Kanayama et al (2000), and Haruno et al. (1999), all of which are statistically modeled.

To give an idea of an output parsed by the current system, an example is given in Table 1.

Table 1: A successful output.

05年度は中途採用を当初計画の20人から最大150人まで拡大。
zero-go-nen-do-wa-chuuto-saiyo-o-tousho-keikaku-no
(0-5-fiscal-year-Topic-midway-employment-Object-initial-plan-of)
-nijuu-nin-kara-saidai-hyakugojuu-nin-made-kakudai
(-20-person-from-at-most-150-person-to-expansion)

内容	機能	文法的役割
05年度	は	話題 (TOPIC)
中途採用	を	目的語 (OBJECT)
当初計画	の	名詞修飾句 (NOMINAL MODIFIER)
20人	から	始点 (POINT OF DEPARTURE)
最大150人	まで	継続終点 (UP-TO)
拡大	(省略)	名詞止め文 (NOUN-ENDING SENTENCE)

The first column in the table contains the content components, the second the functional components, the third the descriptions of the functional roles. The meaning of the parsed sentence is that in the fiscal year of 2005, (the company) expanded the number of midway employment from the initially planned 20 to 150.

The present paper first describes the components of the system and the relations among them, then discusses the pros and cons before ending with a short conclusion.

2. Architecture

The current system is structured in an object-oriented design, comprising four classes (or programs). The main is the *MorphAlgorithm* class, and it is supported by the remaining three classes: the *Phrase*, *Grammar* and *CharIdentifier* classes. The object-oriented design facilitates the creation of classes that represent concepts we are already familiar with, and thus helps us understand the functions of the classes and the interaction between them. Since the current system attempts to parse sentences into phrases, it has classes representing the parsing algorithm, the syntactic unit of phrase, and the grammar containing grammatical information. In addition, the system is provided with a class named *CharIdentifier* so that it is able to recognize the types of characters, because it parses texts transcribed in *Joyo Kanji* (frequently used Chinese characters) wherever applicable, and thus makes use of the orthographic difference in the transcription of the content and the functional parts of phrases. Figure 1 below shows a simplified state chart in UML (Unified Modeling Language) for illustrating the relations among the classes in the current system.

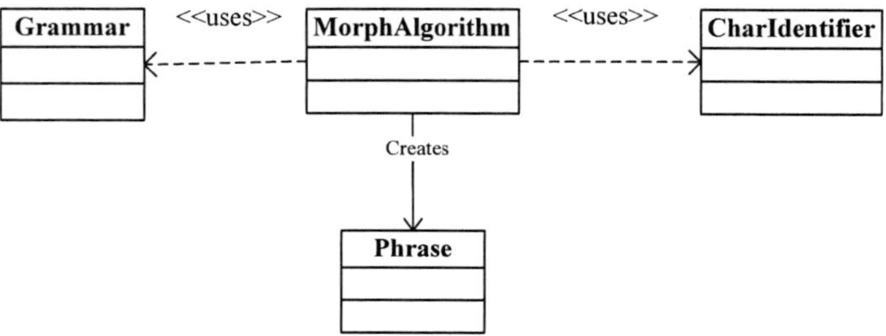

Figure 1: A simplified state chart diagram for the current system.

Below comes a more detailed description of each class in the current system.

2.1. The *MorphAlgorithm* class

The *MorphAlgorithm* class[1] is the main class of the present system that controls the process of recognizing phrases and identifying the functional roles played in the sentences of the text. The target texts are articles in newspapers, magazines, professional journals and public documents that are transcribed wherever applicable by using so called *Joyo Kanji* (frequently used Chinese characters). In such texts, the content parts of phrases are likely to be transcribed in *Kanji* (Chinese characters) or/and *Katakana* (phonetic characters used for transcribing words of foreign origin). At the same time most parts that indicate the functions of phrases are written in *Hiragana* (phonetic characters for transcribing words of Japanese origin). The system utilizes these orthographic features to recognize phrases, and identify the content and the functional parts. In addition, it resorts to another feature characteristic of Japanese (a head-final language) that the functional part is located at the end of a phrase.

The *MorphAlgorithm* class first cleans up the sentences to parse, for instance, by removing a tab stop and a new line characters. All the sentences in the text are appended into a *StringBuffer* instance, and are dealt with one sentence at a time. The algorithm that makes up the backbone of the *MorphAlgorithm* class (illustrated on Appendix A in this paper) is discussed in detail in Alam (2007). The following is a synopsis of the algorithm.

The algorithm first looks for a character or characters that are unacceptable at the beginning of a phrase. Such a character or characters are a period, a comma, a parenthesis and characters indicating a complementizer.[2] After examining these elements, the algorithm yet has to look for another irregular situation before going on to find a typical phrase with the content section consisting of *Kanji* or/and *Katakana*, followed by the functional *Hiragana* part. The irregular case is that a phrase, in particular, the content part begins with a *Hiragana* character. When it finds only one *Hiragana* character followed by a *Kanji* or a *Katakana*, it checks if the *Hiragana* is an honorific prefix. If not, and followed by another *Hiragana*, it keeps reading *Hiragana* characters until it hits a character that is not a *Hiragana*. Then the *Hiragana* sequence is assumed to be a phrase, and sent to the procedure in order to find the functional role of the phrase by its ending part.

When the algorithm does not find a *Hiragana* at the beginning of the phrase, but a *Kanji* or a *Katakana*, it keeps reading it until it meets a character that is not a *Kanji* or a *Katakana*. It

---

[1] The current system is written in Java programming language, in which a software system consists of many sets of programs called *classes*. Each *class* is a model that is a collection of procedures (called *methods*) and data (called *data fields*) used in the procedures. A *class* can be instantiated, and the instance can be used by another *class*. Some *classes* (often called *utility classes*) may never be constructed as instances, but the *methods* may be called and utilized by other *classes*.

[2] A *complementizer* is an element similar to *that* in *I think that many people like the movie.* と (pronounced 'toh') is a complementizer in Japanese. A complementizer cannot appear at the beginning of a phrase in Japanese, a Head-final language.

furthermore checks if the character that is not a *Kanji* or a *Katakana* is other than a *Hiragana* such as a period, a bracket or a comma. If it is, the sequence of *Kanji* or/and *Katakana* is a phrase that has the functional part omitted, and the phrase is marked accordingly (like an example presented in Table 1). When the sequence of *Kanji* or/and *Katakana* is followed by a *Hiragana* or a sequence of *Hiragana*, the phrase is probably a phrase typically found in a text targeted in the present system, and is sent to the procedure in order to find what functional role represented by the *Hiragana* or the sequence of *Hiragana*. As seen above, the *MorphAlgorithm* class is a class that controls the present system.

2.2. The *Phrase* class

The *Phrase* class represents a phrase, a syntactic unit that forms a sentence together with other phrases. A phrase is a group of words that are ofen used together and that have a special meaning and function. Among them are a noun phrase, a verb phrase, a preposition (or postposition) phrase, and a clause phrase. All the phrases can be separated into the content part that contains information on the meaning of the phrase, and the function part that indicates the functional role of the phrase played in the sentence. The function part is located at the end of a phrase in Japanese, a Head-final language. In formal Japanese documents, the content part tends to be transcribed in *Kanji* or/and *Katakana* while the function part in *Hiragana*. The current system has created the *Phrase* class by making use of these generalizations or likelihoods.

The *Phrase* class has many accessor methods, which are shown in Table 2. Whenever the algorithm in the *MorphAlgorithm* class detects the beginning boundary or the ending boundary of a phrase, that position on the sentence is recorded in the current instance of the *Phrase* class by calling the *setter* methods like *setHead* and *setNonhead*, listed in Table 2, and once the process of the current *Phrase* instance is complete, information contained in the instance is printed out by calling the *getter* methods such as *getHead* and *getNonhead*.

At present all the phrase instances processed in the sentence are not stored in a container of a *Collection* class, but once processed (or printed out) they are discarded. There might be a need in the future to store information in all the *Phrase* instances of a sentence, for instance, to identify an embedded clause such as a relative clause and a complementizer phrase or to disambiguate between adverbial and adjectival uses of preposition (or postposition) phrases. The current system can accomodate such a change, but that would require much of semantic study before implementation.

Table 2: Accessor methods in the *Phrase* class.

setters	getters
setHead	*getHead*
setNonhead	*getNonhead*
setGramRole	*getGramRole*
setHeadStart	*getNonheadStart*
setHeadEnd	*getHeadEnd*
setNonheadStart	*setNonheadStart*
setNonheadEnd	*getNonheadEnd*
setPhraseStart	*getPhraseStart*
setPhraseEnd	*getPhraseEnd*

During the process of looking for the beginning and the ending boundaries of the *Phrase* instance, the algorithm of the *MorphAlgorithm* class at the same time attempts to identify the grammatical role in terms of information provided by the *Grammar* class. Once obtained, information on the grammatical function of the *Phrase* instance is stored and printed out by calling the accessor methods in the *Phrase* instance.

2.3. The *Grammar* class

The *Grammar* class provides the *MorphAlgorithm* class with information on the functional roles of the function parts of phrases. For instance, Table 3 lists Case markers registered in the *Grammar* class.

Table 3: Case markers.

Case/ Particles	Pronun- ciation	Functional role(s)
が	ga	Subject marker
を	o	Object marker
は	wa	Topic marker
で	de	Place/Instrument/Conjunctive
へ	e	Goal
から	kara	Point of departure
まで	made	'up to/till'
より	yori	Point of departure (formal or archaic)

In addition, the *Grammar* class registers information on particles denoting conjunction (such as a particle denoting 'and'), clause particles that make up various clauses by immediately following sentences and propositions (such as a particle indicating 'because'), and particles denoting approximation (such as a particle indicating 'about'). See Alam (2007) for the list of all the grammatical information contained in the *Grammar* class.

Table 4 shows the names of the data fields (or data used in the methods) and the methods listed in the *Grammar* class. The prefix + indicates that the data field is a *public* data field while the prefix – a *private* one that is used only inside the *Grammar* class.

As the names of the data fields in Table 4 indicate, the functional particles, suffixes and inflections are first recognized by the number of *Hiragana* characters that make them up, and then are examined for the grammatical roles by calling the *getGrammaticalRole* method.

2.4. The *CharIdentifier* class

The *CharIdentifier* class is a utility class that helps identify the orthographic types of characters. The types identified by the class are *Kanji* (Chinese characters), *Katakana* (phonetic characters used for transcribing words of foreign origin), *Hiragana* (phonetic characters used for transcribing words of Japanese origin, Case markers, inflections, particles, etc.), Arabic numerals, the Roman alphabet, special symbols and punctuations. The methods used for identification are illustrated in Table 5.

Table 4: Data fields and methods in the *Grammar* class.

Grammar
+ONE_CHAR_GRAM_MARKERS
+TWO_CHAR_GRAM_MARKERS
+THREE_CHAR_GRAM_MARKERS
+FOUR_CHAR_GRAM_MARKERS
+FIVE_CHAR_GRAM_MARKERS
-TWO_CHAR_PARTICLES
-TWO_CHAR_VERBAL_SUFFIXES
-THREE_CHAR_PARTICLES
-THREE_CHAR_VERBAL_SUFFIXES
-THREE_CHAR_ADJECTIVE_SUFFIXES
-THREE_CHAR_CONJUNCTIVES
-FOUR_CHAR_PARTICLES
-FOUR_CHAR_VERBAL_SUFFIXES
-FIVE_CHAR_PARTICLES
-FIVE_CHAR_VERBAL_SUFFIXES
-FIVE_CHAR_GRAM_PARTICLES
-CONJ
-ADV
+getGrammaticalRole()
+isIn()

Table 5: Methods in the *CharIdentifier* class.

CharIdentifier
+isNumeric()
+isKatakana()
+isHiragana()
+isKanji()
+isValidChar()
+isComma()
+isPeriod()
+isParen()
+isOpenParen()
+isCloseParen
+isQuote()
+isOpenQuote()
+isCloseQuote()
+isDateAlone()
+isTimeSuffixAlone()
+isTimeNoun()

3. Discussion

The current system, without a dictionary, is fairly successful in parsing texts transcribed wherever applicable by *Joyo Kanji* (frequently used Chinese characters), but it is not able to parse successfully sentences containing successive phrases transcribed in *Hiragana*, because it recognizes the beginning of a phrase by finding a character that is not a *Hiragana*. Therefore, it fails to parse correctly such texts as those found in books for young children that are written without using Chinese characters. For a better treatment, it must be enriched by finding a minimum heuristic way of handling phrases transcribed in *Hiragana* that appear successively. The current system also fails to recognize, for instance, nouns consisting of a mixture of *Kanji* and *Hiragana* characters. As a heuristic means, it would be a good idea to install a special list of such nouns so that they could be recognized as content words.

The present system is a simple and light-weight rule-based analyzer, thus parsing texts at a high speed. It could be embedded in a large-scale system, and be employed in a mode dealing with texts such as articles in newspapers and professional magazines. The larger-scale system, with a dictionary, can come into use whenever having phrases exclusively in *Hiragana*.

Verb phrases appear typically in the form of the verbal stem (or root) transcribed in *Kanji*, followed by the (suffixes and) tense inflection transcribed in *Hiragana*. At present, the current system is equipped with a heuristic means of handling verb phrases, for instance, by listing each possible form. It would be feasible, however, to parse verb phrases fairly accurately, and not in a heuristic manner, because the orders in which the verb stems and the verbal suffixes/inflections occur are predictable. Such a morphological analyzer of verb phrases is under preparation. Once completed, this engine could be incorporated into the current system without difficulty. A foreseeable problem would be to locate a verb phrase. In Japanese, which is a head-final language, verb phrases appear at the end of sentences. This information helps recognize a verb phrase found at the end of a sentence, but verb phrases can appear at the end of clauses as well, for instance, at the end of relative clauses or complementizer phrases. For a better treatment, further linguistic study about clause boundaries would be needed.

Once a morphological analyzer of verb phrases is implemented in the present system, data fields in the *Grammar* class could get rid of much information on verbal suffixes and inflections, and eventually would contain a shorter list of functional elements to examine. As such data fields in the *Grammar* class are at present based on heuristics, the incorporation of a rule-based verb phrase morphological analyzer would transform the current system into a more principle-based system.

4. Conclusion

This paper has focused on the architecture of an analyzer to parse into phrases sentences in texts transcribed wherever applicable in *Joyo Kanji* (frequently used Chinese characters). Such texts are articles in newspapers, professional and technical magazines and government documents. The system is designed so that linguistic components are reflected in the programs. The design is simple and intuitive, and facilitates easy modification and extension. In spite of the limitations, this simple light-weight fast analyzer is fairly successful in recognizing phrases and identifying the functional roles played in the sentences. It could be used for many purposes: for instance, as a component in a larger system, as a tool preparing a dictionary, and as a preliminary analyzer of Japanese sentences.

References

Alam, Yukiko Sasaki. 2007. A Morpho-Syntactic Analyzer of Controlled Japanese. In T. H. King and E. M. Bender, ed., *Parallel Proceedings of GEAF 2007 Workshop*. Stanford, CA: CSLI Publications (CSLI Studies in Computational Linguistics ONLINE: http://csli-publications.stanford.edu/).

Asahara, Masayuki. 2003. *Corpus-based Japanese Morphological Analysis*. Ph.D. Thesis. Nara Institute of Science and Technology.

Fuchi, Takeshi and Shinichiro Takagi. 1998. Japanese Morphological Analyzer Using Word Co-occurrence. *Proceedings of the COLING*, pp. 409-413.

Haruno, Masahiko, Satoshi Shirai, and Yoshifumi Ooyama. 1999. Using Decision Trees to Construct a Practical Parser. *Machine Learning*, 34, 131-149.

Kameda, Masayuki. 1996. A Portable & Quick Japanese Parser: QJP. *Proceedings of the COLING*, pp. 616-621.

Kanayama, Hiroshi, Kentaro Torisawa, Yutaka Mitsuishi and Jun'ichi Tsujii. 2000. A Hybrid Japanese Parser with Hand-crafted Grammar and Statistics. *Proceedings of the COLING*, pp. 411-417.

Kashioka, Hideki, Yasuhiro Kawata and Yumiko Kinjo. 1998. Use of Mutual Information Based Character Clusters in Dictionary-less Morphological Analysis of Japanese. *Proceedings of the COLING*, pp. 658-662.

Kazama, Jun'ichi. 2001. *Adaptive Morphological Analysis with a Small Tagged Corpus*. Master Thesis. University of Tokyo.

Kurohashi, Sadao and Makoto Nagao. 2003. Building a Japanese Parsed corpus — While Improving the Parsing System. In Anne Abeille, ed., *Treebank Building Using Parsed Corpora*, pp. 249-260. Dordrecht, The Netherlands: Kluwer Academic Publishers.

Matsumoto, Yuji, Akira Kitauchi, TatsuoYamashita, Yoshitaka Hirano, Hiroshi Matsuda, Kazuma Takaoka and Masayuki Asahara. 2001. *Morphological Analysis System ChaSen version 2.2.4 Manual*. Nara, Japan: Nara Institute of Science and Technology.

Sekine, Satoshi. 2001. A Fast Japanese Sentence Analyzer. *Proceedings of the First International Workshop on MultiMedia Annotation*.

Suzuki, Hisami, Chris Brockett, and Gary Kacmarcik. 2000. Using a Broad-Coverage Parser for Word-Breaking in Japanese. *Proceedings of the COLING*, pp. 822-828.

Uchimoto, Kiyotaka, Masaki Murata, Satoshi Sekine and Hitoshi Isahara. 2000. Dependency Model Using Posterior Context. *Proceedings of the Sixth International Workshop on Parsing Technologies*, pp. 321-322.

Appendix: Algorithm employed in the *MorphAlgorithm* class (adopted from Alam 2007).

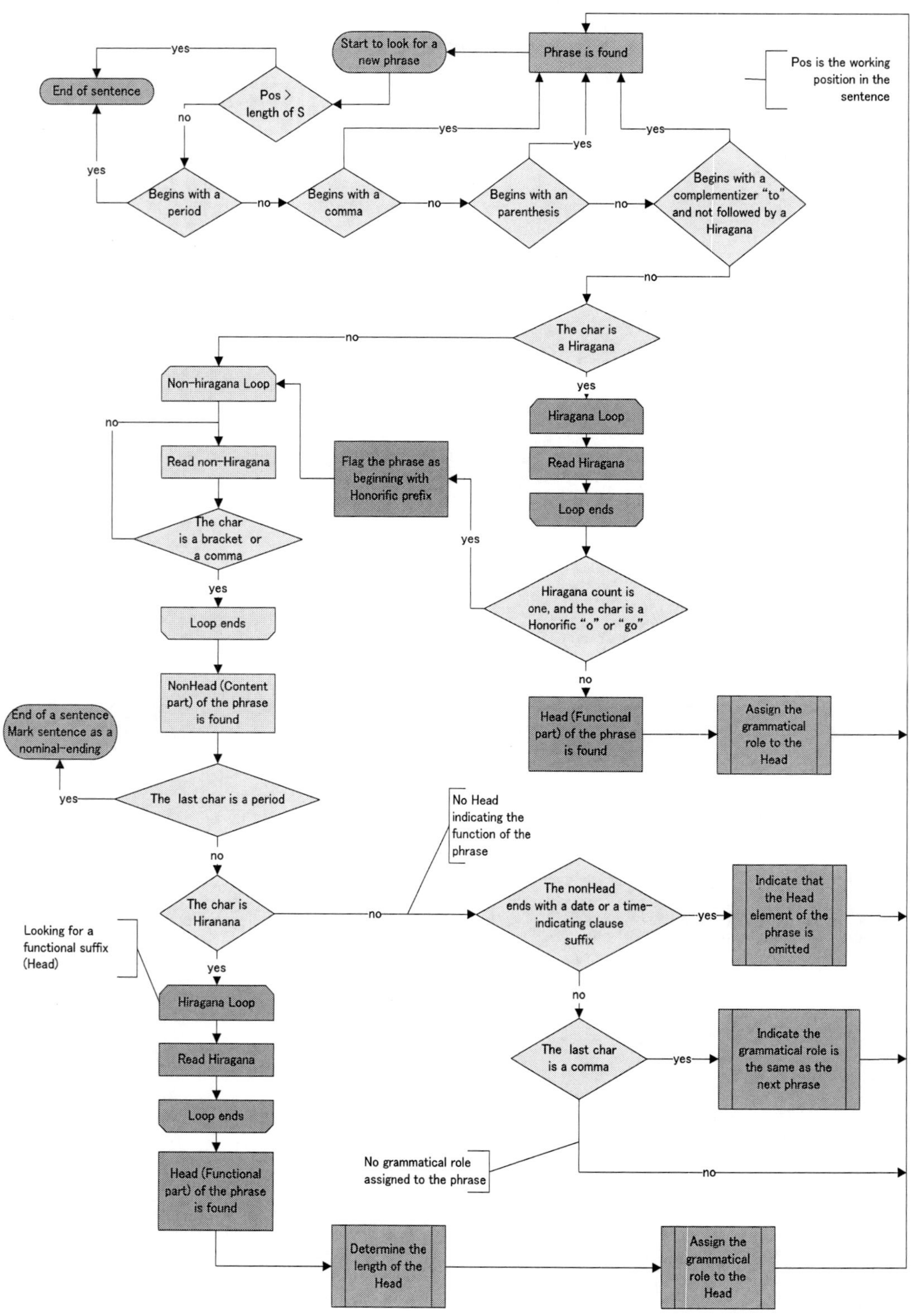

Opinion Extraction based on Syntactic Pieces[*]

Suguru Aoki and Kazuhide Yamamoto

Nagaoka University of Technology,
1603-1, Kamitomioka, Nagaoka, Niigata 940-2188 Japan
{aoki, ykaz}@nlp.nagaokaut.ac.jp

Abstract. This paper addresses a task of opinion extraction from given documents and its positive/negative classification. We propose a sentence classification method using a notion of *syntactic piece*. Syntactic piece is a minimum unit of structure, and is used as an alternative processing unit of n-gram and whole tree structure. We compute its semantic orientation, and classify opinion sentences into positive or negative. We have conducted an experiment on more than 5000 opinion sentences of multiple domains, and have proven that our approach attains high performance at 91% precision.

Keywords: syntactic piece, opinion extraction, sentence classification

1. Introduction

One can easily disseminate information through the Internet, that include their personal opinions, such as reputation and dissatisfaction with products, complaints about services, and so on. Weblogs and message boards in particular have attracted a great deal of attention as a new information source, since they enable us to obtain subjective opinions easily. In order to automatically extract useful information from these sources, various approaches have been proposed. (Inui and Okumura, 2006)

Researchers have been exploring techniques for classifying documents according to sentiment orientation, or positive/negative (p/n) in particular. Turney (2002) extracts phrases containing adjectives or adverbs, and determines their semantic orientation. Further, p/n of a document is judged by computing the average of the semantic orientations. The *NEAR* operator in the Alta Vista search engine is used in the method. If you search a query like *A NEAR B* in Alta Vista, the search engine shows pages containing within near words of each other. However, this operator is not provided in Japanese version.

Wang and Araki (2007) extend Turney's method into Japanese by collecting and using a set of words that contribute significantly to p/n orientation. Fujimura et al. (2004) use corpora divided into p/n words, and statistically classify a document by extracting opinions. These methods provide the semantic orientation only with bag-of-words. A word, however, contains little and partial information. Therefore, we assert that the scope of the process needs to be expanded. Moreover, these methods do not identify reasons for p/n judgment, that is, expressions that cause semantic orientation. For a commercial application, this function is essential in marketing research.

Besides these, other document classification approaches have also been   proposed, which prepare a semantic orientation dictionary in advance. Tateishi et al. (2004) construct this

---

dictionary in advance by extracting opinion triplets that consist of `object name, attribute expression, evaluative expression', and classify documents by using the triplets. The method extracts only expressions that appear in a definite pattern, and it is thus difficult to obtain satisfactory coverage and accuracy. Kobayashi et al. (2005) first extract a few opinion pairs of attribute and value with an anaphora resolution technique, and construct a semantic orientation dictionary of the pairs for a target domain. They then gradually expand the entries of the dictionary from the pair seed. However, if the accuracy of the primary pairs is not adequate, the quality of the dictionary becomes gradually poorer due to gradually involving noises. In addition, making the dictionary domain by domain is very expensive.

In this paper we do not use a word as an unit of tagging information to extract opinions. As other work does, we also think that a document can be classified when we only extract partial sentiment expressions. However, we do not think that bag-of-words approach is not suitable for this task, and we need something else instead. One can see this fact that, for example, the semantic orientation of a word can vary according to a given domain. Let us consider this example; a word `big' is positive when used in sentence such as `this LCD monitor is *big.*', while the word should be judged negative in a sentence such as `that portable audio player is too *big* to me.'

Consequently, we assert that it is necessary to use a longer unit as a sentiment expression instead of using an unit of word in which conventional works do so. In this paper, we propose an opinion-mining method that utilize a new notion of *syntactic piece*. Syntactic piece is a unit of sentiment expression that is suitable for keeping semantic orientation. More explanation of syntactic piece is described later.

2. Syntactic Piece

Syntactic piece and other units are illustrated in Figure 1.

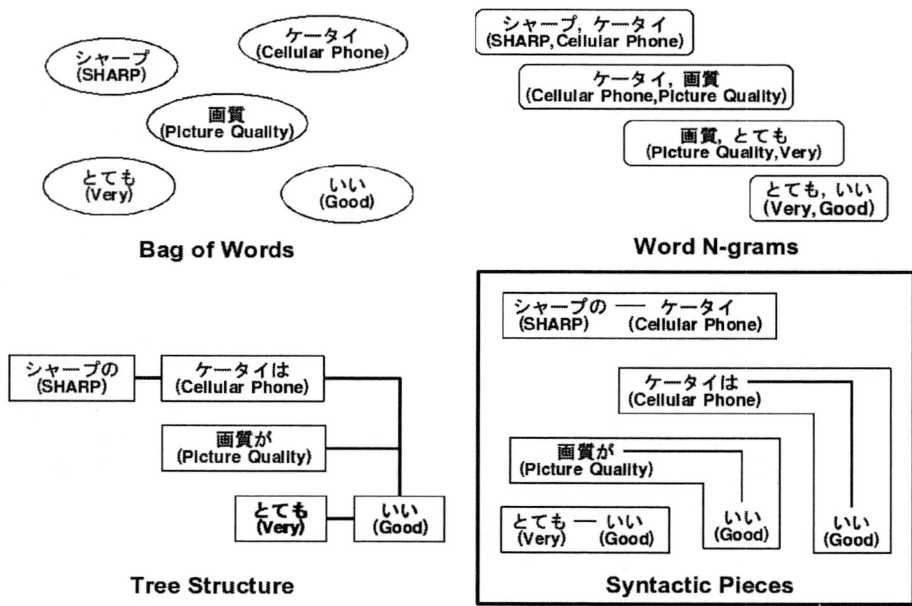

Figure 1: Idea of syntactic piece compared with other units

Syntactic piece is a minimum unit of syntactic structure of an expression. It is defined as a pair consisting of a modifier and a modifiee (modified entity) from dependency analysis result. This pair is expressed as follows.

syntactic piece : modifier ⇒ modifiee

Syntactic piece has several characteristics:

- it is very simple; it is easy, just like n-gram statistics, to extract pieces from any given expression since it requires only (partial) parsing result. In contrast, using the whole syntactic structure for opinion extraction is computationally very expensive. Consequently, we think the notion of syntactic piece is considered to have advantages of both n-gram and (whole) tree structure.
- it contains far more information than n-gram. N-gram is a consecutive sequence that keeps information of local context. It is observed that agglutinative languages such as Japanese and Korean has enormous combination of word sequence, since the word order is relatively free. In such languages n-gram-based model is expected not to work well, and some kinds of syntax should be dealt with.
- it can deal with a chunk of meaning, such as a phrasal idiom; e.g. a Japanese phrase `気-に ⇒ なる' that means `feel uneasy.' Conventional methods have avoided this problem by (1)ignoring them, or (2) importing an idiom dictionary from outside. In contrast, our method gives them the same treatment, hence we do not need such idiom dictionary or we do not need to recognize idioms as they are.

Here we present Japanese patterns of the syntactic piece below:

continuous modification
- **case frame** : noun(-particle) ⇒ predicate
    e.g. 画面-が ⇒ きれい (clear screen)
- **adverbial modification** : adverb ⇒ predicate
    e.g. とても ⇒ おいしい (delicious)

adnominal modification
- **noun modification** : noun-no ⇒ noun
    e.g. キャノン-の ⇒ カメラ (Canon's camera)
- **verbal modification** : verb ⇒ noun
    e.g. くつろげる ⇒ 店 (comfortable shop)
- **adjectival modification** : adjective ⇒ noun
    e.g. おいしい ⇒ ケーキ (delicious cake)
- **compound noun** : noun-noun
    e.g. 携帯-電話 (cellular phone)
- **prefix** : adverb ⇒ prefix-noun
    e.g. 高-画質 (high picture quality)

3. Method

Our opinion extraction model is illustrated in Figure 2.

To begin with, our system extracts syntactic pieces[1] from a training corpus. We then compute a semantic orientation score for each piece, and construct a seed dictionary of the pieces. We then generalize the dictionary by increasing the entries of the pieces that are labeled according to information of the existing pieces. We extend the dictionary employing large texts

---

[1] We may just call *piece* for short hereafter.

of general domains. Finally, we classify a sentence with the dictionary into three types: positive, negative or other.

In this paper we assume that we have a training corpus in which semantic orientation of positive or negative tags are labeled for all sentences. There are no chance that both positive and negative tags are labeled to the same sentence. We also assume that the large amount of texts of general domains, such as newspaper corpus, is available.

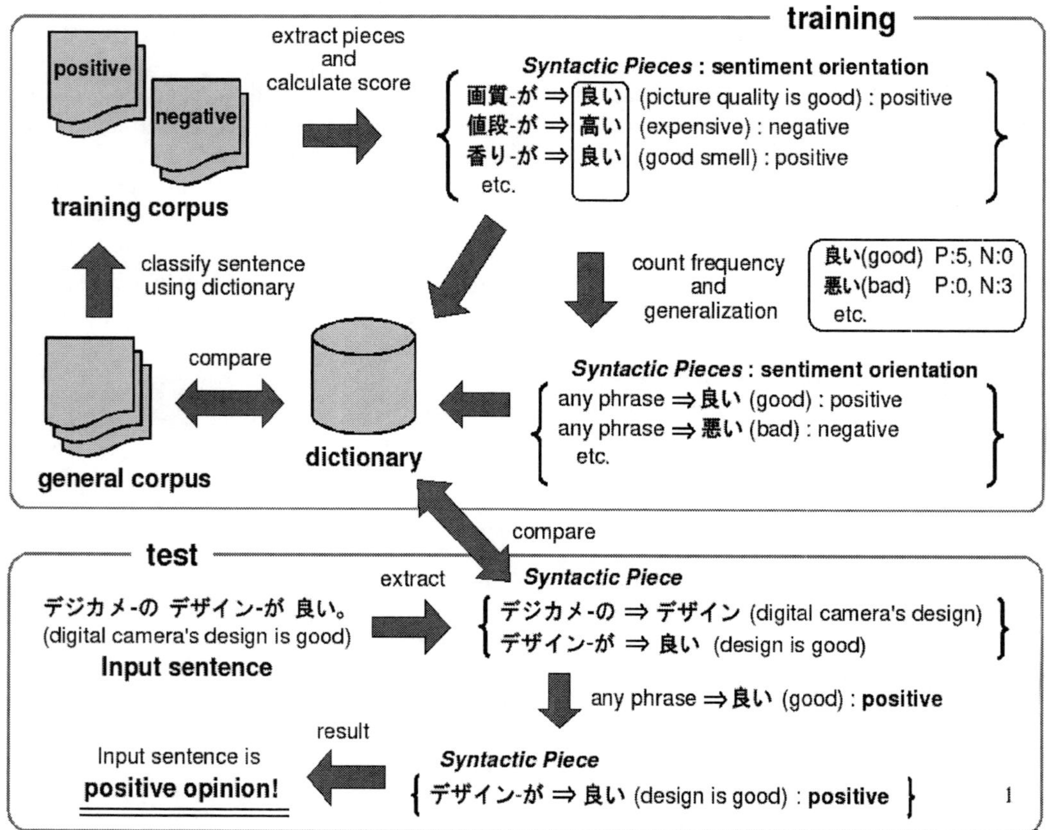

Figure 2: Opinion extraction model

3.1. Syntactic Piece Extraction

First of all, a sentence in the training corpus is analyzed by a dependency parser that creates the dependency structure. We then pick up pairs of modified item and a modifier, for all modifications in the dependency structure. Each pair constitutes a syntactic piece. Sometimes two modifiers, say A and B, modify the same expression, say C. In this case two syntactic pieces, i.e. (A ⇒ C) and (B ⇒ C), are created.

When a given sentence has a positive tag, all syntactic pieces extracted from a given sentence are tagged positive. The same is done for negative case.

As mentioned, we do not need sentences which have no semantic orientation since we use syntactic pieces to classify the sentence into p/n. Moreover, although compound noun is regarded as noun modification of noun, that is the target of syntactic piece extraction, they are not extracted since compound noun seems to have no semantic orientation.

3.2. Semantic Orientation Score

We then compute the semantic orientation score for each syntactic piece extracted from the corpus using a formula seen in Fujimura et al. (2004).

According to Fujimura, a word that has positive semantic orientation should appear in a positive opinion. The same can be said to syntactic piece. Based on this hypothesis, we compute the differences of frequency between positive opinions and negative opinions. If the syntactic piece does not have semantic orientation, the frequency of positive opinions should be the same as the frequency of negative opinions. A positive piece is expected to have a positive value.

Semantic orientation scores for all syntactic pieces are given in the following procedure.

1. prepare text collection each of which has either p or n,

2. extract all syntactic pieces from all texts,

3. count the frequency of p/n opinion for each piece, and

4. calculate the semantic orientation score with the following equation:

$$score(piece_i) = \frac{P(piece_i) - N(piece_i)}{P(piece_i) + N(piece_i)} \qquad (1)$$

$$\left(-1 \leq score(piece_i) \leq 1 \right)$$

where $piece_i$ is a syntactic piece, $score(piece_i)$ is sentiment orientation score of $piece_i$, $P(piece_i)$ is frequency of $piece_i$ appeared in positive opinions, and $N(piece_i)$ is frequency of appeared $piece_i$ in negative opinions. By conducting this process we can automatically construct a syntactic-piece dictionary that has semantic orientation score.

In the conventional methods such as Turney (2002) and Fujimura et al. (2004), document classification is based on statistically extracted keywords, as well as tagged semantic orientation for each word n-gram. Hence, the method depends on the domain of the learning corpus, that is, semantic orientation of a word may change with the domain. For example, a word '高い' in '値段-が ⇒ 高い' (expensive in terms of money) is considered to be negative in general, while the same word in '画素数-が ⇒ 高い' (high picture quality) is considered to be positive.

In contrast, the semantic orientation of syntactic piece is expected to be independent of the domain of learning corpus. This is because, semantic orientation of a syntactic piece lengthens the context than using an unit of word, that enables us clearer semantic orientation. This feature is important since it is not required for our proposed method to consider (i.e. classify and/or identify) domain; it is enough that we prepare pieces with semantic orientation in any domain as many as possible.

3.3. Dictionary Generalization

We first provide syntactic pieces that are extracted from a training corpus. Next we use this seed to label other pieces. Compared with labeling p/n information to words, we need to tag more since the number of syntactic pieces are far more than number of words in general. Therefore it is necessary to extend given information to other unlabeled pieces. Here we will explain how we do that.

As we have mentioned before, semantic orientation of a word may change with a domain in many cases. However, we all know that some words always show only p or n. For example, we see that sentiment orientation of a word '良い(good)' is always positive, even if we do not know what is good. Hence, we generalize the dictionary by identifying such syntactic pieces as '良い'.

We automatically label p/n as follows. When we collect pieces that constitute the same first element (i.e. modifier), and only positive tags are observed in the set, we tag all pieces that has the same first element positive. The similar procedure is conducted for negative tags, and also for the same second element (i.e. modified item) set.

We show how to do this process. Suppose that there are six syntactic pieces that has semantic orientation in the dictionary.

<table>
<tr><td>`画質-が⇒良い'</td><td>`味-が⇒良い'</td><td>`画面-が⇒大きい'</td><td>: tagged positive</td></tr>
<tr><td>(picture quality is good)</td><td>(taste good)</td><td>(big screen)</td><td></td></tr>
</table>

<table>
<tr><td>`騒音-が⇒大きい'</td><td>`デザイン-が⇒悪い'</td><td>`印象-が⇒悪い'</td><td>: tagged negative</td></tr>
<tr><td>(very noisy)</td><td>(poor design)</td><td>(bad impression)</td><td></td></tr>
</table>

	positive	negative	
`*any phrase* ⇒ 良い'	2	0	⇒ tagged **positive**
`*any phrase* ⇒ 大きい'	1	1	⇒ not extracted
`*any phrase* ⇒ 悪い'	0	2	⇒ tagged **negative**

3.4. Sentence Classification

The semantic orientation of a sentence is determined between p/n by extracting syntactic pieces in the given sentence. If syntactic piece appears more than once, the sentence score is calculated by summing up the score of each syntactic piece in the sentence.

$$sentence\_score(S) = \sum_{piece_i \subset S} score(piece_i) \tag{2}$$

$$\begin{cases} if \quad sentence\_score(S) > 0 \Rightarrow positive \\ sentence\_score(S) = 0 \Rightarrow not \quad opinions \\ sentence\_score(S) < 0 \Rightarrow negative \end{cases} \tag{3}$$

Here, $piece_i$ is a syntactic piece in a sentence S, and $sentence\_score(S)$ is its sentence score. The final judgment of semantic orientation is either positive, negative, or neutral (i.e., the sentence is not an opinion sentence). If there is no syntactic piece extracted in the given sentence, the sentence is judged not to be an opinion sentence. And if, the syntactic piece in the sentence is not in the dictionary, the syntactic piece score is 0.

3.5. Dictionary Extension

We have two types of dictionaries: the seed dictionary and the generalized seed dictionary. Although the size of the seed dictionary is small, it is not easy in general to increase learning corpus, when we want to extend the amount of the seed dictionary. Hence, what we do here is to classify other large corpus using the dictionaries to make learning data.

First, we provide a large corpus. This corpus is a collection of raw texts and do not require any tags such as positive or negative. We classify sentences in the corpus using the seed dictionary and the the generalized seed dictionary into either positive, negative or other. We use the classes of positive and negative as tagged data, and the other class is not used. We extract syntactic pieces out of the tagged data, and calculate semantic orientation score from the method explained in section 3.1 and 3.2 using this positive and negative tagged corpus. This is what we call the extended dictionary. Finally, we generalize this extended dictionary.

4. Experiment

In this experiment we have prepared a training corpus that consists of a variety of 13 domains and 5,608 sentences. Statistics of the corpus are presented in Table 1. And we use a general corpus that consists of Weblog texts and million sentences to extend dictionary.

As pre-processing, we analyzed the corpus using CaboCha[1], a Japanese dependency analyzer. Evaluation was performed by 13-fold cross validation, a way of unseen input evaluation, using all domains. The corpus was divided into thirteen domains. We classified sentences in the test data using the dictionary, and evaluated the results by precision and recall values.

Table 1: Number of sentences in training corpus

domain	positive	negative	total
digital camera	533	238	771
PC	112	100	212
soft drink	559	90	649
services	185	271	456
MP3 player	364	231	595
printer	103	177	280
cellular phone	156	73	229
designer goods	221	46	267
shampoo	478	173	651
beer	748	161	909
video game	61	52	113
cosmetics	44	12	56
sweets	322	98	420
total	3886	1722	5608

5. Results and Discussions

Table 2 illustrates the effect of the dictionary extension and generalization. We see from the table that precision is very high, even if we generalize the dictionary. Although we expect before the experiment that the precision sharply or gradually declines with the dictionary generalization, but it has unexpectedly increased. This may imply the robustness of our method against the noise given by the dictionary generalization. One possibility for this surprising result is that there may be low possibility that the syntactic pieces are wrongly tagged thanks to the longer unit.

Other issue is that high precision is attained without domain specification in our method. This should also thank longer processing unit, since it decreases possibility of interference that enables coexistence and no need to switch domains.

On the other hand, the recall is not satisfactory at this time. However, we think that this is an encouraging result since there is an possibility to further extend the dictionary with keeping this precision high, according to the discussion above. Actually, even though we used general corpus consists of weblog, precision and recall have increased.

Table 2: The precision and the recall for sentiment classification

dictionary	precision	recall
seed only	0.85 (752/888)	0.13 (752/5608)
seed + generalization	0.86 (2423/2809)	0.43 (2423/5608)
extended seed	0.82 (1033/1257)	0.18 (1033/5608)
extension + generalization	0.91 (3046/3338)	0.54 (3046/5608)

Table 3 and 4 show an example syntactic piece dictionary. The seed dictionary has about ten thousand pieces. After the dictionary extension, pieces increased to 130,000. We observe that the syntactic piece score was almost `1' or `-1'. This means that the semantic orientation of syntactic piece is aptly separated into p and n. Therefore, this fact have also proven that a unit of the syntactic piece has little ambiguity in deciding semantic orientation.

Table 3: An example of positive sentiment orientation tagged syntactic piece dictionary

pattern	syntactic piece
case frame	コンテンツ-が⇒充実 (contents is enriched) 好感-を⇒持てる (favorable impression) デザイン-が⇒かわいい (design is cute) 動作-が⇒速い (response is quick) 心地⇒良い (feel good)
verbal modification	暖まる⇒エピソード (heart warming episode) 楽しむ⇒方法 (way to enjoy)
adverbial modification	とっても⇒きれい (very beautiful) かなり⇒コンパクト (very compact)
adjectival modification	いい⇒香り (good smell) 高い⇒品質 (high quality) すごい⇒お洒落 (very stylish)
prefix	新-商品 (new product) 省-スペース (small space) 高-機能 (highly functional)

Table 4: An example of negative sentiment orientation tagged syntactic piece dictionary

pattern	syntactic piece
case frame	画質-が⇒良い-ない (picture quality is not good) 使い勝手-が⇒悪い (usability is bad) 消耗-が⇒激しい (very waste) サイズ-が⇒小さい (size is small) 気持ち⇒悪い (feel sick)
verbal modification	違う⇒商品 (different item)
adverbial modification	すぐ⇒壊れる (break at once) かなり⇒高額 (very extensive)
adjectival modification	ぬるい⇒ビール (lukewarm beer) 物足りない⇒感じ (not good enough)
prefix	異-音 (noise) 再-起動 (reboot) 非-表示 (no display)

Table 5 shows the result according to patterns of syntactic piece. We see from Table 5 that case frame patterns and adverbial modification pattern almost fill the system output. Weblogs are unstructured data, it is thus not always true that the attribute is written in the sentence; it may also be written before the sentence instead. It is adverbial modification pattern that accounts for a large percentage of system output. Normally, if contextual processing is conducted, or if an anaphora analysis is performed, we have to identify the attribute. However, we are not concerned with this problem here.

Table 5: The precision and the recall for each pattern of syntactic piece

pattern	precision	recall
case frame	0.82 (417/506)	0.07 (417/5608)
adverbial modification	0.85 (290/340)	0.05 (290/5608)
verbal modification	0.88 (59/67)	0.01 (59/5608)
adjectival modification	0.85 (69/81)	0.01 (69/5608)
prefix	0.67 (16/24)	0.00 (16/5608)

Table 6 shows an example of the generalized dictionary. The generalized seed dictionary has about 7,800 pieces. After the dictionary extension, generalized pieces increased to 33,000. We see that most of the generalized pieces are reasonable, such as positive for beautiful, good taste, and easy-to-use, and negative for no good, bad taste, and troublesome. This observation also supports the high precision.

Table 6: An example of the generalized dictionary

semantic orientation	syntactic piece
positive	*any phrase* ⇒キレイ (beautiful) *any phrase* ⇒使い-やすい (easy to use) *any phrase* ⇒美味しい (good taste) 飲み-やすい (easy to drink) ⇒*any phrase*
negative	*any phrase* ⇒良い-ない (no good) *any phrase* ⇒使い-にくい (hard to use) *any phrase* ⇒まずい (bad taste) いまひとつ (unattractive) ⇒*any phrase* 不具合-が (trouble) ⇒*any phrase*

Table 7 shows the results of each domain using extended dictionary. From results shown in Table 7, it is clear that high precision is obtained regardless of domains. It is also important that as the size increases, the precision also increases.

Table 7: The precision and the recall for sentiment classification using extended and generalized dictionary

domain	precision	recall
digital camera	0.84 (408/484)	0.53 (408/771)
PC	0.90 (109/121)	0.51 (109/212)
soft drink	0.92 (406/441)	0.63 (406/649)
services	0.88 (206/233)	0.45 (206/456)
MP3 player	0.91 (317/350)	0.53 (317/595)
printer	0.91 (117/129)	0.42 (117/280)
cellular phone	0.96 (130/136)	0.57 (130/280)
designer goods	0.95 (156/164)	0.58 (156/267)
shampoo	0.91 (326/358)	0.50 (326/651)
beer	0.96 (544/567)	0.60 (544/909)
video game	0.89 (59/66)	0.52 (59/113)
cosmetics	1.00 (37/37)	0.66 (37/56)
sweets	0.92 (231/252)	0.55 (231/420)

6. Conclusion

This paper presents a new method of opinion extraction. The novel feature of our method is use of its treating unit; *syntactic piece*. Compared with other units such as a single word, n-gram, and a whole tree structure, a notion of syntactic piece collects several advantages in total that others have. Our proposed method achieves high precision, and is domain-independent. Moreover, our approach is able to clearly identify the reasons for positive or negative semantic orientation by observing tags of the pieces.

Although the low recall is observed throughout the experiment this time, several ways are considered to improve recall rate. The biggest issue is that we need to further label pieces by somehow generalizing information in the seed pieces. This is an exciting items and we will tackle this task first as a future work.

List of Tools Used in this Work

1) CaboCha, Ver.0.53, Matsumoto Lab., Nara Institute of Science Technology. http://chasen.org/~taku/software/cabocha/

References

Shigeru Fujimura, Masashi Toyota, and Masaru Kitsuregawa. 2004. A Consideration of Extracting Reputations and Evaluative Expressions from the Web. *Technical Report of the Institute of Electronics, Information and Communication Engineers*, 104:144-146.

Takashi Inui and Manabu Okumura. 2006. Research Trend about Opinions Analysis of the Text. *Journal on Natural Language Processing*, 13(3):201-241.

Nozomi Kobayashi, Ryu Iida, Kentaro Inui, and Yuji Matsumoto. 2005. Opinion Extraction Using a Learning-Based Anaphora Resolution Technique. In *Proceedings of the Second International Joint Conference on Natural Language* Processing, pp. 175-180.

Kenji Tateishi, Toshikazu Fukushima, Nozomi Kobayashi, Tetsuro Takahashi, Atsushi Fujita, Kentaro Inui, and Yuji Matsumoto. 2004. Web opinion extraction and summarization based on viewpoints of products. *Information Processing Society of Japan SIGNL Note*, 2004(93):1-8.

Peter D. Turney, 2002. Thumbs Up or Thumbs Down? Semantic Orientation Applied to Unsupervised Classification of Reviews. In *Proceedings of the 40th Annual Meeting of the Association for Computational Linguistics*, pp. 417-424

Guangwei Wang and Kenji Araki. 2007. Modifying SO-PMI for Japanese Weblog Opinion Mining by Using a Balancing Factor and Detecting Neutral Expressions. In *Proceedings of the North American Chapter of the Association for Computational Linguistics*, pp. 189-192.

BEYTrans: A Free Online Collaborative Wiki-Based CAT Environment Designed for Online Translation Communities[*]

Youcef Bey[a,b], Kyo Kageura[b], and Christian Boitet[a]

[a]Laboratoire LIG-GETALP, L'Université Joseph Fourier, 385, rue de la Bibliothèque.
Grenoble, France.{youcef.bey, christian.boitet}@imag.fr [b]Graduate School of Education
The University of Tokyo, 7-3-1 Hongo, Bunkyo-ku, 113-0033,Tokyo, Japan.kyo@p.u-tokyo.ac.jp

Abstract. This paper introduces BEYTrans (Better Environment for Your TRANSlation), the first experimental environment for free online collaborative computer-aided translation. The requirements and functionalities related to individual translators and communities of translators are distinguished and described. These functionalities have been integrated in a Wiki-based complete environment, equipped with all currently possible asynchronous linguistic resources and translation aids. Functions provided by BEYTrans are also compared with existing CAT systems and ongoing experiments are discussed.

Keywords: Language Resources, Computer-Aided Translation Tools, Translation Memory, Segmentation, Collaborative Translation, Volunteer Translation Communities, Wiki.

1. Introduction

Multilingual information exchange is rapidly increasing on the Internet. A substantial part of this multilingualization is carried out by volunteers (engaged in the translation of documents, articles, reports, etc. as well as the translation/localization of computer software). Many online translation communities are formed by translators, software engineers, and in general people sharing the same motivations and aims. In view of this, various useful projects for online translation communities have emerged. Yakushite.Net is one such example. In Yakushite.Net, the system aims to improve machine translation (MT) performance through the interaction with volunteer translators. Translators contributing in turn can take advantage of MT and other functions provided by Yakushite.Net, while they contribute to the improvement of the system by augmenting its language resources (YAKUSHITE, 2007).

Open environments for developing free online lexical resources also exist. Wiktionary – The linguistic companion of the huge free Wikipedia encyclopedia – is one example (WIKTIONARY, 2007). Papillon, another example, aims also to construct a large-scale, free multilingual lexical database with the help of volunteers (Mangeot, 2002). In addition, free

[*] Acknowledgements: Special thanks go to the DEMGOL organizers at Trieste (Italy), in particular Mr. Giovanni Zorzetti, who helped us to transfer hundreds of multilingual documents by developing special scripts, and Ms. Francesca Marzari, who has devoted much time and effort to evaluating and testing BEYTrans in a real-world environment.

[*] This research is partly supported by grant-in-aid (A) 17200018 "Construction of online multilingual reference tools for aiding translators" by the Japan Society for the Promotion of Sciences (JSPS).

standalone translation memory (TM) systems such as Omega-T are now available (OMEGAT, 2007).

While appreciating the importance of these online environments and systems for directly or indirectly promoting the multilingual exchange of information, we recognize the lack of an integrated environment to help online translator communities in a systematic way. Against this backdrop, a free online computer-aided translation (CAT) environment, BEYTrans (Better Environment for Your TRANSlation) has been developed, and the system is now in its experimental stage. This first experimental version has two levels of functionality. The first level corresponds to the translators, who act as separate entities and need specific functionalities (translation editor, linguistic help, etc.). The second level corresponds to the community, in which translators work as an integrated entity. Both functionalities have been integrated into our system using a collaborative Wiki-based technology which provides to volunteer translators with a user-friendly environment and helps them improve translation consistency (Schwartz et *al.*, 2004) (Augar et *al.*, 2004).

This paper explains the basic background, concepts and functionalities of BEYTrans. In section 2, we describe the flow of linguistic data and the interactions among translators, on the basis of which the system requirements have been identified. Section 3 describes the different functionalities that should ideally be made available to 1) individual translators and 2) translation communities. In section 4, a detailed explanation of BEYTrans and its position among existing CAT environments is given. The system is currently being used experimentally by the DEMGOL project and other communities, which is briefly examined in the final section.

2. Virtual translation network

Online volunteer translators are organized in communities in which they perform translation together or separately, and disseminate multilingual content on the Web. In so doing, they use their private translation environments and communicate frequently with their counterparts (other translators). To build a support system that deals adequately with this situation, for this situation, we need to understand the requirements and the needs of communities, considered as integrated entities, and those of translators, considered as separate entities (Figure 1). In other words, it is important to help translators at two levels: the translator level and the community level. Distinguishing between these two levels allows us to more effectively identify and fulfill existing needs in the translation process.

For example, the translation progress in the context of the ArabicMozilla project (ARABICMOZILLA, 2007) needs to be checked constantly and translators should be kept aware of changes in the content. At the same time, each translator, as individual entity, performs translation separately and sends it to the repository (web location dedicated to the relevant community) where the new content is updated.

The translation process led us to differentiate two categories of practices:

> (i) Individual translators working as separated entities;
> (ii) A translators working as an integrated entities.

The former is related to translator behavior where she/he uses private environment (editors, dictionaries, etc.). The later needs separate functionalities for increasing collaboration and consistency.

The communication and data exchange in ARABICMOZILLA can be schematized as shown in Figure 1. The community itself is divided into three sub-communities and modeled as a network where nodes represent translators and edges represent change and data manipulation – it reflects also the action that data is subjected to – Furthermore, nodes reflect the translator's position and requirements inside her/his community and edges represent the requirements and needs of the community.

For example, translator A adds an entry in the community dictionary (requirement category (i): dictionary addition function). The same translation could be used by B for the translation of a source word (requirement category: (i) search function and (ii) control change function). After that, it could be updated by C (requirement category (i): dictionary update function). Translators D and E may exchange comments about the possible validation of the new entry (requirement category (i): communication). In fact, in the process of translation, these tasks are done manually and still need to be controlled and supported by an integrated environment.

To further clarify our method and show how it applies to the real situation of translation communities in a concrete way, according to these categories of functionalities, we take as an example the ARABICMOZILLA community, in which the translation process is as follows:

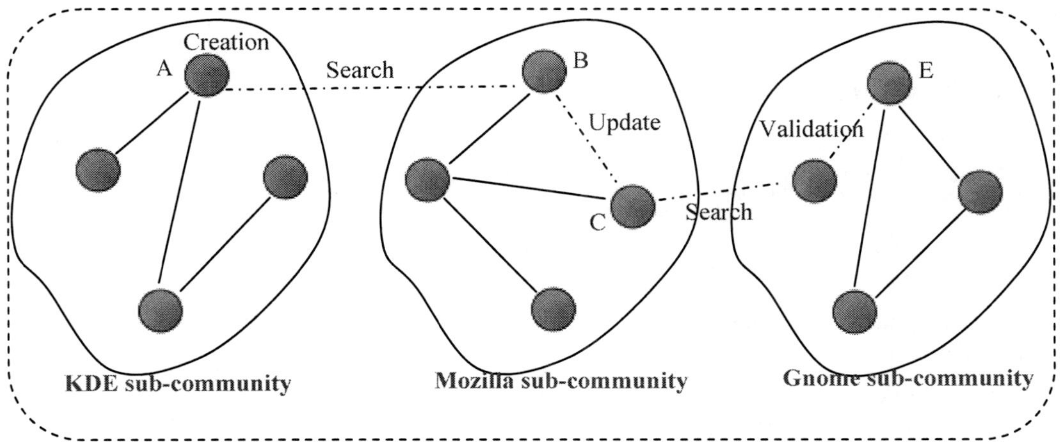

Figure 1: Translator and sub-community interactions in the ARABICMOZILLA project.

The community is comprised of 10–20 volunteer translators (ARABICMOZILLA, 2007). Translators constantly check new English releases; if available, they proceed to the translation/localization into Arabic. In the process, many problems arise. For example, the Arabic script is RTL (Right To Left), hence, translation needs to be tuned with the software compilation. An estimated of 100 strings can be translated in one hour. For example, for the last Gnome release, version 2.18 had about 6,000 extra strings which were translated in 60 hours. The translation was performed by 6 translators and took one month, including checking the translation of the whole text (which contained about 35,000 strings) in order to ensure consistency. As for linguistic resources, translators are very active and have created under Wiki a technical terms dictionary, which contains around 18,000 entries (ARABEYES, 2007). Translators refer sometimes also to commercial standalone dictionaries like the English-Arabic 'Al-warid', which is largely regarded as authoritative in Arabic-English translation.

As is usual in any community, some group-motivated behaviors appear in this translation community. In this case, they are related to the organization of translators and to data manipulation, and reflect separated and group functions. It is very difficult to delimit such behaviors either at translator or group level. But some lacks and needed functionalities are common to this and other communities (FRENCHMOZILLA, W3C, etc.). These functionalities, which correspond to the practices (i) and (ii) cited above, can be categorized as follows:

    a. Functionalities for translator who operates on translation in autonomous way and disposing of private environments (Bey *et al.*, 2006 (a)) (Abekawa *et al.*, 2007).

    b. Functionalities for collaboration and work between translators (Bey *et al.*, 2006 (b)).

In the next section, details of these two categories of practice are described and the specification for functionalities implementation is given.

3. Description of integrated functionalities: the first step toward a solution

In the process of translation, a volunteer translator will want individually exploit the potential of various automatic linguistic functionalities (e.g., dictionaries and MT suggestions) and at the same time interact with her/his counterparts by using community functionalities (e.g. asking for translation community aid when linguistic aids aren't sufficient). From this point of view, translator and community functionalities should be implemented as follows.

3.1. Individual translator functionalities

The environment should be open to all volunteers without any restriction. Individual translators should be able to take advantage at the following different functionalities:

- Text extraction and tokenization: documents to be translated undergo a process of text extraction and tokenization for the identification of Translation Units (TU) (LINGPIPE, 2007) (Walker et al., 2001).

- Linguistic aids: linguistic aids are integrated and activated automatically in an online asynchronous manner (see 4.3).

- Online translator-oriented editor: translators read the source TUs synchronized with their corresponding target TUs and input the translation in the source TU in order, segment by segment, or jumping to the segment they wish to work on. The target TUs are replaced in fact automatically or manually by the "best" pre-translations of MT or TM –

3.2. Translator community functionalities

Extended functionalities for the translation community have been implemented using the Wiki technology. As explained above, Wikis are user-friendly environments that recently have provided to be a great success. Using this technology, any user/translator can upload documents and share them with his/her community; thereby making it possible to implement the following functionalities (Schwartz et al., 2004) (Augar et al., 2004):

- Collaboration: documents of the same community can be grouped in a specific space where they are freely accessible by all translators of the same community. Each translator has an information access that allows her/him to interact with other translators.

- Progression control: collaborative translation needs access control and historic content revision. The progress of the translation can be checked comparing different versions of the same document. Translators can check the content and make comparisons between versions at the sentence or word levels.

The translator and community functionalities outlined above have been combined to produce the integrated collaborative environment BEYTrans, which is described in the next section.

4. BEYTrans: first experimental version

In this section, the position of BEYTrans compared with existing CATs is discussed, and then its concrete application is illustrated.

4.1. Environment features

A first experimental version of BEYTrans has been completed and deployed on the Web (BEYTRANS, 2007). However, it is necessary at this stage to clarify the position of our environment in comparison with other CAT functionalities. The comparison here is limited to Trados™ and Déjà vu™ (TRADOS, 2007) (DÉJÂ VU, 2007), but it could be extended to other CAT environments (CAT-COMPARISON, 2007).

Almost all the individual functionalities are present in these environments. The networked version is absent in Déjà Vu but is available in a separate version of Trados. Our environment integrates the basic translator functionalities for translators and the online collaborative functionalities for communities. Adding to that, all linguistic translation aids are suggested automatically and simultaneously in "proactive" behavior. Furthermore, BEYTrans is platform-independent – translators need only a PC with an Internet connection and browser –

4.2. Translator-oriented edition in a collaborative Wiki environment

The online translation editor has an Excel-like interface where all source and target TUs are displayed in parallel (Figure 2, area I). The editor allows translators to exploit dictionaries and machine translation asynchronously (Figure 2, area II).

Fuzzy matching detection is proposed at the same time the TU is selected in the main grid (Figure 2, area III). In fact, during the translation process, the editor proposes suggestions by computing similarity scores between the current source TU and the TUs stored in multiple translation memories (each translation community has its own TM, which stores previous translations). Accordingly, edition functionalities are important: translators are able to add, delete and split TU cells, which is useful for the manual enhancement of the tokenization (Figure 2, area IV). Translators can however choose the rate of similarity (Figure 2, area V) and fine-tune the environment parameters.

After a translation is complete, BEYTrans creates a new version of the TC (translation companion is an XML structure in which are managed the TUs) and sends it to its repository. As the content is saved in Wiki mode, it is easy to track the modifications by comparison that has been made to a translation, which enhances the efficiency and increases the consistency of the translation. Finally, translators are able to generate a target document that can be directly disseminated, and that also becomes available to readers on the BEYTrans Web site (BEYTRANS, 2007).

Table 1: Comparison of BEYTrans with April Déja Vu™ and Trados™.

	Atril Déja Vu™	Trados™	BEYTrans
Editor			
Looks like	Excel	Word processor	Excel
Bold/Italic/Underline formatting	No	Yes	Yes
Comments on sentence level	No	Yes	Yes
Backup/Restore facilities	No	No	Yes
Connection to Machine Translation	No	Yes	Yes
Translation memory			
Fuzzy matching quality	6/10	9/10	Needs a huge MT but works efficiently
Search results on the same screen	No	Yes	Yes
Difference marking	Yes	Yes	Yes

	No	Yes	Yes
Automatic search	No	Yes	Yes
Multiple Translation Memory	No	Yes	Yes
Percentages shown	Yes	Yes	Yes
Terminology search			
Search results on the same screen	No	Yes	Yes
Multiple words	No	Yes	Yes
Automatic search	No	Yes	Yes
Multiple Terminology databases	No	Yes	Yes
Translation memory management			
Global search/replace	Yes	Yes	Yes
Translation unit edition	Yes	Yes	Yes
Networking			
Collaborative translation	No	Separate networked version	Yes
Networked terminology	No	Separate networked version	Yes

4.3. Linguistic resource functionalities

BEYTrans has been equipped with modules that allow for dictionary management. Functionalities related to dictionary management are as follows:

- Entire dictionary importation: a dictionary in its original format has to be preprocessed and transformed into the XLD format used by BEYTrans importation module, which extracts headwords and their corresponding translations. The newly imported dictionary is also activated automatically, and becomes immediately available to all translators (Bey et *al.*, 2006(a)).

- Progressive dictionary construction: translators are able to create temporary or permanent dictionaries. This process has been made quite simple: translators can specify the community and dictionary name, and can then automatically create a new dictionary for their own use.

- Look-up functions: the search function can be called up manually or automatically during translation. The selection of the TU in the editor area (Figure 2, area I) activates the sentence tokenization and dictionary suggestions.

Direct dictionary creation enhances translators' ability to work on their own data rather than on the data of the whole community. Related look-up functionalities are integrated with the translation aids, which makes it possible to select and update entries "on the fly" while translating.

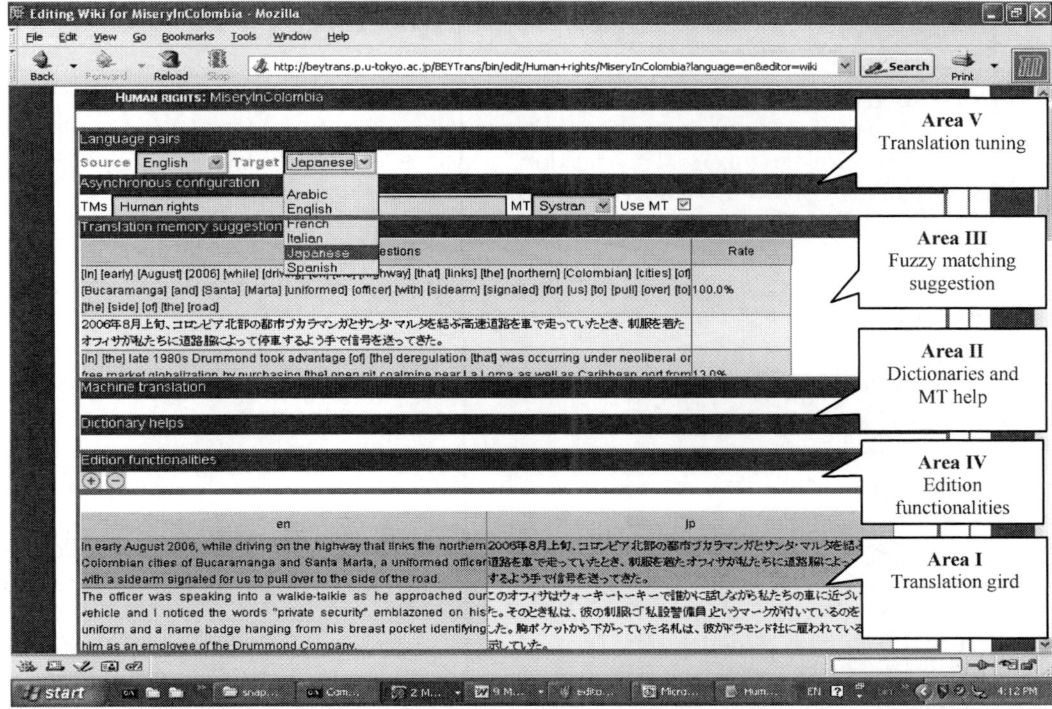

Figure 2: Multilingual online translator-oriented editor.

5. Experimentation

The environment is deployed on the Web for free translation (BEYTRANS, 2007) and is being used experimentally by the DEMGOL translation community (DEMGOL, 2007) and other translation communities. DEMGOL is an Italian research project which aims at the construction of an etymological dictionary of the Greek mythology and Homeric references. It contains about 1200 Italian documents which volunteers are translating into French, and which will later be translated into Spanish.

Beside DEMGOL, there is another ongoing experiment testing of multilingual functionalities in the translation of human rights documents from English into Japanese (Figure 2). Furthermore, as many volunteer communities aren't aware of our environment, we have recently studied the nature of individual and community translation work in ARABICMOZILLA (ARABICMOZILLA, 2007) and introduced our environment to these translators. We have imported an English-Arabic technical dictionary with around 18,000 entries for them to facilitate their work.

6. Conclusion

This paper has described the two levels of functionality in the experimental computer-aided translation environment BEYTrans. The first level corresponds to translators who act as separate entities and need specific functionalities (editors, linguistic help, etc.). The second level corresponds to the community level at which several translators work as an integrated entity (communication, progression control, etc.). Both functionalities have been integrated using a collaborative Wiki-based technology which provides volunteer translators with a user-friendly environment. However, the editor was the most important component for translators. When translators are working on a translation, the system suggests a variety of linguistic aids (dictionaries, glossaries, etc.) and translation suggestions (MT, TM, etc.) to them in an asynchronous and "proactive" manner.

As Wiki-based environments are designed basically to support small documents, in the near future, BEYTrans will be extended for managing and translating high-scale data in multilingual format and will also be enhanced by tackling translator and community problems that are identified from the feedback from different translator communities.

References

Abekawa, T. and K. Kageura. 2007. QRedit: An Integrated Editor System to Support Online Volunteer Translators. *Digital Humanities*. 3-5.

ARABICMOZILLA. 2007. http://www.arabeyes.org/project.php?proj=Mozilla.

ARABEYES. 2007. http://www.arabeyes.org.
DÉJÀ VU. 2007. http://www.atril.com.
Augar, N., R. Raiitman and Z. Wanlei. 2004. Teaching and Learning Online with Wikis. *Proceedings of the 21st Australasian Society for Computers in Learning in Tertiary Education Conference*, Perth, pp. 95-104.

Bey, Y., C. Boitet and K. Kageura. 2006(a). The TRANSBey Prototype: An Online Collaborative Wiki-Based CAT Environment for Volunteer Translators. Yuste, E., Ed., *Proceedings of the 3rd International Workshop on Language Resources for Translation Work, Research & Training (LR4Trans-III). LREC 2006 - Fifth International Conference on Language Resources and Evaluation.* Paris: ELRA / ELDA (European Language Resources Association, European Language Resources Distribution Association), Genoa, Italy. 49-54.

Bey, Y., K. Kageura and C. Boitet. 2006(b). Data Management in QRLex, an Online Aid System for Volunteer Translators. *International Journal of Computational Linguistics and Chinese Language Processing*, 11(4), 349-376.

BEYTRANS. 2007. http://beytrans.p.u-tokyo.ac.jp/BEYTrans/.
CAT-COMPARISON. 2007. http://www.geocities.com/fmourisso/CAT.htm.
DEMGOL. 2007. http://demgol.units.it/show.do?action=base.
DHTMLGRID. 2007. http://sourceforge.net/projects/dhtmlgrid/.
FRENCHMOZILLA. 2006. http://frenchmozilla.online.fr.
LINGPIPE. 2005. http://alias-i.com/lingpipe/demo.html.
Mangeot, M. 2002. An XML Markup Language Framework for Lexical Databases Environments: the Dictionary Markup Language. *Proceedings of International Standards of Terminology and Language Resources Management Workshop*, Spain, pp. 37-44.

OMEGAT. 2007. http://www.trados.com.

PAXHUMANA. 2006. Translation of Various Humanitarian Reports in French, English, German, Spanish. http://paxhumana.info.

Schwartz, L., S. M. Clark Cossarin and J. Rudolph. 2004. Educational Wikis: Features and Selection Criteria. *International Review of Research in Open and Distance Learning*, 1(5), Australia, 95-104.

TRADUCT. 2007. http://wiki.traduc.org.

TRANSLATIONWIKI. 2007. http://www.translationwiki.net.

WIKTIONARY. 2007. http://www.wiktionary.org.

Walker, D. J., D. E. Clements, M. Darwin and J. W. Amtrup. 2001. Sentence Boundary Detection: A Comparison of Paradigms for Improving MT Quality. *Proceedings of the 8th Machine Translation Summit*, Santiago de Compostela, Spain.

YAKUSHITE. 2007. http://www.yakushite.net/cgi-bin/WebObjects/YakushiteNet.woa/wa/main.

A Pregroup Analysis of Japanese Causatives [*]

Kumi Cardinal

Keio University, Shonan-Fujisawa Campus,
Graduate School of Media and Governance
5322 Endo, Fujisawa-shi, Kanagawa 252-8520, Japan
cardinal@sfc.keio.ac.jp

Abstract. We explore a computational algebraic approach to grammar via pregroups. We examine how the structures of Japanese causatives can be treated in the framework of a pregroup grammar. In our grammar, the dictionary assigns one or more syntactic types to each word and the grammar rules are used to infer types to strings of words. We developed a practical parser representing our pregroup grammar, which validates our analysis.

Keywords: pregroup grammar, Japanese causatives.

1. Introduction

Japanese causatives have been analyzed from a number of points of view: transformational, lexical, and movement approaches among others. Here, I propose a computational method for analyzing the different types of causative constructions. Our analysis is based on the notion of pregroup grammar, which has been developed as an algebraic tool to recognize grammatically well-formed sentences in natural languages (Lambek, 1999).

This paper is organized as follows: section 2 introduces the pregroup formalism; section 3 describes the properties and characteristics of Japanese causatives; section 4 presents the analysis of Japanese causatives based on pregroup grammar; and finally, section 5 discusses about the implementation of a practical parser.

2. Pregroup grammar

The main idea of a pregroup grammar, which is shared with other categorial grammars, is to assign one (or more) *compound types* to each word of the language and to check the grammaticality of sentences by doing a calculation on strings of types.

We construct the compound types in the following way: we begin with a partially ordered set $(A, \rightarrow)$ of basic types, the partial order being denoted by the arrow. From the basic types we build simple types by taking adjoints or repeated adjoints. Thus from the basic type a, we obtain the simple types

$$..., a^{ll}, a^{l}, a, a^{r}, a^{rr}, ...$$

Compound types are strings of simple types. We then form the *free pregroup* generated by A, whose elements are compound types.

The only computations required are contractions $a^{l}a \rightarrow 1$, $aa^{r} \rightarrow 1$, and expansions $1 \rightarrow aa^{l}$, $1 \rightarrow a^{r}a$, where a is a simple type.

One can extend the operation $()^l$ and $()^r$ to compound types, by defining

$$1^l = 1 = 1^r,$$
$$(a \cdot b)^l = b^l \cdot a^l,$$
$$(a \cdot b)^r = b^r \cdot a^r.$$

The symbol 1 stands for the empty string of types and will be usually omitted, as will be the dot that stands for multiplication.

What makes free pregroups particularly suitable for computation is the following observation:

SWITCHING LEMMA (Lambek, 1999) *When showing that $x_1 \cdots x_m \to y_1 \cdots y_n$ for simple types x_i and y_i, one may assume without loss of generality that all contractions $a^l a \to 1$ and $aa^r \to 1$ precede all expansions $1 \to aa^l$ and $1 \to a^r a$.*

The importance of the *Switching Lemma* is that it offers a deciding procedure, by a sequence of contractions, when a string of simple types can be rewritten as a single simple type. If expansions were needed in addition to contractions, we could for instance compute a number of expansions, followed by a number of contractions, followed by another series of expansions, and continue and so on in an ever-ending process.

So, for the purpose of sentence verification, expansions are not needed, but only contractions, combined with some rewriting by the partial order of A. Expansions are useful for theoretical purposes, for example to prove the following:

$$a^{rl} = a = a^{lr},$$
$$a \to b \Rightarrow b^l \to a^l,$$
$$a \to b \Rightarrow b^r \to a^r.$$

3.   The structure of causative verbs

In Japanese, the causative is formed by attaching the bound causative morpheme *–(s)ase* to the stem of a verb. If the verb to which it attaches ends in a consonant, the initial consonant *s* of the morpheme is deleted.

In (1b), the causative morpheme is attached to a transitive verb stem, *kak* 'write'. Hanako, the original agent of the transitive verb is designated with the dative particle *ni*.

(1)

    a.   *Hanako ga tegami o kaita.*
            Hanako NOM letter ACC wrote
            'Hanako wrote a letter.'
    b.   *Taroo ga Hanako ni tegami o kak-ase-ta.*
            Taro NOM Hanako DAT letter ACC write-CAUS-PAST
            'Taro made Hanako write a letter.'

The Japanese causative is well known for having two types, the so-called *o*-causative and the *ni*-causative. When the causative morpheme is attached to an intransitive verb, as in (2), the original agent of the verb stem can take either the accusative *o* or the dative *ni*.

(2)

    a.   *Hanako ga aruita.*
            Hanako NOM walked.
            'Hanako walked.'
    b.   *Taroo ga Hanako o aruk-ase-ta.*
            Taro NOM Hanako ACC walk-CAUS-PAST
            'Taro made Hanako walk.'

c. *Taroo ga Hanako ni aruk-ase-ta.*
Taro NOM Hanako DAT walk-CAUS-PAST
'Taro let Hanako walk.'

Kuno (1973), Shibatani (1973), and Kitagawa (1974), among others, have commented on the semantics difference between the *o*-causative and the *ni*-causative. *O*-causatives have been characterized as coercive causatives whereas *ni*-causatives have been referred to as non-coercive causatives. Note that this choice of *o* or *ni* exists only if the verb to which *–(s)ase* is attached is intransitive. If the verb is transitive, the original agent of the verb can appear only with the dative *ni*. This constraint against having two or more accusative cases in the same clause is called the Double-*o* Constraint (Harada, 1973).

4. Computational approach to causative verbs

We shall assign one ore more (compound) types to Japanese words and verify whether a given string of words is a grammatical sentence by performing a calculation in the pregroup.

First, we introduce the following basic types:

π = pronoun;
$\tilde{n}$ = proper name;
n = noun;
s_i = sentence,
  $i = 1$ for the present tense;
  $i = 2$ for the past tense.
c_1 = nominative complement;
c_3 = dative complement;
c_4 = accusative complement;
c_6 = ablative complement.

Concepts describing the grammatical constructions of the language fragment help to choose the basic types and the ordering. However, in selecting basic types, we are primarily interested in their algebraic effectiveness, whether or not they correspond to traditional grammatical categories.

We also postulate $n \rightarrow \tilde{n} \rightarrow \pi$.

We then assign the following types to some representative verbs:

aruku 'walk':	$c_1^r s_1$
kaku 'write':	$c_4^r c_1^r s_1$
otiru 'drop':	$c_6^r c_1^r s_1$
aruk-ase-ru 'walk-CAUS-PRES':	$c_4^r c_1^r s_1, c_3^r c_1^r s_1$
kak-ase-ru 'write-CAUS-PRES':	$c_4^r c_3^r c_1^r s_1$
oti-sase-ru 'drop-CAUS-PRES':	$c_6^r c_4^r c_1^r s_1$

As Harada (1973) notes, *ni*-causatives are possible only when the causee holds control over the action that he/she performs. Since 'to drop' is usually not considered as a self-controllable action, the causative verb *otisaseru* has type $c_6^r c_4^r c_1^r s_1$ but not $c_6^r c_3^r c_1^r s_1$[1].

The typing in the pregroup formalism assumes that the verb is the central point of the sentence. The type of the verb may change depending on the order of the complements.

---

[1] In the context such as where the causer is a film director and the causee an actor, we can imagine that the film director makes the actor/actress act as he/she directs. In this case, we could consider the verb 'to drop' as a self-controllable action and the causative verb *otisaseru* would also take the type $c_6^r c_3^r c_1^r s_1$.

However, to keep our analysis within the scope of this paper, we will consider only the most common word order and we will ignore cases of scrambling.

(3)

    a.   *Hanako ga tegami o kaita.*

$$\tilde{n}\,(\pi^{r}c_1)\,n\,(\pi^{r}c_4)\,(c_4^{r}c_1^{r}s_2) \to s_2$$

        Hanako NOM letter ACC wrote

        'Hanako wrote a letter.'

    b.   *Taroo ga Hanako ni tegami o kak-ase-ta.*

$$\tilde{n}\,(\pi^{r}c_1)\,\tilde{n}\,\,(\pi^{r}c_3)\,n\,\,(\pi^{r}c_4)\,(c_4^{r}c_3^{r}c_1^{r}s_2) \to s_2$$

        Taro NOM Hanako DAT letter ACC write-CAUS-PAST

        'Taro made Hanako write a letter.'

    c.   **Taroo ga Hanako o tegami o kak-ase-ta.*

$$\tilde{n}\,(\pi^{r}c_1)\,\tilde{n}\,\,(\pi^{r}c_4)\,n\,\,(\pi^{r}c_4)\,(c_4^{r}c_3^{r}c_1^{r}s_2)$$

        Taro NOM Hanako ACC letter ACC write-CAUS-PAST

The calculations are performed in the following steps. We take as an example the string of types corresponding to the sentence (3a).

$$
\begin{aligned}
\tilde{n}\,(\pi^{r}c_1)\,n\,(\pi^{r}c_4)\,(c_4^{r}c_1^{r}s_2) \;&=\; (\tilde{n}\,\pi^{r})\,c_1\,(n\,\pi^{r})\,(c_4 c_4^{r})\,c_1^{r}\,s_2 \\
&\to\; 1 \bullet c_1 \bullet 1 \bullet 1 \bullet c_1^{r}s_2 \\
&=\; c_1 c_1^{r}s_2 \\
&\to\; 1 \bullet s_2 \\
&=\; s_2
\end{aligned}
$$

Note that we used the partial order $\tilde{n} \to \pi$ and $n \to \pi$ for the contractions $\tilde{n}\,\pi^{r} \to \pi\,\pi^{r} \to 1$ and $n\,\pi^{r} \to \pi\,\pi^{r} \to 1$.

(4)

    a.   *Hanako ga aruita.*

$$\tilde{n}\,\,(\pi^{r}c_1)\,\,(c_1^{r}s_2) \to s_2$$

        Hanako NOM walked

        'Hanako walked.'

    b.   *Taroo ga Hanako o aruk-ase-ta.*

$$\tilde{n}\,(\pi^{r}c_1)\,\tilde{n}\,\,(\pi^{r}c_4)\,(c_4^{r}c_1^{r}s_2) \to s_2$$

        Taro NOM Hanako ACC walk-CAUS-PAST

        'Taro made Hanako walk.'

    c.   *Taroo ga Hanako ni aruk-ase-ta.*

$$\tilde{n}\,(\pi^{r}c_1)\,\tilde{n}\,\,(\pi^{r}c_3)\,(c_3^{r}c_1^{r}s_2) \to s_2$$

        Taro NOM Hanako DAT walk-CAUS-PAST

        'Taro let Hanako walk.'

In (5), the noncausative verb *otiru* 'to drop' allows either an animate or an inanimate subject. However, the causative counterpart *otisaseru* 'cause to drop' requires an animate object, as shown by the examples in (6).

(5)

    a.   *Taroo ga saka kara otita.*

$$\tilde{n}\,(\pi^{r}c_1)\,\,n\,(\pi^{r}c_6)\,(c_6^{r}c_1^{r}s_2) \to s_2$$

        Taro NOM hill from fell

        'Taro fell from the hill.'

    b.   *Hon ga tana kara otita.*

$$n\ (\pi^r c_1)\ n\ (\pi^r c_6)\ (c_6^r c_1^r s_2) \rightarrow s_2$$

book NOM shelf from fell

'The book dropped off the shelf.'

(6)

    a.   *Ziroo ga Taroo o saka kara oti-sase-ta.*

$$\tilde{n}\ (\pi^r c_1)\ \tilde{n}\ (\pi^r c_4)\ n\ (\pi^r c_6)\ (c_6^r c_4^r c_1^r s_2) \rightarrow s_2$$

        Ziro NOM Taro ACC hill from fall-CAUS-PAST

        'Ziro caused Taro to fall from the hill.'

    b.   **Ziroo ga hon o tana kara oti-sase-ta.*

$$\tilde{n}\ (\pi^r c_1)\ n\ (\pi^r c_4)\ n\ (\pi^r c_6)\ (c_6^r c_4^r c_1^r s_2) \rightarrow s_2$$

        Ziro NOM book ACC shelf from fall-CAUS-PAST

        'Ziro caused the book to drop from the shelf.'

The sentence (6a) with the animate causee is grammatical; the causee (Taro) is understood to have fallen of his own accord, and the causer (Ziro) caused this to happen indirectly. The sentence (6b) is ungrammatical because the causee, *hon* 'book', being inanimate, cannot 'drop on his own accord'.

Our current choice of typing accepts the ungrammatical sentence (6b). We must revise our types and perhaps introduce new types so that our grammar rejects the sentence (6b).

4.1. The attribute

Pregroup grammar handles features such as agreement and number by a proliferation of basic types. Consider the incorrect sentence *I sleeps* where the pronoun *I* has type π_1 and the verb *sleeps* the type $\pi_3^r s$, where π_3 stands for the third person singular. The sentence is incorrect since there is no agreement between the subject and the verb.

(7) **I sleeps*

$$\pi_1\ (\pi_3^r s)$$

However, if the attribute is dropped, the typing is interpreted as a subject followed by an intransitive verb, and therefore the sentence *I sleeps* is accepted.

(8) **I sleeps*

$$\pi\ (\pi^r s) \rightarrow s$$

French nouns and adjectives vary in gender and number. Degeilh et al. (2005) introduce the basic type n_{gn} to denote a complete noun phrase, depending on its gender g and number n. They postulate $n_{gn} \rightarrow n$. The type of a noun is indexed by g, which stands for 1 = masculine or 2 = feminine, and by n, where $n = 1$ means singular and $n = 2$ means plural. Nouns are count nouns or mass nouns; count nouns have type c_{gn} and mass nouns have type m_{gn}.

Consider, for example, the noun phrase *une étudiante* 'a student', where the (feminine) article *une* has type $n_{21}c_{21}^l$ and the (feminine) noun *étudiante* has type c_{21}.

(9) une étudiante

$$(n_{21}c_{21}^l)\ c_{21} \rightarrow n_{21}$$

We can treat the animacy restriction of sentences such as (6) in a similar way that Degeilh et al. (2005) did to handle the gender and number attributes in the French noun phrases. Adding the feature *animate* to our grammar will resolve the problem. We introduce the new basic types

n_a and $\tilde{n}_a$ where $a = 1$ means animate, and $a = 2$ means inanimate. Further, we postulate $n_a \rightarrow n$ and $\tilde{n}_a \rightarrow n$. The basic types π and c_4 will also be indexed by a : π_a and c_{4a}. We also postulate $n_a \rightarrow \pi_a$, $\tilde{n}_a \rightarrow \pi_a$, $\pi_a \rightarrow \pi$ and $c_{4a} \rightarrow c_4$.

(10)

    a.   *Ziroo ga Taroo o saka kara oti-sase-ta.*

$$\tilde{n}\,(\pi^{r}c_1)\,\tilde{n}_1\,(\pi_1^{\,r}c_{41})\,n\,(\pi^{r}c_6)\,(c_6^{\,r}c_{41}^{\,r}c_1^{\,r}s_2) \rightarrow s_2$$

         Ziro NOM Taro ACC hill from fall-CAUS-PAST

         'Ziro caused Taro to fall from the hill.'

    b.   **Ziroo ga hon o tana kara oti-sase-ta.*

$$\tilde{n}\,(\pi^{r}c_1)\,n_2\,(\pi_2^{\,r}c_{42})\,n\,(\pi^{r}c_6)\,(c_6^{\,r}c_{41}^{\,r}c_1^{\,r}s_2)$$

         Ziro NOM book ACC shelf from fall-CAUS-PAST

         'Ziro caused the book to drop from the shelf.'

Although the types c_{42} and c_{41} differ only from one index, they are as different as n and c_{41}. The sequence $c_{42}c_{41}^{\,r}$ does not contract to 1, and so the string of types corresponding to the sentence *Ziroo ga hon o tana kara otisaseta* cannot reduce to the simple type s_2.

The following is another example similar to *oti-sase-ru* 'cause to fall'. The intransitive verb *agaru* 'rise' allows both animate and inanimate subject, but the causative verb *agar-ase-ru* 'cause to rise' requires an animate object.

(11)

    a.   *Taroo ga butai ni agatta.*

$$\tilde{n}\,(\pi^{r}c_1)\,n\,(\pi^{r}c_3)\,(c_3^{\,r}c_1^{\,r}s_2) \rightarrow s_2$$

         Taro NOM stage on rose

         'Taro rose onto the stage.'

    b.   *Maku ga agatta.*

$$n\,(\pi^{r}c_1)\,(c_1^{\,r}s_2) \rightarrow s_2$$

         curtain NOM rose

         'The curtain rose.'

(12)

    a.   *Ziroo ga Taroo o butai ni agar-ase-ta.*

$$\tilde{n}\,(\pi^{r}c_1)\,\tilde{n}_1\,(\pi_1^{\,r}c_{41})\,n\,(\pi^{r}c_3)\,(c_3^{\,r}c_{41}^{\,r}c_1^{\,r}s_2) \rightarrow s_2$$

         Ziro NOM Taro ACC stage on rise-CAUS-PAST

         'Ziro caused Taro to rise onto the stage.'

    b.   **Ziroo ga maku o agar-ase-ta.*

$$\tilde{n}\,(\pi^{r}c_1)\,n_2\,(\pi_2^{\,r}c_{42})\,(c_{41}^{\,r}c_1^{\,r}s_2)$$

         Ziro NOM curtain ACC rise-CAUS-PAST

         'Ziro caused the curtain to rise.'

5. Parsing with pregroups

We implemented a parser to test and judge the accuracy of the proposed approach. We followed the algorithm presented in Degeilh et al. (2005), which solves the decision problem of the theory of pregroups as well as recognition by a pregroup grammar in time proportional to the cube of the length of the input string.

Buszkowski (2001) has shown that pregroup grammars are weakly equivalent to context-free grammars. Context-free parsing algorithms such as the ones proposed by Younger (1967) and Earley (1970) also have complexity n^3, however, the context-free grammar associated with a pregroup grammar would include the whole dictionary in its set of rules. Furthermore, context-free algorithms use a constant factor which must bound the number of symbols and rules of the grammar. In Degeilh et al.'s algorithm, however, the constant depends on a bound for the number of types per word and a bound for their length, so there is no need to restrict oneself to finite dictionaries.

Before presenting their algorithm, let me introduce some technical definitions.

Definition 1. (Degeilh et al., 2005)

i)   Let V be a non-empty set, A a partially ordered set and P the free pregroup generated by A. A *dictionary of vocabulary V with types in P* is a map D from V to the set of subsets of P.

ii)   A dictionary D is *bounded* if there are constants k and l such that for every word $v \in V$ the set $D(v)$ has at most k elements, and each type in $D(v)$ has at most length l. A dictionary D is locally finite if $D(v)$ is finite for all $v \in V$. It is said to be finite if the sets V, A, and $D(v)$ are finite.

iii)   A *type-assignment* for a string $v_1...v_n$ of elements in V is a sequence $t_1...t_n$ of types in P such that $t_i \in D(v_i)$, for $i = 1,..., n$.

iv)   Let a be a simple type in P. A string $v_1...v_n$ of elements in V is a-grammatical if it has a type assignment $t_1...t_n$ such that $t_1...t_n \rightarrow a$. A sequence $v_1...v_n$ is grammatical if it is a-grammatical for some simple type a.

A type checking algorithm provides a solution to the problem of grammaticality for every dictionary D in which the sets $D(v)$ are finite. A type assignment algorithm provides $v_1...v_n$ with associated strings of types from the dictionary. Enumerating all the possible type assignments would not be very efficient: if k_i is the number of elements in $D(v_i)$ then there are $k_1k_2...k_n$ different type assignments for $v_1...v_n$. Degeilh et al.'s recognition algorithm combines type assignment and type checking.

The intuitive idea underlying the algorithm is as follows: we process the string of symbols W $= v_1...v_n$ from left to right, proceeding by stages. At each stage, we choose a symbol v_i represented by its index i, a type t in $D(v_i)$ and a position p in t. We examine the simple type(s) placed just to the left of this position in some type assignment and store it (them) in the memory, where they are kept as a 'left parenthesis' waiting to be contracted with a simple type that might come later. Moreover, each of them could also be a 'right parenthesis' to some earlier simple type, that is, a 'left parenthesis' ready for contraction. In this case, the two types are contracted; this means that the 'left parentheses' awaiting contraction at the earlier stage become available again, that is, they are stored in the memory at the present stage. This defines a function Nlp_{DW} on the set of stages. For further details regarding the Nlp function, please refer to Degeilh et al. (2005).

5.1. Experiment

Sentences of Japanese are written without word boundaries. The use of a morphological analyzer is thus required to identify words and their grammatical category. This preprocessing phase was realized by the use of the Japanese morphological analyzer system Mecab (http://mecab.sourceforge.net/). Mecab's output then served as input to our pregroup parser.

Here, I confined my attention to a minuscule portion of Japanese grammar, focusing on causative constructions. But as the syntactical analysis will become more exhaustive, the introduction of new types will be needed. Hence, the data must be organized in an efficient way; grammatical categories and their corresponding types were organized into a dictionary.

We designed the dictionary so that a sequence of words is a grammatical construction if and only if one of the corresponding strings of types reduces to a basic type, say α. In the case where a word has more than one type, it is sufficient that one of the possible choices yields a string reducing to the basic type α.

Every dictionary that respects this equivalence is said to be *correct* (it recognizes only grammatical constructions) and *complete* (it recognizes all grammatical constructions of the language fragment) (Degeilh et al., 2005).

A correct and complete dictionary satisfies the following robustness properties (Degeilh et al., 2005):

i)   Assigning new types to words:

Suppose a word w has type β and we also give it type α such that $\alpha \rightarrow \beta$, then every string of words that is accepted using β for w is also accepted using α.

ii)   Extensions by new basic types:

One can extend a given set A of basic types, by declaring new types and adding inequalities involving the new types, thus obtaining a larger set of basic types A'. Then the free pregroup P' generated by A' includes the free pregroup P generated by A.

This signifies that we can increase the language fragment by adding new types to the dictionary, without having to repeat verification of correctness and completeness performed before the extension.

6. Conclusion

We proposed a computational approach based on pregroup grammar to analyze causative constructions in Japanese. We introduced basic types and have assigned types to words which allowed us to account for the linguistic data, recognizing grammatically well-formed sentences.

Using the pregroup algorithm proposed by Degeilh et al. (2005), we developed a parser to confirm the validity and the efficiency of our grammar. Furthermore, it would be easy to add new types in the dictionary to cover other grammatical constructions.

Pregroup grammars are particularly well suited for investigating the computational aspect of language processing. The grammar rules are universal: they are the same whatever the language, only the dictionary changes. Moreover, pregroup grammars gain in expressive power by the introduction of a higher number of basic types.

The pregroup formalism may not be as expressive as other formalisms such as the HPSG framework, as it does not provide any structure for the phonological and semantic information, however, it enables us to parse sentences by means of simple calculations. Furthermore, in analyzing a sentence, we go from left to right, imitating the way a human hearer might proceed.

References

Buszkowski, W. 2001. Lambek Grammars Based on Pregroups. In P. de Groote, G. Morrill, and C. Retoré, ed., *Logical Aspects of Computational Linguistics*, 95-109. Springer LNAI 2099.

Cardinal, K. 2002. *An Algebraic Study of Japanese Grammar*. Master's thesis, McGill University.

Degeilh , S. and Preller, A. 2005. Efficiency of Pregroups and the French Noun Phrase. *Journal of Logic, Language and Information*, 14, 423-444.

Earley, J. 1970. An Efficient Context-Free Parsing Algorithm. *Communications of the AMC*, 13(2), 94-102.

Harada, S.I. 1973. Counter-Equi NP Deletion. *Research Institute of Logopedics and Phoniatrics, Annual Bulletin, University of Tokyo*, 7.

Kitagawa. C. 1974. Case Marking and Causativization. *Papers in Japanese Linguistics*, 4, 43-57.

Kuno, S. 1973. *The Structure of the Japanese Language*. No. 3 of Current Studies in Linguistics. The MIT Press, Cambridge, Massachusetts.

Lambek, J. 1999. Type Grammar Revisited. In A. Lecomte, F. Lamarche, and G. Perier, ed., *Logical Aspects of Computational Linguistics*, pp. 1-27. Springer LNAI 1582.

Miyagawa, S. 1980. Complex Verbs and the Lexicon. In Coyote Papers, 1. University of Arizona, Tucson.

Miyagawa, S. 1984. Blocking and Japanese Causatives. *Lingua*, 64, 177-207.

Miyagawa, S. 1986. Restructuring in Japanese. In T. Imai and M. Saito, ed., *Issues in Japanese Linguistics*. Foris, Dordrecht, 1986.

Miyagawa, S. 1989. Structure and Case Marking in Japanese, volume 22 of *Syntax and Semantics*. Academic Press, San Diego.

Shibatani, M. 1973. Semantics of Japanese Causativization. Foundation of Language, 9, 327-373.

Younger, D. 1967. Recognition and Parsing of Context-Free Languages in Time n3. Information and control, 10(2).

Customizing an English-Korean Machine Translation System for Patent Translation[*]

Sung-Kwon Choi, Young-Gil Kim

Natural Language Processing Team, Electronics and Telecommunications Research Institute,
161 Gajeong-dong, Youseong-gu, Daejon, Korea, 305-350
{choisk, kimyk}@etri.re.kr

Abstract. This paper addresses a method for customizing an English-to-Korean machine translation system from general domain to patent domain. The customizing method consists of following steps: 1) linguistically studying about characteristics of patent documents, 2) extracting unknown words from large patent documents and constructing large bilingual terminology, 3) extracting and constructing the patent-specific translation patterns 4) customizing the translation engine modules of the existing general MT system according to linguistic study about characteristics of patent documents, and 5) evaluating the accuracy of translation modules and the translation quality. This research was performed under the auspices of the MIC (Ministry of Information and Communication) of Korean government during 2005-2006. The translation accuracy of the customized English-Korean patent translation system is 82.43% on the average in 5 patent fields (machinery, electronics, chemistry, medicine and computer) according to the evaluation of 7 professional human translators. In 2006, the patent MT system started an on-line patent MT service in IPAC (International Patent Assistance Center) under MOCIE (Ministry of Commerce, Industry and Energy) in Korea. In 2007, KIPO (Korean Intellectual Property Office) tries to launch an English-Korean patent MT service.

Keywords: Machine Translation, Customization, Patent Machine Translation

1. Introduction

An English-Korean machine translation system has been developed in earnest in Korea since 1996. We have applied it to different areas such as web translation (Choi, 1999) and broadcasting subtitle translation (Choi, 2001). Recently, the natural language processing(NLP) of intellectual property documents is attracting many researchers and NLP-related companies, because NLP techniques associated with specificity of patent domain have promise for improving the translation qualtiy.

It is well known that a sentence style and a dominant translation for a word vary with domains. Therefore, if the domain to be translated is fixed to patents, a adaptation of bilingual dictionary to the patent domain and a customization of natural language analyzer to the linguistic specificity of patent style would be one of effective ways to improve the translation quality of MT system. There have been studies concerned specifically with patent MT using these domain-specific advantages (Shinmori et al., 2003; Hong et al., 2005; Kaji, 2005; Shimihata, 2005).

---

[*] This work was supported by the IT R&D program of MIC/IITA, Domain Customization Machine Translation Technology Development for Korean, Chinese, and English.

Though intensive research has been made on patent MT for the domain-specific advantages, there still remain many issues to be tackled. We focus on the several issues that have continusely been problems in existing English-to-Korean MT systems: (1) new terminology construction, (2) patent-specific probabilities of POS tagger, (3) long and complex sentence analysis, and (4) target word selection.

This paper addresses the customization of an English-Korean MT system for patent translation. The English-Korean patent MT system described in this paper is based on an English-Korean MT system developed for the web translation in a general domain. English-Korean patent MT system belongs to basically the pattern-based methodology for machine translation. It has the formalism that does English sentence analysis in which English patent-specific patterns are used, matches the English patent pattern with its Korean patent pattern, and then generates a Korean sentence from it. English-Korean patent MT system consists of an English morphological analysis module based on lexicalized HMM, an English syntactic analysis module by pattern-based full parsing, a pattern-based transfer, and a Korean morphological generation.

According to experience of patent attorneys, it is said that they read about 7 English patent documents to examine one Korean patent document in average. It means that they examine about 1,000,000 English patent documents for new 150,000 Korean patent documents every year. Korean patent attorneys have required any machine translation system to solve language barrier because they prefer reading Korean translated patent documents to reading English patent documents in spite of such linguistic competency as English native speaker.

In this point, th development of the English-Koran patent translation system is closely related to offering of English-to-Korean patent machine translation service through Internet. KIPO (Korean Intellectual Property Office) pushes on with on-line translation service of patent documents by using MT system.

The English-to-Korean patent machine translation system described in this paper was developed by ETRI (Electronics and Telecommunications Research Institute) under the auspices of the MIC (Ministry of Information and Communication, Korea) during 2005-2006. In 2006, the patent MT system started an on-line patent MT service in IPAC (International Patent Assistance Center) under MOCIE (Ministry of Commerce, Industry and Energy) in Korea. In 2007, KIPO (Korean Intellectual Property Office) tries to launch an English-Korean patent MT service.

Section 2 describes the customization processes that relate to new terminology construction, patent-specific probabilities of POS tagger, long and complex sentence analysis, and target word selection, respectively. The experimental work is presented in section 3. Lastly, in section 4, we present some conclusions.

2. Customization Process

Some methods of customization to change general MT system to domain-specific MT system have been introduced. For example, the customization process in SYSTRAN as multilingual MT system consists of the following steps: term extraction, dictionary customization, linguistic customization, and testing/evaluation (Zajac, 2003). Hong (2005) applied such an existing customization process to a Korean-English MT system.

In comparison with the existing customization methods above mentioned, the customization process described in this paper is the first worth-mentioning large-scale customization effort of an MT system for English and Korean.

The customization process for an English-Korean patent MT system includes the following steps: 1) linguistically studying about characteristics of patent documents, 2) extracting unknown words from large patent documents and constructing large bilingual terminology, 3) extracting and constructing patent translation patterns 4) customizing the translation engine modules of the existing general MT system according to linguistic study about characteristics of patent documents, and 5) evaluating the accuracy of translation modules and the translation quality

2.1.Construction of Patent Terminology

The first step of customization process for patent MT system is to gather the existing terms, extract the unknown words from patent documents, and build the bilingual terms. The customization process described in this paper is similar to the method of Kaji(2005), Shimohata(2005), and Kim(2005) in respect of using the monolingual dictionary and the monolingual patent corpus, but our method is different in that it contains a step inverting the existing bilingual terminology with opposite direction. Extraction and construction of terminology might be represented as a following customization process:

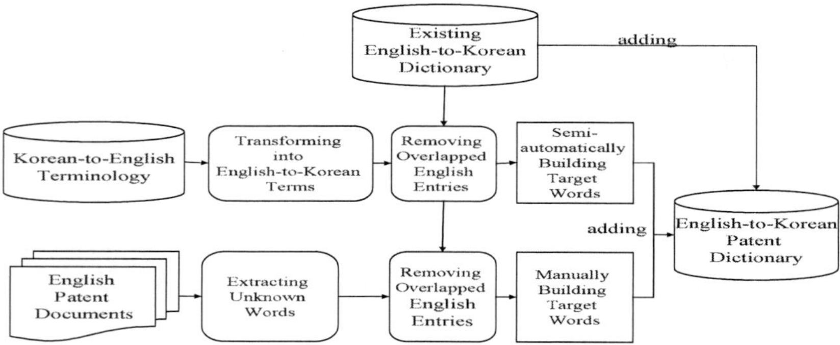

Figure 1: Customization process for building English-Korean patent terminology

   As shown in Figure 1, the patent terminology can be built in two ways. One is to extract the unknown words, remove the overlapped entries, and build manually new bilingual terminology. The other is to build semi-automatically new bilingual terminology, assumed we have the existing bilingual terminology with reverse direction (for example, Korean-to-English terminology). By use of the above customization process, we built semi-automatically 801,046 of new bilingual terminoloy and manually 1,039,189 of new bilingual terminology, that is, 1,840,235 English-Korean terms were totally built for 7 months. 23 people as lexicographers have worked to build the new bilingual terms every day.

Table 1: New English-Korean patent terms semi-automatically built by inverting the existing bilingual terminology

Items	Number of entries
Number of existing Korean-English terminolgy	3,052,655
Number of entries of general-purpose English-Korean dictionary	836,000
New English-Korean terms with the exception of the English terms of existing Korean-English terminolgy overlapped with entries of general-purpose English-Korean dictionary	801,046

Table 1 shows that new 801,046 English-Korean terms were semi-automatically constructed from the existing Korean-English terminology. They are consisted of 207,329 single words and 593,717 compounds.

In addition to new patent terms constructed semi-automatically, we had to extract a number of unknown words from English patent documents and manually build new English-Korean terms, because we had no English-Korean patent corpora.

Table 2: New English-Korean patent terms built manually by use of large English patent documents

Items	Number of entries
English patent documents used	1,001,419
Extracted unknown words	9,662,266
New English-Korean terms	1,039,189

In Table 2, we can know that new 1,039,189 English-Korean terms were built from the very large English patent documents. They consisted of 492,295 single terms and 546,894 compound terms.

In the result, we have now 2,676,235 English-Korean terms including existing 836,000 terms of general-purpose English-Korean dictionary.

2.2. Customization of POS Tagger

We define three customization phases for customizing a general POS tagger based on HMM (Hidden Markov Model) to patent domain, according to the characteristics of English patent document mentioned in the section 2.1:

-   Customization of surface form analysis
    : a tokenization module and/or a morphological analyzer are modified for tokenizing and/or analyzing the peculiar surface forms found in the specific domain.
-   Customization of the lexical information
    : lexical probabilities (output probabilities) are adjusted for holding domain-specific lexical information.
-   Customization of the context information
    : contextual probabilities (transition probabilities) are adjusted for holding the domain-specific contextual information.

In the first phase for customization of surface form analysis, the tokenization module is modified to tokenize and/or chunk very complex symbol words, a chemical formula, a mathematical formula, programming codes, and so on. And our morphological analyzer is improved to assign the estimated part-of-speeches into a compound word connected with hyphen or slash. The estimated part-of-speeches are estimated using the part-of-speeches of its components.

The POS tagging module of English-to-Korean patent machine translation system is based on lexicalized HMM (Pla & Molina, 2005). Therefore, the best simple strategy for the second and third customization phase is retrained from a very large tagged patent corpus. However, there is not a tagged patent corpus and it is also very difficult to construct it. Accordingly, for customizing the lexical and contextual probabilities, we used a raw patent corpus consisting of about one million US patent documents applied for from 2001 to 2005. First, the words of the raw corpus are automatically tagged by our general domain POS tagging system, and then the lexical and contextual probabilities are extracted from the machine-tagged patent corpus. Next, we extracted high-frequent lexical having very different probability with that of the general domain. And we extracted the high-frequent contextual n-grams that didn't appear in the general domain. The extracted lexical and contextual n-grams are tuned by the human experts. For customization of our POS tagger, we tuned about 6,000 lexical and about 1,500 tri-grams.

2.3. Customization of Syntactic Analyzer for Long Sentences

The important syntactic characteristics of the patent document are the frequent use of the patent intrinsic translation pattern and abnormally long sentences. With these as central figures, the main contents of customization of syntax analysis are as follows:

- A build-up and application of the patent translation pattern
  : the patent-specific patterns are manually built up and the processing for the recognition of patterns is performed. The general forms of the patent-specific patterns are composed of lexical words and syntactic nodes. Therefore, for the recognition of the patterns, the lexical words are firstly matched, and then the ranges between the lexical words are parsed. If all ranges are parsed into corresponding syntactic nodes in the translation pattern, the pattern is recognized.
- A large amount of lexical pattern collections and application
  : in the patent documents, the high frequency lexical patterns corresponding to the specific part-of-speech patterns are automatically extracted and are applied to syntactic analysis.
- Performing the coordinate construction recognition for long sentences
  : for the coordinate construction recognition, first, the possible site which can become the initial point, the intermediate point, and an endpoint of the parallel construct. Then, the similarity table between each node is constructed. For the all possible coordinate structures, the coordinate weight is calculated using the similarity table. Finally, the coordinate structure having maximum coordinate weight is selected as a final result. The recognized coordinate construction is chunked to one unit, and accordingly the sentence is simplified.
- Performing the sentence segmentation for the long sentence
  : in case of being too long to analyze the sentence at a time in syntactic analyzer, even after the parallel construction is recognized, the sentence segmentation is performed. The sentence is segmented by recognizing participles or simple sentences.
- Reflecting attachment preferences
  : priority for the attachment of 'for' prepositional phrase and participle is given to the NP attachment than VP attachment.

2.4. Customization of Transfer Module for Target Word Selection

We customized the transfer module for patent document translation. Following customization items for transfer modules were considered:

- The registration of the default target word according to patent technical field
  : In the case that the same source word can be translated into different target word depending on the patent field, the specific value of the 'field' feature is assigned to dictionary.
- The gathering of collocation information for noun/verb with high frequency
  : We use collocation information to select the proper target word depending on the context. The collocation information is used as main knowledge to cope with the problem of the target word selection.
- The implementation of the module to achieve target word selection using collocation information
  : This module carries out the task to select proper target word using collocation information. The approach consists of two levels. In the first step, sense ambiguity of English word is resolved. In the second step, the most suitable Korean target word is selected. To select the most suitable target word, our approach uses multiple knowledge sources such as verb frame patterns, sense vectors based on collocations, statistical Korean local context information and co-occurring POS information. Sense vectors are made using English-Korean parallel corpus. (Lee, 2006)

- The implementation of the interpreter for patent-specific patterns
: The patent-specific patterns were introduced to translate highly frequent expression. Our parser uses these patent-specific patterns in parsing time and then transfer module interprets the patent-specific patterns applied by the parser.

3. Evaluation

3.1. Evaluation of Morphological Analyzer

We evaluated the performance the POS tagger specialized to the patent domain (PatTagger), compared with the performance of our general-purpose POS tagger (GPTagger). For the evaluation, we used 100 sentences of the electrical and electronics field (EEF) among the whole translation evaluation test set. The EEF test set consists of 2,942 words and the number of words per a sentence is 29.42.

Table 3 shows the word accuracy and sentence accuracy of two taggers. From these results we can draw the following conclusions. First, the PatTagger reduced significantly the error tagging about 91% with respect to the GPTagger. Second, PatTagger improved the sentence accuracy with 41% compared with GPTagger. This improvement seems to contribute to the performance improvement of the proposed English-Korean patent translation system.

Table 3: Comparison of the tagging accuracy between GPTagger and PatTager

	GPTagger	PatTagger	
Word tagging accuracy	95.85%	99.62%	Up 3.77%
Sentence tagging accuracy	50.00%	91.00%	Up 41.00%

Table 4 shows the performance improvement factors of PatTagger and the improved word accuracy according to the factors. The improvement factors of PatTagger are three customization phases mentioned in the section 2.2 and construction of terminology mentioned in the section 2.1. The construction of terminology is to add unknown words and their part-of-speeches into morphological analysis dictionary. The performance improvement of word supplement is very low because our POS tagger handles unknown words using suffix analysis as proposed in Brants(2000). From the results of table 4, the customization of lexical and context information is surely needed in order to specialize a general-purpose POS tagger based on HMM to a specific domain.

Table 4: The performance improvement of PatTagger and the improvement of its word tagging accuracy.

The performance improvement factor	The # of tagging error correction	The correction rate	The improvement of word tagging accuracy
Customization of surface form analysis	6	5.41 %	0.20%
Customization of the lexical information	81	72.97 %	2.75%
Customization of the context information	22	19.82 %	0.75%
Construction of Terminology	2	1.80 %	0.07%
Total	111	100.00 %	3.77%

3.2. Evaluation of Syntactic Analyzer for Long Sentences

The evaluation result by the customization of syntactic analyzer is as follows:

Table 5: Evaluation of customization of syntactic analyzer

	Syntactic analysis accuracy	Translation accuracy	Number of translation patterns
General-purpose Syntactic Analyzer	69%	73%	47,413
Customized Syntactic Analyzer	85%	81.6%	75,931
ERR	Up 16%	Up 8.6%	6 months, 3 people per day

In the above table, the syntactic analysis accuracy is calculated by the ratio of the number of correctly analyzed sentences to the number of total sentences[1]. We use the accuracy by the sentence unit instead of the common parsing evaluation metrics by the bracketing match, because the accuracy by the sentence unit shows the direct correlation with the translation accuracy. And the translation accuracy is the comparison result between before and after the customization of syntactic analyzer in the translation system customized for patent documents.

3.3. Evaluation of Transfer Module for Target Word Selection

We compared general-purpose transfer module and patent-specific transfer module for evaluating the performance of target word selection for noun. The test set for the experiment consists of 100 sentences from patent documents. Table 6 shows the experimental results of target word selection of the customized MT system and the non-customized MT system. The performance of customized MT system which has taken customization process for patent document into account overcomes the one of counterpart.

Table 6: Result of target word selection for noun

	Accuracy of target word selection for noun	Percentage of unknown word
General-purpose Transfer Module	71.7%	16.3%
Customized Transfer Module	92.4%	1.5%

3.4. Translation Accuracy

In this chapter, we describe the evaluation about translation quality of English-to-Korean patent MT system. It relates to 5 major patent fields selected from different patent fields. We used the following test sentences, evaluation method and evaluation criterion for translation quality:

- Test sentences
  : translation accuracy was assessed with 100 test sentences randomly extracted from each one of 5 major patent fields (machinery, electronics, chemistry, medicine and computer). The test set was so open that it might reflect a real patent document. Among 100 sentences for each patent field, about 54 sentences were selected from the "detailed description" section of patents, 24 were extracted from the "claim" section, the rest from the "description of the drawing" and the "background of the invention" section. The average length of a sentence was 28.09 words.
- Evaluation criterion:

---

[1] We consider a sentence as correct when the syntactic analysis result of the sentence has a trivial analysis error that dosen't affect the translation result.

Table 7: Scoring criteria for translation accuracy

Score	Criterion
4	The meaning of a sentence is perfectly conveyed
3.5	The meaning of a sentence is almost perfectly conveyed except for some minor errors (e.g. wrong article, stylistic errors)
3	The meaning of a sentence is almost conveyed (e.g. some errors in target word selection)
2.5	A simple sentence in a complex sentence is correctly translated
2	A sentence is translated phrase-wise
1	Only some words are translated
0	No translation

- Evaluation method:
  - 7 professional translators were hired for the evaluation. Ruling out the highest and the lowest score, the scores for each sentence were summed. The method for translation accuracy was as follows:

$$\text{Translation accuracy(\%)} = \sum_{i=1}^{n}(\sum_{j=1}^{5}(score_j/4))/5)/n\times100.0$$, where n is the number of test sentences and $score_j$ is the score evaluated by the j-th professional translator.

The evaluation results for each patent field were as follows:

Table 8: Translation accuracy for each patent field
(Evaluation date: Dec.13, 2006)

Patent field	Average length of a sentence	Translation accuracy higher than 1 score	Translation accuracy higher than 3 scores
Machinery	30.34 words	83.50%	85.00%
Electronics	28.19 words	82.20%	88.00%
Chemistry	29.67 words	82.20%	91.00%
Medicine	26.75 words	81.63%	86.00%
Computer	25.49 words	82.63%	88.00%
Average	**28.09 words**	**82.43%**	**87.60%**

Table 8 shows that the translation accuracy of English-Korean patent MT system was 82.43% on the average. The number of the sentence that were rated equal to or higher than 3 points was 438. It means that about 87.60% of all translations were understandable.

Among the patent fields, the translation of the machinery field was best, while the translation of the medicine field scored worst. The reason for the best scoring of the machinery field is that patent-specific patterns were applied to most of sentences. The medicine field contained, as expected, many unknown words and incorrect target word selection.

Table 9 is the result to compare the translation accuracy before customization with that after customization in the electronic patent document.

Table 9: Comparison of translation accuracy before customization with that after customization in electronic patent document
(Evaluation date: Dec. 13, 2006)

Patent field	Average length of sentence	Translation accuracy before customization	Translation accuracy after customization

| Electronics | 28.19 words | 54.25% | 82.20% |

In Table 9, the difference of translation accuracy between before customization and after customization in electronic patent document was 27.95%. This means that the customization process described in this paper made an important role to enhance the translation qualtiy of English-Korean MT system on patent documents.

4. Conclusion

In this paper we described a method for customizing English-to-Korean machine translation system from general domain into patent domain. The customizing method consists of following steps: 1) linguistically studying about characteristics of patent documents, 2) extracting unknown words from large patent documents and constructing large bilingual terminology, 3) extracting and constructing the patent-specific translation patterns 4) customizing the translation engine modules of the existing general MT system according to linguistic study about characteristics of patent documents, and 5) evaluating the accuracy of translation modules and the translation quality.

The English-Korean patent MT system described in this paper was installed in IPAC (International Patent Assistance Center) under MOCIE (Ministry of Commerce, Industry and Energy) in Korea and provides the patent attorneys and patent examiners with the on-line English-Korean machine translation service for patent documents (http://www.ipac.or.kr). In 2007, KIPO (Korean Intellectual Property Office) is expected to launch its English-Korean MT service.

In near future, we make a plan to evaluate automatically the translation quality like BLEU by building several references and to develop the tool for automatic tuning of bilingual terminology by use of the patent corpus.

References

Brants T. 2000 "TnT – a statistical part-of-speech tagger". *Proceedings of the Sixth Applied Natural Language Processing*, pp. 224-231.

Choi S.K., Kim T.W., Yuh S.H, Jung H.M., Sim C.M. and Park S.K. 1999. English-to-Korean Web Translator: "FromTo/Web-EK", *Machine Translation Summit VII*.

Choi S.K., Yang S.I., Roh Y.H., Lee K.Y. and Park S.K. 2001. English-to-Korean Automatic Caption Translation, *International Conference on the Computer Processing of Oriental Languages*.

Hong M.P., Kim Y.G., Kim C.H., Yang S.I., Seo Y.A., Ryu C. and Park S.K. 2005. Customizing a Korean-English MT System for Patent Translation, *Machine Translation Summit X*, 181-187.

Kaji H. 2005. Domain Dependence of Lexical Translation: A Case Study of Patent Abstract. *Machine Translation Summit X, Workshop on Patent Translation*.

Kim Y.K., Yang S.I., Hong M.P., Kim C.H., Seo Y.A., Ryu C., Park S.K. and Park S.Y. 2005. Terminology Construction Workflow for Korean-English Patent MT. *Machine Translation Summit X, Workshop on Patent Translation*.

Lee K.Y., Park S.K. and Kim H.W. 2006. A Method for English-Korean Target Word Selection Using Multiple Knowledge Sources. *IEICE TRANS. FUNDAMENTALS*, Vol.E89-A, No.6.

Pla F. and Molina A. 2005. Improving Part-of-speech Tagging Using Lexicalized HMMs. *Natural Language Engineering*, 10(2), 167-189.

Shimohata S. 2005. Finding Translation Candidates from Patent Corpus. *Machine Translation Summit X, Workshop on Patent Translation*.

Shinmori A., Okumura M., Marukawa Y. and Iwayama M. 2003. Patent Claim Processing for

Readability - Structure Analysis and Term Explanation, *the Association for Computational Linguistics, Workshop on Patent Corpus Processing.*
Zajac R. 2003. MT Customziation. *Machine Translation Summit Workshop.*

A New Type of NPI Licensing Context:
Evidence from French Subjunctive and *NE Explétif* [*]

Yoon-Hee Choi

Department of French Education

Seoul National University

Seoul 151-742, Korea

youni@snu.ac.kr

Abstract. The purpose of this paper is to propose a new type of NPI licensing context through French subjunctive and *ne explétif.* The distribution of NPIs on previous studies does not exactly correspond to negative function types. French subjunctive and *ne expletif* are good guidelines for reclassifying NPI licensing context. My classification is by a hierarchy of strength in negative force: *overtly negative proposition > negative entailment > negative implicature.* A new type of NPI licensing context is: (i) I-domain for negative implicature (ii) E-domain for negative entailment and (iii) overt negation.

Keywords: NPI licensing context, French subjunctive, *ne explétif,* negative force

1. Introduction

Despite their huge contribution, previous studies on NPI licensing context are problematic in that they treat it as a simple filter. Moreover some contexts are still unexplainable within them. My proposal in this paper can provide an answer of why they license NPIs, also explaining the unexplainable.

  This paper is organized as follows: In section 2, I will briefly present the previous researches. In section 3, I show that French subjunctive is equivalent to nonveridicality specially focusing on its licensing property of weak NPIs. In section 4, I give you the answer of the question "why and where *ne expétif* comes about". In section 5, I will propose a new type of NPI licensing context.

2. Previous Research

Among the studies of NPIs, downward entailment (DE, Ladusaw 1979, cited in 1996) is the first to show the property of NPI licensing context. Later on more accurate properties (Zwarts 1993 cited in Ladusaw 1996 and Nam 1998) were proposed, creating a hierarchy of negative

------

expressions since DE simply distinguishes negation from affirmation. The followings are three negative functions (examples are from Lee 1999).

(1) Three negative functions

（ⅰ）**Downword entailment** If A and B are two Boolean algebras, the function f from A into B
   is polarity reversing iff for any a_1, $a_2 \in A$, if $a_1 \leq a_2$, then $f(a_2) \leq f(a_1)$. e.g. at most (weak)

（ⅱ）A functor f is **anti-additive** iff $f(X \vee Y)=f(X) \wedge f(Y)$. e.g. no, before, every (strong)

（ⅲ）A functor f is **antimorphic** iff f is anti-additive and additionally $f(X \wedge Y)=f(X) \vee f(Y)$.
   e.g. not (the strongest)

Zwarts (1995) added here a weaker function, that is 'nonveridicality' and Giannakodou(2002, 2007) developed it with Greek subjunctive mood. Zwarts' (1995) definition about nonveridicality is as below:

(2) **Nonverdicality**

Let O be a monadic sentential operator. O is said to be veridical just in case $Op \Rightarrow p$ is logically valid. If O is not veridical, then O is nonveridical. A nonveridical operator called averidical iff $Op \Rightarrow \sim p$ is logically valid.

Despite the fact that three negative functions and nonveridicality have been instrumental in our understanding of NPI licensing context, some problems remain unsolved: emotive factive predicates that are veridical but license NPIs (e.g. I am <u>happy</u> to get <u>any</u> ticket), and some nonveridical predicates that partially (e.g. % I <u>hope</u> there is <u>any</u> food left) license NPIs. Moreover there are many examples which do not exactly correspond to the typology based on negative functions. French subjunctive and *ne explétif* can guide us to reconsider the previous unsolved problems about NPI licensing context.

3. French subjunctive and nonveridicality

3.1. French subjunctive, nonveridicality and the weak NPIs

Traditionally indicatives represent the act or state as an objective fact while subjunctives[1] express subjective actions such as will/wanting, emotion, doubt, possibility, necessity, judgement, comparatives. French subjunctive also appears after the conjunctions like 'before',

---

[1] As its name shows, subjunctive is always found in dependent clauses introduced by a subordinate conjunction *que* 'that'.

'except', which license strong NPIs. Intuitively subjunctive is linked with nonveridicality. With this operator, Giannakidou (2007) clearly posits the division between the veridical and the nonveridical in connection with indicatives and subjunctives. If a propositional attitude verb has an availability of at least one truth inference about its complement, it will be veridical and takes the indicative: if not, it will be nonveridical and takes the subjunctive. In this sense, verbs or expressions which license weak NPIs (e.g. will/wanting, emotion, doubt, possibility, necessity, judgement, modal, questions) and even some conjunctions (e.g. before, except) which license strong NPIs are both nonveridical. The example (3) is the usage of the indicative and the subjunctive.

(3) a. Je **désire**   qu'il **vienne**.
    I wish that he come-Sub.
    'I wish that he comes.'
   b. J' **espère** qu'il **viendra**.
    I hope that he come-Ind.-Future.
    'I hope that he will come.'

Why do the pairs (3a)-(3b) take different moods in their complements? Guillaumean concept of *temps opérative* 'operative time' (Guillaume 1970) can give us an answer. According to him, all human mental operations need operative time, though it is very instant, and if we differentiate this time, we can see several phases. From each phase, we can read one's mental state or motive from which a particular expression is produced. In this sense 'Espérer' in example (3b) captures speaker's idea of believing realization of its complement while 'désirer' in (3a) represents speaker's lack of certainty of the subordinate clause. The selection of mood depends on how concrete the speaker feels about what is being said.

Now let me show the examples[2] of French subjunctive (=the nonveridical) licensing weak NPIs. As Lee (1999) argues, we have different forms of strong NPIs '*amu* N *to*' and weak NPIs '*amu* N *i-ra-to*' in Korean. Similarly French has its distinctive form of weak NPIs *qui que ce soit* 'anyone' and its inanimate counterpart *quoi que ce soit* 'anything'.

(4) a. Max est trop honnête pour **désirer**   être   impliqué   dans **quoi que ce soit** de tel.
     Max is too   honest for   to-desire   to-be   implicated in   anything   of such.
     'Max is too honest to want to be involved in any such thing'
   b. Je **doute que** Max fasse **quoi que ce soit** de tel.

---

[2] Examples are from Lee & Larrivée (1999), Vlachou (2003) and the website 'google'.

I doubt that Max do-Sub. anything of such.

'I doubt that Max would do any such thing.'

c. Je **crains que** il ne dise **quoi que ce soit** qui offenserait les banques d'alimentation.

I fear that he *ne explétif* say-Sub. anything which offend-Fut.-anterior the bank-Pl of food.

'I fear to say anything which would offend the banks of food'

d. Cette fois-ci le chauffeur **refuse que** je paye **quoi que ce soit,**...

This time-so the driver refuse that I pay-Sub. anything,...

'This time, the driver refuses to get paid anything from me,...'

e. Ils m'ont laissé seule, **sans que** je sache **quoi que ce soit** sur mes grands parents.

They me had left alone, without I know-Sub. anything about my grand parents.

'They had left me alone, without me knowing anything about my grand parents.'

f. Maintenant, votez pour le chef du forum ! **Avant que** je fasse **quoi que ce soit.**

Now vote-Imp. for the chief of-the forum ! Before I do-Sub. anything.

'Now vote for the chief of the forum ! Before I do anything.'

g. Olivier est **plus grand que qui que ce soit.**

Olivier is more tall than anyone.

'Olivier is taller than anyone.'

In the above examples, the verbs or expressions which take the subjunctive license weak NPIs. The contexts where weak NPIs *amu N-i-ra-to* appears in Korean have a similarity to French subjunctive contexts. Lee (2003) specified in detail the distribution of the weak form *amu N-i-ra-to* in various contexts such as (?)'before' clause, negative predicates, modal, imperative, future tense, generics, *kikkethayya* 'at most', rhetorical questions, questions, conditionals, *?comparatives, ?habitual and universal /generic quantifier. Notice that 'before', negative predicate, rhetorical question and comparatives are supposed to license strong NPIs in negative functions. On this source, I claim that the licensing contexts of NPIs are rather complementary than crystal-clearly divided.

3.2. Unsolved problems: emotive factive predicates and 'hope'

Among the verbs which take the indicative (e.g. assertives, fiction verbs, epistemics, factive verbs, semifactives, Giannakidou 2007), emotive factive predicates in French select subjunctive but do not license NPIs. (5) and (6) are the examples.

(5) Je suis **content** que tu **sois** avec nous.

I am happy that you are-Sub. with us.

'I am happy that you are with us.

(6) * Je suis **content** d'avoir obtenue **quelque ticket que ce soit**.

    I am happy to have get any ticket

    'I am happy to get any ticket.'

However emotive factive predicates in Korean such as *tahaeng-i-ta* 'lucky', *nollap-ta* 'surprising' and *huhoy-ha-ta* 'regret', license weak NPIs form *amu-i-ra-to* 'any', as Lee (1999) observed.

(7) **amu phyo-i-ra-to** kuhae-ss-uni **tahaeng -i- ta**.

    any ticket -be-Dec-C get-Past-since luck -be-Dec

    '(I) am lucky that (I) got any tickets (at all).'

Lee (1999) suggests that emotive factive predicates should be classified as the weakest NPIs since NPI licensibility is not witnessed cross-linguistically. To explain why this kind of variation occurs, he argues that the speaker's real motivation behind the phenomenon of all those polarity-sensitive expressions should be considered. This argument can be supported by Giannakidou (2002) as she proposes 'pragmatic licensing' for a solution of the emotive factive predicates. She notes that it is problematic if we want to maintain a purely semantic account for NPI licensing context since emotive factive predicates are veridical and not downward entailment. That is to say, pragmatic context should be taken into account. On the other hand, nonveridical desiderative predicates 'hope' in English partially license NPIs. (Lee 1999)

(8) % I **hope** to drink **any** beer from any country.

Example (8) show that 'hope' can license weak NPIs only when speaker's negative implicature intervenes in the context. As for (8) it is acceptable only if we imagine that the person involved is a complete alcoholic, or he has been trapped in a boozeless hell for years. This view exactly corresponds to the concept of *temps opératif* presented in 3.1. The above example suggests that the mental operation in *temps opératif* can be differentiated depending on the situations. This view will be developed as 'pragmatic licensing' in section 5. In the next section, we will see how French *ne explétif* is related with negative entailment.

4. *Ne Explétif* and **Negative Entailment**.

In general, French adverb *ne* negates verbs with other reinforcing adverbs such as *pas, point, plus, jamais* etc, (e.g. Je <u>ne</u> bois <u>pas</u> de vin. (I don't drink wine.)) and only *ne* alone can not negate a sentence. So *ne...pas* translates roughly as 'not'. Originally in an Old French *ne* alone was used for negation and *pas* 'step' was used as a minimizer. But through historic change, *pas* is thought to get its negating power from its use for emphasis. Therefore some view *pas* as negative.

On the other hand *Ne explétif* is called "non-negative *ne*", because it has no negative value in and of itself. It is used in situations where the main clause has a weakly negative or uncertainty meaning of fear, warning, doubt. *Ne explétif* appears in a subordinate clause with subjunctive mood, but not all subjunctives can allow *ne explétif*. Accordingly *ne explétif* is a subcase of nonveridicality. Though the appearance of *ne explétif* is not mandatory, it appears in the context where the strong NPIs as well as the weak NPIs are licensed. Thus they do not exactly correspond to three negative functions.

The contexts where *ne explétif* appears are in (9). Some conjunctions such as *à moins que* 'unless' , *avant que* 'before', *sans que* 'without' and comparatives are licensing contexts of strong NPIs while the other conjunctions and verbs take weak NPIs.

(9) **The contexts where *ne explétif* appears**
a. **Verbs/Conjunctions licensing weak NPIs** : avoir peur   'to be afraid', Craindre 'to fear', Douter 'to doubt', Empêcher 'to prevent', Éviter 'to avoid', Nier 'to deny', de peur que 'for fear that', plutôt que 'rather than', de crainte que 'for fear that'
b. **Comparatives/Conjunctions Licensing strong NPIs** : Autre 'other', Meilleur 'better', Mieux 'best', Moins 'less', Pire 'worse', Pire 'worse', Plus 'more', à moins que 'unless', avant que 'before', sans que 'without'

Let's take a look at the usage of ***ne explétif***.

(10) Aidez   -moi   avant que tu   **ne**   parte.
　　 Help-Imp. Me   before   you   *ne explétif* leave-Sub.
　　 "Help me before you leave."
(11) Je crains qu'il **ne**   dise   **quoi que ce soit** qui   offenserait   les   banques
　　 d'alimentation.
　　 I   fear   that   he *ne explétif* say-Sub.   anything   which   offend-Fut-anterior the   bank-Pl
　　 of food.
　　 'I fear to say anything which would offend the banks of food'

Example (10) shows that *avant que* 'before' clause is nonveridical and takes subjunctive and *ne explétif* . This is because in the speaker's hypothetical possible world, the event following 'before' should not be realized until the event of the main clause has happened. *Craindre* 'fear' in (11) also takes subjunctive and *ne explétif* and license weak NPI *'quoi que ce soit'*. Interestingly *ne explétif* is observed in Korean and in Japanese as well[3].

(12) Je crains que vous **ne** preniez froid. (F)

    na-nun ne-ga kamki-ey kelli ci-nun **anh** assul-ka tulyep ta. (K)

    watashi-wa anata-ga kaze-o hiki-wa si-**nai**-ka to sinpai-site iru. (J)

    ≠I fear that you don't catch a cold.

(13) Je désire vous ne prenez pas froid. (F)

    na-nun ne-ga kamki-ey kelli ci anh ki lul palan ta. (K)

    watashi-wa anata-ga kaze-o hika-nai koto-o nozon-de iru.

    ' I hope you don't catch a cold.'

Kinoshita argues that 'fearing something and 'hoping it will not happen' are semantically same. That is, (12) entails (13) in the sentence meaning. To explain her argument, let me write down her hypothesis again.

(14) DÉSIRE NEG . S_i = CRAINDRE S_j

    [Where: $S_i = S_j$; NEG . S_i means the negation of S_i]

If the hypothesis in (14) holds ture, we can presume that (12) is identical with (13). That is, we may also mean (13) only mentioning (12). But to make sure that (13) is involved in the meaning of (12) we need somewhere in (12) some markers. In this sense, NEG in (13) moves to (12) and is transferred into *ne explétif*.

Her argument can be supported by Kadmon & Landman (1993)'s claim. They insist that the relationship between the following example (15)-(16) are not a conventional implicature but an entailment. That is (15) entails (16).

(15) I'm sorry that anybody hates me.

(16) I want for nobody to hate me.

Thus we claim that the context where *ne explétif* appears entails negation in their lexical semantics or expression. In Korean and in Japanese however the context is limited to the following expressions ; *(i) verbs of emotion or feeling which indicate fear or doubt. (ii) expressions with conjunction 'before'.*

---

[3] French and Japanese examples are from Kinoshita (1998).

(17) ubak **-i-ra-to**   o-ci   **anh-ul**   **-ka**   tulyep ta. (K)

(18) hiyou –**de-mo**   **hura**   **nai**   **-ka**   osoroshi i. (J)

    hail -be -Dec –C   come   *ne explétif*   -Comp   afraid-Dec.

    '(I) am afraid it's going to hail.'

(19) te   nai   tul-ci   **anh-ki**   ceney   sicip   ga-ra.

    more   age   get *ne explétif*   before   marriage   go-Imp.

    'Get married before you get older'

(20) kuraku   nara   **-nai**   mae-ni   kaette-kuru no-desuyo.

    dark   become - *ne explétif*   before   return Imp.

    'You must come back home before it gets dark.' (Kinoshita : 1998)

Example (17) *tulyepta* (K) and (18) *osoroshi i*(J) 'afraid' license weak NPIs *N-i ra to* (K)[4],   *N-de-mo* (J) just as *craindre* (F) in (11) licenses weak NPIs *quoi que ce soit*, while (19) *ceney* (K) and (20) *mae-ni* (J) usually license strong NPIs. Then how we can define the context which cause *ne expletif*? Apart from the fact that *ne expletif* -causing contexts in Korean and Japanese do not exactly match to that in French, it is very attractive that this kind of phenomenon happens in different languages. In section 5, I will propose a new type of NPI licensing context with this *ne explétif*-appearing context.

5. A New Type of NPI Licensing Context.

In section 4, I claimed that *ne explétif* is a trace of deletion of negative entailment. This means that all the contexts which cause *ne expletif* entail negation in its lexical expression. Since *ne explétif*-appearing context is the subcase of the subjunctive-appearing context, negative entailment is a subcase of the nonverdical. For more generalization, let me briefly introduce a concept of Martin (1987) as the theoretical background. He argues that *ne explétif* represents a force as a movement from the positive to the negative. That is, *ne explétif* pre-captures movement toward the negative. This can be schematized as in figure 1.

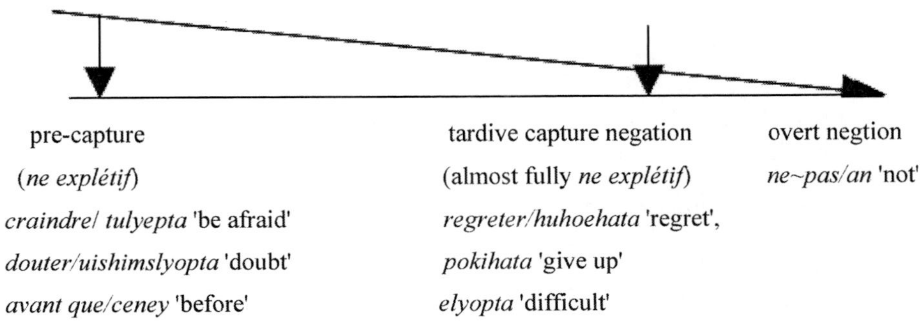

---

[4] K stands for Korean, J for Japanese and F for French.

sans que 'except'   *shillta* 'dislike'

Figure 1: movement toward the negative (Martin 1987)

In figure 1, we see the 'tardive capture' point which is between pre-capture and negation, and French verb *regreter* 'regret' is on that point. *Regreter* 'regret' entails 'hoping not doing' but doesn't take *ne explétif* in its complement. Martin (1987) argues that *ne explétif* occurs only in the context where there exists a contradiction between the real world and the alternative world and where the real world and the alternative world are both the possible world[5]. In other words, the verbs or expressions causing *ne explétif* should presuppose that its complement is neither factive nor non-factive. In case of *regreter*, its complement is factive that is, the truth of which has been already presupposed by the lexical meaning of *regreter*.

Tentatively I will propose a new type of NPI licensing context by a hierarchy of strength in negative force. Lee (1999) already explained that negative entailment is stronger than negative implicature. The negative degree can be shown as follows (Lee 1999):

(21) *overtly negative proposition > negative entailment > negative implicature.*

We argued that some emotive factive predicates and desiderative predicate 'hope' license the weak NPIs only when speaker's pragmatic implicature intervenes. Now let this type of predicates be located in I (mplicature)- domain. As for the predicates or expressions which entail negation in their lexical semantics, let them be located in E (ntailmet)- domain. And I specify E-domain with two sub-domains since all negative predicates do not bring *ne explétif.* I-domain and E-domain can be schematized as in figure 2.

------------------------------------Subjunctive (the nonveridical)-------------------------------------

--negative implicature- -----------negative entailment (b) E-domain ------------------------------------

<--- (b-1) E-*ne explétif* domain--> <------(b-2) E-almost fully---------->

negative *ne* domain

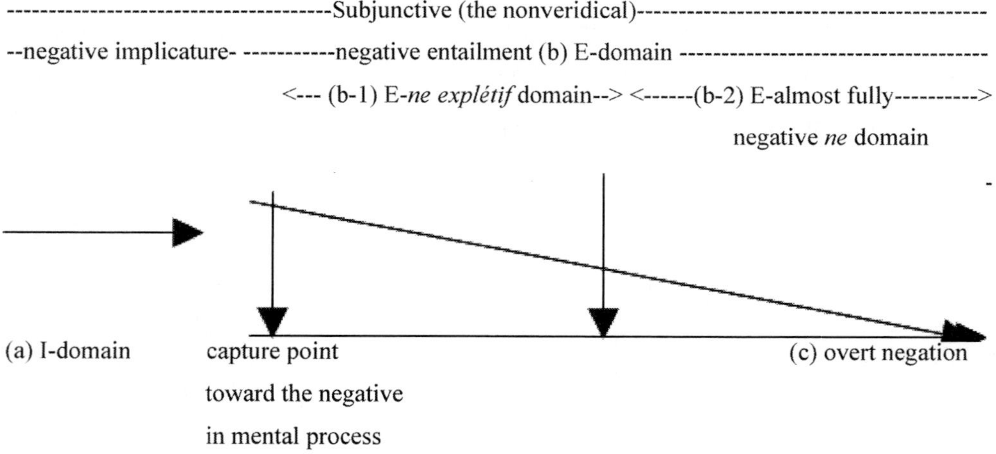

(a) I-domain capture point   (c) overt negation

toward the negative

in mental process

Figure 2 : New type of NPI licensing context by negative force

---

[5] This concept is similar to modal operators.

(a) I-domain: context which holds negative implicature. (i.e. *tahaeng-i-ta* 'lucky', *nollap-ta* 'surprising', hope)

(b) E-domain

(b-1) E-*ne explétif* domain: context of which lexical semantics or expression entail negation but its complement has not been realized yet. (e.g. *craindre/ tulyepta* 'be afraid', *douter/uishimslyopta* 'doubt', *avant que/ceney* 'before', *sans que* 'except', other French contexts which take *ne explétif*)

(b-2) E-almost fully negative *ne* domain: context of which lexical or expression entail negation but its complement is either factive or non-factive. This context does not take *ne explétif*. (e.g. *regreter/huhoehata* 'regret', pokihata 'give up', *elyopta* 'difficult', *shillta* 'dislike')

(c) overt negation (e.g. *ne pas/an*, not)

This new type not only shows the distribution of NPIs in licensing context but also explains why NPIs are licensed in such context. Human thoughts are not clearly divided: positive and negative, strong and weak etc. To understand why the above contexts license NPIs, we should consider 'mental process' up to its production. By this mental process we can approach NPI licensing context more fundamentally.

5. Conclusion

With French subjunctive and *ne explétif,* we could reconsider previous unsolved problems about NPI licensing context. In some languages like French, its grammatical mood can represent speaker's mental process. This fact helps us to understand why French subjunctive corresponds to nonveridical context. On the other hand, It has been shown that emotive factive predicates (e.g. lucky) and nonveridical predicate (e.g. hope) in English can license NPIs only when speaker's negative attitude is implicated. This means that pragmatic factor should be intervened to explain NPI licensing context. Therefore I set up I-domain for negative implicature which is relatively weak in negative force. *Ne explétif* is a good guideline to establish E-domain since I assume that *ne explétif* is a trace of deletion of negative entailment. My new type helps to understand NPI licensing context under the movement from the positive to the negative in our mental process.

REFERENCES

Giannakidou, A. 2002. Licensing and Sensitivity in Polarity Items : from Downward Entailment to (Non)veridicality. *To appear in Chicago Linguistic Society* 39.

--------------------2007. Time for mood: the subjunctive revisited. *To appear in Lingua, special issue on Mood*. Pre-proof draft.

Guillaume, G. 1970. *Temps et Verbe*. Librairie Honoré Champion, Paris.

Kadmon, L. and F. Landman. 1993. Any, *Linguistics and Philosophy.* 16, 353-422.

Kinoshita Hiroaki. 1989. Where Do 《Ne Explétif》 's Come From? *The journal of Wayo Women's University* Vol. 29. 1-14.

Ladusaw, W. 1996. Negation and Polarity Items' in S. Lappin ed., *The Handbook of Contemporary Semantic Theory*. Blackwell. 321-341.

Lee Chungmin. 1996. Negative Polarity Items in English and Korean. *Language Science.* Vol 18. Nos 1-2. 505-523.

------------------. 1999. Types of NPI and Nonveridicality in Korean and other Languages. *UCLA Working Papers in Syntax*. G. Storto ed.

----------------. 2003. Negative Polarity Items in Korean and Japanese: A Contrastive Study," *Icwungenehak*('Bilingualism'), Seoul.

Larrivée, P and Chungmin Lee. 1999. Free-Choice and Negative Polarity Interpretation - A Unified Approach : Evidence from Korean and French. *The Linguistic Society of Korea ed.*, Linguistics in the Morning Calm 4. 497-512.

Martin, R. 1987. *Langage et Croyance -Les 《Universe de Croyance》 dans la Théorie Sémantique*. Pierre Mardaga.

Nam Sengho. 1998. The Typology and Licensin Conditions of Negative Polarity Items (in Korean). *Eoneohag*. The Linguistic Society of Korea 22. 217-244.

Vlachou, E. 2003. Weird polarity indefinites in French. *Linguistics in the Netherlands*, Jonh Benjamins. 189-200.

Zwarts, F. 1995. Nonveridical Contexts. *Linguistic Analysis* 25(3-4). 286-312.

Computing Thresholds of Linguistic Saliency[*]

Siaw-Fong Chung[a] , Kathleen Ahrens[a] Chung-Ping Cheng[b], Chu-Ren Huang[c] , Petr Šimon[c,d]

[a]Graduate Institute of Linguistics, National Taiwan University, No.1, Roosevelt Road, Section 4, Taipei 106, Taiwan.
[b]Department of Psychology, National Chengchi University, No. 64, ZhiNan Road, Section 2, Taipei 11605, Taiwan.
[c]Institute of Linguistics, Academia Sinica, No. 128, Academia Road, Section 2, Nangang, Taipei 115, Taiwan.
[d]TIGP-CLCLP, Institute of Linguistics, Academia Sinica, No. 128, Academia Road, Section 2, Nangang, Taipei 115, Taiwan.
f91142002@ntu.edu.tw, kathleenahrens@yahoo.com, cpcheng@nccu.edu.tw, churen@gate.sinica.edu.tw, petr.simon@gmail.com

Abstract. We propose and test several computational methods to automatically determine possible saliency cut-off points in Sketch Engine (Kilgarriff and Tugwell, 2001). Sketch Engine currently displays collocations in descending importance, as well as according to grammatical relations. However, Sketch Engine does not provide suggestions for a cut-off point such that any items above this cut-off point may be considered significantly salient. This proposal suggests improvement to the present Sketch Engine interface by calculating three different cut-off point methods, so that the presentation of results can be made more meaningful to users. In addition, our findings also contribute to linguistic analyses based on empirical data.

Keywords: saliency, cut-off point, threshold, collocations

1. Introduction

All lexical resources, at the point of their design, will take into consideration whether the resources are useful to a target group. For example, WordNet (Fellbaum, 1998) was originally designed for psychologists, but later was used extensively by computational linguists. Similarly, corpora such as British National Corpus (BNC), the Academia Sinica Corpus of Mandarin Chinese (Chen et al., 1996) and the Gigaword corpus were also designed for the use of target groups such as lexicographers, linguists, language teachers, language learners, etc. These corpora usually provide some forms of statistical analyses so that users will be able to summarize their research results quickly. For example, many corpora provide collocational measures such as Mutual Information values (Church and Hanks, 1989) so that collocated words can be sorted according to their frequency of co-occurrence. Sketch Engine (Kilgarriff and Tugwell, 2001) is a powerful resource which displays search summary in collocated patterns, as well as according to grammatical relations. However, like many other resources, Sketch Engine is unable to determine which of the results in the list are meaningful linguistically.

Therefore, when provided with collocation lists, most linguists report the top "few," based on their preferences. Some linguists report the top one or two and keep the rest in appendixes. In fact, the current search summary from corpora or lexical resources does not give enough

---

[*] We would like to thank Professor Shu-Chuan Tseng for her comments on this paper, and for suggesting the idea underlying third method for calculating cut-off points.

information regarding which of the collocational patterns are significantly different from the bottom words. In this paper, a research question is asked, i.e., whether or not one can select top rankings from linguistic results using principled measures. This selection of top rankings is useful because it will provide an automatic identification of significant linguistic results from the data. This also involves deciding which significant results are likely to be prototypically used in certain linguistic environments (Rosch and Mervis, 1975). In this paper, we propose three methods in which the threshold of linguistic listings can be extracted. In the following section, data presentation in Sketch Engine is first discussed.

2. Data Presentation in the Sketch Engine

Sketch Engine is a system that provides the collocations of words according to grammatical relations. It has been used to analyze large scale corpora data such as the British National Corpus (BNC) and the Chinese Gigaword corpus. The Chinese Sketch Engine was created by Kilgarriff, Huang, Rychly et al. (2005). It has the same function as the English Sketch Engine, which also arranges collocates for query words in grammatical relations. For example, when a query word is searched in Sketch Engine, the system will return with the collocates for this query word. Sketch Engine then arranges them in grammatical relations such as 'objects of the query word,' 'subjects of the query word,' 'modifiers of the query word,' etc.

The following Figure 1 shows an example of the search result for 經濟 *jing1ji4* 'economy' in the Chinese Sketch Engine.

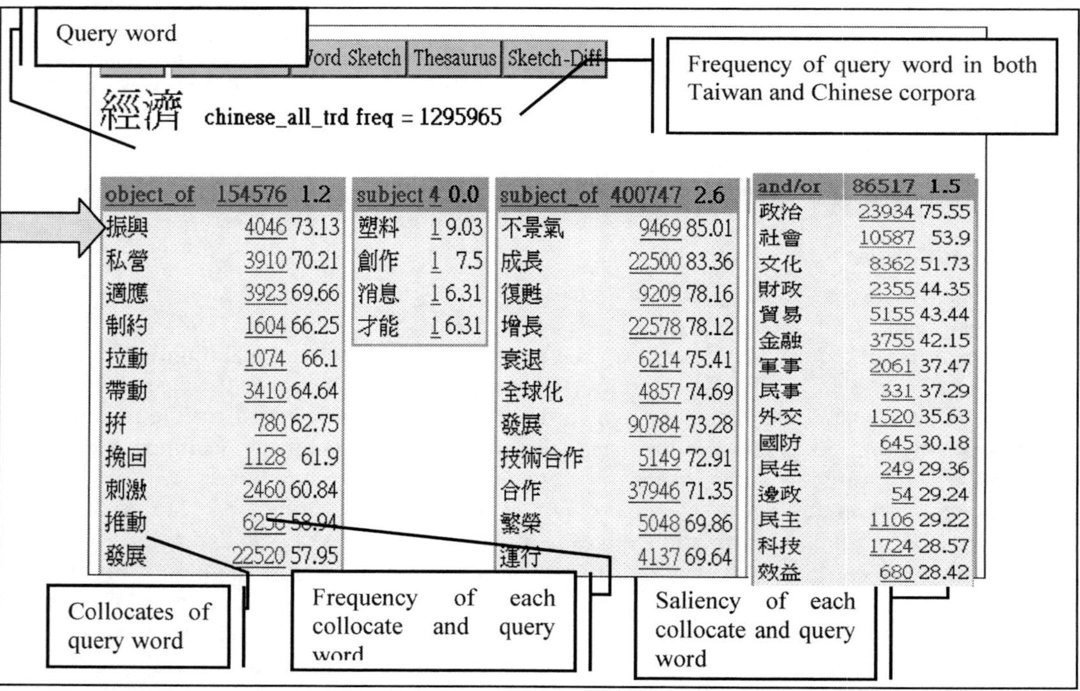

Figure 1: Collocates for the Query Word 經濟 *jing1ji4* 'Economy' in the Chinese Sketch Engine

In Figure 1, the query word and its frequency in the entire Gigaword corpus are shown (i.e. 1,295,965 instances). The frequency for pair of collocates such as 經濟 *jing1ji4* 'economy' and 振興 *zheng4xing4* 'to give life to' under the 'object-of' relation (arrow in Figure 1) is given. In this case, it is 4,046 (in the second column for each relation), indicating that 經濟 *jing1ji4* 'economy' appears as the 'object of' the verb 振興 *zheng4xing4* 'to give life to' 4046 times in the whole Gigaword corpus.

In addition to frequency, Sketch Engine provides an additional score for the ranking of saliency of collocates. This is because Kilgarriff and Tugwell (2001) suggest that frequency alone may not be a reliable score because frequency of the collocates are relative to the number of both words in the whole corpus. Therefore, they suggest using a more reliable account to standardize all frequencies for the collocations based on the overall performance of the collocates in a particular condition. However, while the presentation of saliency in Sketch Engine is robust and useful, it does not indicate which of the collocates in each relation are meaningfully salient.

WordNet (http://wordnet.princeton.edu/) can also display search results based on a "high frequency count" (see Figure 2).

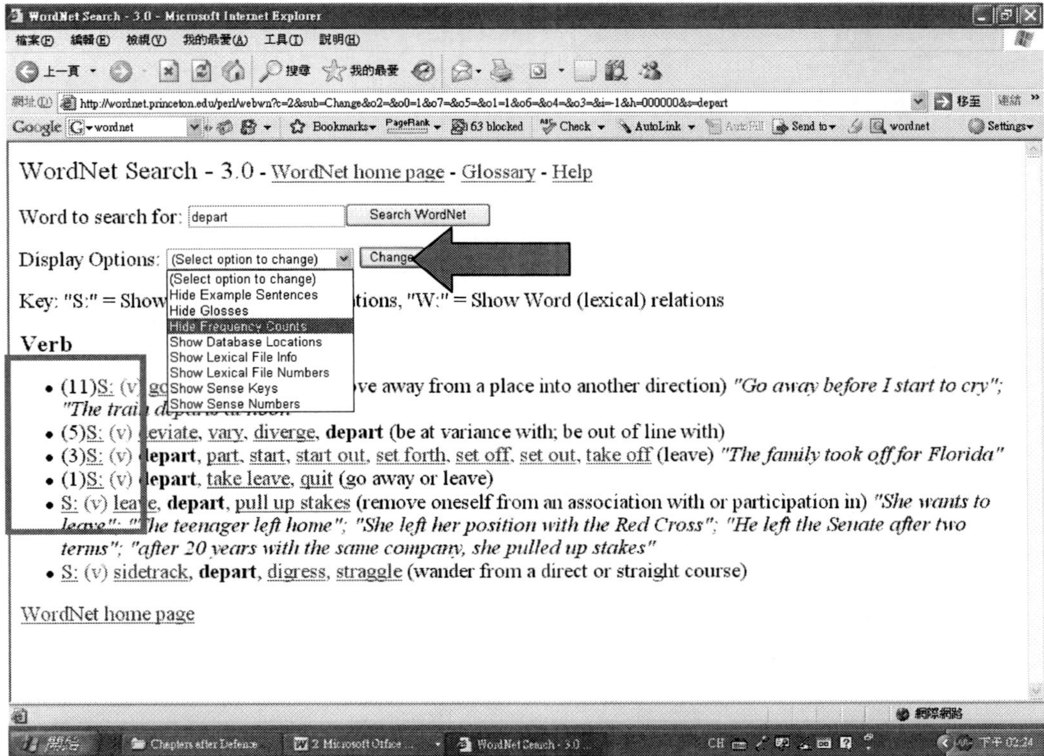

Figure 2: Displayed by Frequency Counts in WordNet 3.0

This frequency count is ordered from the most frequent sense to the least frequent sense (Tengi, 1999) that is computed using a semantic concordance created by Landes, Leacock and Tengi (1999) based on two corpora – the Brown corpus and Stephen Crane's novella entitled *The Red Badge of Courage.*[1]

From Figure 2, one can see that the sense frequencies for 'depart' are 11, 5, 3 and 1. We can see that there is a bigger gap between the frequency of the first sense (11) and the frequency of the second sense (5). Based on this gap, we may say that the first sense is more often used than the second one. It is also possible to say that the first sense is more prototypical than the other

---

[1] Only senses that were found in the two corpora can be shown their frequency counts in brackets.

senses. Therefore, there is possibly a threshold after the first sense to make the first sense more distinctive in use than the others. Therefore, this paper suggests that there should be some objective methods which can help determine the threshold of linguistic listings as such. This paper suggests three methods to find out how many of the top few results should be considered significant in Sketch Engine. These methods are elaborated below.

3.   Computing Thresholds of Linguistic Listings

This paper will discuss three methods. Methods One and Two are based on the characteristics of the distributional listings, which usually follow Zipf's law (Zipf, 1932). Therefore, these two methods will be discussed together in section 3.1 below. Section 3.2 will discuss Method Three, which is different from both methods one and two. Section 4 will present results from all three methods.

3.1. Methods One and Two

Zipf's law states that the most frequent value is most likely to be twice as much as the second most frequent value. For example, when a sample size is large enough, the result of a frequency listing is likely to be in a distributional pattern. For instance, the expression 起飛 *qi3fei1* 'takeoff' in (1) below, has the following collocates from the Sketch Engine (Figure 3).

(1) 但　　在　　台灣　　經濟　　起飛 後　　(Central News Agency of Taiwan)
　　dan4　zai4　tai2wan1　jing1ji4　qi3fei2　hou4
　　but　　at　　Taiwan　　economy　takeoff　after
　　"But after the economy of Taiwan takeoffs…"

The collocates for 起飛 *qi3fei1* 'takeoff' which have similar grammatical relations with 經濟 *jing1ji4* 'economy' (the 'subject' relation) can be seen in Figure 3 (such as 飛機 *fei1ji1* 'airplane,' 班機 *ban1ji1* 'flight,' 跑道 *pao3dao4* 'path' as well as 經濟 *jing1ji4* 'economy'). We can see that in Figure 3, the saliency values of the collocates are arranged in descending order (from 55.67, 48.31, 38.64, and continue on until the lowest value, which is zero).

起飛　chinese_all_trd:taiwan-only freq = 16705

subject	2208	19.6
飛機	514	55.67
班機	225	48.31
跑道	70	38.64
經濟	576	31.78
夢想	27	30.68
客機	51	30.4
滑行道	7	28.31
航機	14	25.19
專機	25	24.33
航空母艦	15	22.34
小時	32	22.24
軍機	15	21.75
戰機	25	21.4
包機	14	21.22
直昇機	17	20.6
航艦	8	20.37
班次	13	20.07
航班	14	18.98
直升機	15	18.38
協和機	3	17.38
基督城	4	17.13
運輸機	8	17.11
志航基地	3	16.29
甲板	5	15.54
機	14	14.79
貨機	5	14.74
佳山基地	2	14.71
才能	27	14.35
回程	4	14.05

Figure 3: Collocates of 'Subjects' of 起飛 *qi3fei1* 'takeoff' in the CNA in the Sketch Engine

Most frequency list follows the pattern of the Zipf's law, where the top few are usually very high and the values will decrease until a state where changes become minimum. For example, for the saliency list in Figure 3, when plotted in graph, the representation can be seen in Figure 4 below. In Figure 4, the x-axis is the 'Chinese subject' and the y-axis is the 'saliency' (Figure 4 uses the rank of the Chinese word to represent the Chinese character – rank 1, 2, 3…). All these Chinese words are the collocates of 起飛 *qi3fei1* 'takeoff.'

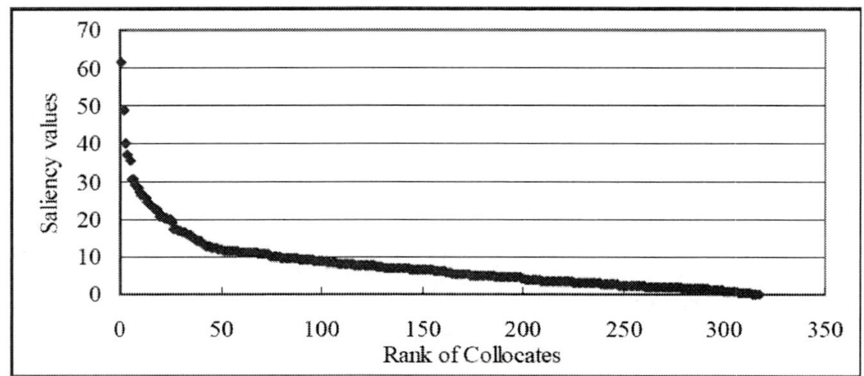

Figure 4: Pattern of Distributional Data for 起飛 *qi3fei1* 'takeoff' **following Zipf's Law**

The function for the type of graph in Figure 4 is such that in (2), where any point in the graph will be (x, f(x)). x is the rank of Chinese subjects on the x-axis and f(x) is the function to calculate the value on the y-axis.

$$f(x) = b(x^a) \quad (2)$$

Using this formula, Methods One and Two will find a point that separates any distributional listing into two lists, i.e., significant and insignificant lists. The purpose of doing this is to find out which among the list should be considered significant and which to be insignificant.

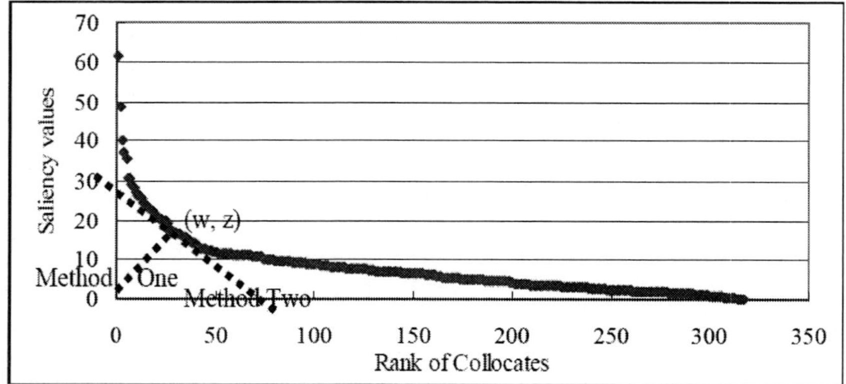

Figure 5: Three Ways to find Threshold Values

Methods One and Two are based on the assumption that there is a point where the curve changes the most when it goes down the y-axis to the x-axis. Methods One calculates the position of (w, z) where it is of shortest distance from (0, 0). This is because when every line departs from the starting point of (0,0), there will be a line that is the shortest distance from the curve. The point where this line touches the curve is the point where the curve changes the most from the y-axis to the x-axis.

Method Two calculates the most slanted slope between the x-axis and the y-axis. When the slope is most slanted, the possibility is high that the curve changes the most at a certain point (w, z). This is because the higher the curve on the y-axis, the more vertical the slope will be. Moreover, the further the curve moves away from (0, 0) on the x-axis, the more horizontal the slope will be. Therefore, the most slanted slope between the vertical and horizontal will be the possible threshold representing where the curve has changed the most.

The formulas for the two methods are shown in (3a) and (3b) below. In these two formula, a and b are the variables in the function of the nonlinear regression $y = b(x^a)$ while i is the threshold value and n is the total number of collocates in the relation.

$$\text{Method One:} \quad i = \left[((-ab^2)^{\left(\frac{1}{2-2a}\right)} \right] \quad (3a)$$

$$\text{Method Two:} \quad i = \left[(-ab)^{\frac{1}{1-a}} \right] \quad (3b)$$

Method Three is elaborated below.

3.2. Method Three

Method Three is called 'mean of means' where series of means will be calculated. For example, for the saliency list in Figure 3, the first mean is the mean of collocates one (55.67) and two (43.81); the second mean is the mean of collocates one (55.67), two (43.81), and three (38.64), i.e., add a new collocate every time. When all means have been calculated for all collocates, an overall mean is obtained from all the means (thus, mean of means). This overall mean will be used as a threshold value for the cut-off point, formulated below.

(4)
Threshold
$$\frac{Mean_1(Saliency_1, Saliency_2) + Mean_2(Saliency_1, Saliency_2, Saliency_3) + \ldots + Mean_n(Saliency_{(n-2)}, Saliency_{(n-1)}, Saliency_n)}{n-1}$$

The computation of mean of means is shown in Figure 6 below.

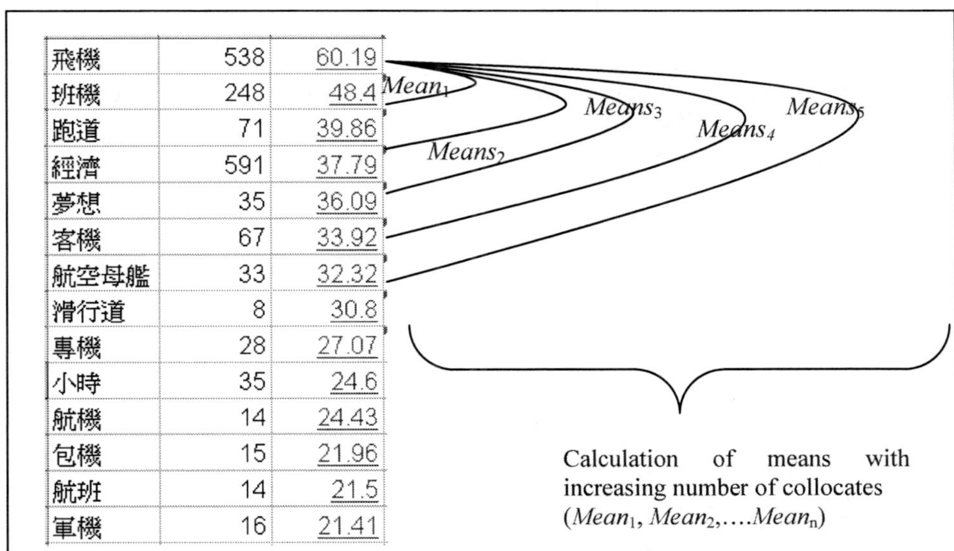

Figure 6: Computing 'Means' for the Collocates of 'Subjects' of 起飛 *qi3fei1* 'takeoff' (CNA)

From Figure 6, we can see that a series of means is produced by increasing the number of collocates each time in the calculation. In the following section, we will discuss the overall results for the three methods.

4. Results

For both Methods One and Two, normalization is used because the ranking in the x-axis (1, 2, 3…) is not comparable to the y-axis (between 0 to about 50).[2] The results for Methods One and Two are shown in Table 1 below for three metaphorical expressions, i.e., 成長 *cheng2zhang3* 'grow/growth,' 起飛 *qi3fei1* 'takeoff' and 癱瘓 *tan1huan4* 'paralytic.' In this table, the first column shows the metaphorical expressions, followed by the total collocates each grammatical relation possesses. "Pseudo-R-square" in column four shows the percentages of the curve that fit the non-linear regression (or in colloquial term, "curve fitting"). For example, the first relation (subject) of 成長 *cheng2zhang3* 'grow/growth' shows a "curve fitting" of 91%. The results for Methods One and Two are given in columns four and five.

Table 1: Calculation of Threshold Values Using Methods One and Two (CNA)

'Types of Metaphorical Expressions'	Relations	Total Collocates	Pseudo-R-square	Method One	Method Two
成長 *cheng2zhang3* 'grow/growth'	Subject	1490	0.906935	5.472613	4.211427
起飛 *qi3fei1* 'takeoff'	Subject	268	0.933048	3.630461	2.926560
癱瘓 *tan1huan4* 'paralytic'	Subject	276	0.935357	4.384251	3.748123
	Modifies	221	0.967868	3.787687	3.173571

The 'subject' relation of 成長 *cheng2zhang3* 'grow/growth' shows to have threshold values above collocate number 5 in Method One and collocate number 4 in Method Two. Similar results can be seen in the examples of 起飛 *qi3fei1* 'takeoff' and 癱瘓 *tan1huan4* 'paralytic' in Table 1 above.

Table 2 provides the mean values in the last column using Method Three. As a comparison, the results for all three methods are shown in Table 2 below. The thresholds are marked by a dotted line across the table after collocate number 4 (Method One), 3 (Method Two) and 89 (Method Three). Only Method Three locates the cut-off collocate at number 89, roughly one third down, from a total 268 collocates.

---

[2] Axis-y: $\dfrac{Collocate_{Rank\ 1\ ...\ Rankn}}{Rank_{n}}$

Axis-x: $\dfrac{Saliency_{1\ ...\ n}}{Sum\ (Saliency_{1},\ Saliency_{2},\ ...\ Saliency_{n})}$

For the axis-y (saliency values), each collocate from rank 1 to *n* will be divided by rank from highest to lowest. For example, if a Chinese word has 200 collocates in a particular relation, the normalization will divide collocates ranked 1 to 200 with 200 (thus, $\dfrac{1}{200}, \dfrac{2}{200}, ... \dfrac{200}{200}$). Therefore, the output of the axis-y is a list of numbers ranging from 0 to 1. As for axis-x, each saliency value will be divided by the sum of all 200 saliency values. The output of the axis-x is also displayed on a scale ranging from 0 to 1 (which is also the percentage of the saliency values).

Table 2: Mean of Means: 'Subject' 起飛 *qi3fei1* 'Takeoff' (CNA)[3]

Collocate Number	Chinese Collocates	English Gloss	Frequency	Saliency	Means
1	飛機 *fei1ji1*	airplane	538	60.19	---
2	班機 *ban1ji1*	airliner	248	48.40	54.30
3	跑道 *pao3dao4*	runway	71	39.86	49.48
4	經濟 *jing1ji4*	economy	591	37.79	46.56
5	夢想 *meng4xiang3*	dream	35	36.09	44.47
6	客機 *ke4ji1*	passenger plane	67	33.92	42.71
7	航空母艦 *hang2kung1 mu3jian4*	aircraft carrier	33	32.32	41.22
8	滑行道 *hua2xing2dao4*	taxiway	8	30.8	39.92
9	專機 *zhuan1ji1*	special plane	28	27.07	38.49
10	小時 *xiao3shi2*	hour	35	24.6	37.10
11	航機 *hang2ji1*	flight	14	24.43	35.95
12	包機 *bao1ji1*	charter plane	15	21.96	34.79
13	航班 *hang2ban1*	flight	14	21.5	33.76
14	軍機 *jun1ji1*	military plane	16	21.41	32.88
15	戰機 *zhan4ji1*	fighter plane	26	21.19	32.10
16	直昇機 *zhi2shen1ji1*	helicopter	18	20.41	31.37
17	班次 *ban1ci4*	flight order	13	19.93	27.85
…..	…..	…..	…….	…..	…….
87	駕駛員 *jia4shi3yuan2*	driver	3	7.94	15.28
88	特號 *te4hao4*	special umber	1	7.85	15.20
89	秋門 *ciu1men2*	a state in Siberia	1	7.83	15.11
90	產業 *chan3ye4*	Industry	15	7.82	15.03
91	雙機 *shuang1ji1*	dual machines	1	7.78	14.95
92	爸爸節 *ba1ba1jie2*	father's day	1	7.66	14.87
…..	…….	…..	…..	…….
…..	…..	…….	…..	……
267	能力 *neng2li4*	capability	1	0.04	7.45
268	目標 *mu4biao1*	goal	1	0.03	7.42
Mean of Means (Threshold)					**15.03**

The annotations to the right of the table read: **Method Two** (pointing between rows 3 and 4), **Method One** (pointing at row 4), and **Method Three** (pointing between rows 89 and 90).

Therefore, from the results, we can see that three different methods provide different threshold values. These methods are useful depending on the purpose of the research. For example, Methods One and Two can be applied to calculating smaller sampling of thresholds (about top 1 to 6) but Method Three allows the calculation of larger sampling of thresholds. For different purposes of linguistic research, these three methods provide choices as to how to select top results using principled methodology.

---

[3] A small number of words in Sketch Engine are wrongly tagged. For example, 秋門*ciu1men2* is a location where the airplane takeoffs but it is wrongly tagged. These errors are due to the problems of Sketch Engine but they will be removed automatically during clustering because they may not fall in any clusters within the list of collocates.

5. Conclusion

In this paper we have proposed three methods to help linguists ascertain which distributional patterns are linguistically meaningful. We suggest calculating a cut-off point for the saliency listings in Sketch Engine, since most empirical studies do not know where to stop when listing results. Most studies tend to list the top few items, and the number of the top few depends on the choice of the researchers. If there are criterion-based methods to find out the thresholds for the linguistic listings, subjectivity will be reduced in terms of choosing which collocational patterns are selected. Furthermore, most lexical resources provide wordlists according to different criteria such as frequency, Mutual Information values, collocation, saliency values, etc. However, a cut-off point for any one of these lists has yet to be suggested. This paper, therefore, deals with the general problems of these listings and suggests three possible ways to solve the problem.

Future work suggests incorporation of the calculation of threshold values in lexical resources such as Sinica Corpus, the English and Chinese Sketch Engine, etc. This proposed idea should contribute to computational linguistic research, linguistic research that relies on statistical methods to analyze linguistic data, and researchers who need to run psycholinguistic experiments related to word meaning.

References

Chen, K.-J. and C.-R. Huang. 1996. SINICA CORPUS: Design Methodology for Balanced Corpora. *Proceedings of the Eleventh Pacific Asia Conference on Language, Information and Computation*, 167-176.

Church, K. W. and P. Hanks. 1989. Word Association Norms, Mutual Information and Lexicography. In the *Proceedings of the. 27th Annual Meeting of ACL*, Vancouver, 76-83

Fellbaum, C. ed., 1998. *WordNet: An Electronic Lexical Database*. MIT Press.

Kilgarriff, A. and D. Tugwell. 2001. WORD SKETCH: Extraction and Display of Significant Collocations for Lexicography. In the *Proceedings of the ACL Workshop on COLLOCATION: Computational Extraction, Analysis and Exploitation*, 32-38.

Kilgarriff, A., C.-R. Huang, P. Rychly, S. Smith, D. Tugwell. 2005. Chinese Word Sketches. In the *Proceedings of Asialex*, Singapore.

Landes, S., C. Leacock, and R. I. Tengi. 1999. Building Semantic Concordance. In C. Fellbaum. Ed., *WordNet: An Electronic Lexical Database*. MIT: Cambridge, Mass. and London, England, 199-216.

Rosch, E. and C. B. Mervis. 1975. Family Resemblances: Studies in the Internal Structure of Categories. *Cognitive Psychology*, 7, 573-605.

Tengi, Randee I. 1999. "Design and Implementation of the WordNet Lexical Database and Searching Software." In Christiane Fellbaum. Ed., *WordNet: An Electronic Lexical Database*. MIT: Cambridge, Mass. and London, England, 105-127.

Zipf, George Kingsley. 1932. *Selected Studies of the Principle of Relative Frequency in Language*. Cambridge (Mass.)

Modality and Modal Sense Representation in E-HowNet[*]

You-Shan Chung, Shu-Ling Huang, and Keh-Jiann Chen

Institute of Information Science, Academia Sinica

128 Academia Road, Section 2, Nankang, Taipei 115, Taiwan

{yschung, josieh, kchen}@iis.sinica.edu.tw

Abstract. This paper explains how we define and represent modality in E-HowNet. Following Lyons (1977, reviewed in Hsieh 2003, among others), we hold that modals express a speaker's opinion or attitude toward a proposition and hence have a pragmatic dimension and recognize five kinds of modal categories, i.e. epistemic, deontic, ability, volition and expectation modality. We then present a representational formalism that contains the three most basic components of modal meaning: modal category, positive or negative and strength. Such a formula can define not only modal words but also words that contain modal meanings and cope with co-compositions of modals and the negation construction.

Keywords: modals, E-HowNet, negation

1. Introduction

E-HowNet, which evolved from HowNet (Dong & Dong 2006), represents an effort to define our knowledge of concepts in the world. Unlike synonym-based frameworks (e.g. WordNet), E-HowNet defines a word by specifying the relationship, as indicated by a set of features, between a core concept to other concepts. Each concept can be further analyzed into atomic meaning units called sememes named after HowNet. Therefore, a word in E-HowNet can be defined with simple concepts, sememes, or a mixture of simple concepts and sememes interacting with features.

E-HowNet has been proved to be capable of dealing with various kinds of concepts, even some very abstract ones, some of which being function words (Chen 2005 et al.) and the comparison construction (Huang et al. 2006), both describing the relationship between concepts. The representation of modality through E-HowNet is informative about the representational capacity of the framework for three reasons. First, modality is a meaning domain suggesting the attitude of the speaker and has a pragmatic dimension. Second, modality is considered a

[*] This research was supported in part by the National Science Council under a Center Excellent Grant NSC 95-2752-E-001-001-PAE and Grant NSC95-2221-E-001-039.

subcategory of function words that also has properties of content words (Chen 2005 et al.). The definition of modality thus provides insights into how words that fall somewhere in the middle on the content-function word continuum are defined. Third, modals' co-occurrences with negation markers show discrepancies between surface structure and meaning, and serve as a on the content-function word continuum are defined. Third, modals' co-occurrences with negation markers show discrepancies between surface structure and meaning, and serve as a testing ground for the defining capability of the framework.

In E-HowNet, the word to be defined is assigned a head, which is semantically and syntactically similar to it. Then, words that describe the head are linked to the head through features. For example, the word 小子 *xiaozi* 'lad' refers to someone who is young. Therefore, we represent the word with the head 人 *ren* 'person' and the modifying word 年幼 *nianyou* 'young'. Since 年幼 *nianyou* refers to the age of the person, the two concepts are linked by the semantic role 'age.' Its representations are as the following, with the first defined by simple concepts and the second by sememes:

(1) 小子 *xiaozi* 'lad'

def: {人:age={年幼}}

def:{human|人:age={child|少兒}}

Eventually, the meaning of words and phrases in E-HowNet will be integrated for the semantic representation of sentences.

The organization of the paper is as follows: In Section 2, we state the definition of modality in E-HowNet. In Section 3, we explain how modals are represented as single words and as components of larger linguistic constituents. In Section 4, we deal with the co-occurrence of negation markers and modals. We show with that E-HowNet is able to cope with meanings that are determined by its relative position with other elements in a sentence. Following that, in Section 5, we conclude that E-HowNet can represent a semantic category like modality that (a) involves pragmatics and (b) belongs to function words but is like content words in some aspects.

2. The scope of modality

Following Hsieh (2005), we do not assume that modals have to be auxiliaries but identify them on semantic grounds. They all refer to speakers' judgment. There are two meanings unanimously recognized as central to modality: epistemic and deontic. The former refers to a speaker's judgment of whether a situation will happen and the latter to a speaker's attitude toward whether something is required to be done. Another two categories admitted by many researchers are words that denote abilities and volition (Hwang 1999, Li 2003, Hsieh 2003, Hsieh 2005). Another modal category that we recognize is expectation, which includes words that describe whether a situation's taking place is expected or not. Below we summarize the five kinds of modal categories adopted by the current study, each followed by some examples:

Epistemic: judgment that something will (not) happen:

> e.g. 絕對 '*juedui* 'absolutely,' 會 *hui* 'will,' 也許 *yiexu* 'maybe,' 不一定 *buyiding* 'not necessarily,' 不可能 *bukeneng* 'impossible,' 未必 *weibi* 'not necessarily'

Deontic: judgment that something is (not) allowed to happen due to the speaker's will or social or ethical reasons:

> e.g. 可以 *keyi* 'may,' 應該 *yinggai* 'be supposed to,' 理當 *lidang* 'be supposed to,' 不該 *bugai* 'be not supposed to,' 不應 *buying* 'be not supposed to,' 不可 *buke* 'may not'

Ability: judgment that someone/something is (in)capable of something:

> e.g. 能 *neng* 'be able to,' 會 *hui* 'can,' 不能 *buneng* 'cannot,' 不會 *buhui* 'cannot'

Volition: judgment that someone is (un)willing to do something:

> e.g. 想 *xiang* 'hope to,' 不想 *buxiang* 'does not want to'

Expectation: judgment that something was (not) expected to happen or someone was (not) expected to do something:

> e.g. 果然 *guoran* 'as expected,' 果真 *guozhen* 'as expected,' 不出所料 *buchusuoliao* 'as expected,' 竟然 *jingran* 'unexpectedly,' 不料 *buliao* 'unexpectedly,' 沒想到 *meixiangdao* 'unexpectedly'

The above examples tell three things about our identification of modals. First, besides auxiliaries, some adverbs are also considered modals, e.g. 果然 *guoran* and 沒想到 *meixiangdao*. Second, like Hsieh (2003), we think that some modals express a positive meaning whereas the others express a negative meaning. The former half of the examples of each modal category is on the positive side whereas the latter is on the negative side. Third, like most researchers, we believe that modals within the same category differ in modal strength (Hwang 1999, Li 2003, Hsieh 2003, Hsieh 2005). Lyons (1977, reviewed in Hsieh 1999) thinks the basic definition of modality is a semantic scope that refers to possibility and necessity, two meanings that differ in strength of assertion. Such a definition suggests that, within the same modal category, modals that express that a judgment is possible is weaker in modal strength than those that express that a situation is necessary. For example, in epistemic modality, the modal 也許 *yiexu* 'maybe' indicates the speaker's speculation that something might happen, whereas the modal 一定 *yiding* 'certainly' conveys the speaker's certainty for something to take place. 一定 *yiding* thus has stronger modal strength than 也許 *yiexu*. Therefore, for each modal category, we adopt two sememes to scale modal strengths:

ish|稍: sememe signaling weak to moderate modal strength.

extreme|極: sememe signaling strong modal strength

3. The representation of modals and words/sentences that contain modal meanings

In Section 2 we have described in brief the representation of meaning in E-HowNet.
We have proposed five modal categories. Besides, we believe that each category consists of modals that express positive and negative meanings. Finally, we give grades for modal strengths. The complete inventory of modal meaning representations is as follows:

Epistemic: possibility={extreme|極}; possibility={ish|稍};
impossibility={extreme|極}; impossibility={ish|稍};
Deontic: allowance ={extreme|極}; allowance ={ish|稍};
disallowance ={extreme|極}; disallowance ={ish|稍};
Ability: capacity={extreme|極}; capacity={ish|稍};
incapacity={extreme|極}; incapacity ={ish|稍};
Volition: willingness ={extreme|極}; willingness ={ish|稍};
unwillingness={extreme|極}; unwillingness={ish|稍};
Expectation: expectedness={extreme|極}; expectedness ={ish|稍};
unexpectedness ={extreme|極}; unexpectedness ={ish|稍};

In the following table we give an example for each modal meaning:

Table 1: Examples of each modal meaning

	strength	negative/positive	example
epistemic	ish|稍	possibility	也許 'maybe'
		impossibility	未必 'maybe not'
	extreme|極	possibility	絕對 'absolutely'
		impossibility	不可能 'impossible'
deontic	ish|稍	allowance	可以 'may'
		disallowance	不用 'do not have to'
	extreme|極	allowance	必須 'must'
		disallowance	不應該 'be not supposed to'
ability	ish|稍	capacity	會 'can'
		incapacity	不克 'not really can'
	extreme|極	capacity	能 'be able to'
		incapacity	不會 'cannot'
volition	ish|稍	willingness	想 'hope to'
		unwillingness	不想 'do not hope to'
	extreme|極	willingness	要 'want to'
		unwillingness	不要 'do not want to'
expectation	ish|稍	expectedness	果真 'really'
		unexpectedness	不料 'unexpectedly'
	extreme|極	expectedness	果然 'as expected'
		unexpectedness	竟 "very unexpectedly"

3.1 The representation for modal words

Some words have modal representation in E-HowNet simply because they are modals. Take 也許 *yiexu* 'maybe,' a word that belongs to epistemic modality, for example. It is an epistemic modal and hence has the meaning of possibility, has a low modal strength and hence is indicated by {ish|稍}, and expresses a positive meaning:

(2) 也許 *yiexu* 'maybe'

def: possibility={ish|稍}

3.2 The representation for compound words that have inherent modal meanings

Modal representations also appear in words that are not modals themselves but have modal implications. For example, in expressing potential forms, we use a modal representation to modify the head, which is a verb:

(3) 信得過 *xindeguo* 'can trust'

def:{believe|相信:capacity={ish|稍}}

3.3 The representation for linguistic constituents that are not modals but have modal meaning

So far, we have talked about the modal representation of either modals or particular forms. In fact, the representation may also appear in any linguistic constituent that contains modal meaning. For example:

(4) 毋遺後患 *wuyihouhuan* 'Get rid of potential threats'

def: {PassOn|留給:possession={mishap|劫難},disallowance={extreme|極}}

4. The interaction between modals and negation markers

The meaning of a modal differs when occurring in different relative positions with the negation marker. Therefore, to show that E-HowNet can capture such meaning shifts is to show that the framework is able to cope with contextual variance and achieves near canonical meaning representation.

The meaning as a result of the interaction between words that mean negation and modals can have two modal strengths: lower and higher on both the positive side and negative side of modal meanings, as shown in the following diagram:

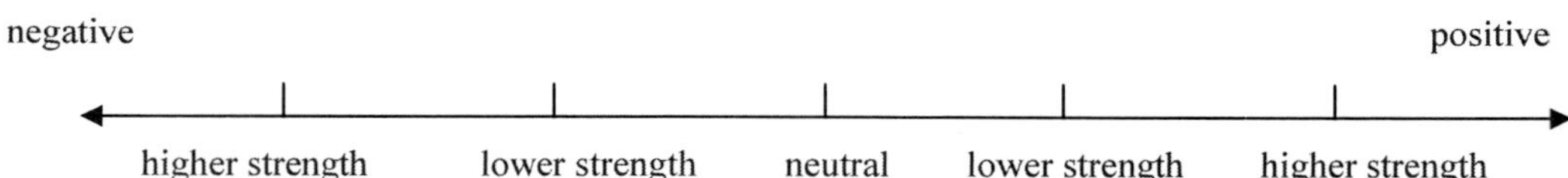

Figure 1: Scale of modal strength

We call modals with weak modal strength (i.e. represented by ish|稍) "ish modals" and modals with strong modal strength (i.e. represented by extreme|極) "extreme modals". According to Li (2003), the combinations (a)*Neg+Mod+V,* (b) *Mod+Neg+V,* and (c) negation forms+V show different behaviors.

Some modals and negation markers can co-occur in the constructions *Neg+Mod+V* and *Mod+Neg+V*; some modals have more than one sense and can occur in a negation construction only under one reading. We will discuss the behaviors of ish modals and extreme modals separately. As will be seen, the two kinds of modals usually experience a shift in modal strength when occurring in the Neg+Mod+V construction but not in the Mod+Neg+V construction.

4.1 The *Neg+Mod+V* construction

4.1.1 Ish modals

If a {ish|稍} type modal co-occurs with a negation marker in the construction *Neg+Mod+V*, the scope of negation is almost always over the modal strength, with the modal meaning negated and turned to carry a {extreme|極} meaning. We call such phenomena a 'scale shift.'

For example, the representation for a sentence like 他不可能來 *Ta bu keneng lai* 'It is impossible for him to come,' which contains the construction *Neg+Mod+V*, would be as below:

(5) 他不可能來

    a bu keneng lai

  he Neg possible come

  'It is impossible for him to come.'

   def:{come|來:agent= {3rdPerson|他人:gender={male|男}}, impossibility=_{extreme|極}}

While 可能 *keneng* is a ish modal, in 不可能 *bu keneng* the value of modal strength becomes {extreme|極}, showing a scale shift.

4.1.2 Extreme modals

Likewise, most of the extreme modals that can occur in the construction have the modal strength negated. For example:

(6) 你不必來

  Ni bu bi lai

  you Neg must come

  'You do not have to come.'

        def: {come|來:agent={listener|聽者},disallowance={ish|稍}}

While 必 *bi* 'must' is an extreme modal, 不必 *bu bi* 'does not have to' is represented with {ish|稍}, indicating a scale shift caused by the negation marker *bu* before the modal.

However, that *bu* before a modal induces a scale shift is not without exceptions. For example, as seen in Table1, the volition modals 要 *yao* 'want to,' which is an extreme modal, and 想, *xiang* 'hope to, which is an ish modal, retain their scale in 不要 *bu yiao* 'do not want to' and 不想 *bu xiang*, 'do not hope to.' We have not come to an explanation of this.

4.2 The *Mod+Neg+V* construction

4.2.1 Ish modals

All ish modals can occur in the construction, which entails the negation of the proposition following the negation marker. For example, 他可能不來 *Ta keneng bu lai* 'He will probably not come' is represented as below:

(7) 他可能不來

 Ta keneng bu lai

 he maybe Neg come

 'He will probably not come.'

  def:{.not.come|來:agent={3rdPerson|他人:gender={male|男}},possibility={ish|稍}}

4.2.2 Extreme modals

All of the extreme modals convey the negation of the proposition after the negation marker. So, 不帶雨傘想必不要緊 (as in 看這大太陽，不帶雨傘想必不要緊 'It should be safe not to bring an umbrella--Look at the shinning sun!') *Bu dai yusan xiangbi bu yaojin* 'It should be safe not to bring an umbrella' is represented as follows:

(8) 不帶雨傘想必不要緊

 Bu dai yusan xiangbi bu yaojin

 Neg bring umbrella must Neg-matter

 'It should be safe not to bring an umbrella.'

  .def: {.not.important|重要:theme={.not.bring|攜帶:patient={tool|用具:telic={obstruct|阻
   止:instrument={~},patient={RainSnow|雨雪}}}},possibility={extreme||極}}

Again, 想必 remains an extreme modal in the Mod+Neg+V construction 想必不要緊 *xiangbi bu yiaojin*.

4.4 Sense ambiguity

We mentioned in the beginning of this section that some modals belong to more than one category but can only occur with the negation marker under one reading. The following is an example:

(9) 他可以開車

 Ta keyi kaiche

 he may/can drive

 'He is allowed/knows how to drive.'

$$\text{def:}\{\text{drive|駕馭:patient=}\{\text{LandVehicle|車}\},\text{agent=}\{\text{3rdPerson|他人:gender=}\{\text{male|}$$
$$\text{男}\}\},\text{allowance=}\{\text{ish|稍}\}\}$$

and

$$\text{def:}\{\text{drive|駕馭:patient=}\{\text{LandVehicle|車}\},\text{agent=}\{\text{3rdPerson|他人:gender=}\{\text{male|}$$
$$\text{男}\}\},\text{capacity=}\{\text{ish|稍}\}\}$$

(10) 他不可以開車

    Ta bu keyi kaiche

    he Neg may drive

    'He is not allowed to drive.'

$$\text{def:}\{\text{ drive|駕馭:patient=}\{\text{LandVehicle|車}\},\text{agent=}\{\text{ 3rdPerson|他人:gender=}\{\text{male|}$$
$$\text{男}\},\text{disallowance=}\{\text{extreme|極}\}\}$$

The 可以 *keyi* 'may/can' in the first sentence can have either a deontic meaning or refers to the ability of the subject. However, the second sentence has to denote a deontic meaning. Some of the modals that show similar behaviors include:

要 *yao* 'will/want to': which belongs to the epistemic, deontic, and volition modality but has to denote an epistemic or deontic meaning in *Mod+Neg+V*.

會: which belongs to either the epistemic or the ability modality but has to denote an epistemic meaning in Mod+Neg+V. For example, 他會不來嗎? *Ta hui bu lai ma* 'Is it possible that he won't come?' can only have an epistemic reading.

5. Conclusion

Our representation of modals shows that E-HowNet is able to cover a meaning domain like modality that has qualities of content and function words and is also linked to pragmatics. It is also shown that the interaction between modals and negation markers and modals can be represented in a coherent way using a few features. This indicates that the framework is also able to represent words that have the same components but which are ordered differently, e.g. words that appear in the *Neg+V+Mod* and the *Mod+Neg+V* construction.

References

Chen, Keh-Jiann, Shu-Ling Huang, Yueh-Yin Shih, and Yi-Chun Chen. 2005. Extended-HowNet: A Representational Framework for Concepts. *Proceedings of OntoLex 2005 - Ontologies and Lexical Resources IJCNLP-05 Workshop*, Jeju Island, South Korea.

Chen, Yi-Jun, Shu-Ling Huang, Yueh-Yin Shih and Keh-Jiann Chen. 2005. The Formulation of Function Word in Extended-HowNet: A Preliminary Study. *Proceedings of The 6th Chinese Lexical Semantics Workshop*. Xiamen University.

Dong, Zhendong and Qiang Dong. 2006. *HowNet and the Computation of Meaning*. New Jersey: World Scientific Publishing.

Hsieh, Chia-Ling. 2003. Chinese Modal Verbs and Modal Adverbs: A Semantic Definition and Categorization. *Proceedings of the 6th World Chinese Teaching Conference*, pp 55-73.

Hsieh, Chia-Ling. 2005. Modal Verbs and Modal Adverbs in Chinese: An Investigation into the Semantic Source. *UST Working Papers in Linguistics*, 1, 31-58.

Hwang, Yu-Chun. 1999. Hanyu Nengyuan Dongci Yuyi Yanjiu (A Semantic Study of Modal Verbs in Chinese). Unpublished M.A. thesis, National Taiwan Normal University.

Li, Renzhi. 2003. *Modality in English and Chinese: A Typological Perspective*. Ph.D. thesis, University of Antwerp.

AutoCor: A Query Based Automatic Acquisition of Corpora of Closely-related Languages [*]

Davis Muhajereen D. Dimalen[a], Rachel Edita O. Roxas[b]

[a] Information Technology Department, School of Computer Studies
Mindanao State University-Iligan Institute of Technology, Tibanga, Iligan City
d_dimalen@yahoo.com
[b] College of Computer Studies, De La Salle University-Manila,
roxasr@dlsu.edu.ph

Abstract. AutoCor is a method for the automatic acquisition and classification of corpora of documents in closely-related languages. It is an extension and enhancement of CorpusBuilder, a system that automatically builds specific minority language corpora from a closed corpus, since some Tagalog documents retrieved by CorpusBuilder are actually documents in other closely-related Philippine languages. AutoCor used the query generation method odds ratio, and introduced the concept of common word pruning to differentiate between documents of closely-related Philippine languages and Tagalog. The performance of the system using with and without pruning are compared, and common word pruning was found to improve the precision of the system.

Keywords: document acquisition, document classification.

1.   Introduction

A corpus is a term used to designate a body of authentic language data that can be used as a basis for linguistic research.[1]   It is also applied to a body of language texts that exist in electronic format. It is estimated that there are currently over 4 billion pages on the world wide web (WWW) covering most areas of human endeavor. And as more information are becoming electronically available on the web, we need more effective methods and techniques to access these information. To date, there has been limited effort in taking advantage of this available information on the web for building natural language resources especially for sparse languages (or minority languages) like Tagalog and other Philippine languages. Unfortunately, to manually collect and organize a language specific corpus over the Web is difficult. The process is tedious and time consuming. To add, an expert in linguistics is needed to manually determine the language where the document collected is written.

---

[*] This project is funded by the Philippine Council for Advanced Science and Technology for Research and Development, Department of Science and Technology, Philippine Government.

[1] Orasan, C. and R. Krishnamurthy 2000. An Open Architecture for the Construction and Administration of Corpora. *Proceedings of the Second International Conference on Language Resources and Evaluation.* pp. 793-800.

A system that automatically acquires language specific documents from the Web is one good solution in corpora building. Creating such a system requires knowledge in information retrieval and natural language processing.

2. Automatic Corpora Builder on a Closed and Open Corpus

Several components are required for an automatic corpora builder: a set of seed documents, a language modeler, a query generator, a web search engine, and a language filter[2].

The CorpusBuilder takes advantage of existing search engine database to collect documents from the web[3]. It iteratively creates new queries to build a corpus in a single minority language. Sets of relevant and non-relevant documents are taken as initial inputs. Relevant documents are those that belong to the target language, while non-relevant documents are other documents that belong to other languages. These documents are used as inclusion and exclusion terms for the query. The query is sent to the search engine and the document that has the highest rank will be retrieved. The document retrieved is processed through the language filter and classified as either relevant or non-relevant document. The newly classified set of documents is the product of the system and is the basis for the next term selection as the system iterates.

CorpusBuilder is a system that automatically builds a minority language corpus. An examination of this corpus showed that the corpus also contained documents in languages that are closely-related to the identified minority language. Specifically, there were documents retrieved that are closely-related Philippine languages to the identified minority language Tagalog. Thus, in this study, we considered the three most closely-related languages in the Philippines, Bicolano, Cebuano and Tagalog, as identified by Fortunato[4], that belong to the Austronesian family of languages. This can be explained by the fact that closely-related languages within the same family of languages exhibit common linguistic phenomena. For instance, there are several Bicolano, Cebuano and Tagalog words which are common to these languages as illustrated in Tables 1 to 3.

Table 1: Words Common to Tagalog and Cebuano.

Tagalog/ Cebuano	English
apo	grandchild
anak	son/daughter
bayaw	in-law
langgam (Tagalog)	ant
langgam (Cebuano)	bird
bangka	sailboat

Table 2: Words Common to Tagalog and Bicolano.

Tagalog/Bicolano	English
hayop	animal
tao	human
langit	heaven
pakpak	wings

---

[2] Ghani, R., R. Jones and D. Mladenic. 2001. Using the Web to Create Minority Language Corpora. *Proceedings of the 10th International Conference on Information and Knowledge Management.* pp. 279 – 286.

[3] Jones, R. and R. Ghani. 2000. Automatically Building a Corpus for a Minority Language on the Web. *In the Proceedings of the Annual Meeting of the Association of Computational Linguistics 2000.* pp. 29-36.

[4] Fortunato, F. T. 1993. *Mga Pangunahing Etnoling-guistikong Grupo sa Pilipinas.* Malate, Manila, Philippines: De La Salle University Press.

pinsan	cousin

Table 3: Words Common to Bicolano, Cebuano, and Tagalog.

Bicolano/Cebuano/Tagalog	English
agaw	snatch
bawi	snatch
kadena	chain
belen	manger

Thus, AutoCor considered closely-related languages rather than a single minority language, and used document classification using common word pruning which has shown to improve the precision of the system.

The corpus that was used in this research contains documents from the web. The corpus contains 4,000 documents, wherein the target or relevant documents were tagged correspondingly, having 250 documents each in Bicolano, Cebuano and Tagalog, and the rest of the documents functioned as the non-relevant documents were in English, Hungarian and Polish. The selection of the set of non-relevant documents was based on similar character sets and the availability of documents.

Figure 1 illustrates the overall architecture of AutoCor on a closed corpus. There are 5 main routines namely, the Language Modeler, Common Word Pruning, the Query Generator, Sampling, and finally the Document Classifier. Each routine is done in sequence. Initially the first routine (Language Modeler) requires initial seed documents for each of the selected closely-related languages (L) and for the other languages (OL). Each language in (L) and (OL) is denoted by the sets $\{L_1...L_n\}$ and $\{OL_1...OL_n\}$, respectively. The "Initial Documents" is defined by the sets (iD_L) and (iD_{OL}) wherein (iD_L) is the set of initial documents in closely-related languages (L) and (iD_{OL}) is the set of initial documents in other languages (OL). The language models are composed of (LM_L) and (LM_{OL}) wherein (LML) is the set of language models for the closely-related languages (L) and (LM_{OL}) is the set of language models for the other languages (OL). The Pruned Language Models are the sets (PLM_L) for the closely-related languages (L) and (PLM_{OL}) for the other languages (OL). The output corpus is composed of a set of documents classified as closely related languages (D_L) and another set of documents classified as other languages (D_{OL}) wherein (D_L) is also equal to the set $\{D_{L1},D_{L2},...,D_{Ln}\}$. Documents are retrieved via Sampling from a Closed Corpus. The system works as follows:

a. Select one seed document each from the set of initial documents in iD_L and the set of initial document in iD_{OL}.
b. Using the seed or initial documents in the target language and other languages, build language models LM_L and LM_{OL} for each of the languages in L and OL.
c. Prune words that are common in the set of language models in LM_L and LM_{OL} and let the PLM_L be the set of pruned language models for L, and PLM_{OL} for OL.
d. Using Odds-ratio, inclusion and/or exclusion terms for the query are determined from PLM_L and PLM_{OL}, respectively.
e. Using the query generated, documents are sampled from the closed corpus that matches the query.
f. The documents retrieved are classified by using a language classifier. Decide whether to add the list of documents in the output corpus, and update the language models in LM_L and LM_{OL}.
g. Repeat step 1 until the stopping criterion is reached.

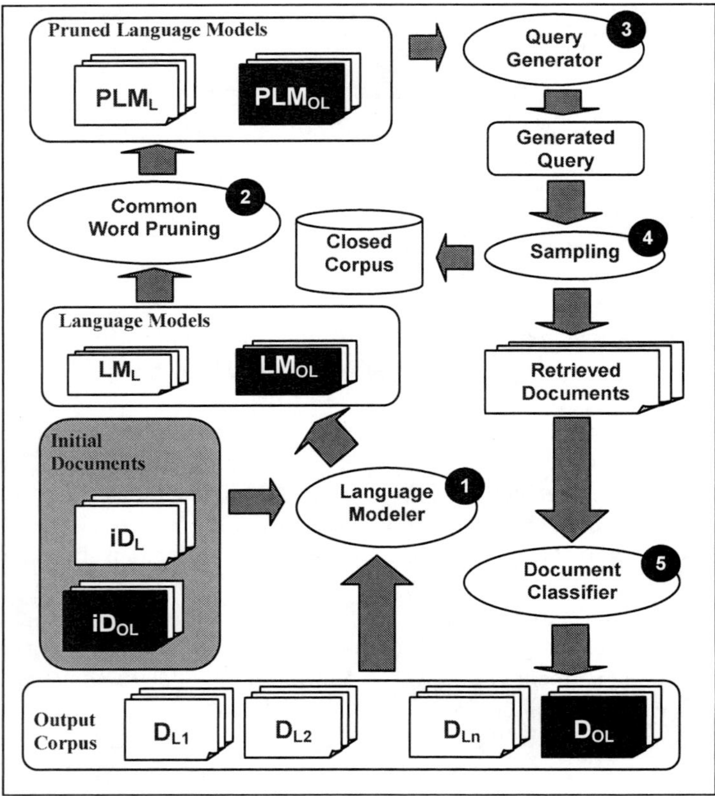

Figure 1: AutoCor on a Closed Corpus.

AutoCor repeats the process of language modeling, common word pruning, automatic query generating, document sampling and document classifying. Stopping criterion is user defined and depends on the number of queries that has to be generated.

AutoCor was extended to access documents from the Web. Information retrieval (IR) on the web poses more challenges as compared to classical IR due to the bulk of information that is available on the web, the heterogeneity of documents, variety of languages, duplication of information, documents having high linkages, ill-formed queries, wide variance of users and specific behavior of the users. The algorithm is similar with that of AutoCor on a closed corpus except that the resource where documents are retrieved is an open corpus or specifically the World Wide Web.

3. Language Modeling

We employed a statistical language modeler using the n-gram distribution-based language modeling. For general text, more training data will always improve a language model (LM). However, as training data size increases, LM size increases which can lead to models that are too large for practical use[5]. Training data is usually biased on its mixture of elements. An automatic language modeling system, that gets its training data from articles in the web recursively, would often process words that are not supposed to be present in the training set, thus, the effect of noise in the LM based on documents from the web must be minimized.

Count cut-off is commonly used to prune language models. The method removes from the LM those n-grams that occur less frequent in the training data, assuming they will be equally

---

[5] Gao, J. and K. Lee. 2000. Distribution-based Pruning of Backoff Language Models. *The 38th Annual Meeting of the Association for Computational Linguistics*. Hong Kong. pp. 579 – 588.

infrequent in all test data. Also, the count cut-off intensifies the bias of the training data. For instance, if we use the bible in training, a word like "sin" may have high frequency in certain chapters but not others. Thus, "sin" can be cut-off in some chapters[5]. These are domain specific issues.

The training set representing a specific language will be processed by a profile generator to generate a profile which will be used for text categorization (see section 5.1 and 5.2). The generation of profile is part of the n-gram distribution based language modeling process.

4.   Common Word Pruning

Pruning language models keeps word n-grams that are more likely to occur in a given document. Early language modeling algorithms remove words that are likely to be infrequent in a test data[5]. AutoCor adopted the idea of pruning but instead of removing infrequent words, words that are common in at least any two documents are removed to maintain a language model containing words that are unique across the language models used by AutoCor. If a common word is found in the target languages, there is no way of identifying to what specific target language the word belongs. Thus, removing common words to all the set of input documents will see to it that the words that are left are words that are unique to each of the set of documents, which are used to model our languages, and will be used in the automatic query generation module.

Documents considered as input are HTML documents. Words such as "about", "us", "contact", and "home" are one of the most common words that appear in most language specific HTML documents. These are called general or standard navigation hyperlinks[6]. Thus, words used as labels to general navigation hyperlinks are also pruned if they appear in any two or more sets of documents.

5.   Query Generation

Odds-ratio (OR) selects the k terms with highest odds-ratio scores. The odds-ratio score for a word w is defined as:

$$\log_2 \left(\frac{P(w \mid \text{relevant doc}) * (1 - P(w \mid \text{non relevant doc}))}{P(w \mid \text{non relevant doc}) * (1 - P(w \mid \text{relevant doc}))} \right)$$

where: P (w | relevant doc) – Probability of a word from a relevant document
P (w | non-relevant doc) – Probability of a word from a non-relevant document

Odds-ratio (OR) achieves very good results compared to other methods such as uniform, term frequency, and RTFIDF.

5.1. Text Categorization on Language Classification

Text categorization is a basic task in document processing. It allows automated handling of enormous streams of documents in electronic form. N-gram based approach is a technique that can be used in text categorization. It is tolerant of textual errors and works very well for language classification and is able to achieve up to 99.8% correct classification[7].

---

[6] Yu, S., D. Cai, J. Wen and W. Ma. 2003. Improving Pseudo-Relevance Feedback in Web Information Retrieval Using Web Page Segmentation. *Proceedings of the twelfth international conference on World Wide Web.* pp. 11 – 18.
[7] Ghani, R., R. Jones, D. Mladenic. 2001. Using the Web to Create Minority Language Corpora. *10th International Conference on Information and Knowledge Management.* pp. 279 - 286.

An N-gram is an n-character slice of a longer string. A string is sliced into sets of overlapping n-grams. Before the string is sliced, blanks are appended at the beginning and end of the string. The following provides examples of bi-grams, tri-grams and quad-grams.

N-gram-based text categorization is based on calculating and comparing profiles of n-gram frequencies (see Figure 2). It first computes for profiles on training set data that represents the various categories or various languages. A new document with an unknown category is processed by the profile generator. The process of computing the profile for the document to be classified is the same as how profiles are created for each of the training sets. Finally, the distance measure, known as the out-of-place measure, between the documents profile and each of the category profiles are computed and the category whose profile has the smallest distance to the document's profile is the selected category of the new document with unknown category[8].

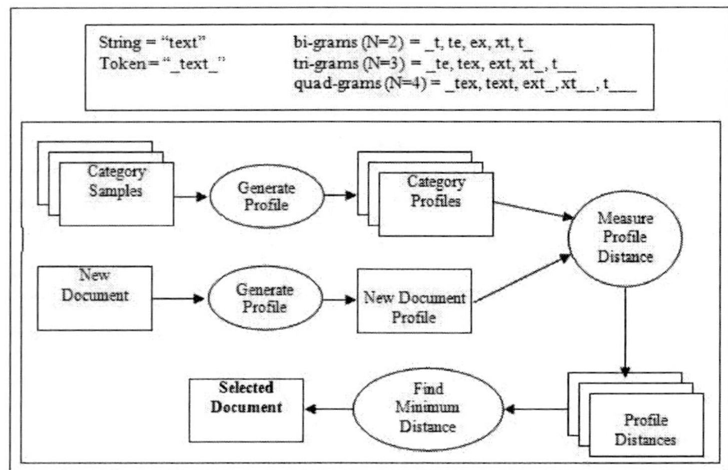

Figure 2: Common Words of Set A, B, C and D.

5.2. Out-of-place Measure Between Two Profiles

The out-of-place measure determines how far out of place an N-gram in one profile is from its place in the other profile. Figure 4 illustrates how the calculation is done using a few sample N-grams. For each N-gram in the document profile, counterparts are matched in the category profile and out-of-place distance is computed. The N-gram "ING" is at rank 2 in the document, but at rank 5 in the category. Thus it is 3 ranks out of place. If an N-gram (such as "ED" in Figure 3) is not in the category profile, it takes some maximum out-of-place value. The sum of all of the out-of-place values for all N-grams is the distance measure for the document from the category[9].

---

[8] Cavnar, W. B. and J. M. Trenkle. 1994. N-gram-based Text Categorization. *Proceedings of Third Annual Symposium on Document Analysis and Information Retrieval.* Las Vegas: NV. pp. 161-175.
[9] Cavnar, W. B. and J. M. Trenkle. 1994. N-gram-based Text Categorization. *Proceedings of Third Annual Symposium on Document Analysis and Information Retrieval.* Las Vegas: NV. pp. 161-175.

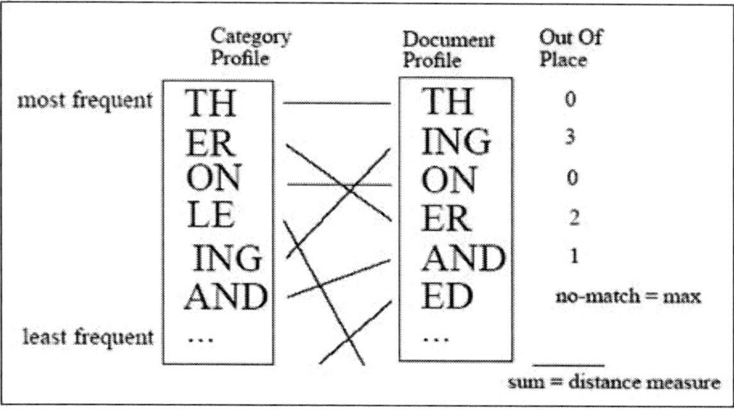

Figure 3: Out-of-place Computation[9].

6.   Results and Discussions

The goal in evaluating an Information Retrieval (IR) system is to measure its effectiveness, that is, the ability of the system to retrieve relevant documents. Specifically, precision and recall are used to measure the effectiveness of an IR system[10].

  Given a set of documents D and a query Q, A is the set of documents retrieved by the system and R is the set of all relevant documents in D. A ∩ R is the set of documents relevant to query Q (see Figure 4).

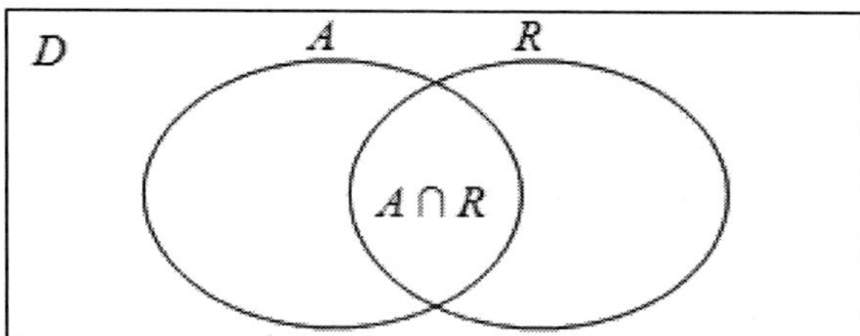

Figure 4: A Diagrammatic View of a Document Collection[10].

The precision of the system is the proportion of retrieved material that is actually relevant. It is the proportion of the items retrieved that are relevant[10]. Precision can be computed by using the following formula:

$$PRECISION = relevant\ retrieved\ /\ total\ retrieved$$
$$= |A \cap R| / |A|$$

Recall is the proportion of relevant material actually retrieved in answer to a search request. It is the proportion of relevant items that are retrieved[10]. Recall can be computed by using the following formula:

$$Recall = relevant\ retrieved\ /\ total\ no.\ of\ relevant\ documents$$
$$= |A \cap R| / |R|$$

---

[10]   Jizba, R. 2004. Measuring Search Effectiveness. [online]. Available: http://www.hsl.creighton.edu/hsl/Searching/Recall-Precision.html. July 15, 2004.

To evaluate performance and efficiency level over a set of N test queries, precision level is averaged at each recall level r. It is the summation of the precision computed per query (level r) wherein the total number of test queries is N:

$$P(r) = \frac{\sum_{i=1}^{N} P(r)_i}{N} \quad \text{Equation 1}$$

If 100% recall is achieved at $i = k$ where in $k < N$ then to compute the average precision, we have:

$$P(r) = \frac{\sum_{i=1}^{k} P(r)_i}{k} \quad \text{Equation 2}$$

The documents were pre-tagged with the language on which the documents were written. The corpus that was used in this research contains documents from the web. The corpus contains 4,000 documents which consist of 250 documents tagged as Bicolano, 250 documents tagged as Cebuano, another 250 documents which are tagged as Tagalog and the rest of the documents were tagged with 3 different languages namely English, Hungarian and Polish. The documents in Bicolano, Cebuano and Tagalog are the target or relevant documents, while the non-relevant documents are documents in English, Hungarian and Polish. The selection of the set of non-relevant documents was based on similar character sets and the availability of documents.

Each of the target languages was tested for query lengths 1 to 5, with 100 generated queries per query length, both with and without pruning. Precision and recall was computed per query, and average precision was computed per query length.

AutoCor on a closed corpus achieved higher average precision with common word pruning for all query lengths 1 to 5, across all the target languages. The highest improvements per language range from 18% to 53% and 19% to 26% for domain and non-domain specific data sets, respectively (DS and NDS); and highest precision values per language range from 21% to 61% and 37% to 51% for DS and NDS data sets, respectively. The results showed that common word pruning improved the precision of the system (Bicolano: with 52.96% highest improvement at query length 4, Cebuano: with 18.00% highest improvement at query length 1, Tagalog: with 19.78% highest improvement at query length 2).

On the other hand, AutoCor on an open corpus yielded the following results: the highest precision values per language range from 14% to 72% and 9% to 61% for DS and NDS, respectively.

These results indicated that the DS data sets yielded better results since the search is more topic-specific and directs the search more effectively. Secondly, the consistent trends of the results show that increasing the query length does not necessarily increase the precision of the system. Thirdly, the test results on the web reveal that using the web as a resource may provide extreme lowest and highest precision values, due to the vast amount of information on the web and their variability.

The test shows that with common word pruning, AutoCor achieves a higher precision than without pruning regardless of query length for all the target languages (Bicolano, Cebuano, Tagalog) that were used during the test. Common word pruning would maintain the language model of each of the target languages to be unique. The results show that with common word pruning, fewer documents in closely-related languages where retrieved since most common words had already been removed in the language models of the target languages. Therefore, the terms that were selected by the query generator for the relevant set are most likely unique to each of the target languages.

Focus on the accuracy of the classifier using common word pruning was made in this study. Although time efficiency in the document classification was not measured in the evaluation of the algorithm, it could be inferred from the minimization of the search space that time efficiency could have been improved by the introduction of common word pruning.

References

Fortunato, F. T. 1993. *Mga Pangunahing Etnoling-guistikong Grupo sa Pilipinas*. Malate, Manila, Philippines: De La Salle University Press.

Gao, J. and K. Lee. 2000. Distribution-based pruning of backoff language models. *The 38th Annual Meeting of the Association for Computational Linguistics*. Hong Kong. 579 – 588.

Ghani, R., R. Jones and D. Mladenic. 2001. Using the Web to Create Minority Language Corpora. *10th International Conference on Information and Knowledge Management*. 279 – 286.

Jones, R. and R. Ghani. 2000. Automatically Building a Corpus for a Minority Language on the Web. *In the Proceedings of the Annual Meeting of the Association of Computational Linguistics 2000*, pp. 29-36.

Orasan, C. and R. Krishnamurthy. 2000. An Open Architecture for the Construction and Administration of Corpora. *In Proceedings of the Second International Conference on Language Resources and Evaluation*. pp. 793 – 800.

Cavnar, W. B. and J. M. Trenkle. 1994. N-gram-based Text Categorization. *Proceedings of Third Annual Symposium on Document Analysis and Information Retrieval*. Las Vegas: NV. pp. 161-175.

Jizba,R.2000.Measuring Search Effectiveness. [online].Available: http://www.hsl.creighton.edu/hsl/Searching/Recall-Precision.html. July 15, 2004.

Yu, S., D. Cai, J. Wen, W. Ma. 2003. Improving Pseudo-Relevance Feedback in Web Information Retrieval Using Web Page Segmentation. *Proceedings of the twelfth international conference on World Wide Web*. pp. 11 – 18.

The Polysemy of *Da3*:
An ontology-based lexical semantic study[*]

Hong, Jia-Fei[a], Chu-Ren Huang[b], Kathleen Ahrens[a],

[a] National Taiwan University, Graduate Institute of Linguistics
No. 1, Sec. 4, Roosevelt Road 106, Taipei, Taiwan R.O.C
[b] Institute of Linguistics Academia Sinica
No. 128, Section 2, Academia Road 115, Taipei, Taiwan R.O.C
{jiafei, churen}@gate.sinica.edu.tw,
kathleenahrens@yahoo.com

Abstract. In this study, we explore the polysemy of *da3* through the ontological conceptual structure found in SUMO. First, we divide several different senses for *da3*, clustering physical event senses and metaphorical event senses. In here, we only focus on physical event senses of *da3*. From the physical event senses of *da3*, we divide them into two main categories: 1) *hit* and 2) *pump*. We then use SUMO ontological concepts to identify these physical senses. Finally, we can observe the common patterns of the "hit" sense group and the "pump" sense group for *da3*.

Keywords: *da3*, Polysemy, ontology, lexical semantics

1. Introduction

In this study, we explore all possible concepts for physical event senses of *da3* through the SUMO ontological concept system (Huang et al. 2004). According to previous work (Gao 2001), *da3* is a basic verb in the large domain of physical action verbs in Chinese, as 1) it refers to the most basic action of the hand; and 2) at the same time it can refer to a wide-range of actions or events that involve physical contact of one kind or another. We will compare her analysis with the analysis we provide based on SUMO.

First, we collect our data from Sinica Corpus and check their senses from Chinese Wordnet. Next, we take these physical event senses of *da3* into SUMO concept system (Huang et al. 2004) to find all possible concepts and distinguish them into different categories. Finally, we analyzed these concepts for semantic features which can help us to compare our analysis with the analysis in Gao's study (2001).

2. Previous research

Regarding verb studies, previous research has focused on VV compound verbs in Modern Chinese (Hong and Huang, 2004), or on near synonyms in Modern Chinese (Chief et al, 2000; Huang et al. 2000; Liu 2002; Tsai, 2002; Huang and Hong, 2005). Also, some scholars have worked on *da3* polysemy analyses. *Da3* is one if the most frequently used verbs, being ranked 16 in the list of most frequently used verbs in Chinese (Bei and Zhang, 1988). Specifically, Gao

---

(2001) explored the semantic properties of *da3* and its prototypical meaning and categorized its semantic representations to show the systematic patterning of its meaning extensions.

3. Motivation and Goals

Language knowledge representation is a manifestation of the systematic contrasts found in human communication, which defies conventional description. Take modal verbs as examples. Modal verbs have similar semantic functions and cannot be easily distinguished in terms of their lexical senses. Therefore, they are considered to be interchangeable. Nevertheless, it is not uncommon that this kind of polysemy always has contrasts in usage, as we can see the contrast between *hui4* (know) and *hui4* (can) below:

(1a) 臺灣廠商到德國開商展時，非常需要**會**德語和中文的人，做為溝通橋樑。

      Tai2 wan1 chang3 shang1 dao4 de2 guo2 kai1 shang1 zhan3 shi2, fei1 chang2
      Taiwan   factory   to   Germany exhibit   time, so

      xu1 yao4 hui4/ * neng2 de2 yu3 han4 zhong1 wen2 de5 ren2, zuo4 wei2
      need   could   German and Chinese   MOD persons, to

      gou1 tong1 qiao2 liang1.
      communicate bridge

      "When Taiwan factories exhibit in Germany, they so need some persons who could speak German and Chinese to communicate with other persons."

(1b) 在上課的時候，他不**會**講德語或中文和學生溝通，因為他怕自己沒辦法完整表達意思。

      Zai4 shang4 ke4 de5 shi2 hou4, ta1 bu2 hui4 jiang3 de2 yu3 huo4
      In   class   MOD time, he will not speak German or

      zhong1 wen2 han4 xue2 sheng1 gou1 tong1, yin1 wei4 ta1 pa4   zi4ji3
      Chinese   with student communicate, because   he worry himself

      mei2 ban4 fa3 wan2 zheng3 biao3 da2 yi4 si1.
      no way   complete   express   meaning.

      "In the class time, he can't communicate with his students in German or Chinese, because he worries that he can't completely express his meaning."

Considering the lexical sense of modal verb polysemy and its natural language use, *hui4* means both "know" or "can". As defined, we notice that they differ from each other, even though they share similar concept.

This paper will investigate the lexical semantic relations between each sense of *da3* polysemy (excluding metaphorical senses) by studying their sense distinction, word formation collocation, and distribution pattern.

4. SUMO

In this study, we use Suggested Upper Merged Ontology (SUMO) to analyze all concepts for *da3*. We find out all possible concepts and divide different them into different categories.

WordNet is inspired by current psycholinguistic and computational theories of human lexical memory (Fellbaum (1998), Miller et al. (1993)). English nouns, verbs, adjectives, and adverbs are organized into synonym sets, each representing one underlying lexicalized concept.

Different semantic relations link the synonym sets (synsets). The version of WordNet that Sinica BOW implemented is version 1.6, with nearly 100,000 synsets.

In Sinica BOW, ach English synset was given up to 3 most appropriate Chinese translation equivalents. In cases where the translation pairs are not synonyms, their semantic relations are marked (Huang et al. 2003). The bilingual WordNet is further linked to the SUMO ontology. We use the semantic relations in bilingual resource to expand and predict domain classification when it cannot be judged directly from a lexical lemma.

5. Data collection

From Sinica Corpus and Gigaword Corpus, we find out several patterns for *da3*. According to the Chinese Wordnet Group analysis (Huang et al., 2003), there are 114 senses which include physical activity senses, metaphor, metonymy and extension senses. In this study, we want to focus on physical activity senses, but not metaphor, metonymy and extension senses. *Da3* has 35 physical event senses listed, along with 79 additional senses. We will take focus on the physical activity senses.

6. Data analysis

The analysis, based on the Sinica Corpus, Gigaword Corpus and the criteria proposed by Huang et al. (2003) to differentiate the lexical meaning, presents several different senses for *da3*.

Table 1: The analysis of *da3* from Chinese Wornet Group

打 1 → da3 ㄉㄚˇ

詞義1：【及物動詞，VC】以手施力使手或手持物撞擊特定對象。{tap,01496422V}
- 例句：男子說完用力的<打>一下桌子，整個桌子馬上變成木屑一片。
- 例句：我用竹棍子用力<打>了竊賊一下，可是，還是被他跑掉了，真是可惜。
- 例句：他用扁骨用力<打>門板好幾下，然後說：我是如此的人嗎？專程來抓你的小辮子？

詞義2：【及物動詞，VC；名詞，nom】用手或手持物打後述對象，使其感到疼痛或受到傷害。{hit,00960484V}
- **義面1：【及物動詞，VC】用手或手持物打攻擊後述對象，使其感到疼痛或受到傷害。{hit,00960484V}**
  - 例句：我跟我姐也是從小<打>到大，越<打>感情越好。
  - 例句：因為他<打>人也是為了完成國家任務，說清楚群眾是會諒解的。
  - 例句：母親忽然沉下臉<打>他一下手背，並告誡他不能指月亮娘娘，會爛耳朵的。
  - 例句：在少年會所第四年時，卑南少年必須接受<打>屁股的儀式，今年這項儀式將開放給遊客體驗，稍稍了解卑南族的斯巴達教育。

- **義面2：【名詞，nom】用手或手持物打攻擊後述對象，使其感到疼痛或受到傷害。{hit,00960484V}**
  - 例句：說謊一臉狡猾，輕輕的對我耳語道：主人，你如果認錯，至少要挨一頓<打>。
  - 例句：這兒的老師也常在學生不乖或考試成績不好時祭出「班法」，給學生一頓好<打>，這一點也令我難以接受。

詞義3：【及物動詞，VC】易碎物品因受到撞擊使破碎。{break,00231588V}
- 例句：在高速公路不知哪裏天上飛來一石，把擋風玻璃<打>成一個小凹洞。
- 例句：在夜裡，我把陶瓷<打>了，天明時我將用它們來聚攏光亮，傳播光亮。

Among these 35 physical activity senses of *da3*, we divide two main physical event senses for *da3*: 1) *hit* and 2) *pump* such as below:

(2) a. 母親忽然沉下臉<打>他一下手背，並告誡他不能指月亮娘娘，會爛耳朵的。

    Mu3 qin1 hu1 ran2 chen2 xia4 lian3 da3 ta1 yi2 xia4 shou3 bei4,

    Mother   suddenly sink down face hit he one time hand,

    bing4 gao4 jie4 ta1 bu4 neng2 zhi3 yue4 liang4 niang2 niang5,

    and   warn   he can't   point moon   queen ,

    hui4 lan4   er3 duo1 de5.

    will decayed ear   MOD.

    "His mother suddenly becomes long-faced and hits him on the back of his hand, then warned him that he will get rotting ears if he points to the moon."

b.這時每一鞭都如<打>在她的身上一般痛楚。

  Zhe4 shi2 mei3 yi1 bian1 dou1 ru2 da3 zai4 ta1 de5

  This time every whipped all like whip she MOD

  shen1 shang4 yi1 ba1 tong4 chu3

  body general pain.

  "At this moment, every whipped whip pains her like she is being whipped."

(3)為了防止車輛陷進沙地，不要把輪胎氣<打>得太足。
  Wei4 le5 fang4 zhi3 che1 liang4 jin4 sha1 di4, bu2 yao4 ba3
  For prevent cars s tuck into sand, don't let

  lun4 tai1 qi4 da3 de2 tai4 zu2.
  tires gas pump too full.

  "Do not pump the tires too full to avoid the cars being stuck in the sand."

Moreover, in "hit" sense of *da3*, we also can divide two different categories: 1) *hand* and *hand holdings* and 2) *force* and *impact*. Then, in the second category, we can divide *force* and *impact* in additional sub-categories: 1) direct contact and 2) contact by injection.

(4)他用力<打>門板好幾下，然後說：我是如此的人嗎？
  Ta1 yong4 li4 da3 men2 ban3 hao3 ji3 xia4, ran2 hou4 shuo1:wo3
  He use force beat door plank several times, then say: I

  shi4 ru3 ci3 de5 ren2 ma5?
  is this MOD man.

  "He beat forcefully the door plank several times and then said: Am I a person like this?"

(5)當靜脈注射毒癮者<打>毒品時，通常是不會馬上把毒品立刻注射進去，而是將針頭插在血管上。
  Dang1 jing4 mai4 zhu4 she4 du2 yin3 zhe3 da3 du2 pin3 shi2,
  When intravenous injection drug addiction person inject drugs time,

  tong1 chang2 shi4 bu2 hui4 ma3 shang4 ba3 du2 pin3 li4 ke4 zhu4 she4
  usually will not at once let drugs immediately inject

  jin4 qu4, er2 shi4 jiang1 zhen1 tou2 cha1 zai4 xie3 guan3 shang4.
  into, instead use needle head insert in blood vessel above.

  "When drug addicts take drugs, they usually rest the needle in the vein instead of injecting the drug directly."

(6)一個滿眼夢想的快樂女孩，因為受傷開刀，要<打>釘子進脊椎，像副衣架一般把彎彎的骨頭撐直。
  Yi2 ge4 man3 yan3 meng4 xiang3 de5 kuai4 le4 nyu3 hai2, yin1 wei4

One   full eyes   dream   MOD happy   girl,   because

shou4 shang1 kai1 dao1, yao4 da3 ding1 zi5 jin4 ji2 zhui1, xiang4 fu4
hurt   operate, will put nail   to   spine, like   set

yi1 jia4   yi1 ban1   ba3 wan1 wan1 de5 gu3 tou2 cheng1 zhi2.
clothes stand in general let   bend   MOD bone   prop   straight.

"A happy girl full of dreams due to an injury happened, has to undergo an operation that
puts nails into her spine to straighten up the wiggled spine, which is very similar to
clothing being hanged on hangers."

We follow these categories to explore the common features for these physical event senses of
da3 in the SUMO concept system.

7. Data analysis

According to Gao's study (2001), she based on sense division principle to analyze *da3*,
generalized the patterns and features of the polysemy of *da3*, and obtained five major categories.

Gao (2001) mentioned the prototypical meaning of *da3*. She talked about in the prototypical
case the most central part of the meaning of *da3* is the physical contact between an agent's
hands and a concrete item. In her paper, she also mentioned that there were three different
semantic elements for *da3* such as 1) *hand, hand holdings* or *instrument*; 2) *force direction* and
3) *impact*.

From all our senses of *da3*, we can divide two main categories: 1) physical event senses such
as *da3 zhuo1 zi5* (to tap the table), *da3 shou3 bei4* (to hit the back of a hand), *ba3 wan3 da3
po4* (to break a bowl)... and so on and 2) metaphorical event senses such as *da3 jiao1 dao4* (to
develop the interpersonal relationship/ to come into contact with), *da3 dian4 hua4* (to call), *da3
ke1 shui4* (to nod)... and so on. However, in this study, we just focus on physical event senses.
Based on Gao's analysis (2001), we know that physical event senses of *da3* include these
features such as hand, hand holdings, instrument; force and impact, so we thoroughly examine
our physical event senses by SUMO concept system. In here, we can observe that there are
several concept of SUMO for physical event senses of *da3* such as below table:

Table 2: SUMO concept for physical event senses of *da3*

The phrase of *da3* in Chinese	Translation in English	SUMO concept
da3 shou3 bei4	to *hit* the back of a hand	impacting
da3 zhuo1 zi5	to *tap* the table	touching
ba3 wan3 *da3* po4	to *break* a bowl	impacting
lun4 tai1 *da3* qi4	to *pump* gas into tire	putting
da3 shi1 li4 kang1	to *inject* silicon	putting

We follow SUMO concept system to obtain these concepts of *da3*. These concepts are such as
impacting, touching, putting. We also know that the SUMO concept identifications correspond
with the divisions and definitions in WordNet. For this reason, we need make sure the WordNet
definitions of these concepts for physical event senses of *da3*.

Table 3: WordNet definition and SUMO concept for physical event senses of *da3*

The English lemma of *da3*	WordNet definition	SUMO concept
hit	deal a blow to, either with the hand or with an	impacting

	instrument	
tap	a light touch or stroke	touching
break	destroy the integrity of; usually by force; cause to separate into pieces or fragments	impacting
pump	deliver forth	putting
inject	force or drive (a fluid or gas) into by piercing	putting

In this way, we obtain the common semantic elements from SUMO concepts for physical event senses of *da3*. The semantic features are hand, instrument, and force. In addition, we can detect when we do these actions, the manners are impact, direct contact or contact by injection. We may visual this as:

(1) Agent + hand, hand holding or instrument --> Patient or Object

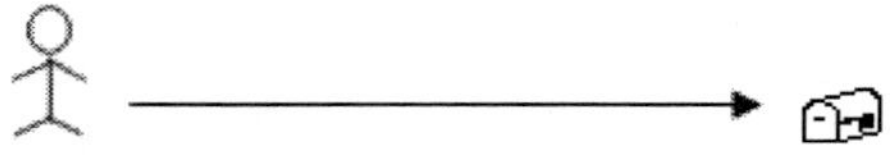

(2) Agent --> impact (direct contact) --> Object

(3) Agent --> force (contact by injection) --> Patient or Object

From the SUMO concept system for the physical event senses of *da3*, we see these concepts imply the following semantic features: hand, hand holdings, instrument; force and impact (direct contact or contact by injection). We use SUMO concept system to find out all possible concepts for the physical event senses of *da3*, while Gao (2001) used semantic features to analyze and explain physical actions of *da3*. Following our analyses, explanations, comparison and demonstrations, we discover that our analyses correspond with Gao's study result for the physical event senses of *da3*.

8. Conclusion

In this study, we explore all possible concepts for physical event senses of *da3* through the SUMO concept system. These concepts imply some semantic features: hand, hand holdings, instrument; force and impact. We use concept-based approach, while Gao (2001) took a semantic-feature-based approach to examine the physical event senses of *da3*. We also compare our analysis with Gao's (2001) and find our results are very similar. This leads us to propose that a concept-base approach is a viable one when exploring the sense of polysemous verbs in Chinese.

References

Bei, Guqin and Xuetao Zhang. eds., 1988. Hanzi Pindu Tognuji – Sucheng Shudu Youxuan Biao (statistics of Chinese Word Frequency – A First Priority Lift for Quick Literacy Reading). Beijing: Dianzi Gongye Chubanshe (Electronics Industry Publishing House).

Chang, Li-li, Chen, Keh-Jiann and Huang, Chu-Ren. 2000. *A Lexical-Semantic Analysis of Mandarin Chinese Verbs: Representation and Methodology. Computational Linguistics and Chinese Language Processing.* Vol.5, No. 1, February 2000, 1-18.

Chief, Lian-Cheng, Chu-Ren Huang, Keh-Jiann Chen, Mei-Chih Tsai and Li-Li Chang. 2000. *What Can Near Synonyms Tell Us. International Journal of Computational Linguistics and Chinese Language Processing.* 5 (1)47-60.

Fellbaum C.. WordNet: An Electronic Lexical Database. Cambridge: MIT Press 1998

Gao, H. H. 2001. Da Polysemy. *The physical foundation of the patterning of physical action verbs, Lund University Press.* 157-204.

Hong, Jia-Fei, Xiang-Bing Li and Chu-Ren Huang. *2004. Ontology-based Prediction of Compound Relations: A study based on SUMO. Presented at PACLIC18.* December 8-10. 151-160. Tokyo: Waseda University.

Huang, Chu-Ren, and Ru-Yng Chang. Sinica BOW (Bilingual Ontological Wordnet): Integration of Bilingual WordNet and SUMO". *Presented at the 4th International Conference on Language Resources and Evaluation (LREC2004).* Lisbon. Portugal. 26-28 May .2004.

Huang, Chu-Ren. Elanna I. J. Tseng, Dylan B. S. Tsai, Brian Murphy. Cross-lingual Portability of Semantic relations: Bootstrapping Chinese WordNet with English WordNet Relations. Languages and Linguistics. 4.3. 2003. 509-532

Huang, Chu-Ren, Kathleen Athens, Li-Li Chang, Keh-Jiann Chen, Mei-Chun Liu, Mei-Chih Tsai. 2000. *The Module-Attribute Representation of Verbal Semantics: From Semantics to Argument Structure.* In International Journal of Computational Linguistics & Chinese Language Processing 5.1: 19-46.

Liu, Mei-Chun. 2002. *Mandarin Verbal Semantic*s: A Corpus-based Approach. 2nd ed., Taipei, Taiwan: Crane Publishing Co.

Miller G. A., R. Beckwith, C. Fellbaum, D. Gross and K. Miller. "Introduction to WordNet: An On-line Lexical Database," *In Proceedings of the fifteenth International Joint Conference on Artificial Intelligence. Chambéry, France.* 28 August- 3 September .1993.

蔡美智. 2002。 講「清楚」、說「明白」—漢語動詞近義、多義、詞義劃分研究。第三屆中文詞彙語意學研討會。台北，南港：中央研究院。

Website Resources

Chinese Word Sketch Engine: http://wordsketch.ling.sinica.edu.tw/
English Word Sketch Engine: http://www.sketchengine.co.uk/
Lexical Data Consortium. 2005. Chinese Gigaword Corpus 2.5.: http://www.ldc.upenn.edu/Catalog/CatalogEntry.jsp?catalogId=LDC2005T14
Sinica Corpus. http://www.sinica.edu.tw/SinicaCorpus/

Ambiguity in the Negative V+bo NP Construction in Taiwanese Southern Min[*]

Huang, Hui-yu

Graduate Institute of Foreign Literatures and Linguistics, National Chiao Tung University,
1001 Ta-Hsueh Road, Hsinchu, Taiwan
s1104029@Gmail.com

Abstract. This paper examines some syntactic and semantic properties of the negative construction V+*bo* NP (VbN) in Taiwanese Southern Min (TSM). It finds out that there are ambiguities between an episode reading and a generic reading in VbN construction which require further investigations and explanations. Therefore, the goal of this paper is to account for the ambiguities lying in the negative VbN construction.

Keywords: negative markers, Taiwanese Southern Min (TSM), ambiguity.

1. Introduction

The V+bo NP is a special negative construction in TSM whose exact syntactic counterpart is not found in Mandarin Chinese. It has been widely acknowledged that the post-verbal negative marker *bo* 'not' in the VbN may form a resultative complement with the preceding verb (e.g. Cheng 1997; Li 1996; Teng 1992). While those works have shed light on the semantic characteristics of *bo*, the VbN construction remains ambiguous between an episode and a generic reading that each needs to be explained. On the episode reading, *bo* expresses the lack of a desired result such as (1). Sentence (1) means that the agent *he* intended to find someone, so he did the finding-event, but failed to find out the person. On the generic reading, the VbN is taken as an association with a potential property, as in (2). It expresses that the agent *he* does not have the ability to do the studying-event well.

(1) I   chue bo lang.
    he find not person
    'He failed in finding the person.'
(2) I   thak bo chhe.
    he study not book
    'He can not study well.'

 The main goal of this paper is to argue that the different interpretations of VbN construction in Taiwanese Southern Min may be due to different structural positions which the post-verbal negative marker *bo* occupies on the ground of Zanuttini's (1997) proposal that argues for there to be different structural positions for two kinds of post-verbal negative markers, namely presuppositional versus non-presuppositional, as stated in (3).

---

[*] This article began as a term paper for my first-year syntax seminar course. I am grateful to C.-S. Luther Liu for his comments of that paper. I am also appreciative of P.-Y. Katherine Hsiao's discussions with me. The author is responsible for all the mistakes in the article and understands further modifications are required in the future.

(3) a. Presuppositional negative markers, which negate a proposition that is assumed in the
       discourse.
    b. Non-presuppositional negative markers, which negate a proposition that does not have
       a special discourse status.

(Zanuttini 1997:
99)

More precisely, *bo* in the episode reading context corresponds to the presuppositional negative
marker whereas *bo* in the generic reading context corresponds to the non-presuppositional
negative marker.

The remaining sections of this article is organized as follows. Section 2 is a summary of
Zanuttini's (1997) analysis of post-verbal negative markers. Section 3 shows an overview of
VbN construction and provides an analysis of the distinction between an episode and a generic
reading. Section 4 briefly reviews previous study on the post-verbal negative *bo*. Section 5
concludes this article.

2. Framework: Zanuttini's (1997) Analysis of Post-verbal Negative Markers

Zanuttini (1997) examines several Romance varieties and offers a systematic investigation of
negative markers. She argues that there are two kinds of post-verbal negative markers. Based
on their contributions to the meaning of the clause, post-verbal negative markers are
distinguished as presuppositional negative markers when they negate a proposition that is
assumed in the discourse, and as non-presuppositional negative markers when they negate a
proposition that does not have a prior discourse grounding. Take (4) as an example.

(4) a. Maria a   mangia *pa/nen* la   carn. (Piedmontese)
       Maria s.cl eats   neg   the meat
       'Maria doesn't eat meat.'
    b. Gianni a   capis   *pa/nen* tut.
       Gianne s.cl understands net   everything
       'Gianni doesn't understand everything.'

(Zanuttini 1997:
67)

In these examples, although there is no apparent difference between the use of *pa* and *nen,* they
indeed contribute different interpretations to the sentences. *Pa* is taken as a presuppositional
negative marker since it negates a proposition assumed in the discourse, whereas *nen* as a non-
propositional negative marker since it does not.

Her syntactic analysis of post-verbal negative markers is essentially based on two findings of
Cinque's work[1]. First, the relative ordering of adverbs in the clause is fixed in the structure.
Second, for each adverb, there is one head position to its immediate right and one head position
to its immediate left.

Regarding the adverbs she mainly considers the ones which occur in lower positions
(compared with those appear in a higher portion in the clausal structure) such as 'already', 'no
more' and 'always' since they are the crucial ones which help determine the distribution of post-
verbal negative markers.

She further proposes that the negative marker occurs in the specifier of a projection labeled
NegP[2]. Assuming this, the NegP-1 is labelled for the projection headed by the pre-verbal
negative marker and the NegPs such as NegP-2, NegP-3, NegP-4 are required for the
projections headed by post-verbal negative markers. The relative order of post-verbal negative

---

[1] For more details, readers are referred to Zanuttini (1997).
[2] Readers for more references are referred to Rizzi (1990), Zanuttini (1997) among others.

markers is determined by virtue of their interaction with the relevant adverbs which occur in lower positions. Apart from these three different structural positions for post-verbal negatives, she implies more NegP projections for post-verbal negative markers are not impossible. The relevant syntactic structure is represented in (5) below.

(5)

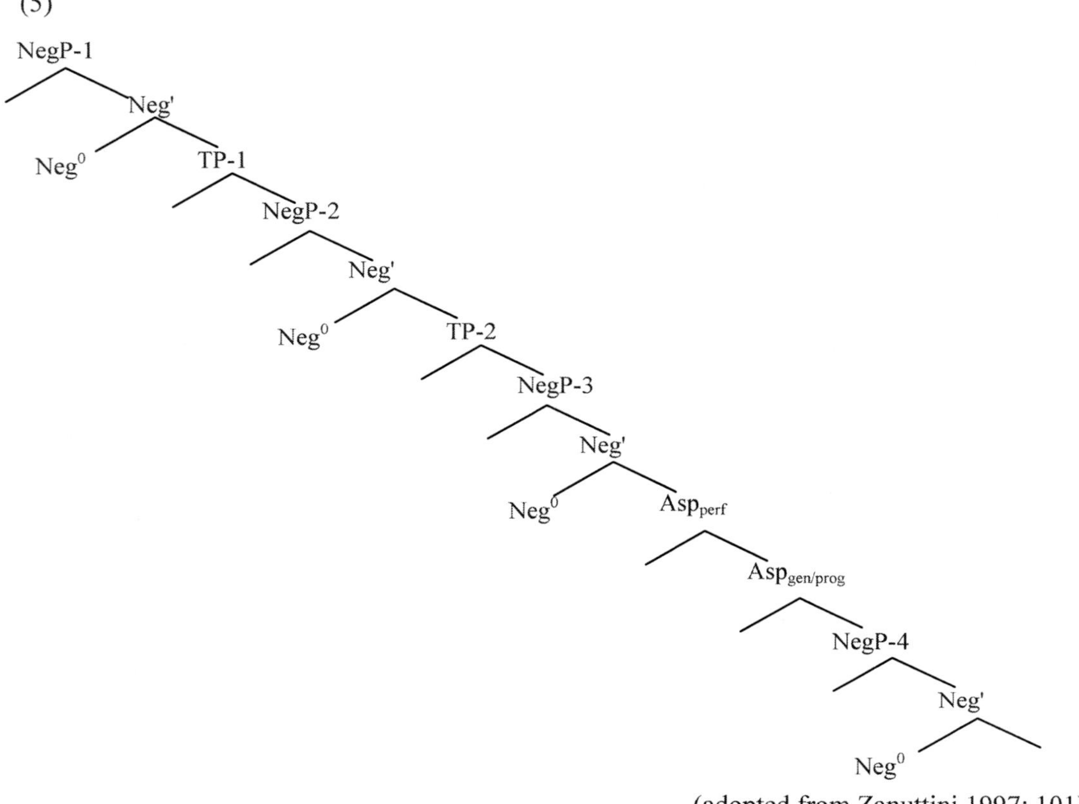

(adopted from Zanuttini 1997: 101)

According to her, NegP-2 is the position for negative markers with a presuppositional reading because of the following reason:

...it is crucial for this type of negative markers to occur above TP-2, the projection that hosts in its specifier and adverbs corresponding to English 'already'. Note that these adverbs also have a presuppositional reading: 'already' presupposes the event and asserts that it has taken place before a certain moment in time. It is tempting to think that it is not a coincidence that both presuppositional negative markers and these adverbs occur in the same portion of clausal structure.

(Zanuttini 1997:100-01)

NegP-3 and NegP-4 are the positions for negative markers with a non-presuppositional reading. This paper will ignore characterization of NegP-3 and NegP-4 since they do not appear to contribute different interpretations to the clause, and hence are irrelevant to clarification of the ambiguities in VbN construction. Instead, attention will be drawn to the distinction between NegP-2 and NegP-4 later in this paper as the former appears to parallel an episode reading while the latter to parallel a generic reading.

3. Overview and Analysis for Taiwanese VbN Construction

3.1.General properties
3.1.1.Syntactic distribution
As noted by Huang (2003), *bo* forms a compound with the preceding verb rather than with the
following noun phrase regardless of an episode or a generic reading. Hence, *bo*+NP can not be
taken as a negative NP, as illustrated in (6-8).

(6) a. I   thak   bo   chhe.
     he study not book
     'He can't study well.'
  b. I chhe thak   bo.
(7) a. Abi chhue bo lang.
     Abi find not person
     'Abi failed in finding the person.'
  b. Abi lang   chhue bo.
(8) a. I   than bo chiN,   ma   chhua bo bo.
     he earn not money also marry not wife
     'He failed in making money and also failed in getting a wife.'
  b. I   chiN   than bo, bo   ma   chhua bo.
     he money earn not wife also marry not

Moreover, the degree adverb *ka* 'more' is compatible with the VbN construction and as it co-
occurs with VbN, this construction will denote a generic reading irrespective of the fact whether
it originally has an episode or a generic reading. To express this, examples in (9-10) show its
original use with an episode reading while examples in (11-12) with a generic reading.

(9) a. In   man bo   kam-a.
     they pick not   tangerine-Suffix
     'They failed in picking tangerines.'
  b. In *kha* man bo kam-a.
     'They are less able to pick tangerines (, comparing with others).'
(10) a. In   lia   bo hi-a.
     they catch not fish-Suffix
     'They failed in catching fish.'
  b. In *kha* lia   bo hi-a.
     'They are less able to catch fish (, comparing with others).'
(11) a. I   thak   bo   chhe.
     he study not book
     'He can't study well.'
  b. I *kha* thak bo   chhe.
     'He is less able to study well (,comparing with others).'
(12) a. Chit-chia ti   chiN bo yu.
     this-CL   pig fry   not oil
     'There is no oil of this pig to be fried.'
  b. Chit-chia ti *kha* chiN bo yu.
     'There is less oil of this pig to be fried.'

We have looked at the distribution of VbN construction and now we will turn to examine its
semantic contribution to the clause.

3.1.2.Semantic properties

Huang (2003) found out a semantic property for VbN construction in which *bo*+NPs only occur
with accomplishment verbs, or activity verbs which are turned into accomplishments by adding
bo+NP. That is, *bo*+NP cannot co-occur with stative verbs which cannot be changed into a telic
event, as shown in (13).

(13) a. *I   ai   bo lang.
          he love not person
          'He failed in loving anyone.'
      b.* I   sioN   bo lang.
          he think   not person
          'He failed in thinking of anyone.'

Furthermore, Cheng (1997) observes more restrictions on verbs in VbN construction. Verbs
which denote 'disposing' meaning such as *be* 'sell', *chhat* 'erase', and *tan* 'throw' are not
compatible with VbN like (14) unless what follows them is concerned with quantity or quality
like (15).

(14) a.* Abing be   bo saN.
          Abing sell not clothes
          'Abing failed in selling any clothes.'
      b.* Abing chhat bo   O-pang.
          Abing erase not blackboard
          'Abing failed in cleaning blackboards.'
(15) a. Abing be   bo chap-niaN saN.
          Abing sell not ten-CL   clothes
          'Abing failed in selling ten suits of clothes.'
      b. Abing chhat bo leng-te O-pang.
          Abing erase   not two-CL blackboard
          'Abing failed in cleaning two blackboards.'

The final set of examples demonstrate that the VbN construction with an episode reading has
a parallel interpretation of Mandarin *mei V-dao N*, where *-dao* serves as a phase marker based
on Chao (1968). This is exemplified in (16-17).

(16) a. I   lim   bo chui. (TSM)
          he drink not water
          'He failed in drinking water.'
      b. Ta mei he-dao   shui. (Mandarin)
          he not drink-PHASE water
(17) a. I   ti   hia   tan bo lang. (TSM)
          he at there wait not person
          'He failed in waiting for the person there.'
      b. Ta zai na-li mei deng-dao   ren. (Mandarin)
          he at   there not wait-PHASE person

Contrarily, on the generic reading the VbN construction does not allow the parallel
interpretation of Mandarin *mei V-PHASE N,* as illustrated in (18b,19b). Rather, they have a
correspondent interpretation of Mandarin *V bu-PHASE N*, as shown in (18c, 19c).

(18) a. I   tso bo tai-tsi. (TSM)
          he do not thing

'He can do nothing well.'
*b. Ta mei zuo-hao   shi-qing. (Mandarin)
    he not do-PHASE thing
c. Ta zuo bu-hao   ren-he shi-qing.
          not-PHASE any   thing
(19) a. Tsit-khu tshan tsing bo mi-kiaN. (TSM)
         this-CL farm grow not thing
         'This farm can't grow anything.'
*b. Zhe-kuai tian-di mei zhong-chu   dong-xi. (Mandarin)
     this-CL   farm   not grow-PHASE thing
c. Zhe-kuai tian-di zhong bu-chu   dong-xi.
                            not-PHASE

Both *bu* 'not' and *mei* 'not' are negative markers used in Mandarin Chinese. Lin (2003) has proposed that *mei* aspectually selects an event as its complement while *bu* aspectually selects as its complement a stative situation that requires no input of energy. Therefore, the comparison between Mandarin and Southern Min negative markers shown above suggests an interesting point that *bo* 'not' in VbN construction has overlapping aspectual properties of *mei* and *bu*.

3.2. The analysis of the distinction between an episode and a generic reading
As we have seen above, there is no apparent syntactic distinction between an episode and a generic reading in VbN construction. They are different only in semantic interpretation   when compared with their counterparts in Mandarin. Under certain circumstances such as cooccurrence of the degree adverb *kha* 'more', the episode reading can be further turned into a generic reading as in (9-10).

Based on the above investigations, I argue that the ambiguity between an episode and a generic reading are due to different heads of NegPs which the negative marker *bo* occupies. To put it more precisely, when *bo* occupies head of NegP-2 it yields an episode reading; when *bo* occupies head of NegP-4 it yields a generic reading. Henceforth I take *bo* with an episode meaning as corresponding to the presuppositional negative marker and *bo* with a generic meaning as corresponding to the non-presuppositional negative marker.

As noted by Zanuttini (1997), TP-2 is the projection which hosts adverbs in its specifier that correspond to English 'already'; therefore, TP-2 presupposes the event and testifies that it has happened before a certain moment of time. As a result of this fact, the negative marker *bo* which occupies head of NegP-2 has the potential for contribution of a telic event, and that makes clauses containing such kind of VbN construction comply with an episode reading. The relevant structure is shown in (20) below.

(20)

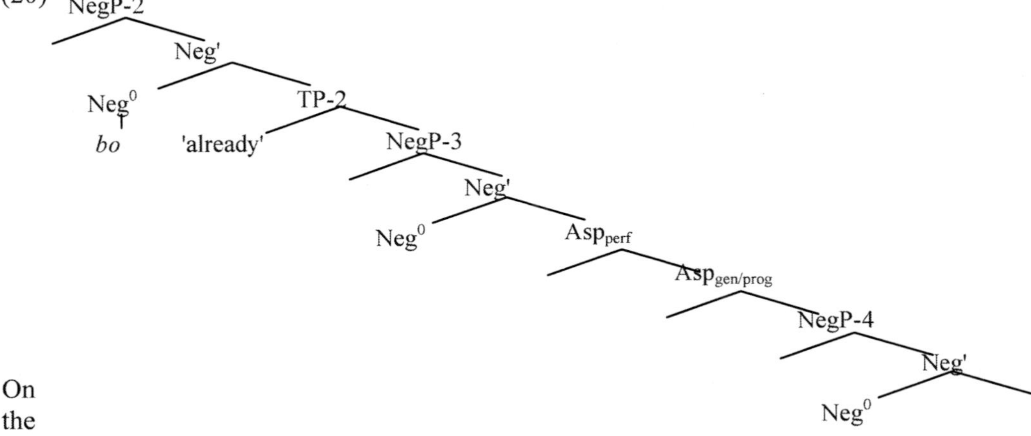

On
the

other hand, when *bo* occupies head of NegP-4, the VbN is associated with a generic reading, as shown in (21).

(21) I   thiaN bo enggi.
     he hear   not English
     'He can't understand English.'

Supporting evidence comes from the interaction between *bo* and the adverb *long* 'always'. (22a) and (23a) are originally with episode readings and (22b) and (23b) are those turned into generic readings.

(22) a. I   khi chhai-chi-a be   bo saN.
        she go market   buy not clothes
        'She failed in buying any clothes in the market.'
     b. I khi chhai-chi-a *long* be bo saN.
        'It's always been the case that she failed in buying any clothes in the market.'
(23) a. I   chha bo Abing-e chu-chi.
        he seek not Abing's address
        'He failed in seeking out Abing's address.'
     b. I *long* chha bo Abing-e chu-chi.
        'It's always been the case that he failed in seeking out Abing's address.'

An adverb like 'always' occurs in the specifier of the projection which Zanuttini (1997) has labeled AspP$_{gen/prog}$, a position lower than TP-2. As shown in (22b) and (23b), *long* 'always' appears to c-command *bo* 'not' so that *long* is structurally higher than *bo* . According to the interpretations, the negation marker *bo* cannot take scope over such adverb. Consequently, *bo* is assumed to occupy a position lower than *long*, namely NegP-4, and yields the clause a generic reading. This is represented in the relevant structure (24) below.
(24)

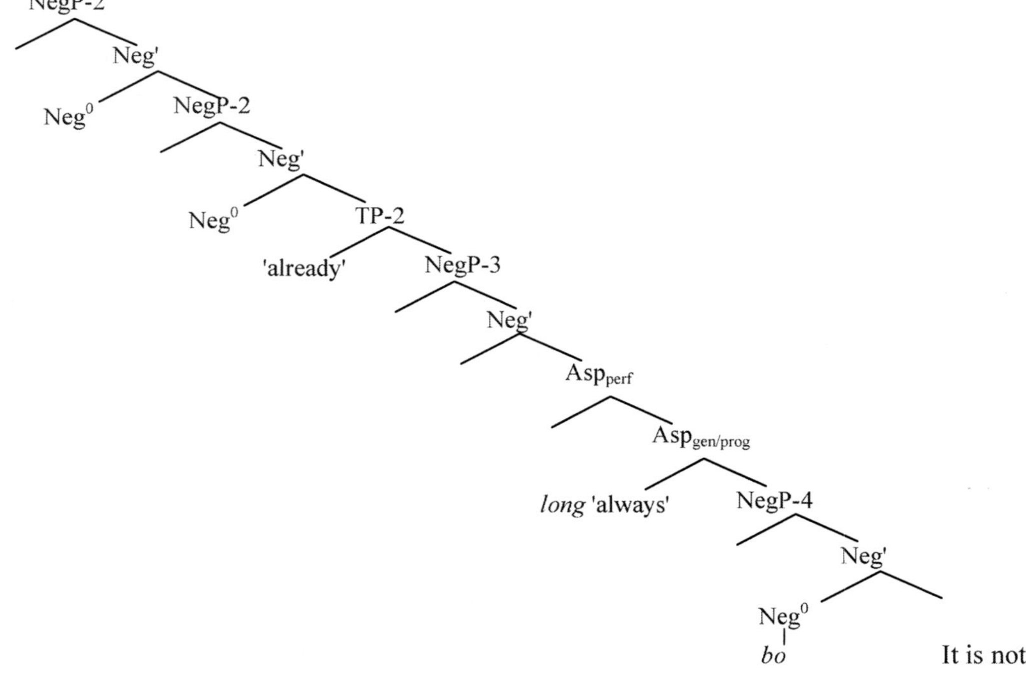

uncommon, as observed by Zanuttini (1997), that the element which is typically used as a presuppositional negative marker can occur in a lower position than 'already'. As this happens, the presuppositional negative marker will contribute a non-presuppositional reading. This may be the reason why an episode reading of *bo* can be turned into a generic usage such as (9-10b, 22-23b) above.

4. Previous Related Study

4.1.Cheng (1997), Li (1996), Teng (1992)'s observations

Cheng (1997), Li (1996) and Teng (1992) claim that *bo* in VbN construction serves as a resultative complement of the preceding verb although they do not give analyses of it. Cheng notices that the V+*bo* or V+*u* construction[3] is ambiguous between potential modality as in (25) and existential aspect as in (26)[4].

(25) a. Q: Chit-chun khi kam be   u mih?
              now   go *kam* buy *u* thing
              'Can you get anything at this hour?'
        b. A: U, be   u.
              U buy *u*
              'Yes, I can.'

(Cheng 1997: 215)

(26) a. Chheh goa cha-hng   be   bo.
           book I   yesterday buy   not
           'I failed to get the book yesterday.'

(Cheng 1997: 212)

Teng takes *bo* as a resultative complement in the following examples (27-29) and calls for a fine analysis of its syntactic characteristics.

(27) Chit-pun chhe hia-ni chhen, li   na-e   khoaN bo?
        this-CL book that   easy   you   how come read   not
        'This is an easy book; how come you don't understand it?'
(28) I   hit-khoan lang   chuat-tui   chhoa bo   sim-pu.
        he   that-kind person absolutely marry not daughter-in-law
        'Nobody could stand being a daughter-in-law to a man like that.'
(29) I-e tian-oe,   goa long   mng bo.
        his telephone   I   always   ask not
        'Nobody could tell me what his telephone number is.'

(Teng 1992: 628)

4.2. Huang's (2003) position on 'bo'

Huang (2003) takes *bo* as forming a resultative compound with the preceding verb instead of forming a negative NP with the following bare noun. Taking this position on *bo*, he implies that *bo* has combined with its preceding verb to form a lexicon verb so that *bo* would not be able to undergo syntactic or semantic operations. However, not only does he give analysis of *bo* but as the previous discussions demonstrate, *bo* should not be taken as a compound with its preceding verb since it has flexibility to occur in different structural positions.

---

[3] . V+*u* is taken as the assertive form of V+*bo* by Cheng.

[4] . In such case, his potential modality corresponds to the generic reading and existential aspect to the episode reading.

4.3. Tang's (1996) analysis

Tang (1996) provides an analysis of *bo* by means of lexicalization. He proposes that *m* 'not' is the only 'simple negation' in Taiwanese Southern Min and that the other negation markers are simply derived from *m* plus other verbs through fusion. Therefore, under his analysis *bo* is composed of *m* and *u* through fusion, where *u* still exists in the underlying form but does not appear in the phonetic form. With this in mind, he claims that we do not need to consider the cooccurrence restriction between *bo* and other syntactic elements; instead, we can predict the syntactic distribution of *bo* simply by investigating its composed element *u*. However, counterexamples arise as in (30-34).

(30) a. *Chit-le   wa-tang lai   u chap-e lang.
      this-CL activity come *u* ten-CL person
      'There came ten people to this activity.'
    b. Chit-le   wa-tang lai   bo chap-e lang.
                       not
      'There came less than ten people to this activity.'
(31) a. *I   chao u lo   a.
      he run *u* way SFP
      'He had ways to go.'
    b. I   chao bo lo   a.
              not
      'He had no way to go.'
(32) a. *Aphang tan   u Abing.
      Aphang wait *u* Abing
      'Aphang succeeded in waiting for Abing.'
    b. Aphang tan   bo Abing.
                not
      'Aphang failed in waiting for Abing.'
(33) a. *Gua chham i   kong u we.
      I   and   he talk *u* word
      'He and I can talk much with each other.'
    b. Gua chham i kong bo   we.
                   not
      'He and I have nothing to talk to each other.'
(34) a. *I   thiaN u li   kong e   we .
      he hear *u* you say   Gen. word
      'He can understand what you say.'
    b. I thiaN bo li kong e we .
            not
      'He can't understand what you say.'

According to these data, the sentences with negative V *bo*+NP construction are syntactically grammatical and to claim that *u* determines the distribution of *bo* would wrongly predict that they are ungrammatical.

5. Concluding Remarks

In this paper, I have argued that the ambiguity of the negative VbN construction in TSM lies within different structural positions which *bo* occupies on the ground of Zanuttini's (1997) analysis of post-verbal negatives. I also examine the diverse syntactic and semantic properties of VbN as well as its interactions with other elements. Apart from the investigation of VbN, I show that some previous study does not give any explanation for the ambiguity which is raised in this paper, and that Huang's (2003) position of *bo* will encounter problems which however might have an explanation from my position. Furthermore, I show that Tang's (1996) analysis of *bo* will fail to explain the counterexamples that I raised. Despite of those advantages, this paper has not provided a full syntactic nor semantic account of how *bo* in TSM comes to NegP-2 and NegP-4 positions. Therefore, further refinement of solutions will be required and we will keep pursuing the negation properties in VbN construction.

References

Chao, Yuen-ren. 1968. *A Grammar of Spoken Chinese.* Berkeley: University of California Press.

Cheng, Robert L. 1997. Taiwanese 'U' and Mandarin 'YOU'. *Taiwanese and Mandarin Structures and Their Developmental Trends in Taiwan III: Temporal and Spatial Relations, Questions and Negatives in Taiwanese and Mandarin,* pp. 191-230. Taipei: Yuan-Liou.

Haegeman, L. 1994. *Introduction to Government and Binding Theory.* 2nd ed.. Blackwell.

Huang, C.-T. James. 2003. The Distribution of Negative NPs and Some Typological Correlates. *Functional Structure(s), Form and Interpretation.* Ed. Andrew Simpson et al. Routledge: Taylor and Francis.

Li, Rulong. 1996. Minnanyu De You He Wu. ['You' and 'Wu' in Southern Min]. *Fangyan yu Yinyun Lunji [Papers on Dialects and Phonology],* pp. 152-58. Hong Kong: T.T. Ng Chinese Language Research Centre of CHUK.

Lin, Jo-wang. 2003. Aspectual Selection and Negation in Mandarin Chinese. *Linguistics,* 41(3), 425-459.

Tang, Ting-chi. 1996. On the Semantics and Syntax of Negatives in Southern Min. *Papers on Southern Min Syntax.* pp. 135-185. Taipei: Student.

Teng, Shou-hsin. 1992. Diversification and Unification of Negation in Taiwanese. *Symposium Series of Institute of History and Philology. Chinese Languages and Linguistics I,* 609-29. Taipei: Academia Sinica.

Rizzi, L. 1990. *Relativized Minimality.* MIT.

Zanuttini, R. 1997. *Negation and Clausal Structure: A Comparative Study of Romance Language.* New York: Oxford University Press.

Time-moving Metaphors and Ego-moving Metaphors: Which Is Better Comprehended by Taiwanese?[*]

May, Hsin-mei Huang & Shelley, Ching-yu Hsieh

Department /Graduate Institute of Foreign Languages and Literature, National Cheng Kung University,
Taxue Road. 1, 70101 Tainan, Taiwan
plum0910@yahoo.com.tw, shelley@mail.ncku.edu.tw

Abstract. This is a semantic pilot study which concentrates on how people in Taiwan process the temporal metaphors, ego-moving metaphor and time-moving metaphor. Motivated by the research of Gentner, Imai, and Boroditsky (2002) in which the English native speakers comprehend ego-moving metaphors faster than time-moving metaphors, the present study attempts to reexamine whether the faster reaction to ego-moving metaphors is shared by both the Chinese native speakers and EFL learners. To achieve the goals, 25 Chinese/English bilinguals are invited to be examined via the16 Chinese and 16 English test sentences. The recordings of their accuracy on each item are served as the databases used to compare with the study of Gentner, Imai, and Boroditsky (2002). The two finding presented here are: (1) when the subjects tested in their native language, Chinese, they process ego-moving metaphors better. (2) when tested in the foreign language, English, they conceptualize time-moving metaphors much better.

Keywords: metaphors, time-moving metaphor, ego-moving metaphor, EFL

1. Introduction

This is a semantic study which attempts to explore how Taiwanese process time metaphors. According to Shuell (1990: 102), "If a picture is worth 1,000 words, a metaphor is worth 1,000 pictures!" By breaking literal meanings, metaphors create thousands of possibilities. The way we structure the thousand pictures relies on conceptual metaphor. Conceptual metaphor is people's underlying cognitive level as the bridge between language and thought. By

---

assimilating the two different domains, conceptual metaphor specifies the concrete idea into abstract entity. In general, conceptual metaphor is the surface structures which make metaphors understandable. (Lakoff and Johnnson, 1980; Goddard, 1998; McGlone, 2007; Charteris-Black & Ennis, 2001). As Lakoff (1993:228) claims, "We do not have detectors for time. Thus, it makes good biological sense that time should be understood in terms of things and motion." That is, the comprehension of the abstract time understood via space is biologically determined.

The two space → time metaphors under examination are time-moving and ego-moving metaphors. Based on the study of Gentner, Imai, and Boroditsky (2002) in which English native speakers conceptualize ego-moving metaphor faster, two research goals are proposed: Chinese native speakers and EFL learners process ego-moving metaphors better. In order to answer the two research questions, this paper is organized as follows, (1) Introduction, (2) the theoretical framework on temporal metaphors, (3) the methodology, (4) results, (5) discussion, and (6) conclusions.

2. Literature review

This study examines how English-Chinese bilinguals in Taiwan structure temporal metaphors. The introduction of the two time metaphors, the different perspective that Chinese and English speakers hold, and the study conducted by Gentner, Imai, and Boroditsky (2002) are covered.

2.1. Sequencing time domain

The two space → time metaphoric systems are ego-moving and time-moving metaphor. The primary difference is that they posit different assignments of front and back in a time line.

Time-moving metaphor

Time-moving metaphors identify the events temporally ordered with another in the time line. In time-moving metaphors, time can be conceived of as preceding and following one another in which time flows from the future via the ego, the point of reference, to the past (Li, 2005; Ahrens and Huang, 2002). In this metaphor, the future is in the back and the past is in the front (Gentner, Imai, and Boroditsky, 2002: 539). For example, 'The final exam is before Thursday' in which 'before', a space term, indicates 'the final exam' is proceeding 'Thursday'. Therefore, the final exam is in the relative the past and Thursday in the relative future. (see Figure 1.)

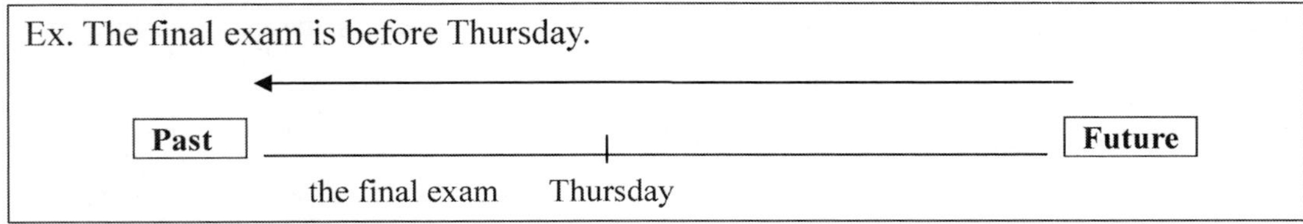

Figure 1. An example of time-moving metaphor

Ego-moving metaphor

Ego-moving metaphor recognizes the event in the time order with the ego/observer. It attributes motion over a landscape to an entity. Li (2005: 16-17) proposes that "the observer comes from the past and moves via the present to into the future, while time as the reference ground remains stationary." Indicated by this metaphor, front is assigned to the future and back to the past (Gentner, Imai, and Boroditsky, 2002: 539). For instance, 'The final exam is before us' in which the space "before" specifies the linear time relationship of "us" as the present time and "the final exam" as the future event. (see Figure 2)

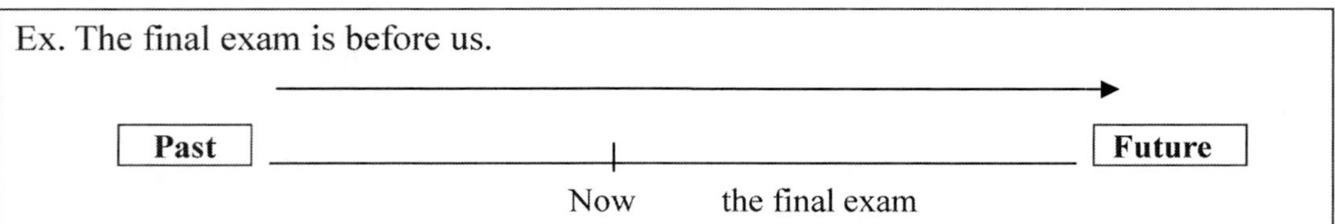

Figure 2. Ego-moving metaphor

2.2. Cultural difference regarding the orientation of the ego

Culture influences people's understanding about the world, as Kövecses (2006: 135) indicates, 'our understandings are mental representations structured by cultural models or frames.' In English, the ego always takes a front-to-the-future orientation. However, in Chinese, ego has dual orientations: a front-to-the-future orientation and a front-to-the-past orientation, while the latter is predominant in Chinese. (Li, 2005: 40). For instance, 'The best is before you.' means that the best is waiting in the 'future.' However, for the Chinese speakers, *qian suo wei jian* 前所未見 'it has never been seen before' refers to the event that has never been seen in the past.

2.3. Gentner, Imai, and Boroditsky's (2002) study on the temporal metaphors

Their research on this topic provides the present study with a theoretical basis. The three experiments conducted show that the English native speakers, apart from relying on an ego-moving framework to interpret time, conceptualize ego-moving metaphor faster than time-moving metaphor. Inspired by their research, the present study aims to reexamine whether it is shared by Chinese native speakers and the EFL learners.

3. Methodology

The present study is conducted to explore how people in Taiwan, who have Chinese as the L1 and English as their foreign language, process time-moving and ego-moving metaphors.

Participants & Materials

The participants are twenty-five English and Chinese bilinguals who are female aged at 31.7. They are chosen, for they have no problem conceptualizing English and Chinese metaphors. Thirty-two test sentences are designed to examine the participants' accuracy. Sixteen of them are in Chinese in which nine used the time-moving metaphors and the others used ego-moving metaphors. As for the other sixteen, they are mostly taken from the study of Gentner, Imai, and Boroditsky (2002) in which eight used the time-moving metaphors and the others used ego-moving metaphors. For example, Christmas is six days ahead of New Year's Day.

Procedures

After the participants read the sample in Chinese and English, they are tested by Chinese test sentences and followed by the English sentences. They see each sentence one at a time by indicating the event 'I will see you' happened in the past or future relative to the reference (4 o'clock). (see Figure 3.) Totally, there are thirty-two such blocks. The arrangement of all the testing sentences is randomized, so the subjects will not notice the two metaphorical types.

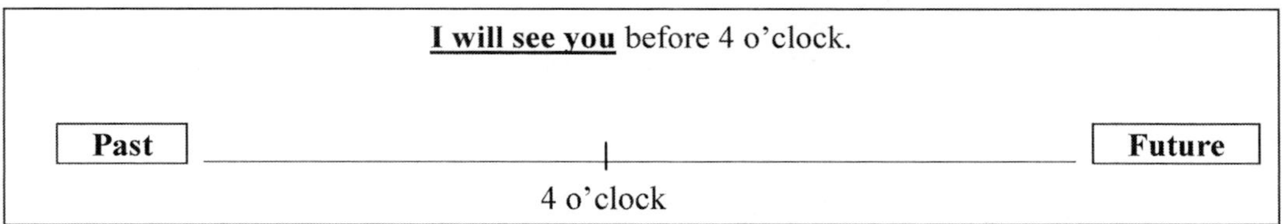

Figure 3. A sample of the English testing sentence.

4. Results

This section is divided into two parts to examine whether the faster reaction to ego-moving metaphors is a shared value for both native speakers and EFL learners.

4.1. Chinese version

The results are summarized in the following figures to verify whether ego-moving metaphors in Chinese are better processed by its native speakers.

The distribution of the participants' accuracy in the two metaphors in Chinese

The following two figures show the distributions of the participants in Chinese time-moving metaphors and Chinese ego-moving metaphors respectively.

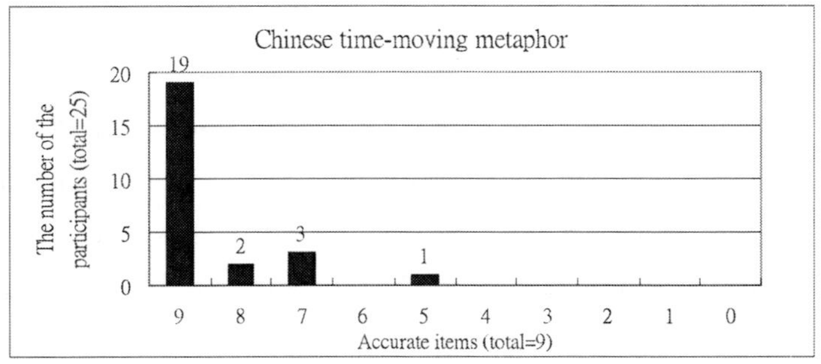

Figure 4. The distribution of the participants in Chinese time-moving metaphors

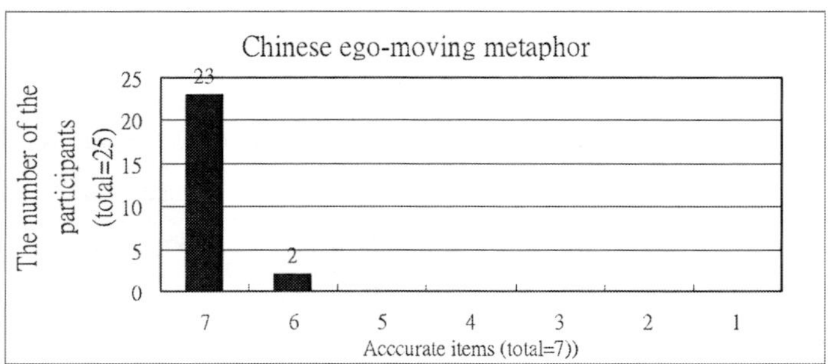

Figure 5. The distribution of the participants in Chinese ego-moving metaphors

From Figure 4, nineteen participants conceptualize all the time-moving metaphors test sentences, accurately; two participants process eight time-moving metaphors accurately, and so on. As shown in Figure 5, twenty-three participants process the seven ego-moving metaphors correctly and the other two process six ego-moving metaphors correctly.

The figures above indicate that ego-moving metaphors are better processed by its Chinese native speakers, so it is consistent with Gentner, Imai, and Boroditsky's (2002) study in which English native speakers process ego-moving metaphors easier.

4.2.English data

This section shows the analysis of the English data by which the easier metaphor for its foreign language learners is presented.

The distribution of the participants' accuracy to the two metaphors in English

Figure 6 and 7 show the distributions of the participants in English time-moving metaphors and English ego-moving metaphors respectively.

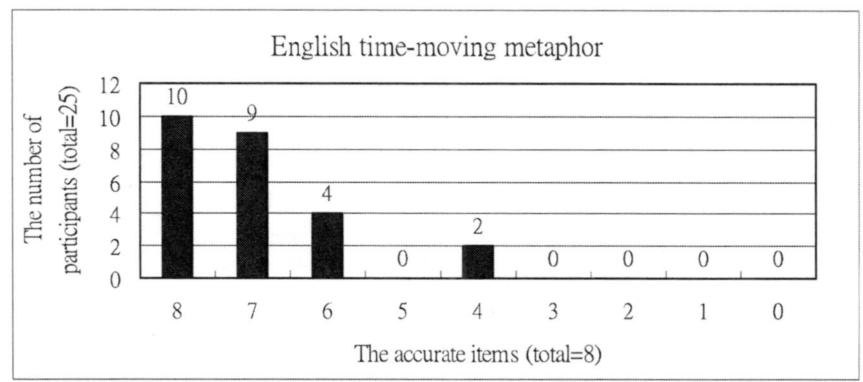

Figure 6. The distribution of the participants in English time-moving metaphors

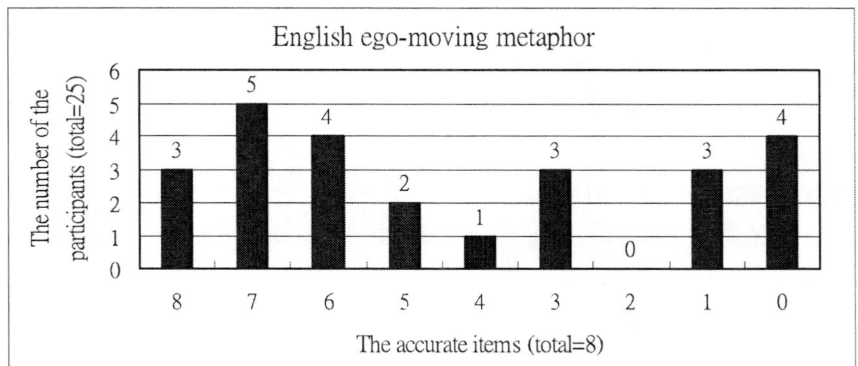

Figure 7. The distribution of the participants in English ego-moving metaphors

From Figure 6, ten participants react accurately to all the time-moving testing sentences, nine participants accurately to seven time-moving metaphors, and so on. As shown in Figure 7, three participants respond accurately to all the ego-moving testing sentences, five accurately to seven ego-moving metaphors, and so forth. Surprisingly, four of the participants entirely fail to process any of the test sentences.

From the two figures presented above, the comprehension of the two metaphors in Chinese version makes a great difference compared with the Chinese version. The participants' processing suggests that English ego-moving metaphors are much harder for its EFL learners. Surprisingly, it contradicts that of Gentner, Imai, and Boroditsky (2002) since the participants process English time-moving metaphors much better.

4   Discussion

This study is compared with that of Gentner, Imai, and Boroditsky (2002). Reduplicating theirs, Chinese native speakers process Chinese ego-moving metaphors better. However, what is contradictory is that EFL learners have a quite hard time processing English ego-moving metaphors.

5.1 Ego-moving metaphors in Chinese are easier for its native speakers

The easiness of Chinese ego-moving metaphors has threefold meanings: people are egocentric, ego-moving metaphors are relative easier, and time-moving metaphors contradict our general direction of time flow.

People's egocentricity

Our body is the reference for describing the world, including time. "The predominance of egocentric reference directions in spatial memory" implies "people's tendency to use egocentric reference systems to code information about their environment" (Waller, Lippa, and Richardson, 2007: 3). Supported by Ahrens and Huang (2002: 491), "we human beings use our body to conceptualize the outside world." Since the way we process time is influenced by egocentricity, ego-moving metaphors appear to be natural and therefore easier.

Ego-moving metaphors as the easier metaphorical type

Based on Gentner, Imai, and Boroditsky (2002:559), ego-moving metaphors identify the time relation between the observer and the event so, it "contains only two points on the time line: an event and an observer" whereas time-moving metaphors specify the time relation between two events "with the ego as the third point." The two-term relation of ego-moving metaphors, which not only involves the ego as the center but also involves only two points in the time line, decreases the degree of processing difficulty.

The contradictory direction of time flow in time-moving metaphor

Li (2005: 15) claims "time that flows from the future to the past is diametrically opposed to our entrenched belief in the direction of the flow of time." The "wrong" direction of time flowing contradicts and therefore interferes with our perception, resulting in increasing the processing difficulty.

5.2 Time-moving in English are easier for its EFL learners

The difficulty of ego-moving metaphors is attributed to two factors: the limited exposure to the target language, and the interference of the participants' first language.

EFL learners' limited exposure to ego-moving metaphors

Learning takes place due to "a structure in semantic memory that specifies the general or expected arrangement of a body of information" (Carroll, 2002:171). People's schemata, the mental representation of a typical instance, are "used in discourse processing to predict and make sense of the particular instance" (Cook, 1994:11).The participants' obscure schemata of ego-moving metaphors makes them fail to fail to structure ego-moving metaphors.

The interference from the participants' first language

Boroditsky (2001: 18) claims that "one's native language appears to exert a strong influence over how one thinks about abstract domains like time." Contrastive Analysis Hypothesis claims that when L2 is learned, the negative transfers from learners' L1 will slow down the speed (Lightbrown and Spada, 2004: 35). English and Chinese as two different languages have different interpretations of time. The differences make the participants confused so that they process ego-moving metaphors with difficulty.

6   Conclusion

This study has two main findings. First, Chinese native speakers, in line with Gentner, Imai, and Boroditsky (2002), process Chinese ego-moving metaphors better, for they are the natural expressions which accord to people's cognitive process. However, inconsistent with Gentner, Imai, and Boroditsky (2002), the Taiwanese, as the EFL learners, process English ego-moving metaphors with great difficulty. This phenomenon points out that the fostering of a foreign language involves the factors, like a great amount of language input and the minimization of the negative transfer from their first language.

References

Ahrens, K. and C. R. Huang. 2002. TIME PASSING IS MOTION. *LANGUAGE AND LINGUISTICS*, 3(3), 491-519.

Boroditsky, L. 2001. Does Language Shape Thought?: Mandarin and English Speakers' Conceptions of Time. *Cognitive Psychology*, 43, 1–22.

Carroll, D. W. 2004. *Psychology of Language*, Fourth Edition. United States of America: Wadsworth.

Charteris-Black, J., and T. Ennis. 2001. A Comparative Study of Metaphor in Spanish and English Financial reporting. *English for Specific Purposes*, 20, 249-266.

Cook, G. 1994. *Discourse and literature: The Interplay of Form and Mind..* Oxford: Oxford University Press.

Creem-Regehr, S. H., J. A. Neil and H. J. Yeh. 2007. Neural Correlates of Two Imagined Egocentric Transformations. *NeuroImage*, 35, 916–927.

Gaddard, C. 1998. *Semantic Analysis*. New York: Oxford University Press.

Gentner, D., M. Imai and L. Boroditsky. 2002. As Time Goes By: Evidence for Two Systems in Processing Space→ Space Metaphors. *LANGUAGE AND COGNITIVE PROCESSES*, 17(5), 537-565.

Kövecses, Z. 2006. *Language, Mind and Culture: a Practical Introduction*. New York: Oxford University Press.

Lakoff, G. and M. Johnson. 1980. *Metaphors We live By.* Chicago: University of Chicago.

Lakoff, G. 1993. The Contemporary Theory of Metaphor. *Ortony. Andre ed., Metaphor and Thought*, Second Edition. Cambridge: Cambridge University Press.

Li, J. E. 2005. *Ying Han 'Qian/Hou' Shi Jian Gai Nian Yin Yu Di Ren Zhi Yan Jiu (The Cognitive Approach of Chinese and English Temporal metaphors on before and after)*. Master thesis. Hua Zhong Normal University.

Lightbown, P. M. and N. Spade. 2004. *How Language Are Learned*, Ninth Edition. New York: Oxford university press.

McGlone, S. T. 2007. What Is The explanatory Value of a Conceptual Metaphor? *Language & Communication*, 27, 109-126.

Radden, G. 2003. The Metaphor TIME AS SPACE Across Languages. *Zeitschrift für Interkulturellen Fremdsprachenunterricht*, 8(2/3), 1-14.

Shuell, T. J. 1990. Teaching and Learning as Problem Solving. *Theory into Practice*, 29, 102-108.

Waller, D., Y. Lippa and A. Richardson. 2007. Isolating Observer-based Reference Directions. *Cognition*, 1, 1-27.

Initialness of Sentence-final Particles in Mandarin Chinese[*]

Xiao-You Kevin Huang

National Tsing Hua University

prince-kevin@yahoo.com.tw

Abstract. This paper gives a thorough investigation into Mandarin sentence-final particles (henceforth SFPs). First I induce core grammatical functions and semantic interpretations of SFPs. Based on Rizzi's (1997) Split CP hypothesis, I make some modifications to accommodate Mandarin SFPs and map them onto separate functional heads within a proper hierarchy. I also examine some empirical evidence of head directionality and tentatively assume Mandarin C is head-initial. To explain the surface head-final order, in light of Chomsky's (2001) Phase Theory and Hsieh's (2005) revised Spell-out hypothesis, I pose a CP complement to Spec movement. Following Moro's (2000) idea, I further claim the motivation behind is to seek for antisymetry.

Keywords: Sentence-final particles, Split CP, Head-directionality, LCA, Antisymmetry, Phase,

1. Functions and Interpretations of SFPs

Based mainly on the studies of Li and Thompson (1982), Chu (1999), and Li (2006), I induce core functions and meanings of the most common SFPs and summarize in the following table with relevant examples given immediately below:

Table 1: Core functions and meanings of SFPs

SFP	Core function and meaning
le	Sentential *le*, differing from aspectual *le*, denotes a "change-of-state," suggesting a previous state changes to the very state to which the sentence ending with *le* refers.
ne	*ne* is closely related to expression of "relevance" and functions as a topic marker.
ba	*ba* lowers the strength of a sentence and display speaker's uncertainty.
a	Normally, *a* reduces forcefulness of the message, as in imperatives or interrogatives.
*ma*1	*ma*1 marks a high degree of the speaker's commitment to the assertion or the speaker's intension to have an action fulfilled in imperative sentences.
*ma*2	*ma*2, though still controversial, is mostly analyzed as a yes-no question particle.
ou	*ou* implies a friendly warning showing concern and caring on the part of the speaker.

(1) a. hua   hong   le.

        flower   red   SFP

        'The flower becomes red.'

---

    b. ta   zhidao zhe   jian   shi   le.
        he   know   this Cl.   incident   SFP
        'He knows the incident (now).'

(2) a. ta   you   san   bu   che   ne!
         he   have   three Cl.   car   SFP
         'He has three cars!'

     b. wo   xihuan zhe   bu   dianying,   ni   ne?
         I   like   this Cl.   movie   you   SFP
         'I like this movie, how about you?'

(3) a. zhe   fu   hua   bucuo   ba./?
         this Cl.   panting   good   SFP
         'This panting is good. / (right)?'

     b. haohao   nianshu   ba!
         hard   study   SFP
         'Study hard, (okay)?'

     c. ni   hui   kaiche ba?
         You   can   drive   SFP
         'You can drive, can't you?'

(4) a. guolai   a!
         come   SFP
         'Come.'

     b. shei   a?
         who   SFP
         'Who?'

(5) a. wo   shuo   jintian   shi   zhouri   ma1.
         I   say   today   is   Sunday   SFP
         'I said today is Sunday!'

     b. zai   he   yi   bei   ma1!
         more   drink one   glass SFP
         'Have one more glass (of wine)!'

(6) ni   shi   xuesheng   ma2?
     you   are   student   SFP
     'Are you a student?'

(7) xiaoxin   ou!
     careful   SFP
     '(Please) be careful!'

2. Structural Mapping of SFPs

Though it is safe to claim that SFPs are the heads of functional projections in CP domain, it is improper to consider that they all occupy the head C position as Mandarin allows sentence-final particle cluster, as in (8).

(8)   hua   hong   le   a./?
          flower   red   SFP   SFP
          'The flower becomes red./?'

Rizzi's (1997) Split CP hypothesis provides a fascinating framework here.

(9) Split CP Hypothesis (Rizzi,1997)
    [Force   Topic*   Focus   Topic*   Fin]

The system is delimited upward by Force, the head encoding "clausal typing" (Cheng, 1997) information; downward by Finiteness, the head differentiating finite and non-finite constructions. Topic and Focus are dedicated to topical and focal interpretations, respectively.

However, this CP system might need some minor modifications to accommodate Mandarin final particles.

According to Li's (2006) proposals, Force should be further split into two distinct heads: Force and Mood. Force head here represents illocutionary force and conveys speech-act information. Mood head instead encodes clause-typing information. This being so, *ma2* as a question particle, though debatable, would belong to Mood.

Haegeman (2002) supports the analysis with evidence. She argues that every clause needs to be typed, but not every clause conveys illocutionary force. For instance, she contends that while matrix clauses are almost always associated with an illocutionary force, embedded clauses are not. Moreover, she finds evidence that "Force," may occupy a lower position than other functional heads such as Topic and Focus. If Li's proposal is right, then, we can maintain Rizzi's assumption that Force is in the highest position and it is Mood that occupies the lower position. And we reach the following hierarchy:

(10) Force > Mood > Fin

Furthermore, following Li (2006), "Degree" is introduced. She argues that Degree head like *ba* and *ma*1 marks scales sentence force. In declarative sentence, with *ba* the speaker is not certain about the factual status of the proposition, whereas with *ma*1 the speaker has a firm judgment. In imperatives and interrogatives, *ba* marks a low degree of the strength of the speaker's intention to have an action carried out or to have the hearer provide an answer and *ma*1 a high degree. Besides, since *a* and *ou* function to strengthen or reduce sentence force as well, they may occupy Degree head position. In short, we can conjecture that Degree is above Force and arrive at the following hierarchy:

(11) Degree > Force > Mood > Fin

Soh and Gao (2004) argue that sentential *le* can be characterized as a "transition marker." Based on them, I call the head position in which it is generated "Trans(ition)". Besides, *le* always follow other SFPs when they co-occur, as in (8). If Chinese CP system is head-initial, which will be discussed later, we might well contend that *le* is structurally the lowest among the SFPs. And the hierarchy in question now extends as below:

(12) Degree > Force > Mood > Trans > Fin

Since *ne* functions to highlight relevance of an utterance and serves as a topic marker, I allocate it to Topic head position. Given Rizzi's (1997) split CP, Topic is located between Force and Finite. Topic must be higher than Trans because as just assumed *le* is the lowest among the SFPs. However, as no enough evidence testifying the relevant order between Topic and Mood in Chinese, I tentatively assume the following structure:

(13) Degree > Force > Mood, Topic > Trans > Finite

Mapping all the final particles onto (13), we ultimately derive a complete hierarchy of SFPs:

(14) Structural mapping of SFPs in Chinese

Degree	>	Force	>	Mood,	Topic	>	Trans	>	Finite
ba, ma1, a, ou				*ma2*	*ne*				*le*

3. Evidence for and against the Initialness Hypothesis

I will first examine some of the evidence provided by Hsieh (2005).

Hsieh (2005) proposes that embedded complementizer *shuo* is head-initial since it precedes its TP complement, as Taiwanese *kong* does, according to Simpson and Wu (2002).

(15) a. wo xiang [CP shuo [TP t ta   shi   taipei   ren]]

  I think   Comp.   he is   Taipei   person

  'I think (that) he is a Taipeier.'

  b. wa xiong [CP kong [TP yi   shi   taipak   lang]]

I   think   Comp. he   is   Taipei   person

'I think (that) he is a Taipeier.'

Nonetheless, the claim is weak as the type of sentence is widely argued to be a dialect of Taiwan Mandarin. That is, it could be a product under the influence of Taiwanese *kong*.

Hsieh (2005) further conjectures the fact that a topicalized wh-word licenses a parasitic gap substantiates the claim that topicalized elements move to the "left" periphery.

(16)   [CP sheme dongxii , [TP ni   mai le PG$_i$ jiu   hui   iong   t$_i$]]

        what   thing   you buy ASP   then would use

        'What thing would you use if you buy?'

However, Tsai (1997b) contends that Chinese topicalization involves base-generation but not movement. To be specific, a null operator is directly merged in Spec-CP, turning its c-command domain into a predicate, predicating of the parallely base-generated topic occupying Spec-TopP. The topic serves to identify the null operator, which in turn controls the empty pronoun in the seeming gap in the comment clause. The evidence comes from the following sentence in which no Complex NP Constraint (CNPC) effect is detected.

(17) [Top Akiu$_i$ (a)], [CP OP$_i$ [DP xuduo [CP e$_i$ chuban e$_j$] de   shu$_j$] dou   mai-de   bu-cho.]

     Akiu Topic   many   publish PNM book all sell—DE not-bad

     'Akiu, many books which (he) published sell well.'

Finally, Hsieh (2005) poses a "CP-sandwiched TP" phenomenon which he believes to confirm the head-complement order, as in (19):

(18)   [C2P [C1P ruguo [TP ni   bu   chifan]] dehua   tC1P] , ...

             if   you not eat-meal   if

        'If you don't have meals, …'

However, a head-final CP system could also reach the same outcome, shown as below:

(19)   [C2P tC1P   ruguo   [C1P [TP ni bu   chifan] dehua]]

Besides, suppose C2 has a feature, assuming it is EPP, which triggers movement, then why TP does not move to [Spec, C1P]? If XP-movement is EPP-driven, we will expect that every C bears an EPP feature. If we are to stipulate that C2 has an EPP while C1 does not, it would be too costly and ill-motivated. Therefore, a feature-driven approach is not favored.

Despite the failure mentioned above, I would tentatively assume Mandarin CP is head-initial. The analysis has an appealing merit, for it gives a uniform account for Chinese phrase structure, as exemplified below:

(20) a. DP, Num(ber)P, and Cl(assifier)P:
          [DP zhe [NumP san [ClP ben [NP shu]]]]
               this   three   Cl.   book
          'these three books'
      b. TP, NegP, AdvP, and Mod(al)P:
          [TP jihui   [NegP bu [ModP hui [AdvP zai [VP lai   le]]]]]
             oppotunity   not   will   again   come   SFP
          'The oppotunity will not come again.'
      c. VP and PP:
          [VP zhu [PP zai [DP sushe]]]
              live   in   dorm
          'live in the dorm'

Moreover, Lin (2006) argues that, driven by feature checking, the vP complement raise to Spec-Asp(ect)P, thus deriving the surface head-final order of AspP as in (21). And the evidence comes from the contrast of CED effect (Huang 1982) shown in (22).

(21)   [TP Zhangsan [AspP [vP xiu   che]   le   tvP]]
              Zhangsan   repair   car   ASP
          'Zhangsan has repaired the car.'
(22) a. Zhangsan   zenmeyang   xiu   che?
          Zhangsan   how   repair car
          'How did Zhangsan repair the car?'
      b. *Zhangsan   zenmeyang   xiu   che   le
          Zhangsan   how   repair car   ASP
          'How did Zhangsan repair the car?'

4. CP-movement Hypothesis

In this section I resort to theoretical apparatus to derive surface head-final order of SFPs. First desiderata is the Chinese CP structure amended from Rizzi (1997), as given (14). To determine word order, Kayne's (1994) Linear Correspondence Axiom (LCA) is also required, given below:

(23) Linear Correspondence Axiom (Kayne, 1994)

A lexical item α precedes a lexical item β iff α asymmetrically c-commands β, or an XP dominating α asymmetrically c-commands β.

Despite its significant success, however, head-complement relation poses problems to LCA because of its mutual c-command configuration, exemplified as (24):

(24)   [XP [X YP]]

(24) will lead to crash at PF for its unlinearizability. Therefore, further syntactic operation is required to fix the flaw, and movement might be an alternative to consider. Suppose (25):

(25)   [XP [YP [XP X tYP]]]

Nonetheless, what is the motivation behind the strategy? And is this kind of "too-local" movement ever legitimate?
The rescue comes from Moro's (2000) idea that movement is driven by the search for antisymmetry. That is, "symmetry-breaking" serves as the driving force of "too-local" movement. The idea is formulated as below:

(26) Movement as a Symmetry-breaking Phenomenon (Moro, 2000)
     Movement is driven by the search for antisymmetry.

If Moro's proposal is on the right track, the motivation and legitimacy of the movement strategy are both ensured.
Our speculation will also proceed under the framework of Chomsky's (2001) widely accepted Phase Theory, stated in (27):

(27) Phase Theory (Chomsky, 2001)
     Syntactic structures are built up in phases (phases referring to vP and CP), and
     once a phase has been produced, the domain/complement of the phase head
     undergoes Transfer/Spell-out to the PF component and the semantic component.

Finally, to avoid elements left untransfered at the phase edge, I resort to Hsieh's (2005) Max-Spell-Out Hypothesis.

(28) The Max-Spell-out Hypothesis (Hsieh, 2005)
     Spell-out the entire phase in the absence of uninterpretable features. In case of
     the presence of uninterpretable features residing at the phase edge, send only the

complement of the phase head to Spell-out.

Equipped with all the theoretical tools we need, we can now work out the surface head-final order of SFPs. Let's take (1a) for example, repeated as (29), and give its derivation process in (30):

(29)   hua   hong   le.
        flower   red   SFP
        'The flower becomes red.'

(30)   a.   [FinP ø [TP hua hong]]
        b.   [TransP [FinP ø [TP hua hong]] le tFinP]
        c.   Spell-out TransP → [ø hua hong le]

FinP moves to the specifier position of Trans head for "symmetry-breaking." Next, the entire TransP is spelled-out in the absence of uninterpretable features. Eventually, the lower copy of FinP gets deleted at PF, and we derive the surface head-final construal, as in (30c).

As for a sentence with a final particle cluster like (8), repeated as (31), the story unfolds roughly the same. The derivational process and structure are given in (32) and (33):

(31)   hua   hong   le   a./?
            flower   red   SFP SFP
            'The flower becomes red./?'

(32)   a.   [TransP le [FinP ø [TP hua hong]]]
        b.   [TransP [FinP ø [TP hua hong]] le tFinP]
        c.   [DegreeP a [TransP [FinP ø [TP hua hong]] le tFinP]]
        d.   [DegreeP [TransP [FinP ø [TP hua hong]] le tFinP] a tTransP]
        e.   Spell-out DegreeP → [ø hua hong le a]

(33)

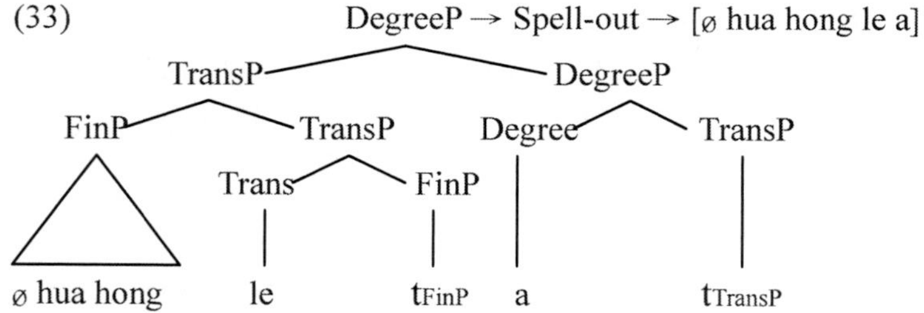

Here, it is dubious why TransP does not undergo Spell-out as in the previous example. Though Hsieh (2005) suggests that ForceP, MoodP (here referred to as MoodP and as TransP), and FinP, are strong phase heads, I prefer to respect Chomsky's (2001) idea that phases are propositional in nature, and conjecture in the split CP domain only the head which can complete a proposition of the entire utterance can count as a phase head.

A "CP-sandwiched TP" is somewhat tricky. Consider (34):

(34) ruguo ni   bu   chifan   dehua, …
     if   you not   eat-meal if
     'If you don't have meals, …'

My solution is that *ruguo* and *dehua* belong to different functional heads and a null C head stands right between them. In this way, the "sandwich relation" is obtaind as follows:

(35) a.   [C3P dehua [FinP ni bu chifan]]
      b.   [C3P [FinP ni bu chifan] [C3P dehua tFinP]
      c.   [C2P ø [C3P [FinP ni bu chifan] [C3P dehua tFinP]]
      d.   [C1P ruguo [C2P ø [C3P [FinP ni bu chifan] [C3P dehua tFinP]]]

Notice that C1 is high enough to asymmetrically c-command C3P; therefore, no movement is required here, respecting Chomsky's (1995) Last Resort Condition.

5. Conclusion

The paper gives a thorough investigation into Mandarin SFPs. Refering to the analyses of Li and Thompson (1982), Chu (1999), and Li (2006), I induce their core functions. From Rizzi's (1997) Split CP I design a Mandarin CP system. According to the mutual scope interaction and word order of SFPs, I map them onto separate functional heads in a proper hierarchy. I also examine evidence about head directionality such as complementizer *shuo*, topicalization, and "CP-sandwiched TP," and find out that they are all refutable. I tentatively assume Mandarin CP is head-initial, which gives a uniform account for Chinese phrase structure. Finally, I exert several theoretical apparatus to derive surface head-final order of SFPs. I employ Kayne's (1994) LCA, and proceed under the framework of Chomsky's (2001) Phase Theory. Resorting to Moro's (2000) idea of "symmetry-breaking" movement and Hsieh's (2005) Max-Spell-out Hypothesis, I contend that FinP moves to a particle's specifier position for the linearization requirement. In the end of derivation the entire phrase is Spelled-out in the absence of uninterpretable features and thus obtaining surface head-final order. The proposal also explains other CP-related phenomena.

Reference

Cheng, L. L.-S. 1997. *On the Typology of Wh-questions*. New York and London: Grand
Publishing.

Chomsky, N. 1995. *The Minimalist Program*. Cambridge, MA, MIT Press.

Chomsky, N. 2001. *Derivation by Phase*. In Michael Kenstowicz ed., Ken Hale: *A Life in
Language*. Cambridge, MA, MIT Press.

Chu, C. C. and T.-J. Chi. 1999. *A Cognitive-functional Grammar of Mandarin Chinese*. Taipei:
The Crane Publishing.

Haegeman, L. 2002. Anchoring to speaker, adverbial clauses and the structure of CP.
GUWPIL 2, 117-180.

Hsieh, F.-F. 2005. Atoms and Particles. Ms., MIT.

Huang, C.T. J. 1982. *Logical Relations on Chinese and the Theory of Grammar*. PhD
Dissertation, MIT.

Kayne, R. 1994. *The Antisymmetry of Syntax*. Cambridge, MA, MIT Press.

Li, B. 2006. *Chinese Final Particles and the Syntax of the Periphery*. The Netherlands:
Leiden University Press.

Li, N. C. and S. A. Thompson. 1981. *Mandarin Chinese*. Berkeley and Los Angeles:
University of California Press.

Lin, T.-H. J. 2006. Complement-to-Specifier Movement in Mandarin Clause. Ms., National
Tsing Hua University.

Moro, A. 2000. *Dynamic Antisymmetry*. Cambridge, MA, MIT Press.

Rizzi, L. 1997. The Fine Structure of the Left Periphery. In *Elements of Grammar*,
ed. by L. Haegeman. 281-337. Dordrecht: Kluwer.

Simpson, A. and Z. Wu. 2002. IP-raising, tone sandhi and the creation of S-final particles:
evidence for cyclic spell-out. *Journal of East Asian Linguistics* 11.1, 67-99.

Soh, H.L. and M. Gao. 2004. Perfective aspect and transition in Mandarin Chinese: An
analysis of double –le sentences. *Proceedings of Texas Linguistics Society* (TLS
8).Somerville, MA, Cascadilla Press.

Tsai, W.-T. D. 1997b. On the Absence of Island Effect. *Tsing Hua Journal of Chinese Studies,
New Series*, 27, 125-149.

A Frame-based Approach to Text Generation[*]

Huong Thanh Le

Faculty of Information Technology, Hanoi University of Technology
1 Dai Co Viet street, Hanoi, Vietnam
huonglt@it-hut.edu.vn

Abstract. This paper is a study on constructing a natural language interface to database, concentrating on generating textual answers. TGEN, a system that generates textual answer from query result tables is presented. The TGEN architecture guarantees its portability across domains. A combination of a frame-based approach and natural language generation techniques in the TGEN provides text fluency and text flexibility. The implementation result shows that this approach is feasible while a deep NLG approach is still far to be reached.

Keywords: natural language interface, text generation, frame-based approach.

1. Introduction

Database management systems (DBMSs) have been widely used thanks to their efficiency in storing and retrieving data. However, retrieving information from database requires users to compose queries in a query language (e.g., QBE or SQL) or to fill some search criteria in the interface (Liu, 1995; Catarci et al., 1997). In addition, traditional DBMSs are still limited by its capability to generate outputs. They normally dump query results in a table or a pre-defined form without any understanding of the meaning of data.

The research on natural language interface to databases has recently received attention from the research communities (Wang et al., 1999; ELF Software Co., 2001; Torgersson and Falkman, 2002; Hallett et al., 2005; Bertomeu, 2006). The purpose of such a natural language interface is to allow users to compose queries in natural language and to receive responses under the form of short answers. The natural language interface is thus preferred than the traditional interface.

A typical natural language interface has to solve two main tasks: (i) translating a natural language query to a query language; and (ii) generating a natural language answer by using information from a query result table. In this paper, we focus on solving the second task. A frame-based approach, which bases on predefined elementary frames and text generation rules to generate new frames and to produce flexible text, is introduced. The implemented system is called Text Generator or TGEN for short.

The remaining sections of this paper are organized as follows: Section 2 introduces the architecture of our proposed Natural Language Interface for Querying Database and Automatically Generating Reports (NLI4DB), in order to get an overview of the TGEN role in the interface. Section 3 describes the rule set used by the TGEN to generate text. Section 4

---

[*] The author gratefully acknowledges the receipt of a grant from the Flemish Interuniversity Council for University Development Cooperation (VLIR UOS) which enabled the research team to carry out this work.

presents the major components and the data flow in the TGEN. In Section 5, two examples are given to illustrate the working process of the TGEN. Our implementation discussion and some experimental results are given in Section 6. Finally, Section 7 concludes the paper and proposes possible future work on this approach.

2. The NLI4DB Architecture

The NLI4DB is a system that is integrated with a traditional database management system to provide a natural language interface for querying database and automatically generating answers. An overview of the NLI4DB architecture is shown in Figure 1.

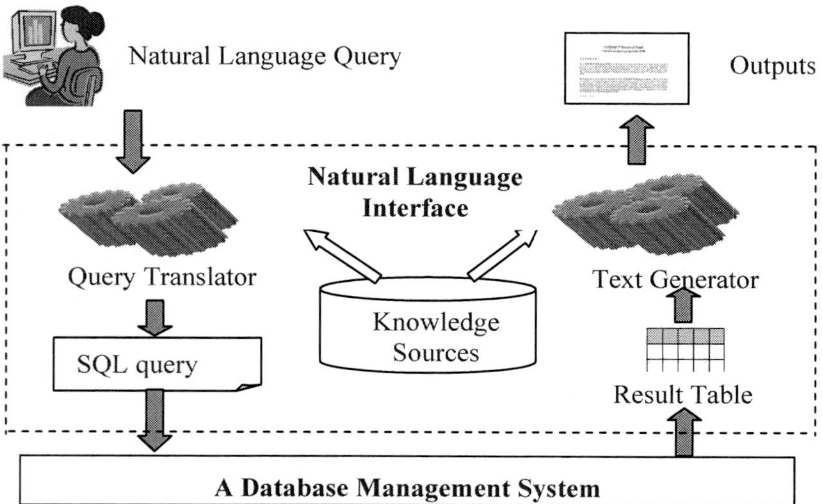

Figure 1: Architecture of the NLI4DB

The NLI4DB consists of two main modules:
- A Query Translator (QTRAN) to translate natural language questions to SQL queries.
- A Text Generator (TGEN) to generate query responses under the form of short answers or summary reports in Vietnamese language.

A natural language question composed by a user is translated into an SQL query by the Query Translator. After that, the Database Management System processes the SQL query and returns the query result in the form of a table. The Text Generator then transforms this result table into a textual answer.

To test the feasibility of the NLI4DB, a specific Database Management System - a student management database – is used. The entity relationship of the database is shown in Figure 2.

Knowledge sources (e.g., syntactic rules and thesaurus) are needed in the working processes of the QTRAN and the TGEN.

The remaining sections present our main focus of this paper - the implementation of the TGEN. The rule set used in generating answers is introduced first.

3. The Grammar used in the TGEN

The TGEN does not generate free texts, but the texts that are based on predefined frames. These frames are typical structures of answers. For example, the frame for an answer of the *List* type is:

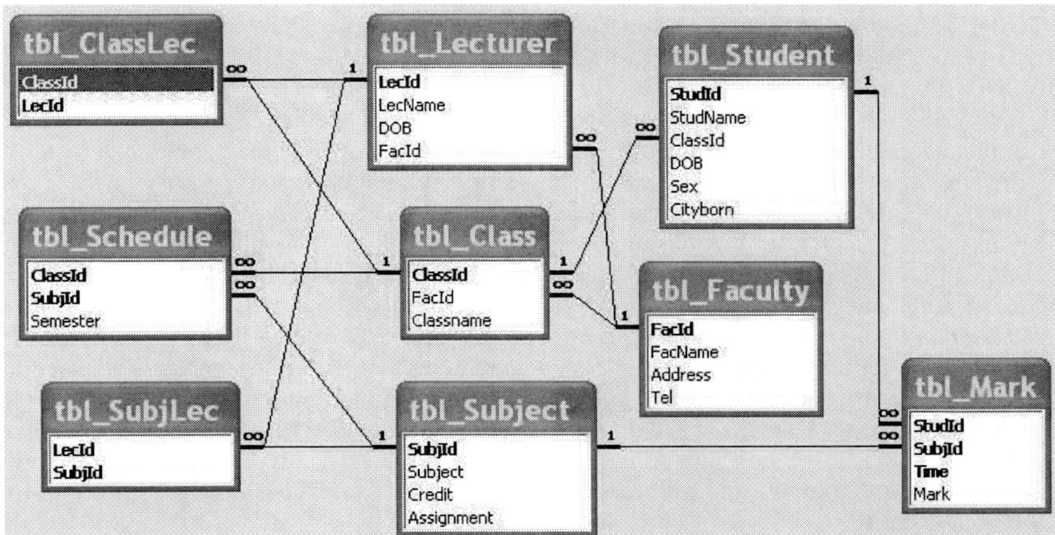

Figure 2 – The entity relationship of the student management database

> *[Noun phrase] [Verb phrase]:*
>   *1. [Item_1]*
>   *2. . . . . . .*
>   *3. [Item_n]*

A *List* answer can also be represented by another frame:

   [Noun phrase] [Verb phrase] [Item_1], …, [Item_n].

Each label *[. . .]* in the frame is a slot that needs to be filled. The *[Noun phrase]* and the *[Verb phrase]* are generated by using the syntactic structure of the user's question. This problem is analyzed in detail in Section 5. The slots *[Item_1], …, [Item_n]* are filled in by values from the result table.

   In order to create the frame set that is used in generating text, we first identify and categorize question types, then we define frames for each question type. The question types that have been considered by us are:

1. Questions that return a single value (e.g., *Who is the leader of the class BK20 in the academic year 2004-2005?*[1]). This question type is called a *Single_value* question.
2. *List* questions (e.g., *Which subjects did the class BK20 study in Semester 1 last year?*)
3. *Statistical* questions (e.g., *Show us the quality of students in the academic year 2005 – 2006.*)
4. *Comparison* questions (e.g., *Compare the percentage of excellent students of the classes BK20 and BK21.*)
5. *Description* questions (e.g., *Give us information about the student Pham Thanh of the class BK20.*)
6. *Evaluation* questions (e.g., *Evaluate the study progress of the student Nguyen Van Minh.*)

The name of a frame is called by its corresponding question type. For example, the frame of a *List* question is a *List* frame.

---

[1] For the convenient, all examples are translated from Vietnamese to English in Sections 3,4 and 5. In Section 6 (Implementation Discussion and Experiments), we present our original examples in Vietnamese and translate them into English.

The TGEN uses a context-free grammar (CFG) to organize generation rules. Each frame in the TGEN is stored in the right hand side (RHS) of a rule, whose left hand side (LHS) is the frame type (e.g., *List* frame, *Comparison* frame). The set of generation rules used in the TGEN is called a rule set.

The LHS of a generation rule can be any non-terminal symbol, whereas the RHS is a combination of non-terminal symbols and terminal symbols. A terminal symbol is a word or a string that appears in the output text. A non-terminal symbol do not appears in the output. Instead, it has to be expanded by other generation rules or to be replaced by a value in the query result. In order to produce flexible output texts, a non-terminal symbol in the RHS of a rule can also be a frame. Only basic frames are manually designed and stored in the system. New frames can be automatically created by connecting or integrating the basic ones. We analyze the *Description* frame to illustrate the organization of our rule set.

The answer for a *Description* question is a text that describes relations among attribute values of one or several entities. In order to keep the generality of the frame set, we design frames for each entity of the database. Each frame consists of all attributes of an entity. During the generation process, if some slots in the frame do not have values to fill in, these slots will be removed from the frame. The following rules are applied to relations among attributes of the *tbl_student* entity.

(1) [frame_student] → *[studname] ([sex]) [vp_studId]. [studname] [vp_DOB], [vp_cityborn].
[studname] [vp_classId].*

(2) [frame_student] → *[studname] ([sex]) [vp_studId]. [studname] [vp_classId]. [studname]
[vp_DOB], [vp_cityborn].*

(3) [vp_studId] → *has the student code [studId]*
(4) [vp_DOB] → *was born on [DOB]*
(5) [vp_cityborn] → *in [cityborn]*
(6) [vp_classId] → *is a student of the class [classId]*
(7) [vp_classId] → *studies in the class [classId]*

In the above rule set, the strings in the square brackets (*[ ]*) are considered as non-terminal symbols; whereas the string that are not in the square brackets are terminal ones.

The rules whose LHS starts with *[frame_* define the structure of a frame. Rules (1) and (2) in the rule set above define two possible structures of the *Description* frame. The non-terminal symbols starting with *[vp_* or *[np_* represent for verb phrases or noun phrases, respectively. The rule set also has an *[s_* symbol, which represents for sentence. The symbols that are in the square bracket and do not start with *[frame_*, *[vp_*, *[np_* and *[s_* are pre-terminal symbols. They represent for entity's attributes and will be replaced by attribute values during the next generating step.

If a *Description* answer describes relations among attribute values of several entities, the system will automatically create a new frame by connecting the frames of these entities through entities' keys.

4. The Text Generator system

The major components and the data flow in the TGEN are shown in Figure 3. The Text Generator is divided into four main components: a Frame Selector, a Slot Filler, a Syntactic Refiner, and an Answer Generator.

4.1.A Frame Selector

This component is used to select frames for the answer. Four factors being considered in selecting frames are: keywords in the user's question, the SQL query[2], the shape of the result table, and values in the result table. Each factor will be analyzed in detail below.

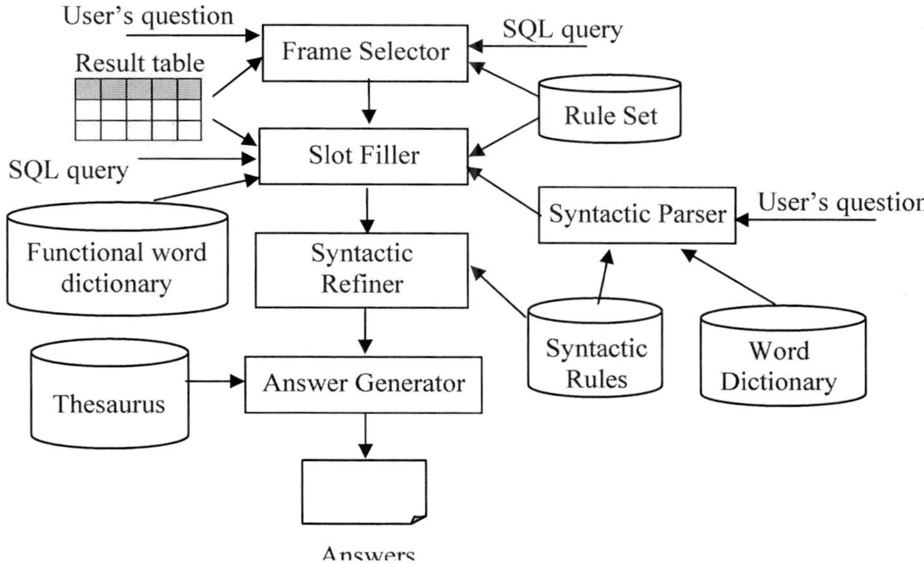

Figure 3: Data flow in the Text Generator

Some user's questions contain keywords that signal their question types. Examples of the keywords are *Compare*, *List*, and *Evaluate*. If these keywords are found in the user's question, the frames corresponding to the detected question type will be chosen.

The shape of the result table can decide the frame type as well.

-   If the result table has only one value, the *Single_value* frame is selected.
-   If the result table has several columns and one row, the *Description* frame is chosen. If the result table is a join among several entities, a join of the corresponding *Description* frames will be established.
-   If the result table has one column and several rows, the *List* frame is chosen.
-   If the result table has multiple rows and columns, the *Statistical* frame or the *Evaluation* frame is the most appropriate.

If the user's question and the shape of the result table do not provide enough information for selecting frames, values in the result table will be used to fill in slots of all candidate frames. The frames whose required slots[3] cannot be filled will be eliminated.

4.2.A Slot Filler

After frames have been selected, the Slot Filler has to generate text using the rule set mentioned in Section 3. This is a top-down generating algorithm.

Our target is to create a variety of output texts, but to keep the algorithm complexity low. Therefore, when selecting rules from the rule set, if two or more rules are satisfied, the rules will be chosen by the following policy:

---

[2] The SQL query is generated by the Query Translator.
[3] A required slot is the slot that must be filled in by text or values. Otherwise, the frame that contains this slot cannot be used.

- All rules whose LHS starts with *[frame_* are chosen. This policy is used to guarantee the flexibility of the output texts
- If the LHS of the rule does not start with *[frame_*, the system will randomly choose one rule among the satisfied rules that have not been used in expanding the chosen frame. If all satisfied rules have been used, they are reselected another round by the same method. This strategy is used to prevent the combination explosion and to make sure that a rule is not repeatedly used all the time.

The Slot Filler needs a functional word dictionary[4] to map values in the result table with frame's slots. For example, the table column *Full name* is mapped with the attribute *studname* of the entity *tbl_student*. Therefore, values in this columns are filled in slots *[studname]* of the considering frames.

Several frame types (e.g., the *List* frame) reuse some parts of the user's question in their content. Therefore, a syntactic parser is integrated with the TGEN to get the syntactic structure of sentences.

The slots that do not have values to fill in will be removed from the frame. This action may cause sentential fragments (e.g., a sentence without a verb phrase) in the output texts. For that reason, the TGEN needs a Syntactic Refiner to solve this problem. The Syntactic Refiner will be introduced next.

4.3. A Syntactic Refiner

The purpose of the Syntactic Refiner is to produce grammatical sentences from the outputs of the Slot Filler. It first parses the outputs of the Slot Filler to detect ungrammatical sentences. In order to do that, the Syntactic Refiner locates positions of NPs and VPs in the Slot Filler's outputs by tracing the applied generation rules. Then, it checks the syntax of sentences given their NPs and VPs.

If a sentence lacks a major part such as an NP or a VP, the Syntactic Refiner will combine it with its adjacent sentences. If it does not succeed, the ungrammatical sentence will be removed from the output texts.

4.4. An Answer Generator

Although the output texts of the Syntactic Refiner are grammatically correct, it may not be fluent. There are some reasons for this problem: the sentences can be too short or too long; some words are repeated several times; etc. The Answer Generator has to refine the texts so that it can be as natural as possible. We only deal with repeated words in this research. The Answer Generator replaces repeated words by its synonym or reference words. A thesaurus, which stores semantic relations among words, is used in this process.

We will illustrate the working process of the TGEN by examples given in Section 5.

5. Examples of the Generating Process

In this section, we consider two examples corresponding to two typical frame types. One frame type does not need syntactic information from user's questions (e.g., the *Description* frame – Example 1), and another frame type does (e.g., the *List* frame – Example 2).

5.1. Example 1

User's question:

(1) *Give us information about student Pham Thanh of the class BK20.*

The result table returned by the SQL query is shown in Table 1 below:

---

[4] The functional word dictionary is used to store relations between a word/phrase and its role in the database. For example, the word *student* corresponds to the entity *tbl_student* in the student management database.

Table 1: The result table returned by the SQL query of Example 1.

Full name	Class	Date of Birth	Sex	Place of birth
Pham Thanh	BK20	24/10/1984	male	Ha Bac

The following steps are carried out by the TGEN:

Step 1: Selecting frames

In this example, the system cannot detect the question type from the user's question. It then looks at the SQL query and finds that all data are attribute values of the entity *tbl_student*. Therefore, it chooses the frame *[frame_student_description]*.

Step 2: Filling in frames' slots

The system finds two frame rules, whose LHS is *[frame_student_description]*. Both of these rules are applied to generate text. The column title *Full name* is mapped with the attribute *fullname* of the entity *tbl_student*. Therefore, the value *Pham Thanh* in the *Full name* column is filled in the slot *[fullname]* of the frames.

The non-terminal symbol *[vp_birthdate]* is expanded by the rule

[vp_birthdate] → *was born on [birthdate].*

The non-terminal symbol *[birthdate]* is replaced by the value *24/10/1984* in the *Date of Birth* column. The same processes are carried out with other slots of the frames.

Step 3: Refining the syntax of sentences

After filling in frames' slots, the system checks the syntax of sentences in these frames. When checking the sentence *[fullname] ([sex]) [vp_studentcode]*, it finds that the slots *[fullname]* and *[sex]* can be filled, but the slot *[vp_studentcode]* cannot. It means that this sentence has a noun phrase, but it does not have a verb phrase. The next sentence in the frame is a grammatical one, and it has the same subject with the ungrammatical sentence. Therefore, the system merges these two sentences into one.

Two output texts are generated after this step:

(1a) *Pham Thanh (male) was born on 24/10/1984 in Ha Bac. Pham Thanh is a student of the class BK20.*

(1b) *Pham Thanh (male) studies in the class BK20. Pham Thanh was born on 24/10/1984 in Ha Bac.*

Step 4: Refining the output texts

The system finds a full name is repeated at the second sentence of both output texts. This situation is not preferred by the system. Therefore, the system replaces the repeated name by a reference string, which is *this student, he/she,* or by the last name of the student.

After being refined by Step 4, the two outputs now becomes:

(1c) *Pham Thanh (male) was born on 24/10/1984 in Ha Bac. He is a student of the class BK20.*

(1d) *Pham Thanh (male) studies in the class BK20. He was born on 24/10/1984 in Ha Bac.*

5.2. Example 2

User's question:

(2) *Who got the mark 10 in the Database subject?*

The syntactic parser integrated in the TGEN determines that the interrogative pronoun *Who* is the noun phrase of the question, and *got the mark 10 in the Database subject* is the verb phrase of the question.

Let us consider the case when the query returns only one value, as shown in Table 2 below:

Table 2: A result table returned by the SQL query of Example 2.

Full name
Nguyen Thuy Linh

In this case, the system chooses the *Single_value* frame (Step 1). To produce an answer, the interrogative pronoun of the question is replaced by the value *Nguyen Thuy Linh* (Step 2). The output of Step 2 is:

(2a) *Nguyen Thuy Linh got the mark 10 in the Database subject.*

Steps 3 and 4 do not modify the above output. Therefore, Sentence (2a) is the final answer.

Consider the case when the result table has several values, as shown in Table 3 below:

Table 3: A result table returned by the SQL query of Example 2.

Full name
Nguyen Thuy Linh
Dinh Thu Van

The four steps being carried out by the TGEN are:

Step 1: Selecting frames

The answer applies the *List* frame.

Step 2: Filling in frames' slots

The VP of the answer is *are*. The NP of the answer will be constructed by the following formula:

[NP1 in plural] [relative pronoun] [VP of the question]

in which the *NP1* is generated as follow:

The system determines where values in the columns *Full name* come from by looking at the SQL query. It returns a pair (entity, attribute), which is (*tbl_student, name*) in this case. The system then interprets the code *tbl_student* to *student* by searching in the functional word dictionary. *NP1* now is *student*. Since the query returns several values, the word *student* is put in the plural form.

Who is chosen to be the *[relative pronoun]* in this example. Therefore, the output of Step 2 is:

(2b) *Students who got the mark 10 in the Database subject are*
    1. Nguyen Thuy Linh
    2. Dinh Thu Van

Sentence (2b) is the final answer since Steps 3 and 4 do not modify the above output.

6. Implementation Discussion and Experiments

A prototype of the TGEN has been implemented for Vietnamese language. Since text generation is our focus in this research, we assume that the Query Translator has already translated the user's question into an SQL query. A Vietnamese syntactic parser (Le et al., 2000) is integrated into the system in order to get the syntactic structure of sentences. The program is written in Java and the database management system is implemented in SQL Server 2000.

The TGEN produces one or several textual answers for a user's question, depending on the number of answer frames a question has. The current version of the system has not evaluated the quality of the answers yet. Instead, all possible answers are displayed in an editable interface so that the user can select, modify, save to file, and print the textual answers.

The word dictionary, the syntactic rules and the thesaurus in the TGEN are domain independent, whereas the rule set and the functional word dictionary are strictly related to the student management domain. To increase the portability of the system, all knowledge sources are stored in separate data files. If the TGEN is applied to other domains, we only need to modify the content of the files corresponding to the generation rule set and the functional word dictionary.

The TGEN architecture can be applied to a variety of other languages. When changing to another language, we only need to change the knowledge sources of the system. These knowledge sources include the syntactic rules, the thesaurus, the generation rule set and the functional word dictionary.

Some experiments with our prototype system are shown below.

Question 1:

(3) *Điểm thi cao nhất trong kỳ thi Tin học học kỳ 1 năm 2006-2007 là bao nhiêu? Ai đạt điểm cao nhất?*

What is the highest mark in the Informatics examination in Semester 1 of the academic year 2006-2007? Who got the highest mark?

The answer for Question 1 is:

(3a) *Điểm thi cao nhất trong kỳ thi Tin học học kỳ 1 năm 2006-2007 là 9. Bành Quỳnh Mai đạt điểm cao nhất.*

The highest mark in the Informatics examination in Semester 1 of the academic year 2006-2007 is 9. Bành Quỳnh Mai got the highest mark.

Question 2:

(4) *So sánh tỷ lệ sinh viên giỏi của lớp BK20 và BK21.*

Compare the percentage of excellent students of the classes BK20 and BK21.

The answer for Question 2 is:

(4a) *Tỷ lệ sinh viên giỏi của lớp BK20 là 20%. Với lớp BK21, tỷ lệ này là 25%. Ta có thể thấy tỷ lệ sinh viên giỏi của lớp BK21 cao hơn lớp BK20.*

The percentage of excellent students of the class BK20 is 20%. With the class BK21, this percentage is 25%. We can see that the percentage of excellent students of the class BK21 is higher than that of the class BK20.

(4b) *Tỷ lệ sinh viên giỏi của lớp BK20 là 20%. Với lớp BK21, tỷ lệ này là 25%, cao hơn so với lớp BK20.*

The percentage of excellent students of the class BK20 is 20%. With the class BK21, this percentage is 25%, higher than that of the class BK20.

7. Conclusions

We described in this paper the TGEN architecture that allows the implementation of a text generator for generating answers from query result tables of a DBMS. The TGEN is not based on a deep natural language generation approach. Instead, it uses a hybrid one. It combines a set of predefined structures with deeper NLG techniques, including (i) using generation rules to generate text; (ii) checking the syntax of sentences; (iii) replacing repeated words by their synonyms or reference words.

The current prototype of the TGEN can produce flexible and grammatical outputs. It proves that a hybrid approach is feasible for this kind of applications while a deep NLG approach is still far to be reached.

To improve the system performance, future work includes: (i) expanding the rule set to deal with a variety of question types; (ii) researching methods to improve the coherence and the fluency of output texts; and (iii) defining criteria to automatically evaluate the outputs.

References

Bertomeu, N., H. Uszkoreit, A. Frank, H-U. Krieger and B. Jörg. 2006. Contextual Phenomena and Thematic Relations in Database QA Dialogues: Results from a Wizard-of-Oz Experiment. *Proceedings of the HLT-NAACL 2006 Workshop on Interactive Question Answering*, New York.

Catarci, T., M. F. Costabile, S. Levialdi and C. Batini. 1997. Visual Query Systems for Databases: A Survey. *Journal of Visual Languages and Computing*, 8(2), 215–260.

ELF Software Co. 2001. *Access ELF: the Amazing Software that Lets you Communicate with Microsoft Access in Plain English*. http://www.elfsoft.com/ns/prodserv.htm (Last Updated: Nov., 2001). ELF Software Co. 210 W 101 St. NYC NY 10025

Hallett, C., R. Power and D. Scott. 2005. Intuitive Querying of E-Health Data Repositories. *Proceedings of the 4th UK e-Science All Hands Meeting*, Nottingham, UK.

Le, H. T., Q.H. Pham and T.T. Nguyen. 2000. An Approach to Automatically Analyze Syntax of Vietnamese Text. *Journal of Informatics and Cybernetics*, 15(4).

Liu, H. 1995. A Visual Interface For Querying a CASE Repository. *Proceedings of 11th International IEEE Symposium on Visual Languages*, Darmstadt, Germany.

Torgersson, O. and G. Falkman. 2002. Using Text Generation to Access Clinical Data in a Variety of Contexts. *Proceedings of MIE2002*, pp. 460-465. IOS Press, 2002.

Wang, S., X. Meng and X. Liu. 1999. Nchiql: A Chinese Natural Language Query System to Databases. *Proceedings of the International Symposium on Database Applications in Non-Traditional Environments* (DANTE'99).

Co-Event Conflation for Compound Verbs in Korean[*]

Jong Sup Jun

Department of Linguistics and Cognitive Science,
Hankuk University of Foreign Studies,
San 89 Wangsanri Mohyunmeon Yonginsi, Kyunggido Korea
drjun@hufs.ac.kr

Abstract. Compound verbs in Korean show properties of both syntactic phrases and lexical items. Earlier studies of compound verbs have either assumed two homonymous types, i.e. one as a syntactic phrase and the other as a lexical item, or posited some sort of transformation from a syntactic phrase into a lexical item. In this paper, I show empirical and conceptual problems for earlier studies, and present an alternative account in terms of Talmy's (2000) theory of lexicalization. Unlike Talmy who proposed [Path] conflation into [MOVE] for Korean, I suggest several types of [Co-Event] conflation; e.g. [$_{\text{Co-Event}}$ Manner] conflation as in *kwul-e-kata* 'to go by rolling', [$_{\text{Co-Event}}$ Concomitance] conflation as in *ttal-a-kata* 'to follow', [$_{\text{Co-Event}}$ Concurrent Result] conflation as in *cap-a-kata* 'to catch somebody and go', etc. The present proposal not only places Korean compound verbs in a broader picture of cross-linguistic generalizations, but, when viewed from Jackendoff's (1997) productive vs. semi-productive morphology, provides a natural account for classifying the compounds that allow *–se* intervention from those that do not.

Keywords: Compound verb, Cognitive semantics, Lexicalization, Conflation, Categorial conversion, Semi-productive morphology

1. Introduction

Compound verbs in Korean pose interesting problems for morphosytax and lexical semantics , in that their distribution is constrained by the interaction between morphology and syntax, which is more or less predictable from meaning. C-H Lee (2006: 129) discusses four types of compound verbs in Korean.

(1) Compound verbs in Korean:
  a. VV type: *ttwi-nolta* 'to run and play'
  b. V-*e*-V type: *ttut-e-nayta* 'to rip off'
  c. V-*ko*-V type: *mil-ko-tangkita* 'to push and pull'
  d. V-*eta*-V type: *tol-ata-pota* 'to look back'

Among these four types, the V-*e*-V type shows certain degree of productivity depending upon kinds of preceding and following verbs, as shown in (2).

---

[*] An earlier version of this paper was presented at Harvard International Symposium on Korean Linguistics 2007. The second stage of Brain Korea 21 project provided me with an ideal atmosphere to work on my research. This work was supported in part by Hankuk University of Foreign Studies Research Fund of 2007.

(2) Elements of V-*e*-V compounds (K-H Kim 1996: 3):
    a. Preceding verbs: *kal-* 'to grind', *kennu-* 'to cross over', *ket-* 'to walk', *kkul-* 'to drag',
        kwulu-'to roll', *nal-* 'to fly', *nayli-* 'to go down', *noh-* 'to put down',
        tul- 'to enter', *olu-* 'to go up', *ttalu-* 'to follow', etc.
    b. Following verbs: *kata* 'to go', *nohta* 'to put down', *mekta* 'to eat', *pota* 'to try', *oluta* 'to
        go up', *ota* 'to come', *cwuta* 'to give', etc.

Among various verbs in (2), *kata* 'to go'as the second verb draws our attention in terms of productivity. Some possible compounds with *kata* are listed in (3).

(3) V-*e*-*kata* (K-H Kim 1996: 3): *kacyekata* 'to take (something) and go', *kechyekata* 'to pass (through)', *kwulekata* 'to go by rolling', *kkwulyekata* 'to be dragged to', *nakata* 'to go out', *nalakata* 'to fly', *naylyekata* 'to go down', *nemekata* 'to go/jump over', *takakata* 'to approach', *ttalakata* 'to follow', *ttekata* 'to scoop up and go', *ttwiekata* 'to run and go', *molyekata* 'to go in a group', *molakata* 'to drive (something/somebody) into some space or situation', *ahpsekata* 'to go forward, to take precedence', *olakata* 'to go up', *capakata* 'to catch somebody and go', *caphyekata* 'to be taken to some place after being caught', *ccochakata* 'to follow', *chacakata* 'to go by searching', etc.

These verbs are basic in form, and are very productive compared with other V-*e*-V compounds. Furthermore, these verbs are particularly important from the perspective of lexical semantics, in that they all have the meaning component of MOVE or GO which is the foundation of all motion events in Talmy's (2000) cognitive theory of lexical semantics.

This paper aims to answer interesting questions about V-*e*-*kata* compounds under the framework of cognitive semantics. Is a V-*e*-*kata* compound a syntactic phrase or a lexical item? Does it show any properties of a phrase? Does it show any properties of a lexical item? How can we understand V-*e*-*kata* compounds from a general perspective of grammar? To answer these qeustions, I present syntactic and lexical properties of V-*e*-*kata* compounds in section 2, problems for C-H Lee's (2006) categorial conversion analysis in section 3, and then my alternative proposal based on Talmy's (2000) theory of lexicalization and Goldberg's (1995) construction grammar in section 4. Section 5 is the conclusion of this paper, and suggests a way of applying the proposed analyses to ontology-building.

2. Syntactic and Lexical Properties of V-*e*-*kata* Compounds

V-*e*-*kata* compounds have dual faces. They show properties of both syntactic phrases and lexical items. A well-known syntactic property of V-*e*-*kata* compounds is the intervention of other morpho-syntactic elements. That is, such elements as a topic marker, delimiters like *–man* 'only' and *–to* 'also', plural/manner markers, and even a case marker can intervene between the V-*e* and -*kata* (K-H Kim 1996, C-S Suh 1996, C-H Lee 2006).

(4) a. salamtul-i   kicha-eyse naylyeka-ss-ta
        people-NOM train-from take.off-Pst-Dec
        'People took off the train.'
    b. salamtul-i kicha-eyse naylye-nun-ka-ss-ta
                            TOP
    c. salamtul-i kicha-eyse naylye-man-ka-ss-ta
                            only
    d. salamtul-i kicha-eyse naylye-to-ka-ss-ta
                           also

    e. salamtul-i kicha-eyse naylye-tul-ka-ss-ta

Plural
f. salamtul-i kicha-eyse naylye-se-ka-ss-ta
Manner
g. salamtul-i kicha-eyse naylye-lul-ka-ss-ta
ACC

Interestingly,–*se* intervention as shown in (4f) is not always possible. Compare the data in (4) with (5).

(5) a. *olakata* 'to go up':
        ola-nun-ka-ss-ta, ola-man-ka-ss-ta, ola-to-ka-ss-ta, ?ola-se-ka-ss-ta, ola-lul-ka-ss-ta
     b. *tulekata* 'to enter':
        tule-nun-ka-ss-ta, tule-man-ka-ss-ta, tule-to-ka-ss-ta, *tule-se-ka-ss-ta, tule-lul-ka-ss-ta
     c. *kacyekata* 'to take (something) and go':
        kacye-nun-ka-ss-ta, kacye-man-ka-ss-ta, kacye-to-ka-ss-ta, *kacye-se-ka-ss-ta, kacye-
lul-   ka-ss-ta

Noticing the difference between (4) and (5), K-H Kim (1996) claims that V-*e-kata* compounds that allow the intervention of –*se* are not (real) lexical compounds. To him, the possibility of –*se* intervention is a good test to show whether a V-*e-kata* compound is a syntactic phrase or a word. Kim's analysis, however, cannot explain that the intervention of –*nun, -man, -to, -lul* is generally allowed for all V-*e-kata* compounds whether they allow –*se* intervention or not.
    A second syntactic property of V-*e-kata* compounds is the –*ki* repetition construction (cf. C-H Lee 2006: 134).

(6) a. salamtul-i   kicha-eyse naylyeka-ss-ta
        people-NOM train-from take.off-Pst-Dec
        'People took off the train.'
     b. salamtul-i kicha-eyse naylyeka-kinun nalyeka-ss-ta
     c. salamtul-i kicha-eyse naylyeka-kinun ka-ss-ta

The –*ki* repetition construcion copies the entire V-*e-ka* complex to focus the verb phrase as in (6b). Crucially, the construction copies only part of the V-*e-ka* complex as shown in (6c), which clearly indicates a syntactic phrasal property of the V-*e-ka* complex
    V-*e-kata* compounds also display properties of lexical items. First, *do-so* substitution for part of the complex is not possible, which suggests lexical integrity.

(7) a. Inho-ka pang-ey tule-ka-ca, Mina-to pang-ey tule-ka-ss-ta
        I-NOM room-into enter.then M-also room-into enter-Pst-Dec
        'Inho entered the room, and Mina also entered the room.'
     b. *Inho-ka pang-ey tule-ka-ca, Mina-to (pang-ey) tule-kulay-ss-ta
     c. Inho-ka pang-ey tule-ka-ca, Mina-to kulay-ss-ta
        'Inho entered the room, and so does Mina.'

(7c) shows that *do-so* substituion is possible only with the entire V-*e-kata* complex.
    Secondly, coordinating parts of V-*e-kata* complexes is not allowed as shown in (8b).

(8) a. Inho-nun satali-lul   ola-ka-ss-ko, Mina-nun naylye-ka-ss-ta
        I-TOP   ladder-ACC go.up-Pst-Dec M-TOP   go.down-Pst-Dec
        'Inho went up the ladder, and Mina went down the ladder.'
     b. *Inho-nun satali-lul ola-(se), (kuliko) Mina-nun naylye-(se)-ka-ss-ta
                                and

Finally, *-si* honorification also suggests that V-*e-kata* compounds are lexical units. According to K-H Kim (1996: 11-12), in a typical syntactic phrase of compound verbs, *-si* honorification is possible with both the preceding and the following verbs.

(9) sensayngnim-kkeyse emeni-lul   osie   mannasi-ess-ta   (syntactic phrase)
      teacher-NOM(Hon) mother-ACC come(Hon) meet(Hon)-Pst-Dec
      'The teacher came and met my mother.'

Unlike typical compound verb phrases, V-*e-kata* compounds allow *–si* honorification only for the second verb as shown in (10).

(10)   a. sensayngnim-i chayk-ul   kacieka-ss-ta
          teacher-NOM book-ACC take.go-Pst-Dec
          'The teacher took the book (and was gone).'
       b. *sensayngnim-kkeyse chayk-ul kaci-si-eka-ss-ta
          teacher-NOM(Hon)   take(Hon).go-Pst-Dec
       c. sensayngnim-kkeyse chayk-ul kacieka-si-ess-ta
          teacher-NOM(Hon)   take.go(Hon)-Pst-Dec
       d. *sensayngnim-kkeyse chayk-ul kaci-si-eka-si-ess-ta
          teacher-NOM(Hon)   take(Hon).go(Hon)-Pst-Dec

As we have discussed so far, V-*e-kata* compounds have both syntactic and lexical properties. K-H Kim (1996) analyzed V-*e-kata* compounds sometimes as syntactic phrases and other times as lexical entries based on the *–se* intervention test; but we have already seen that his analysis faces empirical problems. In the next section, we will see another important approach to V-*e-kata* compounds, i.e. categorial conversion.

3. Categorial Conversion

To explain the dual properties of V-*e-kata* compounds, C-H Lee (2006) proposes an interesting word formation rule based on categorial conversion. According to his proposal, the V-*e* part in

(11)

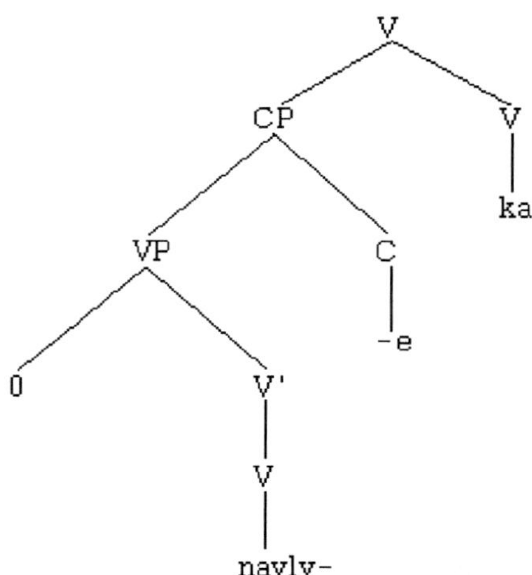

the V-*e-kata* complex begins as a CP complement to *kata* in syntax. For instance, *naylyekata* 'to go down' has the deep structure in (11).

Lee's word formation rule is the lexical operation that refers to the syntactic structure. Hence, the CP in (11) is categorially converted to Adv, and lexicalizes into the V-*e-kata* compound verb. (12) is the result of his categorial conversion and word formation.

(12)

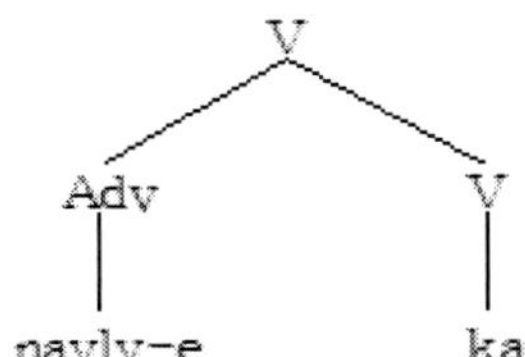

Lee's proposal explains many syntactic and lexical properties of V-*e-kata* compounds, since it allows two different stages, i.e. syntactic and lexical, in the theory. But it is not clear how a lexical operation can look forward at the syntactic structure that is not available in the lexical stage. A possible solution is some sort of backward operation from syntax to the lexicon. This does not provide a natural account, either. We do not know the motivation for this dramatic operation, nor do we understand how one syntactic structure is changed into an inherently different structure after having moved back and forth from syntax to the lexicon, and from the lexicon to syntax.

4. Alternative Proposal: Co-Event Conflation for V-*e-kata* Compounds

My proposed analysis is couched on Talmy's (2000) theory of lexicalization patterns. Talmy has developed an influential lexical semantic theory under a larger framework of cognitive semantics. In his theory, the human cognitive faculty mentally reconstructs a motion event in the external world in terms of primitive notions like [Figure], [MOVE], [Path], [Ground], [Co-Event], etc. In other words, we perceive a motion event as [Figure]'s [MOVE]-ment over (=[Path]) a [Ground] with some [Co-Event].

This cognitive schema provides bases of lexicalization patterns of world languages. For instance, some languages conflate [Path] elements into [MOVE]; another group of languages show the conflation of [Co-Event] into [MOVE], and so on. In Talmy's theory, [Co-Event] is a sub-event that modifies a main event, and includes such semantic fields as Manner, Cause, Precursion, Enablement, Concomitance, Subsequence, etc. The data in (13) show [Co-Event Manner] conflation into [MOVE], and the data in (14) show famous cases of [Path] conflation into [MOVE] in Spanish.

(13)   [Co-Event Manner] conflation into [MOVE]
        a. The rock rolled down the hill.
        b. I ran down the stairs.
        c. I kicked the keg into the storeroom.

(14)   [Path] conflation into [MOVE] (☞ See Talmy's (2000) pp. 49-50 for details.)
        a. La botella entró   a la cueva (flotando)
           the bottle MOVED-in to the cave (floating)
           'The bottle floated into the cave.'
        b. La botella salió   de la cueva (flotando)
           the bottle MOVED-out from the cave (floating)
           'The bottle floated out of the cave.'
        c. La botella pasó   por la piedra (flotando)
           the bottle MOVED-by past the rock (floating)
           'The bottle floated past the rock.'

     d. La botella pasó   por   el tubo (flotando)
       the bottle MOVED-through through the pipe (floating)
       'The bottle floated through the pipe.'

Now, what I propose for Korean V-*e-kata* compounds is the [Co-Event] conflation into [MOVE]. At least three types of [Co-Event] conflation can be found for V-*e-kata* compounds. The first type is the [Co-Event Manner] conflation into [MOVE], where the preceding verb denotes the manner of the main event, as shown in (15).

(15)   [Co-Event Manner] conflation into [MOVE]: *kwulekata* 'to go by rolling', *kkwulyekata* 'to be dragged to', *nalakata* 'to fly', *naylyekata* 'to go down', *nemekata* 'to go/jump over', *ttekata* 'to scoop up and go', *ttwiekata* 'to run and go', *molakata* 'to drive (something/somebody) into some space or situation', *olakata* 'to go up', etc.

Another pattern of lexicalization is the [Co-Event Concomitance] conflation into [MOVE]. Here, the two verbs in the complex denote concomitant events; i.e. they co-occur at an approximately same point of time.

(16)   [Co-Event Concomitance] conflation into [MOVE]: *kacyekata* 'to take (something) and go', *nakata* 'to go out', *ttalakata* 'to follow', *molyekata* 'to go in a group', *ahpsekata* 'to go forward, to take precedence', *ccochakata* 'to follow', *chacakata* 'to go by searching', etc.

A third possible lexicalization pattern is the [Co-Event Concurrent Result] conflation into [MOVE], where the following verb denotes an event that occurs immediately after the event denoted by the preceding verb.

(17)   [Co-Event Concurrent Result] conflation into [MOVE]: *capakata* 'to catch somebody and go', *caphyekata* 'to be taken to some place after being caught'

K-H Kim (1996) also expresses the intuition underlying the second and third generalizations by saying that the event denoted by the first verb is either a co-occurrence or an initiation of the event denoted by the second verb (K-H Kim 1996). Notice that my proposal is different from Talmy's (2000) original suggestion that assumes [Path] conflation for Korean motion verbs.

Manner conflation places the phenomena in a broader picture of cross-linguistic lexicalization patterns. But we still do not understand how to explain all the peculiar phrasal properties of V-*e-kata* compounds. In my proposal, V-*e-kata* compounds are just lexicalized items. They are in some sense the outputs of universal principles that lexicalize concepts into words. Then, how can all the phrasal properties occur? For instance, how is it possible that such elements as a topic marker, delimiters, plural/manner markers, a case marker, etc. intervene between the V-*e* and –*kata*, as discussed in section 2? We also want to know how parts of the entire complex can be repeated in the –*ki* repetition construction.

These questions are taken care of by the idea of the construction grammar (Goldberg 1995). Crucially, Jackendoff (1997), J. S. Jun (2003), and Culicover and Jackendoff (2005) have made an attractive proposal that the basic unit of lexical entries can be anything; i.e. some lexical entries are as big as words, and others are smaller or bigger than words. In this proposal, affixes, inflectional morphemes, derivational morphemes, phrases, sentences, etc. can become legitimate lexical entries. Adopting this innovative view of the lexicon, we can posit a V-*e-kata* construction in (18) as a legitimate lexical entry.

(18)   V-*e-kata* construction as a lexical entry:

      [V [CP [VP [V ___]] [C –*e*]] [V -*kata*]]

What (18) amounts to say is two things: (i) the V-*e-kata* construction is a lexical item; and (ii) this lexical item allows phrasal syntax. The lexical integrity matters only when the lexical item in question is a word. In case the lexical item in question is a construction as in our proposed theory, the lexical integrity does not matter at all, thereby allowing all sorts of phrasal syntax as shown in (19).

(19)

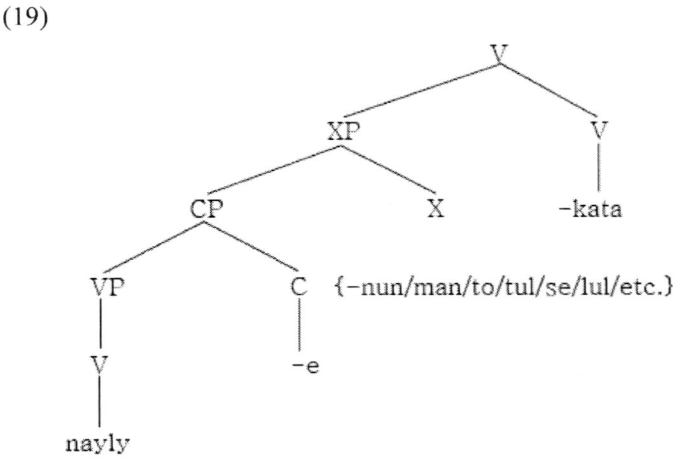

One remaining question is why some verbs allow *–se* intervention while others do not. As we already discussed in section 2, the acceptability of *–se* intervention varies from verb to verb; e.g. *nalye-se-kata* 'to go down',*?ola-se-ka-tata* 'to go up', **tule-se-ka-ta* 'to enter', **kacye-se-ka-ta* 'to take (something) and go'. Here, my working hypothesis is that of all the [Co-Event] conflation types, [Manner] conflation is more basic, and is the target of productive morphology, whereas [Other] conflations are the target of semi-productive morphology suggested by Jackendoff (1997). Since [Manner] conflation is productive, its lexicalized output is a sure compound, thereby allowing *-se* intervention. Since [Other] conflations are not as productive as [Manner] conflation, its lexicalized output has an unclear compound status, thereby disallowing *-se* intervention in general. This hypothesis is supported by the fact that most V-*e-kata* verbs that allow *–se* intervention have the meaning component of [Manner].

5. Concluding Remarks

So far, we have studied the dual nature of V-*e-kata* compounds and some earlier proposals for the problem. My alternative proposal is based on Talmy's (2000) theory of lexicalization patterns and Goldberg's (1995) construction grammar. In my theory, I claim that the lexical properties of a V-*e-kata* complex are due to the fact that it is a lexicalized item that shows [Co-Event] conflation patterns, and that its phrasal properties are due to the fact that it is a construction in the lexicon that allows all sorts of phrasal syntax.

A study of lexicalization patterns is important not only for the theoretical understanding of natural language semantics, but for ontology building as well. Suppose we build a verb ontology for Spanish motion verbs as in (14). Suppose we build a verb ontology for Korean motion verbs. In the initial stage of ontology building, two separate ontologies for two languages are sufficient. But in a more elaborate stage of ontology building, we need to build some sort of general ontology to cover the two languages. One advantage of this approach is that we can include hundreds of other languages in a maximally economical way. My present study opens a direction for such study. That is, instead of building as many ontologies as the languages we study, we build a general ontology that has conceptual primitives like [Figure], [MOVE], [Path], [Ground], [Co-Event], etc. Then, cross-linguistic differences are handled by different lexicalization patterns. This is a promising way of research, and I hope my study of Korean compound verbs guides us to a fruitful inquiry of ontological semantics in the future.

References

Culicover, P. and R. Jackendoff. 2005. *Simpler Syntax*. Oxford: Oxford Univ. Press.

Goldberg, A. 1995. *Constructions: A Construction Grammar Approach to Argument Structure*. Chicago: Univ. of Chicago Press.

Jackendoff, R. 1997. *The Architecture of the Language Faculty*. Cambridge, MA: MIT Press.

Jun, J. S. 2003. *Syntactic and Semantic Bases of Case Assignment: A Study of Verbal Nouns, Light Verbs, and Dative*. Ph.D. Dissertation, Brandeis University.

Kim, K-H. 1996. kuke hapsengtongsa sayngsenguy thongsa uymihakcek haysek [A Syntactic and Semantic Interpretation of the Generation of Compound Verbs in Korea]. *Kwukekwukmunhak* [Korean Language and Literature], 116, 1-37.

Lee, C-H. 2006. V-eV hapsengtongsa hyengseng kyuchikkwa pemcwuthongyong [Word Formation Rule and Categorial Conversion: Focusing on the V-eoV Compound Verb]. *Emunkak* [Language and Literature], 91, 129-161.

Suh, C-S. 1996. *Korean Grammar* (in Korean). Seoul: Hanyang Univ. Press.

Talmy, L. 2000. *Toward a Cognitive Semantics, Vol. II: Typology and Process in Concept Structuring*. Cambridge, MA: The MIT Press.

What Makes Negative Imperative So Natural for Korean [psych-adjective +-*e ha*-] Constructions?[*]

Ilkyu Kim

Department of Linguistics and Cognitive Science
Hankuk University of Foreign Studies
Mohyeon, Yongin, Gyeonggi, 449-791, South Korea
onefinedayjazz@hufs.ac.kr

Abstraction. Regarding Korean psych-adjectives and their -*e ha*- counterparts, e.i., [psych-adjective + -*e ha*-] constructions, what is at issue is how to capture the semantic difference and similarity between the two. Concerning this issue, one of the most controversial and difficult problems is whether the psych-construction has Action (Agency) as part of its meaning. The purpose of this paper is to solve this problem by answering the question why psych-constructions are much more natural when they are used as negative imperative than when they are used as positive imperative. First, in order to figure out why positive imperative is not allowed, we show that –*e ha*- adds the meaning of non-volitional action to psych-adjectives, using Jackendoff's Conceptual Semantics. Secondly, in accounting for why negative imperative is so natural, we show, with Talmy's Force Dynamics theory, what the speaker requires from the hearer is internal volitional action.

Keywords: psych-adjectives, [psych-adjective + -e ha-] constructions, Action, imperative, Conceptual Semantics, Force Dynamics theory

1. Introduction

Korean psych-adjectives and their -*e ha*- counterparts, e.i., [psych-adjective + -*e ha*-] constructions (psych-constructions[1]) have attracted many researchers with respect to their

---

[*] An earlier version of this paper was presented in the weekly meeting of the BK21 research team of Linguistics and Cognitive Science Department at HUFS, October 12. I thank the audiences for comments and questions. I also thank two anonymous reviewers of this paper. All errors and misinterpretations are of course mine.

meaning (e.g. Hong, K-S 1991, Kim, H-S 1989, Kim, K-H 2003, Kim, Y-J 1990, Kim, S-J 1994, Lee & Lee 2005, Nam, S-H 2007, Yeon, J-H 1996). With most semanticists agreeing with the idea that the meanings of the two constructions are certainly different from each other, what is at issue is how to capture the difference and similarity between the two. Regarding this issue, one of the most controversial and difficult problems is whether the psych-construction has Action (Agency) as part of its meaning (Kim S-J 1994).

The purpose of this paper is to solve this problem by answering the question why psych-constructions are much more natural when they are used as negative imperative than when they are used as positive imperative. In answering this question, first, we show that *−e ha-* adds the meaning of non-volitional action to psych-adjectives, thus making the whole construction a kind of action. This characteristic of the psych-construction and its difference from psych-adjectives are captured by Jackendoff's (1990, 2002a, 2002b, 2007) Conceptual Semantics, particularly its mechanism of distinguishing thematic-tier and macrorole tier. Then, we show, with Talmy's (1985, 2003) Force Dynamics theory, in the negative imperative of the psych-construction, what the speaker requires from the hearer is internal volitional action.

The content of the rest of the paper is like the following. In section 2, we will first introduce the concept of Action and Actor on which our analysis is based. Then, in section 3, we will analyze the meaning of psych-constructions, particularly the values they take for the features [VOLITION] and [ACTION], in order to answer our first question: why is positive imperative for psych-constructions impossible or unnatural at least? In doing so, we will focus on the difference between the conceptual structure of psych-constructions and that of psych-adjectives, working under the framework of Jackendoff's (1990, 2002a, 2002b, 2007) Conceptual Semantics. After that, in section 4, we will answer the second question which is, we believe, much more interesting: why is negative imperative for psych-constructions so natural? We will analyze negative imperative of psych-constructions with Talmy's (1985, 2003) force dynamics theory, showing that it can naturally account for why negative but not positive imperative is possible, or at least much more natural, for psych-constructions. In section 5, we support our argument by expanding the scope of predicates that go naturally along with only negative imperative and figuring out their semantic similarity with respect to the features [VOLITION] and [ACTION]. Finally, our conclusion will be given in section 6.

2. Action, Actor and Macrorole Tier

Following Culicover & Wilkins (1986) and Talmy (1985), Jackendoff (1990:128) argues that "conceptual roles fall into two tiers: a *thematic tier* dealing with motion and location, and an *action tier* dealing with Actor-Patient relations."[2] In addition, he adds two more conceptual

---

[1] Throughout this paper, we will call [psych-adjective + *-e ha-*] constructions "psych-constructions" just for convenience.
[2] Later, Jackendoff (2002a) suggests two more tiers, *referential tier* and *information structure tier*.

roles, Experiencer and Stimuls, to the *action tier* and call it *macrorole tier* (Jackendoff 2002b). Now, two conceptual functions are on the level of the macrorole tier: AFF and EXP, each of which takes as its arguments Actor and Patient, and Experiencer and Stimulus.

By postulating the macrorole tier, the traditional notion of Agent can be dissected into a number of independent parts. Jackendoff (1990:129), for example, analyzes the sentence *Bill rolled down the hil.l* like the following.

(1) Bill rolled down the hill.
    Go ([BILL], [DOWN [HILL]])
    a. AFF_{+vol} ([BILL],   )   (willful doer)
    b. AFF_{-vol} ([BILL],   )   (nonwillful doer)
    c. AFF (, [BILL])   (undergoer)

Then, how can we define Action, or the function AFF? Jackendoff (1990, 2002a, 2002b, 2007) suggests the frame *what X did was* ... as a means of testing whether a predicate is Action or not.

(2) a. The ball rolled to the wall.   What the ball did was roll to the wall.
    b. The wind made Bill sneeze.   What the wind did was make Bill sneeze.
    c. Bill entered the room.   What Bill did was enter the room.
    d. The ball was in the corner.   *What the ball did was be in the corner.
    e. The wall surrounded an   *What the wall did was surround an orchard.
       orchard.
    f. Bill owned a VW.   *What Bill did was own a VW.
                          (Jackendoff 2007:198)

Thus, (2a-c) shows *rolled*, *made*, and *entered* are Actions and accordingly, *the ball*, *the wind*, and *Bill* are Actors, while the subjects and the predicates of (2d-f) cannot be Actors and Actions.

3. Why Positive Imperative So Unnatural?

Jackendoff (2007:266) argues that "[i]mperatives require the understood subject YOU to be a volitional Actor." That is, if a word has [+VOLITION, +ACTION] it allows imperative, but if a word does not have [+VOLITION, +ACTION] it cannot. This is why, from syntactic perspective, most Korean verbs can take imperative endings but adjectives cannot. What is interesting is that although there is a variability of acceptability, psych-constructions does not go along naturally, if not impossible, with positive imperative as in (3-4).

(3)   a. *apenim-uy sosik-ul kwungkumhay hay-la!

father-of news-ACC wonder AUX-IMP

'Be curious about father's news.'

  b. *pwulanhay hay.

    be uneasy IMP

    'Don't be uneasy/Be uneasy.'

  c. ?mincwucwuuy-uy cwukum-ul sulphe hay-la!

    democracy-of death-ACC sad AUX-IMP

    'Be sad about the death of democracy!'

(Kim S-J 1994:73)

(4)   a. *simsimhay hay-la!

    bored AUX-IMP

    'Be bored!'

  b. ?*yay-tul-a. sulphe hay-la. apeci-ka tolakasy-ess-ta

    child-PL-VOC sad AUX-IMP father-NOM pass away-PAST-DEC

    'Children. Be sad. Father has passed away.'

  c. ?*ku salam-uy chesa-lul sepsephay hay-la.

    that man-of behavior-ACC sorry AUX-IMP

    'Be sorry for his behavior.'

(Kim S-J 1994:78)

This is very different from other "normal" verbs which allow both positive and negative imperatives very naturally as in (5).

(5) a. Keki ka-la/ka-ci mala.

    there go-IMP/go-COMP NI

    'Do/do not go there.'

  b. Kongpwu hay-la/ha-ci mala.

    study(n) LV-IMP/LV-COMP NI

    'Do/do not study.'

Then, three logically possible reasons why psych-constructions cannot take positive imperative are that they do not have either [+VOLITION] or [+ACTION], or neither of them. Let us look at the features one by one to figure out which value psych-constructions have for each feature. First, as for the feature [VOLITION], we can see psych-constructions have a very low degree of, if at all, volitionality. (6-7) shows various ways to test volitionality of action of the psych-construction.

(6) a. *simsimhay ha-ko siph-ta.

206

bored AUX-COMP want-DEC

'I want to be bored.'

   b. *simsimhay ha-l cwunpi-ka twoye iss-ta.

bored AUX-FUT readiness-NOM become COP-DEC

'I am ready to be bored.'

   d. *simsimhay ha-l nunglyek-i iss-ta.

bored AUX-FUT ability-NOM COP-DEC

'I have ability to be bored.'

   e. *simsimhay hay poa-ss-ta.

bored AUX look-PAST-DEC

'I tried to be bored.'

(Kim S-J 1994:77)

(7) a. ?ku-uy sengkong-ul kippe ha-ca.

he-of success-ACC happy AUX-PROP

'Let's be happy for his success.'

   b. *wuli modwu apenim-uy sosik-ul kwungkumhay ha-ca!

we all father-of news-ACC wonder AUX-PROP

'Let's wonder father's news.'

   c. kohyang-ul kuliwe ha-ca.

hometown-ACC miss AUX-PROP

'Let's miss our hometown.'

(Kim S-J 1994:73)

The above examples show that psych-constructions cannot co-occur with various constructions that imply volitional action, thus do not have [+VOLITION]. In fact, however, there are some cases such as (7c) in which psych-constructions can be used as volitional action.[3] But these cases, as pointed out by Kim S-J (1994), are not normal but either used in special contexts such as literary works or become natural by certain pragmatic factors.[4] Some (e.g. Kim K-H 2003, Hong 1991, Yeon 1996) argue psych-constructions have [+VOLITION] and it is one of the

---

[3] Some other examples are like the following, all from (Kim S-J 1994:75).

   ku salam-ul coha hay-la.
   that man-ACC like AUX-IMP
   'Like the man.'
   yay-tul-a! kippe hay-la. Apeci-ka sala-se tolao-sy-ess-ta.
   child-PL-VOC happy AUX-IMP father-NOM alive-and come back-HON-PAST-DEC
   'Children! Be happy. Father has come back alive.'
   Ku salam-hanthey com mianhay hay-la.
   that man-to a bit feel sorry AUX-IMP
   'Feel sorry for him.'

[4] One pragmatic factor suggested by Kim S-J (1994:75) is whether the hearer can get some benefit by following the speaker's order.

differences between psych-adjectives and their *-eha-* counterparts. In particular, Yeon (1996) does so by insisting acceptability of sentences in (8) which have adverbs *ilpwule/uytocekulo* 'on purpose' in them.

> (8) a. Nay-ka ilpwule/uytocekulo paym-ul mwusewe ha-n-ta.
>
>   I-NOM on purpose/intentionally sneak-ACC afraid AUX-PRES-DEC
>
>   'I am afraid of a sneak on purpose/intentionally.'
>
> b. Nay-ka ilpwule/uytocekulo kohyang-ul kuliwe ha-n-ta.
>
>   I-NOM on purpose/intentionally hometown-ACC miss AUX-PRES-DEC
>
>   'I miss my hometown on purpose/intentionally.'

(Yeon J-H 1996:264)

However, with our linguistic intuition, they are hardly acceptable. Only the possibility of their being acceptable is that the sentences' having some other meaning than what we would normally expect from psych-constructions. That is, if, for instance, the meaning of (8a) is 'I pretended to be afraid of a sneak on purpose', the sentence can be acceptable. But in this interpretation 'my internal psychological state' is out of concern, which is crucial in the original meaning of psych-constructions.

A more difficult issue is whether psych-constructions have [+ACTION], which has caused a lot of conflicts between researchers. While some argue they have action as part of their meaning (e.g. Kim 1990, Lee & Lee 2005, Yeon 1996), others argue they are not actions (e.g. Kim 1994, Hong 1991, Nam 2007). It is important to note that those who maintain psych-constructions have [+ACTION] mostly presuppose their [+VOLITION]. This may be due to the fact that "when the actor of an action is animate, the default interpretation is that the action is performed voluntarily" (Culicover & Jackendoff 2005:427). What we are going to argue, however, is that psych-constructions have [-VOLITION] and [+ACTION] and they take Actor not Experiencer as their subject. Then, two problems are immediately raised both of which are closely related to this issue: 1) what is the evidence of seeing psych-constructions as having [+ACTION] thus taking Actor as their subject? 2) How can we capture the relationship between the meaning of psych-constructions and that of psych-adjectives?

Let us solve the first problem with linguistic data. At first glance, (9), together with (6-7), seems to act as counterevidence to our argument that the psych-construction is some kind of Action, because normal verbs, having action as their meaning, do not have any problem with going along with contexts used in (6-7) and adverbs such as *ellun* 'quickly' and *ppalli* 'quickly' in (9).

> (9) a. *na-nun ellun tungsan-ul cohahay-ssta.
>
>   I-TOP quickly climbing-ACC like-PAST
>
>   'I quickly liked climbing.'
>
> b. *ku-nun ppalli pwukkulewehay-ssta.

208

he-TOP quickly embarrassed-PAST

'He quickly felt shy.'

However, a more elaborate study shows the sentences in (6, 7, and 9) are ungrammatical not because psych-constructions are not actions but because they are not volitional actions. As mentioned above, according to Jackendoff (2002b, 2007), in order for a verb to mean Action whether it is voluntary or not, it must pass the *What X did was* test. We can test whether the psych-construction has action in its meaning by putting them in a similar context. The following is one such test using *X-ka/i han kes-ilakon … ppwun-ita* (*what X did was only*) construction.

> (10) a. Ku-ka han kes-ilakon kunye-lul coha ha-n kes ppwun-ita.
>   he-NOM did COMP-only she-ACC like AUX-PAST COMP only-COP
>   'What he did was only like her.'
>   b. *Ku-ka han kes-ilakon kunye-ka cohun kes ppwun-ita.
>   he-NOM did COMP-only she-NOM like COMP only-COP
>   'What he did was only like her.'

(10a) and (10b) clearly show the difference between psych-adjectives and psych-constructions. The psych-construction *coha ha-* 'like', unlike its counterpart *cohta* 'like', passes the test very successfully, thus showing their having Action as part of their meaning.

Now, we can formalize the conceptual structure of psych-adjectives and psych-constructions and show the relationship between them like the following (of course, one should be much more specific if (s)he wants to give a detailed conceptual structure of the predicates, but for our purpose (11) is specific enough).

> (11) a. Conceptual Structure of the psych-construction *silhe hata* 'dislike'
>   X [(SHOW) [BE/FEEL *silhum* (TOWARD Y)]]
>   X AFF-volition   [Y is not a Patient]
>   b. Conceptual Structure of the psych-adjective *silhta*
>   X BE/FEEL *silhum* (TOWARD Y)
>   X EXP Y

Many researchers (e.g. Kim S-J 1994, Lee & Lee 2005, Nam S-H 2007, Yeon J-H 1996), although they differ from one another in more detail, agree that the meaning of *–e ha-* in the psych-construction is some kind of "externalization of internal feeling" (Yeon J-H 1996:262). We agree with this analysis and use the function SHOW, first proposed by Kim S-J (1994)[5], in

---

[5] The following is what Kim S-J has suggested as the meaning of the psych-construction *silhe hata*:

[EVENT   SHOW (x, [STATE   BE/FEEL (x, [PLACE   AT 싫음][yp])])]

order to capture this meaning. Two important differences should be noted though; first, while Kim S-J argued the macrorole that subject of the psych-construction takes is Experiencer, we argue it is Actor, and secondly, the function SHOW is now parenthesized, which means the psych-construction does not necessarily mean "externalization of internal feeling" any more.; instead, it can just mean just one's internal feeling, without externalizing it, just like psych-adjectives. This can be proved by two facts; first, sentences like (12a) are very natural, and secondly, many psych-constructions can have *na* 'I' as their subject as in (12b-c).

(12) a. Sekhwuni-nun sok-ulo Ciweni-lul pwulewe ha-myenseto ket-ulo-nun
    Sekhwun-TOP inside-to Ciwen-ACC envy AUX-although outside-to-TOP
    pwulewe ha-ci ahn-nun-ta.
    Envy AUX-COMP NEG-PRES-DEC
    'Although Sekhwun internally envies Ciwen, he does not externalize
    his feeling.'

(Kim H-S 1989:203)

    b. nay-ka paym-ul mwusewe ha-n-ta.
    I-NOM Sneak-ACC afraid AUX-PRES-DEC
    'I am afraid of a sneak.'
    c. nay-ka kohyang-ul kuliwe ha-n-ta.
    I-NOM hometown-ACC miss AUX-PRES-DEC
    'I miss my hometown.'

(Yeon J-H 1996:262)

Now, we can answer the question why positive imperative with the psych-construction is unnatural. It is because the construction has [+ACTION] but not [+VOLITION]. But note again that the positive Imperative of the psych-construction is not categorically impossible; instead, there is a variability of acceptability for positive imperative as already shown in (3-4), which seems due to the fact that the construction, after all, is a kind of action and some other out-of-semantic factors discussed above.

4. Why Negative Imperative So Natural?

So far, we have seen why psych-constructions cannot take the positive imperative form. It is because although they have [+ACTION] they lack [+VOLITION] in their meaning which is a crucial element for making imperative possible. What we can expect is, then, negative imperative of psych-constructions must also be unacceptable just like their positive imperative. However, we can see negative imperative forms are much more natural for psych-constructions as in (13).

(13) a. (?)simsimhay ha-ci ma!
    bored AUX-COMP NI
    'Don't be bored!'
  b. yay-tul-a. sulphe ha-ci mala.
    child-PL-VOC sad AUX-COMP NI
    'Children. Don't be sad.'
  c. ku salam-uy chesa-lul sepsephay ha-ci mala.
    that man-of behavior-ACC sorry AUX-COMP NI
    'Don't be sorry for his behavior.'
  d. apenim-uy sosik-ul kwungkumhay ha-ci mala!
    father-of news-ACC wonder AUX-COMP NI
    'Don't be curious about father's news.'
  e. pwulanhay ha-ci ma.
    uneasy AUX-COMP NI
    'Don't be uneasy.'
  f. mincwucwuuy-uy cwukum-ul sulphe ha-ci mala!
    democracy-of death-ACC sad AUX-COMP NI
    'Don't be sad about the death of democracy!'

Sentences in (13) are all counterparts of their positive imperative forms in (3-4). Note that their acceptability or grammaticality is much better than their positive imperative forms. In section 4, we will solve this problem by looking at the verbs in terms of the force dynamics.

4.1 Basic Idea of Force Dynamics in Language

Force dynamics is a semantic category suggested by Talmy (1985, 2003) that captures and generalizes the meanings of a lot of grammatical words, content words, and linguistic constructions with just a few primitives such as Agonist and Antagonist and their relationship with respect to force. The basic type of force interaction is physical interactions and it further extends to physical/psychological, intrapsychological and sociopsychological interactions. Since force-dynamic pattern in the intrapsychological interaction is the most important pattern with regard to our question, let us examine intrapsychological force dynamics in detail. The following is a minimal pair that contrasts force-dynamically neutral expressions with ones that exhibit force-dynamic patterns on the intrapsychological level (Talmy 2003:412):

(14) not VP/refrain from VPing   [*intrapsychological*]
  a. He didn't close the door.
  b. He refrained from closing the door.

First, (14a) is force-dynamically neutral in that no conflicting forces are shown in the linguistic structure. On the other hand, (14b) shows a force interaction occurring within a single psyche; that is, a man urges to close the door without volition, while, at the same time, the same person volitionally inhibits his desire. The key for explaining the intrapsychological force dynamics and the reason that only negative imperative is possible for psych-constructions is the notion of "divided self" (Talmy 2003:431), the state in which both Agonist and Antagonist simultaneously exist within one mind competing each other. The basic idea is like this: "[t]he Agonist is identified with the self's desires, reflecting an inner psychological state. It is being overcome by an Antagonist acting either as blockage ... or as a spur." (Talmy 2003:432) If Antagonist is stronger than Agonist the self *refrain* or *keep oneself from -ing*. On the contrary, if Agonist is stronger than Antagonist, then one *exerts to* VP or *exerts in -ing*. It is important to note that Agonist's desire is without volition while Antagonist's exertion of force is necessarily a volitional act.

4.2 Negative Imperative Presupposes Divided Self!

We are finally ready to answer our question. Negative imperative of psych-constructions, by default, presupposes divided self and Agonist's desire. By uttering negative imperative sentences (cf. (13)), the speaker, with the presupposition above in his/her mind, requires Antagonist, one part of the hearer, to volitionally act against Agonist's desire. For example, (13b) can be roughly paraphrased like this: '(I believe part of you (Agonist) is and keeps trying to be sad, but) do not give in to the desire and overcome Agonist.' Here, what is within the parenthesis is the content of the presupposition, and what the speaker tells the hearer to do is obviously an internal volitional action. In contrast, positive imperative of the psych-construction does not presuppose divided self and just requires the hearer to conduct a non-volitional action.

5. Beyond Psych-constructions: A Typology of Korean Action Predicates

Psych-constructions are not only the predicates that allow only negative imperative. Verbs or constructions that refer to one's physiological actions like *colta*[6] 'drowse', *haphwum hata* 'yawn', *pangkwi kkita* 'fart', *ttelta* 'shiver' also permit only negative imperative as in (16).

    (16) a. *cola-la./col-ci mala.
         drowse-IMP/drowse-COMP NI
         'Drowse./Do not drowse.'
      b. *ttele-la./ttelci mala.
         shiver-IMP/shiver-COMP NI

---

[6] Kim S-J (1994) does not see *colta* as action because it is not volitional. But once we acknowledge the notion of action is divided into two groups according to the feature [VOLITION], we can say the verb is still action even if it is non-volitional.

'Shiver./Do not Shiver.'

We argue this is because these predicates, just like psych-constructions, are non-volitional actions. For example, drowsing and yawning is out of the Actor's control but once the actions (are about to) start, the actor can try to stop doing them with his/her volition. The only difference between the psych-construction and the predicates above is the former can be [-PHYSICAL] when it lacks the function SHOW in its conceptual structure, whereas the latter is always [+PHYSICAL].

Based on the analysis done so far, we can now provide a typology of Korean Action predicates as in Table 1.

Table 1: A Typology of Korean Action Predicates

	+VOLITION	-VOLITION
+PHYSICAL	*ttaylita* 'hit', *chata* 'kick', *ttwita* 'run', etc.	psych-constructions, physiological predicates
-PHYSICAL	*kongpwu hata* 'study', *sayngkak hata* 'think', etc.	(psych-constructions)
Kinds of Imperative Allowed	Both positive and negative imperatives	Only negative imperative

As shown in Table 1, Korean Action Predicates can be divided into four groups according to the criteria of [VOLITION] and [PHYSICAL]. Moreover, regardless of their physicality, they can be further divided into two groups according to their possibility of allowing kinds of imperative: predicates allowing both positive and negative imperatives, and predicates allowing only negative imperative. What is crucial in determining kinds of imperative allowed is the feature [VOLITION]. If the predicate has [+VOLITION] it allows both, whereas if it has [-VOLITION] it only allows negative one.

5. Conclusion

In this paper, we made two main arguments on two interesting phenomena regarding psych-constructions. First, for the phenomenon that psych-constructions cannot take positive imperative, we argued, using Jackendoff's (1990, 2002a, 2002b) conceptual semantics, it is because psych-constructions are actions without volition. Secondly, for the phenomenon that psych-constructions can take negative imperative, we argued, using Talmy's (1985, 2003) Force Dynamics theory, it is because the required action is an internal volitional action. The two different actions within a single psyche were captured by the force dynamic pattern of intrapsychological interactions. And also, we have suggested that not only psych-constructions but other predicates that have non-volitional action as part of their meaning can go naturally along only with negative imperative, thus showing [-VOLITION] and [+ACTION] as the core condition of allowing only negative imperative.

Reference

Culicover, P. W. and R. Jackendoff. 2005. The semantic basis of control in English. In *Simpler Syntax*. Oxford, New York: Oxford University Press.

Jackendoff, R. 1990. *Semantic Structures*. Cambridge, Mass.: MIT Press.

Jackendoff, R. 2002a. *Foundations of Language.* Oxford: Oxford University Press.

Jackendoff, R. 2002b. *Experiencer Predicates, Theory of Mind, and Subjective vs. Objective Valuation*. ms. Brandeis University.

Jackendoff, R. 2007. *Language, Consciousness, Culture: Essays on Mental Structure.* Cambridge: The MIT Press.

Hong, K-S. 1991. Verbal Compounds in English. *Language Research* 32-1, 43-60.

Kim, K-H. 2003. Simli hyengyongsa yenkwu: nonhang kyochey ywuhyengtuluy ehwi uymi kwucolul cwungsimulo (Study of psych-adjectives: focusing on lexical meaning structure of argument changing patterns). *Enehak* 37, 47-68.

Kim, S-J. 1994. *The Lexico-semantic Structure of the Psychological Predicates in Korean.* Seoul National Univ. Ph.D. dissertation.

Kim, Y-J. 1990. *The Syntax and Semantics of Korean Case: The Interaction between Lexical and Syntactic Levels of Representation*. Ph. D. dissertation, University of Victoria.

Lee, I-H and M-H, Lee. 2005. *Simlitongsa-uy uymilon: yenge, hankuke-wa tokile-uy taycoyenkwu* (Semantics of Psych-constructions: comparing English, Korean and German). Seoul: Yeklak.

Nam, J-S. 1993. Hankuke hyengyongsa kwumwunuy thongsacek pwunlywulul wihaye 1: simli hyengyongsa kwumwun (For classifying Korean adjecive constructions 1: psych-adjective constructions). *Language Research* 29-1, 75-106.

Nam, S-H. 2007. *Hankuke Simliswule-uy Nonhang kwuco-wa saken kwuco Hankuke* (Argument Structure and Event Structure of Korean Psych-predicates). Presented at the monthly meeting of the Korean Society for Language and Information, March 24.

Talmy, L. 1985. Force dynamic in language and thought. In *Papers from the Twenty-First Regional Meeting of the Chicago Linguistic Society*. Chicago: Chicago Linguistics Society.

Talmy, L. 2003. Force Dynamics in Language and Cognition. In *Toward a Cognitive Semantics*. Cambridge, Mass.: MIT Press.

Yeon, J-H. 1996. Kwuke Yekyekcwue kwumwundy tayhan pemenecek kwancemuy yenkwu (A study of Korean dative-subject construction on cross-linguistic aspects). *Kwukehak (Korean Linguistics)* 28, 241-275.

On the Syntax and Semantics of the Bound Noun Constructions: With a Computational Implementation*

Jong-Bok Kim and Jaehyung Yang

Kyung Hee University, School of English, jongbok@khu.ac.kr
and
Kangnam University, School of Computer Engineering, jhyang@kangnam.ac.kr

Abstract. The so-called Korean BNC (bound noun construction) displays complex syntactic, semantic, and constructional properties. This paper, couched upon a constraint-based approach, two different syntactic structures for the construction with articulated lexical properties for the BNs and relevant predicates. The paper reports an implementation of this analysis in the LKB (Linguistic Knowledge Building) system and shows us that this direction is robust enough to pare relevant sentences.

Keywords: bound noun construction, complex predicate, implementation

1. Introduction

Bound nouns (BN) exhibit various peculiar properties, not found in common nouns in the language. For example, unlike canonical nouns, bound nouns cannot occur independently: they obligatory select a complement (determiner or sentence). This is rather unusual when considering the language allows most of the arguments to be freely omitted with proper context:

(1) a. *(i) kes
      this thing

    b. *(wuli-ka motu nollass-ten) kes
       we-NOM all surprise-MOD BN
       'the thing that we all surprised'

Bound nouns also place restrictions on the types of their complements. There are at least two different types of BNs with respect to their complements: BNs selecting only a dependent clause (Type I) and those selecting either a dependent clause or a determiner phrase (Type II) (cf. Cha 2001):[1]

(2) a. Type I: cheyk ('pretense'), cwul ('method'), li ('reason'), cek ('experience'), ppen ('being close to doing something'), ba ('way'), etc.

    b. Type II: swu ('possibility'), hwu ('after'), cen ('before'), etc

For example, unlike Type II BN *hwu*, Type I BN *li* selects only a dependent sentence, as observed in the following contrast:

(3) a. [John-i cam-ul ca-n]/ku hwu-ka mwusep-ta
      John-TOP sleep-ACC sleep-MOD/that BN-NOM not.exist-PAST-DECL
      'the time after John was sleeping/after the time'

---

[1]The dependent clause, different from an independent sentence, has the head verb in a dependent verb form. The clause thus cannot be used as an independent sentence. See Kim (2004).

b. [John-i   cam-ul   ca-l]/*ku   li-ka   eps-ess-ta
   John-NOM sleep-ACC sleep-MOD/that BN-NOM not.exist-PAST-DECL
   'It is not possible that John was sleeping'

Bound nouns also place tight restrictions on the verb forms of their sentential complement. In the noun complement construction (NCC), the dependent clause places no strict constraints on the head verb's VFORM value:

(4) [John-i   cam-ul   ca-n/ca-ss-ta-nun]   sasil
    John-TOP sleep-ACC sleep-PNE/sleep-PAST-DECL-PNE fact
    'the fact that John slept

As in (4), the head verb of the dependent clause, functioning as the complement of the factive noun *sasil* 'fact', can be either in a short form *ca-n* or in a full form *can-ss-ta-nun* with the declarative ending. Meanwhile, in the BN construction, the head verb of the dependent clause cannot be in a full verb form: only a short form with restricted tense is allowed:

(5) a. John-un   cam-ul   *ca-n-ta-nun/ca-l/*ca-n
       John-TOP sleep-ACC *sleep-PRES-DECL-PNE/sleep-FUT/*sleep-PRES

       swu-ka   eps-ess-ta
       BN-NOM not.exist-PAST-DECL
       'John couldn't sleep.'

    b. John-un   cam-ul   *ca-n-ta-nun/*ca-l/ca-nun
       John-TOP sleep-ACC *sleep-PNE-DECL-PNE/s*leep-FUT/sleep-PNE

       chey hayess-ta
       BN   did-DECL
       'John pretended to sleep.'

In both cases, the full dependent form (with the declarative marking) is not possible. In addition, the BN *swu* requires the head verb of its complement clause be in the future form, whereas *chey* restricts the dependent verb to be marked with the present tense.

Bound nouns are also peculiar in that they impose restrictions on the types of the predicates following them. For example, the BN *swu* can combine only with the predicate *iss-* 'exist' or *eps-* 'not exist' whereas the BN *li* requires only the latter *eps-*. Also BNs like *tes*, *ppen*, and *ccek* occur only with *ha-* 'do', whereas BNs like *kes* can be followed only by the auxiliary verb *kath-ta* 'seem':

(6) a. [John-i o-l   li-ka]   eps-ta/*iss-ta/*kath-ta
       John-i come-MOD BN-NOM not.exist-DECL/exist-DECL/seem-DECL
       'It is unlikely that John will come.'

    b. [John-i   o-l   tus] ha-ta/*eps-ta/*kath-ta
       John-NOM come-MOD BN do-DECL/not.exist/seem-DECL
       'It seems that John will come.'

    c. [John-i   o-l   kes] kath-ta/*issta
       John-NOM come-MOD BN seem-DECL/exist.
       'It seems that John will come.'

Bound nouns have an additional restriction on the occurrence with case markers, which may be related to the function of the dependent clause:

(7) a. Either NOM or ACC can be attached to the BN: tey ('place'), pa ('way'), ccohk ('side'), etc

    b. Only NOM: nawi ('degree'), li ('reason'), swu ('possibility'), ci ('whether'), etc

    c. Only ACC: tung ('so forth'), yang ('pretense'), cwul ('way'), chey ('pretense'), etc

    d. Only DEL: tus ('seem'), man ('possible'), sang ('seem'), kes ('possible'), etc

The fact that the BNs in (7b) can occur only with NOM and those in (7c) only with ACC can be expected when considering the possible predicate they can be followed. Though all the BNs can occur with a delimiter, those in (7d) allow no case markers at all:

(8) a. pi-ka   o-nun   tus-*ul/*i   ha-ta
       rain-NOM come-PNE BN-ACC/NOM do-DECL
       'It seems to rain.'

    b. John-i   o-l   *kes-i   kath-ta
       John-NOM come-MOD BN-*NOM seem-DECL/exist.
       'It seems that John will come.'

As observed here and in the literature, BNs display complex combinatory possibilities with their complements, case/delimiter markers, and predicates following them. In addition to the constructional properties that each BNC shares, each BN also has its own idiosyncratic lexical properties. This implies that to process these BN constructions with intriguing properties, we need to develop an explicit syntactic and semantic analysis.

2. Syntax and Semantics of the Bound Noun Construction

2.1. Two Different Types

Based on the observations we have seen earlier, one could argue that a BN forms a morphological unit with the following predicate or undergoes a lexical process. However, this fails empirically in several respects: the BN's occurrence with a case or delimiter marker evidences both its syntactic and phonological independence from the following predicate:

(9) a. sensayngnim-i o-si-l   swu-(ka/cocha/man) eps-ta
       teacher-NOM   come-HON-PNE BN-NOM/even/only   not exist
       'It is not possible that the teacher comes.'

    b. sensayngnim-i o-si-l   kes-(to/man) kathta
       teacher-NOM   come-HON-PNE KES-also/only seem
       'It seems that the teacher also will come.'

If one takes the BN with the following predicate as an inseparable lexical unit (e.g., *swu-iss-ta*), we would ignore the traditional wisdom of wordhood and not account for such productive processes.

One basic syntactic property in the BNC is that the BN forms a tight syntactic unit with its complement: no element can intervene between the two:

(10) a. [wuli-ka kwanye   ha-l]   (*cincca) pa-ka   ani-ta
       we-NOM intervention do-MOD really   BN-NOM not-DECL
       'This is not the case where we can intervene.'

    b. [wuli-nun ku-ka   ka-l]   (*cal) cwul-un moll-ass-ta
       we-TOP   he-NOM go-MOD   BN-TOP not.know-PAST-DECL
       'We didn't know that we would leave.'

Further note that there are at least two different types of the BNC. In the *kes* BNC, for example, there is strong syntactic cohesion between the BN and the following predicate. However, such a strong syntactic unity is not found in the *cwul* BNC:

(11) a. pi-ka   o-l   kes (*cengmal) kah-ta
       rain-NOM come-PNE BN really   seem-DECL
       'It seems that it will rain.'

    b. wuli-nun ku-ka   ka-l   cwul-ul/un   (cengmal) moll-ass-ta
       we-TOP   he-NOM go-MOD BN-ACC/TOP really   not.know-PAST-DECL
       'We really didn't know that we would leave.'

These two types are also different with respect to the projection of a full NP. That is, when BNs combine with its complement (dependent clause or determiner), not all can function as a full NP. Observe the following coordination data:

(12) a. *[[sensayngnim-i ka-l   swu] kuliko
        teacher-NOM   go-PNE BN   and

        [haksayngtul-i o-l   swu]] iss-ta
        student-NOM   come-PNE BN   exist
        'The teacher can go and students can come.'

    b. [[sensayngnim-i ka-ko] [hasayngtul-i o-l]   swu] issta
       teacher-NOM   go-or student   come-PNE BN exist

As noted in (12a), the *swu* BNC cannot be coordinated with another BNC. This implies that this type of BNC cannot project a full NP even with its sentential complement. This can be further evidenced by the fact that the BNC cannot be used as an NP fragment, either:

(13) a.*[sensayngnim-i ka-l swu] '(lit.) the possibility that the teacher goes'

    b. [sensangnim-i ka-l hakkyo] 'the school where the teacher will go'

Unlike this, there are examples where the BN with its sentential complement behaves like a constituent:[2]

(14) a. [[aitul-un   ca-nun   chek], [eleu-un cwuk-un chek]] hayessta
        children-TOP sleep-PNE BN   adult   die-PNE pne   did
        'Children pretended to be sleeping whereas adults pretended to be dead.'

    b. [[aitul-un   ka-nun   cwul], [elun-un o-nun   cwul]] alassta
       children-TOP go-sleep-PNE BN   adult-TOP come-PNE BN   know
       '(We) thought that children go while adults come.'

____

[2]Google search provides even a few examples where the BN *swu* projects an independent NP with its sentential complement. However, such examples are hardly found in canonical usages.

These syntactic differences imply that we need both (9a) and (9b) for possible syntactic structures for the Korean BNCs:

(15)   Head-Complement Structure

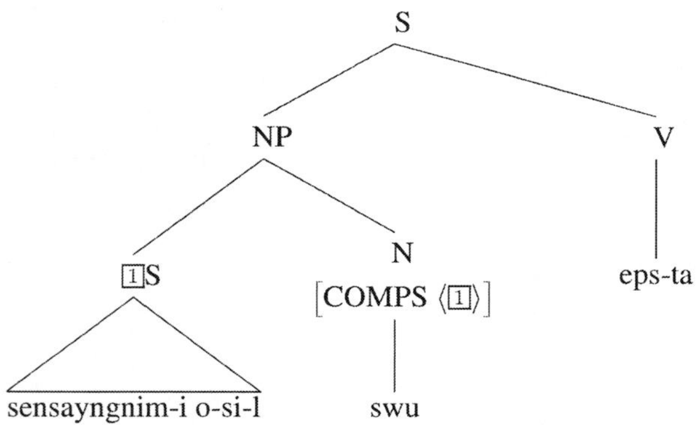

(16)   Complex Predicate Structure:

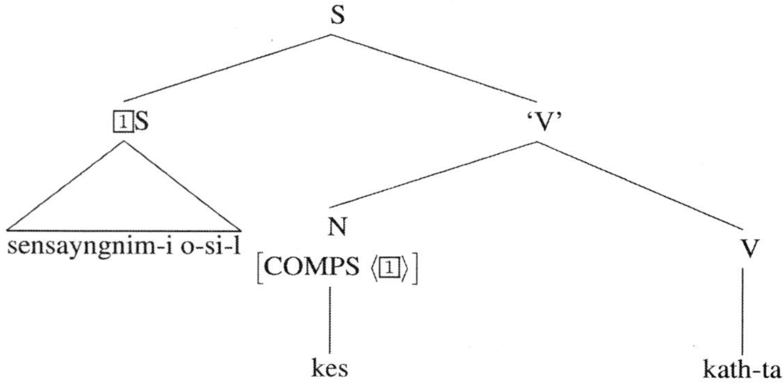

The structure in (15) assumes that the matrix predicate *eps-ta* 'not.exist' selects one argument projected from the BN *swu*. This approach takes the BN, combined with its sentential complement, projects an independent NP. Meanwhile, the structure in (16) assumes that the matrix predicate *kath-* first combines with the BN *kes*, forming a complex-predicate like unit.

2.2.   Head-Complement Type BNC

The structure in (15) is a canonical head-complement phrase licensed by the Head-Complement Rule in (17b). This rule, along with the other grammar rules given here, licenses well-formed phrasal combinations in the language:

(17)   a. Head-Subject Rule:
           XP[*hd-subj-ph*] → ①, **H**$\left[\text{SUBJ } \langle ① \rangle\right]$

       b. Head-Complement Rule:
           XP[*hd-comp-ph*] → ①, **H**$\left[\text{COMPS } \langle ..., ①, ... \rangle\right]$

       c. Head-Modifier Rule:
           XP[*hd-mod-ph*] → $\left[\text{MOD } \langle ① \rangle\right]$, ①**H**

The Head-Subject Rule, generating a *hd-subj-ph*, allows a VP to combine with its subject. The Head-Complement Rule ensures a head to combine with one of its COMPS elements, forming a *hd-comp-ph*. The Head-Modifier Rule allows a head to form a well-formed phrase with an adverbial element that modifies the head, resulting in *hd-mod-ph*.[3]

We also posit the following lexical information for the BN *swu* 'possibility' and *eps-ta* 'not.exist':

(18)

a.
$$\begin{bmatrix} \textit{bn-nonlex} \\ \text{HEAD}\begin{bmatrix} \text{POS } \textit{noun} \\ \text{NFORM } \textit{swu} \end{bmatrix} \\ \text{ARG-ST}\left\langle \text{S}\begin{bmatrix} \text{MOD } \langle\text{N}\rangle \\ \text{IND } s0 \end{bmatrix} \right\rangle \\ \text{SEM}\begin{bmatrix} \text{IND } i \\ \text{RELS}\left\langle \begin{bmatrix} \text{PRED } \textit{possibility} \\ \text{ARG0 } s0 \end{bmatrix} \right\rangle \end{bmatrix} \end{bmatrix}$$

b.
$$\begin{bmatrix} \textit{int-v-bn} \\ \langle\text{eps-}\rangle \\ \text{HEAD}\,|\,\text{POS } \textit{verb} \\ \text{ARG-ST}\left\langle \text{NP}\begin{bmatrix} \text{IND } i \\ \text{FORM } \textit{swu} \end{bmatrix} \right\rangle \\ \text{SEM}\begin{bmatrix} \text{RELS}\left\langle \begin{bmatrix} \text{PRED } \textit{not.exist} \\ \text{ARG0 } i \end{bmatrix} \right\rangle \end{bmatrix} \end{bmatrix}$$

As the lexical information tells us, *swu* is a bound noun selecting a dependent sentence denoting a situation 's0' which functions as its semantic argument. Meanwhile *eps-ta* selects an NP whose FORM value is *swu*.

Together with the grammar system, these lexical entries will project the following structure for a sentence like (9a):

(19)

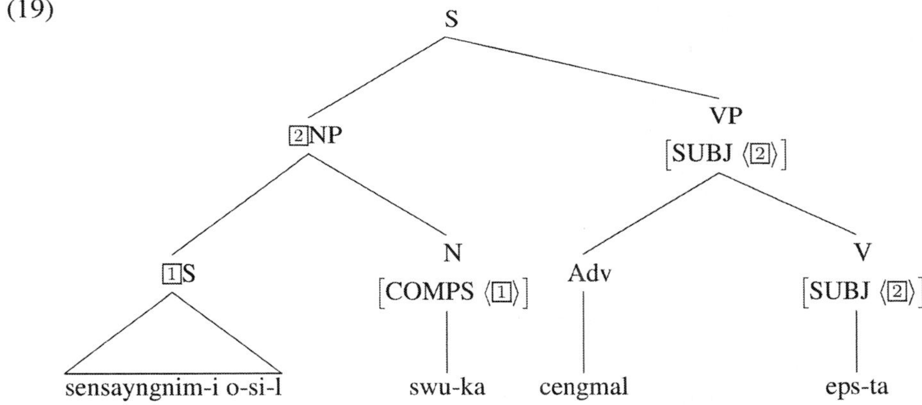

The verb *eps-ta* selects one argument realized as the SUBJ in syntax. In the structure, this verb first combines with the adverb, forming a *hd-mod-ph*. Meanwhile, the BN *swu* combines with its sole complement, the dependent clause marked with a prenominal ending. The resulting NP then will serve as the subject of the verb *eps-ta*. The structure thus involves a canonical head-modifier, head-complement, and head-subject phrase, respectively.

2.3. Complex-Predicate Type BNC

Notice that the language, unlike English, also employs a grammar rule forming a complex predicate like the auxiliary verb construction (AVC). As noted in the literature (cf. Kim (2004)), in the AVC, the main verb and the following auxiliary show a tight syntactic cohesion and form a complex predicate:

---

[3]Note that the grammar rules here place no restriction on the SUBJ value: this allows the head to combine with the subject before combining with a complement. One great advantage of this is to allow sentential internal scrambling with no further operation or mechanism. See Kim (2004), Kim and Yang (2004) for details.

(20) John-i   sakwa-ka/lul   mek-ko   (*cengmal) siph-ess-ta
     John-NOM apple-NOM/ACC eat-COMP really   would.like
     'John would really like to eat apples.'

As argued and shown by Kim and Yang (2004), one effective way of capturing such complex predicate-like properties of the AVC is to introduce the Head-Lexical Rule given in (21):

(21) Head-Lexical Rule:

$$\begin{bmatrix} \textit{hd-lex-ex} \\ \text{COMPS } \boxed{A} \end{bmatrix} \longrightarrow \boxed{1}\begin{bmatrix} \text{LEX} + \\ \text{COMPS } \boxed{A} \end{bmatrix}, \text{H} \begin{bmatrix} \text{AUX} + \\ \text{COMPS } \langle \boxed{1} \rangle \end{bmatrix}$$

The rule specifies that the auxiliary head combines with a lexical (LEX) complement ($\boxed{1}$), and that to the resulting combination the COMPS value ($\boxed{A}$) of this lexical complement is composed.[4] This system, interacting with appropriate lexical entries for auxiliary verbs, will allow the auxiliary verb to combine with the preceding main verb, forming a complex predicate.

We also take BNs like *kes, tus, man* to form a complex predicate with the following predicate. These BNs also display a tight syntactic unit with the following predicates: no elements can intervene between the two.

(22) a. *sensayngnim-i o-si-l   kes cengmal kathta
        teacher-NOM   come-HON-MOD BN really   seem
        'It seems that the teacher will really come.'

     b. *sensayngnim-i o-si-l   tus cengmal hata
        teacher-NOM   come-HON-MOD BN really   do
        'It seems that the teacher will really come.'

The complex predicate analysis can also reflect the mono clausal property with respect to NPI.

(23) a. *John-un [amuwto ossta-ko]   mit-ci   anh-ass-ta
        John-TOP anybody came-COMP] believe-COMP neg-PAST-DECL
        'John didn't believe anybody came'

     b. amwuto o-n   kes kath-ci   anh-ta
        anybody come-MOD BN seem-COMP NEG-DECL
        'It seems that no one has come.'

Given that the expression *kes kath-ci ahn-ta* forms a complex predicate, we could expect the NPI *amwuto* in the same clause.

Just like the Head-Complement type of BNs, the complex-predicate BNs also select a dependent sentence realized as the complement:

(24)
$$\begin{bmatrix} \textit{bn-lex} \\ \langle \text{kes} \rangle \\ \text{HEAD} \begin{bmatrix} \text{POS } \textit{noun} \\ \text{NFORM } \textit{kes} \end{bmatrix} \\ \text{LEX} + \\ \text{ARG-ST} \left\langle \text{S} \begin{bmatrix} \text{MOD } \langle \text{N} \rangle \\ \text{SEM } \boxed{2} \end{bmatrix} \right\rangle \\ \text{SEM } \boxed{2} \end{bmatrix}$$

---

[4]This kind of argument composition is different from the previous analyses, mainly in that the composition happens in syntax rather than in the lexicon.

Notice that there is one difference from BNs like *swu*. That is, complex-predicate BNs are marked as carrying the feature LEX to reflect that it will form a *head-lex-ph*. In addition, its semantics is identified with the complement, reflecting the fact that it behaves like a sentential complementizer, even though it is categorically a noun.

But how about the predicate *kath-ta* 'seem'? Does this select only one argument? Unlike nominal elements, all verbal elements have a subject. What is the subject of this verb? Can it be identical with the subject of the dependent clause? The subject of the dependent clause cannot be identified with that of *kath-ta*. Observe the following between the AVC and the BNC:

(25) a. sensayng-nim-i   o-si-ko   siph-(usi)-ta
          teacher-HON-NOM come-HON-COMP would.like-HON-DECL
          'The teacher would like to come.'

      b. sensayng-nim-i   o-si-l   kes kath-(*usi)-ta
          teacher-HON-NOM come-HON-PNE BN seem-HON-DECL
          'The teacher would like to come.'

If the subject of *kath-* 'seem' is *sensayngnim* 'teacher-HON-NOM, there is no reason why we cannot have the form *kath-usi-ta* as in *siph-usi-ta*. This appears that the BNC does not have any overt subject, but a covert subject not realized in syntax. As a way of reflecting this idea, we posit the following lexical entry for *kath-ta* 'seem':

$$
(26) \quad \begin{bmatrix} \textit{aux-v-bn} \\ \langle \text{kath-} \rangle \\ \text{HEAD} \begin{bmatrix} \text{POS } \textit{verb} \\ \text{AUX } + \end{bmatrix} \\ \text{ARG-ST} \left\langle \text{NP}[\textit{pro}], \begin{bmatrix} \text{IND } \boxed{3} \\ \text{NFORM } \textit{kes} \end{bmatrix} \right\rangle \\ \text{SEM} \begin{bmatrix} \text{RELS} \left\langle \begin{bmatrix} \text{PRED } \textit{seem} \\ \text{ARG0 } \boxed{3} \end{bmatrix} \right\rangle \end{bmatrix} \end{bmatrix}
$$

This lexical entry specifies that the auxiliary verb *kath-ta* selects two arguments: the first one is realized as the *pro* subject whereas the second one is realized as the COMPS whose NFORM value is *kes*.

Given these, we will then have a more elaborated structure like the following for a complex-predicate BNC given in (9):

(27)

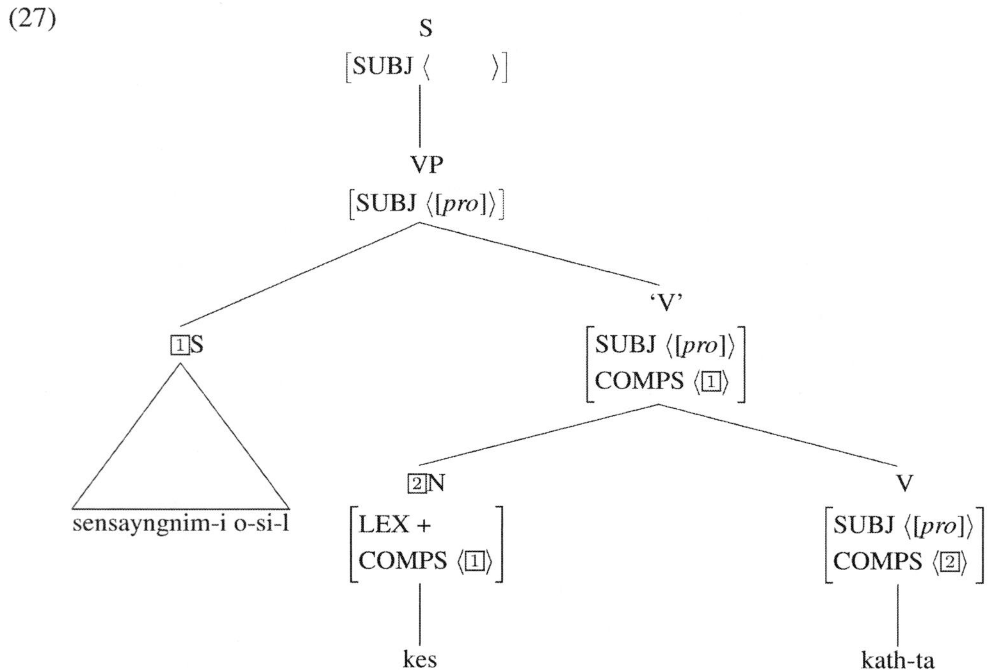

The auxiliary-like verb *kath-ta* takes two arguments. The first argument is the *pro* subject whereas the second argument is the BN *kes*. The verb, combining with this BN complement, forms the complex predicate that inherits the BN's COMPS value. This complex predicate then in turn combines with the dependent sentence, forming a VP with the *pro* subject unsaturated. The language specific rule then allows this VP to project into a complete S.

3.   An Implementation and Concluding Remarks

The analysis we have presented so far has been incorporated into the typed-feature structure grammar HPSG for Korean (Korean Resource Grammar) aiming at working with real-world data. To test the performance and feasibility of the analysis, we have implemented it into the LKB (Linguistic Knowledge Building).[5]

In representing the semantics, we employ Minimal Recursion Semantics (MRS) developed by Copestake et al. (2005). The MRS is a framework for computational semantics designed to enable semantic composition using only the unification of type feature structures (Bender, Flickenger, and Oepen, 2002; Flickinger and Bender, 2003). For example, Figure 1 and Figure 2 are the parsed results for the sentence (9a) and (9b) in our system.

We can see here that the MRS that the grammar generates provides us with enriched semantic information as well. The value of LTOP is the local top handle, the handle of the relation with the widest scope within the sentence. The INDEX value here is identified with the ARG0 value of the *prpstn_m_rel* (propositional message). The attribute RELS is basically a bag of elementary predications (EP) each of whose values is a *relation*.[6] Each of the types *relation* has at least three features LBL, PRED (represented here as a type), and ARG0. For example, we can see that in Fig. 1 the semantic relation *not_exist_rel* selects *possibility* as its ARG1 value. The relation *possibility* also takes the *come_rel* as its argument, inducing the correct semantics. In Fig 2, we can observe

---

[5]The current Korean Resource Grammar has 394 type definitions, 36 grammar rules, 77 inflectional rules, 1,500 lexical entries, and 2100 test-suite sentences, and aims to expand its coverage on real-life data.

[6]The attribute HCONS is to represent quantificational information. The *udef_q_rel* means an undefined quantificational meaning assigned to the unexpressed determiner. See Bender et al. (2002).

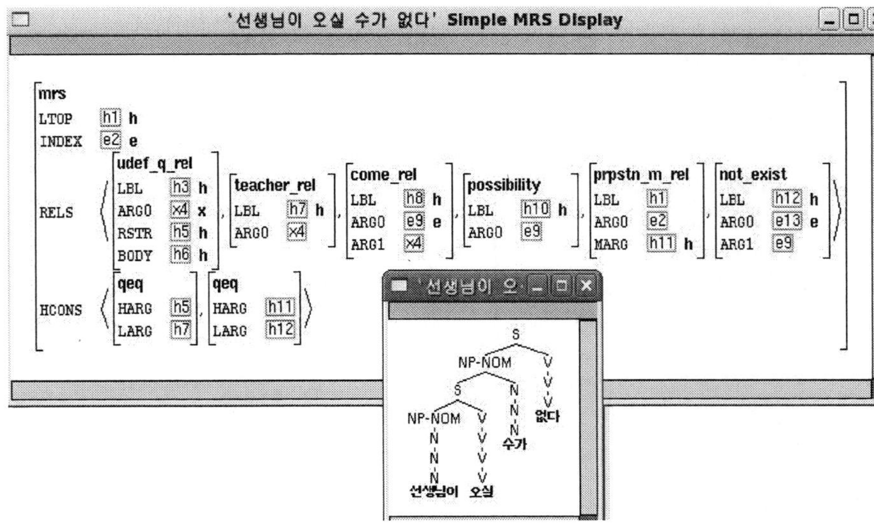

Figure 1: Parsed Tree and MRS for 'There is no possibility that the teacher will come.'

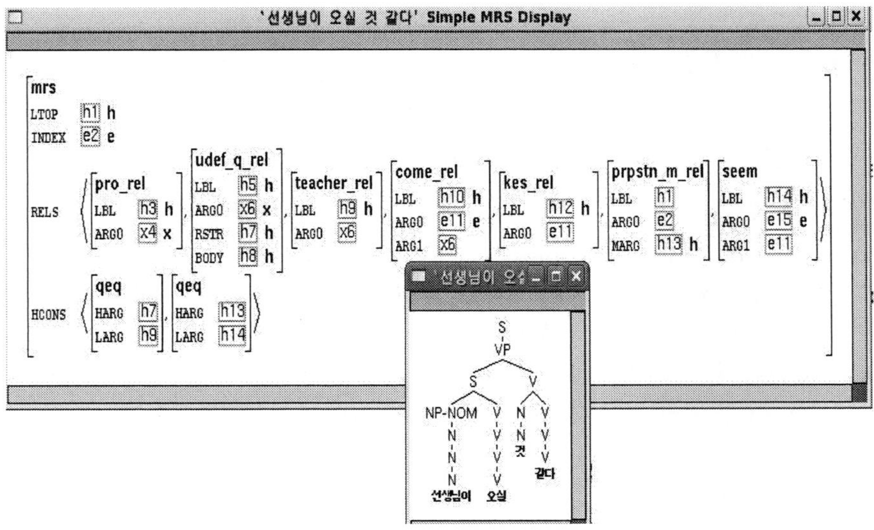

Figure 2: Parsed Tree and MRS for 'It seems that the teacher will come.'

that the ARG1 value of *seem* is 'e9' which is also the ARG0 value of the BN's meaning *kes_rel*. This 'e9' is in fact the event that *come_rel* denotes.

4. Conclusion

The Korean BNC (bound noun construction) display complex syntactic, semantic, and constructional properties. In particular, their combinatorial possibilities with respect to the complement and predicate types call for a much finer-grained syntax. The BNCs can even be classified into two types, depending on the syntactic coherence with the following predicate.

This paper has developed a constraint-based approach that can dissolve such issues. In terms of syntax, we postulated two different syntactic structures: head-complement and complex-predicate structures and then specify articulated lexical properties for the BNs and relevant predicates. This system has been implemented in the LKB system, which gave us robust parsing results for the given sentences.

References

Bender, Emily M., Dan Flickenger, and Stephan Oepen. 2002. The grammar matrix: An open-source starter-kit for the rapid development of cross-linguistically consistent broad-coverage precision grammars. In *Proceedings of the Workshop on Grammar Engineering and Evaluation at the 19th International Conference on computational Linguistics*, pages 8–14, Taiwan. Taipei.

Cha, Jong-Yul. 2001. *Constraints on Clausal Complex Noun Phrases in Korean with Focus on the Gapless Relative Clause Construction*. Ph.D. thesis, UIUC.

Copestake, Ann. 2002. *Implementing Typed Feature Structures*. CSLI Publications, Stanford.

Copestake, Ann, Dan Flickinger, Carl Pollard, and Ivan A. Sag. 2005. Minimal recursion semantics: an introduction. *Research on Language and Computation*, 3(4):281–332.

Flickinger, Dan and Emily M. Bender. 2003. Compositional semantics in a multilingual grammar resource. In *Proceedings of the ESSLLI 2003 Workshop "Ideas and Strategies for Multilingual Grammar Development"*, Vienna, Austria.

Kim, Jong-Bok. 2004. *Korean Phrase Structure Grammar*. Hankook Publishing. In Korean.

Kim, Jong-Bok and Jaehyung Yang. 2004. Projections from morphology to syntax in the korean resource grammar: Implementing typed feature structures. Lecture Notes in Computer Science, Vol.2945, pp.13–24, Springer-Verlag, 2004.2.

Weak Connectivity in (Un)bounded Dependency Constructions[*]

Yong-Beom Kim

Kwangwoon University, Seoul , Korea

ybkim@kw.ac.kr

Abstract. This paper argues that various kinds of displaced structures in English should be licensed by a more explicitly formulated type of rule schema in order to deal with what is called weak connectivity in English. This paper claims that the filler and the gap site cannot maintain the total identity of features but a partial overlap since the two positions need to obey the structural forces that come from occupying respective positions. One such case is the missing object construction where the subject fillers and the object gaps are to observe requirements that are imposed on the respective positions. Others include passive constructions and topicalized structures. In this paper, it is argued that the feature discrepancy comes from the different syntactic positions in which the fillers are assumed to be located before and after displacement. In order to capture this type of mismatch, syntactically relevant features are handled separately from the semantically motivated features in order to deal with the syntactically imposed requirements.

Keywords: Weak connectivity, feature mismatch, missing object construction, passives, topicalized construction, filler, gap, unbounded dependency.

1. Introduction

This paper attempts to deal with filler-gap mismatches found in what Pollard and Sag (1994) calls the weak unbounded dependency construction. One of the key issues in the construction is that there is a feature or category mismatch between the filler and gap, as shown in (1).

(1) a. That John will help us is hard for us to rely on ____.
     b. That Chomsky might be wrong is hard to think of ______.

Prepositions like *on* or *of* would normally be subcategorized to take a nominal complement, but in (1) the filler site for the corresponding gap is occupied by a *that* clause, which would pose a puzzle to a constraint-based analysis as well as to a minimalist approach. This kind of mismatch is not peculiar to the missing object construction (MOC, hereafter). The same kind of mismatch can also be found in a topicalized construction as shown in (2).

(2) a. That some passives lack active counterparts, no theory can capture _____.
     b. *No theory can capture that some passives lack active counterparts.
     c. That some passives lack active counterparts, few teachers were aware of ___.

The verb *capture* does not take as its complement a *that* clause in an ordinary construction as shown in (2b), but in a topicalized construction like (2a), a *that* clause can initiate the construction with the same verb governing the gap site.

This kind of weak connectivity is not restricted to the above two constructions. It can be found in passives as well.

(3) a. That some passives lack active counterparts can be captured by no theory.
     b. That Chomsky might be wrong has never been thought of ___.

---

cf. No one has ever thought (*of) that Chomsky might be wrong.
c. That John will help us may not be relied on.

As shown in (3a) and (3b), a *that* clause can appear as the subject in these passives, but their active counterparts cannot take the clause-type constituent as their complement. There is also a less deviant and less pernicious kind of problem, as in the ordinary missing object construction, as shown in (4)

(4)   a. He/*Him is easy to please ___.
       b. They/*Them will take only five minutes to boil ____.

There arises a case clash between the subject and the corresponding gap in (4) but this issue has been more or less elegantly handled in the framework of HPSG. It is taken care of by requiring not the total identity but a partial identity of feature specifications. However, as we will see in section 2.1, such an account is not still satisfactory.

This paper will argue that the filler-gap relations in these constructions can in general be semantically accounted for, since the categorical mismatch is sometimes inevitable in syntax and should be allowed so far as other components of grammar require such mismatch.

2. Proposals

In this section we will claim that the filler-gap dependency cannot be a relation of total identity between the two elements but one of partial overlap, considering that the features may differ where other grammatical requirements or other structural forces dictate them to be non-identical. One of the proposals in this line of conception has already been presented in PSG framework (See Hukari and Levine (1991)). We will consider missing object constructions, first.

2.1 Missing Object Constructions (MOCs)

Feature mismatches in MOCs can be plainly seen in the examples in (1) through (4) where the 'displaced' main clause subject should be somehow related to the object position of the embedded clause. This construction is relatively easy to deal with since there is a licensing lexical item and its related lexical rule can mediate the feature mismatch. For instance, Hukari and Levine (1991) formulated a rule that ignores [CASE] feature in this construction, and Levine and Hukari (2006, p 355) also suggested a rule as shown in (5)

(5) partial representation of SYNSEM value for *tough* lexical rule

$$
\left[\text{LOCAL} \mid \text{CAT} \quad \left[\begin{array}{ll} \text{HEAD} & \textit{adjective} \\ \text{SUBJ} & <[1]_i >, \\ \text{COMPS} & < ..., \text{VP} \left[\begin{array}{l} \text{INHER|SLASH} \ \{[1]\text{NP}_i \} \\ \text{TO-BIND|SLASH} \ \{[1]_i \} \end{array} \right] > \end{array} \right] \right]
$$

This rule may take care of case clashes between the filler and the gap, since its identity requirement is limited to INDEX value. However, this rule wrongly demands that the filler and the gap should be simultaneously an NP. So the syntactic category mismatch shown in (1a) and (1b) is not taken care of by Levine and Hukari.

This is because the feature specification in the *tough* lexical rule explicitly mentions NP as the SLASH value. To correct this problem, we may loosen the lexical rule to such a degree that the filler and the gap may be minimally different from each other, and thus the SLASH value could be simply a phrase (i.e., XP) instead of an NP. The possible revised lexical rule would contain (6) as the VP specification as the value of COMPS.

(6) VP $\begin{bmatrix} \text{INHER|SLASH } \{ [1]_i \} \\ \text{TO-BIND|SLASH } \{[1]_i \} \end{bmatrix}$

With this revision, we could displace any type of category from the complement position in the MOC, and the sentences like (1a) and (1b) may be licensed by the grammar regardless of whether the preposition licensing the gap in the infinitival phrase can take S as its complement or not[1].

2.2 Passives

The types of passive sentences shown in (3) are not accounted for within the current constraint−based phrase structure grammar. The problems with these examples are twofold: one involves a reanalysis assumption; the other relates to category mismatch as in MOCs. These examples show that passives are not simply a process of demoting and promoting some arguments. If the passive sentences like (3b) and (3c) are to be generated, there should be a process that concatenates *relied* and *on*, in addition to the ordinary passive lexical rule since *rely on* or *think of* cannot be an input the Passive Lexical Rule (PLR) of Sag and Wasow (1999, p235) as it is. Even though the *verb-preposition* sequence can somehow be fed into the Passive Lexical Rule, the least oblique complement cannot be S-bar or S, since it would be governed by a preposition, not by the verb in question, in the active counterpart.

Furthermore, the PRL demotes the first element of ARG-STR value and promotes the least oblique argument in the remainder so that the category next to the main verb becomes the subject in ordinary cases. But this general rule would license the following ill-formed cases shown in (7a), (7b) and (7c). Furthermore, the well-formed ones in (7a'), (7b'), and (7c') are not generated by the PLR.

(7) a. *That John is a liar is not thought.
    a'. It is not thought that John is a liar
    b. *That John is a liar is said.
    b'. It is said that John is a liar.
    c. ?*That John is a liar has never been thought
    c'. That John is a liar has never been thought of.

I assume there is a slight difference in what are presupposed by (7a') and (7c'): (7a') does not carry as much factive presupposition as (7c') does. In order to take care of this situation, some parochial passive rules need to be posited. What is clear is that the Sag and Wasow's (1999) PLR cannot deal with the examples shown above and that it has to be flanked with subsidiary rules. One instance of such rules that can deal with (7c') would look like the one proposed in (8) and this would take care of the two problems: need for reanalysis and categorical mismatch.

In fact, the rule proposed by Sag and Wasow does not take care of the examples in (7a') and (7b'). This cannot be dealt with by a kind of extraposition operation, either, since the (7a) and (7b) are not well-formed sentences. Therefore, the passive forms without prepositions, like *thought* and *said* are to be dealt with separately from the ones with prepositions.

---

[1] This point may be debatable according to the theoretical assumptions within HPSG grammar because this statement is based on a particular theory-internal assumption that SLASH termination at the bottom of the UDC is performed by no special rule but is taken care of by such mechanisms like Argument Realization Principle (Sag and Wasow 1999:402). Then there seems to be no apparatus within this version that can incorporate this generalized category (XP, for instance) into specific rules because a gap is a product of lexicon-internal operation regarding argument structure, but not a rule-to-rule operation. The point is that the lexicon-internal operation cannot deal with generalized categories like XP but full-fledged syntactic categories regarding *part-of-speech* features.

(8) Passive Lexical Rule for some propositional verbs

$$
\left\langle [1],\ \begin{bmatrix} \textit{tv-lxm} \\ \text{AGR-ST} < NP_k,\ \text{PP} \begin{bmatrix} \text{PFORM}\ \alpha \\ \text{P-OBJ}\ NP_i \end{bmatrix} > \end{bmatrix} \right\rangle >\quad \Rightarrow
$$

$$
\left\langle F_{PSP}([1]),\ \begin{bmatrix} \textit{Word} \\ \text{SUB}\ < [\quad]_i > \\ \text{SYN}\ [\text{HEAD}\ [\text{FORM}\ \text{pass}]\,] \\ \text{AGR-ST} < P[\text{PFORM}\ \alpha],\ \text{PP} \begin{bmatrix} \text{PFORM}\ by \\ \text{P-OBJ}\ NP_k \end{bmatrix} \end{bmatrix} \right\rangle >
$$

The rule in (8), first, takes a verb-preposition sequence and changes it to a passive form and concatenates the preposition to the passive form. Second, the prepositional object is promoted to a subject position but the promoted one only carries an index identical to INDEX value of the original object.

So, the passive subject need not match all the feature specifications of the (original) prepositional object. I assume, as Sag and Wasow do, verbal categories (or S) can carry exactly the same type of INDEX specifications as nouns, especially if the nouns are propositional nouns like *fact, proposal, assumption, conception*, etc.

Without this kind of rule, it would be impossible to generate appropriate structures for the above passive tokens[2]. This proposal will eventually deal with what has been put aside for the so-called reanalysis of a verb phrase.

2.3 Topicalized Constituents

Topicalized constituents carry some special discourse functions that make the constituents prominent and such discourse properties seem to be shared by MOCs and Passives as well. Investigating into this discourse property in full length would be beyond the scope of this paper, but I will talk briefly about this property, assuming that the topic phrase, passive subject and MOC's subject act as a *link* between the preceding utterance and the following. Consider the following sentence.

(9) A: What happened to John?
    B: He was hit by a truck.
    Cf. A truck hit him.

(10) A; I hate these math problems.
    B: Yeah, those are very difficult to solve.
    Cf. Yeah, it is very difficult to solve those.

(11) A: We should reexamine various kinds of premises before going any further.
    B: Did you know that John is Brazilian?
    A: John is Brazilian, I have never thought of ____.
    Cf. I have never thought that John is a Brazilian.

What is common among these constructions is that the constituents in question are discourse oriented and, thus, their grammatical functions are somewhat 'diluted' in the sense that the

---

[2] There is a possibility of over-generation of ill-formed structures with this revision and a possible solution to this problem will be mentioned at the end of section 2.3.

phrases in question are not adjacent to their lexical governor. In some cases, the meanings are not identical. For example, the third utterance in (11) is not identical to the compared pair in meaning and it may be the more appropriate form of utterance than the other in this context.

So the category mismatch is somewhat related to non-adjacency to the lexical governor and this is common to many discourse-oriented constructions. So the solution to the mismatch should reflect this property. So the requirement imposed on this construction will be whether it is interpretable on a discourse level as well as on a semantic level. In the same way as we dealted with passives, the rule schema for the topicalized construction should be loosened as shown in (12):

(12) Head-Filler Rule (Revised)

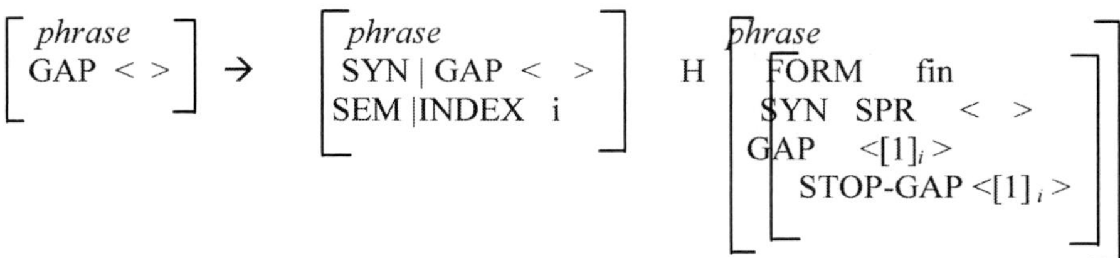

$$\begin{bmatrix} phrase \\ \text{GAP} < > \end{bmatrix} \rightarrow \begin{bmatrix} phrase \\ \text{SYN} \mid \text{GAP} < > \\ \text{SEM} \mid \text{INDEX} \ i \end{bmatrix} \quad \text{H} \begin{bmatrix} phrase \\ \text{FORM} \quad \text{fin} \\ \text{SYN} \quad \text{SPR} \ < > \\ \text{GAP} \quad <[1]_i> \\ \text{STOP-GAP} <[1]_i> \end{bmatrix}$$

What this rule does is to allow the mismatch between the filler and gap as long as they share a certain semantic property, that is, the same index. On a discourse level, some propositions can be referred to by nouns like *the fact, the proposal, the assumption*, and so on. This type of anaphoric reference may be reflected partially in the rule in (12). This formulation of head-filler rule may over-generate some ill-formed sentences like the ones in (13a) and (13c).

(13) a. *That John is Canadian, we put the book on [NP e].
    b. #We put the book on the fact that John is Canadian.
    c. *The table, we put the book [PP e].

In this paper, the solution to this over-generation will be sought based on the (im)possibility of a kind of reference or processing. In (13a), the awkwardness comes from semantic mismatch since the location role imposed by semantics of the verb *put* cannot be satisfied by the noun *fact*. This is why (13b) is also ill-formed. In other word, (13a) is not acceptable for the same reason that (13b) is unacceptable. As for (13c), we would say that there is no known (co-)reference relation between NP and PP, unlike the case of NP and S-bar[3]. Let us compare (13c) with (14):

(14) a. [That John is Canadian]$_i$, we have never thought of [NP e]$_i$.
    b. We have never thought of [the fact]$_i$ [that John is Canadian]$_i$.

The kind of relation that is frequently found between NP and S-bar within or across sentences as shown in (14) cannot be found between NP and PP. We think this is why (13c) is unacceptable.

The loosened head-filler rule in (12), however, may over-generate the ill-formed ones in (15b) and (15c):

(15) a. Him, I very much doubt anyone likes _____.
    b. *Him, I very much doubt nayone likes _____.
    c. *He, I very much doubt anyone likes _____.
    d. He, I very much doubt _____ likes anyone.
    (Levine and Hukari, 2006: 23)

---

[3] The same type of over-generation is expected with passives and MOCs, but we can provide the same kind of solution that is derivable from the filler-gap construction, as we can see regarding the examples in (13).

Since the freer head –filler rule places no restriction on the possibility of diversity in features between filler and the gap, it in fact does generate all the sentences in (15) and it should be restricted or tightened. The dilemma is that we need a rule tighter than the one in (12) while we don't want a rule that is as tight as shown in (16):

$$(16) \quad \begin{bmatrix} phrase \\ \text{GAP} < > \end{bmatrix} \rightarrow [1] \begin{bmatrix} phrase \\ \text{GAP} < > \end{bmatrix} \quad \text{H} \quad \begin{bmatrix} phrase \\ \text{FORM} \quad fin \\ \text{SYN} \quad \text{SPR} \quad < > \\ \text{GAP} \quad <[1]> \\ \quad \text{STOP-GAP} <[1]> \end{bmatrix}$$

A solution to this dilemma may be found by revising the rule in (12) so that the CASE feature should be relevant in this rule. Of course, only nominal (and pronominal) categories will always bear the CASE feature and clauses will never carry any CASE feature. Therefore, we will need a non-defeasible constraint like (17):

(17) (1) No clause-type categories carry the CASE feature.
     (2) Every (pro)nominal categories carry the CASE feature.

Given the above constraints which are needed independently, we can devise a separate schema as shown in (18):

(18) Head-Filler Rule (proposed)[4]

$$\begin{bmatrix} clause \\ \text{GAP} < > \end{bmatrix} \rightarrow \begin{bmatrix} phrase \\ \text{GAP} < > \\ \text{CASE} [2][\beta]/\text{NIL} \\ \text{SEM} | \text{INDEX} \quad i \end{bmatrix} \quad \text{H} \quad \begin{bmatrix} phrase \\ \text{FORM} \quad fin \\ \text{SPR} \quad < > \\ \text{GAP} <[1][\text{CASE} [2]]> \\ \quad \text{STOP-GAP} <[1]> \\ \text{SEM}|\text{INDEX} \quad i \end{bmatrix}$$

By introducing the feature CASE and allowing its value to alternate between a certain value and NIL, the proposed Head-Filler Rule can achieve the effect of collapsing two different rules in conjunction with the constraint stated in (17). One rule will conatain the CASE feature in the filler position and it will generate a clause in which (pro)nominal phrases are extracted; and the other will not carry the CASE feature and it will allow for cases where clauses or non-nominal phrases are displaced.

3. Conclusions

This paper has proposed that categorical mismatch can be accounted for by revising the filler-gap rule or setting up some parochial rules within an HPSG framework. There seem to be a lot of cases that require a detailed refinement or re-examination in the grammar. We also need to tighten up the semantic and pragmatic portion of grammar in order to prevent (over)generation of ill-formed sentences. Especially, more research is also need in the discourse functions of these constructions, which seems to call for a larger paper.

References

Ginzburg, J. and I. A. .Sag 2001. *Interrogative Investigations*. Stanford: Center for the Language and Information.

---

[4] The slash notation in this rule renders one of the the values around it present in the structure.

Hukari, T. and Levine, R. D. 1987. Rethinking Connectivity in Unbounded Dependency Constructions. In Megan Crowhurst ed. *Proceedings of the Sixth West Coast Confernece on Formal Linguistics*, Stanford: Stanford Linguistics Association.

Hukari, T. and Levine, R. D. 1991. On the Disunity of Unbounded Dependency constructions, *Natural Language and Linguistic Theory* 9:97-144.

Jacobson, P. 1984. Connectivity in Phrase Structure Grammar, *Natural Language and Linguistic Theory* 1: 535-581

Levine, R. D. and T. Hukari. 2006. *The Unity of Unbounded Dependency Constructions*, CSLI Lecture Notes #126, Stanford, California: CLSI Publications.

Pollard, C. and I. A. Sag. 1994. *Head-Driven Phrase Structure Grammar*, Center for the Study of Language and Information, Stanford. California: University of Chicago Press.

Sag, I. A. and T. Wasow. 1999. *Syntactic Theory, A formal Introduction*, Stanford University: CSLI Publications.

A Transformation-Based Learning Method on Generating Korean Standard Pronunciation[*]

Kim Dong-Sung[a] and Chang-Hwa Roh[a]

[a] Department of Linguistics and Cognitive Science
Hankuk University of Foreign Studies
San89 Wansanri Mohyunmeon Yonginsi, Kyunggido Korea
{dsk202, rayr}@hufs.ac.kr

Abstract. In this paper, we propose a Transformation-Based Learning (TBL) method on generating the Korean standard pronunciation. Previous studies on the phonological processing have been focused on the phonological rule applications and the finite state automata (Johnson 1984; Kaplan and Kay 1994; Koskenniemi 1983; Bird 1995). In case of Korean computational phonology, some former researches have approached the phonological rule based pronunciation generation system (Lee et al. 2005; Lee 1998). This study suggests a corpus-based and data-oriented rule learning method on generating Korean standard pronunciation. In order to substituting rule-based generation with corpus-based one, an aligned corpus between an input and its pronunciation counterpart has been devised. We conducted an experiment on generating the standard pronunciation with the TBL algorithm, based on this aligned corpus.

Keywords: Transformation-Based Learning, Computational Phonology, Data-oriented Processing, Corpus-based Learning, Pronunciation Generation

1. Introduction

This paper presents a Transformation-Based Learning (TBL) method on generating Korean standard pronunciation. Previous studies on the phonological processing have been focused on the computation of the phonological rule application and the representation of the finite state automata (Johnson 1984; Kaplan and Kay 1994; Koskenniemi 1983; Bird 1995). In case of Korean computational phonology, some former researches have approached the pronunciation generation based on the phonological rules (Lee et al. 2005; Lee 1998)[1]. Unlike previous works, this study suggests a standard Korean pronunciation generation method on the basis of corpus-based and data-oriented TBL learning.

The role of the computational phonology is to generate a legitimate output counterpart of the underlying phonological input. Phonological rules are involved in the process of phonological generation. The SPE style operations on the computational phonology have used the rewriting rule ordering or the finite state transducer (Bird 1995; Bird and Ellison 1994; Gildea and Jurafsky 1996; Kaplan and Kay 1994). Those approaches, however, should reduce complicated

---

[*] This paper was supported by the Second Brain Korea 21.

[1] Anyone can visit the website of Lee et al. (2005) and generate standard pronunciation at *http://urimal.cs.pusan.ac.kr*.

orderings because of huge amount of rewriting rules and rule orderings among themselves (Gildea and Jurafsky 1996). Other differently motivated approaches have suggested the data-oriented models, using a pronunciation corpus to derive legitimate outputs (Daelemans, Gillis and Durieux 1994; Johnson 1984).

In this study, we use the learning method of TBL that was proposed by Brill (1995). We design a set of templates and abstract transformations of possible pronunciations. For the experiments, we set up an aligned corpus between the text based on the Korean standard orthography and the text based on the Korean standard pronunciation. We conducted an experiment on generating the standard pronunciation with the TBL algorithm, using this corpus.

We use the phonotactic constraints to reduce the complexity of TBL process. As noticed in Hayes and Wilson (forthcoming), the phonological feature constraints can reduce the complication of phonotactics. We set up a list of constraints on the phonotatics, which is derived from the phonological features.

The rest of the paper is composed of three parts: Section 2 is to introduce the TBL method into the phonological operation. Section 3 describes the experiment on Korean pronunciation. Section 4 deals with the experiment discussions.

2. TBL Application on the Pronunciation Handling

Rule-oriented processing in phonology has been represented with context-sensitive rewrite rules. For example, Korean underlying stops are realized as unreleased voiceless stops in the word final position. The following example shows the rule application on the voiceless stop /t/.

$$(1)\ t \rightarrow t^\neg /\_\#\ ^2$$

The most popular way of formalizing the phonological rule is to induce two-level formalism in Koskenniemi (1984) and Karttunen (1993), or finite state transducer of Kaplan and Kay (1994). The basic intuition on these operations is that a rule rewrites an underlying string as a surface string, which can be implemented as a transducer that reads a lexical input and writes to a surface tape. [Figure 1] shows an example of this operation using the rule in (1).

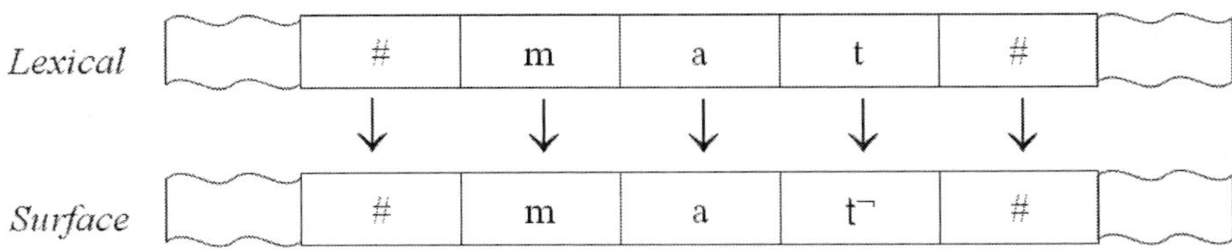

Figure 1: Rule based operation on the phonology

Phonological derivation-based method ought to have the complicated rule ordering systems. A phonological input has the chance of different output realization(s), depending on rule orderings. Computation based on the finite state transducer is so complicated that the processing mechanisms are varied among the researchers. Gildea and Jurafsky (1996) suggest a method to reduce complicated rule ordering.

Another different method is to use the data-oriented approach. Daelemans, Gillis and Durieux (1994) suggest a stochastic method to assign stress, the supra-segmental feature. This approach utilizes stochastic gain of information from a corpus.

TBL is known as learning the most approximate tagging rules from the corpus. TBL is a data-oriented method. It considers every possible transformations of the tagging, using a limited set

---

² For Korean sound and feature system, see Figure 4 and Figure 7 in the next section.

of transformations. The algorithm of TBL needs a small set of templates, abstracted transformations. A phonological input can be transformed into a phonological output. In Korean, the voiceless stop /t/ is varied among [t], [d], and [t], depending environments. Consider the following templates that transform the phonological input.

If the preceding phonological environment is #, then /t/ becomes [t].
If the preceding phonological environment is Vowel, then /t/ becomes [d].
If the following phonological environment is Consonant, then /t/ becomes [t].
If the following phonological environment is #, then /t/ becomes [t˺].

Figure 2: TBL application on the phonological change

TBL method learns the phonological environment, by instantiating the incoming items in the templates. Every possible phonological environment in the template is iteratively tested by filling in every specific phonological input. This method transforms an input into an output, following the list in the template. In some sense, this approach is similar with one in two-level formalism, matching an input and an output. However, TBL needs a learning text (corpus). As Brill (1995) notes, a small amount of training data can resolve a large amount of processing data.

Templates in TBL method have the list of environment which the phonological change must follow. The environment is conceptually the same as a context window in the KeyWord In Context (KWIC). In Figure 3, an example of context window is given.

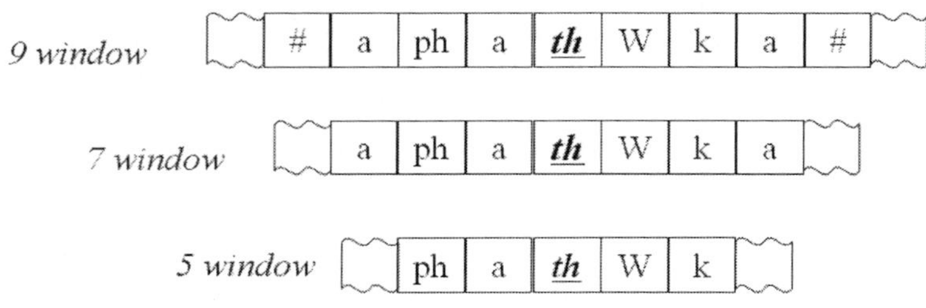

Figure 3: Context Windows in TBL

The phonological features are inter-related with the phonotactic constraints. As Hayes and Wilson (forthcoming) insist, phonological features reduce the phonotactic constraints. Following such idea, we set up constraints on phonotactics, combining the phonological feature systems. This simplifies the search mechanism of TBL processing.

3. Experiments

For the experiment, we set up the corpus which aligns the spoken data from the Sejong corpus and its standard pronunciation. The spoken data has 14,500 ejeols[3] (approximately 60,000 morphemes), which is composed of the transcription in the Korean standard orthography. We converted the data into the standard pronunciation, using Korean standard IPA converter of Lee et al. (2006). For instance, (2a) is converted into (2b) with Korean standard IPA converter.

---

[3] *Ejeol* is the similar with *bunsetsu* in Japanese. *Ejeol* is the terminology for the chunks between spaces in a sentence. For more information, see Sohn (1999).

(2) a. Na-nun cip-e   ka-n-ta.
     I-Top   house-Loc   go-Asp-End[4]
   b. Na-nWn tsi-be   ka-n-da[5]

Following this process, we gathered the aligned corpus as follows.

(3) Na-nun {N.a-n.W.n} cip-e {ts.i-p.e} kan-ta {k.a.n-d.a}

In (3) the convention '-' and '.' split intra syllables and inner syllable structures (onset-rhyme-coda), respectively. The ejeol initial position is marked with '{' and the ejeol final one with '}'. The statistics of the standard pronunciation corpus is that the total phonemes are 106,478 with 7 phonemes per an ejeol and 1.78 phonemes per a morpheme.

For the phonetic purpose, 19 consonants and 10 vowels are used for the Korean pronunciation as follows:

IPA	ARPabet	IPA	ARPabet
p	p	i	i
pʰ	ph	ɛ	E
p*	p*	ɯ	W
t	t	ʌ	A
tʰ	th	u	u
t*	t*	o	o
k	k	a	a
kʰ	kh	ɰ	Y
k*	k*	j	y
s	s	w	w
s*	s*		
tɕ	ts		
tɕʰ	tsh		
tɕ*	ts*		
m	m		
n	n		
ŋ	G		
l	l		
h	H		

Figure 4: ARPabet for Korean pronunciation

Depending on the word positions (either ejeol initial or ejeol final) and syllable positions (onset-rhyme-coda), we gather 600 different phonemic types for the context window. These types are used to induce the template of TBL. The following is an example of TBL template with the very first preceding and the very next following.

> If the preceding phonological environment is #, then /t/ becomes [t].
> If the preceding phonological environment is V, the /t/ becomes [d].
> If the following phonological environment is #, the /t/ becomes [t⁻].

Figure 5: TBL templates

As noted in Figure 3, the phonological environment is similar with a context window. If we enlarge the context window by 4, Figure 5 is changed into Figure 6.

> If the phonological environment with 4 context window is {#,#,_,Vowel$_{Rhyme}$}, then /t/ becomes /t/.
> If the phonological environment with 4 context window is {Vowel$_{Rhyme}$,-,_,Vowel$_{Rhyme}$}, then /t/ becomes /d/.
> ....

Figure 6: Example of 4 context windows TBL

We randomly gathered 1,000 ejeols from the Sejong corpus for the test purpose. Using the aligned corpus, we converted the test material into its pronunciation. We have tested 20, 10, 5, 4, 3, or 2 context windows to see if there is any difference in accuracy. Brill (1995) suggests that TBL also reduce the training size of tagging. We also checked the total training, increasing training size by 1,000 until we reached the total size of the aligned corpora.

Hayes and Wilson (forthcoming) claim that English phonotactics is explainable with 24 different constraints based on phonological features. Phonotactic constraints can reduce the search space of the TBL templates. Because the phonotactic constraint stops to search ill-formed phonotactics in the templates, the wrongly-predicted pronunciation is eradicated.

In Korean, 29 phonemes in Figure 4 have the constraints on the phonotactic placements. The moderate phonological feature set of Korean is as follows.

Table 1: Korean phonological feature system[6]

			p	p*	ph	t	t*	th	k	k*	kh	s	s*	ts	ts*	tsh	m	n	G	l	H
Major Class Features		sonornat	-	-	-	-	-	-	-	-	-	-	-	-	-	-	+	+	+	+	-
		consonant	+	+	+	+	+	+	+	+	+	+	+	+	+	+	+	+	+	+	+
		syllable	-	-	-	-	-	-	-	-	-	-	-	-	-	-	-	-	-	-	-
Consonant Features	Manner Features	continuent	-	-	-	-	-	-	-	-	-	+	+	-	-	-	-	-	-	-	+
		delayed release	-	-	-	-	-	-	-	-	-			+	+	+	-	-	-		
		lateral				-	-	-				-	-	-	-	-		-		+	
	Place Features	coronal	-	-	-	+	+	+	-	-	-	+	+	+	+	+	-	+	-	+	-
		anterior	+	+	+	+	+	+	-	-	-	+	+	-	-	-	+	+	-	+	-
	Subsidiary Features	tense	-	+	+	-	+	+	-	+	+	-	+	-	+	+	-	-	-	-	-
		aspiraion	-	-	+	-	-	+	-	-	+	-	-	-	-	+	-	-	-	-	+

		i	E	W	A	u	o	a	y	w	Y
Major Class Features	sonornat	+	+	+	+	+	+	+	+	+	+
	consonant	-	-	-	-	-	-	-	-	-	-
	syllable	+	+	+	+	+	+	+	-	-	-
Tongue Body	high	+	-	+	-	+	-	-	+	+	+

[6] The feature map is from Shin and Cha (2004).

Features	Features	low	-	-	-	-	-	-	+	-	-	-
		back	-	-	+	+	+	+	+	-	+	+
	Rounded	round	-	-	-	-	+	+	-	-	+	-

What the feature map in Figure 5 specifies is any clusters with consonant and diphthong [yE] cannot be placed next to each other. This cluster is predictable with the phonological feature of *[+cons][-back,-rnd,-syl][+syl]. The constraint restricts under the system in Figure 7. This restriction stops the searching mechanism of TBL since any restricted item is found. We build up the restriction list of 20 constraints.[7]

Generally, the morphological information is pre-requisite for the phonological handling. The phonological change depends on the morphological information; such as irregular verbs, grammatical functions, word classes, etc. Our assumption on the morphological issue is that larger context windows in TBL include more morphological information. We doubted that such information can be replaceable with the size of context window. If the context window is larger, such morphological information is possibly included. We considered two groups of experiments; one with morphological information and the other is without morphological information. We compared the accuracy rate of two groups.

4. Discussion

We use 20, 10, 5, 4, 3, or 2 context windows in the template to see the change in the precision. This test did not contain the morphological information, but only aligned corpus was used.

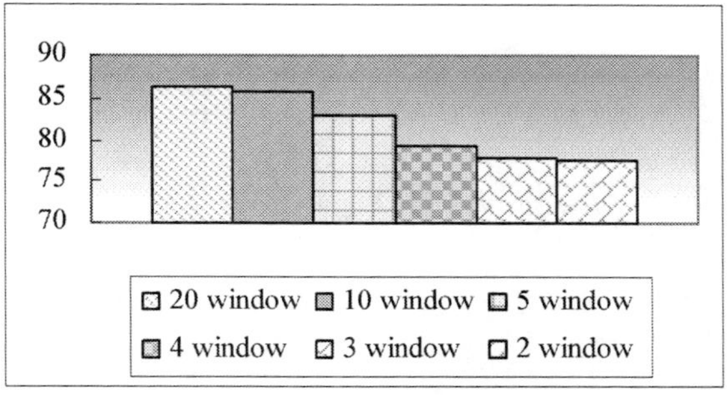

Figure 7: Difference in precision rate without phonological information

The result shows that the context window becomes larger and the precision rate goes up. Consider that an ejeol contains an average of 7 phonemes and each phoneme has an average of 1.78 morpheme(s). 10 and 20 context window contains more than 2 ejeols, which show the better precision rate. This reflects that the morphological information across an ejeol is reflected in the larger windows.

With the morphological information, the precision rate of the experiment is as follows.

---

[7] We used the hand-written constraints. To handle with the phonological feature system, very different computational mechanism is required. Bird (1995) and Bird and Ellison (1994) present a way to compute such features in the logical way. The problem for handling the feature system is to cope with the very complexity of feature systems. Gildea and Jurafsky (1996) use a decision tree to simply handle the feature geometry in phonology, as a way of simplifying the feature systems. We kept it for the future study.

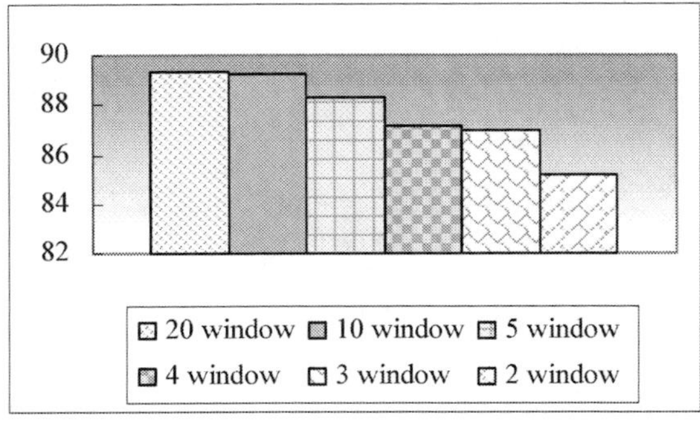

Figure 8: Difference in precision rate with the morphological information

The morphological information provides the phonological process with more information. Thus, there is a rise in the precision rate in case of smaller context windows. Morphological information seems to appropriately contribute on the phonological processing.

In case of phonotactic constraints, there is only 0.2~0.3% rise in the precision rate. The processing time with the phonotactic constraints is shorter than the processing time without it.

Like Brill (1995) experimented on the learning size. We have tested the relationship between the precision rate and the size of the training data. We found out that the precision rate is stable with more than 4,000 training data.

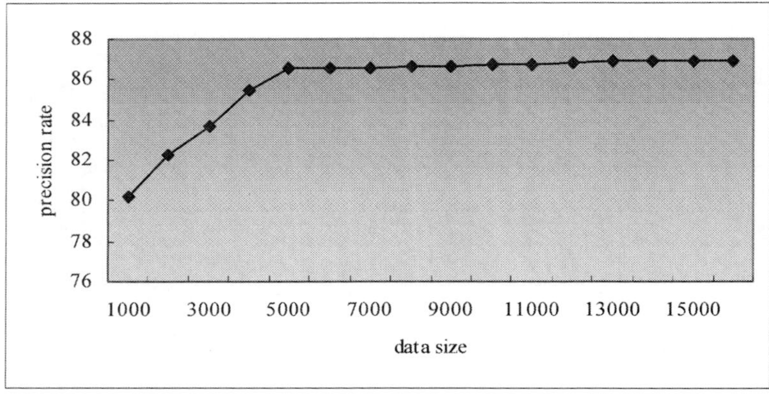

Figure 9: Training data size and precision rate

5. Conclusion

In this paper, we suggest that the TBL method generates the standard Korean pronunciation. We used a corpus and data-oriented transformation method. We found out that the larger context windows in TBL carry more morphological information.

The importance of this study lies in the speech technology. The study of the phonological change is the main topic in the domain of computational phonology. Also, the pronunciation generation is prerequisite to the speech-related technology. In text-to-speech system, the pronunciation generation mechanism provides a system with a better accurate mechanism. Also in speech recognition area, the more advanced pronunciation prediction reveals better recognition results.

The phonological information is related with the morphological encodings; regular vs. irregular, word classes, tagging information of previous word, etc. Such information is essential for the phonological processing. In this study, the concept on context window can cope with morphological information. But this idea needs further exploration.

References

Bird S. 1995. *Computational Phonology*. Cambridge: Cambridge University Press.

Bird S. and T. M. Ellison. 1994. One-level phonology. *Computational Linguistics,* 20(1), 55-90.

Brill E. 1995. Transformation-Based Error-Driven Learning and Natural Language Processing: A Case Study in Part of Speech Tagging. *Computational Linguistics,* 21(4), 543-565.

Daelemans W., S. Gillis and G. Durieux. 1994. The acquisition of stress: A data-oriented approach. *Computational Linguistics*, 20(3), 421-451.

Gildea D. and D. Jurafsky. 1996. Learning bias and phonological-rule induction. *Computational Linguistics,* 22(4), 497-530.

Johnson M. 1984. A discovery procedure for certain phonological rules. *Proceedings of the 10th International Conference on Computational Linguistics and 22nd Annual Meeting of the Association for Computational Linguistics,* pp 344-347.

Hayes B. and Wilson C. forthcoming. A maximum entropy model of phonotactics and phonotactic learning. *Linguistic Inquiry.*

Kaplan R. and M. Kay. 1994. Regular models of phonological rule system. *Computational Linguistics*, 20(3), 331-378.

Karttunen L. 1993. Finite-state constraints. In Goldsmith, ed., *The Last Phonological Rule*, pp 173-194. University of Chicago Press, Chicago.

Karttunen L. 1998. The Proper Treatment of Optimality in Computational Phonology. *Proceedings of the International Workshop on Finite State Methods in Natural Language Processing,* pp 1-12 .

Koskenniemi, K. 1983. *Two-level morphology*. Ph.D. thesis, Department of General Linguistics, University of Helsinki.

Lee G. 1998. Desing and implementation of vocal sound variation rules for Korean Language. *Journal of Korean Informational Society,* 5(3), 851-861.

Lee E. et al. 2005. IPA Converter of Korean Standard Pronunciation. *Proceedings of the Conference of Korean Cognitive Society,* pp 206-211.

Sohn Ho-Min. 1999. *The Korean Language.* Cambridge: Cambridge University Press.

Shin J. and J. Cha. 2005. *Korean Sound System.* Seoul: Hanuk-Munwha-Sa .

Transition and Parsing State and Incrementality in Dynamic Syntax[*]

Masahiro Kobayashi[a] and Kei Yoshimoto[b]

[a]University Education Center, Tottori University, 4-101 Koyama-cho Minami,
Tottori, 680-8550 Japan, kobayashi@uec.tottori-u.ac.jp
and
[b]Center for the Advancement of Higher Education, Tohoku University,
Kawauchi 41, Aobaku, Sendai, 980-8576 Japan, kyoshimoto@mail.tains.tohoku.ac.jp

Abstract.   This paper presents an implementation of a gramar of Dynamic Syntax for Japanese. Dynamic Syntax is a grammar formalism which enables a parser to process a sentence in an incremental fashion, establishing the semantic representation. Currently the application of lexical rules and transition rules in Dynamic Syntax is carried out arbitrarily and this leads to inefficient parsing. This paper provides an algorithm of rule application and partitioned parsing state for efficient parsing with special reference to processing Japanese, which is one of head-final languages. At the present stage the parser is still small but can parse scrambled sentences, relative clause constructions, and embedded clauses. The parser is written in Prolog and this paper shows that the parser can process null arguments in a complex sentence in Japanese.

Keywords: Japanese, Dynamic Syntax, implementation, rule application, null argument

1.   Introduction

Incremental processing of a sentence as it is inputted from left to right has been taken as most accurately simulating human sentence processing. When we attempt theoretically to account for this incrementality of sentence processing, however, we notice that there is a difference between head-initial languages and head-final languages. What we need to take into account is that in head-initial languages, like English, parsers can *look ahead* to syntactic structures to be established to some extent as a word is consumed. By contrast, this is not the case in head-final languages such as Japanese, because in these languages the syntactic positions of NPs remain unfixed until the matrix verb is inputted finally in the sentence. The Dynamic Syntax approach (Kempson, Meyer-Viol, and Gabbay, 2001; Cann, Kempson, and Marten, 2005), which allows the parser to process a sentence in an incremental fashion, has settled this difficulty by adopting structural underspecification. However, Kempson, Meyer-Viol, and Gabbay (2001) and Cann, Kempson, and Marten (2005) do not provide an explicit algorithm for implementation of the framework as formally as Moot (1999) presents *Grail*, the toolkit for a parser of Categorial Grammar Logics. This paper will delineate the basic idea of a parser for Japanese based on the Dynamic Syntax (hereafter, DS) framework, providing the algorithm of the application of lexical rules and transition

---

[*]We would like to thank two anonymous reviewers for valuable comments.
0

rules. This paper will also show that the parser is able to cope with null arguments or empty pronouns in embedded clauses. Currently the parser is implemented in Prolog.

The outline of this paper is as follows: the subsequent section will provide a brief introduction to the DS formalism and address issues of parsing inefficiency and the algorithm of rule application, discussing the previous studies. Section 3 will illustrate the implementation of the DS formalism and our algorithm to process head-final languages like Japanese. Section 4 shows how the parser deals with the complex sentences with empty pronouns. Section 5 will be devoted to the discussion. Section 6 will be a conclusion.

2. Dynamic Syntax and Issues of Implementation

2.1. Formalization and Unfixed Nodes

This subsection presents a brief illustration of the DS formalism. DS is a grammar formalism which allows a parser to process a sentence from the onset word to the final word in an incremental way. The (partial) tree structure grows larger and larger, step by step, by the application of transition rules as well as the word consumption; the initial tree structure T_0 shifts to a subsequent structure T_1, and ultimately to the final tree structure T_n as seen in (1).

(1) $T_0 \Longrightarrow$ rule application $\Longrightarrow T_1 \Longrightarrow \cdots\cdots \Longrightarrow T_{n-1} \Longrightarrow$ rule application $\Longrightarrow T_n$

The tree structure T is a set of nodes in the DS formalism, and the initial tree structure consists of a single node $\{Tn(a), ?Ty(t), \Diamond\}$ (Kempson, Meyer-Viol, and Gabbay, 2001, pp.57) called the root node, where Tn is a predicate which expresses an *address* of a node which includes the variable a indicating that a position of this node has not been specified yet. Moreover, the predicate Tn expresses the relationship between nodes; for instance, $Tn(01)$ is the functor node of $Tn(0)$, $Tn(00)$ is the argument node of $Tn(0)$. $Ty(t)$ is a predicate which expresses the type of the node. The question mark '?' prefixed to $Ty(t)$ is called a *requirement*, which expresses that $Ty(t)$ needs to be satisfied by the end of processing: in this initial state, the goal of processing is to meet the condition that this node is of type t. In this sense, the parsing formalism of DS is called goal-directed. The pointer '$\Diamond$' is used to highlight a node and the lexical rules and transition rules are applied to only pointed nodes.

The lexical items themselves take the form of rules such as **IF** A holds **THEN** execute B **ELSE** execute C. These lexical rules as well as transition rules update the current tree structure to the subsequent structure. We assume the following transition rules in this paper for Japanese; LOCAL *ADJUNCTION, which is used to introduce an unfixed NP for local scrambling to the tree structure; GENERALISED ADJUNCTION for introducing the embedded clause to the tree; *ADJUNCTION for long-distance scrambling; ELIMINATION for the functional application; COMPLETION, used to bring the pointer back to the mother node; THINNING for deleting or satisfying the requirements; LINK ADJUNCTION for introducing the relative clauses to the tree; LINK EVALUATION for building up the semantic representation for relative clause construction; MERGE for the unification of unfixed nodes with the vacuous, fixed nodes.

As we have accounted for, NPs in Japanese need to be kept unfixed until the verb has been consumed when the parser processes a sentence. In (2a) the sentence initial NP is the object of the simple main clause, whereas the first NP of (2b) is the object of the embedded, subordinate clause. However, the parser cannot specify the fixed positions of the initial NP of both (2a) and (2b) when the parser consumes them.

(2) a. Bōru o   John ga   nageta.
         ball ACC John NOM throw-PAST

         "John threw the ball."

b. Bōru o   John ga   nageta   to   Tarō ga   itta.
ball   ACC John NOM throw-PAST COMP Taro NOM say-PAST

"Taro said that John threw the ball."

LOCAL *ADJUNCTION introduces an unfixed node which is immediately dominated by the root node. By contrast, in (2b), first, the unfixed root node of type t for the embedded clause is introduced by GENERALISED ADJUNCTION, then LOCAL *ADJUNCTION introduces an unfixed node which is immediately dominated by the root node of the embedded clause. These unfixed nodes need to find their fixed position by the end of parsing by means of the application of MERGE. Thus, the DS formalism is non-deterministic because the processing of the same sentence initial NP may yield multiple different tree structures. For a more detailed description about the formalism, readers are referred to Kempson, Meyer-Viol, and Gabbay (2001) and Cann, Kempson, and Marten (2005).

2.2. Issues of Implementation

This subsection addresses the issues of implementation of the DS framework. When we try to develop an account of linguistic phenomena with limited data, the paper-and-pencil approach is very inefficient. In implementing the DS framework we have two problems to address. The first issue is how we should handle the unfixed nodes efficiently: in the previous subsection we showed that in some case the sentence initial NP is treated as the locally unfixed node introduced by LOCAL *ADJUNCTION, whereas it is treated as the unfixed node dominated by the type t, an unfixed root node for the subordinate clause, introduced by GENERALISED ADJUNCTION. These unfixed nodes all need to find their fixed positions in the course of processing with the transition rule MERGE or other update processes. Originally Kempson, Meyer-Viol, and Gabbay (2001) deals with nodes in the tree structure as a set and thus it is very inefficient to search the pointed node among a set each time a rule is applied, if we implement the grammar this way. Purver and Otsuka (2003) and Otsuka and Purver (2003) present a generation and parsing model for English, in which the tree structure is represented as a set of nodes in Prolog. Since in Japanese we need to keep some nodes unfixed, this is not so efficient an approach to Japanese. Instead if we try to cope with these nodes as a normal binary tree structure, we will get into trouble. For example, in Prolog the normal binary tree structure is often implemented recursively: `node(s, node(np, [], []), node(vp, [], []))` is the well-known Prolog notation for the tree diagram in which S goes to NP and VP. Unfixed nodes are not easy to be handled in this way. We propose a partitioned-parsing state to cope with these unfixed nodes and MERGE operation.

The second issue this paper addresses is the algorithm of lexical rules and transition rules of DS. DS is a kind of an abstract grammar formalism and in the current framework lexical rules and transition rules are applied arbitrarily: DS does not provide any algorithm to specify which rule is applied when. When the parser processes a Japanese sentence such as simple sentences, relative clause constructions, and complex sentences, we assume that 8 rules are needed to establish the semantic representation as we explained in the previous subsection. If the rules are applied in an arbitrary way, the parser has to compute the repeated permutation of the rules, including vacuous application. This results in very inefficient parsing. Although Purver and Otsuka (2003) and Otsuka and Purver (2003) propose a generation and parsing model based on the DS framework, which is written in Prolog, their parser mainly deals with only English. As we explained, in head-final languages such as Japanese various unfixed nodes are introduced and merged in the course of parsing so that we need a different algorithm. In the subsequent section we propose the algorithm to implement a DS grammar for Japanese, a slightly modified version of Kobayashi (2007).

3. Implementation of DS for Japanese

3.1. Parsing State

This subsection illustrates the parsing state. Our parser consists of a triple $\langle W, S, P \rangle$, where W is a list of words to be consumed (words which have not been processed yet), S is a list of (partial) tree structures which the parser obtains until it processes the current word, P indicates the position at which the pointer exists right now. The initial and final position of the pointer is the root node. The parsing successfully ends if and only if W contains no word to be scanned, and the pointer goes back to the root node of the resulting fixed tree structure; P is `pn(fixed, [root])`, and the semantic formula is built up at the root node. The basic idea of the parsing process, from the initial to the final stage, is shown in (3).

(3) $\langle W_0, S_0, \texttt{pn(fixed, [root])} \rangle \Rightarrow \cdots \cdots \Rightarrow \langle \phi, S_n, \texttt{pn(fixed, [root])} \rangle$

In a triple $\langle W, S, P \rangle$, S consists of a double $\langle R, T \rangle$ where R is a list of rules which has been applied to establish the current tree structure. T consists of a triple $\langle F, G, L \rangle$ where F is a fixed tree structure, G is a tree structure which is introduced by GENERALISED ADJUNCTION rule, and L is a tree structure which is introduced by LINK ADJUNCTION. This definition of the parsing state allows the parser to have additional spaces for unfixed nodes and execute MERGE operation efficiently.

3.2. Algorithm of Rule Application

This subsection describes the algorithm for processing Japanese sentence on the basis of the DS framework. We also take a brief look at the approach to English sentences presented by Purver and Otsuka (2003) and Otsuka and Purver (2003). The basic idea of Purver and Otsuka's approach is to divide transition rules into two groups in order to improve efficiency. One group is `always_rules`, which apply forcibly between the transitions, and the other is `possible_rules`, which do not necessarily apply but can be applied. Since Japanese is a typical head-final language, it is not easy to predict what syntactic structure comes next when the parser processes a sentence in an incremental fashion. To put it another way, the syntactic structure of Japanese is determined (or fixed) by the word the parser has processed to some extent. Japanese is lexically driven in that sense. In order to process Japanese sentences efficiently we need to take into account when lexical rules are applied together with transition rules. Therefore, Purver and Otsuka's approach is efficient to parse English sentences, but it does not apply directly to Japanese. This subsection proposes an algorithm for Japanese, which is a slightly revised version of Kobayashi (2007).

The key idea of this algorithm is that the transition rules are classified into two groups: one is `tree_expansion_rules`, which are used to expand the current tree structure, providing, for example, a new unfixed node; the other one is `node_update_rules` used to update the information of the pointed node and to move the pointer up to the mother node (COMPLETION). `tree_expansion_rules` includes LOCAL *ADJUNCTION, GENERALISED ADJUNCTION, and LINK ADJUNCTION. By contrast, MERGE, LINK EVALUATION, ELIMINATION, THINNING, and COMPLETION belong to `node_update_rules`. The algorithm is illustrated in Figure 1. In `node_update_rules`, rules are applied in the following order; MERGE, LINK EVALUATION, ELIMINATION, THINNING, and COMPLETION. This is because the parser has to establish the semantic representation with ELIMINATION and delete the requirement with THINNING at the current pointed node before the pointer goes up to the mother node (with COMPLETION). `node_update_rules` can vacuously apply, so the tree structure is passed to the next rule without any modification if some of `node_update_rules` cannot apply. As Figure

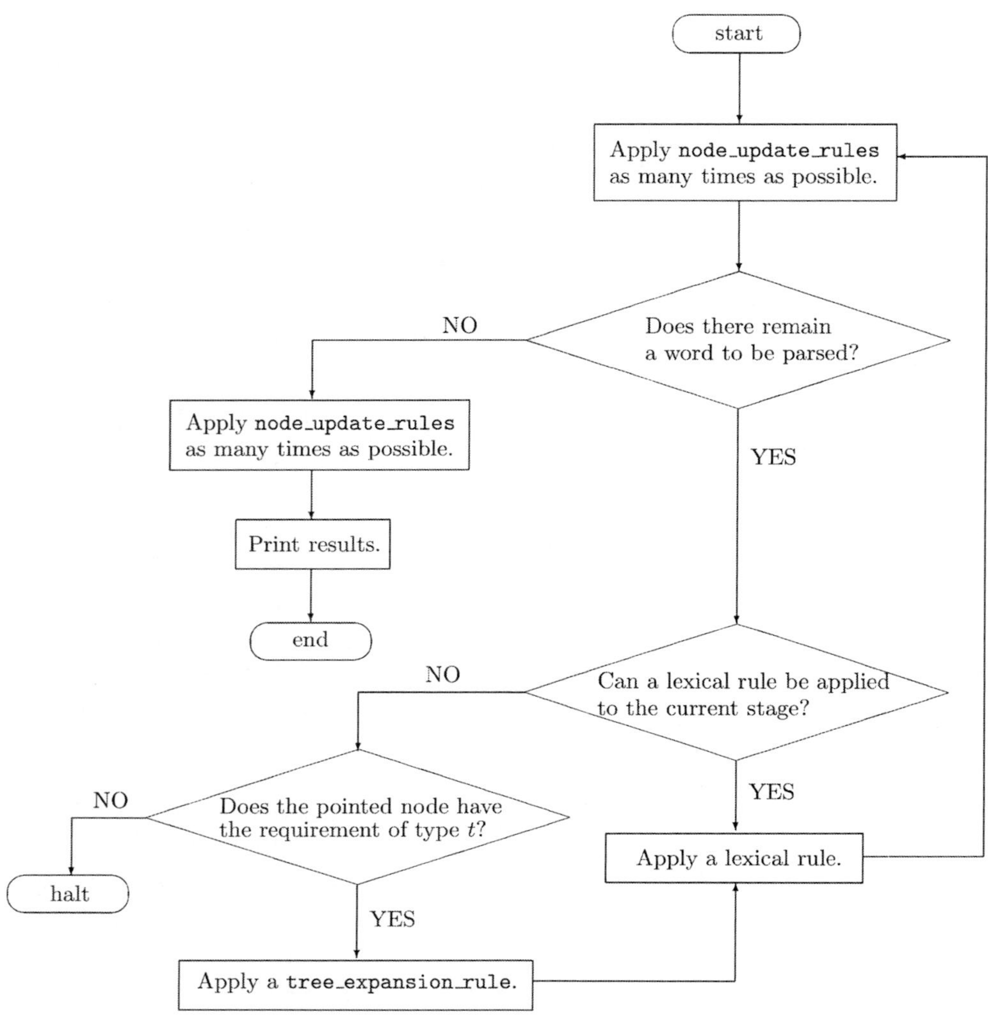

Figure 1: Flow Chart of Algorithm

1 shows, `tree_expansion_rules` apply if a lexical rule cannot apply to the pointed node; `tree_expansion_rules` apply if the parser cannot consume the current word because in DS each lexical item is a lexical rule. This algorithm implements the lexically-driven processing of sentences in Japanese and reflects the prominent difference between English and Japanese.

4. Incremental Processing and Null Arguments

This section shows how the parser works on the basis of the DS framework with special reference to the processing of null arguments. The parser is written in SWI-Prolog on Linux OS. It consists of about 1,200 lines, 41.1 KB except the lexicon. The parser accepts a sentence composed of N words returning N+1 steps, from the initial step to the final one with the semantic representation.

The parser proposed in this paper is still small. Nonetheless, it can parse not only simple sentences but also relative clause constructions, embedded clauses, and scrambled sentences. Let us take a look at how the parser works in processing a simple scrambled sentence (2), repeated here as (4).

(4) Bōru o   John ga   nageta.
    ball   ACC John NOM throw-PAST

   "John threw the ball."

Figure 2 is a successfully parsed output of example (4). As the figure shows, the sentence consists of five words so that the parser returns the six steps with the semantic representation on the last line. In each step, rules which are applied at each stage are listed in the second line. The tree structure is represented in a tab delimited format.

Incremental processing is obviously crucial to word-order phenomena, but it is also important for the parser to specify (or underspecify) null arguments and pronouns in an incremental way. Let us illustrate how the parser works in processing null arguments in embedded clauses and relative clauses. As seen in Kuroda (1965), Hoji (1998) and other studies, many studies in the literature discuss empty categories and null arguments, especially within the framework of generative grammar. As shown by Takahashi (2006, p.1), unlike English, the subject and object NPs can be empty even in the embedded clauses.

(5) John ga   Naomi ni   e   kyōju   ni   e   shōkaisuru to   itta.
    John NOM Naomi DAT   professor DAT   introduce COMP say-PAST

   "John told Naomi that he (or someone) would introduce her (or someone) to the professor."

In (5) the subject and object NPs of the embedded clause are omitted. Missing items can refer to someone in the context, but the salient reading is that the omitted subject refers to the subject of the main clause, *John*, and the missing object refers to the object *Naomi*. In this example, the positions in the fixed tree structure of NPs and null arguments cannot be specified until the verb *introduce* is consumed. Let us show the parsing result of (5) in Figure 3. The figure shows that at step 1 the sentence initial NP *John* is located at an unfixed node which is introduced by LOCAL *ADJUNCTION. Thus this initial NP is tentatively unfixed but will find a fixed position in the main clause (other possibilities cannot survive by the end of parsing). Step 10 is the final stage of the parsing with the semantic representation at the bottom of it. The normal binary tree structure of step 10 is illustrated in Figure 4. As seen in the representation in Figure 3 the parser produced the semantic representation `fo(say(john, introduce(meta_v, meta_v, professor), naomi))` where `meta_v` is a meta variable, which is merged with someone in the context. Although in the framework of generative grammar it has been argued whether ellipsis or empty pronouns are involved in null arguments, DS can process them without setting up a stipulation.

```
?- parse([boru, o, john, ga, nageta], X).

Step 0
Nothing applied.
Pointer: pn(fixed, [root])
Root: [tn([0]), an([?ty(t)]), []]
Gen_adj: []
Linked: link([[], [], []])

Step 1
local_adj, boru applied.
Pointer: pn(fixed, [root, local])
Root: [tn([0]), an([?ty(t)]), [loc([fo(ball), ty(e), ?ty(e)])]]
Gen_adj: []
Linked: link([[], [], []])

Step 2
thinning, o applied.
Pointer: pn(fixed, [root])
Root: [tn([0]), an([\/[1, ty((e->t))], ?ty(t)]), []]
        [tn([0, 1]), an([\/[0, ty(e)], \/[0, fo(ball)], ty((e->t))]), []]
                [tn([0, 1, 0]), an([fo(ball), ty(e)]), []]
Gen_adj: []
Linked: link([[], [], []])

Step 3
local_adj, john applied.
Pointer: pn(fixed, [root, local])
Root: [tn([0]), an([?ty(t), \/[1, ty((e->t))]]), [loc([fo(john), ty(e), ?ty(e)])]]
        [tn([0, 1]), an([\/[0, ty(e)], \/[0, fo(ball)], ty((e->t))]), []]
                [tn([0, 1, 0]), an([fo(ball), ty(e)]), []]
Gen_adj: []
Linked: link([[], [], []])

Step 4
thinning, ga applied.
Pointer: pn(fixed, [root])
Root: [tn([0]), an([\/[0, fo(john)], \/[0, ty(e)], ?ty(t), \/[1, ty((e->t))]]), []]
        [tn([0, 0]), an([fo(john), ty(e)]), []]
        [tn([0, 1]), an([\/[0, ty(e)], \/[0, fo(ball)], ty((e->t))]), []]
                [tn([0, 1, 0]), an([fo(ball), ty(e)]), []]
Gen_adj: []
Linked: link([[], [], []])

Step 5
nageta applied.
Pointer: pn(fixed, [root, 1, 1])
Root: [tn([0]), an([?ty(t), \/[0, fo(john)], \/[0, ty(e)], \/[1, ty((e->t))]]), []]
        [tn([0, 0]), an([fo(john), ty(e)]), []]
        [tn([0, 1]), an([\/[0, ty(e)], \/[0, fo(ball)], ty((e->t))]), []]
                [tn([0, 1, 0]), an([fo(ball), ty(e)]), []]
                [tn([0, 1, 1]), an([fo(lambda(ball, lambda(john, throw(john, ball)))), ty((e->e->t))]), []]
Gen_adj: []
Linked: link([[], [], []])

Step 6
completion, elimination, completion, elimination, thinning applied.
Pointer: pn(fixed, [root])
Root: [tn([0]), an([ty(t), fo(throw(john, ball)), \/[1, fo(lambda(john, throw(john, ball)))], \/[0, fo(john)],
    \/[0, ty(e)], \/[1, ty((e->t))]]), []]
        [tn([0, 0]), an([fo(john), ty(e)]), []]
        [tn([0, 1]), an([fo(lambda(john, throw(john, ball))), \/[1, fo(lambda(ball, lambda(john, throw(john,
        ball))))], \/[1, ty((e->e->t))], \/[0, ty(e)], \/[0, fo(ball)], ty((e->t))]), []]
                [tn([0, 1, 0]), an([fo(ball), ty(e)]), []]
                [tn([0, 1, 1]), an([fo(lambda(ball, lambda(john, throw(john, ball)))), ty((e->e->t))]), []]
Gen_adj: []
Linked: link([[], [], []])

Semantic Representation: fo(throw(john, ball))
```

Figure 2: Parsing Output of (4)

```
?- parse([john, ga, naomi, ni, kyoujyu, ni, shoukaisuru, to, itta], X).

Step 0
Nothing applied.
Pointer: pn(fixed, [root])
Root: [tn([0]), an([?ty(t)]), []]
Gen_adj: []
Linked: link([[], [], []])

Step 1
local_adj, john applied.
Pointer: pn(fixed, [root, local])
Root: [tn([0]), an([?ty(t)]), [loc([fo(john), ty(e), ?ty(e)])]]
Gen_adj: []
Linked: link([[], [], []])


~~~~~~~~~~~~~~~~~~~~~~~~~~~~~~~~~~~~~~~~~~~~~~~~~~~~~~~~~~~~~~~~
~~~~~~~~~~~~~~~~~~~~~~~~~~~~~~~~~~~~~~~~~~~~~~~~~~~~~~~~~~~~~~~~


Step 10
completion, elimination, completion, elimination, completion, elimination, thinning applied.
Pointer: pn(fixed, [root])
Root: [tn([0]), an([ty(t), fo(say(john, introduce(meta_v, meta_v, professor), naomi))), \/[1, fo(lambda(john,
     say(john, introduce(meta_v, meta_v, professor), naomi)))], \/[1, ty((e->t))], \/[0, fo(john)],
     \/[0, ty(e)]]), []]
        [tn([0, 0]), an([fo(john), ty(e)]), []]
        [tn([0, 1]), an([fo(lambda(john, say(john, introduce(meta_v, meta_v, professor), naomi))),
        \/[1, fo(lambda(introduce(meta_v, meta_v, professor), lambda(john, say(john, introduce(meta_v,
        meta_v, professor), naomi))))], \/[1, ty((t->e->t))], \/[0, ty(t)], \/[0, fo(introduce(meta_v,
        meta_v, professor))], ty((e->t))]), []]
                [tn([0, 1, 0]), an([ty(t), fo(introduce(meta_v, meta_v, professor)),
                \/[1, fo(lambda(meta_v, introduce(meta_v, meta_v, professor)))], \/[0, ty(e)],
                \/[0, fo(meta_v)], \/[1, ty((e->t))]]), []]
                        [tn([0, 1, 0, 0]), an([fo(meta_v), ?ty(e)]), []]
                        [tn([0, 1, 0, 1]), an([fo(lambda(meta_v, introduce(meta_v, meta_v, professor))),
                        \/[1, fo(lambda(meta_v, lambda(meta_v, introduce(meta_v, meta_v, professor))))],
                        \/[1, ty((e->e->t))], \/[0, ty(e)], \/[0, fo(meta_v)], ty((e->t))]), []]
                                [tn([0, 1, 0, 1, 0]), an([fo(meta_v), ?ty(e)]), []]
                                [tn([0, 1, 0, 1, 1]), an([fo(lambda(meta_v, lambda(meta_v,
                                introduce(meta_v, meta_v, professor)))), \/[1, fo(lambda(professor,
                                lambda(meta_v, lambda(meta_v, introduce(meta_v, meta_v,
                                professor)))))], \/[1, ty((e->e->e->t))], ty((e->e->t)), \/[0, ty(e)],
                                \/[0, fo(professor)]]), []]
                                        [tn([0, 1, 0, 1, 1, 0]), an([fo(professor), ty(e)]), []]
                                        [tn([0, 1, 0, 1, 1, 1]), an([fo(lambda(professor,
                                        lambda(meta_v, lambda(meta_v, introduce(meta_v, meta_v,
                                        professor)))))), ty((e->e->e->t))]), []]
                [tn([0, 1, 1]), an([fo(lambda(introduce(meta_v, meta_v, professor), lambda(john, say(john,
                introduce(meta_v, meta_v, professor), naomi)))), \/[1, fo(lambda(naomi,
                lambda(introduce(meta_v, meta_v, professor), lambda(john, say(john,
                introduce(meta_v, meta_v, professor), naomi)))))], \/[1, ty((e->t->e->t))], ty((t->e->t)),
                \/[0, ty(e)], \/[0, fo(naomi)]]), []]
                        [tn([0, 1, 1, 0]), an([fo(naomi), ty(e)]), []]
                        [tn([0, 1, 1, 1]), an([fo(lambda(naomi, lambda(introduce(meta_v, meta_v,
                        professor), lambda(john, say(john, introduce(meta_v, meta_v, professor),
                        naomi))))), ty((e->t->e->t))]), []]
Gen_adj: []
Linked: link([[], [], []])

Semantic Representation: fo(say(john, introduce(meta_v, meta_v, professor), naomi))
```

Figure 3: Abbreviated Parsing Output of (5)

$$\{Tn(0),\ Ty(t),\ \Diamond,$$
$$Fo(say(john,\ introduce(V,\ W,\ professor),\ naomi))\}$$

$\{Tn(00),\ Ty(e),\ Fo(john)\}$

$$\{Tn(01),\ Ty(e{\to}t),$$
$$Fo(\lambda x(say(x,\ introduce(V,\ W,\ professor),\ naomi))\}$$

$$\{Tn(010),\ Ty(t),$$
$$Fo(introduce(V,\ W,\ professor))\}$$

$$\{Tn(011),\ Ty(t{\to}e{\to}t),$$
$$Fo(\lambda y.\lambda x.say(x,\ y,\ naomi))\}$$

$$\{Tn(0100),$$
$$Ty(e),\ Fo(V)\}$$

$$\{Tn(0101),\ Ty(e{\to}t),$$
$$Fo(\lambda x.introduce(x,\ W,\ professor))\}$$

$$\{Tn(0110),\ Ty(e),$$
$$Fo(naomi)\}$$

$$\{Tn(0111),\ Ty(e{\to}t{\to}e{\to}t),$$
$$Fo(\lambda z.\lambda y.\lambda x.say(x,\ y,\ z))\}$$

$$\{Tn(01010),$$
$$Fo(W),\ Ty(e)\}$$

$$\{Tn(01011),\ Ty(e{\to}e{\to}t),$$
$$Fo(\lambda y.\lambda x.introduce(x,\ y,\ professor))\}$$

$$\{Tn(010110),\ Ty(e),$$
$$Fo(professor)\}$$

$$\{Tn(010111),\ Ty(e{\to}e{\to}e{\to}t)$$
$$Fo(\lambda z.\lambda y.\lambda x.introduce(x,\ y,\ z))\}$$

Figure 4: Abbreviated Parsing Output of (5)

5. Discussion

In this paper we have accounted for the algorithm of the application of lexical and transition rules and the implementation of the DS parser for Japanese. This section provides a discussion regarding the current DS grammar, one on the implementation and future research. One of DS's goals is to explore language faculty, and our implementation can contribute to the study of this issue by the simulation of human sentence processing. Although this DS Prolog grammar can parse a simple sentence, relative clause constructions, and embedded structure, currently the coverage of this grammar is very small. As future research we would like to integrate a stochastic approach into the system. Another issue to be tackled is how we should deal with pragmatically-related problems such as pronoun resolution. For instance, the parser provides place-holders such as a `meta_v`, but as far as I know there is no research given in the literature about how the parser merges entities in the context with these variables on the basis of the DS framework. This paper deals with only Japanese and we need to make sure whether this algorithm can be applied to other head-final languages such as Korean.

6. Conclusion

This paper presented the basic implementation of the parser based on the DS framework. The lexical rules and transition rules are applied arbitrarily within the current framework, therefore we provided the algorithm of the application of lexical rules and transition rules for head-final languages like Japanese. This parser adopts the partitioned parsing state, which allows the parser to access the pointed node efficiently. The algorithm is implemented in Prolog. This paper also showed that the parser can process empty pronouns in embedded clauses often observed in Japanese.

References

Cann, R., R. Kempson, and L. Marten. 2005. *The Dynamics of Language*. Elsevier, Oxford.

Hoji, H. 1998. Null object and sloppy identity in japanese. *Linguistic Inquiry*, 29:127–152.

Kempson, R., W. Meyer-Viol, and D. Gabbay. 2001. *Dynamic Syntax: The Flow of Language Understanding*. Blackwell Publishers, Oxford.

Kobayashi, M. 2007. Incremental processing and design of a parser for japanese: A dynamic approach. In *Proceedings of the Fourth International Workshop on Logic and Engineering of Natural Language Semantics (LENLS2007)*, pages 261–273.

Kuroda, S.-Y. 1965. *Generative Grammatical Studies in the Japanese Language*. Ph.D. thesis, MIT.

Moot, R. 1999. Grail: An automated proof assistant for categorial grammars. In R. Delmonte, editor, *Proceedings of Venezia per il Trattamento Automatico delle Lingue '99 (VEXTAL99)*, pages 225–261.

Otsuka, M. and M. Purver. 2003. Incremental generation by incremental parsing. In *Proceedings of the 6th Annual CLUK Research Colloquium*, pages 93–100.

Purver, M. and M. Otsuka. 2003. Incremental generation by incremental parsing: Tactical generation in dynamic syntax. In *Proceedings of the 9th European Workshop on Natural Language Generation*, pages 79–86.

Takahashi, D. 2006. Apparent parasitic gaps and null arguments in japanese. *Journal of East Asian Linguistics*, 15:1–35.

A Focus Account for Contrastive Reduplication:
Prototypicality and Contrastivity*

Binna Lee, Chungmin Lee

Seoul National University, 599 Kwanangno, Kwanak-gu Seoul,
51-742, Korea
bin4you8@snu.ac.kr, clee@snu.ac.kr

Abstract. This paper sets forth the phenomenon of Contrastive Reduplication (CR) in English relevant to the notion of contrastive focus (CF). CF differs from other reduplicative patterns in that rather than the general intensive function, denotation of a more prototypical and default meaning of a lexical item appears from the reduplicated form resulting as a semantic contrast with the meaning of the non-reduplicated word. Thus, CR is in concordance with CF under the concept of contrastivity. However, much of the previous works on CF associated contrastivity with a manufacture of a set of alternatives taking a semantic approach. We claim that a recent discourse-pragmatic account takes advantage of explaining the vague contrast in informativeness of CR. Zimmermann's (2006) Contrastive Focus Hypothesis characterizes contrastivity in the sense of speaker's assumptions about the hearer's expectation of the focused element. This approach makes possible adaptation to CR and recovers the possible subsets of meaning of a reduplicated form in a more refined way showing contrastivity in informativeness. Additionally, CR in other languages along with similar set-limiting phenomenon in various languages will be introduced in general.

Keywords: Contrastive Reduplication, Contrastive Focus, contrastivity, pragmatic

1. Introduction

This paper examines the linguistic phenomenon of what is called Contrastive Reduplication (henceforth **CR**) (Ghoemshi et al. 2004) in English. In many works on reduplication patterns, CR has been unfairly regarded as a subclass of mere repetition or lexical duplications that simply function as an intensifier. However, CR is understood to have distinguishable uniqueness apart from the family of reduplication forms shown in various languages which are intensively studied in phonological and morphological aspects. Interestingly, the semantic properties of CR allows itself to be more exposed to our everyday, mundane conversation than to written discourse.

CR is not merely a repetition or duplicated form of a lexical element for the purpose of intensive use. Consider the examples of CR given in (1).[1]

(1) a. I'll make the tuna salad, and you make the SALAD-salad.
    b. Oh, we're not LIVING-TOGETHER-living-together.
    c. My car isn't MINE-mine; it's my parents'.
    d. I had a JOB-job once.
        [a 'real' 9-to-5 office job, as opposed to an academic job]

---

[1] More examples of CR in English discussed by Ghomeshi et al. (2004) can be found in the website
http://www.umanitoba.ca/linguistics/russell/redup-corpus.html

e. Are you LEAVING-leaving?

(from Ghomeshi et al., 2004)

As illustrated in the examples of (1), the reduplicated form *SALAD-salad* has the semantic function of elucidating possible interpretation of a word that is associated with the term in a context. So in (1a), the CR denotes plain, normal salad as opposed to other specific salads (e.g. *chicken salad, shrimp salad,* etc.) overall and (1b) is understood as living together as roommates (which is the general interpretation of living-together) not lovers. Besides the prototypical effect, additional CR semantic properties are that CR is not limited to nouns but can be produced in various lexical categories like verbs (*LEAVING-leaving*) or adjectives (He is *HANDSOME-handsome?*), etc. In other cases, proper names (She's *MARY-Mary?* as in the Mary the speakers know) and lexicalized expressions (*LIVING-TOGETHER-living-together*) are also possible candidates for CR. Likewise, CR has loose morphological restrictions on the construction of the form unlike general reduplication patterns.

Correspondingly, CR is a target for many lexical categories and also functions to determinate the prototypical, default meaning of the reduplicated item it targets and plays to make disambiguation of the distribution of the different senses of the same expression. So it is noteworthy that the semantic influence of this unique duplicated construction is to limit and "to focus the denotation of the reduplicated element on a more sharply delimited, more specialized range." (Ghomeshi et al., 2004; 308)

CR is considered to have a repeated word or a phrase (chunk) within the expression for the semantic effect of contrastiveness in a sense. The reduplicated form is not redundant as it has a construction that contains a repeated form with a distinct use from the unduplicated form. The difference is clearly shown in (2).

(2) a. I'll make the tuna salad, and you make the SALAD-salad.
   b. *I'll make the tuna salad, and you make the salad.

Without the reduplicated form placed in (2b), the sentence is ungrammatical as there exist no semantic effect of differentiation. Thus, this type of reduplicated form differs from other reduplication process in English as emphasizing or intensifying the simple form is not the exact consequence expected. Furthermore, CR is of interest for it displays a narrowing effect to a prototypical variant of the non-reduplicated form.

The primary goal of this paper is to show an account of focus pragmatic framework for the CR in English along with introduction to other types of devices in various languages having resemblance in narrowing semantic effects. We make a distinction from the prior studies of focus by taking a pragmatic-focus framework rather than a semantic one to analyze CR. As the intended meaning of CR is of our interest, the issue of contrastive focus should shed light on this construction. It should be asserted that this type of contrast in informativeness is in concordance with contrastive focus which also requires a set of contrastive sets as alternatives. However, what is exactly contrasted here in meaning in CR remains a vague issue and the rightful approach of contrastiveness and focus should be under consideration in specific details. We argue that a pragmatic reason lies in the contrastiveness in CR, not a semantic one.

The organization of this paper is as follows: The succeeding section introduces previous studies of the CR construction with some insights on contrastive focus. In section 3, the focus semantic approach on CR will be considered in specific details for a more adequate explanation of the phenomenon. Section 4 discusses a pragmatic view on CR with an advantage of the explanation of vagueness in meaning. The final section puts forth the conclusion of this paper with acknowledgment to the significance of the pragmatic approach on CR.

2. Previous works on CR and Prototypicality

What makes CR more intriguing is its semantic distinction from other reduplication patterns. CR can be characterized as a distinctive kind of reduplication phenomena. Majority of the research on reduplication construction crosslinguistically highlighted the phonological and morphological aspects of the construction rather than the semantic or pragmatic effects.[2] Likewise, the analysis of the semantic function of reduplication was limited to diminution and pluralization, and repetition for intensification.

There has been minority report in the linguistic literature on the phenomena of reduplication patterns related to contrastive informativeness (Dray, 1989; Horn, 1992; Ghomeshi et al., 2004). Despite the resemblance in CR with other reduplication phenomena, CR can not be characterized by prosodic features or morphologically-based rules as displayed in complex reduplicated phrased forms like 'Do you *LIKE-'EM-like-'em*?'.

Moreover, the semantic characteristic of CR is to have more focus on the denotation of the reduplicated form with more limited and specialized bounds for meaning. A clearer explanation is given by Horn (1992), He claims: "As a rough approximation, we can say that the reduplicated modifier singles out a member or subset of the extension of the noun [or verb, or adjective, or preposition - JG et al.] that represents a true, real, default, or prototype instance" (p. 48). Thus, CR has a prototypical and focused meaning in contrast. Horn (1992)'s work on CR was fundamentally to categorize the semantics of this pattern into four types; prototypical meaning, literal meaning, intensified meaning, and 'value-added' meaning.[3]

Analyzing CR on account of pragmatic mechanism was also considered by Levinson (2000).Levinson examines the reduplicated structure or repetitions within the framework of his theory of *Generalized Conversational Implicatures* (GCIs).[4] He explains that I-implicature, which is one of the three principles that derives possible implicatures, is the general, default or stereotypical meaning of a linguistic pattern that enables the hearer to clearly understand the utterance of the speaker who aim to clarify oneself from the most simple expression with unmarked uses. On the other hand, the M-implicature denotes that marked constructions are used for reference to non-stereotypical situations. Considering the reduplication phenomenon a marked form of the non-reduplicated one, Levinson seeks a pragmatic account due to

---

[2] Setting aside the CR, in general, reduplication construction is shown in at least six different patterns by Ghomeshi et al. (2004). The instances given below in (i) a~f. are the cases of such.

(i)a. 'Baby-talk' reduplication, e.g., *choo-choo. wee-wee.*

  b. Multiple partial reduplications, e.g., *hap-hap-happy.*

  c. Deprecative reduplication, e.g., *table-shmable.*

  d. 'rhyme combinations': *super-duper, willy-nilly, pall-mall, okey-dokey, hanky-panky,...*

  e. 'Ablaut combinations': *flim-flam, zig-zag, sing-song, pitter-patter, riff-raff, mish-mash...*

  f. Intensive reduplication: *You are sick sick sick!*

[3] Examples below are cases of (ii)a. prototypical meaning, b. literal meaning, c. intensified meaning, and d. 'value-added' meaning. (Ghomeshi et al., 2004)
(ii) a. I want the SALAD-salad.
  b. A: Maybe you'd like to come in and have some coffee?
    B: Yeah, I'd like that.
    A: Just COFFEE-coffee, no double meanings.
  c . I'm nervous but not NERVOUS-nervous.
  d. We're not LIVING-TOGETHER-living-together. We are roommates.

[4] See Levinson (2000) for more adequate explanation on generalized conversational implicatures (GCIs). He characterizes three principles (I, M, Q principles) to explain the pragmatic effect of linguistic structures evoking implicatures.

implicature arising to address CR. His approach is based on pragmatic mechanism which shows the nature of these structures. However, Levinson did not distinguish CR from other reduplication forms which is of our concern in the present paper.

As a lexical word or a phrase may often leave ambiguity or lack in precision, CR could be an option to clarify these cases in means of establishing a prototypical denotation in contrast to a more wider generalization or more limited range of interpretation. This is clear in the examples of (3).

(3) a.   She is just a COW-cow.
    b.   Should I wear a HAT-hat?

As shown, the nouns are in CR forms with the reduplication signaling the default denotation of the lexical item intended. Both the examples in (4a) and (4b) destricts the denotation to a prototypical ones. It is noteworthy that the use of CR is to restrict meaning of a lexical item and that CR can not be constrained to functional items.

In some cases, proper names can also be CR under the condition that the names are to be clearly distinguished from other denotations of the same word the speaker and hearer know. In this instance, prominence and salience may be used as the function to pick out the referent:

(4) a. So was the guy I saw at the gym DAVE-Dave, or just Dave?
    b. Oh, that's BEACON-STREET-Beacon-Street!

In both cases (4a) and (4b), the discourse participants must have a shared background knowledge or information about the denotation of the proper name so the most salient candidate of denotations will be determined as the appropriate meaning. As from such examples, the term 'prototypical' does not predict the observed patterns to be disambiguated as the other CRs and does not independently determines the meaning of this construction as considered in previous analysis. Rather, additional functions make attributions to CR perhaps even intensification, default and salient meanings. One single meaning interpretation can not cover up all the examples of CR found in natural conversation. The issue of the prototype related to CR will be discussed more in the following section.

Moreover, contrastiveness in reduplication exist not only in English but also in other languages as well. For instance, Spanish and Russian also appears to have CR construction. An example of Spanish CR is given below in (5). This duplicated form also displays the real, default and prototypical meaning in the reduplicated form *CASA*.

(5) No es una CASA-casa.
     'This isn't a real [sic] house.'   [Horn 1993: 49]

Additionally, the semantic effect of CR can also be expressed morphologically in some languages just like other reduplication form can be in concordance with morphological forms with symmetric meanings. Poser (1991) claims that the prefix ma- in Japanese can be interpreted as to restrict the denotation to a prototypical meaning. The examples in (6) illustrates this fact.

(6) Japanese prefix ma- (Poser 1991)

mae 'front'	*maNmae* 'right in front'
siro 'winter'	*mafuyu* 'dead of winter'
kita 'north'	*makita* 'due north'
aka 'red'	*makka* 'deep red'

Considering the fact that prefixes may maintain the same semantic function that CR has, other instances of prefixes limiting denotations to the 'true, real, genuine' meaning can be found in other languages. In Korean, the prefixes 'han-', 'cham-', 'cin-' etc. are to be matched with the prototypical denotation of a lexical item.

(7) Korean prefix 'han-', 'cham-', 'cin-'

   yerum 'summer'
   hanyerum 'the peak of summer'

   mosup 'appearance'
   chammosup 'the true look of one's appearance'

   bemin 'culprit'
   cinbemin 'the real culprit'

Thus, CR and prefixes share semantic restrictive function as they have the denotation of limiting effects shown in various languages. Both should be considered as a general phenomenon that is possibly analyzed within a unitary theory of meaning with relevance to contrast in informativeness.

3. Theories of Focus Interpretation and CR

3.1.Contrastive Focus (CF)

A certain form of meaning can represent something more than plainly truth conditions. As of one example, there is a wide range of constructions in English that are known to exhibit some form of focus. In general, focus is featured by a prosodic feature like nuclear pitch accent. While prosodical characters may involve in the combination of focus and meaning interpretation, contemporary theories of focus shed light on the semantic or pragmatic appliance.

Contrastive Focus involves sets of alternatives with great significance to the notion of contrastiveness. However, the contrast of informativeness and the range of alternatives are quite vague and still unclear. Despite the problematic issues that arises in contrastivity, the notion of focus has been widely discussed in the semantic and pragmatic fields with merely dissimilar views on the concept.

Focus interpretation from a semantic perspective shows semantic objects, focus semantic values, which are shaped by construction-specific rules (Rooth, 1992, 1996). This kind of approach take it that intonational focus has a grammatical coordinate which is shaped by rule-based mechanisms. Rooth's (1985, 1992) alternative semantics is also considered to be a semantic approach as the basic idea is to analyze focus items on grounds of question-answer criterion on a rule-based account.

In contrast, pragmatic approach to focus makes no specific reference to linguistic patterns. Rather, pragmatic factors are correlated to the relevant focus optionally (Rooth, 1992; Roberts, 1996). Pragmatic theories exclude focus attached to linguistic items as being focus operators.

Lee (2003) makes a semi-pragmatic proposal with the question-answer criterion still motivated. This testing device is to make a distinction between contrastive topic (CT) and contrastive focus (CF).[5] CF is said to be preceded by an alternative disjunctive question making parallel to the result of producing a set of alternatives.

____

[5] From Lee's (2003) analysis of distinguishing contrastive focus (CF) and contrastive topic (CT), CT is thought to be preceded by a conjunctive question.

In a more recent research, Zimmermann (2006) departs from the previous analysis on focus issues and claims a new discourse-pragmatic account on the phenomenon of contrastivity. He argues that focus should not be related with the terms of contrastivity or exhaustivity on a semantic basis. Approaching CF as a discourse-pragmatic phenomenon, contrastivity signifies that "a particular content, or a particular speech act is unexpected to raise the hearer's attention, and to get him to shift his background assumptions accordingly, is to use additional grammatical marking, e.g. intonation contour, syntactic movement, clefts, or morphological markers." (p.2) To reiterate, CF is largely connect to the background assumptions of discourse participants, especially the information related to the hearer's suppositions. The CF is affirmed in a hypothesis as below:

(8) **Contrastive Focus Hypothesis** (Zimmermann, 2006)
   Contrastive marking on a focus constituent α express the speaker's assumption
   that the hearer will not consider the content of α, or the speech act containing
   α likely to be(come) common ground.

Contrastive Focus Hypothesis suggests that contrastivity does not refer to the contrast in a set of alternatives in the linguistic conditions. Rather, the contrast lies in the information communicated by the speaker in stating a linguistic expression and the expectation of the hearer's assumption. A speaker will apply a contrastive marking on a focus element if assumes that the hearer will not have postulated the assertion or the speech act made by the speaker in advance. See the example in (9).

(9) a. Q: What did you eat in France?   A: *Escargot.*
    b. A: Surely you ate *escargot*? B: No, *Foie gras*, we ate!

In (9a), there exists no contrastive focus on the reply *escargot* as predicted for an appropriate answer is provided as a speech act of a *wh*-question. On the other hand, in (9b), it is assumed that speaker B's answer will not be expected by hearer A as she expects no contradiction and so a contrastive focus is on B's answer *Foie gras*.
   Considering contrastive focus marking as an oppositeness between the knowledge conditions of the participants in a discourse, this view has an advantage over the previous 'alternatives'-based contrastivity of not bearing the burden of manufacturing a set of alternatives in contrast as some data show contrastive foci without explicit optional choices of the same type. CR is also subscribes to be examples of non-productive construction of alternatives in some cases. The position advocated in the present paper is to evaluate the focus of CR from a discourse-pragmatic theory based on Contrastive Focus Hypothesis.

3.2. CR and CF

The semantic association of focus to a set of alternatives provides insights for contrastiveness. CR can be parallel to CF in that contrast in informativeness evokes when reduplication results to a narrow meaning. The semantic characteristic splits between the two as illustrated in the following examples:

(10) a. I didn't give the book to JOHN.   [CF]
        Contrast set: (John, Bill, Dave, Sue,...)
     b. I didn't give the book to JOHN-John.   [CR]
        Contrast set: (John1, John2,...)

(11) a. It wasn't a GOAT.   [CF]
        Contrast set: (goats, horses, pig, sheep ...)
     b. It wasn't a GOAT-goat.   [CR]

Contrast set: (prototypical goats, non-prototypical goats, figurative goats)

(Ghomeshi et, al, 2004)

As shown in the examples (10) and (11), CF and CF shares the semantic effect of contrast in informativeness. The difference between the two lies in what is contrasted. CF indicates the contrast from other words of the compatible type but CR makes contrastiveness within other possible meanings. As mentioned, CF has a narrowing effect in the selection of the denotation of a lexical item.

   The question arises whether to consider the set-shrinking effect of CR as producing a set of alternatives from the consequence of contrastive focus. The duplicated form has a strong intonational focus that is commonly seem in contrastive focus elements. I argue that the function of narrowing down the range of applicable referents of a lexical form should not be interpreted as a consequence of semantic focus but rather a result of pragmatic effect involved. In the next section, the treatment of CR as evoking alternatives from a semantic focus view or analyzing CR on a pragmatic account will be explored.

4. Is the focus on CR semantic or pragmatic?

In this section, we argue that CR does not have a clear set of alternatives in many cases and that the Contrastive Focus Hypothesis has advantage over other focus theories in explaining the semantic gap in a pragmatic perspective.

Some instances of CR seem to suggest that simply the concept of prototypicality *per se* isn't the right diagnosis for the clarification of interpreting the meaning of the contrast. For there seems to be a number of ways on which speakers affirm different interpretations of lexical items reduplicated in CRs. It is unpredictable to catch the subset of a lexicon's extension a speaker means to deliver from conceptual structure alone. Take the example in (11).

(12)   ...you mean thought-about-it-considered-it or just CONSIDERED-IT-considered it.

In (12), rather than the prototypical meaning of the lexical word 'consider' (which is a problematic point itself to take up the possibility of approving verbs as to have a more default, general meaning and the elements of the set of interpretation are unclear with no particularly concrete objects as selective denotations), the context itself supplies possible alternatives meaning in the reduplicated form suggesting applicable range on which meaning is to understand and be recoverable and the intended sense is clear. The interpretation of the reduplicated form must be context-dependent in some way as the salient, default meaning is reflected in the structure. Whitton (2007) provides another instance of where the notion of prototype is problematic as illustrated in (13).

(13) a. "Do you want a bottle of wine?" Mac asks. "I think I'll have a DRINK-drink," I say, and
         when the waiter comes I order a martini.
     b. (around 3 euros a shot and 8 euros a DRINK-drink)
     c. A: What do you wanna get?
         B: I'll probably just get water so if you want a DRINK-drink get whatever you want.
     d. Are you looking for alcohol? Or just a DRINK-drink?

In the examples shown in (13a-d), the CR *drink*-drink has a contrastive interpretation of the non-reduplicated form *drink,* each differently understood in meanings: the CR *drink*-drink can contrast an alcoholic drink from a non-alcoholic one (13a) or a mixed drink from a shot (13b), a soft drink from water (13c), or a non-alcoholic drink from alcohol (13d). The intended default meaning is vague depending solely on the conceptual structure as a context-based interpretation is required essentially.

Additionally, proper names are also possible candidates for being a CR but the criterion for determining the denotations are not normal, default and prototypical meanings but rather the most salient and prominent object that the discourse participants share knowledge about. This is illustrated in example (14).

(14) Do you mean JOHN-John?
           Contrast set:
           (the most salient John we know in this context, other non salient Johns??)

This vagueness of the clear-cut options of the meaning of CR makes an unstable position for the composition of a set of alternatives. If the meaning from the lexical item is determined by factors beside the prototypical meanings, contrast in informativeness arises not by alternative sets but by the speaker and hearer's background assumptions in contexts. Thus, a discourse approach might be favored in explaining these muddy areas.

The Contrastive Focus Hypothesis makes clarification of the CR as the supposition of the discourse participants about the common assumptions within the linguistic context displays an important role pragmatically. Not only CR but the other languages that take prefixes as the similar device to restrict the denotation of a duplicated word to prototypical meaning also can be implied to go under the pragmatic account that the interlocutors background assumptions are factors of focusing elements on the marked form.

What should be significant here is that the application of a marked structure over an unmarked structure must come with pragmatic effects in terms of an informational excess for the hearer. Thus this should be not be acknowledged in a stipulation of a set of alternatives in the linguistic item as contrastive focus reading requires the presupposed set to be a set containing more than one element.

5.Conclusion

This paper sets forth the CR construction on a discourse-pragmatic focus account. CR has distinctive semantic interpretation due to a limiting effect on the denotation of a lexical element. As a corollary, CR seems to play the role of determining possible interpretation of a lexical form a hearer should decide from a set-shrinking effect. Contrast in informativeness arises due to the restriction on the denotation of the non-reduplicated form.

The notion of contrastivity here should not be considered as making a set of alternatives from a lexical item. Rather contrastivity arouses due to pragmatic factors like the speaker's assumption about the hearer's expectation of information on a focus constituent. The speaker will use a contrastive focus marking in a linguistic expression if he or she assumes that the hearer will not by fully aware of the assertion of the expressed form or speech act. Contrastive Focus Hypothesis makes possible explanation not only for CRs but also the prefixes in some languages that shows corresponding semantic effects in showing contrastivity. The present paper does not discuss issues concerning the extended research on the correlation with focus and prototypicality for generalization in various languages which will be left for further research.

References

Dray, N. 1987. *Doubles and Modifiers in English.* Unpublished M.A. thesis, University of Chicago.

Ghomeshi, J. and R. Jackendoff and N. Rosen and K. Russell. 2004. Contrastive Focus Reduplication in English (the salad-salad paper). *Natural Language and Linguistic Theory* 22: 307-357.

Horn, L. 1993. *Economy and Redundancy in a Dualistic Model of Natural Language.* SKY: The Linguistic Association of Finland.

Lasersohn, P. 1999. Pragmatic halos, *Language* 75: 522-551.

Lee, C. 2003. Contrastive Topic and/or Contrastive Focus. Bill McClure ed., *Japanese/Korean Linguistics* 12. CSLI, Stanford.

Levinson, S. 2000. *Presumptive Meanings*: The Theory of Generalized. Conversational Implicature. The MIT Press: Cambridge.

Poser, W. 1991. *Japanese periphrastic verbs and noun incorporation.* Unpublished manuscript, Stanford University.

Rooth, M. 1992. A theory of focus interpretation. *Natural Language Semantics*: 75-116.

Rooth, M. 1996. Focus. In S. Lappin ed., *Handbook of Contemporary Semantic Theory.* Oxford: Blackwell, 271-297.

Whitton, L. 2007. The Function of English Contrastive Reduplication: Evidence from Homonyms. Paper presented at the Linguistic Society of America (LSA) Annual Meeting, Anaheim, CA..

Zimmermann, M. 2006. Contrastive Focus. In Fanselow, G., Fery, C. & Krifka, M. eds., *Working Papers of the SFB632, Interdisciplinary Studies on Information Structure (ISIS).* Potsdam: University publishing house Potsdam.

Gei^{3}ta^1 in Taiwan Mandarin--- A Particular Construction[*]

Chiachun Lee

Nan-Jeon Institute of Technology, Department of Applied English,
737-46, No.178. Chaochin Rd. Yianshui Town, Tainan County. Taiwan
chiachun@njtc.edu.tw

Abstract. The present paper investigates a particular structure in Taiwan Mandarin, "(NP) + (intensifier) + gei^{3}ta^1 "give him/it"+ adjective" in terms of construction grammar. The structure is mostly observed in utterances of younger generation. Though it is not regarded as a grammatical or standard structure, it is still a register of language. The structure lays emphasis on speaker's attitude toward an undesired, unpleasant event. In most cases, the attitude tends to be negative. The events or propositions must have existed or been completed. The adjectives compatible with this structure belong to category of higher degree. The grammatical usage illustrates semantic bleaching of gei^{3}ta^1. And the changes from giving to a grammatical particle denoting subjective belief is a kind of subjectification. Moreover, ta^1 could refer to events or situation expressed by a more complicated grammatical structure, or denotes nothing as a dummy word. Though many previous studies paid attention to the newly developed structure resulted from language contact, the adequate account was not provided. It is hoped through this investigation, we will get a better understanding of this particular structure.

Keywords: gei^{3}ta^1, construction meaning, speaker's subjective attitude/belief, negative, event

1. Introduction

Taiwan Mandarin is the result of language contact between Mandarin Chinese and Taiwanese Southern Min(TSM). There have been plenty of investigations on novel usages brought about by influence from TSM, including Kubler(1985), Tsai(2002) and Zeng(2003). However, these previous investigations mainly focus on the differences between Mandarin and Taiwan Mandarin. Few efforts were made to provide an adequate account on these newly emerged sentence structures. In the present paper, I am going to be concerned with one particular construction which are newly developed structure. In modern Taiwan Mandarin there are two particular structures evoking gei^{3}ta^1. One is descriptive expressions, "gei^{3}ta^1 + adjective". The other one is resultative structure, "verb + gei^{3}ta^1 + complement". These two sentence structures could be regarded as the result of language contact. The former structure is more novel and is confined in ordinary utterances of younger generation. Instead of their content meaning of a giving verb and the third person pronoun, gei^{3}ta^1 function like an infix for the purpose of denoting speakers' undesired and unpleasant attitude toward on the event mentioned. The corresponding combination of giving word and the third person pronoun in TSM do not have the similar function. Thus, he present paper aims at pinning down the function and features conveyed by the construction "(NP) + (intensifier) + gei^{3}ta^1 + adjective" in TM from the perspective of construction grammar proposed by Goldberg(1995, 2006). Through careful investigation on this novel structure, it is proven once again that language has its own life. It will be influenced by surrounding languages and has its own development. The data used as examples are attracted from, mainly blogs, internet and radio programs in Taiwan. The

---

[*] I would like to express my heartfelt thanks to the anonymous reviewers for comments and suggestions on the earlier abridged version of this paper. Needless to say, I am solely responsible for any infelicities.

paper is organized by the following parts. Chapter 2 tackle with the function and features of the structure "(NP) + (intensifier) + *gei³ta¹* + adjective", including its syntactic variations and features of the compatible adjectives, the function of *gei³ta¹*, the reference of *ta¹*. Chapter 3 is conclusion.

2. The structure "*gei³* + *ta¹* + adjective" in TM

2.1 Construction meaning

Based on Goldberg (2006), grammatical constructions are conventionalized pairings of form and function. She claims that constructions bear specific function, especially idiosyncratic structure.[1] While verbs are important in semantics of a construction, construction also denotes certain kind of meaning. Moreover, CG claims that different surface structure spells different meaning. Furthermore, CG also take information structure and pragmatics into consideration. In the step of mapping from semantics to syntax, not all roles in frame are necessarily profiled in surface structure. Some could be omitted if they are recoverable from the context or they are of no importance in information.

In this study, I am going to investigate the newly developed construction in terms of CG on account of the following reasons. First, this construction is signified by its characteristics. This structure amplifies speaker's emotive evaluation on undesired or unpleasant event or situation. The event or situation must be realis. That is to say that, it must be fact. Second, the adjectives compatible with this structure must be adjectives with higher degree. General adjectives are seldom found in this structure.

There are two kinds of special structures evoking "*gei³* + *ta¹*"[2] in TM. Type I, descriptive expressions, "*gei³ta¹* + adjective" and "*gei³ta¹* + verb". The other one is resultative structure, "verb + *gei³ta¹* + complement". In the present study, the focus is on "*gei³ta¹* + adjective". The core part of the structure is "*gei³ta¹* + adjective". By adding adverbs there are several variations[3]:

1. *gei³ta¹* + *ge⁰* + N
    a. *Wo³ zhan⁴zai⁴ yuan² di⁴ bu⁴ zhi¹dao⁴ yiao⁴ shuo¹ sha²,*
    I stand at original place NOT know will speak what
    zhen¹shi⁴ gei³ta¹ ge⁰ bu⁴ yu³ zhi⁴ pien⁴
    really GEI TA CL   not give place comment
    Standing at the original place without knowing what to say, I really do not intend to give any comment.
    b. *Wo³jüe²de² jin¹tian¹zhen¹de⁰hen³gei³ta¹ge⁰ jin⁴bao⁴*
    I feel today really very GEI Ta CL surprise
    Today, I really feel very much surprised.
2. *gei³ta¹* + ADJP
    a. *ta¹ suo³xue²de⁰ fan²wei² zhen¹de⁰ shi⁴ you³dian³ gei³ta¹   za²*
    he learn field really be a little GEI TA complicated
    What he learned was a little complicated.
3. *fei¹chang²* + *gei³ta¹* + ADJ
    a. *jin³ji² xun²zhao³ … (fei¹chang² gei³ta¹ jin³ji²)*
    urgent look for (very much GEI TA urgent
    Look for something in emergency. (Extremely in emergency)
4. (*zhen¹de⁰* +) *you³dian³*+ *gei³ta¹* + ADJ
    a. *Tian¹yu³chuan²shuo¹ …   zhen¹de⁰you³dian³ gei³ta¹ wu²liao² shuo¹*
    Tianyuchanshuo(a puppet play)   really a little   GEI TA boring speak
    Tianyuchanshuo is really very boring.

---

[1] For more details, please take reference to Goldberg (2006:6, 7).

[2] The character of third person pronoun is "他"or "它". "他" is human 3ʳᵈ person pronoun. "它" usually denotes unanimated objects/matters or animated animals, excluding human. Though there are different characters presenting different gender of the third person personal pronouns, the male third person pronoun is more general than female one, especially in informal situations. Thus, in original data both "他"and "它" are observed.

[3] I use Hanyu Pinyin for transliteration of Chinese words. Some function lexemes are not clearly explained. Instead, I use capitalized letters, such as CL is classifier, LE is a marker indicating the completion of event or changes. LA is a sentence final particle. NOM is nominalization marker. NOT is negation.

5. *zhen^{1}de^0 + gei^{3}ta^1 + you^{3}dian^3* + ADJ

    a. *shuo^1 zhen^{1}de^0 ni^{3}de^0 fan^{3}ying^4 zhen^{1}de^0 you^{3}dian^3 gei^{3}ta^1 chi^{2}dun^4 le^{0}shuo^1*

  speak the truth   your reaction really a little   GEI TA slow LE speak

    To tell the truth, your reaction is really a little slow.

6. *zhen^1(shi^4) + gei^{3}ta^1 + you^{3}gou^4* + ADJ

    a. *kuang^{2}dao^1 zhen^{1}de^{0}shi^4 gei^{3}ta^1 you^{3}gou^4 shuai^4 de^0 la^0*

    Kuangdao^4 really   be GEI TA very much handsome DE LA

    Kuangdao is really handsome.

In the 1st token, *gei^3* is a verb of giving. The noun following *gei^{3}ta^1* is the theme transferred. The goal of giving action is *ta^1*. The three internal arguments of giving verb are realized, though the theme transferred is abstract. These themes are nominalized by the classifier *ge^0*. This structure could be regarded as residue of original functions as a giving verb. In the other variations, the constituent following *gei^{3}ta^1* is no longer a noun, instead, these elements compatible could be adjectives. Thus, *gei^3* is not a verb and *ta^1* not a goal. In the first type of variations *gei^{3}ta^1* is obligatory because *gei^3* is still a main verb in the clause while in the other variations it is no longer essential. Thus, there are some changes in syntax and semantics in *gei^3* and *ta^1*. That will be investigated in the later section. With regard to the other variations, the syntactic distribution could be summarized as the following pattern:

      (3) (*zhen^1/zhen^{1}de^0/ zhen^{1}shi^4/ zhen^{1}de^{0}shi^4* 'truly, really'+) *gei^{3}ta^1* (+ *fei^{1}chang^2*'very much'/ *you^{3}dian^3* a little'/ *you^{3}gou^4*'enough') + ADJ

"*zhen^1/zhen^{1}de^0/ zhen^{1}shi^4/ zhen^{1}de^{0}shi^4*" emphasizes the validity of the following evaluation. In our data, *gei^{3}ta^1* must go after this type of adverbs. Moreover, their syntactic position must precede adverbs modifying adjectives, including *fei^{1}chang^2/ you^{3}dian^3/ you^{3}gou^4*. The relative position between *gei^{3}ta^1* and intensifier is more flexible. These degree adverbs come before or follow after *gei^{3}ta^1*.

The structure in question is featured with the following quality. First, the structure expresses speaker's subjective evaluation. Second, the goal of evaluation is factivity. Third, the adjectives tend to be negative in most cases, though the positive ones are compatible.

The concept of subjectivity here is defined as that a construction or a particular item should make reference to speaker for its interpretation. Take the following pair of sentences as a example (Smet and Verstraete, 2006: 367).

    (4)a. Mum <u>won't</u> let us go out tonight. I asked her but she said we had partied more than enough this week.

      b. Judith <u>won't</u> be late. She never is.

In (4) a, *won't* expresses Mum's unwillingness to give permission to them to go out at night. In(4) b, *won't* describes speaker's judgment on the matter that whether Judith is likely to be late or not. The speaker reasons on the basis of Judith's previous behavior. Because it "refers to a judgment by the speaker rather than an action or a characteristic of one of the clausal participants" (Smet and Verstraete, 2006: 367), sentence (b) is subjective while sentence (a) is not. In the concept of subjectivity the speaker should be included in the interpretation. Take the following "minimal pair" sentences as examples.

    (5) a. *ta^1 suo^{3}xue^2 de^0 fan^{2}wei^2 zhen^{1}de^0 shi^4 you^{3}dian^3 gei^{3}ta^1 za^2*

      He learning NOM field   really   a little GET TA complicated

      What he learned was a little complicated.

      b. *ta^1 suo^{3}xue^{2}de^0 fan^{2}wei^2 zhen^{1}de^0 shi^4 you^{3}dian^3 za^2*

      He learning NOM field   really   a little   complicated

      What he learned was a little complicated.

    (6) a. *Ah! Kai^1 Xiao^{3}hei^1 chu^{1}qü^4 you^{3}dian^3 gei^{3}ta^1 wei^{2}xian^3*

      Ah! Drive Xiaohei   out   have a little GEI TA danger

      Ah! Driving Xiaohei(black car) is a kind of danger.

      b. *Ah! Kai^1 Xiao^{3}hei^1 chu^{1}qü^4 you^{3}dian^3 wei^{2}xian^3*

      Ah! Drive Xiaohei   out   have a little danger

      Ah! Driving Xiaohei(black car) is a kind of danger.

In these minimal pair sets, sentences b are more general while sentences a manifests the emphasis of speaker's emotion. Though sentences b also indicates speaker's evaluation on the matter talked about, the addition of *gei3ta1* specifies the matter being judged. In (5) a the evaluation of "complication" is based on speaker's understanding of his field of study, and in (6) a "danger" is a judgment from speaker's

---

[4] Kuangdao is a character in a puppet play.

knowledge of the car or of the person will drive the car. The interpretation of the evaluation should make reference to speaker's understanding of the real world.

2.2 The adjectives in the construction

As far as the adjectives are concerned, only intransitive adjectives are observed, for examples, wu^2liao^2 boring, chi^2duen^4 slow (in thought or action), za^2 complicated, $bu^2iao^4lian^3$ shameless, $bu^4shuang^3$ angry, wue^2xian^3 dangerous, jin^3zhang^1 nervous. From the data, it is observed that about 70% of the predicates observed in our data are negative while approximately 30% of these adjectives are positive.

Table 1: The percentage of adjective quality

	number	percentage	examples
negative adjectives	120	70%	$bu^4shuang^3$ not well, chi^2duen^4 slow (in thought or action), $bu^2iao^4lian^3$ shameless, wue^2xian^3 dangerous
positive adjectives	48	30%	$shuai4$ handsome, $xing^4fu^2$ happy, hao^3kan^4 beautiful, $haoi^3ting^1$ pleasant to hear
total	168	100%	

In this construction, gei^3 and ta^1 do not keep their respective original function. It carries more grammatical meaning, especially pragmatically. On the one hand, gei^3ta^1 could be regarded as an expletive. In English, there is also expletive to stress the emotion of speaker, such as *bloody* in *per-bloody-haps, inde-bloody-pendent.* Macmillian(1980) claims that infixing is emotive stress amplifier and semantically neutrual. The additional insertion entails emotive factors, such as taboo violation, vehemence, (dis)approval, playfulness and irritation. On the contrary, Adams(2001, 2004) argues that the inserts add lexical meaning to their matrices in addition to emotive intensity. In addition to emotional intensity, it also conveys lexical meaning, such as humor, which depends on its relationship to verbal context at the same time. Growing numbers of examples suggest that the rules of infixing and interposing are changing and more flexible. gei^3ta^1 in TM, like *bloody* in English functions as an expletive to stress emotion. It seems that gei^3ta^1 is empty in meaning. But through careful investigation, it implies lexical meaning.

The differences between sentences of these "minimal pairs" lie in the attachment of gei^3ta^1. There is no difference in lexical meaning between the two sentences of the same pair. That means gei^3ta^1 is not an obligatory. Like the expletive in English, gei^3ta^1 not only involves the amplification of speakers' emotion, it also has its own lexical meaning. With regard to its function as an emotive stress amplifier, gei^3ta^1 changes a detached report of an event into an expression of personal involvement, especially speakers' unpleasant and undesired feeling. In these pairs of sentences above, sentence a conveys more than sentence b in terms of speakers' subjective attitude and emotive reaction toward the event being mentioned.

According to Shetter(2000), Spanish, French and German have ethical pronoun to express speakers' caring. However, in other languages ethical pronoun is first person pronoun. Fogsgaard(2005) claims that what the ethical dative does is "to introduce the enunciator directly in the reference scene of the utterance and so put an extra stress on the interest taken in that scene, the evaluation regarding the emotional importance of the event." Gei^3ta^1 involves two subparts in meaning. One is the source, that is the speaker. The other is the goal of giving, the event or situation being evaluated. In spite of the loss of content meaning of gei^3ta^1, the addition of it reminds addressee the existence of addresser and event. Gei^3 Ta^1 is somewhat like an ethical dative which highlights speaker's implication.

Traugott(2003:125) interprets subjectivity as the way in which natural languages, in their structure and their normal manner of operation, provide for the locutionary agent's expression of himself and his own attitudes and beliefs. Finegan (1995) holds that language expresses not only objective consideration on preposition but also speakers' perspective, affect and epistemic modality. In addition to stress on speaker's subjective emotion, the structure in question profiles speaker's position in utterance reference scene by which speaker has much closer correlation with his utterances.

2.3 The reference of ta^1

Though gei^3ta^1 carries more pragmatic function, in order to have sufficient understanding about its essence, it is absolutely crucial to figure out its lexical meaning. The reference of ta^1 will be discussed firstly. Regarding to the antecedent of pronoun, *ta^1* in our data are classified as pleonastic and referential. There are two kinds of linguistic references, exophora and endophora. Exophora is reference to something extralinguistic. For example,

(10) *that chair over there is John's*

The words "that" and "there" in the above example are exophoric because they indicate the direction of the chair referred to. Endophora is to something intralinguistic, i.e. in the same text.

(11) I saw Pam yesterday. She was lying on the beach.

In the sentence "she" is intralinguistic because it refers to "Pam" in prior expression. Based on the data, referential *ta^1* could be a type of endophora. It could refer to something else already mentioned in the preceding utterances. Observation shows that the referential *ta^1* refers to events, propositions or situations. According Gundel et al.(2004), events, as well as facts, propositions, situations and other 'higher-order' entities are often introduced into discourse by non-nominal constituents like clauses, sequences of clauses and verb phrase. Similarly, the references of *ta^1* are expressed by more complicated and higher constituents.

(12)a. *Zhe^4 ci^4 de^0 ban^1 jü^4 hen^3 duo^1 ren^2 dao^2*

    This time DE class gathering very many people reach

    zhen^1 shi^4 gei^3 ta^1 you^3 yi^4 dian^3 jing^1 yia^2

    really GEITA a kind of surprising

    Many people took part in classmates reunion. It really makes me surprised

b. *Ming^2 tian^1 zhong^1 wu^3 shi^4 wuo^3 gen^1 xi^3 huan^1 de^0 nü^3 hai^2*

    tomorrow noon be I and like DE girl

    di^4 yi^1 ci^4 dan^1 du^2 Yüe^1 hui^4, gei^3 ta^1 fen^3 jin^3 zhan^1

    the first time separately date GEITA very nervous

    I am going to have a date with the girl I love at noon tomorrow. It makes me very nervous.

The reference of *ta^1* in a is a fact that many classmates attended classmate reunion. Similarly, *ta^1* in c refers to one's first date with the girl he likes. Both events in b and c are presented by clause.

Asher(1993) regards that eventualities have a relatively high degree of world immanence, since such entities have spatialtemporal location and causal efficacy. Because of the high degree of world immanence, eventualities are available to immediately subsequent with *ta^1*. Thus, in summary, *ta^1* is an event-related argument. Moreover, the events denoted by *ta^1* are interpreted as reason contributing to the final result, such as sentence (13) or a matter or issue on which speakers to make a comment, sentence (14) b.   .

(13) *Ting^1 lao^3 yin^1 yüe^4 de^0 xia^2 chan^3,*

    Listen to old music DE result

    jiu^4 shi^4 hui^4 muo^4 ming^2 gei^3 ta^1 shang^1 gan^3 qi^3 lai^2

    JIU BE will without any reason GEITA sad   start to

    The result of listening to old music is starting to get sad without any reasons.

(14) *XX gou^4 wu^4 wan^3 yie^4 you^3 gou^4 gei^3 ta^1 bu^4 zhuan^1 yie^4*

    xx buy objects webpage enough GEITA NOT professional

    xx shopping webpage is very unprofessional.

In terms of information structure, presentation of a clausally introduced entity within the topic of an utterance is one of the ways to promote salience, and bring the entity into focus. *Gei^3 ta^1*, the repetition of the event mentioned previously not only indicates reasons or topics but also emphasize speaker's attitude, feeling.

The pleonastic *ta^1* could not find any antecedent to refer to, even in the whole context.

(15) a. *wuo^4 hu^3 cang^2 long^2 zhen^1 de ^{0} gei^3 ta^1 chao^1 hao^3 kan^4*

    Crouching Tiger, Hidden Dragon truly   GEITA very nice see

    Crouching Tiger, Hidden Dragon is really a good movie

b. *tai^2 wan^1 ba^1 dian^3 dang^3 lian^2 xü^4 jü^4 zhen^1 shi^4 gei^3 ta^1 bu^4 hao^3 kan^4*

    Taiwan 8 o'clock   soap opera   really GEITA NOT nice watch

    In Taiwan the soap opera at eight o'clock was really bad.

3. Conclusion

"(NP) + (intensifier) + *gei^3 ta^1* + adjective" is a newly developed expression which is frequently observed in utterances spoken by younger generation in Taiwan. In comparison with the corresponding expressions in Mandarin, the usage of *gei^3 ta^1* amplifies speaker's emotional attitude, mostly negative. In some cases, the third person pronoun could refer to an event or situation but in other cases *ta¹* does not denote anything like a dummy word. The path of change could roughly depicted as:

transfer of object > evaluative situation > textual/metalinguistic meaning >

subjective attitude toward proposition

The adequate and explicit path of grammatical change needs deeper investigation. On the other hand, there is still another way to account the change. One of the reviewer suggests that *gei³ta¹* could be analyzed semantically as a two-place predicate with an event argument and an individual argument, representing as the following :

lamda lamda_x [SP_NEG_ATT(e) & High-Degree (e) & Theme (e,x)]

The reason why *gei³ta¹* is followed by adjective is that the degree of the event must be specified as a high scale. The analysis provides another perspective to explain this structure. It deserves further investigations. Moreover, the motivations for the change are also another issue which deserve further research. It is assumed that the newly developed structure originates from Taiwan Southern Min because in Taiwan Mandarin the functions of *gei³* could correspond to *ka⁷* in TSM. However, the adequacy of the assumption needs further study.

References

Asher, Nicholas. 1993. *Reference to Abstract Objects in Discourse.* Boston: Dordrecht, Kluwer Academic.

Finegan. E. 1995. Subjectivity and Subjectivisation: an Introduction. In *Subjectivity and Subjectivisation* eds. by Stein and Wright. pp. 1-15. Cambridge: Cambridge University Press.

Fogsgaard, Lene.(2005) Enunciation and emotion: grammatical devices for emotion coding in language. From: http://www.hum.au.dk/semiotics/pdf/emotion_dev.pdf

Kubler. Cornelius.C. 1985a. *The development of Mandarin in Taiwan: a case study of language Contact.* Taipei: Student Book Co. Ltd.

Kubler. Cornelius C. 1985b. The influence of Southern Min on the Mandarin of Taiwan. *Anthropological Linguistics.* Vol. 27. . 156-176.

Heine, Bernd., Ulrike Claudi, and Friederike Hünnemeyer. 1991. *Grammaricalization: a Conceptual Framework.* Chicago: University of Chicago Press.

Goldberg, Adele E.1995. *Constructions: A Construction Grammar Approach to Argument Structure.* Chicago and London: The University of Chicago Press.

_______________ 2000. Patient arguments of causative verbs can be omitted: the role of information structure in argument distribution. *Langauge Science 23.* 503-524.

_______________ 2002. Surface Generalizations: an alternative to alternations. *Cognitive Linguistics.*

_______________ and Ray Jackendoff.2004. The English resultative as a family of constructions. *Language* 80.532-568.

_______________2005a. Argument realization: the role of constructions, lexical semantics and discourse. FactorsIn Östman, Jan-Ola (ed. and introd.); Fried, Mirjam (ed. and introd.), *Construction Grammars: Cognitive Grounding and Theoretical Extensions.* 17-43. Amsterdam, Netherlands: Benjamins.

_______________ 2005b. Constructions, lexical semantics and the correspondence principle: Accounting for generalizations and subregularities in the realization of arguments Nomi Erteschik-Shir and Tova Rapoport eds., *The syntax of aspect.* Oxford University Press.

_______________ 2006. *Constructions at work: The nature of generalization in language.* New York: Oxford University Press.

Gundel, Jeanette; Hedberg, Nancy; Zacharski, Ron. 2004. Pronouns without explicit antecedents: How do we know when a pronoun is referential? In Branco, António (ed. and foreword); McEnery, Tony (ed. and foreword); Mitkov, Ruslan ed. and foreword, *Anaphora Processing: Linguistic, Cognitive and Computational Modelling.* Amsterdam,

Netherlands: Benjamins. 351-64. CILT Amsterdam, Netherlands: Amsterdam Studies in the Theory and History of Linguistic Science IV: Current Issues in Linguistic Theory.

Macmillan, James B. 1980. Infixing and interposing in English. *American Speech* 55, 163-183.

Lord, Carol, Foong Ha Yap, and Shoichi Iwasaki. 2002. Grammaticalization of 'give': African and Asian perspectives. In: Ilse Wischer and Gabriele Diewald eds., *New reflections on grammaticalizaiton* (Topological Studies in Language 49), 217-235. Amsterdam/Philadelphia: John Benjamins.

Shetter, William Z. 2000. My dogs died on me. Pronoun of 'caring". http://home.bluemarble.net/~langmin/miniatures/ethical.htm

Smet, Hendrik De. & Verstraete, Jean-Christophe. 2006. Coming to termswith subjectivity. *Cognitive Linguistis* 17-3: 365-392.

Traugott, Elizabeth Closs. 1987. From less to more situated in language: The unidirectionality of semantic change. Papers from the Fifth International Conference on English Historical Linguistics. Ed. by Sylvia M. Adamson. Vivien Law. Nigel Vincent, and Susan M. Wright. Amsterdam: Benjamins.

Traugott, Elizabeth Closs. 1989. On the rise of epistemic meanings in English: an example of subjectification in semantic change. *Langauge* 65:31-55.

Traugott, Elizabeth Closs and Ekkehard König. 1991. The semantics—pragmatics of grammaticalization revisited. In *Approaches to grammaticalization*. Vol.1 ed. by ElixabethCloss G\Traugott and Bernd Hein. Amsterdam/Piladelphia: John Benjamins Publishing Company. 189-218.

Traugott, Elizabeth Closs and Richard B. Dasher. 2002. *Regularity in semantic change.* Cambridge: Cambridge University Press.

Traugott, Elizabeth Closs. 2003. From subjectification to intersubjectification. *Motives for language change.* ed. by Kickey, Raymond. Cambridge, New York Cambridge University Press. 124-139.

Tsai,Mei-chih.2002.Yiou^{4}tai^{2}wan^{1}guo^{2}yü^{3}de^{0}yü^{3}fa^{3}te^{4}dian^{3}kan^{4}gong^{4}tong^{2}yü^3, fang^{1}yian^2 zhi^1 hu^{4}dong^4. On the interaction between pidgin and dialects from the perspective of grammatical features of Taiwan Mandarin. *Papers from The 4th International Conference on Taiwan Language and Teaching.* 1-25.

Zeng, Sin-Yi. 2003. *Dangdai Taiwan Guoyude Jyufajiegou. The syntax structures of contemporary Taiwanese Mandarin.* Master thesis. National Taiwan Normal University. Graduate Institute of Teaching Chinese as a second language.

Implementation of Presence and Absence of Blocking Effects: A Categorial Grammar Approach to Chinese and Korean[*]

Yong-hun Lee

Dept. of English Lang. & Lit. Chungnam Nat'l Univ. & Hannam Univ.
220 Gung-dong, Daejeon 305-764, Korea
ylee@cnu.ac.kr

Abstract. Among the languages that allow long-distance reflexives, some languages have blocking effects, whereas others don't. The goal of this paper is to provide computational algorithms that can handle presence and absence of blocking effects of long-distance reflexives. We will examine the blocking effects in Chinese and Korea and develop computational algorithms for handling blocking effects in those two languages. The algorithms will be developed by incorporating Chierchia's Binding Theory into Steedman's Combinatory Categorial Grammar (CCG). Through the analyses and implementations, this paper illustrates how blocking effects can be implemented computationally.

Keywords: long-distance reflexive, blocking effects, Chinese, Korean, CCG

1. Introduction

In some languages, long-distance reflexives are allowed in addition to their sentence-bound counterparts. Among the languages that allow long-distance reflexives, some languages have blocking effects, but others don't. Chinese is one language that has blocking effects and the sentence (1) demonstrates an example of blocking effects (Cole, et al., 2000:14).[1]

(1)   Blocking Effect in Chinese
        Zhangsan$_i$ renwei wo$_j$ zhidao Wangwu$_k$ xihauan   ziji$_{*i/*j/k}$
        Zhangsan   think   I   know   Wangwu   like   self
        'Zhangsan thinks I know Wangwu likes self.'

Here, the reflexive *ziji* cannot refer to *Zhangsan* because *wo* blocks co-reference between *ziji* and *Zhangsan*. Let's compare this sentence with (2). (2) is the Korean counterpart of sentence (1).[2]

---

[1] Cole et al. (2000) included state-of-art introduction to long-distance reflexives, and various approaches to long-distance reflexives are tried by Pica (1987), Manzini & Wexler (1987), Battistella (1989), Katada (1991), Haung & Tang (1991), Cole & Sung (1994), etc. Discussions on Chinese long-distance reflexives are contained in Huang (1982), Hung (1984), Tang (1989), Haung & Tang (1991), among others.

[2] We have similar phenomenon in the following sentence (Moon, 1996:15).

(i) *John$_i$-un* [*nay$_j$-ka caki$_{i/*j}$-lul*   *ttayli-ess-ta-ko*]   *syangkakha-n-ta.*
    John.TOP I.NOM   self.ACC   beat.PAST.DECL.COMP   think.PRES.DECL
    'John thinks that I beat him.'

Here, the reflexive *caki* can refers to *John* across the pronoun *nay*. If Korean had blocking effects, this phenomenon would be impossible since the pronoun *nay* blocks the co-referential relations between *caki* and *John*.

(2)   No Blocking Effect in Korean
        Chelsoo$_i$-nun   [*nay$_j$-ka*   [*Younghee$_k$-ka   caki$_{i/*j/k}$-lul co.aha-n-ta-ko*]
        Chelsoo.TOP   I.NOM   Younghee.NOM self.ACC   like.PRES.DECL.COMP
        a(l)-n-ta-ko]   *sayngkakha-n-ta.*
        know.PRES.DECL.COMP think.PRES.DECL
        'Chelsoo thinks that I know that Younghee likes him/herself.'

As the co-reference relations in (2) indicate, *caki* CAN refer to *Chelsoo*, though *nay* is located between them. Therefore, we can say that there is no blocking effect in Korean long-distance reflexives.

The goal of this paper is to provide computational algorithms that can handle presence and absence of blocking effects. The algorithms will be developed by combining Steedman (1996, 2000)'s Combinatory Categorial Grammar (CCG) and Chierchia's Binding Theory, which will be called a CCG-like system.

This paper is organized as follows. In Section 2, Categorial Grammar and Chierchia (1988)'s Binding Theory will be introduced. Section 3 introduces a CCG-like system and demonstrates how blocking effects can be handled in the CCG-like system. Section 4 provides computational algorithms for presence and absences of the blocking effects, and Section 5 summarizes this paper.

2. Binding Theory in Categorial Grammar

Categorial Grammar was first introduced by Ajdukiewicz (1935) and later modified and advanced by Bar-Hillel (1953), Curry & Feys (1958), and Lambek (1958). In this framework, we have two basic categories *n* and *s*, and other categories come from the combinations of these two categories. All the syntactic phenomena are described and analyzed by the functor-argument relations of the constituents.

Steedman (1996, 2000) extended previous studies in Categorial Grammar and developed Combinatorial Categorial Grammar (CCG). The most important characteristic of his system is that predicate-arguments relations are projected by the combinatory rules of syntax, and other operations are based on these predicate-arguments relations (Steedman, 2000:38). The most fundamental combinatory rule is functional application, which is delineated in (3). Here, *f* is the semantic interpretation of the functor category, and *a* is that of the argument.

(3)   Functional Application (Steedman, 1996:13)
        a. $X / Y :f$ Y $:a$ $\rightarrow$ X : fa (>)
        b. Y $:a$ $X \backslash Y :f$ $\rightarrow$ X : fa (<)

Chierchia applied Categorial Grammar to explain Binding phenomena in English, and he described syntactic constraints of reflexives and pronominals as follows (Chierichia, 1988:134).

(4)   Binding in Categorial Grammar
        a. A reflexive must be bound to an F-commanding argument in its minimal NP
             or S domain.
        b. A non-reflexive pronoun must not be co-indexed with anything in its minimal NP
             or S domain.
        where F-command is simply c-command at function-argument structure.

Agreement in number and gender must hold between pronouns and their antecedents, in order to pronouns can refer to their antecedents. The constraint for checking agreement is stated in (5a).

FT(*n*) in (5b) has three information: *n* is the index of the NP, *gndr* is gender, and *nmbr* is number (Chierchia, 1988:132).

(5)   Agreement-Checking Algorithm
      a. FT(*n*)≈FT(*m*): The features associated with *n* are non-distinct from those associated with *m*.
      b.
$$FT(n) = \begin{pmatrix} n \\ gndr \\ nmbr \end{pmatrix}$$

For example, the FTs of three different NPs *John*, *himself*, and *her* can be stated as follows.

(6)
$$FT(1) = \begin{pmatrix} John_1 \\ 1 \\ male \\ 3 \end{pmatrix} \qquad FT(2) = \begin{pmatrix} himself_2 \\ 2 \\ male \\ 3 \end{pmatrix} \qquad FT(3) = \begin{pmatrix} her_3 \\ 3 \\ female \\ 3 \end{pmatrix}$$

Chierchia introduced resolution algorithms for pronouns in English based on the combinatorics, and they are enumerated in (7). Here and throughout, integers will be used as names for the categories mentioned in the rules.

(7)   Chierchia's Algorithms (1988:138-9)
      a. $TV_0 + NP_1 \Rightarrow IV_2$

        (i) $LPS(0) \cap LPS(1) = \varnothing$ non-coreference
        (ii) $SLASH(2) \cap (LPS(1) \cup LPS(2)) = \varnothing$ crossover
        (iii)$SLASH(2) = SLASH(0) \cup SLASH(1)$ slash-percolation
        (iv)$LPS(2) = LPS(0) \cup LPS(1)$ LPS-percolation

      b. $S/NP_{n\;0} + NP_{n\;1} \Rightarrow S_2$

        (i) $LPS(2) = \varnothing$ A-opacity boundary
        (ii) $SLASH(2) \cap (LPS(1) \cup LPS(2)) = \varnothing$ crossover
        (iii)$SLASH(2) = SLASH(0) \cup SLASH(1)$ slash-percolation
        (iv) $n_{+refl} \notin LPS(0) \cup LPS(1)$ reflexive

      c. $IV/IV_0 + IV_1 \Rightarrow IV_2$

        (i) $LPS(2) = LPS(0)$ A-opacity boundary
        (ii) $SLASH(2) \cap (LPS(1) \cup LPS(2)) = \varnothing$ crossover
        (iii)$SLASH(2) = SLASH(0) \cup SLASH(1)$ slash-percolation
        (iv) $n_{+refl} \notin LPS(1)$ reflexive

      d. Reflexives
        (i) $A_{n\,[+refl]\,\in\,LPS} \Rightarrow A_{n\,\notin\,LPS}$
        (ii) conditions: (a) $A = IV, TV$ (b) $FT(A) \approx FT(n)$
        (iii)translation: $\lambda x_n [A'(x_n)]$

3. Analyzing Blocking Effects with Category

3.1. A CCG-like System

The system that this paper develops is a CCG-like system, which has been introduced in Lee (2002a, 2002b, 2003a, 2003b). It is basically an incorporation of Chierchia's ideas into Steedman's Combinatory Categorial Grammar (CCG). This system is similar to Steedman's system in that surface combinatorics triggers other operations, especially reflexive resolution algorithms in this paper. It is different from Steedman's in that it uses attribute-value ordered pairs (**avop**) in (8) to describe syntactic dependencies of constituents. The six attributes are explained in (9).

(8)   Structure of Attribute-Value Ordered Pair
        <PHON,CAT,(AGR),TRANS,NPS,(SLASH)>

(9)   Six Attributes
        a. PHON
                (i)   phonological/morphological form
                (ii) concatenates a word to a stream of words
        b. CAT
                (i)   has categorial information
                (ii) such as S, NP, S\NP, and so on
        c. AGR
                (i)   agreement feature
                (ii) index, type, gender, and number
        d. TRANS
                (i)   semantic interpretation
                (ii) based on Montagovian semantics
        e. NPS (NP Index Store)
                (i)   something like a Cooper-storage
                (ii) stores indexes of NP
        f. SLASH
                (i)   similar to that of HPSG
                (ii) deals with crossover phenomena

The functional application on the CAT values triggers operations on TRANS and NPS values, and all the reflexives are resolved by these operations. NPS is similar to Chierchia's LPS, but different in (i) that NPS stores the indexes for other types of NPs in addition to pronouns and (ii) that NPS is not local. That is, the indexes stored in NPS can be percolated up beyond the minimal S domain. AGR and SLASH are parenthesised in (8), because the values for these two attributes will be omitted from the actual representations.

  The reflexive resolution algorithms in the CCG-like system can be described as follows. Each constituent in the input sentence is combined with the others by functional applications in (3). After this combination, if there is [+refl] in the NPS store, it triggers reflexive resolution algorithms. The resolution algorithms perform some operations on TRANS and NPS values, and all the reflexives are resolved with their antecedents.

3.2. Blocking Effects in the CCG-like System

Now, let's see how presence and absence of blocking effects can be handled in the CCG-like system. First, in order to process long-distance reflexives, Chierchia's algorithms in (7) must be revised slightly. Among the conditions that are enumerated in (7), the conditions that prohibit long-distance reflexives are (7bi) and (7biv). Both conditions say that reflexives must be resolved in the minimal S domain, and that [+refl] indexes cannot be percolated up beyond the minimal S boundary. In order to handle sentences in (1) and (2), these conditions have to be deleted. (10) and (11) are the algorithms after this revision. (10) is for Chinese and (11) is for Korean.

(10)   Revised Chierchia's Algorithms for Chinese
          a. $(S\backslash NP_n)/NP_n + NP \Rightarrow S\backslash NP$
               0   1   2

               (i) $NPS(0) \cap NPS(1) = \varnothing$ non-coreference
               (ii) $SLASH(2) \cap (NPS(1) \cup NPS(2)) = \varnothing$ crossover
               (iii)$NPS(2) = NPS(0) \cup NPS(1)$ NPS-percolation
               (iv)$SLASH(2) = SLASH(0) \cup SLASH(1)$ slash-percolation
          b. $NP_n + S\backslash NP_n \Rightarrow S$
             0   1   2

               (i) $SLASH(2) \cap (NPS(1) \cup NPS(2)) = \varnothing$ crossover
               (ii) $NPS(2) = NPS(0) \cup NPS(1)$ NPS-percolation
               (iii)$SLASH(2) = SLASH(0) \cup SLASH(1)$ slash-percolation
          c. Reflexives
               (i) A $\Rightarrow$ A
                    n [+refl] $\in$ NPS $n \notin$ NPS

               (ii) conditions: (a) $A = S\backslash NP$ (b) $FT(A) \approx FT(n)$
               (iii)translation: $\lambda x_n [A'(x_n)]$

(11)   Revised Chierchia's Algorithms for Korean
          a. $NP + (S\backslash NP_n)\backslash NP_n \Rightarrow S\backslash NP$
             0   1   2

               (i) $NPS(0) \cap NPS(1) = \varnothing$ non-coreference
                (ii) $SLASH(2) \cap (NPS(1) \cup NPS(2)) = \varnothing$ crossover
               (iii)$NPS(2) = NPS(0) \cup NPS(1)$ NPS-percolation
               (iv)$SLASH(2) = SLASH(0) \cup SLASH(1)$ slash-percolation
          b. $NP_n + S\backslash NP_n \Rightarrow S$
             0   1   2

               (i) $SLASH(2) \cap (NPS(1) \cup NPS(2)) = \varnothing$ crossover
               (ii) $NPS(2) = NPS(0) \cup NPS(1)$ NPS-percolation
               (iii)$SLASH(2) = SLASH(0) \cup SLASH(1)$ slash-percolation
          c. Reflexives
               (i) A $\Rightarrow$ A
                    n [+refl] $\in$ NPS $n \notin$ NPS

               (ii) conditions: (a) $A = S\backslash NP$ (b) $FT(A) \approx FT(n)$
               (iii)translation: $\lambda x_n [A'(x_n)]$

(7c) is deleted here, since we will not use this category combinatorics. Note that the conditions
(7bi) and (7biv) are deleted in (10) and (11). Also, note that NP follows $(S\backslash NP_n)/NP$ in (10a) but
NP precedes $(S\backslash NP_n)\backslash NP$ in (11a). This is just a language-specific property.

   Revised algorithms in (10) and (11) are for handling long-distance reflexives. Now, it's time to
develop algorithms for handling blocking effects. For this purpose, this paper adopts Reflexive-
Antecedent Pairing Algorithm in (12) that are developed in Lee (2002b, 2003a).

(12)   Reflexive-Antecedent Pairing Algorithm
          For the reflexive r and all the potential antecedents a, make a pair '$r = a$' if category of
          a is NP.

These processes start from the closest antecedent from the reflexive r and continue until all the
possible antecedents are exhausted. In addition to this algorithm, to handle differences between

Chinese and Korean, we have algorithms in (13) and (14) for blocking effects.

(13)   Blocking Effect Algorithm for Chinese
        When we meet a reflexive-antecedent pair whose agreement feature is not compatible,
        delete all the reflexive-antecedent pairs after this pair.

(14)   Blocking Effect Algorithm for Korean
        When we meet a reflexive-antecedent pair whose agreement feature is not compatible,
        delete only this reflexive-antecedent pair and comparison processes continue.

Now, let's take (1) and (2) again, and see how these algorithms work.
   First, according to the algorithm in (12), Reflexive-Antecedent Pairs for sentence (1) and (2)
can be calculated as in (15) and (16).

(15)   Reflexive-Antecedent Pairs for (1) (Step I)
        a. ziji   =   Wangwu
        b. ziji   =   wo
        c. ziji   =   Zhangsan

(16)   Reflexive-Antecedent Pairs for (2) (Step I)
        a. caki-lul   =   Younghee-ka
        b. caki-lul   =   nay-ka
        c. caki-lul   =   Chelsoo-nun

Then, compatibility between the reflexive and its antecedents are checked from (a) to (c).
Because the reflexive and the antecedents in (15b) and (16b) are not compatible, (15b) and
(16b) are deleted as in (17) and (18).

(17)   Reflexive-Antecedent Pairs for (1) (Step II)
        a. ziji   =   Wangwu
        b. ~~ziji   =   wo~~
        c. ziji   =   Zhangsan

(18)   Reflexive-Antecedent Pairs for (2) (Step II)
        a. caki-lul   =   Younghee-ka
        b. ~~caki-lul   =   nay-ka~~
        c. caki-lul   =   Chelsoo-nun

Because we meet a Reflexive-Antecedent Pair whose agreement feature is not compatible,
Blocking Effect Algorithms in (13) and (14) are applied, and we reach the final results as in (19)
and (20).

(19)   Reflexive-Antecedent Pairs for (1) (Final)
        a. ziji   =   Wangwu
        b. ~~ziji   =   wo~~
        c. ~~ziji   =   Zhangsan~~

(20)   Reflexive-Antecedent Pairs for (2) (Final)
        a. caki-lul   =   Younghee-ka
        b. ~~caki-lul   =   nay-ka~~
        c. caki-lul   =   Chelsoo-nun

Following the Reflexive-antecedent Pairs in (19), (21) is analyzed as in (22), where (21) is the same sentence as (1) except that bracketed numbers are added by superscription. These numbers refer to morphological/phonological forms of each lexical item. Note that the algorithm in (10c) is applied to the $S\backslash NP_3$ node. By (10ci), 4_{+refl} is deleted from the NPS. (10cii) is satisfied because the current category is $S\backslash NP$. By (10cii), the semantic interpretation of the $S\backslash NP_3$ node is changed from $like'(x_4)$ into $\lambda x_4[like'(x_4, x_4)]$. After this node meets *Wangwu*, *ziji* is resolved only with *Wangwu*, as $like'(w,w)$ indicates.

(21)　　[1]Zhangsan_i　[2]renwei　[3]wo_j　[4]zhidao　[5]Wangwu_k　[6]xihauan [7]ziji*_i/*_j/k
　　　　Zhangsan　　think　　I　　know　　Wangwu　　like　　self
　　　　'Zhangsan thinks I know Wangwu likes self.'

(22)
$$\langle[1]+\ldots+[7],S,think'(z,\,\hat{}\,know'(I,\,\hat{}\,like'(w,w))),NPS:1_{+name},2_{+pron},3_{+name}\rangle$$

$$\langle[1],NP_1,z,NPS:1_{+name}\rangle\langle[2]+\ldots+[7],S\backslash NP_1,think'(\,\hat{}\,know'(I,?like'(w,w))),NPS:2_{+pron},3_{+name}\rangle$$

$$\langle[2],(S\backslash NP_1)/S,think',NPS:1\rangle\langle[3]+\ldots+[7],S,know'(I,\,\hat{}\,like'(w,w)),NPS:2_{+pron},3_{+name}\rangle$$

$$\langle[3],NP_2,I,NPS:2_{+pron}\rangle\langle[4]+\ldots+[7],S/NP_2,know'(\,\hat{}\,like'(w,w)),NPS:3_{+name}\rangle$$

$$\langle[4],(S\backslash NP_2)/S,know',NPS:2\rangle\langle[5]+\ldots+[7],S,like'(w,w),NPS:3_{+name}\rangle$$

$$\langle[5],NP_3,w,NPS:3_{+name}\rangle\qquad\langle[6]+[7],S\backslash NP_3,\lambda x_4[like'(x_4,x_4)],NPS:3\rangle$$

$$\langle[6]+[7],S\backslash NP_3,like'(x_4),NPS:3,4_{+refl}\rangle$$

$$\langle[6],(S\backslash NP_3)/NP,like',NPS:3\rangle\langle[7],NP_4,x_4,NPS:4_{+refl}\rangle$$

Likewise, (23) can be analyzed into either (24) or (25), based on the Reflexive-Antecedent Pairs in (20). Here also, (23) is the same sentence as (2) except that bracketed numbers are added by superscription for morphological/phonological forms.

(23)　　[1]*Chelsoo_i-nun* [[2]*nay_j-ka* [[3]*Younghee_k-ka*　　[4]*caki_i/*_j/k-lul*　[5]*co.aha-n-ta-*[6]*ko*]
　　　　Chelsoo.TOP　I.NOM　Younghee.NOM　self.ACC　　like.PRES.DECL.COMP
　　　　[7]*a(l)-n-ta-*[8]*ko*]　　　　　　[9]*sayngkakha-n-ta.*
　　　　know.PRES.DECL.COMP think.PRES.DECL
　　　　'Chelsoo thinks that I know that Younghee likes him/herself.'

(24)
$$\langle[1]+\ldots+[9],S,think'(c,\,\hat{}\,know'(I,\,\hat{}\,like'(y,y))),NPS:1_{+name},2_{+pron},3_{+name}\rangle$$

$$\langle[1],NP_1,c,NPS:1_{+name}\rangle\langle[2]+\ldots+[9],S\backslash NP_1,think'(\,\hat{}\,know'(I,\,\hat{}\,like'(y,y))),NPS:2_{+pron},3_{+name}\rangle$$

$$\langle[2]+\ldots+[8],S',know'(I,\,\hat{}\,like'(y,y)),NPS:2_{+pron},3_{+name}\rangle\langle[9],(S\backslash NP_1)\backslash S',think',NPS:1\rangle$$

$$\langle[2]+\ldots+[7],S,know'(I,\,\hat{}\,like'(y,y)),NPS:2_{+pron},3_{+name}\rangle\langle[8],S'\backslash S,\lambda\phi[\phi],NPS:\varnothing\rangle$$

$$\langle[2],NP_2,I,NPS:2_{+pron}\rangle\langle[3]+\ldots+[7],S\backslash NP_2,know'(\,\hat{}\,like'(y,y)),NPS:3_{+name}\rangle$$

$$\langle[3]+\ldots+[6],S',like'(y,y),NPS:3_{+name}\rangle\langle[7],(S\backslash NP_2)\backslash S',know',NPS:2\rangle$$

$$\langle[3]+\ldots+[5],S,like'(y,y),NPS:3_{+name}\rangle\langle[6],S'\backslash S,\lambda\phi[\phi],NPS:\varnothing\rangle$$

$$\langle[3],NP_3,y,NPS:3_{+name}\rangle\qquad\langle[4]+[5],S\backslash NP_3,\lambda x_4[like'(x_4,x_4)],NPS:3\rangle$$

$$\langle[4]+[5],S\backslash NP_3,like'(x_4),NPS:3,4_{+refl}\rangle$$

$$\langle[4],\mathrm{NP}_4,x_4,\mathrm{NPS}:4_{+\mathrm{refl}}\rangle\langle[5],(\mathrm{S\backslash NP}_3)/\mathrm{NP},\mathrm{like'},\mathrm{NPS}:3\rangle$$

(25)

$$\langle[1]+\ldots+[9],\mathrm{S},\mathrm{think'}(c,{}^{\wedge}\mathrm{know'}(\mathrm{I},{}^{\wedge}\mathrm{like'}(y,c))),\mathrm{NPS}:1_{+\mathrm{name}},2_{+\mathrm{pron}},3_{+\mathrm{name}}\rangle$$

$$\langle[1]+\ldots+[9],\mathrm{S},\lambda x_4[\mathrm{think'}(c,{}^{\wedge}\mathrm{know'}(\mathrm{I},{}^{\wedge}\mathrm{like'}(y,x_4)))](c),\mathrm{NPS}:1_{+\mathrm{name}},2_{+\mathrm{pron}},3_{+\mathrm{name}}\rangle$$

$$\langle[1]+\ldots+[9],\mathrm{S},\mathrm{think'}(c,{}^{\wedge}\mathrm{know'}(\mathrm{I},{}^{\wedge}\mathrm{like'}(y,x_4))),\mathrm{NPS}:1_{+\mathrm{name}},2_{+\mathrm{pron}},3_{+\mathrm{name}},4_{+\mathrm{refl}}\rangle$$

$$\langle[1],\mathrm{NP}_1,c,\mathrm{NPS}:1_{+\mathrm{name}}\rangle\langle[2]+\ldots+[9],\mathrm{S\backslash NP}_1,\mathrm{think'}({}^{\wedge}\mathrm{know'}(\mathrm{I},{}^{\wedge}\mathrm{like'}(y,x_4))),\mathrm{NPS}:2_{+\mathrm{pron}},3_{+\mathrm{name}},4_{+\mathrm{refl}}\rangle$$

$$\langle[2]+\ldots+[8],\mathrm{S'},\mathrm{know'}(\mathrm{I},{}^{\wedge}\mathrm{like'}(y,x_4)),\mathrm{NPS}:2_{+\mathrm{pron}},3_{+\mathrm{name}},4_{+\mathrm{refl}}\rangle\langle[9],(\mathrm{S\backslash NP}_1)\backslash\mathrm{S'},\mathrm{think'},\mathrm{NPS}:1\rangle$$

$$\langle[2]+\ldots+[7],\mathrm{S},\mathrm{know'}(\mathrm{I},{}^{\wedge}\mathrm{like'}(y,x_4)),\mathrm{NPS}:2_{+\mathrm{pron}},3_{+\mathrm{name}},4_{+\mathrm{refl}}\rangle\langle[8],\mathrm{S'\backslash S},\lambda\phi[\phi],\mathrm{NPS}:\varnothing\rangle$$

$$\langle[2],\mathrm{NP}_2,\mathrm{I},\mathrm{NPS}:2_{+\mathrm{pron}}\rangle\langle[3]+\ldots+[7],\mathrm{S\backslash NP}_2,\mathrm{know'}({}^{\wedge}\mathrm{like'}(y,x_4)),\mathrm{NPS}:3_{+\mathrm{name}},4_{+\mathrm{refl}}\rangle$$

$$\langle[3]+\ldots+[6],\mathrm{S},\mathrm{like'}(y,x_4),\mathrm{NPS}:3_{+\mathrm{name}},4_{+\mathrm{refl}}\rangle\langle[7],(\mathrm{S\backslash NP}_2)\backslash\mathrm{S'},\mathrm{know'},\mathrm{NPS}:2\rangle$$

$$\langle[3]+\ldots+[5],\mathrm{S},\mathrm{like'}(y,x_4),\mathrm{NPS}:3_{+\mathrm{name}},4_{+\mathrm{refl}}\rangle\langle[6],\mathrm{S'\backslash S},\lambda\phi[\phi],\mathrm{NPS}:\varnothing\rangle$$

$$\langle[3],\mathrm{NP}_3,y,\mathrm{NPS}:3_{+\mathrm{name}}\rangle\langle[4]+[5],\mathrm{S\backslash NP}_3,\mathrm{like'}(x_4),\mathrm{NPS}:3,4_{+\mathrm{refl}}\rangle$$

$$\langle[4],\mathrm{NP}_4,x_4,\mathrm{NPS}:4_{+\mathrm{refl}}\rangle\langle[5],(\mathrm{S\backslash NP}_3)/\mathrm{NP},\mathrm{like'},\mathrm{NPS}:3\rangle$$

In (24), note that the algorithm in (11c) is applied to the S\NP₃ node, and *caki* is resolved only with *Younghee*. In (25), the algorithm in (11c) is applied to the S\NP₁ node, and *caki* is resolved only with *Chelsoo*.

4. Implementation of Blocking Effects

Now, it's time to develop algorithms for handling blocking effects. Those algorithms can be divided into two steps. The first one is to calculate reflexive-antecedent pairs such as those in (15) or (16), and the second step is to filter out the reflexive-antecedent pairs whose agreement feature is not compatible. (26) is the algorithm for calculating reflexive-antecedent pairs. That is, (26) is an implementation of idea in (12).

(26)   Algorithm for Reflexive-Antecedent Pairing

```
function set reflexive_antecedent_pairing(int i, int j, int k)
var
     string rPHON, aPHON;
     set RAPairs;
begin
     RAPairs := {};
     r := k;
     rPHON := PHON(Lex[NPs[r]]);
     for a from j to i step ?1 do
         begin
             aPHON := PHON(Lex[NPs[a]]);
             RAPairs := RAPairs + 'rPHON=aPHON';
         end;
     return(RAPairs);
end;
```

Here, Lex[] is an array where every lexical item is stored, and NPs[] is an array where all the NPs are stored. That is, NPs[] corresponds to NPS in the analyses in (22), (24), and (25). k refers to the position of the reflexive in NPs[]. Searching domain for possible antecedents is from NPs[i] to NPs[j]. The algorithm searches this domain backwards, i.e., from NPs[j] to NPs[i], and makes a Reflexive-Antecedent Pair 'rPHON = aPHON'. Here, rPHON is the phonological/morphological form of the reflexive, and aPHON refers to that of the possible antecedents. Then, the algorithm adds this pair to RAPairs, where all the reflexive-antecedent pairs are stored. After all the NPs are exhausted, the algorithm returns RAPairs.

The next step is to check agreement feature of each pair in RAPairs, to rule out the pairs where the reflexive and a possible antecedent are not compatible. (27) and (28) are those algorithms, where (27) is the implementation of (13) and (28) is that of (14).

(27)   Algorithm for Blocking Effects (Chinese)

```
function set Chinese_blocking_effects (set ra)
var
    boolean flag;
    string RAString, RARefl, RAAnte;
    set RAPairs, RASet;
begin
    flag := true;
    RAPairs := ra;
    RASet := {};
    while flag = true and RAPairs is not exhausted do
        begin
            get one RAString from RAPairs;
            RARefl := reflexive form of RAString;
            RAAnte := antecedent form of RAString;
            if (FT(RARefl)?FT(RAAnte)) flag := false;
            if (flag = true) then RASet := RESet + RAString;
        end;
        return(RASet);
end;
```

(28)   Algorithm for Blocking Effects (Korean)

```
function set Korean_blocking_effects (set ra)
var
    boolean flag;
    string RAString, RARefl, RAAnte;
    set RAPairs, RASet;
begin
    flag := true;
    RAPairs := ra;
    RASet := {};
    while RAPairs is not exhausted do
        begin
            get one RAString from RAPairs;
            RARefl := reflexive form of RAString;
            RAAnte := antecedent form of RAString;
            if (FT(RARefl)?FT(RAAnte)) flag := false;
            if (flag = true) then RASet := RESet + RAString;
            if (flag = false) then flag := true;
        end;
        return(RASet);
end;
```

If the agreement feature between the reflexive and its possible antecedent is not compatible, *flag* is set to be false. When *flag* is false, different actions are taken between Chinese and Korean. In Chinese, as the algorithm in (27) demonstrates, we get out of the while loop, and returns the reflexive-antecedent pairs whose agreement feature is compatible up to now. In Korean, as the algorithm in (28) shows, we filter out only that reflexive-antecedent pair, and continue comparison processes until all the pairs in RAPairs are exhausted. Along with these algorithms, we can handle presence and absence of blocking effects in Chinese and Korean effectively.

5. Conclusion

In this paper, we have developed algorithms for handling blocking effects of long-distance reflexives. Chinese has blocking effects, but Korean doesn't have. We found that long-distance reflexives in these languages can be analyzed efficiently in the CCG-like system and that the presence and absence of blocking effects can be implemented by some operations on the reflexive-antecedent pairs.

References

Ajdukiewicz, K. 1935. Die Syntaktische Konnexitat. *Studia Philisophica*, 1, 1-27.

Bar-Hillel, Y. 1953. A Quasi-arithmetical Notation for Syntactic Description. *Language*, 29, 47-58.

Battistella, E. 1989. Chinese Reflexivization: A Movement to INFL Approach. *Linguistics*, 27, 987-1012.

Chierchia, G. 1988. Aspects of a Categorial Theory of Binding. In R. Oehrle et al. eds., *Categorial Grammars and Natural Language Structures*, 125-51. Dordrecht: R. Reidel.

Cole, P., G. Hermon, and J. Huang. 2000. Introduction: Long-Distance Reflexives, the State of the Art. *Syntax and Semantics*, 33, xiii-xlvii.

Cole, P. and L. Sung. 1994. Head Movement and Long-distance Reflexives. *Linguistic Inquiry* 21, 1-22.

Curry, H. and R. Feys. 1958. *Combinatory Logic*. Vol. 1. Amsterdam : North Holland.

Huang. J. 1982. *Logical Relations in Chinese and the Theory of Grammar*. Ph.D. thesis. MIT.

__________. 1982. On the Distribution and Reference of Empty Pronouns. *Linguistic Inquiry*, 15, 531-574.

Huang, J. and L. Liu. 2000. Logophoricity, Attitude, and *Ziji* at the Interface. In Cole, P., G. Hermon, and J. Huang. 2000. *Syntax and Semantics* 33, 141-195.

Huang, J. and J. Tang. 1991. On the Local Nature of the Long-distance Reflexive in Chinese. In Koster, J. and E. Reuland, eds., *Long-distance Anaphora*, 263-282. Cambridge: Cambridge University Press.

Katada, F. 1991. The LF Representation of Anaphors. *Linguistic Inquiry*, 22, 287-313.

Lee, Y. 2002a. Implementation of Long-distance Reflexives in Korean. *Proceedings of the 16th Pacific Asia Conference on Language, Information, and Computation (PACLIC-16)*, 296-307.

______. 2002b. Resolving A Korean Reflexive Cakicasin: A Categorial Grammar Approach. *Studies in Linguistics Science*, 32(1), 55-77. UIUC, Urbana.

______. 2003a. Bound vs. Long-distance Reflexives in Korean: A Categorial Grammar Approach. In G. Iverson and S. Ahn, eds., *Explorations in Korean Language and Linguistics*, pp. 423-41. Seoul : Hankook Publishing Co.

______. 2003b. *Anaphora Resolution Algorithms with Category: English and Korean*. Ph.D. thesis. University of Illinois at Urbana-Champaign.

Lambek, J. 1958. The Mathematics of Sentence Structure. *American Mathematical Monthly*, 65, 154-170.

Manzini, M and K. Wexler. 1987. Parameters, Binding Theory, and Learnability. *Linguistic Inquiry*, 18, 414-444.

Moon, Seung-Chul. 1996. *An Optimality Approach to Long Distance Anaphors*. Ph.D. thesis. University of Washington. Seoul: Thaehaksa.

Pica, P. 1987. On the Nature of Reflexivization Cycle. *Proceedings of NELS*, 17, 483-499. GLSA, University of Massachusetts at Amherst.

Steedman, M. 1996. *Surface Structure and Interpretation*. Cambridge, MA: MIT Press.

__________. 2000. *The Syntactic Process*. Cambridge, MA: MIT Press.

Tang, C. 1989. Chinese Reflexives. *Natural Language and Linguistic Theory*, 7, 93-121.

Mining Parallel Text from the Web based on Sentence Alignment [*]

Bo Li, Juan Liu and Huili Zhu

School of Computer Science, Wuhan University
Wuhan, 430072, China
whulibo@gmail.com, liujuan@whu.edu.cn

Abstract. The parallel corpus is an important resource in the research field of data-driven natural language processing, but there are only a few parallel corpora publicly available nowadays, mostly due to the high labor force needed to construct this kind of resource. A novel strategy is brought out to automatically fetch parallel text from the web in this paper, which may help to solve the problem of the lack of parallel corpora with high quality. The system we develop first downloads the web pages from certain hosts. Then candidate parallel page pairs are prepared from the page set based on the outer features of the web pages. The candidate page pairs are evaluated in the last step in which the sentences in the candidate web page pairs are extracted and aligned first, and then the similarity of the two web pages is evaluate based on the similarities of the aligned sentences. The experiments towards a multilingual web site show the satisfactory performance of the system.

Keywords: Parallel Corpus, Web Mining, Sentence Alignment, Information Extraction

1. Introduction

Data-driven methods take a more important place in the research field of natural language processing nowadays, which calls an urgent need for enough parallel corpora with high quality. Parallel corpora made up with text in parallel translation are the foundational resource in data-driven natural language processing, which has a direct impact on the effectiveness of this kind of technologies such as statistical machine translation (Brown et al., 1990), cross-lingual information retrieval (Davis and Dunning, 1995; Landauer and Littman, 1990; Oard, 1997) and automatic lexical acquisition (Gale and Church, 1991b; Melamed, 1997). But it is disappointed that there are only a few parallel corpora publicly available today and most of them are small in size, specializing in narrow areas or out-of-date. It will cost too much time and human labor to construct parallel corpora with big scale and high quality, which constraints the increase of parallel corpora. The rapid development of the Internet and the intense intercourse between countries gives hope that we can construct parallel corpora automatically from the web. Through the rough observation, it is found that there are many web sites containing web pages in parallel translation. Based on the above considerations, we present a novel tool called Parallel Web Corpus Construction system (PWCC) to mine parallel corpora automatically from the web, which may help to facilitate the construction of parallel corpora with much less cost.

  The PWCC system uses a four-step process to fetch parallel corpora from the web. In the first step, a tool called web spider is employed to fetch all the web pages from specific hosts which

---

[*] The work was finished while the first author visited Wuhan Office of Comet Electronics Hong Kong.

probably contain high-quality parallel web pages. The software WebZip[1] is utilized to fetch web pages in the PWCC system. In the second step, candidate parallel web page pairs are prepared from the raw web page set based on the outer features of the web pages. The third step is the key of the whole system, in which the candidate parallel web page pairs produced by the second step are evaluated and the actually parallel pairs are saved. The evaluation module first extracts the sentences from each candidate page pair and aligns them, and then the similarity of the web pages in a pair is evaluated based on the similarities of the sentences which have been aligned. The sentences are aligned based on the length correlation criterion and the sentence similarity is measured by a novel strategy we design. We also design a novel strategy for evaluating the web page similarity based on the aligned sentence similarities. The last step is to save the parallel web pages. It can be concluded from the results of the experiments that the PWCC system is a high-performance and reliable tool for automatically constructing parallel corpora from the web.

The structure of the paper is as follows. The PWCC architecture is introduced in Section 2. The strategy for candidate parallel pair preparation is described in Section 3. The evaluation process is discussed in Section 4 which is the key section of the paper. We practice the experiments and discuss the results in Section 5. The paper is concluded in Section 6.

2. System Architecture

The PWCC system implemented as a four-step process is designed for automatically mining the web for parallel corpora (Figure 1). The first step of the system is the web page fetching process which downloads all the web pages from the hosts specified by the user. In the experiment section, the site of the ministry of foreign affairs of China is selected to be crawled because this site contains a great amount of parallel web pages with high quality. There have already been some free tools to do this work, and the software WebZip is chosen for the PWCC system. The candidate parallel page pairs are prepared in the second step of PWCC. The pairing process mainly relies on the similarity of the URLs, and also some other features such as web page size and anchor text are considered too. The candidate page pairs are then evaluated by the third step

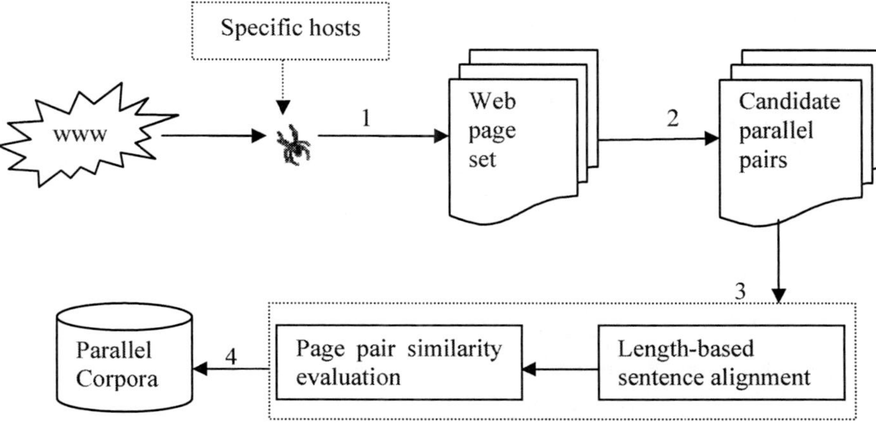

Figure 1: The architecture of the PWCC system

---

[1] http://www.spidersoft.com/

which is also the most important module of PWCC. In this step, the text from the candidate web page pairs is aligned at sentence level first based on the length correlation criterion, and then the similarity of the web pages is measured by combination of the similarities of the sentences that have been aligned. The truly parallel web pages are saved at last.

3. The Candidate Pair Preparation Module

Having been fetched from the web, the web page set consisting both Chinese web pages and English web pages is paired up. Each page is made up of one page from the Chinese page set and one from the English page set. It is important to pair them efficiently and effectively. The number of all the web pages is rather large, so it not only can save much time and RAM space to pair the pages up but also can save a great deal of time for the candidate parallel page pair evaluating step by effective pairing. Moreover, the candidate parallel page pair evaluation step can produce high recall and high precision at a higher probability given the candidate page pairs which are more parallel. There are about two types of methods to pair the web pages up in previous work. One is to pair web pages according to the similarity of the URLs and other features and the other is to simply treat each page from the Chinese page set and each page from the English page set as a candidate pair. It is clear that if the web page set is large, it may be inappropriate to adopt the latter idea because it will produce too many pairs for the evaluation step to process. For the former idea, previous work mostly utilizes the concept of similarity of character strings. They first detect the patterns indicating the language version such as *e, eng* and *english* in the URL string according to a pattern list and then use classic algorithms such as the *minimal edit distance* algorithm to measure the similarity of the two URLs. One notable drawback of the existed strategies is that they seldom consider for the deep characters of the URLs and simply treat them as strings. We design a novel candidate page pair preparation algorithm for the problem, which is more powerful than the methods in previous work, and meanwhile its time complexity is considerably low. The algorithm is based on the following assumptions:

    Assumption 1: Parallel web pages have the most *common paths* and similar *dictionary depths*.
    Assumption 2: Parallel web pages have similar file size.
    Assumption 3: Parallel web pages have similar anchor texts.

In *Assumption 1*, the *common paths* mean the common dictionaries the URLs of two web pages share, and the *directory depth* is the layer where the web page lies. For example, we consider two web pages:

    Chinese web page P1 URL: *http://www.fmprc.gov.cn/chn/wjdt/zyjh/t263606.htm*
    English web page P2 URL: *http://www.fmprc.gov.cn/eng/wjdt/zyjh/t264261.htm*

The number of *common paths* between page *P1* and page *P2* is 2 which are the directories *wjdt* and *zyjh*, and the difference of *directory depths* between page *P1* and page *P2* is 0, because the *directory depth* of page *P1* is 4 and that of page *P2* is 4 too. In *Assumption 2*, the file size is the size of the pure HTML file not including files such as images and audios embedded in the web page. In *Assumption 3*, the anchor text is the text shown at a hyper link, which usually gives the user relevant descriptive or contextual information about the content of the link's destination.

Based on the above assumptions, the strategy we use in the PWCC system is as follows:

For each page *C* in the Chinese page set *C-set*, we find the pages in the English page set *E-set* which can most probably constitute candidate pairs with the page *C*. We select first according to the *common paths* measure. The English pages *Es* which have the most *common paths* with the page *C* are selected first. Then the English pages *Es* are filtered by the *directory depth* criterion. For convenience, the *directory depth* difference between web page *A* and *B* is denoted as *DD(A, B)* and it is clear than *DD(A, B)=DD(B, A)*. The *directory depth* filter step is as follow: if two pages *E1* and *E2* in *Es* have different *directory depth* differences with the page *C* and we suppose *DD(E1, C)>DD(E2, C)*, we delete *E1* from *Es*. At last, we filter *Es* based on the file size and anchor text criterion. Anchor text is usually a good and brief summary of the content, so parallel web pages should have similar anchor texts. An easy strategy is designed to evaluate the similarity of the anchor texts in the PWCC system. A bilingual anchor text wordlist which contains words and phrases in parallel translation such as names, place names, duty names, company names and organization names is manually built first. For two anchor texts, if a word or phrase occurs in one anchor text and the bilingual wordlist but its translation in the wordlist doesn't occur in the other anchor text, the two anchor texts are not likely to be the anchor texts of parallel web pages. For each page E in *Es,* if the file size of E and C is too different or the anchor texts of E and C are not similar, the page E is excluded from *Es.* When each page C in the Chinese page set *C-set* is processed, we add the corresponding English page set *Es* to the Chinese-English page pair table *Tce.* The whole process is described in the algorithm in *Appendix A.*

For each page E in the English page set *E-set,* we perform the similar operation as above and then we can construct another page pair table *Tec.* At last, we can combine *Tce* and *Tec* to get the final candidate parallel page pair set.

4. The Candidate Pair Evaluation Module

The candidate pair evaluation module is the key of the PWCC system. This module consists of a two-step process. The module first aligns the text extracted from the candidate web page pair at sentence level and then evaluates the similarity of the web pages based on the similarities of the aligned sentences. If the similarities of the web page pairs exceed certain threshold, they are treated as parallel wed pages to be saved.

4.1. Sentence Alignment

As the first step of the candidate pair evaluation module, the process of sentence alignment tries to align the sentences extracted from the huge amount of web pages. For the purpose of similarity evaluation in the next step, only coarse alignment is needed here and the alignment process should be designed to work as effectively as possible. There are usually two different strategies for aligning sentences in the parallel text, one is lexicon-based [Wu, 1994] and the other is based on the length correlation of the parallel sentences [Gale and Church, 1991a]. The lexicon-based methods can usually produce aligned sentence pairs with high precision, but the drawbacks of this kind of methods are obvious too. It will cost much time to prepare the fundamental resources such as the bilingual dictionary for the operation, and the operations such as text preprocess and word segmentation are time-consuming too. Compared to the lexicon-based methods, the length-based strategy can achieve a considerably high precision with much less time and space cost. The length-based strategy is used in the PWCC system.

Given a pair of parallel text, the length-based methods would choose the alignment that maximizes the probability over all possible alignments which can be denoted as

$$\arg\max_{A}\Pr(A\,|\,T_1,T_2) \tag{1}$$

where A is an alignment, and T_1 and T_2 are the English and Chinese text respectively. An alignment A is a set consisting of $L_1\&L_2$ pairs where each L_1 or L_2 is an English or Chinese passage. It is usually hard to calculate from the formula (1), so the approximation of the probability can be made that the probabilities of the individual aligned pairs with an alignment are independent, which can be described as

$$\Pr(A\,|\,T_1,T_2)\approx\prod_{(L_1\&L_2)\in A}(L_1\,\&\,L_2\,|\,T_1,T_2)\approx\prod_{(L_1\&L_2)\in A}(L_1\,\&\,L_2\,|\,l_1,l_2) \tag{2}$$

where l_1 and l_2 are the lengths of passages L_1 and L_2 respectively. For the English text, the length means the count of the characters in the text. The length of the Chinese text should be counted as twice of the count of the Chinese characters in the text. Then the problem of maximizing the probability of the alignment given two pieces of text in the formula (2) can be transformed to the minimum problem

$$\arg\max_{A} \Pr(A \mid T_1, T_2) \approx \arg\max_{A} \prod_{(L_1 \& L_2) \in A} (L_1 \& L_2 \mid l_1, l_2)$$
$$= \arg\min_{A} \sum_{(L_1 \& L_2) \in A} -\log \Pr(L_1 \& L_2 \mid l_1, l_2) \tag{3}$$

The minimization problem in the formula (3) can be implemented in a dynamic programming way.

4.2. Similarity Evaluation

After the above sentence alignment process, the aligned sentences should be utilized to evaluate the similarity of the web pages. It is intuitive that if two pieces of text are in parallel translation, the aligned sentences from them should be roughly in parallel translation too. And the similarity of the sentences is easier to measure than that of the web pages containing the whole text. For example, sentence *S1* in English and sentence *S2* in Chinese are the sentences to be evaluated,

S1: For <u>the first time</u> in <u>three decades</u> <u>Afghanistan</u> is <u>holding</u> <u>parliamentary</u> <u>elections</u>.

S2: <u>阿富汗</u> 将 <u>举行</u> <u>三百年</u> 来 的 <u>首次</u> <u>议会</u> 选举。

The word boundaries of languages such as Chinese and Japanese are not clear, so the process of word segmentation should be practiced on *S2* first. Then we can see that the two sentences *S1* and *S2* have many words in parallel translation such as the pair *Afghanistan* and *阿富汗*. The similarity of the sentences *S1* and *S2* can be measured by the number of words in parallel translation they have. It is clear that a bilingual dictionary is needed here. We have also found that some words such as *in, for* in English and *的, 将* in Chinese have little impact on the meaning of the sentences and sometimes will confuse the similarity evaluation process, so we should remove this kind of words in the evaluation process.

It is supposed that the sentence(s) *SA* in language *A* and the sentence(s) *SB* in language *B* are from a candidate web page pair and have been aligned in the sentence alignment step. The sentences *SA* and *SB* are preprocessed by modules such as word segmentation if needed. Then a strategy is designed to evaluate the similarity of the sentences *SA* and *SB*.

For each word *WA* in the sentence *SA,* if one of its translations in the bilingual dictionary occurs in the sentence *SB,* the *translation count* will be added by 1; else the *translation count* is minus by 0.2. Then the similarity of *SA* and *SB* is given by

$$sim(SA, SB) = \frac{translation\ count}{\max(length(SA), length(SB))} \tag{4}$$

where *sim(SA,SB)* is the *sentence similarity* of the sentence(s) *SA* and the sentence(s) *SB, length(SA)* and *length(SB)* are the count of the words in *SA* and *SB* respectively, the value of the function *max(langth(SA),length(SB))* is the bigger one between *length(SA)* and *length(SB)*. The value of the *sentence similarity* is between 0 and 1. The bigger the value is, the more similar the two sentences are.

The strategy for evaluating the *sentence similarity* has been illustrated above, and then we need to evaluate the similarity of the text extracted from the candidate parallel web pages based on the *sentence similarity*. By the sentence alignment process, the candidate parallel text is divided into aligned sentences in two languages. There are many *sentence similarities* for a candidate web page pair, which are denoted as SS_1, SS_2, SS_3, ..., SS_n. For a candidate parallel page pair, if the similarities of too many aligned sentences are low, we filter this candidate page pair which is not likely to be parallel directly. Because SS_p and SS_q *(p≠q)* are produced independently, the similarity of the candidate web pages can be estimated as

$$similarity = \prod_{i=1}^{n} SS_i \qquad (5)$$

In order to facilitate the calculation process, we transform the similarity criterion to its logarithm style which is

$$\log similarity = \sum_{i=1}^{n} \log SS_i \qquad (6)$$

The *log similarity* in the formula (6) is a number no more than 0. The threshold for the value in the PWCC system is set to *log 0.65* based on the experiments and our experience.

5. Experiments and Discussions

In this section, experiments are designed to examine the performance of the system. First, two widely used evaluation standards in the information retrieval field are introduced, which are also applicable in our case. In our experiments, *precision* is defined as the proportion of page pairs in parallel translation to the total page pairs that are produced by PWCC. *Recall* is defined as the proportion of page pairs in parallel translation produced by the PWCC system to the total parallel page pairs in the whole web page set.

The factor *number of pairs in parallel translation* must be calculated from the human annotated page pairs, so we invite a native Chinese having learned English for many years to help to annotate these page pairs. To calculate the *recall,* we need to know the total number of parallel pairs in the page set. It is hard to count out the actual number of the parallel pairs in the page set because the web page set is really too large. We build a relatively small test set to test the *recall* of the PWCC system.

The PWCC system first fetches all the web pages from specific hosts. In the experiments, the web spider software WebZip is set to crawl the website of the ministry of foreign affairs of China (http://www.fmprc.gov.cn) which contains a great amount of high-quality Chinese and English web pages in parallel translation. Through the rough observation, most of the web pages in this site are news or governmental archives in both Chinese and English, so the text extracted from the web pages is formal and suitable for auto process by the computer. A web page set containing 40262 Chinese web pages and 17324 English web pages is fetched by the web spider[2]. Some preprocess technologies are practiced on the page set, and then the web pages left are processed by the candidate pair preparation module. After that, the text is extracted from these candidate pairs omitting html tags, advertisements and so on and evaluated by the candidate pair evaluation module. The time it costs is also considerably short. To examine the *precision* of the system, a subset of 400 pairs are selected from all the pairs PWCC produces. A Chinese who has learned English for many years and has a fluent English tongue is asked to annotate the subset, and it is found that 379 pairs in the subset are actually in parallel translation, which accounts for a *precision* of 94.8%. For evaluation of the *recall,* a human-annotated web page pair set is needed here. We construct a web page pair set consisting of 320 parallel page pairs and 80 nonparallel pairs. This web page set is evaluated by the PWCC system and 299 out of the 320 actual parallel pairs are recognized as parallel by the system, which accounts for a *recall* of 93.4%. Both the *precision* and the *recall* show the outstanding performance of the PWCC system. Based on the analysis of the page pairs which are actually parallel but PWCC

---

[2] The web page set constructed by us has been used in some other experiments before the work in this paper.

considers nonparallel and the page pairs which are actually nonparallel but PWCC considers parallel, we find that most of these pages contain many sentences with similar length, which always brings some problems to the length-based sentence alignment module. But fortunately this kind of web pages only occupy a very small proportion of the whole page set, and will not significantly influence the performance of the system.

6. Conclusion

The PWCC system designed to fetch parallel text from the web is introduced in this paper. The system first uses the web spider to fetch all the web pages from some hosts given by the user, and then candidate parallel web page pairs are prepared by the candidate pair preparation module based on features such as URL and file size. In the last step, candidate parallel web page pairs are evaluated by the sentence alignment-based strategy. We design novel strategies for the second and the third steps, which are then proved to be rather efficient by the experiments. The PWCC system is useful and reliable for automatically constructing parallel corpora from the web.

References

Brown, P. F., J. Cocke, S. D. Pietra, V. J. D. Pietra, F. Jelinek, J. D. Lafferty, et al. 1990. A Statistical Approach to Machine Translation. *Computational Linguistics,* 16(2), 79-85.

Davis, M. and T. Dunning. 1995. A TREC evaluation of query translation methods for multi-lingual text retrieval. *Proceedings of The 4th Text Retrieval Conference (TREC).*

Gale, W. A. and K. W. Church. 1991a. A program for aligning sentences in bilingual corpora. *Proceedings* of *The 29th Annual Meeting of the ACL,* Berkeley, CA

Gale, W. A. and K. W. Church. 1991b. Identifying word correspondences in parallel texts. *Proceedings of The 4th DARPA Workshop on Speech and Natural Language.*

Landauer, T. K. and M. L. Littman. 1990. Fully automatic cross-language document retrieval using latent semantic indexing. *Proceedings of The 6th Annual Conference of the UW Centre for the New Oxford English Dictionary and Text Research,* UW Centre for the New OED and Text Research, Waterloo, Ontario.

Melamed, I. D. 1997. Automatic discovery of non-compositional compounds in parallel data. *Proceedings of The 2nd Conference on Empirical Methods in Natural Language Processing (EMNLP-97),* Brown University.

Oard, D. W. 1997. Cross-language text retrieval research in the USA. *Proceedings of The 3rd DELOS Workshop.*

Wu, D. 1994. Aligning a parallel English-Chinese corpus statistically with lexical criteria. *Proceedings of The 32nd Annual Meeting of the ACL,* Las Cruces, NM

Appendix A: The Algorithm for Preparing Candidate Parallel Page Pairs

```
for each page C in C-set
{
    maxCommonPath = -1;
    directoryDepthDifference = 100;
    // clear the E-set object
    E-set = null;
    for each page E in E-set
    {
        // CP(E, C) is the count of common paths between page E and C
        if(CP(E, C) > maxCommonPath)
        {
            // LD(E, C) is the file length difference between page E and C
            // AS(E, C) is the similarity of the anchor texts of E and C
            if(LD(E, C) < 20kB && AS(E, C) == true)
            {
```

```
            maxCommonPath = CP(E, C);
            // DD(E, C) is the directory depth difference between page E and C
            directoryDepthDifference = DD(E, C);
            E-set = null;
            Add E to E-set;
        }
    }
    else if(CP(E, C) == maxCommonPath)
    {
        if(DD(E, C) < directoryDepthDifference)
        {
            if(LD(E, C) < 20kB && AS(E, C) == true)
            {
                directoryDepthDifference = DD(E, C);
                E-set = null;
                Add E to E-set;
            }
        }
        else if(DD(E, C) == directoryDepthDifference)
        {
            if(LD(E, C) < 20kB && AS(E, C) == true)
            {
                Add E to E-set;
            }
        }
    }
}
// each page in E-Set can constitute a candidate parallel page pair with C
Add (C, E-set) to Tce;
}
```

The Excessive Structural Article in Mandarin —
Study of *dao*（到）[*]

Hsiu-Ying Liu

Asia University, 500, Liufeng Rd., Wufeng Hsiang, Taichung County, Taiwan

violet@asia.edu.tw

Abstract. The present paper targets on the excessive structural article *dao* in the "X[1] + *dao* + *si*" phrases, aiming to see the possible generation of the excessive meaning. The generation of excessiveness will be analyzed from the aspect of cognition, including conceptual structure and metaphor. It will be concluded that the position indicated by *si* in concept plays a crucial, which then tells the importance of collocation. What is more, the comparison of *dao* and Southern Min *kah* will be made to see the degree of grammaticalization of *dao*.

Keywords: excessive structural article, conceptual structure, metaphor

1. Introduction

It is not easy to explain "extent" since it is somewhat abstract; however, extent seems to exist in our daily lives. Everything bears a relation to extent: the redness of roses, the extent of saltiness, or even the maturity of a man. Mentioning extent, *hen* is always the term for use in Mandarin, such as *Ta hen mei* 她很美 (She is very beautiful). However, *hen* cannot indicate the highest extent. To show excessiveness, there is a construction which is popular with the young generation in Taiwan nowadays. The excessive construction is structured as "X + *dao* + *si*", and it pragmatically emphasizes the speaker's subjective emotion.

> (1) 我　今天 累　到　死
> *wo　jin-tian lei　dao　si*
> I　　today tired DAO die　　　"I'm extremely tired today."

The phrase is always used to indicate the very high extent of a certain state; therefore, we name the construction "the excessive construction" and *dao* the excessive structural particle, which appears in sentences mainly to link the word or phrase that precedes it to the elements that immediately follows it. In example (1), *dao* links the predicate *lei* and the complement *si*.

  As for the excessive construction, *dao* is worthy of discussion. *Dao* originally is a spatial term indicating "arrive at". Since we failed to find *dao*'s use as an extent marker in ancient Mandarin, it might be until this modern time it is used to indicate excessive extent. How could a spatial term derive extent meaning? In addition, *dao* is not obligatory; that is, it could be omitted.

> (2) 我　今天　累 死 了
> *wo　jin-tian lei　si　le*
> I　　today tired die ASP　　"I'm extremely tired today."

---

[1] The symbol X refers to either a verb or an adjective.

As a result, there is coexistence of "X *dao si*" and "X *si*". Does the appearance of *dao* imply some other meaning different from "X *si*"?

The paper works on the excessive structural particle *dao* in Taiwan Mandarin. The data are collected mainly from *google* search engine. The main discussion falls on how *dao* derives from a spatial word to an excessive structural particle. We will look into the conceptual structure of the construction, in hopes to see the operation of human cognition and the generation of excessive meaning. The paper will be organized as follows. Section 2 briefly reviews the literature. The theoretical framework adopted in this paper is introduced in section 3. Section 4 presents the discussion which mainly focuses on the generation of excessive *dao*. A comparison between *dao* and Southern Min *kah* will be made in section 5, and the last section provides a summary and a tentative conclusion.

2. Literature View

The typical structural article in Mandarin is *de*, which has some variants, i.e. 得, 的. According to the discussions on *de*, it could be an extent structural particle, as in the expressions "*Hao de hen* 好得很(Very good)! " Comparing with the great number of papers about *de*, there is no considerable amount of studies regarding the excessive structural particle *dao*, possibly because of the lack of long history. *Dao* as an extent marker is not listed in dictionaries, neither classic nor modern ones. Indeed, the term "excessive structural particle" is first proposed here. As to *dao*, Huang (1984), by looking into modern Mandarin, discusses the extent use of "V(Adj) + *dao* + ..." construction. Indicating the reaching to a certain extent, the construction takes the following kinds of predicates.

> A) gradable adjectives
>> *leng   qing   dao   le   ji-dian*   冷清到了極點
>> cold clear   DAO ASP   very end   "It's extremely desolate."
> B) psych verbs
>> *pei-fu   dao   le   ji-dian*   佩服到了極點
>> admire DAO   ASP   very end   "admire someone very much"
> C) verbs denoting change or action
>> *ji-hua   dao   yi-ding cheng-du le*   激化到一定程度了
>> agitate DAO certain extent   ASP   "agitate to some extent"

Liu (2006) studies the degree modification of adjectives in Mandarin Chinese, and the *dao*-clause is discussed. As to the following sentence, Liu states that the *dao*- clause offers an endpoint which is neither temporal nor locative but an extent of height.

> (3) *Yuehan gao   dao   keyi   mo   dao   tianhuaban* 約翰高到可以摸到天花板
> John   tall DAO   able touch-arrive   ceiling
> "John is tall enough to touch the ceiling."

He treats the *dao*- clause the adjectival construction, and the thesis mainly discusses its interaction with the degree modifier *guo*. His discussion regarding incompatibility of *guo* and the *dao*- clause is not the concern here; however, he contributes to point out that the *dao*- clause displays the properties of a complement and semantically is a "scale adjuster". In addition, the *dao*- clause possesses the ability "to saturate and restrict the degree argument of adjectives and alter the limit of the scale structure of associated adjectives." Li (2006) studies the rich polysemies of the motion verb *kao* in Taiwanese. She offers a complete discussion on the derivations of excessive *kah* from *kao* (see CHART 1), and it reveals that cognitive operations (i.e. metaphor and metonymy) play crucial roles.

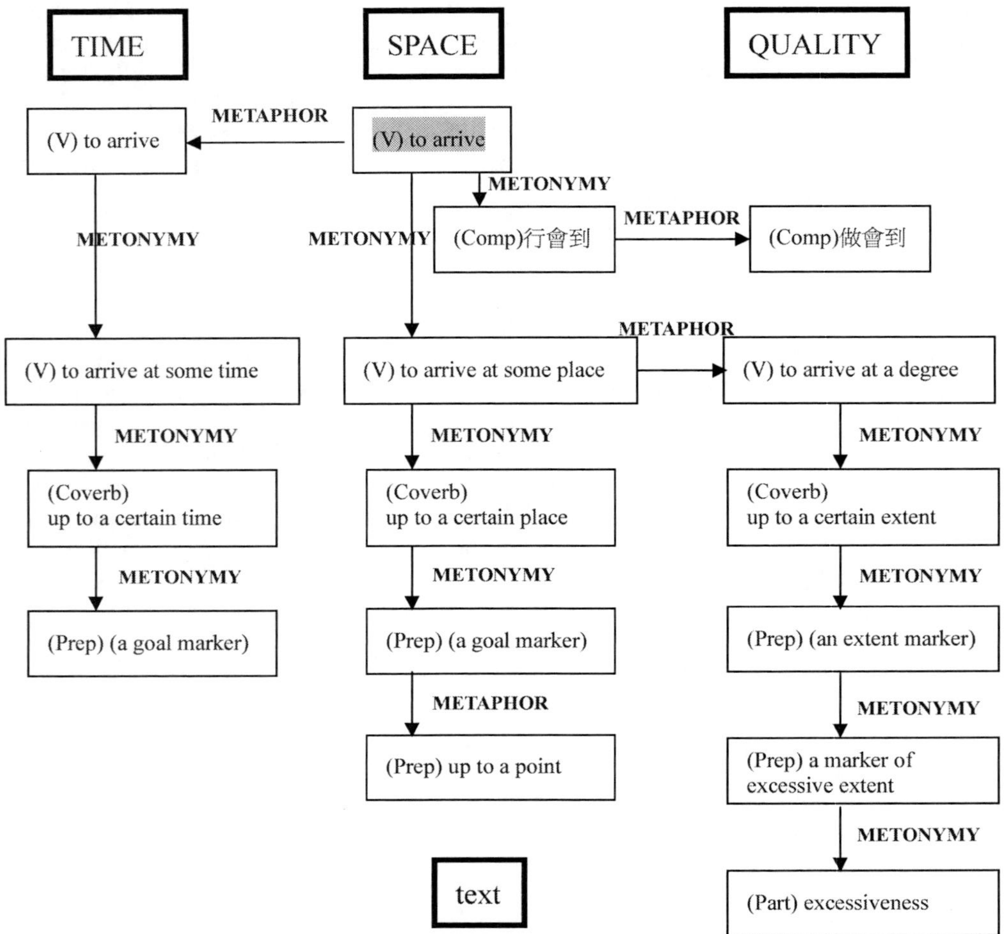

The two papers working on Mandarin point out the extent meaning of *dao*; nonetheless, there is no mentioning of the derivation of excessiveness. To complement this gap, the present study will trace the possible derivational routes of excessive *dao*. Li's analysis of *kah* would be referred. However, in her study, the metaphorical extensions are not presented in details; what is more, collocation is not mentioned in her study. In my opinion, collocation is the key that brings the grammaticalization. Basically, when two or more words appear together with a very high frequency, there will be syntactic or semantic changes of the composed terms. Therefore, in this study, collocation and metaphor extension will be carefully examined. The proposition is: the complement *si* is the key that brings the excessive meaning to *dao*. In concept, *dao* takes *si* as the goal; *si* stands for the very end in conceptual structure (Liu 2006), which further metaphorically means "excessive extent". The high-frequency occurrence of *dao* with *si* later makes *dao* change from a content spatial word to an excessive structural particle.

3. Theoretical Background

Since the conceptual structure of *dao* will be examined first, the introduction of Conceptual Structure is necessary. Conceptual Structure, by definition, is an autonomous level of cognitive representation (Ray Jackendoff 1983,1987,1990), representing concepts in terms of a small number of conceptual primitives, such as GO, STAY, BE, etc. The theory of conceptual structure is decompositional since it decomposes meanings in terms of conceptual primitives. It is also conceptualist because it identifies meanings with concepts, i.e. mental entities. In addition, in its origin, conceptual structure is localistic, for it elaborates the idea that notions of location and movement are central in the semantic analysis of verbs and sentences. Since the verb indicating "arrive" involves spatial movement, the conceptual structure of it should be examined.

The theory of metaphor is also necessary for review here, for the conceptual metaphor (Lakoff & Johnson 1980) of *si* will be discussed. In cognitive linguistics, conceptual metaphor refers to the understanding of one conceptual domain in terms of another, for example, we understand time in terms of space (e.g. *Time flies.*) *Si* evokes the concept of life, which is metaphorically regarded as a journey.

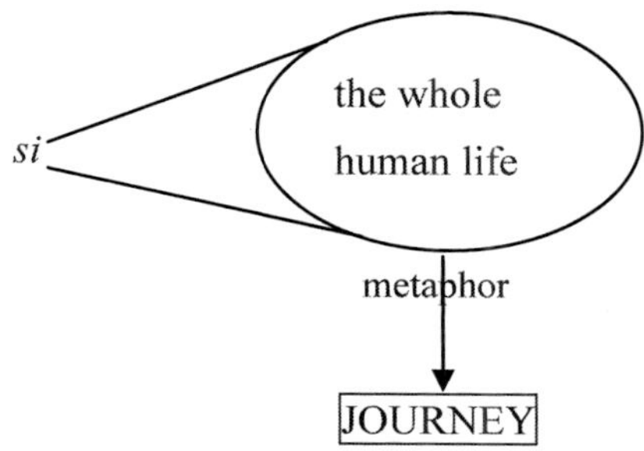

The journey metaphor requires a source and a goal, and it is *si* that plays the role of goal.

Basically, both *dao* and *si* undergo grammaticalication. In historical linguistics, grammaticalisation refers to a process of linguistic change by which a content word (lexical morpheme) changes into a function word or further into a grammatical affix. It also includes the processes of phonological reduction and semantic bleaching. Therefore, either metaphor or metonymy could be regarded as a kind of grammaticalization since it, most of the time, brings semantic bleaching.

4. Main Discussion
4.1 *Dao*
In Taiwan Mandarin, the phrase X-*dao-si* is popular with the young generation. And in many informal situations, the construction is used to express the highest of a state.

(4) *jing-ming yi   jie   re   dao   si*   精明一街熱到死
jing-ming first street   hot   DAO death
"It is extremely hot on Jing-ming lst Street.

(5) *na shi wu-liao dao   si   de   jing-dian*   邢是無聊到死的景點
that be boring DAO death   tourist place
"That is an extremely boring place for visiting."

(6) *Tou-lan de xia-chang jiu shi qi-mo-kao mang-dao- si* 偷懶的下場就是期末忙到死
lazy   outcome   be final exam busy DAO death
"Laziness will make you awfully busy during the final exam."

In these expressions, *dao* plays the part of structural particle.

To trace the origin, *dao*, a motion verb, prototypically refers to "arrive at".

(7) *Wo yi   dao   Taipei le*   我已到台北了
    I already DAO   Taipei   ASP   "I've arrived at Taipei."

Through grammaticalization, it also takes the use as a preposition which introduces a goal.

(8) *Ta   zou   dao Taipei.*   他走到台北
    He walk DAO Taipei.   " He walks to Taipei."

By way of metaphor, *dao* then is extended to the temporal domain.

(9) *Ta   deng dao wu   dian*   他等到五點
    He   wait   DAO   five o'clock   "He waited until five o'clock."

This metaphorical extension is a natural process in human cognition. The cognitive process is "concrete ⇨ abstract", and SPACE is a concrete source that further extends to abstract TIME.
  As a motion verb, *dao* basically requires three theta roles. Mostly, motion verbs involve change of position and assign three theta roles: theme, source and goal. Theme is obligatory whereas the other two are optional.

(10) <u>*che zi* zou le</u>   車子走了
<u>The car</u> is gone.   (theme)

(11) <u>*ta*</u>   *qu*   <u>*Taipei*</u>   她去台北
<u>She</u> went to <u>Taipei</u>.   (theme, goal)

(12) <u>*ta*</u>   *li-kai* <u>*Taipei*</u>   他離開台北
<u>He</u> left <u>Taipei</u>.   (theme, source)

(13) <u>*ta*</u>   *cong* <u>*Taipei*</u> *zou   dao* <u>*Kaohsiung*</u>   他從台北走到高雄
<u>He</u> walked from <u>Taipei</u> DAO <u>Kaohsiung</u>.   (theme, source, goal)

Without prepositional source and goal assigners (*from, to*), a verb itself also could do the assigning. Some verbs assign SOURCE (e.g. *li-kai* 離開), and some assign GOAL to the objects (e.g. *qu* 去). Adopting Jackendoff's Lexical Conceptual Structures (LCS), a motion verb could be conceptualized as "AGENT MOVE/GO VIA PATH". The path TO highlights the source whereas FROM emphasizes the goal. Based upon Jackendoff's, the conceptual structure of *dao* would be AGENT/THEME MOVES TO A GOAL. As to the goal, it prototypically refers to a concrete location and later metaphorically extends to abstract TIME and STATE.

TIME: (14) *Tie-ta   de shi-jian dao*   <u>*23:00*</u>   鐵塔的時間到 23:00
         tower   time   DAO   23:00
         "The tower is not closed until 23:00."

STATE: (15) *Ta   dao   <u>lao</u>   dou hai-shi xing-nan* 他到老都還是型男
         he DAO   old   all   still dandy man
         "He will always be a dandy man."

A stative goal is regarded as a result and hence the phrases after *dao* are resultative complements. Being preceded by a predicate, *dao* gradually becomes a proposition. The prepositional *dao* preserves the thematic properties of the verbal *dao*. First, it assigns GOAL to the object. In addition, the goal could be a location, time, or a state.

LOCATION: (16) *Ta   zou   dao Taipei*   他走到台北
　　　　　　　he walk   DAO Taipei.
　　　　　　　" He walks to Taipei."

TIME:　　　(17) *Ta   deng   dao   wu   dian*   他等到五點
　　　　　　　He   wait   DAO five o'clock
　　　　　　　"He waited until five o'clock."

STATE:　　　(18) *Ta ku   dao*   *yan-jing hong zhong* 她哭到眼睛紅腫
　　　　　　　he cry DAO   eye   red   swelling
　　　　　　　"She cried so heavily that her eyes are inflamed."

Conceptually, *dao* is like a goal indicator. When it is an extreme state that plays the role of goal, the excessive *dao* appears. In other words, the excessive meaning of *dao* is mainly brought by the element(s) following it. Then, how does *si* derive such a meaning? Many scholars study X-*si* construction, but only few touches this issue. Liu (2002) states that the excessive *si* is derived via metaphor; Chu (2006) proposes it is human's traditional concept about death that makes *si* excessive. In my opinion, however, there is a more convincing way for explanation. Similar to Liu, I also adopt metaphor; but differently, the metaphor on discussion is more directly related to excessiveness.

4.2 *Si*

Si originally refers to "death". The excessive meaning of it probably is made possible through conceptual metaphor. Human life is always conceptualized as a journey; therefore, there is always the expression "*zai rensheng de lutu shang* 在人生的旅途上 (in the journey of life)" uttered. A journey, basically, has a starting place and a destination, corresponding to SOURCE and GOAL. And in this life journey, death plays the very end.

Accordingly, the conceptual structure of *si* is AGENT/THEME MOVES TO THE **END** OF A GOAL. Generally, arriving at a destination might not imply an end. V-*si*, differently, has an inherent end which makes the whole process bounded. Analyzing it from the aspect of climbing up a building, the entering into a building exemplifies the former conceptual structure, in which the building refers to the goal, the final destination. Climbing up to the top floor, the end of the building, takes the second conceptual structure.

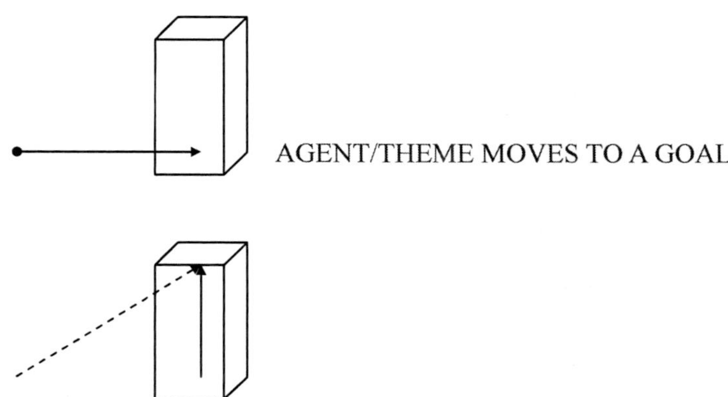

291

The second not only mentions the result but also amplifies the inner state of this result. And taking the excessive meaning, *si* could be an degree adverb or a complement.

ADVERB: (19) *Ta si ai qian*   他死愛錢
         he SI love money
         "He likes wealth a lot."

COMPLEMENT: (20) *Ta mang si le*   他忙死了
         he busy SI ASP
         "He is awfully busy."

        (21) *Tian-qi leng dao si* 天氣冷到死
         Weather cold DAO SI
         "It is extremely cold."

4.3 *Dao-si*: The Emergence of Excessiveness

According to *Wikipedia*, the free encyclopedia, it is now commonly proposed that grammaticalization is a function of frequency of use. It is hypothesized that words found together with a high frequency come to be cognitively processed as single units, and that these units then evolve as individual words. In colloquial Taiwan Mandarin, *dao* is always combined with *si* to indicate the excessiveness of a state. The combination will gradually fix *dao* to an excessive complement, which then makes *dao* an excessive structural particle linking the predicate and the complement. To process the construction, the predicate first invokes a scale, *dao* makes the pointer move, and the occurrence of *si* leads the pointer to the highest volume.

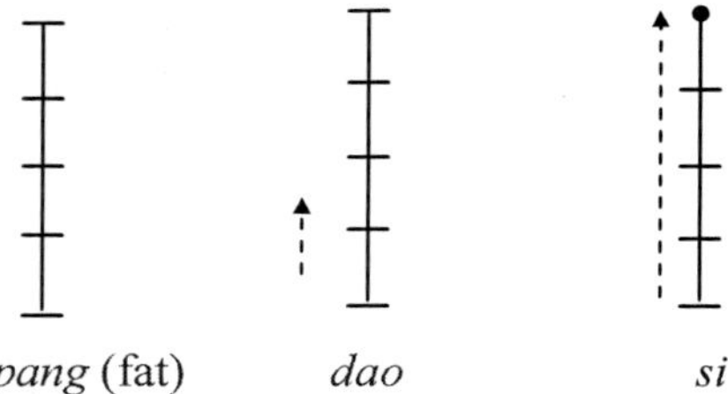

Once when *dao* is so closely linked to the excessive meaning that it takes over the semantic meaning of the complement, *si* could be deleted. As a result, *dao* could appear independently as a final particle (see section 5).

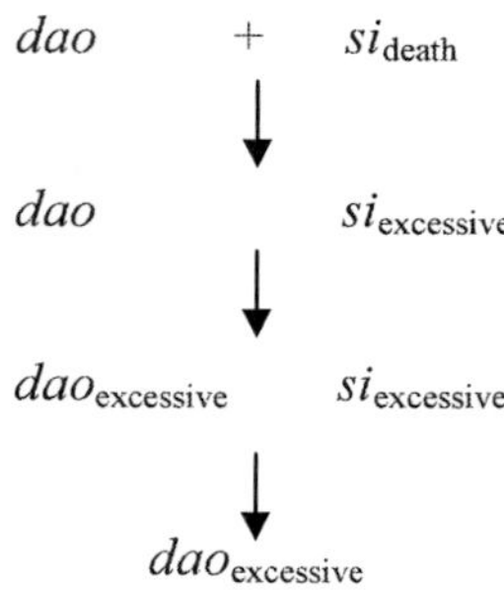

4.4 With or Without *Dao*

It has been mentioned that the X-*dao-si* construction coexists with the X-*si* one, which seems to make the appearance of *dao* less significant. If the existence of *dao* makes no difference, why is there still the X-*dao-si* construction prevailing? In my opinion, an expression with *dao* is somewhat different from that without *dao*. The two structures seem to share the same meaning – excessiveness; however, *dao* appears to emphasize more the excessive state. First, the two *sis* are phonologically different. Through my personal observation, *si* in X-*dao-si* is more stressed. On the other hand, *si* in X-*si* construction cannot be strongly stressed, probably because of the following *le*. X-si always takes *le* at the end to be the aspect marker. Differently, there is always a period put at the end of V-*dao-si* phrase. Therefore, the sentence final *si* could be prolonged and results in stronger emotion.

   Cognitively, *dao* might more directly link the predicate and *si* (do something until dying). The associating process then progresses smoothly and can successfully express the extent the speaker intends to tell. Without *dao*, the predicate and *si* usually cannot be associated directly, for example, it is hard to combine *shuai* (handsome) with death. This then requires more processing time and the dramatic effect is reduced.

5. Degree of Grammaticalization

In some dialects, the excessive structural article would further grammaticalized to a final particle. Basically, a final particle is more grammaticalized than a structural one, for the later more or less obeys the original syntactic requirements. *Dao*, as a verb, takes two arguments. Being a structural particle, the argument after *dao* is still required, but not limit to nouns only. The structural particle *dao* could also take a clausal complement.

> (22) *Ta   dao gong-yuan*　　他到<u>公園</u>　　　(noun)
> 　　 he DAO park　　　　　"He arrived at the park."

> (23) *Ta　　 xia dao　　 shou jiao fa-ma*　他嚇到<u>手腳發麻</u>　(clause)
> 　　 he frighten DAO　 hand foot benumbed
> 　　 "He is so frightened that his limbs are benumbed."

Quite the other way, as a final particle, everything following DAO should be left out, which makes it a little deviate from the original syntactic structure. The following presents the possible grammaticalization process of motion terms:

VERB ➲ PREPOSITION ➲ STRUCTURAL PARTICLE ➲ FINAL PARTICLE

Mandarin *dao* is still on the middle way of grammaticalization and cannot be used as a final particle. However, the excessive structural particle in Southern Min, *kah*[4], can appear at the end.

> (24) *Sui*[2]　　 *kah*[4]!　　水kah!
> 　　 beautiful DAO
> 　　 "Very beautiful!"

> (25) *Soe*　　[2] *kah*[4]!　　衰kah!
> 　　 unlucky DAO
> 　　 "Very unlucky!"

Basically, this grammaticalization process might occur in two situations. First, when the combination of the structural particle *dao* and *si* appears with a very high frequency, people are able to predict what is followed while hearing *dao*. In such a circumstance, the elements after *dao* are unnecessary. Second, the grammaticalization happens when there is no excellent word to describe the state. Beside *si*, there are various expressions which could be filled in the complement slot, and most of them refer to extremely miserable situation.

(26) *san³ kah⁴ hoo⁷ kui² liah⁴ khi⁰* 窮到予鬼掠去
 poor DAO ghost catch go
 "extremely poor"

(27) *soe¹ kah⁴ chhua³-sai²* 衰到挫屎
 unlucky DAO take shit
 "extremely unlucky"

(28) *leng² kah⁴ beh⁴ kau³ pe⁷* 冷到欲哭爸
 cold DAO want cry father
 "awfully cold"

There might be cases in which the extremeness is too high to be described by any word, just like a girl is so beautiful that no word fits for admiration. Since it's hard to find a good expression to accurately express the situation, the speaker will make a pause after *kah*, trying to make long the time for finding a suitable phrase. The pause then becomes a period when *kah* becomes a final particle.

6. Conclusion

In this paper, we examine both *dao* and *si* in the modern popular X-*dao-si* construction. The structural particle *dao* is derived from the arriving *dao* through grammaticalization. And the excessive meaning of *dao* mainly comes from its adjacent element, namely, *si*. *Si*, by symbolizing the very end of the life journey, metaphorically indicates excessiveness. And its high-frequency occurrence with *dao* makes the excessive meaning spread to *dao*.

 It is not specific that the motion verb denoting to "arrive at" becomes an excessive structural particle because there are many southern dialects displaying such a phenomenon. However, dialects might differ in the degree of grammaticalization. Through a comparison between Mandarin *dao* and Southern Min *kah*⁴, we find that *kah*⁴ is more grammaticalized.

VERB ➲ PREPOSITION ➲ STRUCTURAL PARTICLE ➲ FINAL PARTICLE

Mandarin ——————————————————————▶

Southern Min ————————————————————————————————▶

References

Jackendoff, Ray. 1983. *Semantics and Cognition.* Cambridge, MA: MIT Press.

Jackendoff, Ray. 1987. *Consciousness and the Computational Mind.* Cambridge, Mass.: MIT Press, 356.

Jackendoff, Ray. 1990. *Semantic Structures.* Cambridge, Mass.: MIT Press, 322.

Lakoff, George and Mark Johnson. 1980. *Metaphors we live by.* University of Chicago Press, Chicago.

Liu, Cheng-Hui. 2002. *Hanyu Dongbu Jiegou Lishi Fazhan* 漢語動補結構歷史發展 *(Historical Development of Mandarin Verb-Complement Construction).* Taipei: Hanlu Book Ltd. (翰蘆圖書公司)

Liu, Chi-Ming. 2006. *Degree Modification of Adjectives in Mandarin Chinese*. Master Thesis. Taiwan: Ching-Hua University.

Liu, Hsiu-Ying. 2006. Jinji de Piaobai – Chutan "SI" de Yufahua Guocheng yu Jixing Buyu de Yongfa 禁忌的漂白－初探「死」的語法化過程與極性補語的用法 (Taboo Purification – Grammaticalization of the Excessive Complement SI), the EACL volume, *Chinese linguistics in Budapest*.

Huang, Hua. 1984. "Dong (Xing)+Dao+…" de Jiegou Fenxi 動(形)+到+…"的結構分析 (Analysis on the "Verb (Adj.)+DAO+…" Construction), *Tianjin Shida Xuebao* (天津師大學報) 5, 620-635.

Zhu, Sai-Ping. 2006. Chengdu Buyu yu Jizhi Yiyi de Huode – yi "SI" Lei Ci Weili 程度補語與極致意義的獲得－以"死"類詞爲例 (Extent Complement and Excessive Meaning—Study on Words Related to SI), *Wenchou Shifan Xueyuan Xuebao* (溫州師範學院學報), Vol. 27, No.6, 26-30.

Using Non-Local Features to Improve Named Entity Recognition Recall[*]

Xinnian Mao[1], Wei Xu[1], Yuan Dong[1, 2], Saike He[2], and Haila Wang[1]

[1]France Telecom R&D Center (Beijing), Beijing, 100080, P.R.China

{xinnian.mao, wxu.ext, yuan.dong,haila.wang}@orange-ftgroup.com

[2]University of Posts and Telecommunications, Beijing, 100876, P.R.China

yuandong@bupt.edu.cn; hsk000@gmail.com

Abstract. Named Entity Recognition (NER) is always limited by its lower recall resulting from the asymmetric data distribution where the *NONE* class dominates the entity classes. This paper presents an approach that exploits non-local information to improve the NER recall. Several kinds of non-local features encoding entity token occurrence, entity boundary and entity class are explored under Conditional Random Fields (CRFs) framework. Experiments on SIGHAN 2006 MSRA (CityU) corpus indicate that non-local features can effectively enhance the recall of the state-of-the-art NER systems. Incorporating the non-local features into the NER systems using local features alone, our best system achieves a 23.56% (25.26%) relative error reduction on the recall and 17.10% (11.36%) relative error reduction on the F1 score; the improved F1 score 89.38% (90.09%) is significantly superior to the best NER system with F1 of 86.51% (89.03%) participated in the closed track.

Keywords: Named Entity Recognition, Non-local Feature, Conditional Random Field

1. Introduction

Named entity recognition (NER) is a subtask of information extraction that seeks to locate and classify predefined entities, such as names of persons, locations, organizations, etc. in unstructured texts. It is the fundamental step to many natural language processing applications, like Information Extraction (IE), Information Retrieval (IR) and Question Answering (QA). Most empirical approaches currently employed in NER task make decision only on local context for extract inference, which is based on the data independent assumption (Krishnan and Manning, 2006). But often this assumption does not hold because non-local dependencies are prevalent in natural language (including the NER task). How to utilize the non-local dependencies effectively is a key issue in NER task. Unfortunately, few researches have been devoted to this issue, existing works mainly focus on using the non-local information for further improving NER label consistency.

There are two methods to use non-local information. One is to add additional edges to graphical model structure to represent the distant dependencies and the other is to encode the non-locality with non-local features. However, in the first approach, heuristic rules are used to find the dependencies (Bunescu and Mooney, 2004; Sutton and McCallum, 2004) or penalties for label inconsistency are required to handset ad-hoc (Finkel et al., 2005). Furthermore, high computational cost is spent for approximate inference. In order to establish the long dependencies easily and overcome the disadvantage of the approximate inference, Krishnan and Manning (2006) propose a two-stage approach using Conditional Random Fields (CRFs) with extract inference. They represent the non-locality with non-local features, and extract the non-local features from the output of the first stage CRF using local context alone; then they incorporate the non-local features into the second CRF. But the features in this approach are

---

only used to improve label consistency.

To our best knowledge, up to now, non-local information has not been explored to improve NER recall in previous researches; on the other hand, NER is always impaired by its lower recall due to the imbalanced distribution where the *NONE* class dominates the entity classes. Classifiers built on such data typically have a higher precision and a lower recall and tend to overproduce the *NONE* class (Kambhatla, 2006). In this paper, we employ non-local information to recall the missed entities. Similar to Krishnan and Manning (2006), we also encode non-local information with features and apply the simple two-stage architecture. Different from their work for improve label consistency, their features are activated on the recognized entities coming from the first CRF, the non-local features we design are used to recall more missed entities which are seen in the training data or unseen entities but some of their occurrences being recognized correctly in the first stage, our features are fired on the raw token sequence directly with forward maximum match. Compared to their non-local information extracted from training data with 10-fold cross-validation, our non-local information is extracted from the training date directly; our approach obtaining the non-local features is simpler. Moreover, we design different non-local features encoding different useful information for NER two subtasks: entity boundary detection and entity semantic classification. Our features are also inspired by Wong and Ng (2007). They extract entity majority type features from unlabelled data with an initial maximum entropy classifier. Our approach is validated on the third International Chinese language processing bakeoff (SIGHAN 2006) MSRA and CityU NER closed track, the experimental results show that non-local features can significantly improve the recall of the state-of-the-art NER system using local context alone.

The remainder of the paper is structured as follows. In Section 2, we introduce the first stage CRF with local features alone; then we describe the second stage CRF using non-local features we design in Section 3. We demonstrate the experiments in Section 4 and we conclude the paper in Section 5.

2. Our Baseline NER System

To validate the effectiveness of our approach of exploiting non-local features, we need to establish a baseline with state-of-the-art performance using local context alone. Similar to (Krishnan and Manning, 2006), we employ two-stage architecture under conditional random fields (CRFs) framework. In the first stage, we build the baseline with local features only, and then we build the second NER system with non-local features. We will introduce them step by step.

2.1. Conditional random fields

We regard the NER task as a sequence labeling problem and apply Conditional Random Fields (Lafferty et al., 2001; Sha and Pereira, 2003) since it represents the state of the art in sequence modeling and has also been very effective at NER task. It is undirected graph established on G = (V, E), where V is the set of random variables $Y = \{Y_i|1 \leq i \leq n\}$ for each the n tokens in an input sequence and $E = \{(Y_{i-1}, Y_i) | 1 \leq i \leq n\}$ is the set of $(n - 1)$ edges forming a linear chain. Following Lafferty et al. (2001), the conditional probability of the state sequence (s1, s2...sn) given the input sequence (o1, o2...on) is computed as follows:

$$P_\Lambda(s \mid o) = \frac{1}{Z_o} \prod_{c \in C(s,o)} \exp(\sum_{t=1}^{T} \sum_{k=1}^{K} \lambda_k f_k(s_{t-1}, s_t, o, t)) \quad (1)$$

Where f_k is an arbitrary feature function; and λ_k is the weight for the feature function; it can be optimized through iterative algorithms like GIS (Darroch and Ratcliff, 1972) and IIS (Della Pietra et al., 1997). However recent research y been shown that quasi-Newton methods, such as L-BFGS, are significantly more efficient (Byrd et al., 1994; Malouf, 2002; Sha and Pereira, 2003).

2.2. Local features

The fist stage CRF labels for token directly depends on the labels corresponding the previous and next token, namely C_{-2}, C_{-1}, C_0, C_{-1}, C_2, $C_{-2}C_{-1}$, $C_{-1}C_0$, C_0C_{-1}, C_1C_2, and $C_{-1}C_1$, where C_0 is the current character, C_1 the next character, C_2 the second character after C_0, C_{-1} the character preceding C_0, and C_{-2} the second character before C_0. In addition, the first CRF used the tag bigram feature. Although these local features are simple, they give us state-of-the-art baseline using local information alone as described in Section 4.

2.3. Low recall in NER task

As Kambhatla (2006) points out that NER system typically have a higher precision and a lower recall and tends to overproduce the NONE class because the *NONE* class dominates all other classes in the task. In natural language, different sentences contain different useful contextual information; the missed entities are happened when their context surroundings are not indicative enough for the statistical-based approaches (including the CRFs) to make a correct decision. When we analyze these missed occurrences of the missed entities further, we can put them into three groups. The first is the seen entities in the training data; the second is the unseen occurrences, but some other occurrences of the entities have been correctly recognized in certain indicative context surroundings. The third is the unseen occurrences with no any occurrences recognized correctly. In NER task, considering influences between extractions can be very useful, if the context surrounding one occurrence of a token sequence is very indicative of it being an entity, then this should also influence the tagging of another occurrence of the same token sequence in a different context that is not indicative of entity (Bunescu and Mooney, 2004). So if we consider the non-local dependencies between the same entities, some of these missed occurrences will be recognized correctly. We will describe how to capture the non-locality to recall more missed entities in Section 3.

3. Recalling Missed Entities with Non-local Features

In natural language, difference sentences contain different useful context information; the missed entities happen when their context surroundings are not indicative enough for the first stage CRF to make correct decisions. If the context surrounding one occurrence of a token sequence is very indicative of it being an entity, then this should also influence the labeling of another occurrence of the same token sequence in a different context that is not indicative of entity (Bunescu and Mooney, 2004). So considering the non-local dependencies between the same entities can be very useful, if these non-local dependencies are incorporated into the CRF model, some of the missed entities will be recalled correctly.

3.1. Flow chart using non-local features

Figure 1 shows the flow using non-local features in two-stage architecture under CRFs framework. The first CRF is trained with local features alone as baseline (described in Section 2), and then we test the testing data with the first CRF and get the entities plus their type from the output. The second CRF utilizes the non-local features derived from the entity list which is merged by the output of the first CRF from the testing data and the entities extracted directly from the training data. To provide flexible and general conclusion, we only use non-local information found in labeled training data and test data rather than external knowledge sources, such as post-of-speech, gazetteers, external lexica and etc.

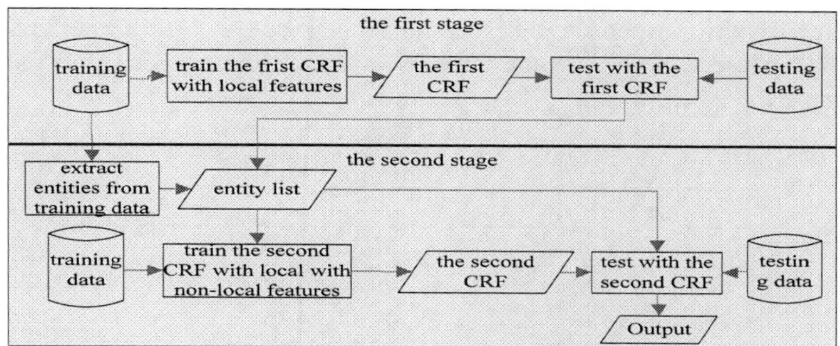

Figure 1. The flow using non-local features in two-stage architecture

3.2. Four kinds of non-local features

We design four kinds of non-local features which encode different useful information for the two NER subtasks, i.e. entity boundary detection and entity semantic classification, the non-local features are fired on the token sequences if they are matched with certain entity in the entity list in forward maximum matching (FMM) way. I will describe them one by one as follows.

Entity-occurrence features (F1): These refer to the occurrence information assigned to the token sequence which is matched with the entity list exactly. These features capture the dependencies between the identical candidate entities; which results in the same candidate entities of different occurrences can be recalled favorably.

Token-position features (F2): These refer to the position information (start, middle and last) assigned to the token sequence which is matched with the entity list exactly. These features enable us to capture the dependencies between the identical candidate entities and their boundaries.

Entity-majority features (F3): These refer to the majority label assigned to the token sequence which is matched with the entity list exactly. These features enable us to capture the dependencies between the identical entities and their classes, so that the same candidate entities of different occurrences can be recalled favorably, and their label consistencies can be considered too.

Token-position & entity-majority features (F4): These features capture non-local information from F2 and F3 simultaneously. They take into account the entity boundary and semantic class information at the same time.

These non-local features are applied in English NER in one-step approach (Krishnan and Manning, 2006; Wong and Ng, 2007), they employ these features to improve entity consistence among their different occurrences. These features are assigned to token sequences that are matched exactly with the (entity, majority-type) list in forward maximum matching (FMM) way. During training or testing, when the CRFs tagger encounters a token sequence $C_1...C_n$ such that $(C_k...C_s)$ $(k{\geq}1,\ s {\leq}n)$ is the longest token sequence existing in the entity list; the correspondent features will be turned on to each token in $C_k....C_s$. For example, considering the following sentence: *我(wo) 爱(ai) 北(bei) 京(jing) 天(tian) 安(an) 门(men)(I love Beijing Tiananmen)*. If (*北京, Maj-LOC*), (*京, Maj-LOC*), and (*天安门, Maj-LOC*) are presented in the *(entity, majority type)* list, the features below will be turned on as table 1 shows.

Notice that the feature turned on for 京is *E-Maj-LOC*, not *B-Maj-LOC*, because the longest matching sequence is 北京. Different from (Krishnan and Manning, 2006; Wong and Ng, 2007), they only assign the majority type information, like *Maj-Loc,* to each token in matched candidates, boundary information like *B, I* and *E* is ignored, it is acceptable because they utilize these features only for English corpora, and the boundary information can be captured by the capitalization characteristics. But in Chinese NER, NED is more difficult than NEC, so we assign the boundary information, representing with *B, I* and *E*, to each token in the matched candidates. Please note that not all matching token sequences are true candidates. The false candidates come from two aspects: the first is the boundaries are correct, but the occurrences are common words[1]; the second errors come from FMM, so the features are soft constraints.

Table 1. Example for Token-Majority-Type features

Token	Entity-Majority-Type Feature
我	-
爱	-
北	B-Maj-LOC
京	E-Maj-LOC
天	B-Maj-LOC
安	I-Maj-LOC
门	E-Maj-LOC

4. Experiments

4.1. Corpus analysis

Our investigation is based on the MSRA and CityU datasets from the NER closed track of the third International Chinese language processing bakeoff (SIGHAN 2006) (Levow, 2006); its goal is to perform NER on three entity classes: PERSON, LOCATION and ORGANIZATION. We give up the LDC corpus because it is initially designed for ACE Evaluation and the definition of named entity is different from traditional definition. The named entities in SIGHAN training data sets are labeled in IOB-2 format, we covert the corpus to OBIE as a pre-processing, because some existing work and our experiments show that OBIE scheme outperforms other formats when applying machine learning to NER. In OBIE format, tokens outside of entities are tagged with *O* (*NONE* class), while the first token in an entity is tagged with B-k to begin class k, the token inside the entity is tagged with I-k and the end token in the entity is tagged with E-k; single-token entity is labeled as B-k.

General information for each dataset appears in Table 2. It also summarizes the statistic information of seen and unseen entities in the test sets. A seen named entity in test set means that it exists in its correspondent training data set. From the table, we can find that the proportion of seen entities is very high. 71.86% of named entities in MSRA test data can be found in MSRA training data, while 73.53% for CityU corpus. In fact, most of named entities may appear frequently in our generally lives. To make use of existing named entities in training data is crucial to improving capability to capture seen entities and thereby unseen entities, since many models consider the possibilities of labels in context. We also see an interesting phenomenon in MSRA corpus that many named entities are consecutive without punctuations, especially the person names. Particularly, in MSRA testing data, nearly 20% named entities appear consecutively. It brings great difficulties for NER system to capture such entities separately.

Table 2. Corpus overall statistics

	#(W)	#(E)	#(C)	#(S)
MSRA (Training)	1.3M	75060	10.93%	---
MSRA(Testing)	100k	6190	19.68%	71.86%
CityU (Training)	1.6M	112347	10.13%	---
CityU (Testing)	220k	16407	9.60%	73.53%

#(W): the size of words; (E): the size of entities;#(C): the proportion of the consecutive entities; #(S): the proportion of the seen entities

4.2. Problems of NER with only local information

---

[1] For the string 两岸, when it refers to Mainland and Taiwan, it is an entity, when it refers to the bank of rivers, it is a common word.

Table 3 displays the performance on MSRA and CityU NER closed track. The F0 row lists the precision, recall and F-measure (β=1) got by the first CRF (described in Section 2) using local features alone. The score makes the first CRF rank the top position on the MSRA and the second on the CityU in SIGHAN bakeoff (Levow, 2006)[2]. It shows that our baseline has achieved the state-of-the-art performance. However, comparing the recall with the precision on each dataset, we find that the performance is impaired by the relatively low recall. To investigate the causes of this problem, we analyze the missed entities further. We categorize them into two classes, seen and unseen in training data. Five kinds of statistic information are collected and listed in F0 column in table 4. (1) The number of different missed named entities; (2) The times of missing occurrences; (3) The number of different missed named entities which are detected correctly at least once; (4) The times missing occurrences under the case of (3).

From (1) and (2) measurements of the seen entities in the F0 column in table 4, we find that there are many seen named enmities are missed. Though identifying unseen named entities is more difficult than seen named entities, the boldfaced number indicates that about 10% (24 of 254) for MSRA and 23% (111 of 476) for CityU of unseen and missed named entities have been labeled out correctly for at least once. The difficulty to capture unseen named entities in training data is because of the nature of machine learning techniques. However, the statistical results in Table 4 show there is a great potential (200+48)/(200+330)=47% for MSRA and (384+396)/(384+1144)=51% for CityU, to improve recall by enhancing the capture of seen named entities and making use of labeled outputs from test data to capture more unseen named entities. What is more, performance can be improved further when more named entities are labeled correctly, because many models, such as CRF, assign labels according to the possibilities of whole sequence.

4.3. Influence of using non-local features in NER

After we feed the non-local features (described in Section 3) to the second CRF, we test it on the testing data of MSRA and CityU again. Table 3 lists the performance got by each kind of feature configurations. F0 means the first CRF (baseline) using local features alone, and the F0+Fi (i=1, 2, 3, 4) means the second CRF using local features (F0) as well as the non-local features Fi. From the table 3, we can conclude that exploiting non-local information is a good choice to recall more missed entities. Comparing with the baseline using only local context, the recalls of NER systems are improved after taking non-local information into account by - 0.34%~3.76% on MSRA, 2.92%~3.68% on CityU. And the overall F-measures increase by - 0.54%~2.19% and 0.72%~1.27% on MSRA and CityU each. The MSRA performance got by F0+F1 decrease slightly because there are many consecutive entities in the testing data. Since F1 does not encode boundary and class information, more entity tokens are recalled, but their boundaries or classes are wrong. After we implement a post-processing step with person name list extracted from the MSRA training data to separate the consecutive candidate entities, the performance lists with F0+F1 (PP) increases. The performance difference among F1, F2, F3 and F4 are mainly because they encode different useful non-local information as described in Section 3.2. For F1, it only encode whether a token sequence is an entity. No boundary and class are considered which are represented in F2 and F3 respectively, so F2 and F3 both achieve high performance than F0, and F4 consider both boundary and class simultaneously, so it is the best choice of exploiting non-local information to improve NER recall. We can not compare between F2 and F3 directly because boundary detection and semantic class classification are the two different sub-tasks in NER.

The performance difference between the performance on CityU and MSRA come from two folds. One is because CityU testing data contains more seen entities than that of MSRA since the seen entities can be captured easily by the non-local features. The other is because MSRA data sets contain much more consecutive named entities than CityU. Since NER with non-local information prefers to dig out more and thereby longer named entities, it may tend to label more

---

[2] The best F1-score on MSRA and CityU is 86.51% and 89.03% respectively.

continuous named entities as a single named entities and introduce more errors damaging both in recall and precision.

Table 3. NER performance on MSRA and CityU

Corpus	System	P	R	F
MSRA	F0	90.58	*84.04*	**87.19**
	F0+F1	89.81	83.70	86.65
	F0+F1(PP)	89.40	85.46	87.39
	F0+F2	89.73	85.96	87.81
	F0+F3	90.58	87.16	88.84
	F0+F4	91.01	*87.80*	**89.38**
CityU	F0	92.48	*85.43*	**88.82**
	F0+F1	90.73	88.35	89.53
	F0+F2	90.96	88.83	89.88
	F0+F3	90.90	88.65	89.76
	F0+F4	91.09	*89.11*	**90.09**

Then, we investigate the situation of missed seen and missed unseen named entity in NER with non-local information by filling the Table 4. F0 is the first CRF (baseline) using local features alone, and the F0+Fi (i=1, 2, 3, 4) means the second CRF using local features (F0) as well as the non-local features Fi. The four same measurements are used as described in Section 4.2. Compared with the numbers in F0 column, significant reduction of missing of seen entities is achieved by adding non-local features. What is more, the hit of unseen entities is also increased as we predicted in previous analysis.

Table 4. Analysis of missed named entities with non-local information

Corpus		F0	F0+F1(PP)[3]	F0+F2	F0+F3	F0+F4
Seen (MSRA)	1	109	28	26	33	29
	2	200	158	74	83	75
	3	*45*	*13*	*14*	*15*	*17*
	4	*126*	*86*	*45*	*45*	*47*
Unseen (MSRA)	1	254	198	202	229	224
	2	330	484	246	275	270
	3	*24*	*1*	*0*	*0*	*0*
	4	*48*	*2*	*0*	*0*	*0*
Seen (CityU)	1	216	87	87	88	86
	2	384	149	149	152	148
	3	*118*	51	55	56	54
	4	*243*	94	105	109	119
Unseen (CityU)	1	476	356	348	355	350
	2	1144	704	696	702	693
	3	111	12	6	9	5
	4	396	17	12	15	11

5. Conclusions and Future Work

In this paper, we propose an approach of exploiting non-local information to improve NER recall. To our best knowledge, our work is the first attempt to utilize non-local information to improve NER recall, our work demonstrates that non-local information are effective to recall the missed entities which are seen in training data or unseen but some occurrences of these unseen

---

[3] We do not perform post-processing step on CityU testing data

entities have been recognized correctly with local context alone. We also compare the different kinds of non-local features which fit to different NER sub-tasks and find that non-local feature considering the boundary and class information simultaneously is the best. Our approach is language independent, due to lack of annotated corpora of other languages, the experiments have only been conducted on Chinese corpora, and related experiments on other languages can be done in the future.

References

R. Bunescu and R. J. Mooney. 2004. Collective information extraction with relational Markov networks. *Proceedings of the 42nd ACL*, pp. 439–446.

R.H. Byrd, J. Nocedal and R.B. Schnabel. 1994. Representations of quasi-Newton matrices and their use in limited memory methods. *Mathematical Programming*, (63):129-156.

J.N. Darroch and D. Ratcliff. 1972. Generalized iterative scaling for log-linear models. *The Annals of Mathematical Statistics*, 43 (5):1470-1480.

J. Finkel, T. Grenager, and C. D. Manning. 2005. Incorporating non-local information into information extraction systems by gibbs sampling. *Proceedings of the 42nd ACL*, pp. 363–370.

N. Kambhatla. 2006. Minority Vote: At-Least-N Voting Improves Recall for Extracting Relations. *Proceeding of the 44th ACL*, pp. 460–466.

V. Krishnan and C. D Manning. 2006. An Effective Two-Stage Model for Exploiting Non-Local Dependencies in Named Entity Recognition. *Proceedings of the 44th ACL*, pp. 1121–1128.

J. Lafferty, A. McCallum, and F. Pereira. 2001. Conditional Random Fields: Probabilistic models for segmenting and labeling sequence data. *Proceedings of the 18th ICML*, pp. 282–289. Morgan Kaufmann, San Francisco, CA

G. Levow. 2006. The Third International Chinese Language Processing Bakeoff: Word Segmentation and Named Entity Recognition. *Proceedings of SIGHAN-2006*, pp. 108-117. Sydney, Australia.

R. Malouf. 2002. A comparison of algorithms for maximum entropy parameter estimation. *Proc. of CoNLL-2002*, 49-55. Taipei, Taiwan.

S.D. Pietra, V. Della Pietra, and J. Lafferty, 1997. Inducing features of random fields. *IEEE Transactions on Pattern Analysis and Machine Intelligence*, 19(4):380-393, 1997.

F. Sha and F. Pereira. 2003. Shallow parsing with conditional random fields. *Proc. of HLT/NAACL-2003*, 213-220. Edmonton, Canada.

C. Sutton and A. McCallum. 2004. Collective segmentation and labeling of distant entities in information extraction. *In ICML Workshop on Statistical Relational Learning and Its connections to Other Fields*.

Y. CH. Wong and H. T. Ng. 2007. One class per named entity: exploiting unlabeled text for named entity recognition. *Proc. of IJCAI-2007*. 1763-1768. India.

Analysis of Indirect Uses of Interrogative Sentences Carrying Anger [*]

Hye-Jin Min and Jong C. Park

Computer Science Division EECS Department, KAIST
373-1 Guseong-dong, Yuseong-gu Daejeon 305-701 South Korea
{hjmin, park}@nlp.kaist.ac.kr

Abstract. Interrogative sentences are generally used to perform speech acts of directly asking a question or making a request, but they are also used to convey such speech acts indirectly. In the utterances, such indirect uses of interrogative sentences usually carry speaker's emotion with a negative attitude, which is close to an expression of anger. The identification of such negative emotion is known as a difficult problem that requires relevant information in syntax, semantics, discourse, pragmatics, and speech signals. In this paper, we argue that the interrogatives used for indirect speech acts could serve as a dominant marker for identifying the emotional attitudes, such as anger, as compared to other emotion-related markers, such as discourse markers, adverbial words, and syntactic markers. To support such an argument, we analyze the dialogues collected from the Korean soap operas, and examine individual or cooperative influences of the emotion-related markers on emotional realization. The user study shows that the interrogatives could be utilized as a promising device for emotion identification.

Keywords: Interrogative sentences, Wh-words, Emotion identification, Anger

1. Introduction

Every utterance has its illocutionary force that makes the hearers to act a certain behavior, in accordance with the speaker's intentions, such as assertives, directives, commissives, expressives and declarations (Austin, 1962; Searle, 1969). The actions induced by such intentions, or speech acts, are systematically related to particular types of a sentential form uttered by the speaker (Levelt, 1989). However, these relations do not appear quite strict because speech acts with a particular sentential form could be dependent upon prosodic and paralinguistic devices. For instance, interrogative sentences are not only used for asking a question or making a request directly to the hearers, but also perform speech acts indirectly, including rejection, refutation, and reproach. In particular, in an utterance, such indirect speech acts could also carry the speaker's psychological attitude (Kim, 2003), as shown in the following utterance.

(1) A: 어서 그에게 가서 잘못을 사과해.
   (Promptly apologize to him for your fault.)[1]

---

[*] This research was performed for the Intelligent Robotics Development Program, one of the 21st Century Frontier R&D Programs, and Brain Science Research Center, funded by the Ministry of Commerce, Industry and Energy of Korea.

[1] The transcriptions in English are placed in round brackets.

B: 사과라구요? 내가 <u>왜</u> 사과하는데요? 잘못한 사람이 <u>누군데</u>?
(Apology? <u>Why</u> do I have to apologize to him? <u>Who</u> did something wrong?)

Example (1) contains the interrogatives '왜(why)' and '누군데(who)' to convey an indirect speech act that the speaker B rejects the proposal of the speech partner A, carrying a negative attitude in the utterance. Similarly, in the most utterances of soap opera, the indirect speech act with such psychological attitudes is much closer to the negative emotion, such as anger, than to the positive emotion, such as joy. In contrast to this realization by the interrogatives, the distinction of anger from joy is known as a difficult problem in emotion identification with speech signals, which are actively utilized as an important information source in the most studies for emotion recognition. The speech signals for anger and joy have quite similar pitch and intonation. Thus, if we identify certain types of interrogative sentences related to a negative psychological attitude and make the patterns from those types, emotion identification from speech signals could perform better with the help of the patterns.

In this paper, we analyze interrogative sentences with psychological attitudes, especially related to the speaker's anger. We first describe the interrogatives for their underlying effects on emotions in utterance, and other emotion-embedded expressions, such as adverbial words, demonstrative expressions, syntactic markers and discourse markers. Such expressions are often used alone to convey the speaker's emotions, but they could be used in interrogative sentences so as to expose the emotions more clearly. We look into the individual or cooperative uses of interrogatives and the emotion-embedded expressions, in order to classify the characteristic patterns related to the emotion of anger.

In order to analyze interrogatives, we collect utterances from the scripts of romantic soap operas that show rich emotional expressions in Korean. We examine the collection of utterances to see how such interrogative sentences influence the process of identifying the speaker's anger, and then confirm the influence through a user study of tagging emotions to utterances in the same domain. As a preliminary result from the user study, we constructed patterns of sentences and their speech acts carrying particular emotions. We believe that such patterns could be utilized as a high quality resource to identify the emotion and the mood of dialogues with precision.

The rest of this paper is organized as follows. Section 2 shows previous researches for the linguistic elements that express the speaker's emotions. Section 3 analyzes the linguistic structures of interrogative sentences as well as other linguistic components in contexts, especially focusing on an indirect speech act with emotional attitudes. Section 4 describes a user study of emotion tagging and its preliminary result. Section 5 discusses complex cases in interrogative sentences. Finally, Section 6 concludes the paper.

2. Background

There have been many researches on linguistic elements in the Korean spoken language related to the speaker's psychological attitudes. (Jang, 1998) examined the actual function of 'Wh-words' in a spoken language corpus, who asserted that the frequencies of 'what' and 'where' as an exclamation and an infinite in a real utterance is not so low and even higher than those of 'what' and 'where' as a standard interrogative. The collected examples show that these interrogatives function as exclamations expressing the instant senses or abrupt emotions. (Jung, 2005) analyzed the meaning of the interrogative 'what' by classifying it as a basic meaning for standard questions and an extended meaning for discourse markers. According to her classification, three meanings of 'what' as a discourse marker are related to emotions of the speaker. First, when it is utilized for emphasis it contains regretfulness. Second, it is a marker for surprise by the unexpected information. Third, when the speaker does not accept the current situation emotionally, it served as a marker for disappointment or abandonment. (Kim, 2003) regarded some interrogatives as modal interrogatives when they are used in special interrogative questions with indirect speech acts. These researches show that the usages of 'Wh-words' or interrogatives are not just limited to the basic and standard questions, but many of them are used to convey the speaker's psychological attitude.

Exclamations, adverbial or demonstrative expressions that function as discourse markers also express the speaker's diverse psychological attitude such as persistence, surprise, hedge, and so on (Byron and Heeman, 1997; Kang, 2002). These expressions do not affect the informative meaning of the utterances but convey additional emotional meanings or attitudes along with it. In addition, special endings of questions with indirect speech acts such as rhetorical questions, echo questions, or imperative questions influence the expression of negative attitudes such as refutation, rejection, or suspicion (Jeon, 1996; Kim, 1999) The ending in rhetorical-echo questions functions as a syntactic marker indicating that the sentence is in the form of an ending and that it is a repeated expression of the previous utterance. In the case of imperative questions, the ending serves as a marker for emphasizing the given action.

All these researches reveal that there are some linguistic elements in the spoken language that describe the speaker's emotional attitude, but their main focus has not been on emotional attitudes. Neither have the relations among these components been discussed systematically. It is hard to see how all these co-occurring components in utterances affect the speaker's emotional attitude at a glance, but there could be at least some characteristic patterns. In this paper, we analyze these linguistic components together as they are used in utterances and examine how much these components influence the process of recognizing the speaker's emotion, especially anger, by focusing on interrogative sentences.

3. The Structure of the Interrogative Sentences Related to Anger

3.1. Interrogative sentences and interrogatives

The expected action of the hearer when the speaker is asking a question is to provide some information for the speaker. However, if the sought information is already accessible to both the speaker and the hearer, the real intention of the speaker would be different from simply asking for it. In such a case, the interrogative is utilized in order to emphasize the intention. For example, the speaker B produces an utterance in the form of an interrogative sentence to emphasize refutation against A's assertion in (1). The interrogative pronoun 'who' in the second one has its antecedent in the context as opposed to those of standard questions. Although B knew who did something wrong, B asked such a question to convey the negative attitude to A. The interrogative pronoun 'who' refers to B and what B actually believes is the opposite of the mentioned information in such a question. The corresponding declarative sentence could be that '잘못한 사람이 내가 아니다' (I didn't do anything wrong)' by substituting '누구'(who) with '나'(I) and negating the predicate '인데'(be). The speaker could express the same meaning with such a declarative sentence without losing the denotative meaning of the original utterance. However, the connotative meaning of the utterance such as anger in this case may be lost.

From this observation, we looked further into other interrogatives related to anger by collecting 100 short dialogues from the scripts for soap opera with two genre, teen-agers and romance. Each dialogue consists of one speaker's turn that includes at least one utterance expressing the speaker's anger[2], and its preceding and following turns that support the fact that the utterance expresses the anger. We then found out that the frequency of the interrogative sentences with negative attitudes such as denial, refutation, persistence, reproach and oppressive order is quite high, approximately twenty percent, in the turn of the speaker, who expresses his or her anger. The utterance in (2) is one of the examples that we collected, which contains the interrogatives, with the Wh-words 'where' and 'how'.

---

[2] We utilized descriptive information such as facial expressions, emotion words or behaviors within the scripts to choose the utterance with anger.

(2) 동규: 대체 화안당이 <u>어디</u> 붙어 있는 거야?
　　　네비게이션에도 안 뜨는 촌구석을 <u>어떻게</u> 찾아가라구?
　　(Dong-kyu: <u>Where</u> in the world is hwaan-dang located ?
　　<u>How</u> can I find out such a small place not listed in the GPS navigation device?)

Dong-kyu is having a difficulty in finding a place called hwann-dang, although he knew its address and the way to reach it in the situation. It is obvious that the two interrogative sentences are not utilized for asking but for emphasizing his annoyance. In a way similar to the case of 'who', the second sentence with 'how' could be related to the declarative sentence, '네비게이션에도 안 뜨는 촌구석을 찾을 수 없네(I can't find such a small place not listed in the GPS navigation device)' by negating the predicate and having the declarative ending. Figure 1 shows the frequency of 'Wh-words' in the dialogues we have collected.

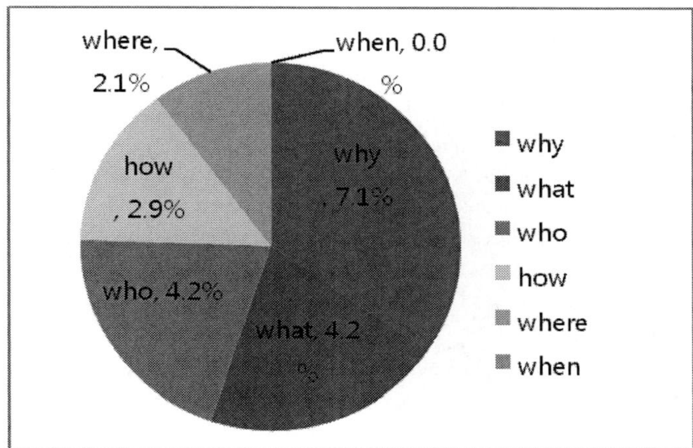

Figure 1: Frequency of Wh-words

3.2. Other emotion-embedded expressions with interrogative sentences

One of the major reasons that people get angry is that they find out something or someone blameworthy by their standards of judgment (Ortony et al., 1988). So when they express their anger, some specific words or phrases that are related to the degrees of the standards of judgment appear in their utterances. Such degrees could be measured as the amount of the blameworthy actions or deepness of each action's blameworthiness. Adverbs or demonstrative expressions have properties that can infer the degree of blameworthiness within the interrogative sentences. For example, the adverb '자꾸/맨날(so many times)' shows that the action in the utterance is repetitive and that its amount exceeds the speaker's acceptable standards. '아예(why don't you)' in (3b) indicates that the predicate in the utterance is regarded as an extremely unacceptable behavior, so the degree of the blameworthiness is quite high.

(3c) shows the role of the demonstrative expression '그렇게(so)' in the utterance. It comes with the interrogative adverb '왜(why)', and the connoted meaning is the same as that of '매우(very)' (Shin, 1993). It decides the degree of the blameworthiness, in this case, '비뚤어지다(being bully)'. In the opinion of the speaker's opinion, the degree of blameworthiness of the hearer exceeded some limits, so she chose to use such a word. All these expressions let the hearer notice that his or her action is not acceptable to the speaker more clearly with the interrogatives.

(3) a. 황회장: 너 지금 할애비한테 반항하는 거여? 맞고 할텨? 그냥 할텨?

(President Whang: Are you defying me now? Will you do it after getting spanked?
Or just do it?)
동규: <u>아 글쎄</u> 그 촌구석에 있는 집을 왜 <u>자꾸/맨날</u> 탐내시<u>냐구요</u>?
300 년 된 종택이라 팔 수도 없다잖아요!
(Dong-kyu: <u>Ah</u>, why do you keep craving for the house in such a small village
<u>so many times</u>?
They can't even sell it because of its long historical background!)
b. 수하: 남의 걸 허락없이 왜 뒤져요? 정말 이상한 사람이야!
(Sue-ha: Why did you search for my stuff without my permission? You are so weird!)
동규: 누가 뭘 뒤졌다고 그래요? 연락처 알라고 잠깐 본 건데? 아, 울컥하네.
왜에? <u>아예</u> 훔쳤다고 하지?
(Dong-kyu: Who searched for what? I just took a quick look to find your phone-number.
I'm so annoyed. Why? <u>Why don't you</u> say I stole it?)
c. 수하: 부모님 밑에서 부족한 거 없이 잘 자란 애가 왜 <u>그렇게</u> 비뚤어진 건데?
왜? 애기씨 소리 못 들어서 서운해?
(Sue-ha: How come you are <u>so</u> bully despite being raised under such caring and rich parents?
Why? Are you sad that you are not called as a princess?)
준희: <u>허!</u> 누가 그딴 소리 듣고 싶대? 웃겨 진짜!
(Jun-hee: <u>Huh!</u> Who would like to hear such a sound? That's so ridiculous!)

Exclamations as discourse markers are often located either in the front or at the back of the interrogative sentences. They also work as clues for indirect speech acts related to an emotional attitude with those sentences. In fact, emotional exclamations apparently function as markers expressing the emotions such as '하하' and '히히' for joy or '에고' and '어이' for sadness (Nam and Ko, 1985). Likewise, exclamations '아(ah)' and '글쎄(well)' in (3a) and '허(huh)' in (3c) are the clues that indicate their utterances carry the spearker's anger. However, these might express several emotions depending on the co-occurring utterances, so we should analyze not only the exclamations but also other kinds of information such as interrogatives and speech acts. For example, the discourse marker '글쎄(well)' is used both when the speaker highlights her strong opinion against the thought of the addressee and when the speaker must answer with uncertainty, so it's hard to identify the speaker's emotion with only the presence of '글쎄(well)'. However, it could be utilized to strengthen the speaker's refutation in connection with the following rhetorical echo question. Further cases of when it is still necessary to consider contextual information such as the previous or following utterances will be discussed in Section 5.

The speaker often repeats the hearer's former question to emphasize her anger. In this case, the special ending with the role of repetition is attached to the verbs or adjectives in the utterance of the speaker like '-라구요' in (1). The ending belongs to '-다고(-tako)', which syntactically makes a sentence end (Jeon, 1996). Jeon examined the functions of this type of ending and she argued that one of the functions is to indicate the speaker's refutation or denial. She explained why the speaker utters this way instead of just directly mentioning a refusal according to the politeness principle (Leech, 1983). By uttering that way, the speaker can unload the hearer's burden. However, when the speaker wants to express the anger at the hearer, she also takes this kind of repercussive question with other linguistic expressions that we have discussed so far. Dong-kyu's utterance in (3a) is one example containing the adverb and the discourse marker. Therefore, repercussive questions with –tako ending that indicating a refusal or denial also express the speaker's anger with the help of other linguistic device such as interrogatives, discourse markers. Table 1 summarizes some of these linguistic elements in Korean.

Table 1: Interrogatives and emotion-embedded expressions for anger

Adverbial words	자꾸/맨날 (so many times), 아예,

	감히(dare)
Demonstrative expressions	그렇게/그런/그딴(so), 이딴(this)
Discourse markers	아(ah), 글쎄(well), 허/흥(huh), 뭐(what)
-Tako endings	-라고/라구, -다고, -라고/라구/다고 그래(요)

4. User Study and the Results

In order to examine the real influence of the interrogative sentences on identifying the speaker's anger, we took a test tagging utterances within the scripts for soap opera, with the same genre as we analyzed. We first collected segments of a script that includes a situation where one of the speakers uses interrogative sentences when he or she expresses his or her anger. Each segment is either a whole scene or part of a scene. Then we converted the interrogative sentences into declarative sentences and made a copy of each segment including converted declarative sentences (CS) instead of interrogative sentences (IS). The conversion rules are as follows.

[1] If a sentence is a rhetorical question, we remove the interrogative and negate the meaning of the sentence manually. In case of the interrogative 'who' we substitute it with a relevant antecedent. We then convert the ending of the sentence for the question into the one for the declarative.

[2] If there are discourse markers, adverbial words, and demonstrative expressions near the interrogative sentence, we remove them. For example, the converted utterance of Jun-hee in (3c) is "난 그런 소리 듣고 싶지 않아 (I don't like to hear about it)" by substituting '누가(who)' with '난(I)' and by removing the exclamation '허(Huh)'.

We asked 20 subjects to judge whether the speaker is angry in the given example utterances by assigning the intensity of the anger on a seven-point Likert scale-based questionnaire. We divided the subjects into two groups where one group takes utterances with original interrogative sentences and the other group takes the ones with converted declarative sentences. Figure 2 shows two different kinds of utterances with the same denotative meanings and Figure 3 shows the screen shot of the test page. Subjects can tag the intensity of the anger by the drop-down box. The subject in Figure 3 tagged the last two sentences so the outline of the boxes became pink. During the test, they did not know about the actual intention of the test.

수하: 남의 걸 허락없이 왜 뒤져요?

정말 이상한 사람이야!

동규: 누가 뭘 뒤졌다고 그래요?

연락처 알라고 잠깐 본 건데?

아, 울컥하네.

왜에? 아예 훔쳤다고 하지?

(a) The original interrogative sentences

수하: 남의 걸 허락없이 뒤지시다니 좀 이상한 분이시네요.

동규: 내가 핸드백을 뒤진게 아니고, 연락처 알라고 잠깐 본 거에요.

아, 기분 안좋네요.

훔쳤다고 하시다니.

(b) The converted declarative sentences

Figure 2: A sample set of utterances for test (in Korean)

Figure 3: The screen shot of the test page (in Korean)

We performed an independent T-test ($p < 0.05$, two-tailed). The total number of the interrogative sentences we used for the test was 29; the mean values of IS and CS were 3.81 and 2.89, respectively; and their standard deviations were 1.60 and 1.536, respectively. The result was found to be statistically significant at the 0.05 level (df: 508, $p < 0.05$). Table 2 shows part of the sentences that are statistically significant.

Table 2: Statistically significant sentences

Original interrogative sentences	Mean (CS)	Mean (IS)	Std. D (CS)	Std. D (IS)	p-value
은심: 물만 먹어도 살찌는걸 나보고 어쩌라고? (Eun-sim: Since I get fat by drinking just water, what am I supposed to do?)	2.30	5.10	1.947	2.132	0.007
동규: 주인이 안 판다는데 그럼 어떡하라구요? (Dong-kyu: Since the owner has not the least intention of selling it, What can I do?)	1.40	2.70	0.699	0.949	0.03
수하: 남의 걸 허락없이 왜 뒤져요? 정말 이상한 사람이야! (Sue-ha: Why did you search for my stuff without my permission? You are so weird!)	2.70	3.85	0.675	1.226	0.01
동규: 왜에? 아예 훔쳤다고 하지? (Dong-kyu: Why? Why don't you	2.30	4.00	0.675	1.333	0.02

just say I stole it?)					
동규: 휴지통에 홀라당 버린 사람이 누군데 그래요? (Dong-kyu: Who threw it away in the garbage bin?)	2.20	4.50	1.135	1.9	0.04
수하: 도망이라뇨? 내가 왜 도망을 치는데요? 잘못한 사람이 누군데? (Sue-ha: Running away? Why should I run away? Who did something wrong?)	3.10	4.40	1.449	1.188	0.014

As shown in Table 2, the utterances with the interrogatives '왜(why)' and '누구(who)' are more significant in order to judge how much the speaker gets angry than any other interrogatives. In addition, if such utterances appear consecutively, the subjects tend to tag the intensity of the speaker's anger far higher.

5. Discussion

Through a statistical evaluation, we found that some interrogative sentences play a significant role when the speaker expresses her anger. This shows that there are some relations among such linguistic components so the combinations of the components are useful for identifying the emphasized emotional attitude in utterances. From this point, we can create patterns for the interrogative sentences carrying anger. We identify some general rules from the example and encode them with regular expressions. For example, once the expression (\s*\S*)*누군데\s*\S* is created by looking into the sentence '잘못한 사람이 누군데?', it can also be made to account for other sentences, for instance, '휴지통에 홀라당 버린 사람이 누군데 그래요?' with a special ending such as '-그래요'. In order to consider discourse markers or adverbial and demonstrative expressions, patterns could be extended by accommodating spaces for them. These patterns from such sentences may work as an effective device for identifying the speaker's underlying intentions as well as subtle emotional changes more precisely by distinguishing them from negated declarative sentences.

It is still too early to say that they are more important than the corresponding declarative sentences that the speaker expresses her anger directly with explicit emotional words, but interrogative structures are employed to ask the hearer to pay more attention to the speaker and allow the hearer to have some time to anticipate the following utterance of the speaker as shown in (4).

(4) a. 동규: 진짜 그것뿐이에요? 찬민이 좋아하는 마음 조금도 없어요?
   (Dong-kyu: Is really that all? Don't you like Chan-min at all?)
   b. 수하: 내가 그 인간을 왜 좋아해요?
   (Sue-ha: Why Do I like the jerk?)
   c. 하나도 안 좋아해.
   (I don't like him at all.)
   d. 지금 같아선 황동규 씨 보다 백배 천배 만배 더 싫구만!!
   (I hate him hundred, thousand, and million times more than Mr. Whang Dong-kyu!)

The declarative sentence (4d) is the most obvious one that expresses Sue-ha's refutation among her utterances (4b) ~ (4d). However, she didn't say (4d) in the first place because by adopting the interrogative sentence first and having the same verb as Dong-kyu's utterance, she can connect her utterance with his more naturally. In addition to it, she can emphasize her emotion gradually with three consecutive sentences without losing his attention.

Since interrogative sentences that express the speaker's emotion are highly dependent upon their context, we also need to consider the preceding or the subsequent utterance. By the turn-taking rule, if the speaker does not assign the right to speak to the hearer, even if she utters until she reaches the normal transition-relevance place in the question (Levelt, 1989), she might not expect the hearer to answer her question. Furthermore, if the hearer, who is also the following speaker, does not produce the utterance that is relevant to the adjacency pair as an answer for the speaker's question, the current speaker's communicative intention is not related to the question but interpreted as an indirect assertion or reproach. This is more apparent in the case where the utterances between the speaker and the hearer are in the form of an interrogative sentence consecutively as in (3b), (3c) and (4).

From such clues, we can also build inter-sentential patterns identifying the speaker's angry emotion. There are some general rules in the use of inter-sentences. First, the main verb or adjective is repeated when the hearer utters after the speaker's normal question. Second, if the speaker takes two interrogative sentences consecutively with '왜(why)' and '누구(who)' or '뭐(what)', the sentence with '왜(why)' is followed by the one with '누구(who)' or '뭐(what)'. Example (1) shows these rules. The main verb '사과하다(apologize)' is repeated and the interrogative sentence with '왜(why)' is preceded. If the second interrogative sentence with '누구(who)' is followed by it, it seems to be an awkward sequence. Figure 4 shows the schematic diagram of the inter-sentential pattern by applying the rules.

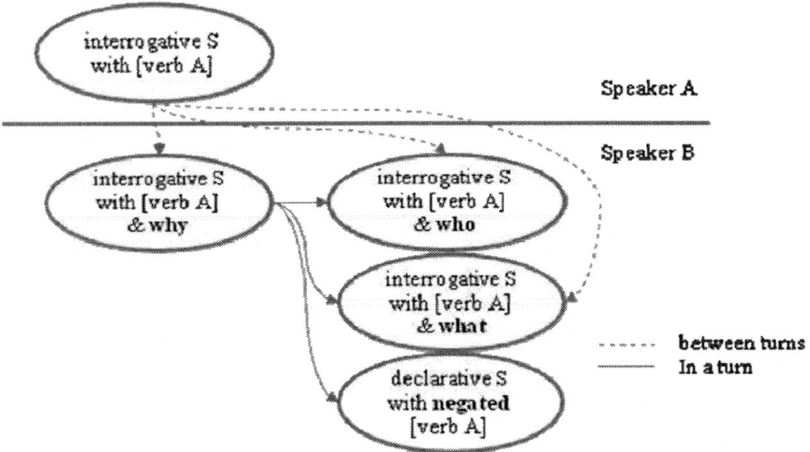

Figure 4: Inter-sentential pattern

6. Conclusion

In this paper, we analyzed interrogative sentences that convey the speaker's emotion of anger. The result from the user study shows that rhetorical questions with Wh-words 'who' and 'why' are statistically significant. We believe that this is a substantiated finding that is novel in emotion identification, to the best of our knowledge. We also believe that patterns from such sentences with the help of emotion-embedded expressions could be utilized as a high quality resource to identify anger. However, the correlation between these sentences with other utterances that use different sentential forms in the context may also affect the speaker's emotions. In addition, emotions resulting from the relative meaning of verbs or adjectives depending on the individual's point of view may influence the identification in real utterances. Further study is necessary for the proper contextual setting.

References

Austin, J.L. 1962. *How To Do Things With Words*. Oxford:Clarendon Press.

Byron, D.K. and P.A. Heeman. 1997. Discourse Marker Use in Task-Oriented Spoken Dialog. *Proceedings of Eurospeech'97*, pp. 2223-2226.

Chang, S.-W. 1998. The Study of the Actual Usage of the Korean Wh-words. *Korean Journal of Linguistics*, 23(4), 691-708. (In Korean)

Jeon, H.-Y. 1996. On Pragmatic Functions of '-tako'-ending Repercussive Question. *Korean Journal of Linguistics*, 21(3), 889-991. (In Korean)

Jung, E.-H.. 2005. The Study of an Interrogative 'Mua' in Korean. *Journal of Korean National Language and Literature 35,* 110-131. (In Korean)

Kang, W.-W. 2002. A Comparative Study on Characteristics of 'a' and 'eo'. *Language Research 12,* 241-257. (In Korean)

Kim, J.-H. 1999. The Interpretation of Wh-words in Echo Questions. *Eneohak* [Linguistics], 25, 77-100. (In Korean)

Kim, S.-H. 2003. A Study on the Modal Interrogative in Special Interrogative Sentence. *Hangeul* [Korean languages], 259, 115-140. (In Korean)

Leech, G. 1983. *Principles of Pragmatics*. London: Longman.

Levelt, W. J. M. 1989. *Speaking: From Intention to Articulation*. The MIT Press.

Nam K.-S. and Y.-G. Ko. 1985. *Pyojunkukeyomunbubnon* [Korean Standard Grammar]. The Top Press.

Ortony, A., G.L. Clore, and A. Collins. 1988. The *Cognitive Structure of Emotions*. Cambridge University Press.

Searle, J. R. 1969. *Speech Acts*. Cambridge University Press.

Shin, J.Y. 1993. Deixis in Spoken Language. *Eohakyeungoo* [Linguistics Study]. 363-380. (In Korean)

Hierarchical Structure in Semantic Networks of Japanese Word Associations [*]

Maki Miyake[a], Terry Joyce[b], Jaeyoung Jung[c], and Hiroyuki Akama[c]

[a]Osaka University, 1-8 Machikaneyama-cho, Toyonaka-shi, Osaka, 560-0043, Japan
[b]Tama University, 802 Engyo, Fujisawa-shi, Kanagawa-ken, 252-0805, Japan
[c]Tokyo Institute of Technology, O-okayama, Meguro-ku, Tokyo, 152-8552, Japan

mmiyake@lang.osaka-u.ac.jp
terry@tama.ac.jp
{catherina, akama}@dp.hum.titech.ac.jp

Abstract. This paper reports on the application of network analysis approaches to investigate the characteristics of graph representations of Japanese word associations. Two semantic networks are constructed from two separate Japanese word association databases. The basic statistical features of the networks indicate that they have scale-free and small-world properties and that they exhibit hierarchical organization. A graph clustering method is also applied to the networks with the objective of generating hierarchical structures within the semantic networks. The method is shown to be an efficient tool for analyzing large-scale structures within corpora. As a utilization of the network clustering results, we briefly introduce two web-based applications: the first is a search system that highlights various possible relations between words according to association type, while the second is to present the hierarchical architecture of a semantic network. The systems realize dynamic representations of network structures based on the relationships between words and concepts.

Keywords: Network analysis, Graph clustering, Japanese word associations.

1. Introduction

As an approach to deepening our understanding of lexical knowledge, many areas of cognitive science, including psychology and computational linguistics, are seeking to unravel the rich networks of associations that connect words together. Key methodologies for that enterprise are the techniques of graph representation and their analysis that allow us to discern the patterns of connectivity within large-scale resources of linguistic knowledge and to perceive the inherent relationships between words and word groups.

---

[*] This research has been supported by the 21st Century Center of Excellence Program "Framework for Systematization and Application of Large-scale Knowledge Resources". The authors would like to acknowledge here the generosity of the Center. The first and second authors have been supported by Grants-in-Aid for Scientific Research from the Japanese Society for the Promotion of Science (research project number 19700238 to first author and 18500200 to the second). In addition, the authors wish to express their thanks to Professor Shun Ishizaki for permission to use his Associative Concepts Dictionary in this study.

Although studies applying versions of the multidimensional space model, such as Latent Semantic Analysis (LSA) and multidimensional scaling, to the analysis of texts have been fairly fruitful, the methodologies of graph theory and network analysis are particularly suitable for elucidating the important characteristics of semantic networks.

Recently, a number of studies have applied graph theory approaches in investigating linguistic knowledge resources (Church and Hanks, 1990; Dorow, Widdows, Ling, Eckmann, Danilo and Moses, 2005; Steyvers and Tanenbaum 2005; van Dongen, 2000; Watts and Strogatz, 1998). For instance, Dorow, et al (2005) utilize two graph clustering techniques as methods of detecting lexical ambiguity and of acquiring semantic classes instead of word frequency based computations.

This paper applies graph theory and network analysis methods to the analysis of semantic network representations of Japanese word associations. After briefly outlining the two separate Japanese word association databases used—the Associative Concept Dictionary (Okamoto and Ishizaki, 2001) and the Japanese Word Association Database (Joyce, 2005, 2006, 2007)—the paper calculates some basic statistical features, such as degree distributions, clustering coefficients and the average clustering coefficient distribution for nodes with degrees. We also apply the recently developed Recurrent Markov Clustering (RMCL) algorithm (Jung, Miyake and Akama, 2006) which enhances the bottom-up classification method of the basic MCL algorithm by making it possible to adjust the proportion in cluster sizes. Given this greater control over cluster sizes, the RMCL clearly provides a very appealing approach to the automatic construction of condensed network representations, which, in turn, can facilitate the creation of hierarchically-organized semantic spaces as a way of visualizing large-scale linguistic knowledge resources.

2.   Building Semantic Network Graphs of Japanese Word Associations

This section outlines the semantic network representations of the Japanese word association databases. Specifically, the section briefly describes two separate databases of Japanese word associations—the Associative Concept Dictionary (ACD) and the Japanese Word Association Database (JWAD)—and the semantic network representations created from them.

2.1. Existing word association norms

As frames of reference concerning the scales of the two Japanese word association databases, it worth noting that large-scale, comprehensive word association normative data has existed for some time for English. For example, Moss and Older (1996) collected between 40-50 responses for some 2,400 words of British English, while Nelson, McEvoy and Schreiber (1998) compiled perhaps the largest database of American English covering some 5,000 words with approximately 150 responses per item. Notwithstanding the early survey by Umemoto (1969), which gathered free associations from 1,000 university students for a very small set of 210 words, clearly there has been a serious lack of comparative databases of Japanese word associations. Both the ACD and the JWAD seek to redress this situation, especially the ongoing JWAD project which is committed to constructing a large-scale database for its current survey corpus of 5,000 basic Japanese kanji and words.

2.2. Associative Concept Dictionary

Okamoto and Ishizaki (2001) created the Associative Concept Dictionary (ACD), which is organized as a hierarchal structure of higher/lower level concepts. The data consists of 33,018 word association responses provided by 10 respondents according to specified response categories for 1,656 nouns. By excluding response words with a frequency of 1 and a clustering coefficient of 0, 9,373 words were selected for use in creating a semantic network representation.

2.3.Japanese Word Association Database

The Japanese Word Association Database is being constructed as part of a project to investigate lexical knowledge in Japanese by mapping out Japanese word associations (Joyce, 2005; 2006; 2007). While the particular task—specifying in advance the associative relationship for responses—employed in creating the ACD can arguably be justified in terms of constructing a dictionary of associated concepts, the data provides little insight into the rich and diverse nature of word associations. Accordingly, the JWAD employs the free word association task in collecting association responses. Also in contrast to the ACD, which only examined nouns, the JWAD is surveying words of all word classes. Version 1 of the JWAD consists of a random sample of 2,099 items from the survey corpus of 5,000 basic Japanese kanji and words that were presented to up to 50 respondents. For the JWAD network, only words with a frequency of 2 or more were selected, which resulted in set of 7,966 words to be clustered.

3. Analyses of the Network Structures

As already suggested, graph representations and the techniques of graph theory and network analysis are particularly promising techniques with which to examine the intricate patterns of connectivity within large-scale linguistic knowledge resources. For instance, Steyvers and Tenenbaum (2005) conducted a noteworthy study that examined the structural features of three semantic networks. By calculating a range of statistical features, including the average shortest paths, diameters, clustering coefficients, and degree distributions, they observed interesting similarities between the three networks in terms of their scale-free patterns of connectivity and small-world structures.

Following their basic approach, we analyze the characteristics of the two semantic network representations of Japanese word associations by calculating the statistical features of degree distribution and clustering coefficient—an index of the interconnectivity strength between neighboring nodes in a graph.

3.1.Degree distribution

From their computations of degree distributions, Balabasi and Albert (1999) suggest that the degree distribution, P(k), for scale-free network structures will correspond to a power law, which can be expressed as $P(k) \approx k^{-r}$.

Figure 1 presents degree distributions for word occurrences in the two semantic networks, which indicate that P(k) conforms to a power-law in both cases (with exponent values, r, of 1.8 for the ACD (panel a) and 2.3 for the JWAD (panel b). In the case of the ACD, the average degree value is 19.96 (0.2%) for the complete semantic network of 9,373 nodes, while the average degree value is 3.67 (0.05% for 7,966 nodes) in the JWAD's case. The results clearly indicate that the networks exhibit a pattern of sparse connectivity; in other words, that they possess the characteristics of a scale-free network.

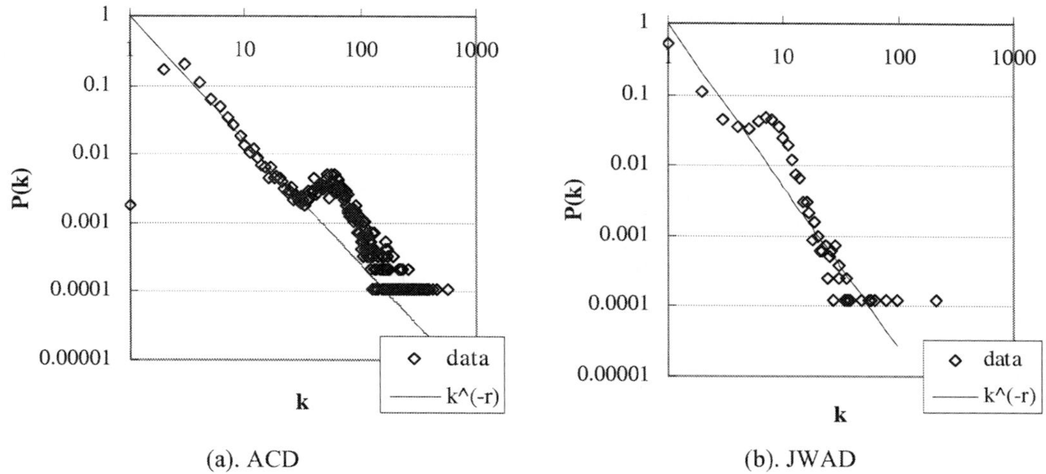

(a). ACD   (b). JWAD

Figure 1: Degree distributions for the two semantic networks

3.2. Clustering coefficient

In their social network study investigating the probabilities that an acquaintance of an acquaintance is also an acquaintance of yours, Watts and Strogatz (1998) advocate the notion of clustering coefficient as an appropriate index of the degree of connections between nodes. In this study, we define the clustering coefficient of n nodes as:

$$C(n) = \frac{\text{number of links among n's neighbors}}{N(n) \times (N(n)-1)\,/\,2}$$

where N(n) represents the number of adjacent nodes. Accordingly, a clustering coefficient is a value between 0-1.

Moreoever, Ravasz and Barabasi (2003) introduce the notion of clustering coefficient dependence on node degree as an index of the hierarchical structures found in real networks—such as the WWW, the Actor Network based on the www.IMDB.com database—which are based on the hierarchical model of $C(k) \approx k^{-1}$ (Dorogovski, Goltsev, & Mendes, 2001). Specifically, the hierarchical nature of a network can be characterized by using the average clustering coefficient, C(k), of nodes with k degrees, which will follow a scaling law such as $C(k) \approx k^{-\beta}$, where β is defined as a hierarchical exponent.

Figure 2 presents results of scaling C(k) with k for (a) ACD and (b) JWAD. The dashed line in (a) has a slope of -1, while the fitting exponent, β, is 0.6 for JWAD. The solid lines correspond to the average clustering coefficient. In the case of the ACD, the average clustering coefficient is quite high at 0.35, which can be regarded as indicating the small-world property. In the case of the JWAD, the average clustering coefficient is 0.04, which indicates that the complete network basically consists of many star graphs connected together. As both networks conform well to a power law, we may conclude that both networks have intrinsic hierarchies.

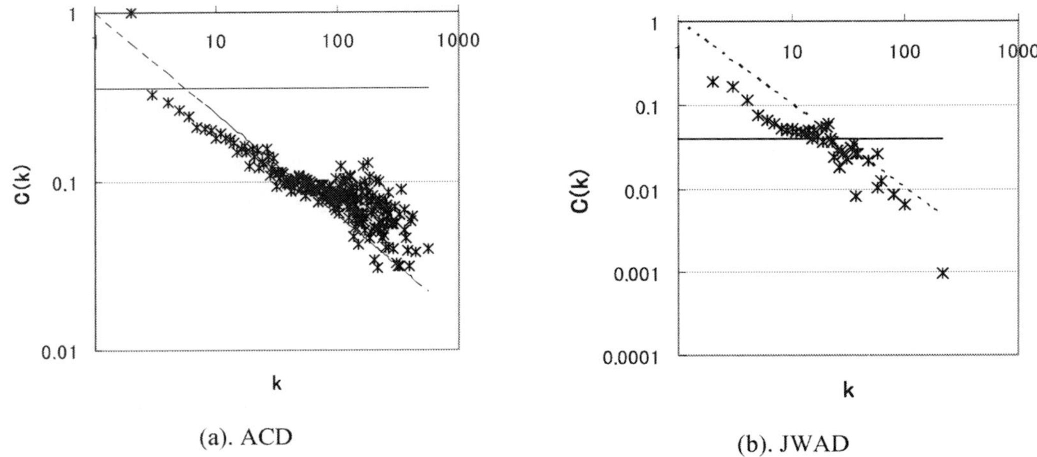

(a). ACD   (b). JWAD

Figure 2: Clustering coefficient distributions for the two semantic networks

4. Graph Clustering: Recurrent Markov Clustering

4.1. Algorithm

Jung, et al. (2006) have recently proposed an improvement to Markov Clustering (MCL), called Recurrent Markov Clustering (RMCL), which provides for greater control over the sizes of clusters by making it possible to adjust graph granularity and, thus, the generality of concepts. MCL is an effective method for the detection of patterns and clusters within large and sparsely connected data structures. The first step in the MCL consists of sustaining a random walk across a graph by 'expansions'. The recurrent process incorporates feedback about the states of overlapping clusters prior to the final MCL output stage. This reverse tracing procedure is a key feature of the RMCL making it possible to generate a virtual adjacency matrix for non-overlapping clusters based on the convergent state that emerges from the MCL process. The resultant condensed matrix provides a simpler graph that can highlight the conceptual structures that underlie similar words.

4.2. Results

The RMCL algorithm is realized as a series of calculations executed with gridMathematica. Taking the JWAD as an example of the calculation steps in the RMCL, Figure 3 presents the transition in cluster sizes as a function of the MCL process. Starting from the adjacency matrix for co-occurrences, the MCL process finally generated a nearly-idempotent stochastic matrix at the 19th clustering stage with 1,441 hard clusters, where the average number of cluster components is 5.6 with a standard deviation (SD) of 3.1. In contrast, the RMCL resulted in just 759 hard clusters with an average of 1.9 cluster components (SD = 1.5). Among the representative nodes for RMCL clusters, 1,176 nodes (83%) were found to be words that had been presented as stimulus words. Figure 4 presents MCL and RMCL cluster sizes for both the ACD and the JWAD, which illustrate the transitions occurring in downsizing the networks generated from graph clustering. Figure 5 plots the number of components for both MCL and RMCL clusters as a function of frequency. In the case of the ACD, the MCL resulted in 1,408 hard clusters (average cluster size = 6.7, SD = 8.6), while the RMCL resulted in 118 hard clusters, where the average number of cluster components was 11.9 with a rather high SD of 68.6.

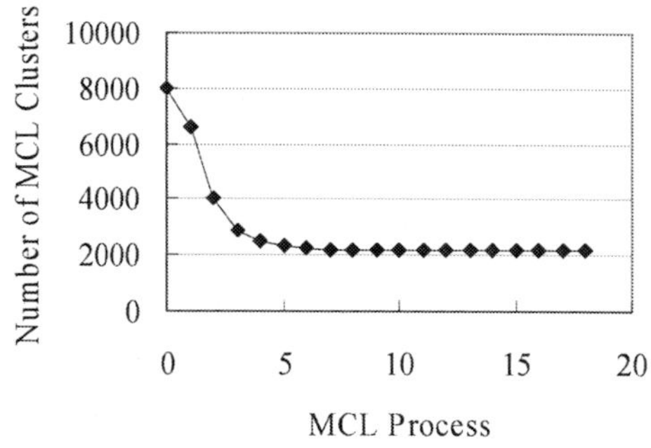

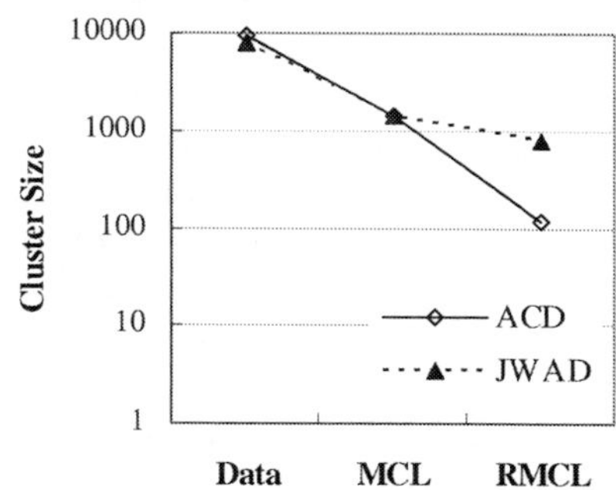

Figure 3: Cluster size transitions during MCL process

Figure 4: Cluster sizes for MCL and RMCL

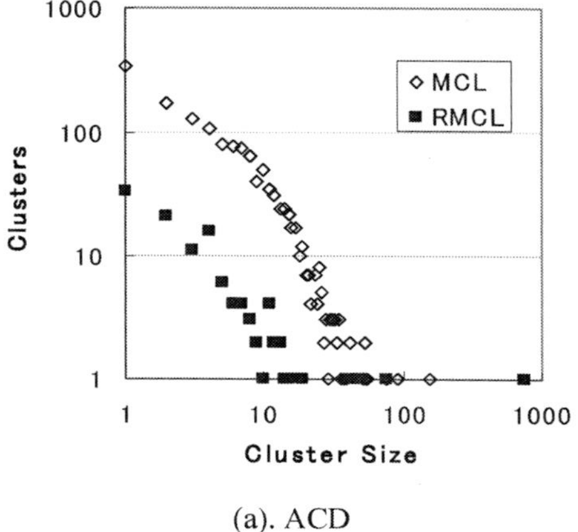

(a). ACD

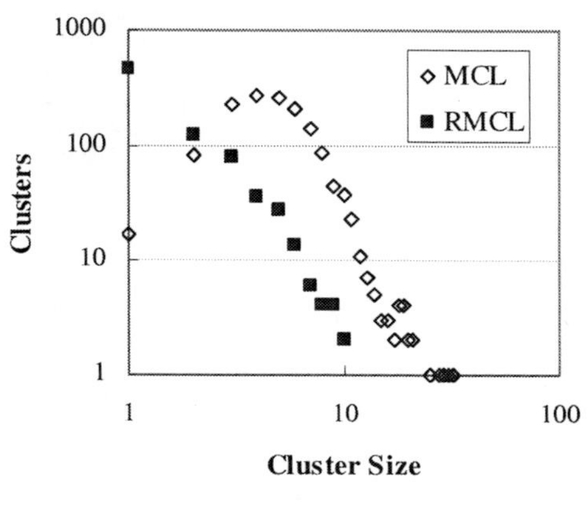

(b). JWAD

Figure 5: Component size distributions for both the MCL and the RMCL

5. Applications of the RMCL

As Widdow, Cederberg, and Dorow (2002) astutely observe, graph visualization is a particularly powerful tool for representing the meanings of words and concepts. In order to utilize the MCL and RMCL clustering results of the networks, we have developed two web-based applications implemented by webMathmatica: the first is an 'Associative Composition Support System (ACSS)' to search for free association words according to different types of association information, while the second is 'RMCLnet' which elucidates the hierarchical architecture of large-scale networks.

5.1. The Associative Composition Support System

The free web-based ACSS proposed by Jung *et al.* (2006) seeks to promote associative thinking ability, and so, in turn, to foster language learning and creativity. ACSS is developed based on a database that makes it possible to retrieve three types of associative information such as word-based, concept-based and group-based associations. Such associative information is apparently sufficient to support system users in improving their associative thinking and creativity by encouraging them to move beyond literal, direct and superficial aspects to richer, freer, and more inspired conceptual associations. The variety of links between words can foster free, flexible, integrative, and imaginative thinking, while simultaneously encouraging users to discover the implicit relevance of words and even to occasionally fill in the semantic gaps between words with imaginative creations.

Figure 6 presents a screen shot of the main page for the ACSS system. Users can access the online system at http://atheneum.dp.hum.titech.ac.jp/semnet/ACSS/index.jsp. The entire interface on the user side is controlled by Javascript. When retrieval requirements are sent to the remote web server, search results are calculated in real-time by WebMathematica through the JSP and Mathematica kernel. The database was constructed in the form of a semantic network and is stored on the web server after calculating original Japanese word associations with GridMathematica. System users can input any two words to see three types of association information.

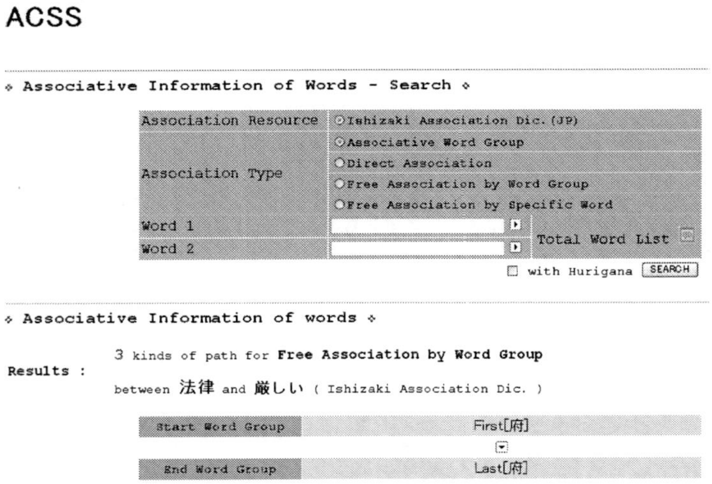

Figure 6: Screen shot of the GUI to the ACSS system

5.2.RMCLnet

Graph visualization of the semantic structures generated through MCL and RMCL clustering is implemented with webMathematica, employing basic techniques drawing on java servlet/JSP technology (Miyake, 2006). webMathematica can handle interactive calculations and visualization is realized by integrating Mathematica with a web server. The web server employs Apache2 as its http application server and Tomcat5 as a servlet/JSP engine. The URL for RMCLnet is http://perrier.dp.hum.titech.ac.jp/semnet/RmclNet/index.jsp.

Clustering results from both the MCL and RMCL processes can dynamically represent the relationships between words, with MCL components possibly corresponding to concepts (Figure 7). The implementation method is quite straightforward, as it is sufficient to simply store the multiple files that are created automatically when the RMCL process is executed. The system can simultaneously represent results for both the ACD and the JWAD, making it possible to examine the structural similarities and differences between the two semantic networks, which can yield interesting insights into the nature of word associations and how graph clustering functions.

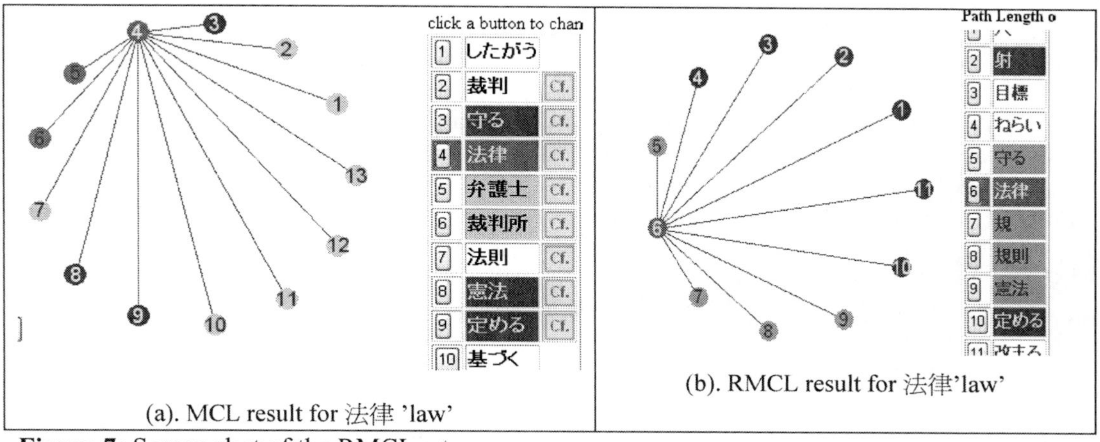

(a). MCL result for 法律 'law'

(b). RMCL result for 法律 'law'

Figure 7: Screen shot of the RMCLnet

6. Conclusions

In summary, this paper has reported on the application of graph clustering methodologies to the analysis of semantic network representations of Japanese word associations. After outlining two separate large-scale databases of Japanese word associations, the paper analyzed the characteristics of two semantic network representations of Japanese word associations. In addition to the calculation of degree distributions for the networks, which indicate that the networks are scale-free, average clustering coefficient distributions for nodes were found to conform to a power law, indicating that the networks have hierarchical organizations. Moreover, the ACD was found to have a high average clustering coefficient value, suggesting the small-world property, while the lower value for the JWAD network suggests it has less interconnectivity.

Finally, we briefly introduced two web-based applications as examples that utilize RMCL clustering results. The network representation application is useful in elucidating the structures within hierarchically-organized semantic spaces, which makes it an especially appealing approach to the visualization of large-scale linguistic knowledge resources.

References

Barabasi, A.L. and R. Albert. 1999. Emergence of scaling in random networks. *Science,* 286, 509-512.

Church, K.W. and P. Hanks. 1990. Word association norms, mutual information, and lexicography. *Computational Linguistics,* 16, 22-29.

Dorogovtsev, S.N., A.V. Goltsev and J.F.F. Mendes. 2001. Pseudofractal Scall-free Web. *e-print cond-mat/0112143*.

Dorow, B., D. Widdows, K. Ling, J. Eckmann, D. Sergi and E. Moses. 2005. Using Curvature and Markov Clustering in Graphs for Lexical Acquisition and Word Sense Discrimination. *Proceeding of the Second Workshop of the Meaning Project.*

Jung, J., M. Miyake and H. Akama. 2006. Recurrent Markov Cluster (RMCL) Algorithm for the Refinement of the Semantic Network, *International Conference on Language Resources and Evaluation.* pp.1428-1432.

Jung, J., M. Miyake, N. Makoshi and H. Akama. 2006. Development of a Web-based Composition Support System: Using Graph Clustering Methodologies Applied to an Associative Concepts Dictionary. *Proceedings of the Sixth IEEE International Conference on Advanced Learning Technologies,* pp.431-435.

Joyce, T. 2005. Constructing a Large-scale Database of Japanese Word Associations. In K. Tamaoka, ed., *Corpus Studies on Japanese Kanji (Glottometrics 10)*. pp. 82-98. Hituzi Syobo and RAM-Verlag.

Joyce, T. 2006. Mapping Word Knowledge in Japanese: Constructing and Utilizing a Large-scale Database of Japanese Word Associations. *Proceedings of the Large-Scale Knowledge Resources Symposium*, pp.155-158.

Joyce, T. 2007. Mapping Word Knowledge in Japanese: Coding Japanese Word Associations. *Proceedings of the Large-Scale Knowledge Resources Symposium*, pp. 233-238.

Miyake, M. 2006. Implementing a Semantic Network of the Synoptic Gospels based on Graph Clustering, *IPSJ SIG Computers and the Humanities Symposium*, 161-165.

Moss, H. and Older L. 1996. *Birkbeck Word Association Norms*. Psychological Press.

Okamoto, J. and S. Ishizaki. 2001. Associative Concept Dictionary and its Comparison Electronic Concept Dictionaries. *PACLING2001,* 214-220.

Ravasz, E. and A.L. Barabasi. 2003. Hierarchical Organization in Complex Networks. *Physical Review E*, 67, 026112.

Umemoto, T. 1969. *Word Association Norms: Free Associations from 1,000 University Students.* (in Japanese). Tokyo Daigaku Shuppankai.

Steyvers, M. and J.B. Tenenbaum. 2005. The Large-Scale Structure of Semantic Networks: Statistical Analyses and a Model of Semantic Growth, *Cognitive Science,* 29(1), 41-78.

van Dongen, S. 2000. *Graph Clustering by Flow Simulation*. Ph.D. thesis, University of Utrecht.

Vechthomova, O., D. Gfeller, J.-C. Chappelier and P. De Los Rios. 2005. Synonym Dictionary Improvement through Markov Clustering and Clustering Stability. *International Symposium on Applied Stochastic Models and Data Analysis*, 106-113.

Watts, D. and S. Strogatz. 1998. Collective Dynamics of 'Small-world' Networks, *Nature*, 393, 440-442.

Widdows, D., S. Cederberg and B. Dorow. 2002. Visualisation Techniques for Analysing Meaning. *Proceeding of the Fifth International Conference on Text, Speech and Dialogue,* pp.107-115.

Japanese Expressions that Include English Expressions [*]

Masaki Murata[a], Toshiyuki Kanamaru[a], Koichirou Nakamoto[b], Katsunori Kotani[a],
and Hitoshi Isahara[a]

[a]National Institure of Information and Communications Technology,
3-5, Hikaridai, Soraku-gun, Kyoto, 619-0289, Japan
{murata, kanamaru, isahara}@nict.go.jp, kat@khn.nict.go.jp
[b]Osaka University of Foreign Studies,
8-1-1 Aomatani-Higashi, Minoh, Osaka, 562-8558, Japan
nobi@sings.jp

Abstract: We extracted English expressions that appear in Japanese sentences in newspaper articles and on the Internet. The results obtained from the newspaper articles showed that the preposition "in" has been regularly used for more than ten years, and it is still regularly used now. The results obtained from the Internet articles showed there were many kinds of English expressions from various parts of speech. We extracted some interesting expressions that included English prepositions and verb phrases. These were interesting because they had different word orders to the normal order in Japanese expressions. Comparing the extracted English and katakana expressions, we found that the expressions that are commonly used in Japanese are often written in the katakana syllabary and that the expressions that are not so often used in Japanese, such as prepositions, are hardly ever written in the katakana syllabary.

Keyword: English expression, katakana expression, newspaper article, Internet

1. Introduction

We often see English expressions inserted in Japanese sentences, such as "コンサート in 東京" ("コンサート"=concert, "東京"=Tokyo). We extracted such expressions that were written in kanji, katakana, hiragana, and Roman alphabet characters or combinations of these characters from articles in the Mainichi Shinbun (a major daily Japanese language newspaper) and on the Internet. From the same sources, we also extracted expressions that used katakana characters instead of English characters, such as "博覧会イン京都" ("博覧会"= exposition, "イン"=in, "京都"=Kyoto). The study of such expressions is useful for linguists studying the development process of languages (Ito (2001), Daulton (2003), and Murata et al. (2004)).

2. Automatic extraction of English and Katakana expressions

We used computers to extract candidate expressions in Japanese that included English expressions from Mainichi Shinbun articles published between 1991 and 2005 and from about 2 GB of Internet articles. We then checked the candidate expressions by hand to select the actual expressions we would use in our research.

We initially extracted expressions from Mainichi Shinbun articles. We took only the expressions that contained brackets. This is because expressions that include English

---

expressions in Japanese sentences often appear in brackets. We automatically extracted expressions that satisfied the following conditions: i) included both Japanese characters in hiragana, katakana, and kanji and characters in the Roman alphabet, ii) the adjacent characters to English expressions are Japanese characters, or English expressions appear at the beginning of the expressions or the end of the expressions, iii) the second to last characters of the English expression were not capitalized, and iv) English expressions that consisted of more than one character. The condition ii) is used because there were many cases where the expressions were just replaced with Japanese expressions such as "過労死 (karoushi) 病" ("過労死"="overwork death", "karoushi" is the reading of "過労死", "病"=disease), and we excluded such expressions. The condition iii) is used because there were many cases where expressions consisted of capitalized characters that were probably abbreviations, such as "OPEC" and "ASEAN", and we excluded such expressions. We used only the cases were an English expression inserted into a Japanese sentence consisted of one word. This is because English expressions that consist of multiple words are often quotations of English phrases or sentences and are not expressions where the Japanese and English languages merge. We extracted expressions that did not contain appropriate spaces, such as "Welcometo". We did not use expressions where the English expression was a noun, a proper noun, a symbol, or adjective that was modified by adding the Japanese suffixes "na" (for an adjective) and "suru" (for a verb). This is because the deleted expressions are popular in the conventional Japanese language. (In this study, we extracted "de", although it is not English but French. This is because its frequency is high and it is also an interesting expression.)

We arranged the final list of expressions in order of frequency (see Table 1). "V", "AJ", "AV", "PP", "CJ", "AR", "PO", and "PH" (in the table below) indicate verbs, adjectives, adverbs, prepositions, conjunctions, articles, possessive pronouns, and phrases, respectively.

Next, we extracted expressions from articles on the Internet. We used the same conditions as above and one additional condition: the first character of an English expression at the beginning of the sentence had to be capitalized. The results are shown in Table 2. Here, the extracted results are arranged by parts of speech. The table shows the English expression, its frequency, and some examples for each expression. In the example, the corresponding part of the English expression is marked with a *. Table 2 shows the results in descending order of frequency. The table only contains expressions that appeared more than 10 times.

Finally, we extracted from Mainichi Shinbun and Internet articles Japanese expressions that contained katakana expressions. We next constructed a list of the English expressions written in katakana characters. Using only katakana expressions, we compiled a list of expressions in order of frequency (Tables 3 and 4).

We plotted graphs showing the average (we call it *average value*) of the average, mode, and median years when the extracted expressions appeared (Figures 1 and 2). In the figures, each expression is displayed in ascending order of the average value. We added the total number of expression and the average value to each expression in the figures. Therefore, expressions that appeared in the earlier years are displayed higher on the graph, while expressions that appeared in the later years are displayed lower.

3.   Discussion

Table 1 shows that English prepositions have been used for more than 10 years. The use of the expression "in" rapidly increased in 1994. After that, it appeared more than 10 times each year. "Let's" has also been used for more than 10 years; however, it stopped appearing in 2000. The prepositions "at", "of", "with", "from", "by", "of", "with", "from", "by", and "to" have been also used for a relatively long time.

We extracted various English expressions that form various parts of speech from articles on the Internet (Table 2). Prepositions appear the most frequently, followed by conjunctions. Adjectives are third. After that, in descending order of frequency, come phrases, adverbs,

Table 1: English expressions in Mainichi Shinbun articles

1991			1992			1993			1994			1995		
in	PP	2	in	PP	4	Lets	PH	1	in	PP	12	in	PP	21
Lets	PH	1	The	AR	1	in	PP	1	the	AR	1	and	CJ	1
at	PP	1	Handy	AJ	1	vs	PP	1	my	PO	1	From	PP	1
de	PP	1	New	AJ	1	with	PP	1	by	PP	1	by	PP	1
vs	PP	1	of	PP	1				de	PP	1	from	PP	1
									to	PP	1	to	PP	1
												with	PP	1

1996			1997			1998			1999			2000		
in	PP	15	in	PP	28	in	PP	21	in	PP	22	in	PP	19
Dear	AJ	3	With	PP	2	de	PP	6	de	PP	3	de	PP	9
Thats	PH	2	Dear	AJ	1	The	AR	3	My	PO	2	at	PP	2
New	AJ	2	Jr	AJ	1	Lets	PH	1	vs	PP	2	from	PP	2
Lets	PH	1	for	PP	1	ing	CJ	1	Its	PH	1	with	PP	2
de	PP	1	vs	PP	1	By	PP	1	New	AJ	1	and	CJ	1
to	PP	1	with	PP	1	for	PP	1	ing	CJ	1	by	PP	1
vs	PP	1	Forever	AD	1	to	PP	1	or	CJ	1	to	PP	1
with	PP	1				with	PP	1	from	PP	1			
Be	V	1												

2001			2002			2003			2004			2005		
in	PP	32	in	PP	13	in	PP	17	in	PP	12	in	PP	12
de	PP	6	de	PP	7	de	PP	5	de	PP	6	with	PP	3
New	AJ	2	New	AJ	2	by	PP	4	of	PP	2	Good	AJ	1
from	PP	2	and	CJ	1	Jr	AJ	1	From	PP	1	New	AJ	1
to	PP	2	from	PP	1	The	AR	1	Jr	AJ	1	The	AR	1
the	AR	1	with	PP	1				New	AJ	1	my	PO	1
Thats	PH	1							to	PP	1	the	AR	1
Whats	PH	1												
Digital	AJ	1												
can	AX	1												
De	PP	1												
With	PP	1												
for	PP	1												
vs	PP	1												
again	AD	1												

Table 2: English expressions on the Internet

Prepositions (34 types, 16352 tokens in total)				
in	4852	キャンペーン ∗ 渋谷 (campaign * Shibuya)	with	533 [PERSON] ∗ オーケストラ ([PERSON] * orchestra)
by	2504	現地レポート ∗ [PERSON] (on-site report * [PERSON])	for	461 データ ∗ ピアノ・レッスン (data * piano lesson)
vs	1894	[PERSON] ∗ [PERSON]	to	360 固定電話 ∗ 固定電話 (fixed-line phone * fixed-line phone)
de	1290	メール ∗ ゲット！ (mail * get!)	from	354 文部科学省の働き ∗ [PERSON] (activities of Ministry of Education, Culture, Sports, Science and Technology * [PERSON])
in	1276	ジャズ トリオ ∗ 神戸 (jazz trio * Kobe)		
vs	888	山形市民 ∗ 天童市民 (Yamagata citizens * Tendo citizens)		

Table 2: English expressions on the Internet (cont.)

Prepositions (34 types, 16352 tokens in total) (cont.)					
by	269	医療施設 ⋆ [ORGANIZATION] (medical facility ⋆ [ORGANIZATION])	new	72	⋆ アルバム (⋆ album)
at	254	忘年会 ⋆ 難波 (year-end party ⋆ Namba)	Online	67	⋆ 作文教室 (⋆ writing class)
vs.	254	湘南 ⋆ 新潟 (Shonan ⋆ Niigata)	back	65	⋆ ナンバー (⋆ number)
de	240	ねっと ⋆ しょっぷ (net ⋆ shop)	Free	52	⋆ 座談室 (⋆ round-table meeting room)
on	189	奥津 ⋆ メディア (Okutsu ⋆ media)	New	74	⋆ ステッカー (⋆ sticker)
From	145	⋆ こうち (⋆ Kochi)	all	50	⋆ ほっかいどう (⋆ Hokkaido)
of	77	編集部 ⋆ 速報ニュース (editorial office ⋆ breaking news)	more	47	⋆ レッドハットニュース (⋆ Red Hat news)
By	75	⋆ [PERSON]	free	45	⋆ 素材 (⋆ material)
to	60	ドア ⋆ ドア (door ⋆ door)	public	42	⋆ 参加 (⋆ entry)
For	44	⋆ ビギナース (⋆ beginners)	next	41	個展 ⋆ 開催 (personal exhibition ⋆ holding)
To	42	⋆ 軽井沢 (⋆ Karuizawa)	Open	40	⋆ フォーラム (⋆ forum)
with	42	[PERSON] ⋆ [PERSON]	Weekly	39	⋆ レポート (⋆ report)
By	27	⋆ 監督 (⋆ director)	active	35	⋆ 手段 (⋆ measures)
About	26	⋆ 文学部 (⋆ literature department)	close	34	全て ⋆ です (be all ⋆)
about	25	⋆ 海洋堂 (⋆ Kaiyodo)	good	34	⋆ ウェイキ (⋆ wake)
for	25	コンサート ⋆ [ORGANIZATION] (concert ⋆ [ORGANIZATION])	Dear	33	⋆ [PERSON]
on	24	アンケート集計 ⋆ ネット (summary of questionnaire ⋆ network)	Special	29	⋆ キャンペーン (⋆ campaign)
Vs.	21	⋆ [ORGANIZATION]	Digital	27	⋆ 出力 (⋆ output)
since	20	⋆ 平成11年9月27日 (⋆ September 27, 1999)	cool	27	⋆ ブランド (⋆ brand)
at	20	コンテスト ⋆ [LOCATION] (contest ⋆ [LOCATION])	official	26	⋆ サイト (⋆ site)
With	17	⋆ [PERSON]	Personal	25	⋆ モデル (⋆ model)
from	17	独り言 ⋆ [PERSON] (soliloquy ⋆ [PERSON])	Cool	24	⋆ サイト (⋆ site)
by.	14	⋆ [PERSON]	Jr.	24	⋆ 選手権 (⋆ championship)
In	13	⋆ [LOCATION]	Back	23	⋆ モデル (⋆ model)
			Next	23	⋆ シーズン (⋆ season)
Conjunctions (4 types, 3458 tokens in total)			virtual	23	⋆ 体験 (⋆ experience)
or	2236	交換 ⋆ 差し上げます (exchange ⋆ give)	weekly	22	⋆ パッケージ (⋆ package)
and	641	[PERSON] ⋆ [PERSON]	Happy	21	⋆ 懸賞らいふ！ (⋆ days with prize)
or	541	おかゆ ⋆ ご飯 (porridge ⋆ rice)	digital	20	⋆ 回路 (⋆ circuit)
and	40	パスタ ⋆ ワイン (pasta ⋆ wine)	mobile	20	⋆ 端末 (⋆ terminal)
			special	20	⋆ 企画 (⋆ enterprise)
Adjectives (59 types, 3066 tokens in total)			Best	19	⋆ 記録 (⋆ record)
new	582	⋆ おまかせプラン (⋆ prepared plan)	happy	18	⋆ ハート (⋆ heart)
New	399	⋆ ぐるりん阿蘇 (⋆ touring Aso)	Mobile	17	⋆ 端末 (⋆ terminal)
main	158	⋆ 作品 (⋆ work)	closed	16	⋆ 会議 (⋆ meeting)
open	133	⋆ 会議 (⋆ conference)	Jr	16	⋆ フルート教室 (⋆ flute class)
online	130	⋆ 雑誌 (⋆ magazine)	Virtual	15	⋆ ゼミ訪問 (⋆ visit to seminar)
good	111	⋆ 性能バランス (⋆ performance balance)	inline	15	⋆ 画像 (⋆ image)
No	72	⋆ 残業DAY (⋆ overtime working day)	personal	15	⋆ ホームページサーバ (⋆ homepage server)
Super	72	⋆ アモルファス (⋆ amorphous)	Good	14	⋆ リフォーム (⋆ reform)
			Hot	14	⋆ リスト (⋆ list)
			Monthly	14	⋆ セミナー (⋆ seminar)
			short	14	⋆ ブーツ (⋆ boots)
			Big	13	⋆ プレゼント (⋆ present)
			Easy	13	⋆ 登録 (⋆ registration)
			Global	13	⋆ 企業 (⋆ company)
			offline	13	⋆ 状態 (⋆ status)
			Hyper	12	⋆ 和紙 (⋆ Japanese paper)

Table 2: English expressions on the Internet (cont.)

Adjectives (59 types, 3066 tokens in total) (cont.)					
super	12	＊ 特急 (* limited express)	only	63	土日 ＊ (Saturdays and Sundays *)
Daily	11	＊ ランキング (* ranking)	all	50	同業者 ＊ (* peer)
High	11	＊ レベル (* level)	off	30	５００円 ＊ (500 yen *)
			only	16	英語 ＊ (English *)

Phrases (23 types, 909 tokens in total)			Articles (3 types, 364 tokens in total)		
Welcometo	294	＊ 腕時計資料室 (* wrist watch archives)	The	201	＊ 沖縄 (* Okinawa)
What's	114	＊ けいば (* horse race)	the	115	＊ 古書 (* old book)
Let's	75	＊ スタート！ (* start!)	The	48	＊ 日本列島 (* Japanese archipelago)
Presentedby	34	＊ 関東バス (* Kanto Bus)			
writtenby	32	＊ [PERSON]	Possessive pronouns (4 types, 357 tokens in total)		
Lets	31	＊ テニス！ (* play tennis!)	My	181	＊ コレクション (* collection)
Howto	29	＊ アクセス (* access)	My	77	＊ ページ (* page)
Producedby	29	＊ [ORGANIZATION]	my	69	＊ テーマ (* theme)
Writtenby	28	＊ [PERSON]	my	30	＊ ページ (* page)
producedby	27	＊ [ORGANIZATION]			
photoby	25	＊ [ORGANIZATION]	Verbs (9 types, 246 tokens in total)		
welcometo	24	＊ 情報科学部 (* information science department)	start	56	＊ インターネット (* Internet)
Poweredby	23	＊ [PERSON]	Welcome	48	＊ えひめ (* Ehime)
Backto	22	＊ 広県大ＨＰ (* Hiroshima Prefecture University homepage)	Do	29	＊ 中国茶 (* Chinese tea)
It's	18	＊ オススメ!! (* recommended!!)	welcome	28	＊ [ORGANIZATION]病院 (* [ORGANIZATION] hospital)
postedby	17	＊ [PERSON]	Get	25	＊ 懸賞 (* prize)
foryou	15	メッセージ ＊ (* message)	love	22	＊ 熊本電波 (* Kumamoto radio wave)
presentedby	14	＊ [ORGANIZATION]	enjoy	16	＊ 講座 (* course)
Textby	12	＊ [PERSON]	Welcome	12	＊ [ORGANIZATION]ホームページ (* [ORGANIZATION] homepage)
what's	12	＊ ろうきん？ (* Labour Bank?)	Love	10	＊ みやざき (* Miyazaki)
Whats	12	＊ ろうきん (* Labour Bank)			
That's	11	＊ インタビュー (* interview)	Suffixes (2 types, 202 tokens in total)		
howto	11	＊ 物 (* related things)	ing	148	俳句 ＊ (haiku *)
			ing	54	職 ＊ 全国版求人情報 (work * job information for all regions)
Adverbs (7 types, 593 tokens in total)					
up	208	9,000円 ＊ (9,000 yen *)	Interrogative pronouns (1 type, 10 tokens in total)		
off	131	10パーセント ＊ (10 percent *)	What	10	＊ 共栄会 (* Kyoueikai)
not	95	＊ オススメ (* recommended)			

Table 3: Katakana expressions in Mainichi Shinbun

1991			1992			1993		
アップ (up)	AD	11	デジタル (digital)	AJ	11	アップ (up)	AD	21
ニュー (new)	AJ	7	スーパー (super)	AJ	7	スーパー (super)	AJ	8
グローバル (global)	AJ	5	ニュー (new)	AJ	7	デジタル (digital)	AJ	6
スーパー (super)	AJ	3	アップ (up)	AD	7	ジュニア (junior)	AJ	4
デジタル (digital)	AJ	3	パーソナル (personal)	AJ	6	ニュー (new)	AJ	4
ジュニア (junior)	AJ	2	オール (all)	AJ	3	ザ (the)	AR	3
パーソナル (personal)	AJ	2	ジュニア (junior)	AJ	3	オール (all)	AJ	3
ベスト(best)	AJ	2	ノー (no)	AJ	3	オンライン (online)	AJ	2
ザ (the)	AR	1	ベスト(best)	AJ	3	グローバル (global)	AJ	2
ハウツー (how to)	PH	1	オープン (open)	AJ	2	ザッツ (that's)	PH	1
オープン (open)	AJ	1	グローバル (global)	AJ	2	オープン (open)	AJ	1
オール (all)	AJ	1	スペシャル (special)	AJ	2	ハンディー (handy)	AJ	1
ノー (no)	AJ	1	ハイパー (hyper)	AJ	2	バーチャル (virtual)	AJ	1
ウエルカム (welcome)	V	1	ハウツー (how to)	PH	1	フリー (free)	AJ	1
			アンド(and)	CJ	1	ベスト(best)	AJ	1
			ウェルカム (welcome)	V	1	イン (in)	PP	1
						オンリー (only)	AD	1

Table 3: Katakana expressions in Mainichi Shinbun (cont.)

1994			1995			1996		
アップ (up)	AD	22	オール (all)	AJ	20	アップ (up)	AD	20
デジタル (digital)	AJ	14	デジタル (digital)	AJ	12	デジタル (digital)	AJ	19
スーパー (super)	AJ	12	アップ (up)	AD	12	グローバル (global)	AJ	10
オール (all)	AJ	4	スーパー (super)	AJ	9	スーパー (super)	AJ	8
オンライン (online)	AJ	3	グローバル (global)	AJ	5	オール (all)	AJ	6
グローバル (global)	AJ	3	オンライン (online)	AJ	4	バーチャル (virtual)	AJ	5
ジュニア (junior/Jr.)	AJ	3	オープン (open)	AJ	3	ニュー (new)	AJ	4
オープン (open)	AJ	1	ニュー (new)	AJ	3	オープン (open)	AJ	2
オフライン (offline)	AJ	1	イン (in)	PP	2	オンライン (online)	AJ	2
ニュー (new)	AJ	1	イッツ (it's)	PH	1	ジュニア (junior)	AJ	2
ノー (no)	AJ	1	ハウツー (how to)	PH	1	ビッグ (big)	AJ	2
バーチャル (virtual)	AJ	1	レッツ (let's)	PH	1	ベスト (best)	AJ	2
パーソナル (personal)	AJ	1	キッズ (kids)	AJ	1	イン (in)	PP	2
ベスト (best)	AJ	1	ジュニア (junior)	AJ	1	ザ (the)	AR	1
ウェルカム (welcome)	V	1	スペシャル (special)	AJ	1	アクティブ (active)	AJ	1
エンジョイ (enjoy)	V	1	ビッグ (big)	AJ	1	クローズ (close)	AJ	1
アゲイン (again)	AD	1	ベスト (best)	AJ	1	スペシャル (special)	AJ	1
			イング (ing)	CJ	1	ハイパー (hyper)	AJ	1
			ウエルカム (welcome)	V	1	マイ (my)	PO	1
			サポート (support)	V	1			

1997			1998			1999		
デジタル (digital)	AJ	42	デジタル (digital)	AJ	27	デジタル (digital)	AJ	39
アップ (up)	AD	22	グローバル (global)	AJ	15	グローバル (global)	AJ	31
グローバル (global)	AJ	18	アップ (up)	AD	10	スーパー (super)	AJ	10
スーパー (super)	AJ	14	スーパー (super)	AJ	9	アップ (up)	AD	10
オール (all)	AJ	11	オール (all)	AJ	8	オール (all)	AJ	9
バーチャル (virtual)	AJ	8	ニュー (new)	AJ	6	オンライン (online)	AJ	8
ニュー (new)	AJ	5	バーチャル (virtual)	AJ	3	ジュニア (junior)	AJ	6
オープン (open)	AJ	2	モバイル (mobile)	AJ	3	バーチャル (virtual)	AJ	3
オンライン (online)	AJ	2	オンライン (online)	AJ	2	キッズ (kids)	AJ	2
ビッグ (big)	AJ	2	キッズ (kids)	AJ	2	ネクスト (next)	AJ	2
スペシャル (special)	AJ	1	ジュニア (junior)	AJ	2	マンスリー (monthly)	AJ	2
ノー (no)	AJ	1	ノー (no)	AJ	2	モバイル (mobile)	AJ	2
メイン (main)	AJ	1	アクティブ (active)	AJ	1	ニュー (new)	AJ	1
モバイル (mobile)	AJ	1	ディジタル (digital)	AJ	1	ノー (no)	AJ	1
イン (in)	PP	1	ナイス (nice)	AJ	1	ハッピー (happy)	AJ	1
			ベスト (best)	AJ	1	ベスト (best)	AJ	1
			マンスリー (monthly)	AJ	1	エンジョイ (enjoy)	V	1
			イン (in)	PP	1			
			フォーエヴァー (forever)	AD	1			

2000			2001			2002		
デジタル (digital)	AJ	46	グローバル (global)	AJ	24	グローバル (global)	AJ	18
グローバル (global)	AJ	23	デジタル (digital)	AJ	17	デジタル (digital)	AJ	17
スーパー (super)	AJ	17	スーパー (super)	AJ	12	ジュニア (junior)	AJ	8
オール (all)	AJ	10	アップ (up)	AD	12	アップ (up)	AD	8
アップ (up)	AD	8	ベスト (best)	AJ	5	スーパー (super)	AJ	7
モバイル (mobile)	AJ	7	ジュニア (junior)	AJ	4	ニュー (new)	AJ	7
オンライン (online)	AJ	5	オール (all)	AJ	3	オンライン (online)	AJ	5
バーチャル (virtual)	AJ	4	オンライン (online)	AJ	3	スペシャル (special)	AJ	3
ジュニア (junior)	AJ	3	バーチャル (virtual)	AJ	3	モバイル (mobile)	AJ	3
ニュー (new)	AJ	3	モバイル (mobile)	AJ	3	オール (all)	AJ	2
ハイパー (hyper)	AJ	3	イン (in)	PP	3	キッズ (kids)	AJ	2
キッズ (kids)	AJ	2	アクティブ (active)	AJ	2	ノー (no)	AJ	2
アクティブ (active)	AJ	1	キッズ (kids)	AJ	2	バーチャル (virtual)	AJ	2
ノー (no)	AJ	1	ザ (the)	AR	1	イン (in)	PP	2
マンスリー (monthly)	AJ	1	クローズド (closed)	AJ	1	フォーエバー (forever)	AD	2
イン (in)	PP	1	ハンディー (handy)	AJ	1	アクティブ (active)	AJ	1
オンリー (only)	AD	1	フリー (free)	AJ	1	ビッグ (big)	AJ	1
			マイ (my)	PO	1	ベスト (best)	AJ	1
			アゲイン (again)	AD	1	ウェルカム (welcome)	V	1
			オンリー (only)	AD	1			

Table 3: Katakana expressions in Mainichi Shinbun (cont.)

2003			2004			2005		
デジタル (digital)	AJ	30	スーパー (super)	AJ	33	スーパー (super)	AJ	28
ベスト (best)	AJ	30	ベスト (best)	AJ	29	ベスト (best)	AJ	28
スーパー (super)	AJ	28	デジタル (digital)	AJ	24	デジタル (digital)	AJ	22
グローバル (global)	AJ	10	グローバル (global)	AJ	13	グローバル (global)	AJ	14
ジュニア (junior)	AJ	7	オール (all)	AJ	7	オール (all)	AJ	13
ニュー (new)	AJ	6	バーチャル (virtual)	AJ	4	ノー (no)	AJ	11
オンライン (online)	AJ	4	モバイル (mobile)	AJ	3	ジュニア (junior)	AJ	5
バーチャル (virtual)	AJ	3	アンド (and)	CJ	1	マイ (my)	PO	5
イン (in)	PP	2	ディジタル (digital)	AJ	1	オンライン (online)	AJ	3
オール (all)	AJ	2	ニュー (new)	AJ	1	モバイル (mobile)	AJ	3
マイ (my)	PO	2	ビッグ (big)	AJ	1	バーチャル (virtual)	AJ	2
フロム (from)	PP	1	マイ (my)	PO	1	バイ (by)	PP	1
モバイル (mobile)	AJ	1						

Table 4: Katakana expressions in articles from the Internet

Adjectives (40 types, 64867 tokens in total)				
デジタル (digital)	15319	* 処理 (* treatment)	ウィークリー	20 * 検索 (* retrieval)
オンライン (online)	12223	* 写真集 (* photo collection)	(weekly)	
メイン (main)	7982	* 曲選出 (* music selection)	スーパ (super)	19 * 熱分析システム
フリー (free)	3953	* 素材 (* material)		(* heat analysis system)
ベスト (best)	3543	* 盤 (* album)	アクティヴ (active)	10 * 発想 (* idea)
モバイル (mobile)	3230	* 端末 (* terminal)		
ディジタル (digital)	2241	* 画像 (* image)	Adverbs (5 types, 23258 tokens in total)	
スペシャル (special)	1677	* 料金 (* fee)	アップ (up)	19615 何点 * (how many points *)
グローバル (global)	1636	* 企業 (* company)	オフ (off)	3373 日本語入力 *
ホット (hot)	1578	* 情報 (* information)	オンリー (only)	(Japanese-language input *)
アクティブ (active)	1442	* 商社 (* trading company)		243 読み物 * (reading *)
スーパー (super)	1395	* 不況 (* depression)	アゲイン (again)	26 長野 * (Nagano *)
ジュニア (junior)	1247	* 選手権 (* championship)	オンリィ (only)	1 [PERSON] * ([PERSON] *)
オフライン (offline)	769	* 質問フォーム		
		(* questionnaire form)	Prepositions (6 types, 1816 tokens in total)	
クール (cool)	754	* 解説 (* comment)	イン (in)	1214 探検隊 * [LOCATION]
ハンディ (handy)	574	* 機 (* machine)		360 (expedition * [LOCATION])
バーチャル (virtual)	569	* 博物館 (* museum)	デ (de)	129 ねっと * わーく (net * work)
ビッグ (big)	517	* 当選 (* win)	アバウト (about)	66 * 八日市 (* Yokaichi)
ハッピー (happy)	499	* [ORGANIZATION]	フロム (from)	24 * 沖縄推進機構
ニュー (new)	481	* 軽量骨材		23 (* Okinawa Initiative)
		(* lightweight aggregate)	オブ (of)	良品 * 京都
オフィシャル (official)	384	* 応援歌 (* fight song)		(good item * Kyoto)
インライン (inline)	343	* 入力 (* input)	トゥ (to)	フロム市長 * 職員
パーソナル (personal)	287	* 感覚 (* sense)		(from the Mayor * officers)
オール (all)	269	* 専任教師		
		(* full-time teacher)	Verbs (3 types, 741 tokens in total)	
ショート (short)	269	* 丈 (* length)	エンジョイ	611 * ふくい (* Fukui)
クローズ (close)	264	* 状態 (* status)	(enjoy)	
グッド (good)	260	* ぐんまの新鮮野菜	ウェルカム	73 * へいあん (* Heian)
		(* fresh vegetables in Gumma)	(welcome)	
パブリック (public)	236	* 空間 (* space)	ウエルカム	57 * 東久留米
ハイパー (hyper)	186	* 調査隊 (* expedition)	(welcome)	(* Higashikurume)
ノー (no)	178	* 試験 (* examination)		
デイリー (daily)	160	* 情報 (* information)	Possessive pronouns (1 type, 270 tokens in total)	
マンスリー (monthly)	91	* 壁紙 (* wallpaper)	マイ (my)	270 * 切手 (* stamp)
ネクスト (next)	81	* 牌 (* tile)		
ハンディー (handy)	73	* 機器 (* device)	Articles (1 type, 178 tokens in total)	
クローズド (closed)	57	* 期間 (* period)	ザ (the)	178 なるほど * 信州
イージー (easy)	30	* 操作 (* operation)		(I see. * Shinshu)
エクストラ (extra)	21	* 告知ページ		
		(* information page)		

Table 4: Katakana expressions in articles from the Internet (cont.)

Phrases (3 types, 83 tokens in total)		Suffixes (1 type, 28 tokens in total)	
レッツ (let's)	73 ★不動産 (* real estate)	イング (ing)	28 遊★ (play *)
ザッツ (that's)	8 ★下町考		
	(* thinking about downtown)		
ウェルカム トゥ	2 ★お台場ラジオ会館		
(welcome to)			

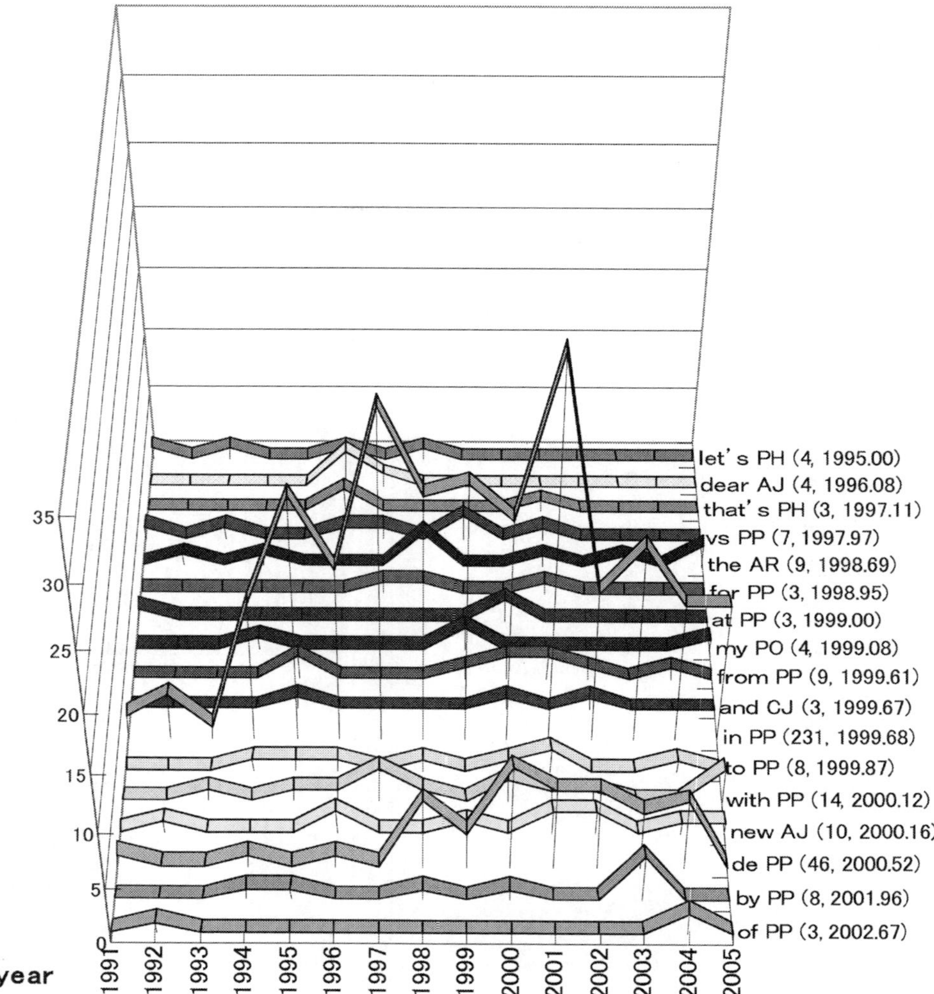

Figure 1: Change in the number of English expressions in Mainichi Shinbun (The two numbers in the parentheses indicate the total number of expressions and the average value of appeared years.)

articles, possessive pronouns, suffixes, verbs, and interrogative pronouns.

The expressions using prepositions, phrases, and verbs from articles on the Internet (Table 2) have a word order that is different from the usual Japanese language word order. For example, "キャンペーン in 渋谷" ("キャンペーン"=campaign, "渋谷"=Shibuya (location name)), "What's けいば" ("けいば"="horse race"), and "Welcome えひめ" ("えひめ"=Ehime (location

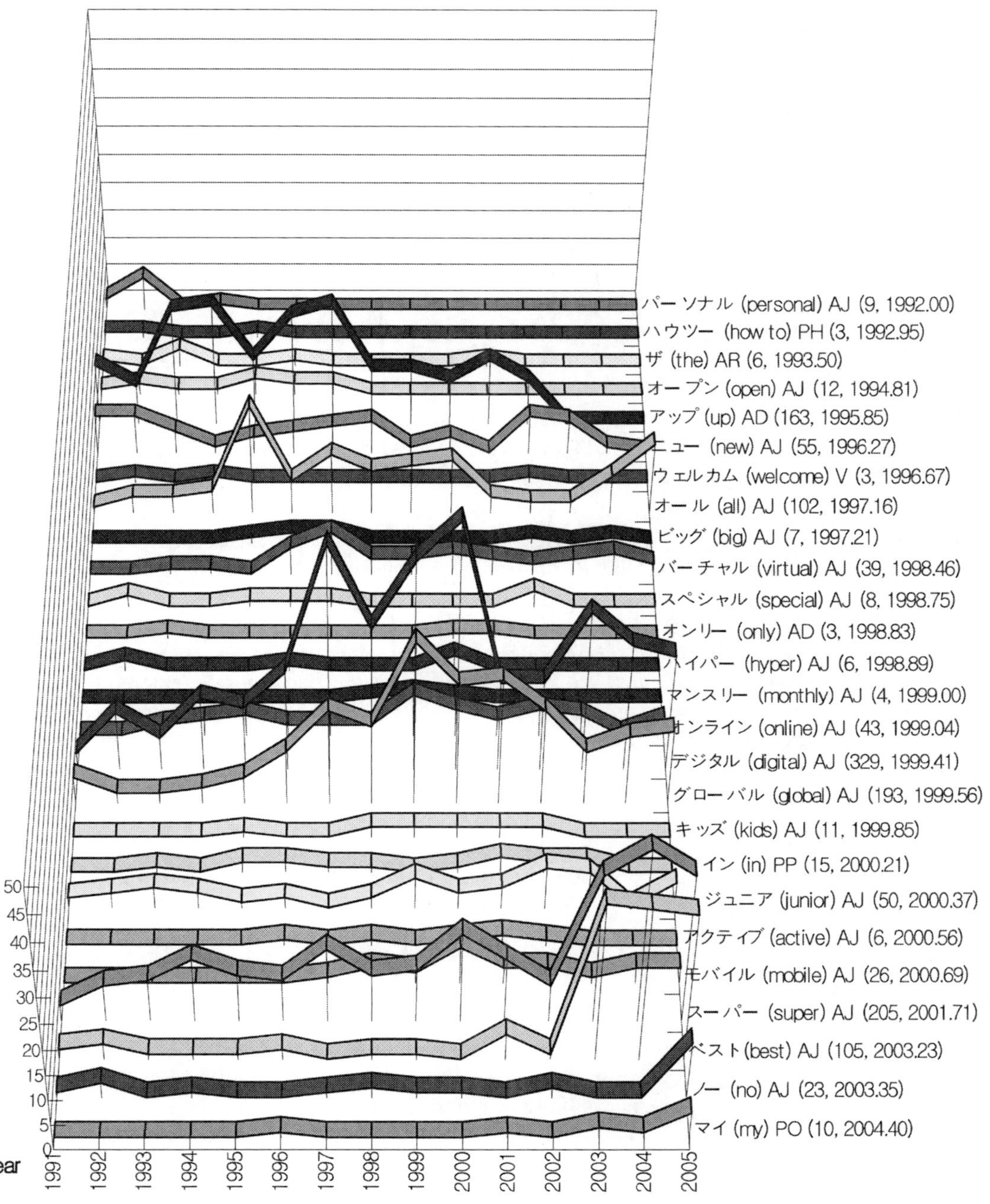

Figure 2: Change in the number of Katakana expressions in Mainichi Shinbun (The two numbers in the parentheses indicate the total number of expressions and the average value of appeared years.)

name)). The Japanese standard word order is "渋谷でのキャンペーン" ("渋谷"=Shibuya (location name)), "での"=in, "キャンペーン"=campaign), "けいばとは何" ("けいば"="horse race", "とは"=be, "何"=what), and "えひめへようこそ" ("えひめ"=Ehime(location name),

"へ"=to, "ようこそ"=welcome), respectively. The reason for the change in word order is because in English the important thing is usually at the beginning of a sentence, so it is convenient to construct compact expressions in this way.

This kind of the word order difference has already been seen in Japanese expressions of Chinese origin, such as "於東京" ("於"=in, "東京"=Tokyo), "必履修" ("必"=require, "履修"="take a course"), and "対テロ" ("対"= against or to, "テロ"=terror). Expressions like "キャンペーン in 渋谷" are possibly due to the tolerant and flexible characteristic of Japanese language which permits expressions like "於東京".

Table 3 shows the frequency with which katakana expressions appear in Mainichi Shinbun articles. Adjectives and adverbs have appeared with high frequencies for a long time. The table shows that katakana expressions containing adjectives and adverbs have been used more often then other parts of speech. The article "the" and the verb "welcome" have been used for a long time.

By comparing the frequency of English expressions with that of katakana expressions using the data in Tables 2 and 4, we found that adverbs and adjectives, such as "アップ" (up) and "デジタル" (digital), that are often used in Japanese are often expressed using katakana and that prepositions that are not used so often in Japanese are not often expressed using katakana. That is, we found a trend in which English expressions that have been used often in Japanese are likely to be expressed with katakana and English expressions that have not been used often in Japanese are likely to be expressed using the Roman alphabet.

We can see many English expressions in the parts of speech that are not adjectives and adverbs. These are prepositions, conjunctions, phrases, articles, possessive pronouns, suffixes, verbs, and interrogative pronouns. We think these expressions have not yet entered the Japanese language, and they are new expression styles. In terms of adjectives and adverbs, we can see many English expressions for the adjectives "new" and "old" and the adverbs "all" and "not". Thus, the adjectives and adverbs may be special expressions.

4. Conclusions

We extracted Japanese expressions that included English expressions from Mainichi Shinbun articles that appeared over a 15-year period and from 2 GB of Internet articles. We found that the preposition "in" has been used often for more than ten years. We extracted from Internet articles many kinds of English expressions that contained various parts of speech. We also extracted interesting expressions that used English prepositions or verb phrases. These interesting expressions had different word orders to ordinary Japanese sentences. From comparing the extracted English and katakana expressions, we suggest that English expressions that are common in Japanese are likely to be written in katakana and that English expressions that are not common in Japanese are likely to written in the Roman syllabary.

References

Ito Masamitsu. 2001. The Judgment Standard for Distinguishing Loan Words of Western Origin from Western Words in Japanese Pop Songs, *Mathematical Linguistics*, Vol.23, No.2, 110-131. (in Japanese)

Daulton Frank. 2003. Loanwords in the Media, *Annual report of Ryukoku University International Center*, Vol.12, 59-72.

Murata Masaki, Mika Shindo, Qing Ma and Hitoshi Isahara. 2004. Conversion between English Parts of Speech Using a Word Dictionary, *The 25th Conference of the International Computer Archive of Modern and Medieval English* (ICAME25), 78-79.

Two Types of Complex Predicate Formation:
Japanese Passive and Potential Verbs [*]

Hiroaki Nakamura

Japan Coast Guard Academy, Department of Liberal Arts,
5-1, Wakaba-cho, Kure City, Hiroshima, 737-8512, JAPAN
nakamura@jcga.ac.jp

Abstract. This paper deals with the complex verb formation of passive and potential predicates and syntactic structures projected by these verbs. Though both predicates are formed with the suffix *-rare* which has been assumed to originate from the same stem, they show significantly different syntactic behaviors. We propose two kinds of concatenation of base verbs and auxiliaries; passive verbs are lexically formed with the most restrictive mode of combination, while potential verbs are formed syntactically via more flexible combinatory operations of function composition. The difference in the mode of complex verb formation has significant consequences for their syntactic structures and semantic interpretations, including different combination with the honorific morphemes and subjectivization of arguments/adjuncts of base verbs. We also consider the case alternation phenomena and their implications for scope construals found in potential sentences, which can be accounted for in a unified manner in terms of the optional application of function composition.

Keywords: Complex predicates, passive verb, potential verb, honorification, subjectivization, Combinatory Categorial Grammar.

1. Introduction

Syntax and semantics of complex verbs have long been the focus of attention in Japanese linguistics. This paper proposes a new approach to the formation of passive and potential verbs, both of which include the auxiliary verb *-rare*, and explore the relationship between the complex verb formation and projections of syntactic structures. The auxiliary verb *-rare* has been assumed to be semantically ambiguous among passive, potential, spontaneous and honorific interpretations. We will take up the passive and potential interpretations of the auxiliary verb, and argue that there is a crucial difference between the two use of this verb. First, observe the sentence in (1):

(1) Kurisumasu-ni-wa   takusan-no   keeki-ga   taber-are-ru.
    Christmas-at-Top   a lot of   cake-Nom   eat-Can/Pass-Pres
    'At Christmas, a lot of cakes are/can be eaten.'

(1) can be interpreted as passive on one reading, i.e., a lot of cakes are eaten at Christmas. On another reading, (1) is taken to be a statement of the possibility; we (or arbitrary people) can eat a lot of cakes at Christmas.

The multiple usages of the auxiliary verb -*rare* has been assumed to be due to the common origin, sharing the meaning of spontaneity (*get, become*, etc.), though there are different hypotheses concerning which use is original. The interpretations of -*rare* are ambiguous in some cases and it is necessary to take contextual information into account. We will argue, however, that the two complex verbs must be derived in a completely different manner, exploring the interactions between the word formation and honorification or choice of subjects in sentences projected from them. Honorification is a device to indicate that the speaker feels respect for the person referred to by the grammatical subject or object, using the discontinuous honorific morpheme comprising the prefix *o-* and the verb -*ni-nar* (a kind of auxiliary verb). This morpheme combines with (actually wrap) verbal roots (infinitives) without changing the argument structures of the latter. (2) illustrates the subject honorification we address in this paper. Hereafter, HP stands for the honorific prefix (*o-*) and HS the honorific suffix (-*ninar*).

(2) Sensei-wa   keeki-o   o-tabe-nina(r)-tta.
     Sensei-Top cake-Acc HP-eat-HS-Past
     'Sensei ate a cake.'

Interestingly, the passive and potential complex verbs, both of which are formed by the concatenation with the auxiliary verb -*rare*, shows different processes of honorification. The honorific morpheme wraps derived complex passive forms, while it wraps only base verbs, and -*rare* follows the derived honorific forms in the potential verb formation. Compare the following examples:

(3) a. Sensei-wa   okusama-ni   o-sikar-are-nina(r)-tta.
        teacger-Top wife-BY   HP-reproach-Pass-HS-Past
        'The teacher was reproached by his wife.'

     b. Sensei-wa   okusama-o/-ga   o-sikar-ninar-(ar)e-nai.
        teacher-Top wife-Acc/-Nom   HP-reproach-HS-Can-Neg-Pres
        'The teacher cannot reproach his wife.'

This paper provide a new account for the relation between syntactic structures and the complex verb formation, in which passive and potential complex verbs are formed in a completely different manner. We discuss how subjects with a wide variety of semantic relations to base verbs are derived in potential constructions and consider the properties of (major) subjects in stative sentences, the license of which should be distinguished from that of ordinary subjects.

2. Framework: Combinatory Categorial Grammar

In this paper we adopt a mildly context-sensitive grammar, Combinatory Categorial Grammar (henceforce, CCG; see Steedman 1996, 2000, Baldridge 2002, among others) as a descriptive framework. 'Mildly context-sensitive' means that this grammar formalism allows associativity (rebracketing) and permutativity (reordering) among the modes of combination, in addition to the standard context-free concatenation (application). The combinatory rules allowing such flexible combinations are often said to be too strong in generative capacity, and quite often derive illicit strings in some languages. For example, it has been pointed out that the non-associative and permutative mode (for the mixed composition rules) is not necessary for English grammar, but necessary to derive some constructions in Dutch. To constrain the applicability of rules, Baldridge (2002) and Steedman & Baldridge (2007) propose to use modalized slashes in combinatory rules, so that the applicability of rules can be lexically controlled. The Multi-modal CCG defines the hierarchy of modes as in (6):

(4)

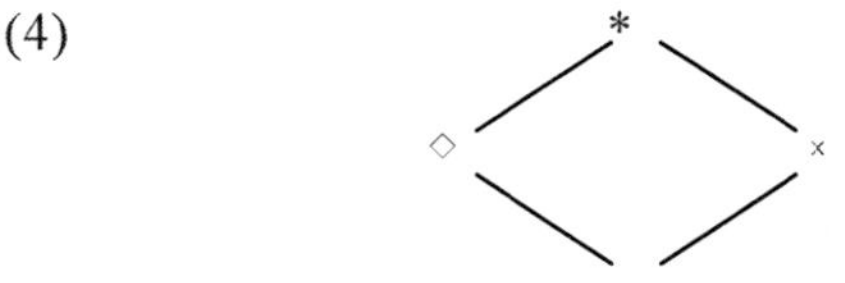

    * non-permutative/non-associative
    ◇ associative/non-permutative
    ˟ non-associative/permutative
    · associative/permutative

The * modality is the most restricted and allows only functional application. The $^\diamond$ modality permits order-preserving associativity in derivation. The mode · is placed at the bottom of hierarchy, which indicates that it is the most permissive one, inheriting the properties of all the others. Then we have the following list of combinatory rules:

(5)   a.   (>) X/Y Y $\Rightarrow$ X
     (<) Y $X\backslash Y$ $\Rightarrow$ X
   b.   (>B) $X/_\diamond Y$ $Y/_\diamond Z$ $\Rightarrow$ $X/_\diamond Z$
     (<B) $Y\backslash_\diamond Z$ $X\backslash_\diamond Y$ $\Rightarrow$ $X\backslash_\diamond Z$
   c.   (>B$_\times$) $X/_\times Y$ $Y\backslash_\times Z$ $\Rightarrow$ $X\backslash_\times Z$
     (<B$_\times$) $Y/_\times Z$ $X\backslash_\times Y$ $\Rightarrow$ $X/_\times Z$
   d.   (>T) X $\Rightarrow$ $Y/_i(Y\backslash_i X)$
     (<T) X $\Rightarrow$ $Y\backslash_i(Y/_i X)$
   e.   LWRAP: Y $X\downarrow_\diamond Y$ $\Rightarrow$ X

We will simply omit the symbol '*' in the derivations hereafter. The harmonic composition rules in (5b) allows associativity, while the disharmonic, mixed composition rules in (5c) allow permutation of elements in input strings. The input to the type-raising in (5d) does not make reference to any slashes, but the slashes in the output category must have the same mode, and the subscript *i* stands for a variable over modes. CCG has no (left) wrap rules as in (5e) but we will use the wrapping rule as in (5e) only for expository purposes when the honorific morpheme combines with verbs, and assume that it may participate in harmonic composition.

3. Derivations of Passive and Potential Complex Verbs

In this section, let us consider how to derive the two complex verbs, especially addressing the interaction with honorification. We also examine the subject selection in sentences projected from these complex predicates (especially in potential constructions), which is proved to be a direct consequence of the concatenation we propose shortly. First let us start with the fact that the discontinuous honorific form wraps the complex passive verbs, whereas it wraps only the base infinitive of potential verbs.

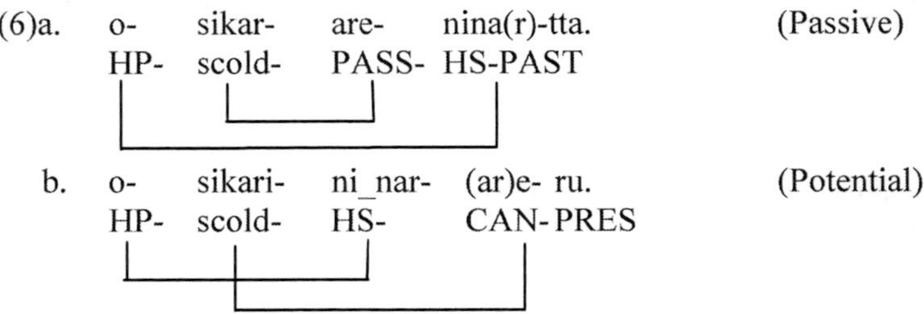

(6)a.   o-   sikar-   are-   nina(r)-tta.   (Passive)
    HP-   scold-   PASS-   HS-PAST

  b.   o-   sikari-   ni_nar-   (ar)e- ru.   (Potential)
    HP-   scold-   HS-   CAN-PRES

The dependency relations between corresponding morphemes can be shown respectively as in (6). We should notice the change in argument structures through the concatenation. In (6a), the honorific expressions mark the derived external argument of the passive verb *sikar-are* 'reproached', which was originally the theme argument of the base verb, as the person the speaker has respect for. Since this change of argument structure is not derived syntactically, the derivation of passive verbs must be treated in the lexicon. In examples and derivations, the respected referents are indicated with underlines annotated with H if necessary. In (6b), the relation between discontinuous honorific expressions and that between the base and potential verbs may be said to show crossing dependencies. The base verb is wrapped by the honorifics first and the derived form *o-sikari-ninar*, is followed by the potential auxiliary verb. We assume that the original external argument of infinitive is suppressed/demoted and the original theme is promoted to the outermost argument in the argument structure of a passive, whereas such argument change does not occur in that of a potential verb. The derivation of a passive verb with honorifics can be shown as in (7) where the passive complex verb is formed by a lexical operation, and honorification may apply to it in syntax.

(7) sikar-   -(r)are   o...nar
     reproach(x)(y)   Pass   HP+HS
     ——————————————————<Lex.
       sikar-are: *be_reproached*(y)(x)
     ————————————————————————<W
       o-sikar-are-ninar: *be_reproached*(y)($\underline{x}_H$)

The subject of a potential construction is often difficult to distinguish from that of passive, as illustrated in (1), where the theme of the original base verb is the subject in both readings, but we can see a significant difference in subject selection between two constructions. In potential sentences, any argument or adjunct can be subjectivized, as illustrated in (8), the derivation of which will be explored in the following section.

(8) a. <u>Kono resutoran-ga</u>/-de   oisii   keeki-o/-ga   taber-are-ru.
       this restaurant-Nom/-Loc delicious cake-Acc/-Nom   eat-Can-Pres
       'This restaurant is such that people can eat delicious cakes there.'

    b. <u>Kono naifu-ga</u>/-de   katai niku-o/-ga   kantan-ni kir-(rar)e-ru.
       this-knife-Nom/-By   leathery meat-Nom/-Acc easily   cut-Can-Pres
       'This knife is such that people can cut leathery meat easily with it.'

It should be noticed that adjuncts cannot be subjectivized in passive sentences. The examples in (8) remind us of the missing object constructions in English. In fact, any argument/adjunct can become a subject in tough-type sentences in Japanese. The only candidate for the syntactic structure of these sentences can be derived by via null operator movement in the government-binding theory, as shown in (9). Here let us assume that adjuncts are optional arguments to the verb following Marten (2002), McConnell-Ginet (1982), Steedman (1996).

(9) [Kono naifu-ga   [$_{CP}$ OP$_i$ [$_{IP}$ PRO$_{arb}$ katai-niku-o t_i kir] -(ar)e-ru].
    this knife-Nom   leathery meat-Acc cut- Can-Pres

The direct movement of the adjunct to the subject position is not allowed in the theory, so the null operator must be posited in its base position and be moved up to associate the matrix subject with the proper semantic role (i.e., instrumental). Because the null operator movement is a kind of *wh*-movement, adjuncts as well as arguments can be moved to the [Spec, CP] position. It is not clear, however, how the structure like (9) can provide a proper interpretation compositionally, which is considered in section 4. Sentences like (8) suggest that the argument structures are not changed as seen in the passive case (7), so we can infer that the potential complex verb is derived syntactically. Observe the formation of the potential verb with honorifics in (10).

(10)

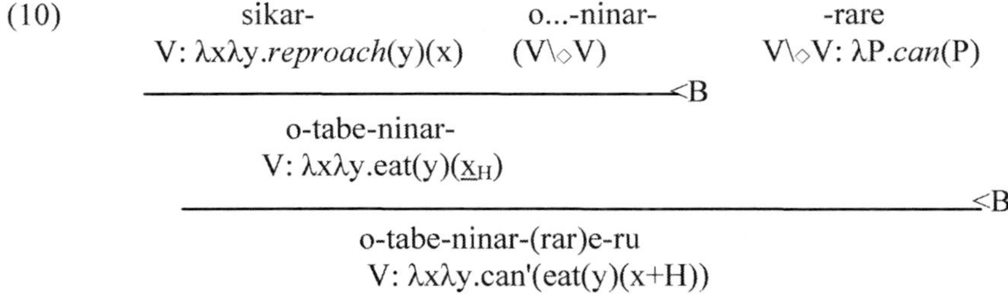

In derivation (10), the base verb *-tabe* combines with/wrapped by the honorific morpheme first, postponing the concatenation with arguments/adjuncts lexically or optionally specified. The information of arguments/adjuncts can be passed along to the resulting complex form. Then the honorific base verb combines with the potential auxiliary verb by composition. The complex potential verb with the honorific morpheme actually conveys information of arguments or adjuncts which were not consumed throughout the formation. This will explain the occurrence of multiple nominative terms in potential constructions, which is not allowed in passive sentences. Notice that any absorption of arguments or externalization of internal arguments does not occur here. The information of semantic roles of a base verb are simply passed up via a device like the slash-feature passing mechanism. This operation must be carried out in syntax.
   Here let us consider the examples of case alternation like (11).

(11) a. Taroo-ga   eigo-o   hanas-(ar)e-ru.
         Taroo-Nom   English-Acc   speak-Can-Pres
         'Taroo can speak English.'

     b. Taroo-ga   eigo-o   hanas-(ar)e-ru.
         Taroo-Nom   English-Acc   speak-Can-Pres
         ibid.

There is no semantic difference between (11a) and (11b) (but we will see a difference in scope interpretation in the next section). In (11a) with the accusative object, the arguments combine with the base verb in the order lexically specified. On the other hand, in (11b) with the nominative object, the base verb 'speak' combines with the potential verb, which assigns the nominative case to the object as a stative verb (because stative verbs has no ability to assign accusative case). This alternation is not allowed in passive sentences because passive verbs are lexically specified to consume arguments by the most restrictive mode of operation, which results in obligatory case absorption. The * modality in the category of passive verbs allows only the applicative rule. On the other hand, the potential verb are lexically specified as having less restrictive modality. Naturally, we can conclude that the potential suffix are allowed to concatenate in both the * and $^{\diamond}$ mode, exactly as in the tough-sentences in (12).

(12) a. It is easy to play the sonata with the violin.
     b. This violin is easy to play the sonata with.

(13) a. It seems to need repainting this wall.
     b. This wall seems to need repainting e.

In (a) sentences, the accusative case is assigned to the object in situ by the infinitive. In (b) sentences, the information of missing objects is passed up to the top of complement clauses. It should be noticed that the matrix subjects are licensed by the embedded clauses with missing objects (i.e., open propositions, ignoring agent arguments of infinitives). The point is the optionality of the application of function composition/slash-feature passing operation. This optionality is not available for the passive verb formation which is lexically specified to undergo the most restrictive combination. The hierarchy for slash modalities can account for the difference in availability of case alternation between passive and potential verbs.

4. Selection of Subjects and its Implications

In this section let us extend the analysis proposed in the previous section and derive potential sentences including subjects with various semantic roles. We proposed that passives are formed only by application while potentials are formed by application or composition. Therefore, only the theme arguments of base verbs can be subjects in passive sentences, as expected. So the problem may happen only if the base verbs have more than one objects like ditransitive verbs. On the other hand, any argument or adjunct can be subjectivized in potential sentences, which we want to explain. Let us take a look at derivation (14) as a first approximation:

$$
\begin{array}{llll}
(14) & \text{kono naifu-ga} & \text{yasai-o} & \text{kantan-ni} & \text{o-kiri-ninar-(ar)e-ru} \\
& \text{this knife} & \text{vegetables} & \text{easily} & \text{HP-cut-HS-Can-Pres} \\
& N_{Nom} & N_{ACC} & VP\backslash VP & (((S\backslash N_{PRO})\backslash \diamond N_{Inst})\backslash N_{Acc} \\
& & & & \lambda x.\lambda y.can'(cut'(y)(\underline{PRO_H})(with\_x)
\end{array}
$$

$$\overline{\qquad\qquad\qquad\qquad\qquad\qquad\qquad\qquad\qquad} {}^{<B}$$

$$S\backslash NP_{Inst}: \lambda x.can'(cut'(vegetables)(\underline{PRO_H})(with\_x)$$

As mentioned above, we take adjuncts to be of *e*-type as optional arguments to base verbs, not of $<<e,t>,<e,t>>$ type, which is assigned to typical verb phrase modifiers. Notice that the accusative object can be marked with nominative if function composition is applied before it is consumed by application. Composition rule can be generalized as (15), so that we can easily transmit any number of arguments/adjuncts to the resulting category. Then the features of missing instrumental and theme arguments may be inherited to the predicate phrase.

(15) Backward Composition (<B):[1]

    $Y\backslash Z\$ \quad X\backslash Y \Rightarrow X\backslash Z\$$

    where the symbol $Z\$$ stands for Z and all lefttward-looking functor categories into Z.

In derivation (14) we encounter another problem. The derived predicate phrase is the functor looking leftward for the adjunct which seems to convey oblique case, but the corresponding subject is marked with nominative case, so case conflict arises here. This is a very important point to be accounted for to deal with the notion of subject in stative sentences in languages like Japanese. In the generative grammar tradition, the notion of major subject has been appealed to, which is not directly licensed by the argument structure of a verb, but by a whole predicate phrase containing some gap. Typical example of a sentence containing the major subject can be shown in (16), which has been referred to as a so-called multiple subject construction.

---

[1] The \$-convention is defined as in (i)

(i) The \$ convention

For a category α, $\{\alpha\$\}$, (respectively, $\{\alpha/\$\}$, $\{\alpha/L\$\}$) denotes the set containing α and all functions (respectively, leftward functions, rightward functions) into a category in $\{\alpha\$\}$(respectively, $\{\alpha/\$\}$, $\{\alpha/L\$\}$). (Steedman 2000:42)

(16) Souru-ga   jinkoo-ga   ooi.
      Seoul-Nom   population-Nom   many-Pres
      'Seoul is such that its population is large.'

The argument structure of the predicate *ooi* 'be many' is saturated by the second subject.   The hearer, however, takes the leftmost nominative phrase *Souru-ga* to be a kind of subject which denotes a property of Seoul. As the interpretation of (16), Seoul is a member of the set denoted by the clause 'jinkoo-ga   ooi' (a set of cities with a large population). Suppose that *jinkoo* 'population' is a relational noun, and, roughly, it is of type <e,e>, a function from individuals to individuals. It takes some individual (a city/country/area) and returns its population as a value. Therefore, (16) has the structure as illustrated in (17):

(17) [Seoul-ga   [$_{<e,t>}$ [e's jinkoo-ga] ooi]]
        S/(S\NP$_{-Case}$):   S\NP$_{Gen}$:
        λP:P(*Seoul*)   λx.*be_many* (*population_of_*x)
      ——> inferential application
              S: *be_many*(*population_of*(*Seoul*))

We assign the special lifted category, S/(S\NP$_{-Case}$) to the major subject like *Souru-ga* in (17), which is licensed by an open proposition containing at least one gap inside. This category ignores or circumvents case mismatch, which is caused by and inherited from a missing argument/adjunct. So the application of the major subject with the typed-up category to the open proposition is not purely grammatical, but inferential (subjects should have the property denoted by the remaining phrases). This application is licensed by inference or the set-inclusion relation, something like that Seoul (denoting a set of sets) should include a set of individuals with a large population. This category for major subjects as in (17) can be assigned only to the subjects of stative sentences in languages like Japanese.
   Potential constructions are stative in that they denote some potentials/abilities belonging to the referents of subjects, and their subjects can or must be lifted as S\(S/NP) by definition. On the other hand, since passives usually denotes events, they are not stative and their subjects are not allowed to have this category for the subjects. We conclude the derivation of (14) as shown in (18):

(18) kono naifu-ga   yasai-o   kantan-ni   o-kiri-ninar-(ar)e-ru
                         ——
      S/(S\NP$_{-Case}$):   S\NP$_{Inst}$: λx.*can'*(*cut'*(*vegetables*)(<u>PRO</u>$_{H}$)(with_x)
      λP:P(*this_knife*)
      ——>
              S: λx.*can'*(*cut'*(*vegetables*)(<u>PRO</u>$_{H}$)(*with_this_knife*)

The sentence means that this knife has the property that arbitrary people can cut vegetables easily with it. The flexibility of subject selection in potential constructions can be accounted for in terms of more general property of subjects in stative sentences. Their subjects are lifted to denote a set of properties, and simply licensed by open propositions syntactically and semantically.
   Let us see one consequence of our analysis. Tada (1992) points out that Case alternations in potential sentences result in the difference in quantifier scope. Observe the difference in scope interpretation illustrated by (19a) and (19b):

(19) a. John-ga   migime-dake-o   tumur-e-ru-koto
         John-NOM   right-eye-only-ACC   close-can-fact
         'John can close only his right eye.'   (can > only, only > ?*can)

b. John-ga   migime-dake-ga   tumur-e-ru-koto
   John-NOM   right-eye-only-NOM   close-can-fact   (only > can, *can > only)

The dominant reading of (19a) with the accusative object is that John can close only his right eye (i.e., he can wink his right eye). When marked with nominative case, the theme argument in (19b) must take scope over the potential verb. Sentence (19b) implies that he cannot close his left eye. He tries to explain the difference in scope in (19) in terms of movement of the object, which cannot apply to the similar difference in (20).

(20) a. Kono resutoran-dake-de   50-nin-ga   suwar-(ar)e-ru.
         this   restaurant-only-In   50-Clas-Nom   sit-Can-Press
         '50 people can sit in this restaurant.'   (can > only, only > ?*can)

     b. Kono resutoran-dake-ga   50-nin-ga   suwar-(ar)e-ru.
         this restaurant-only-Nom   50-Clas-Nom   sit-Can-Pres
         '50 people can sit in this restaurant'   (only > can, *can > only)

(20b) implies that there is no other restaurant which can accommodate 50 people. Tada's analysis cannot account for the difference in interpretation between (20a) and (20b) because NP-movement should not be used to move adjuncts to the Spec-IP position. Our function composition account can easily deal with the contrasts found in (19) and (20) in a unified way because this operation does not distinguish arguments and adjuncts if we take adjuncts to be optional arguments of predicates.

5. Conclusion

 We compared the passive and potential verb formation, and explored their implications for the interactions with honorification and subjectivization. Though the same suffix *-rare* is used to derive both the passive and potential constructions, they show completely different syntactic behaviors. We noted the different morphological processes of honorification and proposed that passive predicates are formed by the most restrictive combinatory mode in the lexicon, application, whereas potential verbs are formed by composition, which permits associativity. We discussed some syntactic consequences of our proposed analysis, including subject selection in these constructions and quantifier scope construals in potential constructions. Our analysis of the potential verbs using function composition allows a wider variety of arguments and adjuncts to become the subjects of potential sentences. We have shown that it also accounts for the interaction of case alternations and scope interpretations found only in potential constructions.

References

Brown, P. F., S. A. Della Pietra, V. J. Della Pietra and R.L. Mercer. 1993. The Mathematics of Machine Translation: Parameter Estimation. *Computational Linguistics*, 19(2), 263-311.

Baldridge, J. and G-J. Kruijff. 2002 Multi-Modal Combinatory Categorial Grammar. Proceedings of 10th Annual Meeting of the EACL.

Huck, G. J. 1988. Phrasal Verbs and the Categories of Postponent in Oehrle, R. and E. Back, eds. *Categorial Grammars and Natural Language Structures*, 249-263. D. Reidel.

Marten, L. 2002. *At the Syntax-Pragmatics Interface: Verbal Underspecification and Concept Formation in Dynamic Syntax*. Oxford University Press.

McConnell-Ginet, S. 1982. Adverbs and Logical Form: A Linguistically Realistic Theory. *Language* 58, 144-184.

Mihara, K. and T. Hiraiwa. 2006. *Shin-Nihongo-no Toogo-koozo--Minimarisuto Puroguramu-to*

Sono Ooyoo. Syoohaku-sya.

Steedman, M. 1996. *Surface Structure and Interpretation.* MIT Press.

Steedman, M. 2000. *The Syntactic Process.* MIT Press.

Steedman, M. and J. Baldridge. (to appear) Combinatory Categorial Grammar. In: R. Borsley and K. Borjars eds., *Non-Transformational Syntax.* Blackwell.

Tada, Hiroaki. 1992. Nominative Objects in Japanese. Journal of Japanese Linguistics 14, 91-108.

Acquisition of Named-Entity-Related Relations for Searching[*]

Tri-Thanh Nguyen and Akira Shimazu

Japan Advanced Institute of Science and Technology
1-1, Asahidai, Nomi, Ishikawa, 923-1292, Japan
{t-thanh,shimazu}@jaist.ac.jp

Abstract. Named entities (NEs) are important in many Natural Language Processing (NLP) applications, and discovering NE-related relations in texts may be beneficial for these applications. This paper proposes a method to extract the ISA relation between a *"named entity"* and its *category*, and an IS-RELATED-TO relation between the *category* and its related object. Based on the pattern extraction algorithm *"Person Category Extraction"* (PCE), we extend it for solving our problem. Our experiments on Wall Street Journal (WSJ) corpus show promising results. We also demonstrate a possible application of these relations by utilizing them for semantic search.

Keywords: Named-entity-related relations extraction, information extraction, pattern extraction, algorithm, semantic search.

1. Introduction

Text documents often contain valuable relations among entities. For example, in the sentence taken from the WSJ corpus:

> There's a generally more positive attitude toward the economy, said Bette Raptapoulos, analyst for Prudential-Bache Securities Inc., ...　　　　(1)

there are relations: "Bette Raptapoulos" **is-a** analyst, and analyst **for** "Prudential-Bache Securities Inc."

Such relations may be beneficial in many NLP applications, such as for answering *Who* and *List* questions, e.g., "Who is *Bette Raptapoulos?*" or "Give me the list of *analyst for Prudential-Bache Securities Inc.*"

Relations in text documents can be extracted by pattern extraction as in (Brin 1998). (Brin 1998) presented Dual Iterative Pattern Relation Extraction (DIPRE), and used DIPRE to extract ⟨*author, title*⟩ tuples describing the relation: the author of the book *title* is *author*. Based on Brin's model, (Agichtein and Gravano 2000) presented the *Snowball* system to extract ⟨*organization, location*⟩ tuples indicating that the headquarters of *organization* is in *location*. (Nguyen and Shimazu 2007) developed the PCE system for extracting ⟨*person, category*⟩ tuples describing that the *person* is-a *category*.

This study proposes to automatically extract quadruples ⟨*ne, category, related-to, object*⟩ describing that the named entity *ne* ISA *category*, and the *category* IS-RELATED-TO *object*. We call such relations *"named-entity* is-a *category"* relation, and *"category* related-to *object"*

---

[*] This study was supported by Japan Advanced Institute of Science and Technology, the 21st Century COE Program: "Verifiable and Evolvable e-Society".

relation. The *related-to* and *object* of a quadruple may be null. We extend PCE algorithm to extract quadruples, and build a semantic search system to utilize extracted quadruples for answering some types of questions.

The remainder of this paper is organized as follows: Section 2 summarises some related work. Section 3 describes the original PCE algorithm and our extraction model. Section 4 gives a possible application of the extracted quadruples; Section 5 presents experiments and evaluation; Conclusions are given in the last section.

2. Related work

(Brin 1998) presented the DIPRE algorithm for extracting relations, and used DIPRE to extract (*author, title*) tuples having the relation: the author of the book *title* is *author*. Starting with a small number of (*author, title*) seed tuples, DIPRE finds the occurrences of tuples in order to generate new patterns. New patterns are, again, used to extract further (*author, title*) tuples. The DIPRE algorithm is graphically depicted in Figure 1.

Based on DIPRE, (Agichtein and Gravano 2000) introduced another method of generating new patterns, and developed the Snowball system for extracting (*organization, location*) tuples expressing the relation: the headquarters of *organization* is in *location*.

Current Named Entity Recognition (NER) systems often operate based on a predefined set of named entity classes, and assign a unique class to a discovered named entity (Chieu and Tou 2003). This is not natural, since the potential classes of named entity is large, and a named entity may belong to more than one class. For example, a person named entity may be both "*executive vice president*" and "*chief financial officer*" as expressed in the sentence: "Daniel Akerson, executive vice president and chief financial officer, said MCI's growth is being fueled by …" With the purpose of extending the number of named entity classes, (Nguyen and Shimazu 2007) proposed the "Person Category Extraction" (PCE) algorithm to automatically extract fine-grained categories of person Named Entities from text corpora. Based on DPIRE, (Nguyen and Shimazu 2007) introduced new types of patterns based on part-of-speech (POS) and chunk tags. One more proposal of their study which improved the perfomance of PCE a lot was the use of a validation function in the extraction procedure. Details of the PCE algorithm are provided in Section 3.1.

3. Extraction system

In this section, we describe the original PCE algorithm, and our extension for extracting ⟨*ne, category, related-to, object*⟩ quadruples.

4. PCE algorithm

The PCE algorithm is depicted in Figure 2, and the description is given in Figure 3. Starting with two seed *patterns*, PCE extracted ⟨*person, category*⟩ tuples. The extracted tuples were used to extract *occurrences* of ⟨*person, category*⟩ tuples in texts for generating new patterns. Again, new patterns were used to extract new tuples. The process terminated when no more patterns were produced. A pattern is defined as a 4-tuple:

(*order,   person_slot,   middle, category_pattern*),

where *order* (a Boolean value) indicates the occurrence order of *person* and

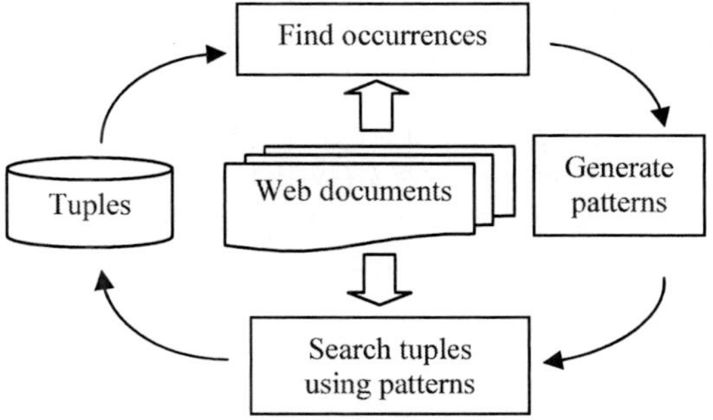

Figure 1: The DIPRE model.

category in a sentence; *person_slot* is a slot which will be replaced with a person named entity; *middle* is the string surrounded by *person* and *category*; *category_pattern* is defined as:

$$category\_pattern := noun\_phrase_1 \text{ (and } noun\_phrase_2)?^1$$

where *noun_phrase_i* is a regular expression that matches a noun phrase with added POS tags.

In order to extract new ⟨*person, category*⟩ tuples, for every sentence *s*, from a pattern (whose *order* is true), and for each person NE *named_entity* in *s*, we construct a regular expression:

  * *named_entity middle category_pattern* *

If *s* matches the above regular expression, the ⟨*person, category*⟩ tuple is extracted according to the algorithm in Figure 4, where *is_valid(category)* is a function that returns true if *category* is a sort of 'person', and false otherwise. The purpose of this function is to ignore unexpected matches, i.e., matches that give incorrect tuples. The *is_valid* function operates based on the fact that if a *person* is-a *category,* then the *category* must be a sort (or subtype) of person. Since a *category* is a sort of person is equivalent to the *category* is a *hyponym* of person (or person is a hypernym of the *category*), this constraint is checked by using WordNet (Fellbaum 1998) which contains hyponymic and hypernymic relations among concepts. When *order* is false, *named_entity* and *category_pattern* are switched. PCE can extract two tuples from a match, if there are two.

Occurrences: An occurrence of a ⟨*person, category*⟩ tuple is defined as a 4-tuple:

  (*order, person, middle, category*),

where *middle* is a string surrounded by *person* and *category*. An occurrence of a (*person, category*) tuple is extracted if a sentence *s* matches the regular expression:

  * *person middle category* *

or

  * *category middle person* *

After extracting occurrences from the text corpus, they are used to generate new patterns. However, a *middle* of an occurrence is not necessarily reliable, (Nguyen and Shimazu) proposed a method to retain reliable ones based on two criteria: *repetition* and *diversity* as follows:

Repetition of a *middle* (repetition(*middle*)) is the number of times the *middle* appears between the *person* and *category* of (*person, category*) tuples of same *person*.

Diversity of a *middle* (diversity(*middle*)) is the number of times the *middle* appears between the *person* and *category* of (*person, category*) tuples of different *persons*.

A *middle* that has repetition(*middle*)>threshold$_R$ seems reliable and is kept. A pattern seems specific if it is generated based on tuples of a *person*, so only *middles* that have diversity(*middle*)>threshold$_D$ are kept to make the generated patterns general (Condition 1).

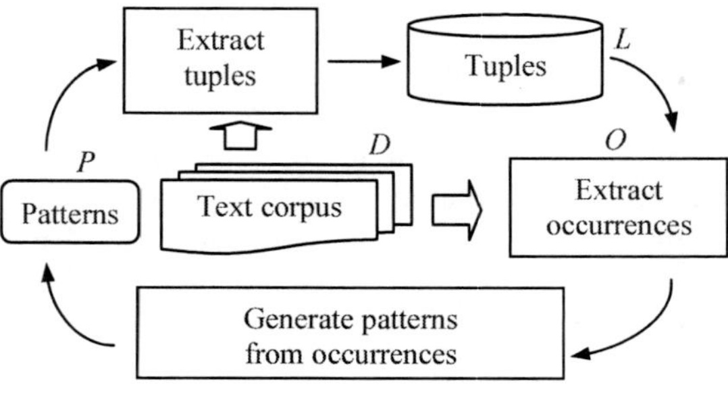

Figure 2: The PCE model.

---

[1] '?' stands for there is zero or one. Since PCE works on sentences which has been parsed by a shallow parser, each sentence contains POS and chunk tags. In this paper, we ignore POS and chunk tags in all regular expressions for readability.

If a *middle* contains a verb phrase, the verb phrase should express the relation *person* is-a *category* (Condition 2).

These two conditions are used in the pattern generation procedure as described in Figure 5. In the experiments, for the simplity, $threshold_R$ and $threshold_D$ are set to the same value which was called *threshold* for short.

Pattern types: Patterns whose *middles* are generated directly from the *middles* of occurrences are called *exact patterns*. Exact patterns are relately reliable, howerver, they have low coverage. In order to increase the coverage, (Nguyen and Shimazu 2007) introduced two more types of patterns, i.e., *sketch* and *extended sketch* patterns. An example of *middle* of an exact pattern with *order* true is:

$$\text{``] ,/, [NP ABC/NNP] [NP 's/POS ''} \tag{2}$$

The exact pattern with *middle* (2) can match the sentence:

$$\text{[NP Harvey/NNP Dzodin/NNP] ,/, [NP ABC/NNP] [NP 's/POS vice/NN president/NN] ...} \tag{3}$$

However, this pattern can not match a similar sentence that describes the "director" of another company, e.g., IBM, in the same syntax as (3):

```
Input: Text corpus D; Seed pattern set Ps
Output: The list L of quadruples
Preprocessing: Find NEs in every sentence by an NER;
     Remove sentences that contain no person NE.
     Add part-of-speech (POS) and chunk tags for every sentence by a
     shallow parser;
1. P← Ps;  L ← ∅;
2. Extract the list L' of quadruples from sentences that match a
   pattern in P; L ← L + L';
   Let D' be list of sentences from which quadruples in L' were
   extracted, D ← D - D';
   If D is empty then return;
3. Extract the list of occurrences O of quadruples in D;
4. Generate new patterns set P' from O;  P ← P';
   If P is empty then return; else go to Step 2;
```

Figure 3: PCE algorithm.

```
1. Generate categoryᵢ by removing all POS tags in noun_phraseᵢ.
2. If  is_valid(categoryᵢ), then
     Generate person ne by removing all POS tags in named_entity to
     form a ⟨person, categoryᵢ⟩ tuple;
     Return ⟨person, category⟩ tuples;
```

Figure 4: ⟨*person, category*⟩ extraction from a match.

```
1. Group all occurrences in the list O by order and middle;
   Let the resulting groups be O₁, O₂, ..., Oɴ;
2. For each group Oᵢ, if the middle satisfies the two conditions,
   then generate a new pattern:
      (order, person_slot, middle, category_pattern)
```

Figure 5: Pattern generation procedure.

[NP Alan/NNP Baratz/NNP] ,/, [NP IBM/NNP] [NP 's/POS director/NN] ...   (4)

If *middle* (2) is modified so that its pattern can match (4), then expected relations in both (3) and (4) can be extracted. In order to do this, (2) is converted into a *template* that can match other sequences having similar structure. Concretely, nouns, adjectives, cardinals and articles in a *middle* are replaced with a variable $*word* that matches a word. Below is the template constructed from the *middle* (2):

   "] ,/, [NP $*word*/NNP] [NP 's/POS "   (5)

This template was called the *sketch* of a *middle*. A new pattern type whose the *middle* is replaced with a *sketch* was called *sketch pattern*. Details about the extended sketch patterns and other information can be seen in (Nguyen and Shimazu 2007).

4.1. Named entity category object extraction

The purpose of PCE is to extract ⟨*person, category*⟩ tuples, in which *category* can be used as the fine-grained type of person, so the set of NE types can be expanded by automatically extracting from texts. When we extract the tuple ⟨"Bette Raptapoulos", 'analyst'⟩ from (1), we only have information: "Bette Raptapoulos" **is-a** 'analyst'. If we can extract the relation: 'analyst' **for** "Prudential-Bache Securities Inc.", we will have complete information about "Bette Raptapoulos". Since PCE can be used to extract tuples of other NE types, such as *organization* and *location*, we propose to extend the PCE to extract ⟨*ne, category, related-to, object*⟩ quadruples describing the relations: *ne* is-a *category*, and *category related-to object* (or related-to relations for short).

From our observations, the related-to relations can be expressed in the following ways:

a) The *category* and *object* are linked by a preposition: "*category preposition object*", e.g., "analyst **for** Prudential-Bache Securities Inc."

b) The *category* and *object* are connected by a possessive apostrophe: "*object's category*", e.g., "Semi-Tech**'s** chief executive officer". This can be interpreted as "*category* of *object*", e.g., "chief executive officer of Semi-Tech".

c) The *object* and *ne* are linked by a preposition: "*category ne preposition object*", e.g., "… said economist David Littmann of Manufacturers National Bank…", from which an expected quadruple is ⟨"David Littmann", 'economist', 'of', "Manufacturers National Bank"⟩.

d) The *object* is embedded in *category*, e.g., "IBM president". This can also be interpreted as "*category* of *object*", e.g., "president of IBM".

e) The related-to relation is implicitly expressed, e.g., "Mr. Baird, who heads the Manhattan U.S. attorney's securities-fraud unit, denied the quote …", from which an expected quadruple is ⟨'Baird', 'header', 'of', "securities-fraud unit"⟩.

Since case e) does not have fixed expressions, we do not treat such cases. In case d), because *object* is already embedded in *category*, we do not need to extract the *object*. For cases a), b) and c), we build regular expressions to extract the *object*. We modify the procedure in Figure 4 to extract ⟨*ne, category, related-to, object*⟩ quadruples instead of ⟨*ne, category*⟩ tuples. Let *category_str* be the string containing the *category*, the regular expressions corresponding to each case are (we omit POS and chunk tags for readability):

a) * *category_str preposition noun_phrase* *

b) * *noun*_phrase**'s** *category_str* *

c) * *named_entity preposition noun_phrase* *

After extracting a valid *category* and an *ne* (Step 2 of Figure 4), if the current processing sentence matches one of the above regular expressions, the *object* is produced by removing POS tags in *noun_phrase*; *related-to* is the *preposition* after removing POS tags in cases a) and c); *related-to* is 'of' in case b), then, ⟨ne, category, related-to, object⟩ quadruples are returned instead of tuples. If no regular expressions match the current processing sentence, the *object* and *related-to* are null.

We call our new algorithm NECOE which stands for "Named Entity Category Object Extraction".

5. Utilizing quadruples for semantic search

The extracted ⟨ne, category, related-to, object⟩ quadruples are valuable for NLP applications. In this section, we use them for answering some types of questions. If *ne* in a quadruple is a person, the quadruple helps answer the query: "Who is *ne*?". If *ne* is of another type, such as *organization* or *location*, the quadruple helps answer the query: "What is *ne*?" For answering the question, we just search for a quadruple having the same *ne* as that of the question. If a quadruple is found, then the answer is:

> *ne* is a *category related-to object*.

The extracted quadruples also help answer *list* questions, e.g., "Give me the list of analyst for Prudential-Bache Securities Inc." The general form of this question type is "Give me the list of *category* [*related-to object*]", where the part in square brackets is optional. For answering this question type, we search for the list L of quadruples having the same *category* (*related-to* and *object*) as those of the question. The answer is the list of *nes* of quadruples in L.

If *related-to* of a question is 'of', we also search for quadruples whose *object* is embedded in *category* (case (d) as discussed in Section 3.2). For example, if the question is "Give me the list of president of IBM", we also search for quadruples whose *category* is "IBM president".

6. Experiments and evaluation

Since person related questions takes a large portion among NE-related questions, as seen in Text Retrieval Conference (TREC) 9 question-answering track[2], our experiments concentrated on extracting person named-entity-related relations.

6.1. Dataset

We used the same corpus as that used in (Nguyen and Shimazu 2007), i.e., the Wall Street Journal (WSJ) corpus which consists of 595 files. After extracting the body part and removing other parts, e.g., the headers, a plain text collection of nearly 3 million sentences with the size of 308 MB was produced. From this text collection, a test set of 1,000 sentences was randomly selected. From the test set, 385 "*ne* is-a *category*" relations (called is-a relation for short) were manually extracted. Among 385 is-a relations, 199 relations had additional related-to relations. The distribution of related-to relations according to cases discussed in Section 3.2 is given in Table 1. In the preprocessing step of the algorithm in Figure 4, all NEs in this plain text collection were tagged by LingPipe[3]. After removing sentences that contain no person NE, a collection of 667,981 sentences was produced (we call this big-dataset). Next, OpenNLP[4] was used to add POS and chunk tags for the big-dataset.

---

[2] http://tangra.si.umich.edu/clair/NSIR/cgi-bin/trec-question.cgi?collection=9&script=html/nsir.cgi
[3] http://www.alias-i.com/lingpipe/index.html
[4] http://opennlp.sourceforge.net

Table 1: The distribution of related-to relations.

Case	a)	b)	c)	d)	e)
%	74.87	17.74	2.05	3.59	2.05

Table 2: Results of experiments.

Is-a relations					
Pattern	NECOE-NoValidation			NECOE		
	P(%)	R(%)	F(%)	P(%)	R(%)	F(%)
Seed	89.03	35.84	51.11	99.26	35.06	**51.82**
Exact	63.41	72.47	67.64	94.48	75.58	**83.98**
Sketch	62.88	74.81	68.33	94.50	80.26	**86.80**
Related-to relations					
	P(%)	R(%)	F(%)	P(%)	R(%)	F(%)
Seed	92.13	41.21	**56.94**	97.53	39.70	56.43
Exact	79.34	48.24	60.00	97.03	49.25	**63.97**
Sketch	76.64	52.76	62.50	96.64	57.64	**72.33**

6.2. Experiments and evaluation

Besides NECOE, we also extended the baseline program in (Nguyen and Shimazu 2007) to extract quadruples, and called this program NECOE-NoValidation, since it had no category validation function. We ran NECOE on the big-dataset to get patterns. These patterns are used to extract quadruples on the test set for evaluation. Since a *related-to* relation was extracted after an is-a relation was extracted, we evaluated the results of the two relations in quadruples separately.

PCE used a *threshold* in the pattern generation procedure, and the proper value of threshold selected from experiments was 3. In our experiments, we also set the value of this threshold to 3. The results of our experiments are shown in Table 2. Since extended sketch patterns did not increase the coverage much, we do not show their results.

Figure 6 shows the growth of the number of extracted quadruples and distinct categories from the big-dataset. The figure shows that the number of actual categories (40761) is relatively large.

Though sketch patterns help to extract only 5.5% of the total extracted quadruples, their discovered categories comprise 24% of total distinct categories.

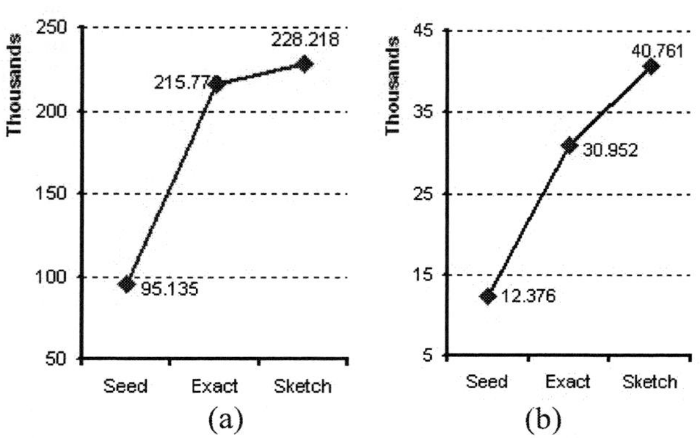

Figure 6: The growth of extracted quadruples (a) and distinct categories (b).

Top ranked	President (22679), Chairman (12835), Analyst (6729), Vice President (6011), Director (5821), Chief Executive Officer (5326), Judge (5050), Dr. (4931), Rep. (3479)
Bottom ranked	part-time CIA employee (1), partnership analyst (1), parliament deputy (1), parts marketing administrator (1), patent specialist (1), personal translator (1), freight carrier (1)
Related-to relation	managing director of investment bank, vice president for economic research, president of Trans World International Inc., deputy of Japanese equities, manager of sales

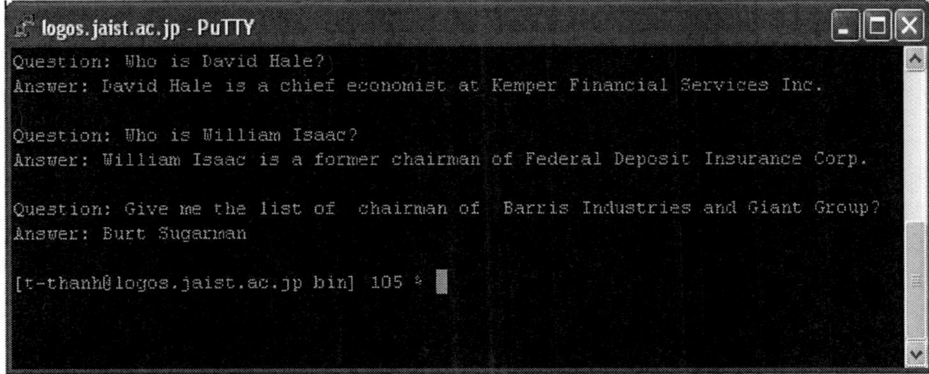

Figure 7: The prototype of a semantic search system.

Table 3 lists some top, bottom ranked categories along with their frequencies, as well as some related-to relations extracted by NECOE.

From our observations, the reason that decreases the precision of related-to relations is derived from the extraction of incorrect is-a relations. The precision of related-to relations is 100%, if it is calculated on correctly extracted is-a relations. Since the related-to relations has a relatively large portion in is-a relations that can not be extracted by PCE, this is the reason that decreases the recall of related-to relations.

Figure 7 introduces the prototype of a semantic search system that utilizes the relations in quadruples extracted from the WSJ corpus.

7. Conclusion

In this paper, we proposed a method for automatically extracting from text documents ⟨*ne*, *category*, *related-to*, *object*⟩ quadruples describing that "*ne* ISA *category*", and "*category* IS-RELATED-TO *object*". We extended PCE algorithm to extract these quadruples. Our experiments on the Wall Street Journal corpus obtained relatively good results.

We also utilize the extracted quadruples in a semantic search system for answering some types of questions.

Our algorithm can be applied to extract quadruples of other NE types, such as *organization* and *location*.

References

Agichtein, E. and L. Gravano, 2000. Snowball: Extracting Relations from Large Plaintext Collections. *Proceedings of the 5th ACM International Conference on Digital Libraries*, pp. 85-94.

Brin, S., 1998. Extracting Patterns and Relations from the World Wide Web. *Proceedings of the 6th International Conference on Extending Database Technology*, pp. 172-183.

Chieu, H. and N. Tou, 2003. Named Entity Recognition with a Maximum Entropy Approach, *Proceedings of Conference on Computational Natural Language Learning 2003 (CoNLL-2003)*, pp. 160-163.

Fellbaum, C., editor, 1998. WordNet: An Electronic Lexical Database and Some of Its Applications, *MIT Press*.

Nguyen, T. T. and A. Shimazu, 2007. Automatic Extraction of the Fine Category of Person Named Entities from Text Corpora. *IEICE Transactions on Information and Systems, Special section on Knowledge, Information and Creativity Support System*, Vol. E90-D, No. 10, 1542-1549.

Bracketing Input for Accurate Parsing [*]

Yongkyoon No[a]

Chungnam National University
220 Koong-dong, Yuseong-gu, Taejeon, Korea
yno@linguist.cnu.ac.kr

Abstract. Syntax parsers can benefit from speakers' intuition about constituent structures indicated in the input string in the form of parentheses. Focusing on languages like Korean, whose orthographic convention requires more than one word to be written without spaces, we describe an algorithm for passing the bracketing information across the tagger to the probabilistic CFG parser, together with one for heightening (or penalizing, as the case may be) probabilities of putative constituents as they are suggested by the parser. It is shown that two or three constituents marked in the input suffice to guide the parser to the correct parse as the most likely one, even with sentences that are considered long.

Keywords: manually parsed corpus, Probabilistic Context Free Grammar, Korean syntax, bottom-up chart parser, pre-annotated input, Paak, KWGInterpreter

1. Introduction

Syntactic parsers often produce parses many of whose parts are correct but which do contain partially inaccurate structures. To attain a high level of precision and recall, serious research has to be conducted and just about every kind of research in this field may well benefit from a moderate amount of manually parsed, i.e, correctly parsed, sentences.

When it comes to the Korean language, a widely available, yet dependable corpus of parsed sentences is something that has yet to be constructed. In this paper, we describe a move that will help build a parsed corpus of about one thousand sentences. Our idea here is to use an initial stage probabilitic CFG parser with a partially bracketed input. This work is inspired by Pereira and Schabes (1992), who use bracketed sentences to induce grammar rules automatically.

We will describe our initial stage parser, *Paak*, in Section 2. How the input string with some bracketings are processed in this parser is described in the next section. Section 4 gives algorithms for keeping track of the bracketing information and for affecting the probabilities of constituents, which conform to, are consistent with, or contradict the information annotated in the input. The performance gains at each degree of bracketing information are estimated in Section 5, where it is shown that no more than two pairs of bracketings suffice to yield the correct parse of a sentence of length twenty.

2. The probabilistic CFG parser *Paak*

Paak is a probabilistic parser of the Korean language with a set of context-free grammar rules. It relies on a tagger of Korean for its analysis of input string into the smallest units of syntactic

---

[*] I am grateful to one of the anonymous referees of the Program Committee of PACLIC 21, who gave me useful comments.

processing.[1] The tagger uses fifty three tags, many of which correspond to parts-of-speech. *Paak* has 45 preterminal symbols and 20 nonterminals. Currently it has just over three hundred PCFG rules.

The parser is a probabilistic parser implemented in Java. The implementation basically follows Charniak(1993: 1.4). It is a bottom up parser. Its grammar rules have been extracted from a very small hand-parsed corpus of twenty sentences.

3. Adding constituent structures to the input string

The parser takes an input file and gives an output file. Its input file normally consists of sentences of the language. What we suggest is add information about the input sentence's constituent structures so as to guide the parser to its correct parse.

The input string itself may have bracketings added to them. Adding bracketings to a string of words would be the easiest way of annotating their syntactic structure.

(1) a. 일상생활에 지장이 있는 정도는 아니라지만, 오른쪽 목과 어깨의 통증으로 고생이 심하다.
   b. (일상생활에 지장이 있는 정도는 아니라)지만, (오른쪽 목과 어깨의 통증)으로 고생이 심하다.
   c. (일상생활에 지장이 있는 정도는 아니라)지만, (오른쪽 (목과 어깨)의) 통증으로 고생이 심하다.
   d. ((((((일상생활)에) (지장이) 있는) 정도)는 아니라)지만), ((((오른쪽 ((목과 어깨))의) 통증)으로) ((고생이) 심하다).)

The first string above, (1a), has no information added. It is the kind of input string ordinary parsers would expect. (1b) has two constituents marked with pairs of parentheses. The next string has three constituents marked and the last, (1d) has all its nonlexical constituents marked. None of these strings mark their constituents with labels, however.

We are to allow our parser to process all of the input types given in (1). A special provision has to be made in order to distinguish the ordinary characters `(' and `)' from our metacharacters for marking the boundaries of constituents.

The parser ought to identify the metacharacters and their positions and then has to remove them before it passes them to the tagger. The parser will make use of the partial constituency information in calculating the input's constituents. If the constituent being built by the parser at a given point is one of the spans indicated by the bracketings, its probability is to be heightened. If the constituent being built is in conflict with a bracketing marked in the input, its probability is to be lowered. As the probability of a parse is the product of the probabilities of all its parts, making a constituent's probability higher or lower directly affects the probability the parse of the whole sentence ends up getting.

4. Algorithms

Getting the parser to make use of preannotated constituency involves two sorts of algorithms. The first is to identify the positions of the opening and closing brackets in such a way that they correspond to boundaries of the words to be fed to the parser. As the words to be fed to the

---

[1]   The lemmatizing POS tagger of the language is being serviced at `http://linguist.cnu.ac.kr:8080/servlets/KWGInterpreter`. Its properties are described in No(2007).

parser are only available after the tagger performs analysis on the input string, and as the bracketings need to be removed before the input string is submitted to the tagger, the task of assigning correct positions to the brackets is not trivial.

The second algorithm concerns affecting the probabilities of constituents built by the initial stage parser with the constituency information gathered by our first algorithm. We describe these in turn.

4.1 Mapping positions across the tagger

The Korean language has many clitics. Its orthographic convention allows much freedom in tokenizing its words. Sequences of words are required to be written without intervening spaces and some sequences are allowed to be written with or without intervening spaces. Thus, sentence (1a) would have eleven groups in ordinary writings, as their boundaries are indicated with integers in (2).

However, as many of these groups have more than one word in them, the result of tagging the sentence would be twenty three words. This situation is illustrated with integers indicating word boundaries in (3).

(2) 0 일상생활에 1 지장이 2 있는 3 정도는 4 아니라지만, 5 오른쪽 6 목과 7 어깨의 8 통증으로 9 고생이 10 심하다. 11

(3) [0] 일상 [1] 생활 [2] 에 [3] 지장 [4] 이 [5] 있는 [6] 정도 [7] 는 [8] 아니라 [9] 지만 [10] , [11] 오른 [12] 쪽 [13] 목 [14] 과 [15] 어깨 [16] 의 [17] 통증 [18] 으로 [19] 고생 [20] 이 [21] 심하다 [22] . [23]

The task for the parentheses identifier, let us call it **g2w**, is to map 0 to [0], 1 to [3], 2 to [5], and so on, given the tokenization in (2). This is straightforward when parentheses appear only at group boundaries: the tagger analyzes each group of words into words, the number of which is easy to count. The parenthesis at position p of the input string marks position $[\sum_{i=0}^{p-1}$ number-of-words in $g_i]$ of the output of the tagger (or, of the input to the parsing component).

However, many syntactic boundaries may well fall within a group. The group *ilsangsaynghwaley*(일상생활에) has a constituent boundary before the postposition *ey*(에), *cengtonun*(정도는) has one between the noun *cengto*(정도) and the delimiter *nun*(는), the group *anilaciman*(아니라지만) contains two verbs, the second verb taking a clause as its complement; only the noun in the noun-postposition group *ekkayuy*(어깨의) is a part of the conjunction *mokkwa ekkay*(목과 어깨), and hence, the group has a boundary before the postposition; similarly for *thoncungulo*(통증으로).

Group-internal parentheses present a difficulty in specifying **g2w**: the portion flanked by two boundaries (i.e., parentheses or a space) may turn out to be any number of word tokens. We avoid this difficulty by imposing the following constraint on the user:

Constraint
Group-internal parentheses are assumed to be dense. An internal parenthesis is interpreted as separating the n-th word from $(n + 1)$-th, only when there are $n - 1$ preceding group-internal parentheses.

Put in other words, the first parenthesis after the beginning of a group is taken to be marking the boundary between the first word of the group and the following words. The second parenthesis is taken to be marking the boundary between the second word of the group and the following words, and so on.

While group-internal boundaries may mark the end of a phrase, it does not seem to be the case that there are group-internal boundaries that mark the beginning of a phrase. The orthographic conventions of the language are such that all beginnings of phrases fall at a group boundary.[2]

This finding makes it easier to specify the boundaries-mapping function **g2w**.

> 1. Initialize a string, **trimmedGroup**, a stack, **aStack** and a list, **aList**.
> 2. Split the input string (possibly with brackets) into an array of   strings, using the space character as the pivot.
> 3. For each string in the array, count the number of closing parentheses in   it and split it into a second-order array, this   time using the regular expression [)]*, as the pivot.
> 4. For each position i in the first-order array, for each position j in the second-order array do:
>   (i) for each opening parenthesis in array[i][j] create a span (i, j, -1, -1) and push it onto **aStack**.
>   (ii) for each closing parenthesis in array[i][j] pop a span from the stack. Set the span's third and fourth arguments to be i and j, respectively. Store the resulting span in **aList**.
>   (iii) strip all opening parentheses off of array[i][j] and concatenate it with **trimmedGroup**.
> 5. Add **trimmedGroup** to the array of strings to be submitted to the tagger.

When the loop above has iterated through the input, **aList** ends up with as many spans as there are pairs of brackets in the input. The annotation-free input string, built by concatenations of **trimmedGroup**, is passed to the tagger, which outputs word tokens of the following form:

(4) (MassNoun 일상 daily_life) (ProcessNoun 생활 NA) (PO 에 GR) (MassNoun 지장 interference) (PN 이 GR) (vrel 있 exist) (VAdjunctNoun 정도 extent) (Delimiter 는 GR) (viq 아니 be_not) (vadv EMPTYSTEM say) (COMMA , comma) …

The tagger organizes word tokens into groups, as is dictated by the original input's groupings of words. Thus, how many words there are in each group can be kept in an array. Call it **convert**. The integer in **convert**[k] indicates that the (k + 1)-th group of the original input has this many words in it.

With the help of **convert**, the first and third terms of each span in **aList** are now updated. Each span, <start, startoffset, end, endoffset> is replaced with a new span, <convert[start], startoffset, convert[end], endoffset>.

4.2 Making the probabilities of constituents sensitive to bracketings

A bottom-up probabilistic parser calculates the probability of each constituent based on its subconstituents' probabilities. It simply multiplies over all its subconstituents' probabilities. We modify this part of the parser's behavior in such a way that it multiplies the resulting probability with a huge number in case the constituent to be formed matches one of the spans in the list of the designated spans.[3] A constituent matches a span iff its start position is the same as the latter's (start + startoffset) and its end position is the same as the latter's (end + endoffset).

A spurious constituent can be penalized by a further move of dividing, rather than multiplying, its probability with a huge number. Spurious constituents are a proper subset of constituents that

---

[2] The only exception seems to be the ones involving opening quotation marks.

[3] The probability of the putative constituent would be between 0 and 1. If this constituent is among the constituents marked in the input, its probability is to be multiplied by 1000000. It might suffice to give such a constituent the probability of 1.0.

fail to match a span in the list. As the annotations in the input string are partial, there could be constituents that do not match any of the spans but are indeed licit.

The constituents to be penalized are then those which conflict with a span in the list. A constituent c conflicts with a span s if either (i) c starts before s and ends in the middle of s or (ii) c starts in the middle of s and ends after s.[4]

These are cases of crossing brackets used as a measure of parser correctness. See Carroll, Briscoe and Sanfilippo (1998) and Jurafsky and Martin (2000: 464).

5. Gains of annotated input

We tested the modified parser with six sentences of various lengths and differing levels of annotation. The sentences are:

[A] kimkunthaynun cikumto komunhwuyucungul alhnunta.
　　김근태는 지금도 고문후유증을 앓는다.
[B] kunun kokaylul cayensulepkey tollici moshanta.
　　그는 고개를 자연스럽게 돌리지 못한다.
[C] hanchamul tallita poni eyncini simhakey ttellinta.
　　한참을 달리다 보니 엔진이 심하게 떨린다.
[D] kulena hakkyochukun uyhokul cosahaci anhko sinssilul cokyoswulo thukchayhayssta.
　　그러나 학교측은 의혹을 조사하지 않고 신씨를 조교수로 특채했다.
[E] hakkyochukun ohilye 3 kaywel twi yellin 228 cha isahoyeyse cangyunsunimul isacikeyse
　　학교측은 오히려 3 개월 뒤 열린 228 차 이사회에서 장윤스님을 이사직에서
　　hayimhayssta.
　　해임했다.
[F] ilsansaynghwaley cicangi issnun cengtonun anilaciman, olunccok mokkwa ekkayuy
　　일상생활에 지장이 있는 정도는 아니라지만, 오른쪽 목과 어깨의
　　thongcungulo kosayngi simhata.
　　통증으로 고생이 심하다.

Table 1, in the following page, gives the result.

It can be seen from the table that two pairs of bracketings are enough to guide the parser to the unique correct parse, in most of the cases. The only sentence the parser fails to give the correct parse as its most likely parse is Sentence F in Table 1, which is our example (1). Marking two of its constituents in its input, as in (\ref{neckshoulder}b), produces a wrong parse. See (6) below. Marking three, as in (1c), is enough. The most likely parse turns out to be the correct one, important part of which is shown in (7). In both parses, the sentential adjunct *ilsangsaynghwaley cicangi issnun cengtonun anilaciman*(일상생활에 지장이 있는 정도는 아니라지만) is assigned the same structure, which is judged correct. We present only the main clause portions, namely the subtree rooted by the lower **rootclause** node in (5).

Table 1. Number of total parses and rank of the correct parse

---

[4] As a span has offsets stored in it in addition to its start and end positions, c conflicts with s in either of the following cases:

(i)　　c.start $<$ s.start $+$ s.startoffset $\wedge$ s.start $+$ s.startoffset $<$ c.end$\wedge$ c.end $<$ s.end $+$ s.endoffset

(ii)　　c.start $>$ s.start $+$ s.startoffset $\wedge$ s.end $+$ s.endoffset $>$ c.start $\wedge$ c.end $>$ s.end $+$ s.endoffset

(b=*k* stands for the number of bracket pairs in the input; * indicates either no parse produced or no attempt to parse made)

sentence	# of groups	# of words	Total parses			Rank of correct parse		
			b=0	b=1	b=2	b=0	b=1	b=2
A	4	8	2	*	*	1	*	*
B	5	10	34	220	172	8	10	1
C	6	9	22	13	*	7	1	*
D	8	17	*	20	*	*	1	*
E	11	21	*	38	*	*	1	*
F	11	23	*	*	1020	*	*	3

(5)

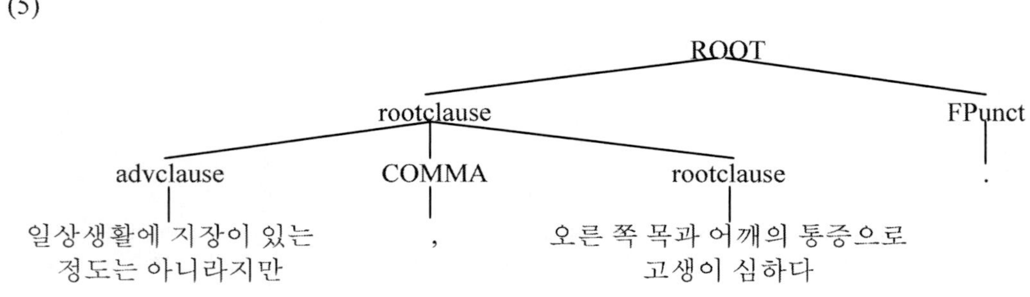

(6)

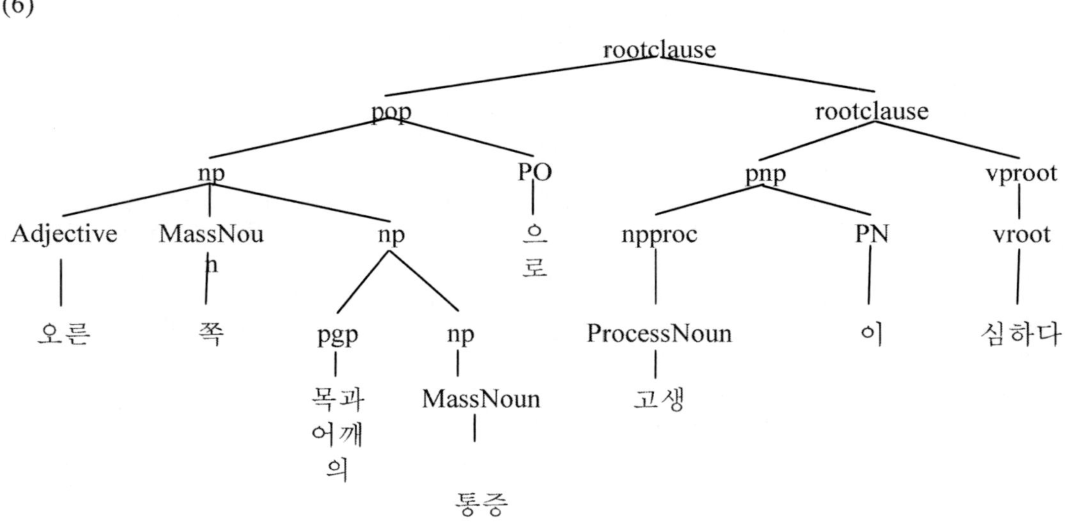

(7)

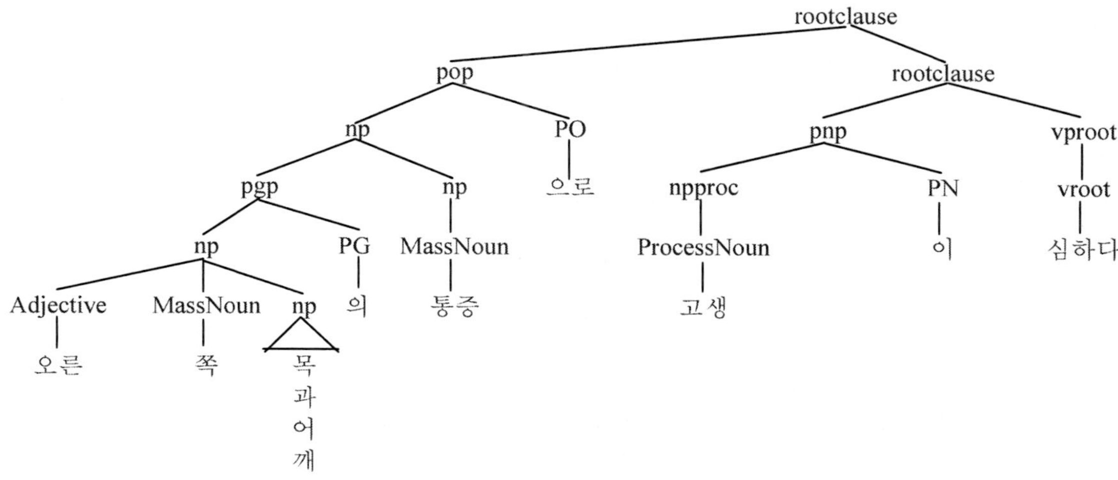

6. Conclusion

We have shown that accurate parses of the kind one would like to have in a manually parsed corpus can be obtained with bracketings added to the input string. The somewhat involved work of keeping track of bracketings in a language like Korean whose orthographic convention requires a sequence of words written in a single group, has been carried out. The number of constituents to be annotated in this fashion has proven small, which is good news to developers of parsed corpora. A parser, such as *Paak*, with this functionality certainly facilitates development of moderate-sized corpora, which in turn will be used to get better probabilities of its CFG rules.

References

Carroll, John, Ted Briscoe, and Antonio Sanfilippo. 1998. Parser Evaluation: A Survey and a New proposal. In *Proceedings, First International Conference on Language Resources and Evaluation*, pp. 447--54. European Language Resources Association.

Charniak, Eugene. 1993. *Statistical Language Learning*. The MIT Press.

Jurafsky, Daniel and James~H. Martin. 2000. *Speech and Language Processing: An Introduction to Natural Language Processing, Computational Linguistics, and Speech Recognition*. Prentice-Hall, Inc.

No, Yongkyoon. 2007. KWGInterpreter: a lemmatizing POS tagger for the Korean language. *Proceedings of the 2007 Joint Conference of LAK, MLSK, and KSLI*, pp. 86--94. Linguistic Association of Korea.

Pereira, Fernando and Yves Schabes. 1992. Inside-outside Reestimation from Partially Bracketed corpora. In *27th Annual Meeting of the Association for Computational Linguistics*, . 128--135. ACL.

Case, Coordination, and Information Structure in Japanese [*]

Akira Ohtani[ab] and Mark Steedman[a]

[a] School of Informatics, University of Edinburgh,
2 Buccleuch Place, Edinburgh, EH8 9LW, Scotland, United Kingdom
[b] Faculty of Informatics, Osaka Gakuin University,
2-36-1 Kishibe-minami, Suita, Osaka 564-8511, Japan
{aotani, steedman}@inf.ed.ac.uk

Abstract. This paper investigates the nature of Japanese argument cluster (Steedman 2000b). Based on Combinatory Categorial Grammar, a type-raising analysis of case particles which captures some aspects of the information structure in Japanese is discussed, including contrastive interpretation of coordination, *wh*-constructions, and some theme and rheme-related grammatical phenomena. These observations offer further support for the study of syntax, semantics, and phonology interface and the earlier analysis of English information structure.

Keywords: argument cluster, Japanese case particles, information structure, Combinatory Categorial Grammar (CCG), coordination, *wh*-constructions, multiple-*ga*, theme, rheme

1. Introduction

Steedman (2000b: p.172) accounts for a number of facts about "non-constituent" coordination in Japanese by allowing type-raised subject and object *NPs* in Japanese to combine not only by forward application to the verb (>), as in (1b) below, but also by forward-composition (>**B**), as in (1c) below, under the framework of Combinatory Categorial Grammar:

(1)   a. Ken-ga   Naomi-wo   tazune-ta.
           Ken-NOM   Naomi-ACC   visit-PAST

            'Ken visited Naomi.'   (Steedman 2000b: p.172, (3a))

b.
$$\frac{\overline{\text{Ken} - \text{ga}}^{>T} \quad \overline{\text{Naomi} - \text{wo}}^{>T} \quad \overline{\text{tazune} - \text{ta}}}{\underline{S/(S\backslash NP_{nom})} \quad \underline{(S\backslash NP_{nom})/((S\backslash NP_{nom})\backslash NP_{acc})} \quad \underline{(S\backslash NP_{nom})\backslash NP_{acc}}}$$
$$\frac{}{S\backslash NP_{nom}}{}^{>}$$
$$\frac{}{S}{}^{>}$$

c.
$$\frac{\overline{\text{Ken} - \text{ga}}^{>T} \quad \overline{\text{Naomi} - \text{wo}}^{>T} \quad \overline{\text{tazune} - \text{ta}}}{\underline{S/(S\backslash NP_{nom})} \quad \underline{(S\backslash NP_{nom})/((S\backslash NP_{nom})\backslash NP_{acc})} \quad \underline{(S\backslash NP_{nom})\backslash NP_{acc}}}$$
$$\frac{}{S/((S\backslash NP_{nom})\backslash NP_{acc})}{}^{>B}$$
$$\frac{}{S}{}^{>}$$

                                       (Steedman 2000b: p.172, (3b))

[*] We are indebted to Takeo Kurafuji and an anonymous PACLIC21 reviewer for their invaluable comments on an earlier version of this paper. Our thanks also go to Yoshiyasu Shiraii, the president of Osaka Gakuin University. All remaining inadequacies are our own.

The derivation in (1b) is isomorphic to a standard phrase structure analysis, as in (2a) below. However, the derivation in (1c) allows the *NPs* to compose *non-standard* constituent cluster, as shown in (2b):

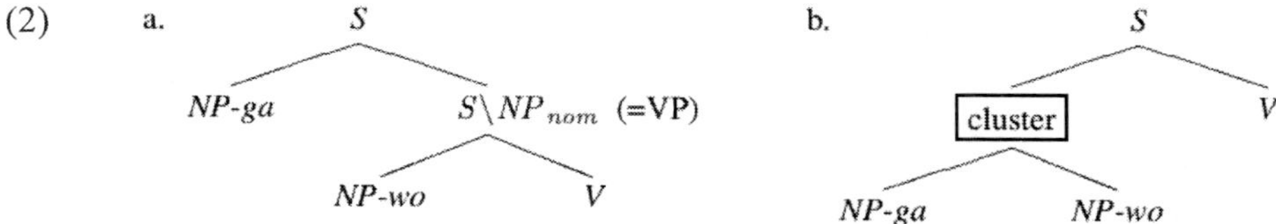

In this paper, we discuss the nature of non-standard constituent cluster in Japanese. Based on Combinatory Categorial Grammar (CCG) (Steedman 1996, 2000b, Steedman and Baldridge 2007), we propose a type-raising analysis of case particles which captures some aspects of the information structure in Japanese/Korean.[1] This account of the information structure of argument clusters offers further support for the earlier analysis of English information structure.

2. A CCG Analysis of Gapping

2.1. Gapping Revisited

One motivation for the non-standard structure in (2b) is the tendency of argument clusters to act like constituents under coordination, and the relation of this phenomenon to the base order of constituents across SOV, VSO and SVO language and/or construction (Ross 1970). Ross's generalization follows as a theorem from the axioms of CCG, as illustrated by Japanese gapping construction like (3a) and the possibility of the non-standard constituent illustrated in (1c) as its part, as in derivation (3b):

(3)   a. [Ken-ga   Naomi-wo] [Erika-ga   Sara-wo] tazune-ta.
             Ken-NOM Naomi-ACC Erika-NOM Sara-ACC visit-PAST

            'Ken visited Naomi, and Erika, Sara.'   (Steedman 2000b: p.172, (4))

b. Ken — ga Naomi — wo Erika — ga Sara — wo   tazune — ta

$$\frac{\overline{S/((S\backslash NP_{nom})\backslash NP_{acc})}^{>\mathbf{B}} \quad \overline{S/((S\backslash NP_{nom})\backslash NP_{acc})}^{>\mathbf{B}} \quad \overline{(S\backslash NP_{nom})\backslash NP_{acc}}}{\dfrac{\overline{S/((S\backslash NP_{nom})\backslash NP_{acc})}^{\phantom{<\Phi>}}}{S}}$$

                                                        (Steedman 2000b: p.172, (4))

The possibility of semantically surface-compositional syntactic derivations like this is one of the main theoretical attractions of CCG. The availability of two different derivations in (1b) and (1c) for sentences like (1a) allows us to consider the possibility that they are semantically and pragmatically distinct in some way.

There are some specific properties of gapping that are interesting in this respect. See below:

(4)   KEN visited NAOMI, and ERIKA <u>visited</u> SARA..   (Capitals for stress in English)

In English, the second occurrence of the verb *visited* in (4) can be gapped. The arguments left in the gapped conjunct are in a contrastive relation to the correspondents in the full conjunct.[2]

Note that the same intuition is hold for Japanese gapping sentence in (3a), repeated as (5):

---

[1] Steedman (2000b) deals exclusively with Japanese data. We also use Japanese data mainly by assuming that Japanese and Korean pattern together in grammatical phenomena discussed in this paper.
[2] This is reflected in the intonation aspect of gapping, which requires that both remnants and the correspondents they are contrasted with carry pitch-accents (Sag 1976).

(5)   KEN-ga   NAOMI-wo   <u>tazune</u>, (soshite) ERIKA-ga   SARA-wo   tazune-ta.
       Ken-NOM Naomi-ACC visit   and   Erika-NOM Sara-ACC visit-PAST
       'Ken visited Naomi, and Erika visited Sara.'   (Capitals for accent in Japanese)

Apart from the direction of gapping, two pairs of subject and object *NPs* in (5) are mutually in a contrastive relation.

The involvement of contrast in the argument clusters in (5) suggests a deeper link between such clusters and the concept of information structure. In particular, it is natural to assume that derivation (1c), rather than (1b), applies in the case where the *NPs* are an information unit such as the "theme" or "rheme" in the sense of Steedman (2000a, 2000b). We will return to this question in section 3.

2.2. Clustering with Case Particles

Before going into further discussion of information structure, we will review the combinatory mechanism of argument cluster formation.

The full derivation of (1c) using the case-particle categories in (7) is as follows:

$$
(6) \quad
\begin{array}{c}
\underline{
\begin{array}{cc}
\underline{\text{Ken}} & \underline{-\text{ga}} \\
N & (S/(S\backslash NP_{nom}))\backslash N
\end{array}
\quad
\begin{array}{cc}
\underline{\text{Naomi}} & \underline{-\text{wo}} \\
N & ((S\backslash NP_{nom})/((S\backslash NP_{nom})\backslash NP_{acc}))\backslash N
\end{array}
\quad
\underline{
\begin{array}{c}
\text{tazune} - \text{ta} \\
(S\backslash NP_{nom})\backslash NP_{acc}
\end{array}}
}
\end{array}
$$

(6) Ken $-ga$: N, $(S/(S\backslash NP_{nom}))\backslash N$ → $S/(S\backslash NP_{nom})$ (<)
Naomi $-wo$: N, $((S\backslash NP_{nom})/((S\backslash NP_{nom})\backslash NP_{acc}))\backslash N$ → $(S\backslash NP_{nom})/((S\backslash NP_{nom})\backslash NP_{acc})$ (<)
tazune $-ta$: $(S\backslash NP_{nom})\backslash NP_{acc}$
→ $S/((S\backslash NP_{nom})\backslash NP_{acc})$ (>B)
→ S (>)

(7)   a. -ga := $(S\backslash\$/(S\backslash\$NP_{nom}))\backslash N$
       b. -wo := $(S\backslash\$/(S\backslash\$NP_{acc}))\backslash N$

The categories in (7) are schematized using the "$-convention" (Steedman 2000b: p.42, (32)). For example, the category $S\backslash\$NP_{nom}$ denotes the set of leftward-looking function categories whose domain is $\$NP_{nom}$ and whose range is a set $S\backslash\$$ defined as the recursive transitive closure over S and all leftward functions onto $S\backslash\$$.

Thus, *-ga* has the following lexical categories:

(8)   -ga := $\{(S/(S\backslash NP_{nom}))\backslash N, ((S\backslash NP_{acc})/((S\backslash NP_{acc})/NP_{nom}))\backslash N, \dots\}$

(The first category applies to standard SV intransitive and SOV transitive verbs. The second category is that of the nominative first argument of an OSV verb.)

The categories in (7) allow case-marked *NPs* to compose to form clusters in many orders. Thus we have the following examples:[3]

(9)   a. KEN-ga   NAOMI-ni   (soshite), ERIKA-ga   SARA-ni   Anna-wo   syoukai-shi-ta.
           Ken-NOM Naomi-DAT and   Erika-NOM Sara-DAT Anna-ACC introduction-do-PAST
           'Ken introduced Anna to Naomi, and Erika introduced Anna to Sara.'

       b. ??KEN-ga Anna-wo NAOMI-ni (soshite), ERIKA-ga Anna-wo SARA-ni syoukai-shi-ta.

(10)   a. ??KEN-ga Anna-ni NAOMI-wo (soshite), ERIKA-ga Anna-ni SARA-wo syoukai-shi-ta.
           'Ken introduced Naomi to Anna, and Erika introduced Sara to Anna.'

       b. KEN-ga NAOMI-wo (soshite), ERIKA-ga SARA-wo Anna-ni syoukai-shi-ta.

---

[3] In (11), to avoid entering into the "focus" or "rheme" relation, we mark the subject with *wa*, which is interpreted as "topic" or "theme" in the sense of Bolinger (1965) and Steedman (2000a, 2000b).

(11) a. Anna-wa KEN-ni NAOMI-wo (soshite), ERIKA-ni SARA-wo syoukai-shi-ta.
          'Anna introduced Naomi to Ken, Sara to Erika.'

      b. Anna-wa NAOMI-wo KEN-ni (soshite), SARA-wo ERIKA-ni syoukai-shi-ta.

(12) ANNA-ga KEN-ni NAOMI-wo (soshite), JOE-ga ERIKA-ni SARA-wo syoukai-shi-ta.
      'Anna introduced Naomi to Ken and Joe introduced Sara to Erika.'

The arguments of ditransitive verb *syoukai-suru* 'introduce' can be treated in essentially the same way, the only difference being that the arguments are in a contrastive focus relation between a subject and on indirect object *NP* in (9), a subject and on direct object *NP* in (10), an indirect and a direct object *NP* in (11), and among three *NPs* in (12). We can also give the derivation of cluster, for example, (11a) and (12) are derived as the following (13a) and (13b), respectively.

(13) a.

$$
\frac{
\frac{\text{Anna — wa}}{S/(S\backslash NP_x)} \quad
\frac{\text{Ken — ni} \qquad \text{Naomi — wo}}{(S\backslash NP_{nom})/(((S\backslash NP_{nom})\backslash NP_{acc})\backslash NP_{dat})} {}^{>\mathbf{B}} \quad
\frac{\text{Erika — ni} \qquad \text{Sara — wo}}{(S\backslash NP_{nom})/(((S\backslash NP_{nom})\backslash NP_{acc})\backslash NP_{dat})} {}^{>\mathbf{B}} \quad
\frac{\text{syoukai — shi — ta}}{((S\backslash NP_{nom})\backslash NP_{acc})\backslash NP_{dat}}
}{
\dfrac{\dfrac{(S\backslash NP_{nom})/(((S\backslash NP_{nom})\backslash NP_{acc})\backslash NP_{dat})}{S\backslash NP_{nom}} {}^{>}}{S} {}^{>}
}{}^{<\Phi>}
$$

      b.

$$
\frac{
\frac{\text{Anna — ga Ken — ni Naomi — wo}}{S/((S\backslash NP_{nom})\backslash NP_{acc})\backslash NP_{dat}} {}^{>\mathbf{B}} \quad
\frac{\text{Joe — ga Erika — ni Sara — wo}}{S/((S\backslash NP_{nom})\backslash NP_{acc})\backslash NP_{dat}} {}^{>\mathbf{B}} \quad
\frac{\text{syoukai — shi — ta}}{((S\backslash NP_{nom})\backslash NP_{acc})\backslash NP_{dat}}
}{
\dfrac{S/((S\backslash NP_{nom})\backslash NP_{acc})\backslash NP_{dat}}{S} {}^{>}
}{}^{<\Phi>}
$$

The awkwardness of sentences (9b) and (10a) remains unexplained. We assume that this is an information-based "heaviness" effect. These sentences induce the whole of arguments contrast reading as (12), supporting our claim that the cluster can be composed with a serial *NPs* type-raises by case particles.

This claim is supported by parallel heaviness-sensitive constraints on the remnants of gapping and right node raising in English (cf. Abbott (1976)):

(14) a. #ANNA introduced NAOMI to KEN, and JOE, SARA to ERIKA.

      b. ANNA introduced her MOTHER to KEN, and JOE, his FATHER to SARA.

(15) a. #KEN gave NAOMI an APPLE, and ERIKA, SARA a FLOWER.

      b. KEN gave a TEACHER an APPLE, and ERIKA, a POLICEMAN a FLOWER.

We leave the question of the precise semantic and/or pragmatic origin of such "heaviness" effects for further research.

The next section links the syntactic argument cluster with the concept of information structure.

3. *Wh*-constructions

3.1. *Wh*-question

Utterance meaning consists of information structure and propositional content. Information structure characterizes the relation of components of propositional content to the context of utterance (Halliday 1967, Hajičová, Skoumalová and Sgall 1995), notably with respect to what already is common ground (Clark 1996), and what the utterance itself causes to become common ground (Steedman 2007) content of utterance. Much work has been done on the determination of information structure: here we only mention the test using question-answer pairs to identify the "rheme", as the answer to a *wh*-question. Thus, to the question in (16a) below, we can obtain the answer (16b) in which only *nezumi* 'mouse' is rhematic, either in the context of a discussion of a small set of animals, e.g. in discussing a pet shop, as in (17), or by (in the sense of Lewis (1979) and much subsequent literature) "accommodating" such a set..

(16) a. Dono doubutsu-ga youzinbukai-desu-ka?
    which animal-NOM cautious-COP -Q

    'Which animal is cautious?'

  b. Nezumi-ga youzinbukai-desu.
    mouse-NOM cautious-COP

    'It is a mouse that is cautious.'

(17) pet shop: {bird, gold fish, mouse, dog}

We can also obtain the following answer in (18) to the same question (16a), when a larger set of animals is either available, as in (19), or accommodated:

(18) Nezumi(-to) hitsuji-ga youzinbukai-desu.
  mouse-and sheep-NOM cautious-COP

  'It is a mouse and a sheep that are cautious.'

(19) zoo: {lion, tiger, bear, mouse, sheep, … }

The derivation without forward composition is as follows:[4]

$$(20)\quad \frac{\dfrac{\overline{N:mouse(x)}^{\text{nezumi}} \quad \overline{CONJ}^{\text{to}} \quad \overline{N:sheep(x)}^{\text{hitsuji}}}{N:mouse_{conj}\,sheep(x)}_{<\Phi>} \quad \overline{(S/(S\backslash NP))\backslash N:\lambda Q\lambda P\exists x[Q(x)\ \&\ P(x)]}^{\text{ga}} \quad \overline{S\backslash NP:cautious(x)}^{\text{youjinbukai desu}}}{\dfrac{S/(S\backslash NP):\lambda P\exists x[mouse_{conj}\,sheep(x)\ \&\ P(x)])}{S:\exists x[mouse_{conj}\,sheep(x)\ \&\ cautious(x)]}}$$

Japanese nouns have no distinction on number morphology, and singular and plural are expressed with the same form. Thus, *dono doubutsu* 'which animal(s)' in the question in (16a) is ambiguous and it is not clear whether it requires a unique individual or a plurality of individuals. The answers in (16b) and (18) giving an exhaustive listing reading are often distinguished as "restrictive focus", presupposing a set specified in discourse of which the constituent is a member (Erteschik-Shir 1997).

 In contrast, the present theory follows Steedman (2000a, 2000b) in assuming that restrictive and nonrestrictive rhemes are semantically and grammatically indistinguishable, and only differ in the nature of the context in which they are uttered. We draw the following distinctions:

(21) a. A theme is a part of the meaning of an utterance that the speaker claims some participant in the conversation supposes (or fails to suppose) **already** to be common ground;

  b. A rheme is a part of the meaning of an utterance that the speaker claims some participant in the conversation **makes** (or fails to make) common ground.

Thus, the theme is a predication over the existing context or common ground, and the rheme seeks to effect an update on the context or common ground.

3.2. Multiple *Wh*-question

In section 2.1, we adopted Steedman's claim that Japanese gapping sentence (3a), repeated in (22) below, is argument cluster coordination (Steedman 2000b: p.172), and claimed on the basis

---

[4] The semantics of *to* 'and', *conj*, is tentative.

of an analogy with gapping in English that the coordinated clusters admit a contrastive interpretation:

(22) [KEN-ga   NAOMI-wo] [ERIKA-ga   SARA-wo] tazune-mashi-ta.
      Ken-NOM Naomi-ACC Erika-NOM Sara-ACC visit-POLITE -PAST
      'Ken visited Naomi, and Erika, Sara.'   (Steedman 2000b: p.172, (4), slightly modified)

In support of this analysis, consider the multiple *wh*-question (23), with the common ground in (24) and the corresponding list-pair answer (22).

(23) Dono gakusei-ga dono sensei-wo   tazune-mashi-ta-ka?
      which who-NOM which teacher-ACC visit-POLITE -PAST -Q
      'Which student visited which teacher?'

(24) students: {Ken, Erika}   teachers: {Naomi, Sara}

(22) can be the answer to the *wh*-question, and hence the relevant part of the sentence is considered to admit rheme interpretation from the view point of information structure.

Steedman and Baldridge (2007) point out that the following alternatives to (22) are also possible:

(25) a. [Naomi-wo Ken-ga,] [Sara-wo Erika-ga]   tazune-ta.
         Naomi-ACC Ken-NOM Sara-ACC Erika-NOM visit-POLITE -PAST
         'Ken visited Naomi, and Erika, Sara.'
      b. ?[Naomi-wo Ken-ga,] [Erika-ga Sara-wo] tazune-ta.
              (Steedman & Baldridge 2007: p.34, (94) and (95), gloss and derivation are omitted.)

Sentence (25) is most natrual as an answer to the following order-variant multiple *wh*-question:

(26) Dono sensei-wo   dono gakusei-ga tazune-mashi-ta-ka?
      which teacher-ACC which who-NOM visit-POLITE -PAST -Q
      'Which student visited which teacher?'

(23) and (26) differ only in the order of *wh*-words. Most speakers consider (25a) a natural answer to (26), whereas (25b) sounds awkward as an answer for both (23) and (26). Moreover, (25a), in turn sounds awkward for the question in (23).

The clusters in (25b) have different types as follows, according to the present theory:

(27) a. *Naomi-wo Ken-ga* $:= S/((S\backslash NP_{acc})\backslash NP_{nom})$
      b. *Erika-ga Sara-wo* $:= S/((S\backslash NP_{nom})\backslash NP_{acc})$

It follows that they cannot under the present theory conjoin at all. We conjecture that the marginal acceptability of (25b) depends on some process distinct from simple constituent coordination, perhaps the same process as that involved in English medial verb-gapping. The nature of that process remains a topic for further research.

With regard to marked and unmarked answers of multiple *wh*-questions, Kuno (1982: p.141, (9)) argues that the fronted *wh*-word represents the key for sorting relevant pieces of information in the answer. While not going into an in-depth survey of his analysis, we suggest that it is the differing *types* of the *wh*-questions in (23) and (26) and of the clusters in their respective expected answers in (22) and (25a) that determine their implications for (sorting), and that the reason why (25b) sounds awkward is that it is consistent with *no* sorting key of the kind that Kuno postulates.

3.3. Clefting

The bracketed clusters in the following several instances of cleft sentences in (29) from (28) are rhemes, while the *-no-wa*-marked constituents are themes:

(28)   Anna-ga   Ken-ni   Naomi-wo   syoukai-shi-ta.
        Anna-NOM Ken-DAT Naomi-ACC   introduction-do-PAST

        'Anna introduced Naomi to Ken.'

(29)   a. Anna-ga   syoukai-shi-ta   no-wa   [Ken-ni   Naomi-wo] da.
            Anna-NOM   introduction-do-PAST NM-TOP Ken-DAT Naomi-ACC COP

            'It is Naomi to Ken that Anna introduced.'

        b. Ken-ni syoukai-shi-ta no-wa [Anna-ga Naomi-wo] da.
            'It is Anna Naomi that introduced to Ken.'

        c. Naomi-wo syoukai-shi-ta no-wa [Anna-ga Ken-ni] da.
            'It is Anna to Ken that introduced Naomi.'

        d. Syoukai-shi-ta no-wa [Anna-ga Ken-ni Naomi-wo] da.
            'It is Anna Naomi to Ken that introduced.'
            (NM: nominalizer   Note. English translations are all ungrammatical.)

From the point of view of X-bar theory, these constituents are hard to account for. Takano (2002) calls these elements "surprising constructions" and claims that they are formed by otherwise anomalous movement of an element to another element that does not dominate it.

We note the great interest of Takano's (2002) data including clefts, merely noting that the participation of such non-standard constituents in the grammar of information structure is a prediction from the assumptions of CCG, rather than a surprising anomaly at odds with the theory of grammar.

Since we have assumed that there are several ditransitive verbs in Japanese, with different "scrambled" argument orders, there is in fact more than one possible derivation for the above sentences, with different verb categories for *syoukai-shi-ta*. We assume that these variants differ in the sorting presuppositions identified by Kuno, but have not yet investigated this question in detail.

The following example discussed by in Takano (2002) is interesting in this connection:

(30)   *Bill-ga   Mary-ni   ageta to   omotteiru no wa John-ga   hon-wo   da.
        Bill-NOM Mary-DAT gave that think   NM TOP John-NOM book-ACC COP

        (Lit.) 'It is John a book that thinks that Bill gave to Mary.'
        ('John thinks that Bill gave a book to Mary.')   (Takano 2002: p.245, (8), Gloss is mine.)

Tanako claims that the ungrammaticality of (30) is due to a clausemate condition on movement. The implication of Takano's observation in present terms is either that *Bill-ga Mary-ni ageta to omutteiro no wa* cannot form a constituent of type $(NP \backslash NP_{nom}) \backslash NP_{acc}$, or that the copula does not have a category that can apply to the cluster *John-ga hon-wo*. We note that in English, multiple *wh*-questions like the following, which would violate such a clausemate condition seem grammatical, if strained.

(31)   What did who think that Bill gave Mary?

We therefore assume that it is the category of the copula that imposes this limitation, as it does in English:

(32)   a. It is John who thinks that Bill gave Mary a book.

        b. It is a book that John thinks that Bill gave Mary.

        c. *It is John a book that thinks that Bill gave Mary.

4. Other Rhematic Constructions

4.1. Multiple-*ga*

In section 3.1, we discussed the pragmatics of exhaustive list readings, using example (16b), repeated as (33) below:

(33)   [Nezumi-ga] youjinbukai.
        mouse-NOM cautious
        'It is a mouse that is cautious.'   (Slightly modified.)

Japanese and Korean has a construction that generates more than one nominative/subject. The following is the instances of such a construction:

(34)   [Tokai-ga] nezumi-ga   youjinbukai-desu.
        city-NOM mouse-NOM cautious-COP
        'It is a city where mouse is cautious.'

(35)   [Yoru-ga] tokai-ga nezumi-ga youjinbukai-desu.
        night-NOM city-NOM mouse-NOM cautious-COP
        'It is the night when mouse is cautious in a city.'

The bracketed sentence-initial *NP-ga* is obligatorily marked with focus or "rheme" if the predicate of a sentence presents a state or a habitual/generic action (Kuno 1973). The following *NPs* cannot be marked with rheme although the *NPs* are in serial and they can be if in the sentence-initial. The reason why these *NPs* cannot compose a cluster is reduced to their categorial status. They are adjunct, not arguments led by type-raiser particles. The derivation, for example, of (34) is as follows:

(36)

$$\frac{\dfrac{tokai-ga}{S/S:\lambda Q\exists y[city(y)\ \&\ about(y,Q)]}\quad \dfrac{\dfrac{nezumi-ga}{S/S\backslash NP:\lambda P\exists x[mouse(x)\ \&\ P(x)]}\quad \dfrac{youjinbukai}{S\backslash NP:cautious(x)}}{S:\exists x[mouse(x)\ \&\ cautious(x)]}{}^{>}}{S:\exists y[city(y)\ \&\ about(y,\exists x[mouse(x)\ \&\ cautious(x)])]}{}^{>}$$

In (36), in addition to the type-raiser as in (37a), we introduce the other type of *ga* in (37b):

(37)   a. -ga := $(S/(S\backslash NP_{nom}))\backslash N:\lambda Q\lambda P\exists x[Q(x)\ \&\ P(x)]$
        b. -ga := $(S/S)\backslash N:\lambda Q\lambda P\exists x[Q(x)\ \&\ about(x,P)]$

Successive layers of *ga*-marked *NPs* shown in (34) and (35) are derived recursively with predication function given by (37). With regard to multiple subjects, a number of linguists, e.g. Kuno (1973)(S), Fukui (1986)(V') and Kuroda (1988)(VP), have proposed adjunction analysis, which we broadly follow.

4.2. A Lexicalized Subjectivization

To capture syntactic, semantic and pragmatic characters of multiple-subject construction, we propose two types of *ga*. This brings a right prediction on the so called *subjectivization* (Kuno:1973).

Kuno (1973) claim that in most multiple subject, there is a genitive-head relation between two adjacent just as inside a single noun phrase. Without going into the detail of Kuno's transformation-based mechanism, which deriving a nominative phrase from the genitive phrase by adjoining to S-node, let us see the application of subjectivization to (35):

(38)   a. Yoru-ga tokai-ga nezumi-{ga/*no} youjinbukai.
           b. Yoru-no tokai-ga nezumi-{ga/*no} youjinbukai.
           c. Yoru-no tokai-no nezumi-{ga/*no} youjinbukai.
           d. Yoru-ga tokai-no nezumi-{ga/*no} youjinbukai.

In (38), the innermost *NP* cannot be replaced with genitive case marker *no*, and this distinction between outer and innermost *ga* obviously coincide with classification of *ga* in (37). We propose the lexicalized subjectivization under the framework of CCG by assuming the following *no* category:

(39)   -no := $(N/N)\backslash N : \lambda P \exists y \exists x [P(x) \ \& \ about(x, y)]$

The following is, for instance, the derivation for the sentence in (38d) (Semantics is omitted).

$$
\begin{array}{c}
(40) \quad
\begin{array}{cccccccc}
\text{Yoru} & ga & \text{tokai} & no & \text{nezumi} & ga & \text{youjinbukai.} \\
\hline
N & (S/S)\backslash N & N & (N/N)\backslash N & N & (S/(S\backslash NP_{nom}))\backslash N & S\backslash NP_{nom}
\end{array}
\end{array}
$$

Derivation (40):

Yoru	ga	tokai	no	nezumi	ga	youjinbukai.
N	$(S/S)\backslash N$	N	$(N/N)\backslash N$	N	$(S/(S\backslash NP_{nom}))\backslash N$	$S\backslash NP_{nom}$

with the reductions:

S/S (from Yoru ga, <); N/N (from tokai no, <); N (<); $S/(S\backslash NP_{nom})$ (<); S (>B); S (>).

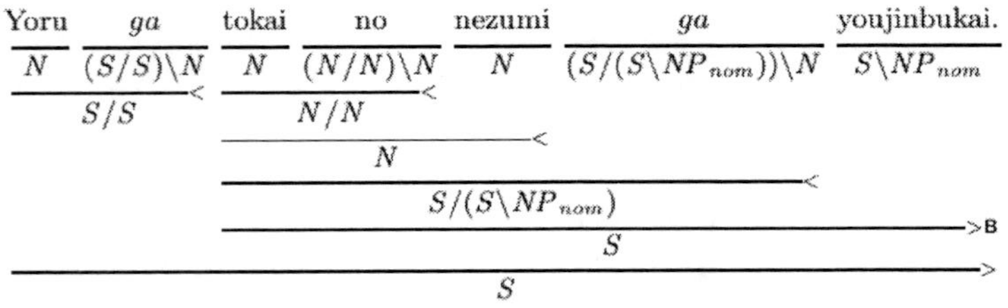

Note that *ga* in (37b) and *no* in (39) differ in their combinatorics of syntactic categories but combinatory process and semantics is substantially the same.

On this point, it may be thought that both (37b) and (39) are only recasting under the CCG framework the mechanism of multiple nominative against V' and multiple genitive against N' case licensing proposed by Fukui (1986). However, our motivation for some parallels between adjoining *ga* and genitive *no* is based on the semantics that is exactly the heart of this phenomenon. The semantics that we described for these categories are the same as Latin *de* as in the book title *De Magnete*.

5. Concluding Remarks

The basic intuition that we pursue in this paper comes from Dowty's (1988) and Steedman's (2000b) analysis of the argument cluster coordination. At first we suggest that the coordinated parts admit a contrastive interpretation based on the analogy of English gapping interpretation. Next we show that unlike English, Japanese allows more than one argument to appear in the focus position with composing a cluster. Then we explore some focus-related grammatical phenomena with discussing evidences linking the CCG analysis of argument cluster with the theory of information structure.

We believe that these observations will be helpful to the study of syntax, semantics, phonology interface and the theory of information structure in universal grammar.

References

Abbott, B. 1976. Right Node Raising as a Test for Constituenthood. *Linguistic Inquiry*, 7(4), 639-642.

Bolinger, D. 1965. *Forms of English*. Cambridge, Massachusetts: Harvard University Press.

Clark, H. 1996. *Using Language*. Cambridge: Cambridge University Press.

Dowty, D. 1988. Type-Raising, Functional Composition, and Nonconstituent Coordination. In R. T. Oehrle, E. Bach and D. Wheeler, eds., *Categorial Grammars and Natural Language Structures*, 153-198. Dordrecht: Reidel.

Erteschik-Shir, N. 1997. *The Dynamics of Focus Structure*. Cambridge and New York: Cambridge University Press.

Fukui, N. 1986. *A Theory of Category Projection and Its Applications*. Ph.D. thesis, Massachusetts Institute of Technology.

Hajičová, E., H. Skoumalová and P. Sgall. 1995. An Automatic Procedure for Topic-Focus Identification. *Computational Linguistics*, 21(1), 81-94.

Halliday, M. 1967. Notes on Transitivity and Theme in English, PartII. *Journal of Linguistics*, 3(2), 199-244.

Kuno, S. 1973. *The Structure of the Japanese Language*, Cambridge, Massachusetts: The MIT Press.

Kuno, S. 1982. The Focus of the Question and the Focus of the Answer. In R. Schneider, and K. Tuite and R. Chametzky, eds., *Papers from the Parasession on Nondeclaratives, Chicago Linguistic Society*, pp. 105-157.

Kuroda, S.-Y. 1988. Whether We Agree or Not: A Comparative Syntax of English and Japanese. In W. J. Poser, ed., *Papers from the Second Workshop on Japanese Syntax*, 103-143.

Lee, K. 2000. A CCG Fragment of Korean. *Proceedings of the Fourteenth Pacific Asia Conference on Language, Information, and Computation*, 219-229.

Lewis, D. 1979. Scorekeeping in a Language Game. *Journal of Philosophical Logic*, 8(1), 339-359.

Ross, J. R. 1970. Gapping and the Order of Constituents.In M. Bierwisch and K. Heidolph, eds., *Progress in Linguistics*, 249-259. The Hague: Mouton.

Sag, I. A. 1976. *Deletion and Logical Form*. Ph.D. thesis, Massachusetts Institute of Technology.

Steedman, M. 1996. *Surface Structure and Interpretation*, Cambridge, Massachusetts: The MIT Press.

Steedman, M. 2000a. Information Structure and Syntax-Phonology Interface. *Linguistic Inquiry*, 31(4), 649-689.

Steedman, M. 2000b. *The Syntactic Process*, Cambridge, Massachusetts: The MIT Press.

Steedman, M. 2007. Surface Compositional Semantics of Intonation. Submitted.

Steedman, M. and J. Baldridge. 2007. Combinatory Categorial Grammar. Unpublished manuscript, Draft 5.0. March 27, University of Edinburgh and University of Texas.

Takano, Y. 2002. Surprising Constituents. *Journal of East Asian Linguistics*, 11(3), 243-301.

Automatic Acquisition of Lexical-Functional Grammar Resources from a Japanese Dependency Corpus[*]

Masanori Oya* and Josef van Genabith*

*National Centre for Language Technology and School of Computing,
Dublin City University, Dublin, Ireland
{moya, josef}@computing.dcu.ie

Abstract. This paper describes a method for automatic acquisition of wide-coverage treebank-based deep linguistic resources for Japanese, as part of a project on treebank-based induction of multilingual resources in the framework of Lexical-Functional Grammar (LFG). We automatically annotate LFG f-structure functional equations (i.e. labelled dependencies) to the Kyoto Text Corpus version 4.0 (KTC4) (Kurohashi and Nagao 1997) and the output of of Kurohashi-Nagao Parser (KNP) (Kurohashi and Nagao 1998), a dependency parser for Japanese. The original KTC4 and KNP provide unlabelled dependencies. Our method also includes zero pronoun identification. The performance of the f-structure annotation algorithm with zero-pronoun identification for KTC4 is evaluated against a manually-corrected Gold Standard of 500 sentences randomly chosen from KTC4 and results in a pred-only dependency f-score of 94.72%. The parsing experiments on KNP output yield a pred-only dependency f-score of 82.08%.

Keywords: Lexical-Functional Grammar, Japanese, automatic linguistic resource acquisition, zero-pronoun identification

1. Introduction

We present a method to automatically annotate Lexical-Functional Grammar (LFG)-style functional structure equations (labelled dependencies) on the unlabelled Kyoto University Text Corpus version 4 (KTC4) (Kurohashi and Nagao 1997), to acquire more abstract and (somewhat) less language-dependent LFG f-structure representations for Japanese sentences. We apply the algorithm to enrich the output of a Japanese dependency parser (Kurohashi-Nagao Parser, KNP) (Kurohashi and Nagao 1998), to construct f-structure representations for KNP output; the enriched parser output is available for further cross-linguistic research or applications such as machine translation.

Our annotation method is based on the assumption that non-configurational, relatively free word-order languages, of which Japanese is one example, do not require phrase structure trees as an indispensable level of linguistic representation. Rather, the rich morphological information on each unit in a sentence, along with the unlabelled dependency between syntactic units in KTC4 and KNP output, provides us with as much information as what can be deduced from phrase-structure trees in other configurational, fixed word-order languages.

Our method provides zero pronoun identification as a preliminary process for long distance dependency (LDD) resolution, based on the morphology of verbs and on the probability of subcategorization frames, associated with particular verbs.

This paper has the following structure: in Section 2 we summarize the background of this research, including LFG and related work. In Section 3, we describe in detail our method of automatic annotation of f-structure functional equations on KTC4, and show how we approach the problem of zero-pronoun identification and present results of our f-structure annotation and

---

* We gratefully acknowledge support from Science Foundation Ireland grant 04/IN/I527 for the research reported in this paper.

parsing experiments. We discuss the overall results and their implications in Section 4, and conclude in Section 5.

2. Background

2.1 Lexical-Functional Grammar

Lexical-Functional Grammar (LFG) (Bresnan 2001; Dalrymple 2001) is a syntactic theory in which there are two levels of representation: c-structures are phrase-structure trees, and f-structures are attribute-value matrices encoding abstract grammatical relations such as subject, object, oblique or adjunct, mapped from the c-structure through functional equations annotated to c-structure nodes. Figure 1 is the c-structure for the sentence "Taro went to Seoul", and Figure 2 is the f-structure for the same sentence:

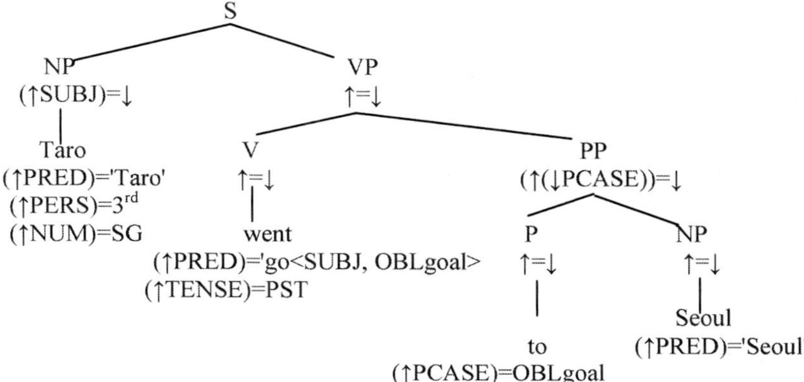

Figure 1: The c-structure for "Taro went to Seoul".

Figure 2: The f-structure for "Taro went to Seoul".

C-structures capture language-specific properties, such as word order and the hierarchical grouping of phrases, while f-structures are more abstract and somewhat more language-independent representations of surface grammatical relations (labelled dependencies). LFG is used in various fields of NLP research, such as Machine Translation (Owczarzak et al. 2007) or Question Answering (Judge et al. 2006).

2.2 Automatic Induction of LFG Resources

Treebank-based automatic acquisition of deep linguistic resources has been one of the important topics in the field of NLP (Hockenmeier et al., 2002; Cahill et al. 2002; Miyao et al. 2003). It is expected to overcome the shortcomings of manual production of linguistic resources: manual development is time-consuming, expensive and limited in terms of coverage. Ideally, automatic methods are expected to be able to induce linguistic resources that are deep, including not only syntactic properties of given sentences but also semantic properties such as predicate-argument structures and long-distance dependencies (LDDs). Several methods to achieve this goal have been developed to date, based on different grammatical formalisms like Combinatory Categorial Grammar (CCG) (Steedman, 2000), Head-Driven Phrase Structure Grammar (HPSG) (Pollard and Sag, 1994), and LFG. For example, Hockenmaier and Steedman (2002) presented an algorithm to translate the Penn-II Treebank into a CCG-style Treebank. Miyao and Tsujii (2005) developed probabilistic models for parsing with HPSG grammars acquired from the Penn-II treebank. Cahill et al. (2002, 2003, 2004) developed a method for automatic annotation of LFG f-structure on the Penn-II Treebank. The approach of Cahill et al. (2002, 2003, 2004) is as follows: first, LFG functional equations are automatically annotated on the phrase-structure trees in the English treebank. The equations specify the constraints on the f-structure mapping from the c-structure. The equations are collected and sent to a constraint solver to generate f-structures for these sentences. Long-distance dependencies (LDD) are resolved on f-structures using LDD path frequencies acquired from the f-structure annotated treebank and automatically acquired subcategorization frames (O'Donovan et al. 2004). This method has been applied to several languages other than English, including Chinese and German (Burke et al. 2004; Cahill et al. 2003).

3. Acquisition of LFG Resources from a Japanese Text Corpus

A wide-coverage LFG grammar for Japanese (Masuichi et al.2003) has been manually developed in the ParGram project (Butt et al. 2002) along with grammars for a number of other languages. To the best of our knowledge our research is the first method for the automatic treebank-based acquisition of deep Japanese LFG resources, focusing on morphological information and on unlabelled dependency relationships among the syntactic units in a sentence, as provided by an existent wide-coverage Japanese corpus.

We use KTC4 as the corpus from which wide-coverage LFG resources are acquired. The method we develop implements the idea that the part-of-speech tags on each morpheme and the unlabelled dependency tags on each syntactic unit in KTC4 provide us with enough information for constructing what Cahill et al. (2003, 2004) call "proto" f-structures for the texts in the corpus, without employing context-free grammar syntactic trees. This idea is inspired by the difference in the type of syntactic information encoded in the English Penn treebank (Marcus et al. 2004) and that in the Japanese text corpus. This difference reflects language-particular properties of Japanese. Japanese is a non-configurational language which has relatively free-word order and where grammatical functions of syntactic phrases are shown not by the word order (as in English), but by the morphology of each syntactic phrase, such as case particles for specifying the grammatical function of an NP (e.g., the case particle "-wo" specifies that the noun phrase with this particle is an OBJ of the verb on which this noun phrase is dependent), or verbal inflections for specifying tense or modal information, and sometimes for the distinction between relative clauses and sentential modifiers. According to this morphological information and unlabelled dependency links as represented in KTC4, f-structure functional equations are automatically annotated on each syntactic unit of the sentences in KTC4; these equations are sent to a constraint solver to construct the f-structures for these sentences.

3.1 Automatic Annotation of f-Structure Functional Equations to KTC4 Representations

This section describes how the method developed in this research augments KTC4 unlabelled dependency representations with the information necessary to construct "proto" f-structures, through f-structure functional equations which are resolved by a constraint solver.

KTC4 encodes morphological and syntactic information by tags in the format displayed in Figure 3, for the example sentence "*Taro ga souru ni itta* (Taro went to Seoul)". The parenthesized lines provide glosses in English, which are not contained in KTC4:

#S-ID:950101001-001
* 0 2D
太郎 たろう * 名詞 人名 * * (*Taro Noun Person***)
が   が   * 助詞 格助詞 * * (*ga particle case* **)

* 1 2D
ソウル そうる ＊名詞 地名 ＊＊　　　　　(*souru "Seoul" * Noun Place***)
に ＊ 助詞　格助詞 ＊＊　(*ni particle　　Case***)
* 2 -1D
行った いった 行く 動詞 ＊子音動詞 過去形 (*itta "went"　Verb * ConsonantStem pst*)
EOS

Figure 3: KTC4 annotation for the sentence "Taro ga souru ni itta (Taro went to Seoul)"

The first line in Figure 3 is the sentence ID. Lines which start with a star are the first lines of syntactic units. The representations also specify the unit ID number and the target unit ID number of the unit on which this unit is dependent, and the character after the target unit ID specifies the type of dependency: D denotes a direct dependency, P a coordinate relation and A an apposition. Note that apart from this, dependencies are unlabelled. If the unit does not have any target unit, then it is the root unit of the sentence, and this is indicated by "-1D".

The f-structure functional annotation algorithm assumes that each one of the syntactic units in the KTC4 representation corresponds to one sub-f-structure and that they combine with each other according to the unlabelled dependency relation provided in the KTC4 representation, to constitute one f-structure for the sentence as a whole. In other words, what is projected from one node in a phrase-structure tree of a configurational language, such as English, is projected from one syntactic unit of Japanese. The labels in the dependencies in the f-structure representation (i.e. the LFG grammatical functions) are captured from the morphological particle information in the KTC4 representation. For example, the first syntactic unit (indexed 0) in Figure 3 contains the case-particle "-ga" which is a subject marker for a noun, and this unit depends on the last syntactic unit (indexed 2), meaning that the information in the first unit provides the value of a SUBJ attribute in the f-structure associated with the head verb (indexed 2). The second syntactic unit (indexed 1) contains the case-particle "-ni" which signals that the syntactic unit functions as an oblique argument of the predicate. The last syntactic unit (indexed 2) has a morpheme whose part of speech is verb. Since its inflection form is the past form, the tense value is past. As it does not have any morpheme which specifies the statement type and style, by default this sentence is a declarative statement in plain style. The dependency relation tag (-1D) specifies that it does not have any target unit on which it is dependent, hence this unit is the root unit of the sentence. From these pieces of information, the f-structure annotation algorithm automatically annotates each syntactic unit with appropriate equations for its grammatical function, for its predicate value, and for some other lexical values such as tense.

For the example sentence in Figure 3 above, the first unit is annotated as the subject of the sentence, the second unit is the oblique-case marked argument, and the last unit is the main predicate of the f-structure of the whole sentence. The output of the annotation algorithm is shown in the Figure 4, and the f-structure generated from these functional equations by the constraint solver is shown in Figure 5:

#S-ID:950101001-001
* 0 2D
太郎 たろう ＊名詞 人名　＊＊　　　　(Taro　Noun　Person **)
が　　が　　＊ 助詞 格助詞 ＊＊　　　(ga　　　particle Case **)
F0:pred ='Taro',
F0:case='ga',
F2:subj=F0,
* 1 2D
ソウル そうる ＊名詞 地名 ＊＊　　　　(souru "Seoul"　* Noun Place**)
に ＊ 助詞　格助詞 ＊＊　(ni particle　　Case**)
F1:pred='Seoul',
F1:case='ni',
F2:obl=F1,
* 2 -1D
行った いった 行く 動詞 ＊子音動詞 過去形 (itta 'went' iku Verb * ConsonantStem pst)

F2:pred='iku',
F2:tns='pst',
F2:stmt='decl',
F2:style='plain'.
EOS

Figure 4: KTC4 annotation for the sentence "Taro ga souru ni itta (Taro went to Seoul)" with functional equasions.

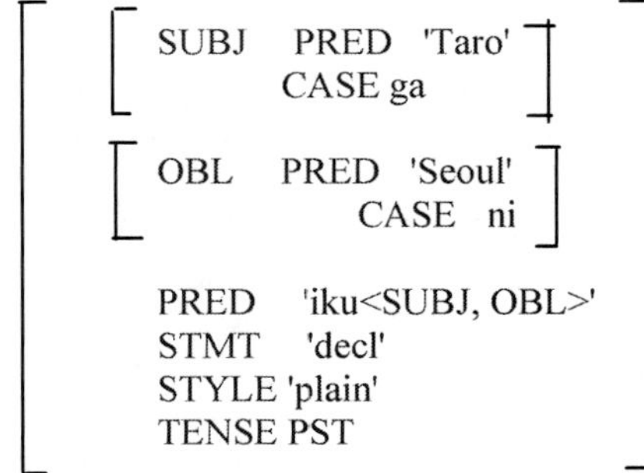

Figure 5: The f-structure for the sentence "Taro ga souru ni itta (Taro went to Seoul)"

The advantage of this method is that the annotation algorithm can be applied not only to the tagged sentences in KTC4, but also to raw texts using JUMAN (a Japanese morphological analyzer), and the KNP parser. This is because KTC4 has been developed along with the development of the KNP parsing system (Kurohashi and Nagao 1998). Using the method on JUMAN-KNP output, we can annotate KNP parser output with LFG f-structure functional equations. The f-structures from parser output can be employed in various applications such as Machine Translation or Question Answering.

Table 1 evaluates the f-structures generated by the method against a 500-sentence gold standard. Details are described in Section 3.3. Overall weighted precision for all features is 95.66%, recall 86.02% and f-score 90.59%:

Table 1: Evaluation results for all features without zero pronoun identification:

Feature	Precision	Recall	F-score	Feature	Precision	Recall	F-score
adj	644/668 = 96	644/662 = 97	97	obj_p	1005/1053 = 95	1005/1033 = 97	96
adjform	207/208 = 100	207/209 = 99	99	obl	321/346 = 93	321/577 = 56	70
asp	120/121 = 99	120/121 = 99	99	padj	1080/1135 = 95	1080/1118 = 97	96
case	990/1065 = 93	990/1088 = 91	92	pfrm	96/96 = 100	96/96 = 100	100
caus	8/8 = 100	8/8 = 100	100	progform	120/121 = 99	120/121 = 99	99
cj	350/361 = 97	350/356 = 98	98	ptrav	394/395 = 100	394/398 = 99	99
comp	300/308 = 97	300/325 = 92	95	prtcj	0/0 = 0	0/29 = 0	0
coord_form	125/162 = 77	125/158 = 79	78	prtcnj	1/1 = 100	1/2 = 50	67
copulaform	105/109 = 96	105/109 = 96	96	prtcs	124/126 = 98	124/129 = 96	97
exrl	0/0 = 0	0/32 = 0	0	rel	281/337 = 83	281/287 = 98	90
mod	66/67 = 99	66/70 = 94	96	sadj	236/246 = 96	236/270 = 87	91
nadv	83/83 = 100	83/83 = 100	100	stmt	1380/1477 = 93	1380/1421 = 97	95
neg	145/151 = 96	145/151 = 96	96	style	1398/1472 = 95	1398/1418 = 99	97
negform	140/151 = 93	140/151 = 93	93	subj	283/288 = 98	283/1418 = 20	33
nform	32/33 = 97	32/32 = 100	98	sufvform	67/67 = 100	67/67 = 100	100
noda	28/34 = 82	28/34 = 82	82	tns	767/770 = 100	767/875 = 88	93
nsa	908/910 = 100	908/915 = 99	100	topic	330/345 = 96	330/350 = 94	95

num	27/30 = 90	27/27 = 100	95		vform	502/507 = 99	502/508 = 99	99
obj	410/414 = 99	410/558 = 73	84		voice	91/96 = 95	91/96 = 95	95

3.2 Zero-Pronoun Identification

The language-particular properties of Japanese mentioned above allow us to induce LFG resources from the KTC4 corpus or KNP parser output. However, zero-pronouns cause a major problem for the method. Along with ordinary pronouns, Japanese has zero pronouns, which have no morphological or phonological realization but, for all intents and purposes, function as pronouns in other languages. Since they are used quite often both in spoken and written Japanese, identification of them is one of the issues in Japanese NLP (Kawahara et al. 2004a, 2004b, among others). Moreover, zero pronoun identification is required to resolve LDDs which is one of the important research topics in automatic induction of deep linguistic resources.

Cahill et al. (2004) present a method to automatically obtain approximations of LDD resolution for LFG resources acquired from a treebank. It uses verb subcategorization frames and LDD paths between coindexed materials (e.g., wh-phrase and its gap), both of which are extracted from the f-structures automatically generated for the Penn-II treebank.

Since KTC4 does not annotate zero pronouns on all the texts (only about 5,000 sentences are annotated with zero pronouns), LDD resolution based on KTC4 necessarily is divided into two steps: the first is zero-pronoun identification and the second is their resolution. The method we have presented in Section 3.1 does not detect the presence of zero pronouns. Hence, we have devised an additional method, making use of morphological and syntactic information in the corpus, in order to identify zero pronouns. If the method is able to identify zero pronouns in the KTC4 corpus, then it can also be applied to the output of KNP, which also does not identify zero pronouns. In this paper we concentrate on zero pronoun identification. Zero pronoun and LDD resolution will be addressed in future research.

3.3 Experiment 1: Zero Pronoun Identification in KTC4

The quality of the f-structures automatically acquired from KTC4 is evaluated against gold-standard f-structures which are manually created for a set of 500 test sentences randomly chosen from the first half of KTC4 (Table 1). 200 sentences randomly chosen from the second half of KTC4 are used as a development set. For both the development and test sets, f-structure functional equations are annotated automatically by the method without zero-pronoun identification and then their f-structures are manually corrected. The zero pronouns in the 500 Gold Standard f-structures are added manually, based on the context in which each of them appeared in the original text, verbal morphology, and A Japanese Lexicon (Ikehara et al. 1999), a hand-coded Japanese case-frame dictionary. Table 2 shows the numbers of the core arguments in the Gold Standard f-structures and the numbers of zero pronouns of each core argument (SUBJ, OBJ, OBL).

Table 2: The numbers of the core arguments and the numbers of zero pronouns of each core grammatical function in the Gold standard f-structures:

Grammatical functions	token numbers	token numbers of pro
SUBJ	1411	1121 (approx. 79% of all SUBJ)
OBJ	536	122 (approx. 22% of all OBJ)
OBL	568	199 (approx. 35% of all OBL)

We have developed five methods for zero pronoun identification. The **first method** is the Null method, which ignores zero pronouns and nothing is added to the f-structure annotation output.

The **second method** is the Simplistic method, which simply adds zero pronouns SUBJ-pro, OBJ-pro and OBL-pro whenever full NPs with the particle "-ga", "-wo" or "-ni" are missing for local verbs, regardless of the case frame of the verb.

The **third method** is the Morphological method, which uses a list of verbs whose morphology specifies their transitivity. The list is automatically constructed from KTC4 (except for the Gold Standard sentences), based on the morphology of the verbs. For some Japanese verbs, morphological information of the verb indicates unambiguously whether it is a transitive or intransitive verb. Verbs which end with "su", whether su is the verb-ending morpheme or part of the verb-ending morpheme, are all unambiguously transitives. For those verbs which are unambiguously transitives, if they appear in KTC4 without an object NP, then an object zero pronoun OBJ-pro is assumed to be present. F-structure equations are added automatically   which specify that the verb takes an object whose predicate value is "pro".

The **fourth method** is the probabilistic method, which uses a list of verbs with high transitivity rate (the rate that each verb appears with an OBJ NP dependent on it). The problem of the morphology-based method 3 is its low coverage. The total number of verb types in KTC4 is 3506, and the total number of verb tokens is 95383. The number of morphologically unambiguously transitive verb types which have their intransitive counterpart is 1286, and their token number is 33911. As for the other 2220 verb types (61472 verb tokens), their morphology does not tell us their valency.

KTC4 does not annotate the text with tags which specify the valency of verbs. Therefore, an approach must be developed to determine the valency of verbs which are not unambiguously marked by their morphology, and one of the possible approaches to achieve this task is to look at the syntactic environment in which the verb appears; e.g., we can estimate the probability that a verb whose morphology does not specify its valency is used transitively in the corpus. The phrase "used transitively in the corpus" means that the verb takes a noun phrase which is dependent on the verb and the noun phrase has the case particle "-wo". If the probability that a verb lemma is used as a transitive verb is higher than a certain threshold, and if it appears without object in a given sentence, then the appropriate f-structure equations are automatically added to the f-structure for the sentence. The list of verbs and their transitivity rate is automatically acquired from the second half of KTC4, which does not contain Gold Standard sentences. The threshold is 0.3 in this experiment, i.e., the list includes verbs whose transitivity rates are above 0.3.

The **fifth method** is a combination of methods 3 and 4: add to the list of method 3 those verbs whose morphology does not specify their transitivity but that have a high transitivity rate.

In all methods, 500 f-structures generated by different zero-pronoun identification methods are converted into dependency triples of a grammatical function, a predicate and its argument: for example, a dependency triple "subj(go, Taro)" which is obtained from a sentence "Taro went to Seoul" means that the subject of the verb "go" is "Taro". The triples are compared with the dependency triples of the Gold Standard f-structures, and the precision, recall and f-score for each grammatical function are calculated using the software of Crouch et al. (2002).

Table 3 shows the evaluation results of the five methods. The figures in the parentheses are recall, precision and f-score of zero pronouns only. "Pred-only" means the result includes the precision, recall and f-score of dependency triples of the predicates, arguments and adjuncts in the 500 test sentences, but not atomic features such as tense, mood, aspect features.

In all methods except for Method 1, SUBJ-pro is added simplistically; since every verb subcategorises for a subject, hence if a clause lacks a subject NP, then pro-SUBJ is added into the clause. However, this result does not yield 100% accuracy because of the wrong annotation of functional equations, especially those on nominal predicates functioning as sentential adjuncts, hence more cleaning up operations are required.

From all the results, method 5 performs best for OBJ zero pronoun identification. The results of zero pronoun identification for OBL are lower than that for OBJ, because of the ambiguity of "ni" marked NPs. This particle can be used as the OBL case marker, or as a postposition which functions as a temporal or a locative adverbial.

Table 3: Results of Experiment 1

		Precision	Recall	F-score
Method 1 (null)	Pred-only	95.71	75.18	84.22
	SUBJ	97.56(0)	19.84(0)	32.97(0)
	OBJ	98.79(0)	73.16(0)	84.06(0)
	OBL	93.31(0)	58.05(0)	71.57(0)
Method 2 (simplistic)	Pred-only	78.22	95.51	86.01
	SUBJ	98.64(98.91)	97.38(97.60)	98.00(98.25)
	OBJ	39.47(14.13)	97.67(95.80)	56.22(24.62)
	OBL	39.25(19.10)	89.94(88.46)	54.65(31.41)
Method 3 (morphological)	Pred-only	95.75	92.69	94.2
	OBJ	92.83(71.55)	88.01(58.04)	90.35(64.09)
	OBL	92.48(88.05)	68.28(28.36)	78.55(42.90)
Method 4 (probabilistic)	Pred-only	95.76	92.92	94.32
	OBJ	97.97(87.09)	77.99(18.88)	86.94(31.03)
	OBL	82.17(63.92)	82.32(67.30)	82.24(65.56)
Method 5 (combination)	Pred-only	95.08	94.37	94.72
	OBJ	93.26(76.29)	91.59(72.02)	92.41(74.09)
	OBL	84.46(68.65)	81.97(66.34)	83.19(67.47)

Results for Method 5 for all features (rather than pred-only) are as follows: precision is 95.61%, recall 94.68% and f-score 95.15%. Compared to Table 1, this shows a marked increase due to the effect of zero-pronoun identification.

3.4 Experiment 2: Zero Pronoun Identification in KNP Parser Output

Experiment 2 explores how the methods in Experiment 1 can identify zero pronouns in raw texts, using KNP, a Japanese dependency parser. We stripped off the dependency and other tags in the 500 Gold Standard sentences and parsed them with KNP. The parser output is automatically annotated with f-structure functional equations, and zero pronouns are identified using the same methods as in Experiment 1. The output f-structures are converted into triples and compared to the Gold Standard triples. Table 4 shows the results of each method. The general tendency of recall, precision and f-scores of SUBJ are the same as Experiment 1:

Table 4: Results of Experiment 2

		Precision	Recall	F-score
Method 1 (null)	Pred-only	83.57	79.06	72.37
	SUBJ	79.93(0)	16.59(0)	27.47(0)
	OBJ	89.63(0)	66.54(0)	76.37(0)
	OBL	85.38(0)	51.64(0)	64.35(0)
Method 2 (simplistic)	Pred-only	67.96	82.77	74.64
	SUBJ	89.60(92.16)	88.84(90.93)	89.21(92.04)
	OBJ	35.88(12.88)	88.90(87.41)	51.12(22.45)
	OBL	34.68(16.63)	79.89(78.36)	48.36(27.43)
Method 3 (morphological)	Pred-only	83.28	80.74	81.99
	OBJ	85.26(65.95)	77.63(43.35)	81.26(52.31)
	OBL	84.96(82.85)	61.69(27.88)	71.47(41.72)
Method 4 (probabilistic)	Pred-only	83.13	80.62	81.86
	OBJ	89.31(84.00)	70.30(14.68)	78.67(24.99)
	OBL	72.82(53.33)	72.44(57.69)	72.62(55.42)
Method 5 (combination)	Pred-only	82.91	81.27	82.08
	OBJ	85.82(68.91)	77.99(44.75)	81.71(54.23)
	OBL	72.82(56.33)	72.44(57.69)	72.62(57.00)

4. Discussion

Method 5 yields the best pred-only f-score for both KTC4 and KNP parser output. The experiments show that the morphology-based approach and the probability-based approach improve the f-scores of the annotation algorithm in terms of the pred-only f-scores of the sentence as a whole.

However, these two approaches do not yet identify zero pronouns as precisely as expected, and the improvement remains moderate; for example, the f-score of zero-pronoun OBJ in Method 5 in parsing is only slightly above 82%.

5. Conclusion

This paper presents a method for automatically acquiring LFG resources from the KTC4 Japanese text corpus and KNP parser output along with a basic zero-pronoun identification method. The performance of the f-structure annotation algorithm for KTC4 is evaluated against a manually-corrected Gold Standard of 500 sentences randomly chosen from KTC4 and the evaluation results in a pred-only dependency f-score of 94.72%. The parsing experiments on KNP output yields a pred-only dependency f-score of 82.08%. The results show that LFG resources automatically acquired from a Japanese text corpus can be improved through zero-pronoun identification.

References

Bresnan, J. 2001. *Lexical-Functional Syntax*. Blackwell Publishers, Oxford.

Burke, M., A. Cahill, M. McCarthy, J. van Genabith, and A. Way. 2002. Evaluating Automatic F-Structure Annotation for the Penn-II Treebank. *Proceedings of TLT 2002, Treebanks and Linguistic Theories*, pp. 42-60.

Burke, M., O. Lam, A. Cahill, R. Chan, R. O'Donovan, A. Bodomo, J. van Genabith and A. Way. 2004. Treebank-based Acquisition of a Chinese Lexical-Functional Grammar. *Proceedings of the 18th Pacific Asia Conference on Language, Information and Computation (PACLIC-18)*, 161-172.

Burke, M., A. Cahill, M. McCarthy, R. O'Donovan, J. van Genabith and A. Way. 2004. Evaluating Automatic F-Structure Annotation for the Penn-II Treebank. *Journal of Language and Computation; Special Issue on "Treebanks and Linguistic Theories"*, eds., E. Hinrichs and K.Simov, Kluwer Academic Press, 523-547.

Butt, M., H. Dyvik, T. H. King, H. Masuichi, and C. Roher. 2002. The Parallel Grammar Project. *Proceedings of COLING-2002 Workshop on Grammar Engineering and Evaluation*, pp. 1-7.

Cahill, A., M. McCarthy, J. van Genabith, and A. Way. 2002. Automatic Annotation of the Penn-II Treebank with LFG F-Structure Information. *Proceedings of Third International Conference on Language Resources and Evaluation, Las Palmas, Spain, June 5th, 2002*, pp. 8-15

Cahill, A., M. Forst, M. McCarthy, R. O' Donovan, C. Rohrer, J. van Genabith and A. Way. 2003. Treebank-Based Multilingual Unification-Grammar Development. *Proceedings of the Workshop on Ideas and Strategies for Multilingual Grammar Development*, at the 15th European Summer School in Logic Language and Information, pp.17-24.

Cahill, A., M. Burke, R. O'Donovan, J. van Genabith and A. Way. 2004. Long-Distance Dependency Resolution in Automatically Acquired Wide-Coverage PCFG-Based LFG Approximations. *Proceedings of the 42nd Annual Meeting of the Association for Computational Linguistics*, pp. 320-327.

Crouch, R., R. M. Kaplan, T. H. King, and S. Riezler. 2002. A Comparison of Evaluation Metrics for a Broad-Coverage Stochastic Parser. *Proceedings of the "Beyond PARSEVAL" Workshop at the 3rd International Conference on Language Resources and Evaluation (LREC'02), Las Palmas, Spain*.

Dalrymple, M. 2001. *Lexical-Functional Grammar*. Academic Press, London.

Hockenmaier, J. and M. Seedman. 2002. Acquiring Compact Lexicalized Grammars from a Cleaner Treebank. *Proceedings of Third International Conference on Language Resources and Evaluation, Las Palmas, Spain, June 5th, 2002*, pp. 1974–1981.

Ikehara, S, M. Miyazaki, S. Shirai, A. Yokoo, H. Nakaiwa, K. Ogura, Y. Ooyama, and Y. Hayashi. 1999. *Nihongo Goi Taikei*. "A Japanese Lexicon". Iwanami Shoten, Tokyo.

Judge, J., A. Cahill and J. van Genabith. 2006. QuestionBank: Creating a Corpus of Parse Annotated Questions. *Proceedings of the 21st International Conference on Computational Linguistics and the 44th annual meeting of the ACL*, pp. 597-504.

Kawahara, D. and S. Kurohashi. 2002. Fertilization of Case Frame Dictionary for Robust Japanese Case Analysis. *Proceedings of the 19th International Conference on Computational Linguistics*, pp. 425-431.

Kawahara, D. and S. Kurohashi. 2004a. Zero Pronoun Resolution Based on Automatically Constructed Case Frames and Structural Preference of Antecedents. *Proceedings of the 1st International Joint Conference on Natural Language Processing (IJCNLP-04)*, pp.334-341,

Kawahara, D. and S. Kurohashi. 2004b. Improving Japanese Zero Pronoun Resolution by Global Word Sense Disambiguation. *Proceedings of the 20th International Conference on Computational Linguistics (COLING2004)*, pp.343-349.

Kawahara, D. and S. Kurohashi. 2005. Gradual Fertilization of Case Frames. *Journal of Natural Language Processing,* vol.12, no.2, 109-131.

Kudoh, T. and Y. Matsumoto. 2002. Japanese Dependency Analysis using Cascaded Chunking. *Proceedings of the 6th Conference on Natural Language Learning 2002 (COLING 2002 Post-Conference Workshops)*, pp. 63-69.

Kurohashi, S. and M. Nagao. 1997. Kyoto daigaku text corpus project. *Proceedings of the Third Conference of Natural Language Processing*, pp.115-118.

Kurohashi, S. and M. Nagao. 1998. Building a Japanese Parsed Corpus while Improving the Parsing System. *Proceedings of the 1st International Conference on Language Resources and* Evaluation, pp. 719-724.

Marcus M., G. Kim, M. A. Marcinkiewicz, R. MacIntyre, A. Bies, M. Ferguson, K. Katz, and B. Schasberger. 1994. The Penn Treebank: Annotating Predicate Argument Structure. *Proceedings of the ARPA Workshop on Human Language Technology.* Princton, NJ., pp. 110-115.

Masuichi, H., and T. Okuma. 2003. Japanese Parser on the Basis of the Lexical-Functional Grammar Formalism and its Evaluation. *Journal of Natural Language Processing* vol. 10, pp. 79-109.

Miyao, Y. and J. Tsujii. 2005. Probabilistic Disambiguation Models for Wide-Coverage HPSG Parsing. *Proceedings of the 43rd Annual Meeting on Association for Computational Linguistics, Ann Arbor, Michigan.* pp. 83-90.

O'Donovan, R. 2006. *Automatic Extraction of Large-Scale Multilingual Lexical Resources.* Ph.D. thesis, Dublin City University.

O'Donovan, R., M. Burke, A. Cahill, J. van Genabith, and A. Way. 2004. Large-Scale Induction and Evaluation of Lexical Resources from the Penn-II Treebank. *Proceedings of the 42nd Annual Meeting of the Association for Computational Linguistics (ACL-04)*, July 21-26, Barcelona, Spain, pp. 368-375.

Owczarzak, K., J. van Genabith, and A. Way. 2007. Labelled Dependencies in Machine Translation Evaluation. *Proceedings of ACL 2007 Workshop on Statistical Machine Translation*, pp. 104-111.

Pollard, C., and I. A. Sag. 1994. *Head-Driven Phrase Structure Grammar*. Chicago: University of Chicago Press.

Steedman, Mark. 2000. *The Syntactic Process*. The MIT Press, Cambridge Mass.

Yoshioka, T., H. Yoshimura, H. Masuichi and T. Okuma. 2003. A Proposal for Experience Knowledge Recycle System. *Proceedings of the 17th Annual Conference of the Japanese Society for Artificial Intelligence, 2003.*

Semi-Automatic Annotation Tool to Build Large Dependency Tree-Tagged Corpus[*]

Eun-Jin Park[a], Jae-Hoon Kim[b], Chang-Hyun Kim[a], and Young-Kill Kim[a]

[a]1 Dongsam-Dong, Youngdo-gu, Busan, 606-791, KOREA,
[b]161 Gajeong-Dong, Yuseong-gu, Daejeon. 305-700, KOREA
jhoon@mail.hhu.ac.kr, {ejpark,chkim,kimyk}@etri.re.kr

Abstract. Corpora annotated with lots of linguistic information are required to develop robust and statistical natural language processing systems. Building such corpora, however, is an expensive, labor-intensive, and time-consuming work. To help the work, we design and implement an annotation tool for establishing a Korean dependency tree-tagged corpus. Compared with other annotation tools, our tool is characterized by the following features: independence of applications, localization of errors, powerful error checking, instant annotated information sharing, user-friendly. Using our tool, we have annotated 100,904 Korean sentences with dependency structures. The number of annotators is 33, the average annotation time is about 4 minutes per sentence, and the total period of the annotation is 5 months. We are confident that we can have accurate and consistent annotations as well as reduced labor and time.

Keywords: Annotation (tagging) tool, Workbench, Error Editor, Corpus construction.

1. Introduction

More recently, a large corpus annotated with linguistic information is used in natural language processing. By using this corpus, natural language processing systems have learn some linguistic phenomena automatically. Building such a corpus, however, is an expensive, labor-intensive and time-consuming work. Furthermore, maintaining consistency of a constructed corpus is difficult. Therefore, we need an annotation tool for improving annotation efficiency and maintaining consistency. To help such work, some annotation tools (Atalay, 2003; Lim, 2002; Morton, 2003; Day, 1997; Brants T. and Plaehn, 2000) have already been used. In this paper, we describe an annotation tool for building a Korean dependency tree-tagged corpus with linguistic information about the segmentation of word phrases (called eojeols in Korean), part-of-speech (POS) tags, boundaries of chunks, and dependency links and relations. We design an annotation tool so that an annotator can carefully investigate them and edit errors on them through a GUI. We also design it so that errors in low level processing like POS tagging might not be propagated to higher level processing step like parsing. Moreover, the tool is characterized by the following features; 1) It is independent of special applications like information extraction. 2) It focuses on localizing errors to modules as far as possible, such as morphological analyzers. It can make annotators find and pay attention to errors related to the modules easily. 3) It has an error checking function to make possible that errors can not be stored as it can be. 4) It promptly shares annotated information among annotators so that annotators can keep consistency with others' annotation within a working group. 5) It has a user-friendly interface.

This paper is organized as follows: In Section 2, we introduce other annotation tools for establishing corpora In Section 3, we describe the architecture of our annotation tool for

---

building a Korean dependency tree-tagged corpus. In Section 4 and 5, we explain the implementation details of our tool and guide process of the annotation using our tool, respectively. Finally, we draw conclusions, and discuss future works in Section 6.

2. Related Works

Several annotation tools (Atalay, 2003; Day, 1997; Lim, 2002; Morton, 2003; Day, 1997; Brants T. and Plaehn, 2000; Carletta, 2002) have been developed and used in several projects (KIBS, 2005; Marcus, 1994; SEJONG, 2005). In this section, we briefly introduce such annotation tools for building a tagged corpus: Alembic workbench (Day, 1997), WorkFreak (Morton, 2003) and a semi-automatic tree annotating workbench (Lim, 2002) developed in the Sejong Project (SEJONG, 2005).

2.1.Alembic Workbench

Alembic Workbench (Day, 1997) developed at MITR[1] is the system which annotates named-entity for an effective information extraction system. It supports multi-languages and SGML formats. Also it learns the user's working pattern to construct the corpus semi-automatically. It helps annotators by graphic user-interface. This system had been upgraded and released as Callisto[2] in 2004. In spite of such upgrade, this system is not yet for general purpose, only information extraction. Furthermore, adapting it to Korean requires preprocessing like morphological analysis and POS tagging.

2.2.WordFreak

WordFreak[3] (Morton, 2003) is a java-based linguistic annotation tool designed to support automatically annotating linguistic data and it employs active-learning for the human correction of automatically annotated data. It annotates several linguistic information like syntactic structure, named-entity and anaphoric information, etc. It provides automatic taggers for tokenization, POS tagging, chunking, full parsing, and name finding through OpenNLP[4] project and also automatically annotates linguistic information by learning the user pattern of work. And it can extend its component to other languages like Korean easily, but also requires preprocessing like morphological analysis and POS tagging for each language.

2.3.Korean semi-automatic tree annotation workbench

In this section, we will describe the workbench (Lim, 2002) which is building a Korean dependency tree-tagged corpus. It extracts various syntactic patterns from the constructed corpus based on the selected features, and automatically applies the extracted syntactic patterns to the appropriate states. It provides an integrated environment for searching, converting and editing Korean parsing tree corpus in the Sejong project (SEJONG, 2005). However, it is for a stand-alone system, but not for a multi-user system, and then cannot share annotated information instantly. It is improper for building a large-scale corpus.

3. Annotation Tool for Building a Korean Dependency Tree-Tagged Corpus

Our work annotates naturally-occurring text for linguistic structure. Most notably, we produce skeletal dependency trees with links and relations showing rough syntactic and semantic information called Korean dependency tree-tagged corpus. We also annotate text with

---

[1] http://www.mitre.org/tech/alembic-workbench/
[2] http://callisto.mitre.org/
[3] http://wordfreak.sourceforge.net/
[4] http://opennlp.sourceforge.net/

segmentation of word phrases (eojeols in Korean), POS tags, and chunk annotation. In this section, we describe the architecture of our annotation tool, called PPeditor, for establishing the Korean dependency tree-tagged corpus. It is designed for editing dependency trees generated from a Korean dependency parser (Kim, 1994), that is, our method for building a corpus is semi-automatic. It also is designed for sharing annotated results through a database (DB) promptly so that many annotators can work simultaneously to keep consistency of dependency tree-tagged corpus.

3.1.Architecture of PPeditor

Figure 1 shows the overall architecture of PPeditor consisting of a sentence analyzer, an annotation tool, and a DB. The sentence analyzer comprises four components: a morphological analyzer, a POS tagger, a partial parser and a dependency parser. The morphological analyzer segments a sentence into a sequence of morphemes and the POS tagger assigns POS tags to morphemes reflecting their syntactic category. The partial parser called a chunker uses a sequence of POS tags provided by a tagger and identify boundaries of syntactic groups like noun and verb groups having linear structures. The chunker preserves all the previously added information in the sentence and only creates the boundaries of constituents called chunks. Finally the dependency parser generates explicit dependency links that show the head-dependent relations between chunks.

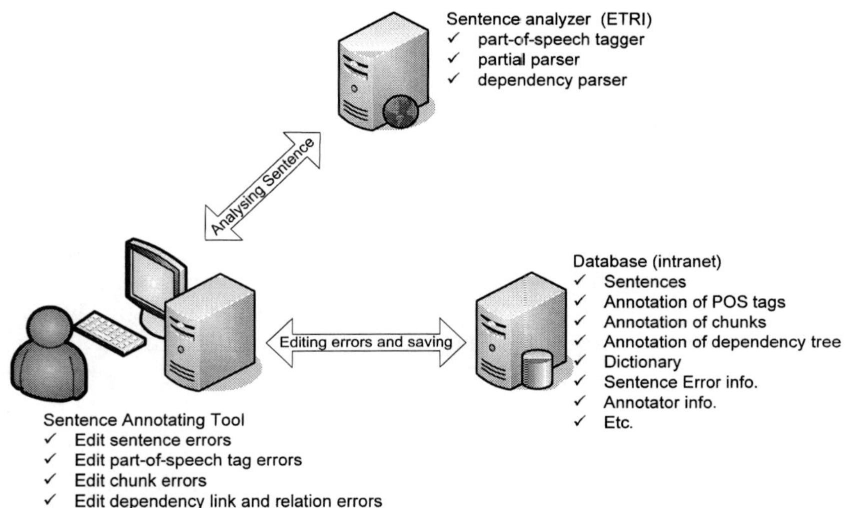

Figure 1: Architecture of PPeditor

The annotation tool helps annotators with editing several kinds of errors (spelling errors, spacing errors, segmentation errors, POS tagging errors, chunking errors, dependency structure errors), and so it is called an error editor also. The DB saves several kind of information on original sentences, annotations for the sentences, dictionaries, annotators, etc.

The annotation flow is as follows;
1. select a sentence from the DB.
2. send it to the sentence analyzer.
3. analyze it by the sentence analyzer.
4. receive analysis results from the sentence analyzer.
5. display the results in GUI.
6. observe errors on the results.
7. edit the errors.
8. repeat 2 through 7 until all the errors are corrected.
9. save the annotation results to the DB.

Step 8 is very important because the errors are propagated to the higher levels. Namely, errors of POS tagging is reflected into the partial parsing and syntactic parsing. The higher level analysis of sentences must be processed again if errors in the low level analysis are corrected. By doing this, the propagated errors are automatically disappeared and then the efficiency is improved greatly.

3.2. Graphic user interface of the PPeditor

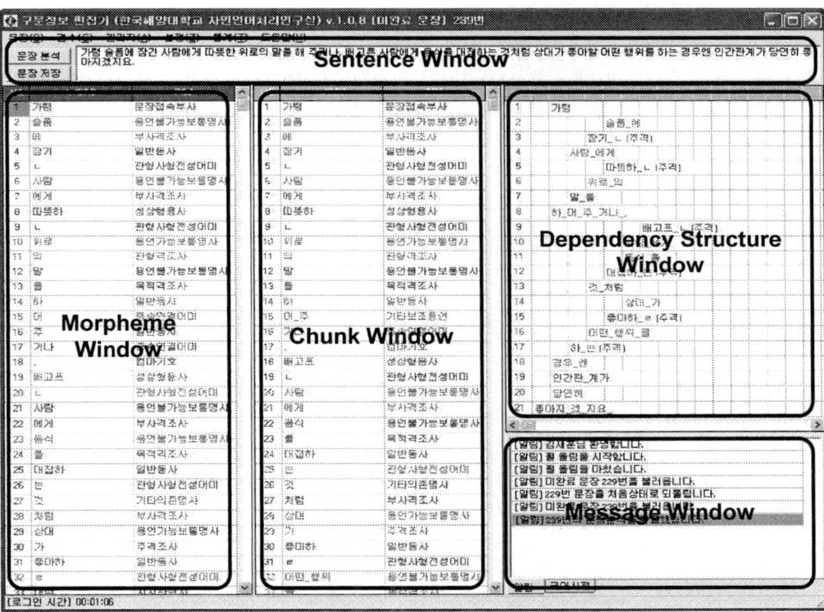

Figure 2: GUI of the error editor

GUI (Graphical User Interface) of the annotation tool is consisting of a main menu, a sentence window, a morpheme window, a chunk window, a dependency structure window, and a message window. Each window displays information on sentences, morphemes, chunks, dependency structures, and messages, respectively. Table 1 shows relations between kinds of errors and windows. On the sentence window, errors on spelling and spacing of words are observed and corrected. On the morpheme window, errors on POS tags and segmentation of eojeols are edited. On the chunk window and the dependency structure window, errors on boundaries of chunks and on dependency structures, which comprise dependency links and relations, are rectified.

Table 1: Relations between kinds of errors and windows

Error	Window
spelling	sentence
spacing	
segmentation	morpheme
POS tag	morpheme / chunk
boundary of chunks	chunk
link with head	dependency structure
dependency relation	

Basic functions of an editor are insertion, deletion, and substitution of objects, and these functions are also basic in editing. For expert users, our system adopts hot keys for every function to improve the efficiency, for example, CTRL-I for insertion of a morpheme or a chunk. All mappings of hot keys and their functions are skipped due to limitation of space. To minimize typing errors on each window, combo-boxes are employed for editing POS tags and dependency relations.

3.3. Functions of PPeditor

Figure 3 shows the structure of PPeditor. The function of PPeditor is classified as the communication function, error edit function, guideline function, and corpus release function. All of the functions are connected with the user interface.

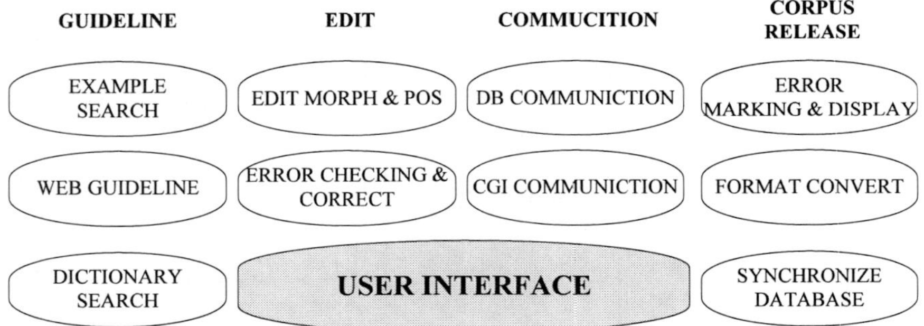

Figure 3: Functions of the PPeditor

The communication function is to communicate with the sentence analyzer and the data base. The communication of the sentence analyzer, which uses the CGI (Common Gateway Interface), is to send the sentence to the analyzer and receive the result of it. Therefore, it can freely set up in the different operating system or the computer system. The MySQL, which is connected with client by ODBC, was used as the data base which store sentences and the results of the annotation.

It is the basic function of PPeditor to correct the errors. It provided the functions of general editor which are insertion, deletion, and addition. But, it has some features which are not provided in the general editor. First, it automatically modified the errors which are repetitively caused by the sentence analyzer. Second, if the error of low step is removed, the result of correction will be reflected to high step in this system. Because the errors of the low step (ex: morphological analysis) are delivered to the high step (ex: syntax analysis). For example, the spelling errors at the sentence affect the morphological analysis and the syntax analysis. Third, it provides user to searching the similar language phenomenon or the similar contexts. There are a lot of ambiguous expressions in natural language. The annotator is able to keep consistency about them by using this function. Fourth, errors are not stored in the data base by checking the errors. The annotator may ignore simple error when he worked lots of time. Fifth, it helps the annotator search the dictionary and examples which are annotated by other annotators. He needs data such as a dictionary although he is familiar to his mother tongue. Sixth, there is focus function which highlights the current position. There is a lot of information on the screen, so he loses his position easily. Plate (i.e., photograph) captions appear underneath the figure, as can be seen in Plate 1. The plates and photographs should be centered.

The guideline function is studying skills for annotating sentences. This includes function of example search, web guideline, and dictionary search. Web guideline is online tutorial to help annotator. The example search is searching examples which are annotated sentences by other annotators. This function is very useful to keep constancy by searching the result of annotation.

The corpus release function is to exchange the results of annotation among annotation groups. It includes the function of format conversion which converts from database to text, and the function of synchronizing data among databases. And also it includes the function of error display which had marked by gaugers who review the dependency tree-tagged corpus. This helps annotator find error position easily.

4. Annotation of the Korean Dependency Tree-Tagged Corpus

Using our tool, we had annotated 100,904 Korean sentences of which all are over 20 words with syntactic structures, which comprise segmentation of eojeols, POS tags of morphemes and chunks, boundaries of chunks, dependency links and relations. 33 annotators, who are trained over 1 month, had worked for 5 months. There are 3 annotation subgroups, which worked 20,000, 40,000, and 40,000 sentences, respectively. Each group has local database and synchronizes their annotated sentences to central database server every 2 weeks. Figure 4 shows the organization of annotation subgroups and a central database server.

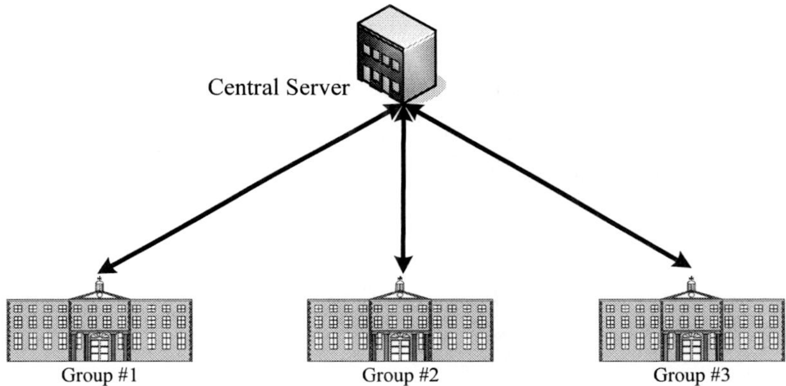

Figure 4: The organization of annotation subgroups

4.1. A scenario for annotating a corpus

The user level consists of gauger, advisers, annotators, and administrators. Most important users for annotating a corpus are annotators and advisers. In the normal case of annotation, an annotator works according to the workflow as mentioned in Section 3.1. In the case, some sentences extracted from running text are very difficult to annotate linguistic information; the annotator asks helps to advisers who are experts on annotations or well-educated corpus linguists. The advisers should hold profound knowledge in linguistics and could explain complex linguistic phenomena. Mostly one among senior annotators is in charges of the advice. Figure 5 shows this flow.

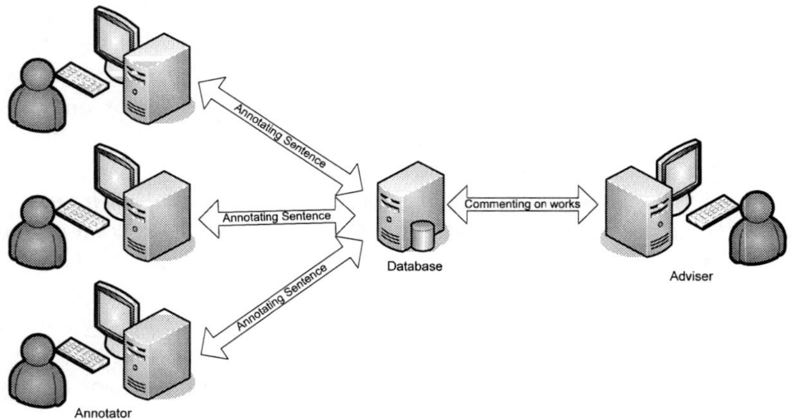

Figure 5: The scenario for annotating a sentence

Several annotators can access one record of the DB simultaneously. This causes problems when one sentence is annotated by two or more annotators. To avoid this problem, we use the 'status' field of the 'sent' table. If one annotator holds a sentence to work, the status of the sentence must be changed into 'reserved'. If the work is done, the status is recovered to the original status or is changed into other statuses.

4.2. The scenario for gauging a corpus

There is one gauger in the project, and each group has one adviser. The adviser examines annotated sentences so that errors can be reduced. If the adviser finds any errors on annotations, they explain the errors, give a guideline for removing the errors, and then ask the annotator of the annotations to remove the errors. We randomly selected the samples of annotated sentences every two weeks at the ratio of 1% and examine the quality of them. If an annotator cannot satisfy the accuracy rates of 99.9%, the adviser commands him to review all his sentences. Otherwise the adviser sends them to the gauger who gauges the sentences once more. This cross validation keeps the high reliability of the corpus. Figure 6 shows the scenario for gauging a corpus.

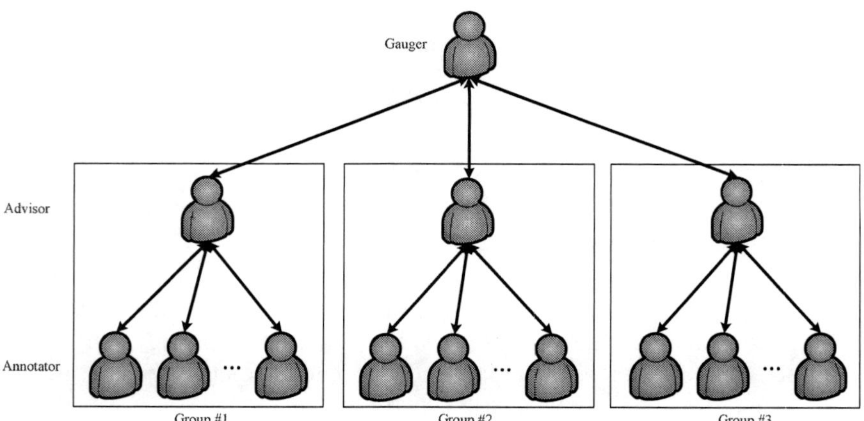

Figure 6: The scenario for gauging a corpus

4.3. Annotating the sentences

Table 2 shows the statistics on our annotated corpus, which consists of 100,904 Korean sentences with dependency structures. The average number of eojeols, morphemes, and chunks per sentence is 22, 43, and 36, respectively. A sentence has 22 eojeols on average and each eojeol has 1.9 parts-of-speech and 1.6 chunks on average. We commit 33 annotators to this work, which has taken 5 months. Each annotator has annotated 3,317 sentences on average and the average working time is 4 minutes and 32 sec on average (see Table 3). As we consider the length of the sentence, over 22 eojeols, the result is remarkable.

Table 2: Statistics on our annotated corpus

	Total	Average
eojeols	2,186,060	22
morphemes	4,344,200	43
chunks	3,644,790	36

Table 3: The Working Time & Num. Of sentence

Annotator No.	Num.	Average Time	Annotator No.	Num.	Average Time	Annotator No.	Num.	Average Time
#1	3,791	3:11	#12	2,018	3:14	#23	1,833	4:23
#2	6,780	3:36	#13	950	3:59	#24	2,364	3:40
#3	3,831	4:56	#14	4,565	4:16	#25	5,189	3:56
#4	3,193	4:25	#15	4,179	3:01	#26	2,757	4:28
#5	2,067	2:38	#16	5,131	3:28	#27	3,116	3:58
#6	3,082	4:43	#17	2,719	3:06	#28	2,100	3:46
#7	1,082	7:38	#18	1,770	4:36	#29	1,997	3:53
#8	2,415	4:10	#19	5,762	3:36	#30	4,567	3:48
#9	2,574	4:52	#20	1,548	4:47	#31	3,157	4:39
#10	7,017	4:30	#21	2,516	4:36	#32	1,131	3:11
#11	6,534	4:57	#22	6,454	3:02	#33	1,280	5:10

5. Conclusions and Future works

In this paper, we describe PPeditor which is the annotation tool for building Korean dependency tree-tagged corpus. The tree-tagged corpus contains many kind of linguistic information about segmentation of eojeols, POS tags of morphemes, boundaries of chunks, and dependency structures with heads and relations. Annotation of linguistic information using PPeditor means correcting the errors occurred in the sentence analyzer. Compared with other annotation tools, the tool is characterized by the following features: independence of applications, localization of errors, powerful error checking, instant annotated information sharing, and user-friendly.

Using our tool, we have annotated 100,904 Korean sentences with dependency structures. The number of annotators is 33, the average annotation time is 4 minutes per sentence, and the total period of the annotation is 5 months. We are confident that we can have accurate and consistent annotations as well as reduced labor and time.

In the near future, we will improve the function of automatic error-correction using machine learning techniques like transformation-based learning (Brill, 1995) and also add the function of detecting error-prone context automatically. We expect that these functions will not only reduce repetitive works, but also improve efficiency and effectiveness of annotations.

References

Atalay, N. B., Oflazer, K. and Say, B.: The Annotation Process in the Turkish Treebank. *Proceedings of the EACL Workshop on Linguistically Interpreted Corpora, Budapest, Hungary* .2003.

Brants T, and Plaehn, O.: Interactive corpus annotation. *Proceedings of the Second International Conference on Language Resources and Engineering* (LREC 2000) .2000. 453-459

Brill, E.: Transformation-Based Error-Driven Learning and Natural Language Processing: A Case Study in Part-of-Speech Tagging. *Computation Linguistics Vol. 21(4):* .1995. 543-565

Carletta, J., McKelvie, D., Isard, A., Mengel, A., Klein, M. and Mller, M. B.: *A generic approach to software support for linguistic annotation using XML. G. Sampson & D. McCarth Eds., Readings in Corpus Linguistics, Continuum International* .2002.

Day, D., Aberdeen, J., Hirschman, L., Kozierok, R., Robinson, P. and Vilain, M.: Mixed-Initiative Development of Language Processing Systems. *Proceedings of the ANLP* .1997. 348-355

Day, D., Aberdeen, J., Hirschman, L., Kozierok, R., Robinson, P., and Vilain, M.: Mixed-Initiative Development of Language Processing Systems. *Proceedings of the Applied Natural Language Processing* .1997. 348-355

KIBS, http://kibs.kaist.ac.kr/, Korea Information Base System .2005.

Kim, C.-H., Kim, J.-H., Seo, J. and Kim, G. C.: A Right-to-Left Chart Parsing for Dependency Grammar using Headable Path. *Proceeding of the 1994 International Conference on Computer Processing of Oriental Languages* .1994. 175-180

Lim, J.-H., Park, S.-Y., Kwak, Y.-J., Rim, H.-C., Kim, U.-S. and Kang, B.-M.: Semi-Automatic Tree Annotators Using Statistical Syntactic Patterns. *Proceedings of the 14th Conference of Hangul and Korean Information Processing* .2002. 343-350

Marcus, M., Kim, G., Marcinkiewicz, M., MacIntyre, R., Bies, A., Ferguson, M., Katz, K. and Schasberger, B.: The Penn Treebank: Annotating Predicate Argument Structure. *Proceedings of ARPA Human Language Technology Workshop* .1994.

Morton, T. and LaCivita, J.: WordFreak: An Open Tool for Linguistic Annotation. *Proceedings. of the NAACL* (2003) 17-18

Ngai, G., and Florian, R.: Transformation-Based Learning in the Fast Lane. *Proceedings of the NAACL* (2001) 40-47

SEJONG, http://sejong.or.kr/english/, The 21st Century Sejong Project .2005.

Multiple Sluicing in English[*]

Myung-Kwan Park and Jung-Min Kang

Department of English, Dongguk University
3-ga 26, Pil-dong, Chung-gu, Seoul, 100-715, Korea
parkmk@dongguk.edu,shinyminny@hanmail.net

Abstract. This paper explores the nature of multiple sluicing in English, which has two or more remnant wh-phrases in clause edge position. At the beginning part of the paper we argue against Nishigauchi's (1998) and Lasnik's (2007) Gapping analysis of multiple sluicing, which says that two remnant wh-phrases each actually occupies the left and right edge of a clause, with the in-between string of words undergoing Gapping. We rather argue that multiple sluicing in English is the same kind as found in Bulgarian and Serbo-Croatian. In other words, multiple sluicing in English is also derived by multiple wh-fronting which otherwise does not apply. We demonstrate that some important properties of the construction noted by Lasnik (2007) under the Gapping approach to it can be accounted for in a principled way by our proposed analysis.

Keywords: multiple sluicing, multiple wh-movement/fronting, sluicing, TP/IP-deletion, multiple pair or pair-list reading, Gapping, rightward focus movement, Wh-QP interaction, locality, clause-boundedness

1. Introduction

Human languages enjoy the common rule of economy: when some word or words are repeated, we do not verbally pronounce what is repeated. This linguistic phenomenon is called ellipsis or, in more technical terms, deletion, which is to delete or suppress the phonological features of repeated word/words in the course of syntactic derivation.

  Deletion is known to be rather widely available to the relevant contexts in English. It has been noted that there are three types of ellipsis depending on what constituent undergoes deletion: (i) VP ellipsis (or maybe vP ellipsis); (ii) NP ellipsis (in the DP system); (iii) T/IP ellipsis. What draws particular attention recently among the three types of ellipsis is the last kind, where wh-movement is mandatory before TP is elided. T/IP ellipsis or what Ross (1969) calls sluicing is illustrated by the following example:

(1) John met <u>someone</u>, but I don't know [CP [**who**] [TP ~~John met t~~]]

The fact that wh-movement feeds sluicing raises a question of whether in contrast to English with single wh-fronting, multiple sluicing (sluicing with multiple survivors) is possible in languages with multiple wh-fronting. Bulgarian and Serbo-Croatian, which allow for multiple wh-fronting, make a test case for this question, and indeed multiple sluicing is attested in these two languages as follows:

(2) <u>Njakoj</u> vidja <u>njakogo</u>, no ne znam   [**koj**] [**kogo**] [~~vidja~~]   Bulgarian
      someone saw someone,   but not I-know   who whom   saw   Richards (1997)
(3) <u>Neko</u>   je vidio <u>nekog</u>,   ali ne znam   [**ko**] [**koga**] [~~je vidio~~] Serbo-Croatian
      someone is seen someone, but not I-know who whom   is seen   Stjepanovic (2003)

Returning to English, a question that arises is whether multiple sluicing is allowed in non-multiple wh-fronting languages like English. Bearing on this question, Bolinger (1978:109) reports several examples like (4), which is quite similar in appearance to those involving multiple sluicing as in Bulgarian and Serbo-Croatian.

(4) I know that in each instance <u>one of the girls</u> got something <u>for one of the boys</u>. But [**which**] [**for which**]   Bolinger (1978: 109)

Incidentally, Bolinger notes that a certain restriction applies to the formation of more than one remnant wh-phrase. In particular, the second remnant wh-phrase is required to be PP, not DP, which is shown by the contrast between grammatical (4) and ungrammatical (5):

(5) *I know that in each instance <u>one of the girls</u> got something <u>for one of the boys</u>. But [**which**] [**which**]

The purpose of this paper is to probe into the nature of examples like (4). In particular, we will investigate whether examples like (4) are analyzed on a par with corresponding examples in Bulgarian and Serbo-Croatian. Although both Nishigauchi (1998) and Lasnik (2007) take a different tack, we will argue in this paper that peculiar properties of examples like (4) can be accounted for by the hypothesis that they are genuine instances of multiple sluicing.

2. A Gapping analysis of multiple sluicing in English: Nishigauchi (1998) and Lasnik (2007)
When we suppose that examples like (4) in English are genuine multiple sluicing which is derived by deleting a TP after multiple wh-fronting occurs out of it, an immediate problem facing us is why the example without TP deletion as in (6) is ungrammatical:

(6) *They didn't tell me [**which**] [**for which**] got something

The following pair also makes the same case. If it is true that (7) is derived by TP deletion after multiple wh-fronting, what rules out the example (8) without the supposed TP deletion?

(7) ?<u>One of the students</u> spoke <u>to one of the professors</u>, but I don't know [**which**] [**to which**]
(8) *<u>One of the students</u> spoke <u>to one of the professors</u>, but I don't know [**which**] [**to which**] spoke

To resolve this problem, Nishigauchi (1998) suggests that examples like (4) and (7) are not really multiple sluicing, but a kind of Gapping constructions. In this analysis, while the first wh-phrase is in Spec of CP, the second occupies some other position at the right edge of the clause, which can be represented roughly as follows:

(9) I know that in each instance <u>one of the girls</u> got something <u>for one of the boys</u>. But [**which**] g~~ot something~~ [**for which**]

If the example (4) results through the derivation represented in (9), it is taken not to involve multiple wh-fronting.

Lasnik (2007) renders further support to Nishigauchi's (1998) analysis of apparent multiple sluicing in English as involving Gapping by showing that the second wh-phrase in this construction exhibits the same properties as the second element in the Gapping construction does: it undergoes rightward focus movement. In this connection, Lasnik provides three pieces of evidence for the rightward focus movement hypothesis of the second wh-phrase.

First, the contrast between (10) and (11), and also between (12) and (13) shows that the second wh-phrase in the apparent multiple sluicing construction is required to be PP, but it cannot be DP:

(10) ?<u>Someone</u> talked <u>about something</u>, but I can't remember [**who**] [**about what**]
(11) ?*<u>Someone</u> saw <u>something</u>, but I can't remember [**who**] [**what**]
(12) ?Mary showed <u>something</u> <u>to someone</u>, but I don't know [**exactly what**] [**to whom**]
(13) ?*Mary showed <u>someone something</u>, but I don't know [**exactly who**] [**what**]

The contrast between PP and DP as the second wh-phrase in these examples is understood as saying that only the former can undergo rightward focus movement.

However, it has often been noted that DP can be shifted rightwards when it counts as 'heavy'. In the same vein with this finding, Lasnik notes that (14b) is ungrammatical because the second light DP wh-phrase cannot undergo rightward focus movement as in (14a). In contrast, as the second heavy DP wh-phrase can undergo rightward focus movement as in (15a), (15b) is ruled in:

(14)a. ?***Who** bought yesterday [**what**]
    b. ?*<u>Someone</u> bought <u>something</u>, but I don't know [**who**] [**what**]
(15)a. Which linguist criticized yesterday [**which paper about sluicing**]
    b. ?<u>Some linguist</u> criticized (yesterday) <u>some paper about sluicing</u>, but I don't know [**which linguist**] [**which paper about sluicing**]

Second, as Merchant (2001) notes, one striking fact about multiple sluices is that they tend not to be separated by a tensed clause boundary, which is what we learn from the example (18). This restriction does not hold for regular wh-movement as in (16) and (17):

(16) Which one of the professors did the students say that Mary spoke to
(17) The students said that Mary spoke to <u>one of the professors</u>, but I can't remember [**which professor**] the students said that Mary spoke to
(18) *<u>One of the students</u> said that Mary spoke <u>to one of the professors</u>, but I don't know [**which student**] ~~said that Mary spoke~~ [**to which professor**]

Lasnik (2007) interprets this restriction differently by saying that it in fact obtains because the second wh-phrase in the apparent multiple sluicing construction is subject to the Right Roof Constraint (Ross (1967)), which roughly says that a rightward focus moved element cannot move out of a finite clause. In Lasnik's terms, (18) is ungrammatical because the second wh-phrase *to which professor* has to move illicitly out of the embedded finite clause before Gapping applies.

Third, the clause with apparent multiple sluicing cannot be construed as a complex one containing an embedded finite clause, which is attributed to the Right Roof Constraint. As noted by Nishigauchi (1998), (19) is interpreted as (20), but not as (21):

(19) Mary said <u>everybody</u> talked <u>about something</u>, but I want to know [**who**] [**about what**]   Nishigauchi (1998)

(20) Mary said <u>everybody</u> talked <u>about something</u>, but I want to know [**who**] talked [**about what**]

(21) Mary said <u>everybody</u> talked <u>about something</u>, but I want to know *[**who**] Mary said e talked [**about what**]

Lasnik (2007) develops an ingenious test by using anaphor binding to confirm Nishigauchi's finding. He first notes that in (22) the remnant remaining after regular sluicing can contain an anaphor, bound via 'reconstruction', whose antecedent is in the deleted context.

(22) ?Everyone_i said that some pictures of himself_i hung on certain walls, but I'm not sure [**how many pictures of himself_i**]

With apparent multiple sluicing as in (23), however, acceptability degrades considerably:

(23) ?*Everyone_i said that <u>some pictures of himself_i</u> hung <u>on certain walls</u>, but I'm not sure [**how many pictures of himself_i**] [**on which walls**]

For the sake of anaphor binding, the deleted part is required to include the matrix subject *everyone_i*, which is the antecedent of the reflexive. In that case, however, the second remnant wh-phrase *on which walls* would have to move of the embedded finite clause, inviting a violation of the Right Roof Constraint.

3. Some problems with the Gapping analysis of multiple sluicing

Despite several new insightful findings that the Gapping analysis of apparent multiple sluicing makes possible, it confronts some problems. First, the restrictions on Gapping do not apply to multiple sluicing in an identical fashion. Notably, Gapping occurs in limited coordination contexts as in (24) (Johnson (1996/2003)):

(24)a. Betsy likes cats and Liz likes dogs
   b. Julie put out the trash, or Andrew put out the recycling bin
   c. First Sarah bought a car, then Liz bought a garage
   d. ?*Vivek likes Chinese action films, but Nishi likes sci-fi movies
   e. *Sam ate something, but Mittie ate nothing
   f. *Some ate nattoo today, because others ate natto yesterday

It occurs only when the two clauses are strictly parallel in terms of structure and interpretation. It cannot occur in coordinate *but* clause as in (24d-e), nor in adjunct clause as in (24f). Nor does it occur in the structural context of (25) because the clause where Gapping applies is not parallel to the corresponding first conjunct in terms of embedding:

(25) *John saw Bill, and Tom said that Mary saw Susan

However, multiple sluicing can occur in the structural contexts where Gapping is banned. The representative examples of multiple sluicing, which are repeated from the above, show that multiple sluicing can occur in the *but* and embedded clauses:

(4) I know that in each instance <u>one of the girls</u> got something <u>for one of the boys</u>. But [**which**] [**for which**]   Bolinger (1978:109)

(7) ?<u>One of the students</u> spoke <u>to one of the professors</u>, but I don't know [**which**] [**to which**]

Lasnik (2007)

Second, there is another difference between multiple sluicing and Gapping in terms of the category of the second remnant. As shown in (26), the second remnant is a wh-phrase.

(26) I know that in each instance <u>one of the girls</u> got something <u>for one of the boys</u>. But they didn't tell me [**which**] [**for which**]

A question is raised whether the second remnant can be a non-wh-phrase as found in the Gapping construction. Lasnik (2007) importantly notes that this is not possible as in (28). This is unexpected given the example (27), where ***about phonology*** can be focus moved rightwards, thereby potentially being survived as the second remnant in the multiple sluicing construction:

(27) **Who**$_i$ did Mary talk to t$_i$ t$_j$ yesterday [**about phonology**]$_j$?
(28) I know who Mary talked to yesterday about phonology, ?*but I don't know [**who**] [**about semantics**]

Note, however, that typical instances of Gapping allow the first remnant to be a wh-phrase, and the second one to be a non-wh-phrase, as follows:

(29)a. Which boy read Hamlet, and [**which girl**] [**Macbeth**]?
    b. Which boy talked about baseball, and [**which girl**] [**about ballet**]?
    c. ?Which boy did Mary talk to about music, and [**which girl**] [**about movies**]?

Third, the Gapping analysis of apparent multiple sluicing predicts that when the second remnant is forbidden from undergoing rightward focus movement, it is not possible to produce examples with multiple sluicing. One relevant test case is the exceptionally Case-marked element, which is known not to undergo rightward focus movement, as in (31):

(30) I believe <u>the politician with high profile in international affairs</u> to be dishonest
(31) *I believe to be dishonest <u>the politician with high profile in international affairs</u>

It seems that this structural context, however, can feed multiple sluicing, as follows:

(32) <u>One of the boys</u> believes <u>behind one of the trees</u> to be the best place to hide, but I don't know [**which**] [**behind which tree**]
(33) <u>One of the RAs</u> expects <u>from one of the cells</u> to emerge a tiny being, but I don't know [**which**] [**from which cell**]

In this section it has been noted that the Gapping analysis of apparent multiple sluicing faces some non-trivial problems. Instead of resolving these problems under the Gapping analysis, we will pursue an alternative analysis of multiple sluicing in English.

4. Towards a 'canonical' multiple sluicing analysis

The analysis we are exploring is that the two wh-phrases in the multiple sluicing construction both are in Spec of CP. The first one undergoes typical wh-movement into Spec of CP, and then the second one tucks into the position using the mode developed by Richards (1997). Multiple wh-fronting then feeds TP deletion. The derivation along this line of analysis can be represented below:

(34) ?<u>One of the students</u> spoke <u>to one of the professors</u>, but I don't know [**which**]ᵢ [**to which**]ⱼ [t̶ᵢ̶ ̶s̶p̶o̶k̶e̶ ̶t̶ⱼ̶]

Our proposed analysis has to account for the three properties of multiple sluicing noted under the Gapping approach to it: (i) remnants are only wh-phrases; (ii) the second remnant wh-phrase is a 'heavy' constituent; (iii) multiple sluicing only occurs in a simple clause.

The first property of multiple sluicing follows without any stipulation from the proposed analysis. Since it is assumed that two remnants undergo movement into Spec of CP before TP deletion applies, they have to be wh-phrases.

However, the assumption that two remnants undergo movement into Spec of CP in the multiple sluicing construction raises a question of why two wh-phrases cannot move into Spec of CP in the sentence without TP deletion. The examples, repeated below, make the point:

(7) ?<u>One of the students</u> spoke <u>to one of the professors</u>, but I don't know [**which**] [**to which**]

(8) *<u>One of the students</u> spoke <u>to one of the professors</u>, but I don't know [**which**] [**to which**] spoke

To understand the contrast between (7) and (8), we first need to assume a certain theory of how wh-movement proceeds. We adopt the recent theory of wh-movement advanced by Richards (1997/2001) and Pesetsky (2000). According to them, the difference in overt and covert wh-movement is not due to the presence or absence of wh-movement itself, but to the application of the copy deletion operation afterwards. Both overt and covert wh-movement apply "overtly," and the first is realized apparently when the tail of the movement is deleted, but the second is realized when the head of the movement is deleted. The thing which determines which copy is deleted is a strong feature. When the probe has a strong EPP feature, the tail of the movement undergoes copy deletion. Otherwise, the head of the movement does.

Assuming this theory of wh-movement, we return to the contrast between (7) and (8). In the latter case, the first but not the second wh-phrase is associated with the strong feature of the probe. Hence the tail of the first wh-phrase undergoes copy deletion, while the head of the second wh-phrase does so. (8) is ruled out because not the head but the tail of the second wh-phrase undergoes copy deletion.

Turning to the former case of multiple sluicing, what distinguishes (7) from (8) is that the tail position of the second wh-phrase is included within the TP constituent affected by the more general operation of (canonical) deletion. In this structural context, if its head is deleted by the copy deletion operation, the second wh-phrase will violate the Recoverability condition on deletion. To avoid this result, its head survives instead, while its tail is part of TP deletion, yielding the multiple sluicing construction. In a nutshell, the head copy not associated with a strong feature can be realized just when the tail copy is included within the constituent undergoing deletion.

We now move on to the second property of the multiple sluicing construction: the second remnant wh-phrase is a 'heavy' constituent. We do not have in hand a good account for the property, but the previous note or formulation regarding it will be helpful in understanding it. First, reporting the contrast between (4) and (5), repeated below, Bolinger (1978) notes that as for (5), "it illustrates a kind of homonymic conflict under the worst possible conditions of repeated accents. Even without accent problem ..., similar repetitions are avoided elsewhere. ....":

(4) I know that in each instance <u>one of the girls</u> got something <u>for one of the boys</u>. But [**which**] [**for which**]

(5) *I know that in each instance <u>one of the girls</u> got something <u>for one of the boys</u>. But [**which**] [**which**]

In (4), homonymic conflict does not arise when the second wh-phrase is PP. Nor does it arise in (15b), repeated below, where the second heavy wh-phrase ensures distinctness from the first wh-phrase.

(15)b. ?<u>Some linguist</u> criticized (yesterday) <u>some paper about sluicing</u>, but I don't know [**which linguist**] [**which paper about sluicing**]

Moreover, on the basis of the contrast between (4) and (5) as well as other various constructions, Richards (2006) proposes a ban on structurally adjacent DPs, which he calls a Distinctness Condition.

(35) Distinctness

If a linearization statement $<\alpha, \alpha>$ is generated, the derivation crashes.

This condition rejects trees in which two nodes that are both of type α are to be linearized in the same phase. Though it can rule out the basic case in (5), however, the condition as it is is too strong, in that it rules out (15b) wrongly. In this sense Bolinger's account for the contrast between (4) and (5) based on the intuitive notion of homonymic conflict seems to be on the right tract.

We now turn to the third property of the multiple sluicing construction: multiple sluicing only occurs in a simple clause. As we saw above, in Lasnik's (2007) analysis this locality restriction of the multiple sluicing construction is ascribed to the fact that the second wh-phrase undergoes rightward focus movement obeying the Right Roof Constraint before Gapping applies. Although some problems were already raised with the Gapping analysis of multiple sluicing in the previous section, there still seems to be another problem with this analysis's treatment of the locality restriction. In particular, it is to be noted that the similar locality restriction holds in the multiple sluicing construction of some languages which disallow rightward focus movement; for example, in Korean and Japanese, which are head-final languages. The following examples in Korean make a case:

(36)a. <u>nuwkuwnka-ka</u>   <u>etten iyaki-ul</u>   malhayss-ciman,
      someone   -Nom some story-Acc said   -but
      na-nun [**nuw-ka   etten iyaki**-inci]   kiekha   mos-ha-nta
       -Top   who-Nom   which story-Comp   remember not   do
      'Someone told some story, but I cannot remember who which story.'
    b. *Mary-ka   <u>nuwkuwnka-eykey</u> [John-i   <u>etten umsik-ul</u>
       -Nom   someone-to   -Nom   some food-Acc
      cohahanta-ko] malhayss-ciman, kunye-nun [**nuwkuw-eykey**
      like-Comp]   said-but   -Top   whom-to
      etten umsik-inci]   kiekhaci   mos hanta
      which food-Q   remember   not   do
      'Mary said to someone that [John liked some food], but Mary cannot remember to whom which food.'   (modeled on Takahashi's (1994) Japanese example)

The contrast between (36a) and (36b) bears on the question of whether the two remnants are separated by a tensed clause boundary in their launching positions before they undergo wh-movement. The fact that the locality restriction holds even in rightward movement-forbidding languages does not provide a direct argument against Lasnik's account for the restriction in English. However, it is desirable to seek after a more general account for the locality restriction in multiple sluicing.

Unlike Lasnik (2007), we attribute the locality restriction in multiple sluicing to the fact that indefinite expressions in the antecedent clause are quantificational; hence they are subject to the well-known clause-bound condition when they take scope at Logical Form (May (1985); Hornstein (1995)). We demonstrate this idea with the example dealt with by Nishigauchi (1998), repeated from the above:

(19) Mary said <u>everybody</u> talked <u>about something</u>, but I want to know [**who**] [**about what**]

We represent (19) in a more detailed manner as (37), with some names of the constituents we will use for our description below:

(37) Mary said <u>everybody</u> talked <u>about something</u>,   [antecedent clause]
        <indefinite correlate>   <indefinite correlate>
    but I want to know [**who**]ᵢ [**about what**]ⱼ [~~tᵢ talked tⱼ~~]   [ellipsis clause]
        <corresponding wh>/<corresponding wh>

In (37) the correlate ***everybody*** in the antecedent clause takes scope in the clause where it appears. Furthermore, in compliance with the scope parallelism condition (Fox and Lasnik (2003); Merchant (2001; to appear)), the corresponding multiple wh-phrases in the ellipsis clause take scope parallel to the indefinite correlates in the antecedent clause. In this way we can ensure that the elided constituent in the antecedent clause of (37) is a simple clause.

There are, however, the multiple sluicing constructions where two indefinite expressions in the antecedent clause are apparently existential, as in (38), which is cited from Lasnik (2007):

(38) Mary said that <u>one of the students</u> spoke <u>to one of the professors</u>, but I can't remember [**which**]ᵢ [**to which**]ⱼ [~~(?*Mary said that) [tᵢ spoke tⱼ]~~]

If existentially quantified expressions can take freer scope than universally quantified ones as argued by Pesetsky (1987) and Reinhart (1997), the unacceptability of (38) with the complex TP deleted is unexpected, which raises a problem with our proposed analysis.

To resolve this problem, we rely on Nishigauchi's (1998) report that the multiple sluicing construction tends to yield multiple pair reading in which the two fronted remnant wh-phrases are interpreted pair-wise. In this respect the sluiced clause of (7), repeated below, is similar to the multiple wh-construction as in (39), which also allows a multiple pair reading of the two wh-phrases:

(7) ?<u>One of the students</u> spoke <u>to one of the professors</u>, but I don't know [**which**] [**to which**]
(39) **Which student** spoke **to which professor**?

Comorovski (1996) makes the important note that when (39) is interpreted with a multiple pair reading, the first wh-phrase has the following properties:

(40)a. It has universal force.
    b. It must be d(iscourse)-linked.

If this is true, then we are ready to account for the unacceptability of (38) with a complex sluiced clause. Since it has universal force, being quantificational, the first remnant wh-phrase of (38) obeys the clause-bound condition in taking scope. The scope parallelism condition then requires that the preceding correlate indefinite expression in the antecedent clause takes scope parallel to the remnant wh-phrase. Hence the contrast between (41) and (42), corresponding to (38):

(41) Mary said that <u>one of the students</u> spoke <u>to one of the professors</u>, but I can't remember [**which**]$_i$ [**to which**]$_j$ [t̶$_i$-̶s̶p̶o̶k̶e̶-t̶$_j$]
(42) ?*Mary said that <u>one of the students</u> spoke <u>to one of the professors</u>, but I can't remember [**which**]$_i$ [**to which**]$_j$ [(̶M̶a̶r̶y̶ ̶s̶a̶i̶d̶ ̶t̶h̶a̶t̶)̶ ̶[̶t̶$_i$-̶s̶p̶o̶k̶e̶ ̶t̶$_j$]̶]

It is to be noted that unlike the multiple sluicing construction, the following multiple wh-construction is grammatical even when it is interpreted with a multiple pair reading:

(43) [**Which student**]$_i$ [did Mary say [t$_i$ spoke [**to which professor**]] ?

This is because this construction is not subject to the scope parallelism condition. In (43) the moving wh-phrase **which student** can take scope at the embedded clause and then undergo further movement into Spec of the matrix CP (Saito and Murasugi (1992)). In other words, it can take cyclic movement which consists of QR followed by wh-movement.

  However, in the antecedent clause of (42) the typical quantified expression takes scope by making a non-cyclic, one-fell-swoop movement (May (1985)). Therefore, the ellipsis clause is construed as a simple clause because otherwise the antecedent and ellipsis clauses in the multiple sluicing construction will violate the scope parallelism condition. To be short, the size restriction on the elided constituent in multiple sluicing is attributed to the scope parallelism condition as well as the clause-bound condition on quantificational expressions.

  We now turn to another example the unacceptability of which the Gapping analysis of multiple sluicing blames for a violation of the Right Roof Constraint, (18), repeated below:

(18) *<u>One of the students</u> said that Mary spoke <u>to one of the professors</u>, but I don't know [**which student**] s̶a̶i̶d̶ ̶t̶h̶a̶t̶ ̶M̶a̶r̶y̶ ̶s̶p̶o̶k̶e̶ [**to which professor**]

In our present approach, (18) is analyzed on a par with the following example reported by Dayal (2002), which is unacceptable when it is construed with a multiple pair reading:

(44) **Which student** believes that Mary read **which book**?

(18) exhibits the same pattern with the following example discussed by Sloan (1991), which is ruled out when it has multiple pair interpretation between the universal quantifier and the trace of the wh-phrase:

(45) **Which book** does **every student** believe that Mary read?

It seems that the conclusion drawn from these examples is that a usual universal quantifier or universally interpreted wh-phrase has a local relation with another wh-phrase when they produce pair-wise interpretation. The former functions as a distributor, and the latter as a share associated with it. As both distributor and share are quantificational, they have to take scope in the clause where they are generated. It is still not clear how multiple pair interpretation is derived, but it seems right to say that the interpretational operation that yields multiple pair interpretation, like the absorption operation proposed by Higginbotham and May (1981), calls for a locality or clause-bound condition. We leave for future study the elaboration on this issue.

5. Conclusion

The recent Gapping approach to multiple sluicing has made an important contribution to the understanding of it. The approach uncovers the following properties of the multiple sluicing construction. First, remnants are only wh-phrases. Second, the second remnant wh-phrase is a 'heavy' constituent. Third, multiple sluicing only occurs in a simple clause. Despite the contribution the Gapping approach has made, we have tried to show that it confronts several problems which seem not easy to overcome in keeping with the approach.

We rather have argued that two remnant wh-phrases in multiple sluicing reside in Spec of CP. In other words, multiple sluicing in English constitutes a rare instance which is fed by multiple wh-fronting. It has also been demonstrated that our proposed approach can provide a non-ad-hoc, principled account for the properties of the construction noted by Lasnik (2007) under the Gapping analysis. In particular, the locality restriction on multiple sluicing, that is, the fact that multiple sluicing only occurs in a simple clause, follows from two things. One is the scope parallelism condition which applies to ellipsis constructions in general. The other is multiple pair interpretation available to the multiple sluicing construction which obtains when the first remnant wh-phrase with universal force functions as a distributor, while the second remnant wh-phrase with existential force functions as a distributor share.

References

Barrie, Michael. 2005. Control and wh-infinitivals. New Horizons in the Grammar of Raising and Control. Harvard University.

Bolinger, Dwight. 1978. Asking more than One Thing at a Time. In *Questions*, ed. Henry Hiz, 107-150. Dordrecht: Reidel.

Comorovski, Ileana. 1996. *Interrrogative Phrases and the Syntax-Semantics Interface.* Dordrecht: Kluwer Academic Publishers.

Dayal, Veneeta. 2002. Single-pair vs. Multiple-pair Answers: Wh in-situ and Scope. *Linguistic Inquiry* 333:512-20.

Fox, Danny and Howard Lasnik. 2003. Successive-cyclic movement and island repair: The difference between sluicing and VP-ellipsis. *Linguistic Inquiry* 34:143-154.

Higginbotham, James and Robert May. 1981 Questions, Quantifiers and Crossing. *The Linguistic Review* 1:41-79.

Hornstein, Norbert: 1995. Logical Form: From GB to Minimalism. Oxford: Blackwell.

Johnson, Kyle. 1996/2003. In search of the middle field. Unpublished manuscript. University of Massachusetts at Amherst.

Lasnik, Howard. 2007. Multiple Sluicing. An handout given in LING 819 Spring 2007. University of Maryland.

May, Robert. 1985. *Logical Form: Its Structure and Derivation.* Cambridge, Mass.: MIT Press.

Merchant, Jason. 2001. *The Syntax of Silence: Sluicing, Islands, and the Theory of Ellipsis.* Oxford: Oxford University Press.

Merchant, Jason. To appear. Variable island repair under ellipsis. In *Topics in Ellipsis*, ed. Kyle Johnson. Cambridge: Cambridge University Press.

Milsark, Gary. 1977. Toward an explanation of certain peculiarities of the existential. construction in English. *Linguistic Analysis* 3:1-30.

Nishigauchi, Taisuke. 1998. 'Multiple Sluicing' in Japanese and the functional nature of wh-phrases. *Journal of East Asian Linguistics* 7:121-152.

Pesetsky, David. 1987. Wh-in-situ: Movement and Unselective Binding. In *The Representation of (In)definites*, ed. by Eric Reuland and Alice ter Meulen, 98-129. Cambridge, Mass: MIT. Press.

__________. 2000. *Phrasal Movement and Its Kin*. Cambridge, Mass.: MIT Press.

Reinhart, Tanya. 1997. Wh-in-situ in the Framework of the Minimalist Program. *Natural Language Semantics* 6:29-56.

Richards, Norvin. 1997. *What Moves Where When in Which Language?* PhD, MIT, Cambridge, Mass.

Richards, Norvin. 2001. *Movement in Language*. Oxford: Oxford University Press.

__________. 2006. A Distinctness condition on linearization. Ms. Department of Linguistics and Philosophy, MIT, Cambridge, Mass.

Ross, John Robert. 1967. *Constraints on Variables in Syntax*. Doctoral dissertation, MIT, Cambridge, Mass. Published as *Infinite Syntax*! Norwood, N.J.: Ablex (1986).

__________. 1969. Guess who? In *Papers from the Fifth Regional Meeting of the Chicago Linguistic Society*, ed. Robert I. Binnick, Alice Davison, Georgia M. Green, and Jerry L. Morgan, 252-286. Chicago Linguistic Society, University of Chicago, Chicago, Ill.

Saito, Mamoru and Keiko Murasugi. 1992. Quasi-Adjuncts as Sentential Arguments. In *Proceedings of the Western Conference on Linguistics* (WECOL) 6.

Sloan, Kelly. 1991. Quantifier-wh interaction. In *MIT working papers in linguistics* 15,. 219-237. Department of Linguistics and Philosophy, MIT, Cambridge, Mass.

Stjepanovic, Sandra. 2003. Multiple wh-fronting in Serbo-Croatian matrix questions and the matrix sluicing construction. In *Multiple Wh-fronting*, ed. Cedric Boeckx and Kleanthes K. Grohmann, 255-284. Amsterdam: John Benjamins.

Takahashi, Daiko. 1994. Sluicing in Japanese. *Journal of East Asian Linguistics*. 3:263-300.

Prosodic Annotation in a Thai Text-to-speech System[*]

Siripong Potisuk

Department of Electrical and Computer Engineering
The Citadel, The Military College of South Carolina
171 Moultrie Street
Charleston, South Carolina 29409 USA
siripong.potisuk@citadel.edu

Abstract. This paper describes a preliminary work on prosody modeling aspect of a text-to-speech system for Thai. Specifically, the model is designed to predict symbolic markers from text (i.e., prosodic phrase boundaries, accent, and intonation boundaries), and then using these markers to generate pitch, intensity, and durational patterns for the synthesis module of the system. In this paper, a novel method for annotating the prosodic structure of Thai sentences based on dependency representation of syntax is presented. The goal of the annotation process is to predict from text the rhythm of the input sentence when spoken according to its intended meaning. The encoding of the prosodic structure is established by minimizing speech disrhythmy while maintaining the congruency with syntax. That is, each word in the sentence is assigned a prosodic feature called strength dynamic which is based on the dependency representation of syntax. The strength dynamics assigned are then used to obtain rhythmic groupings in terms of a phonological unit called foot. Finally, the foot structure is used to predict the durational pattern of the input sentence. The aforementioned process has been tested on a set of ambiguous sentences, which represents various structural ambiguities involving five types of compounds in Thai.

Keywords: Text-to-speech, Prosody.

1. Introduction

Presently, widespread use of text-to-speech technology is limited by its inability to produce high-quality speech. That is, intelligibility and naturalness of synthetic speech is still not quite at the level acceptable by human listeners. In particular, the naturalness issue can be attributed to the lack of sophisticated prosody-generating scheme.

Prosody is often described as a suprasegmental feature of speech (a term for describing phonological features of those aspects of speech that involve more than single consonants or vowels). Acoustically speaking, prosody can be defined as change in the fundamental frequency (F_0), timing, and amplitude of a speech signal. Speakers control the prosody of an utterance in order to signal linguistic and affective information. Linguistic prosody is used by speakers to signal

---

[*] The author would like to thank the Citadel Foundation for its financial support in the form of a presentation grant.

grammatical information at the syllable, word, or sentence level (e.g., stress, intonation). Affective prosody, on the other hand, is used to convey information that indicates speaker's intentions, attitudes, or emotional states. In addition to linguistic and affective information, prosody can also be used to convey non-linguistic information concerning speaker's personal characteristics such as age, gender, idiosyncrasy, speaking style, and physical condition. Such characteristics may or may not be under the speaker's volitional control. It is part of the intelligibility and naturalness of his/her speech. This paper will deal with linguistic prosody only.

The role of linguistic prosody in spoken language is similar to that of punctuation in written language. Punctuation is used to divide a stream of text into smaller segments such as a phrase, clause, or sentence, and thus, helps readers interpret the message according to the intention of the writer. Likewise, prosodic information helps listeners interpret a spoken utterance in the way the speakers intends. The need for punctuation or prosody can be attributed in part to the inherent ambiguity of natural language.

Intuition tells us that intelligibility and naturalness of speech can be attributed to prosody. Some words in an utterance are louder and longer than others. Because function words are acoustically less prominent than the semantically important content words, such as nouns and verbs, we can prosodically distinguish them. Pauses tend to be inserted at certain points in the utterance, and words at the end of the utterance are likely to be lengthened. This suggests the existence of prosodic constituents that are used in the overall prosodic structure or melody of an utterance. Linguists have posited units such as syllables, prosodic words, phonological phrases, and intonational phrases.

The use of prosody by speakers, in attempting to sound intelligibly and naturally, can be best exemplified by considering its use in ambiguous sentences. When two sentences are segmentally identical, a problem of identifying the correct meaning arises for listener, especially when the contextual information is not adequate. In such cases, the listener can make use of another type of information, namely prosody. The question arises, from the speaker's point of view, as to how this information is decoded or associated with different meanings. At an abstract level, a commonly accepted hypothesis is that there is a direct relationship between the syntactic structure of a sentence and its prosodic structure as suggested by Selkirk (1984), and Nespor (1986). This hypothesis implies that an ambiguous sentence will have a different prosodic structure for each syntactic structure, and as such it can be used to determine the correct meaning. At the phonetic level, the speaker tends to manipulate the acoustic correlates of prosody, such as F_0, segmental and pause duration, amplitude, and spectrum of the speech signal in order to signal prosody. The listener, in turn, will try to translate changes in these physical correlates into abstract linguistic concepts in order to arrive at the intended meaning of the utterance.

As in human speech, it is believed that prosodic information can help improve performance of a text-to-speech system. Prosodic information is particularly helpful in generating synthetic speech because of lexical and structural ambiguities of written forms. Prosodic information could be used by computers to generate phonetically similar, but syntactically different utterances.

In the following sections, a novel method for annotating prosody in a text-to-speech system will be described. The process will be abstractly described and demonstrated by using structurally ambiguous sentences involving different types of compounds in Thai. Vongvipanond (1993) concluded that compounds are a major cause of structural ambiguity in Thai and often create problems because of their high frequency of occurrence. Compounding is the most widespread word formation process in Thai. Structural ambiguities often result from compounds because Thai words lack inflectional and derivational affixes to indicate, for example, subject-verb agreement. Nevertheless, compounds can be prosodically distinguished from syntactic phrases by differences in stress patterns. In addition, the process of generating durational patterns for the utterance based on the prosodic annotation process will also be described.

2. Text Processing

Text processing is considered one of the many important aspects of a text-to-speech system involving language modeling. A language model often consists of a grammar written using some formalism which is applied to a sentence by utilizing some sort of parsing algorithm. One popular example is a set of context-free grammar (CFG) production rules, which is based on a phrase-structure representation of syntax by Chomsky (1963), can be used to parse sentences in the language defined by that grammar. A phrase-structure grammar uses a phrase-structure tree (PS-tree) to describe the groupings of words into the so-called *constituents* at different levels of sentence construction. A PS-tree shows which items go together with other items to form tight units of a higher-order, a distributional characteristic of a grouping within a larger grouping. Syntactic class membership is a way of labeling syntactic roles in a PS-tree because a PS-tree does not and cannot specify the types of syntactic links existing between two items in a natural and explicit way. Another approach to syntactic parsing is based on dependency grammar. A dependency grammar describes the syntactic structure of a sentence by using a dependency tree (D-tree) to establish dependencies among words in terms of head and dependents. A D-tree shows a relational characteristic of the syntactic representation in the form of hierarchical links between items, i.e., which items are related to which other items and in which way. In contrast to PS-tree, class membership is not specified in a D-tree. Instead, a D-tree puts a particular emphasis on specifying in detail the type of any syntactic relation between two related items. Such syntactic relations are, for example, predicative, determinative, coordinative relations, etc.

From the above contrastive description of the two approaches to representing the syntax of natural languages, one can draw the following conclusion. The phrase-structure representation is suitable for languages like English, which have a rigid word order and a near absence of syntactically driven morphology. On the other hand, the dependency representation is suitable for languages like Latin or Russian, which feature an incredibly flexible (but far from arbitrary) word order and very rich systems of morphological markings. Word arrangements and inflectional affixes are obviously contingent upon relations between words rather than upon constituents.

In this paper, we argue for the choice of dependency representation of grammar for Thai. We also adopted an alternative formalism, a constraint dependency grammar (CDG) proposed by Potisuk (1996). Thai is the official language of Thailand, a country in the Southeast Asia region. The language is spoken by approximately 65 million people throughout different parts of the country. The written form is used in school and all official forms of communication.

We believe that a CDG parser appears to be an attractive choice for analyzing Thai sentences considering vantage points from both written and spoken language processing aspects of an automatic system. CDG parsers rule out ungrammatical sentences by propagating constraints. Constraints are developed based on a dependency-based representation of syntax. The motivation for our choice of dependency grammar, instead of phrase-structure grammar, stems from the fact that it appears that Thai syntax might be better described by the former representation.

Difficulties in parsing Thai sentences using traditional CFG parsers arise for the following reasons. First, Thai sentences do not contain delimiters or blanks between words. Unlike English, Thai words in a sentence are not flanked by a blank space. Words are concatenated to form a phrase or sentence without explicit word delimiters. This creates a problem for the syntactic analysis of Thai sentences because most parsers operate on words as the smallest syntactic unit in a sentence. To overcome this problem, a word segmentation module must be added to the front end of the parser. This solution, in turn, creates a new problem. Instead of analyzing a single sentence, a parser must now analyze multiple sentence hypotheses comprising a combination of all possible words generated by the word segmentation algorithm. Secondly, Thai words lack inflectional and derivational affixes. Since words in Thai do not inflect to indicate their syntactic function, the position of a word in a sentence alone shows its syntactic function. Hence, syntactic relationships are primarily determined by word order, and structural ambiguity often arises. Thirdly, inconsistent ordering relations within and across phrasal categories characterize Thai sentences. While a noun, the head of a noun phrase, always precedes its modifying adjectives and determiners, the verb phrase exhibits less consistency. Although a verb, the head of the verb phrase, always precedes its object, its modifying auxiliaries can either precede or follow it. In addition, constituents that optionally occur with the head in both noun and verb phrases, such as determiners and quantifiers, tend to be less consistent in their ordering as well. Lastly, Thai sentences sometimes contain discontinuous sentence constituents in their construction. In grammatical analysis, discontinuity refers to the splitting of a construction by insertion of another grammatical unit. In other words, discontinuity occurs when the elements which make up the constituents are interrupted by elements of another constituent in a sentence.

Given the aforementioned properties of Thai sentences, a CDG parser offers many advantages over traditional CFG parsers in order to overcome the difficulties in parsing Thai. For one thing, CDG is capable of efficiently analyzing free-order languages because order between constituents is not a requirement of the grammatical formalism. Since Thai exhibits significant word order variation, using CFG to describe Thai is cumbersome because numerous rules would be needed to cover all possible configurations of a constituent. Secondly, The CDG approach provides a uniform mechanism of constraint propagation for each knowledge source, i.e., lexical, syntactic, semantic, and pragmatic information, in resolving ambiguities during parsing. The constraints for each knowledge source can be independently developed and applied. A CFG parser, on the other hand, does not provide a good coordinating scheme because it is incapable of selectively invoking different knowledge sources. Concerning the need to analyze multiple sentence hypotheses, our CDG parser allows efficient processing in the form of a constraint network consisting of a directed acyclic word graph augmented with parse-related information. Multiple sentence hypotheses are thus processed simultaneously by pruning the network through the propagation of various constraints. The network also provides a much better representation than a list of sentence hypotheses because it reduces redundancy and compactly represents the set of sentence hypotheses, thereby reducing the storage requirement. Due to the scope of the paper, a description of the basics of CDG parsing of Thai will be omitted. Interested readers are referred to the paper by Potisuk (1996) for a discussion of the basic framework and a parsing example. After all the constraints are propagated across the constraint network and filtering is completed, the network provides a compact representation of all possible parses. Syntactic ambiguity is easy to spot in the network. If multiple parses exist, then additional constraints, such as semantic constraints, can be propagated to further refine the analysis to the intended meaning of the input sentence. The resulting parse trees are then ready to be prosodically annotated. The annotation process is described next.

3. Prosodic Annotation

Prosodic annotation or encoding provides to the prosody-generating module in a text-to-speech system relevant information that adequately captures the essence of the prosodic structure of the input sentence or text. Prosodic encoding usually involves the process of predicting prosodic labels for the input sentence according to the intended meaning. The labeling criteria provide a mechanism for mapping abstract prosodic labels into a sequence of acoustic correlates of prosody. As a result, prosodically-labeled sentences contain information concerning the correspondence between the phonological and phonetic attributes of the prosodic structure of utterances and their intended meanings. Prosodic labels should be chosen to represent abstract linguistic categories of prosody, such as rhythmic groupings (or phrasing) and prominence. Also, they should be chosen such that they are used consistently within and across human labelers, and they make the automatic labeling process tractable and consistent. An example of a prosodic labeling system for English speech is described next.

Price et al. (1991) proposed a labeling system consisting of seven labels, called prosodic break indices. These break indices express the degree of perceived decoupling or separation between every pair of words in an utterance. A boundary within a clitic group (e.g. determiner-noun, two-word verb, etc.) is indicated by a 0 break index; a normal word boundary by a 1; a boundary marking a minor grouping of words by a 2; an intermediate phrase boundary by a 3; an intonational phrase by a 4; a boundary marking a grouping of intonational phrases by a 5; and a sentence boundary by a 6. In terms of prominence, prominent syllables in an utterance are indicated by P1 for a major phrasal prominence; P0 for a lesser prominence; C for contrastive stress; and S for syllables with no prominence. Price demonstrated that these metrics could be used effectively by human labelers to determine how speakers encode prosodic cues for structural ambiguities in structurally ambiguous sentences.

In this paper, we modified the Price's methods in the development of our prosodic encoding scheme for Thai to accommodate the use of dependency grammar formalism. The encoding of the prosodic structure is accomplished by annotating each word in the sentence with a prosodic feature called strength. We describe next how the strength features are derived and compare them with Price's break indices.

The strength feature is chosen based on the dependency representation of syntax. According to the congruency model of syntax and prosody used by Bailly (1983), a relation of dominance between two adjacent lexical items can be established based on their positions in the D-tree. Figure 1 illustrates the four basic configurations of relational marks between adjacent lexical items in a D-tree. ID or independence indicates no direct link between the two items; IT or interdependence indicates the dependence of the two lexical items on the same governor; LD or left dependence indicates the dependence on the following word; RD or right dependence indicates the dependence on the preceding word. It is noted that LD and RD are relational marks between two lexical items at different levels of the D-tree while ID and IT are at the same level.

In addition, we have developed a new set of relational marks called strength dynamics in order to take into account the information about the lexical category of each word in addition to its position in the D-tree. Lexical category information is important because it is related to the stress placement rules in spoken language. Content words are usually stressed; function words are usually unstressed.

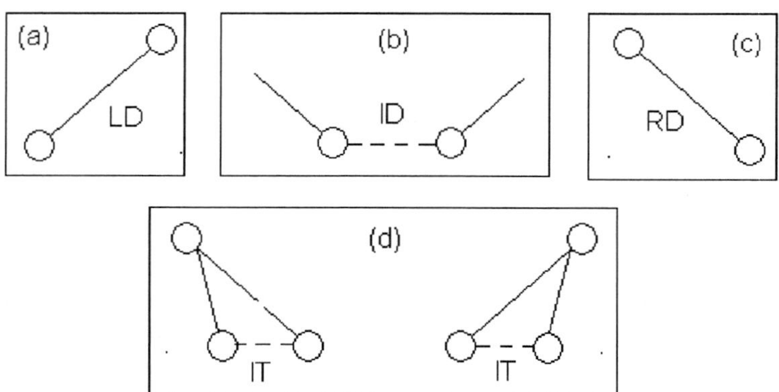

Figure 1: The four basic configurations of the relational marks in the dependency tree: (a) left dependence (LD), (b) independence (ID), (c) right dependence (RD), and (d) interdependence (IT).

There are four levels of strength dynamics: strong dependence (SD), dependence (DE), independence (ID), and strong independence (SI). SD describes a strength dynamic at the word boundary within a clitic group, within a compound, between a content and a function word, or between two function words that are interdependent (i.e., both depend on the same governor). DE describes strength dynamic at minor phrase boundaries, i.e., between a subject noun phrase and a verb phrase, between a verb and an object noun phrase, or between two content words. ID describes strength dynamic at major phrase boundaries (intonational phrases). And, SI describes strength dynamic at the sentence boundary.

Like the break indices used in Price's labeling system, these strength dynamics indicate the degree of connection between the present and the preceding words in an input sentence. They are similar in a sense that both represent the relationship between two adjacent words in a sentence. The stronger the dependency strength is, the smaller the break index. Nonetheless, the strength dynamic has an added benefit in terms of the lexical category information. In addition to the strength feature, a word at the end of a phrase or an utterance will receive the feature *'final'* to indicate that it is affected by the final lengthening effect. Final lengthening is always accompanied by a pause. A word with a *'final'* feature also automatically receives a strength dynamic of ID or SI.

In addition, we utilize a prosodic encoding scheme that integrates both syntactic and rhythmic constraints. That is, the prosodic structure of an utterance is established by minimizing speech disrhythmy while maintaining the congruency with syntax.

Speech is rhythmical not only because of the pattern of sounds and pauses, but also because of the regular recurrence of strongly accented sounds in a series. For example, in a stressed-time language, it is observed by Gee (1983) that speakers tend to produce stressed syllables at a regularly spaced interval of time while they tend to pause according to the syntax of the utterance. The pause distribution seems to be ruled by syntactic constraints. Speech rhythm is also a psychological correlate of speech timing (an objective instrumental measurement of the duration of segments, syllables, etc.) Thus, in a stressed-time language, stress, pause and relative syllable durations interact to form speech rhythm. In addition, the phonology and syntax of the language affect the description of speech rhythm as well.

Thai has a stress-timed rhythm according to Luangthongkum (1977). This means that stressed syllables in Thai are perceived to be isochronous (i.e., they recur approximately at equal intervals of time). A phonological unit called foot is used to describe rhythmic groupings within an utterance. A foot is one of many prosodic constituents and is an elementary unit of the prosodic structure in addition to a syllable. A foot is neither a grammatical nor a lexical unit. The domain of a foot extends from a salient (stressed) syllable up to but not including the next salient syllable. A pause is considered a salient syllable, and the beginning of an utterance is always preceded by a pause. It should be noted that a rhythmic pause has a syntactic function, but a disfluency or hesitation pause does not.

In her analysis of Thai rhythm, Luangthongkum posited five foot structures: | S | = one-syllable foot, | S W | = two-syllable foot, | S W W | = three-syllable foot, | S W W W | = four-syllable foot, | S W W W W | = five-syllable foot, where S and W indicate salient (stressed) and weak (unstressed) syllables, respectively. The four-syllable and five-syllable feet are very rare and are omitted from further discussion. Note that foot boundaries are usually inserted in front of the salient syllables.

Based on the discussion above, the strength dynamics assigned earlier can be used to obtain the information about the foot structure using the following rules. Since we only distinguish between two classes of stress, the salient syllable immediately after a weak syllable receives a strength dynamic of SD. A word before a pause receives a strength dynamic of DE as well as the *'final'* feature. A word after a pause receives a strength dynamic of SI if it is in the utterance-initial position; otherwise, it receives a strength dynamic of ID.

4. Prediction of Durational Patterns

First, we describe the criteria for obtaining duration and pause information from the above strength features (through the derived foot structure). These criteria establish the correspondence between the phonological (strength dynamics) and the phonetic (acoustic correlates) attributes of prosody.

At an abstract level, Luangthongkum assumed that each rhythmic foot is arbitrarily three units long, regardless of the number of syllables comprising the foot. This suggests that as the number of unstressed syllable in the interval increases, a tendency toward equality on inter-stress intervals causes both the stressed and unstressed syllables to become shorter. Thus, the relative syllable duration for each type of rhythmic foot can be abstractly described as follows:

$$| S | \quad \rightarrow \quad | 3|$$
$$| S\ W | \quad \rightarrow \quad | 2 : 1 |$$
$$| S\ W\ W | \quad \rightarrow \quad | 1\tfrac{1}{2} : \tfrac{3}{4} : \tfrac{3}{4} |.$$

Phonetically, a rhythmic foot is not isochronous. The duration of a foot will differ somewhat depending upon the phonetic structure of the syllables comprising it. Thus, the acoustic realization of a rhythmic foot will be different from the above abstract description. The following is a set of rules proposed by Laungthongkum to predict how syllable durations in each type of foot are realized acoustically. The derived or predicted syllable durations were based on her acoustic analysis of read speech.

| 3 | $\rightarrow$ | 2 | if the foot is in an utterance-initial position.

| 3 | $\rightarrow$ | 4 | if the foot is in an utterance-final position and it does not have a CVS structure.

| 2 : 1 | $\rightarrow$ | 2 : 2| if the salient syllable has a CVS structure; or the weak syllable is the first element of a compound that does not have a CVS structure; or both the salient syllable and the weak syllable are function words.

| 1½ : ¾ : ¾ | $\rightarrow$ | 1⅔ : 1⅔ : 1⅔ | if the salient syllable has a CVS structure; or it is in an utterance-initial position; or it is a function word and the two weak syllables are two function words or a function word and a linker syllable.

The above approach has been tested on a set of ambiguous sentences, which represents various structural ambiguities involving five types of compounds in Thai: noun-noun, noun-propernoun, noun-verb, noun-verb-noun, and verb-noun. Figure 2 depicts the process of predicting durational patterns from strength dynamics for two hypotheses of an ambiguous sentence of the type noun-verb compound, / k□□ŋphèt mâak paj /.

Table 1 lists all types of ambiguous test sentences. There are two test sentences for each type of ambiguity resulting in a total of 10 sentence types for the whole set. These sentences are composed of only monosyllabic words. No polysyllabic words were used because structural ambiguity in Thai does not usually involve polysyllabic words.

5. Conclusion

We have described our preliminary work on prosody modeling to improve intelligibility and naturalness of synthetic speech produced by a Thai text-to-speech system. Such improvement will undoubtedly make this type of speech technology more attractive and acceptable to human listeners. This paper describes the prosody annotation process in which the foot structure (the rhythm of the utterance) is obtained from text. The derived foot structure is then used to predict the durational pattern of the utterance. This prediction of prominence and phrasing patterns from text in general only operates on single sentences. Whether this technique can be extended to a different prosodic level as in conversational, discourse, or spontaneous communication remains the subject of future investigation. Modeling the discourse effects of prosody is inherently a difficult problem because of a high level of variability in speaker's choices. Furthermore, a design of robust system for describing discourse prosody would not be considered important unless speech synthesis is used in more conversational applications instead of an interaction involving simple questions and declarative sentences.

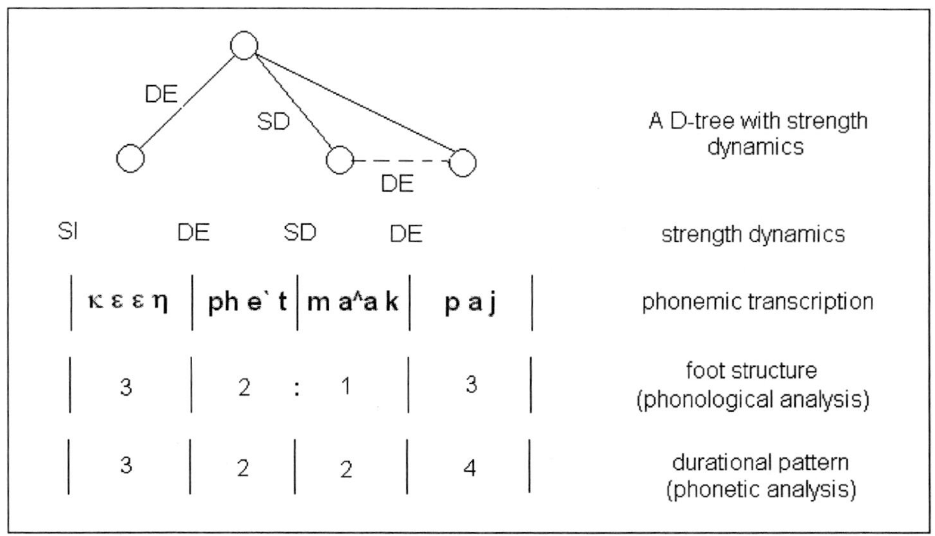

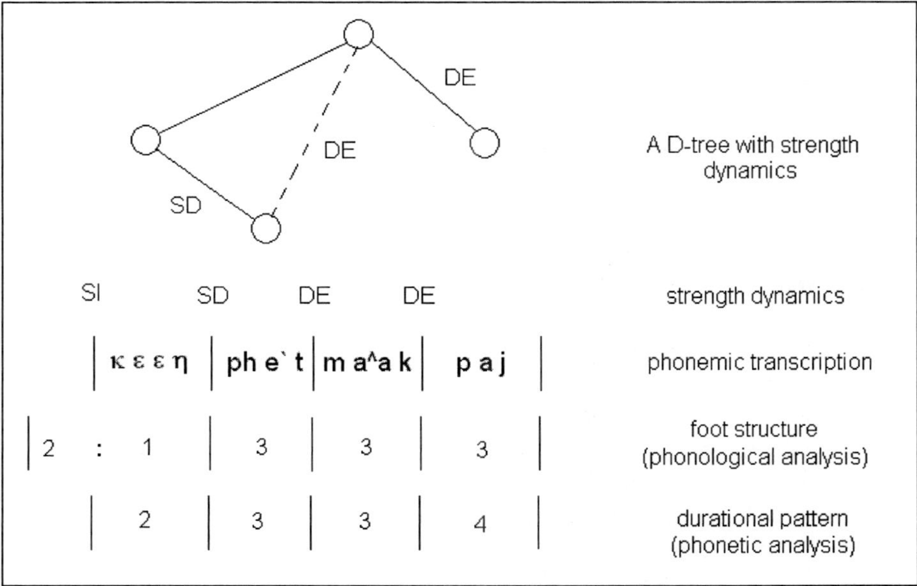

Figure 2: A prediction of durational patterns for two sentence hypotheses of an ambiguous sentence, / k□□ŋ phèt mâak paj /. The top panel indicates the first interpretation, 'the curry is too spicy'. The bottom panel indicates the second interpretation, 'there is too much curry.'

Table 1: A list of ambiguous test sentences used for testing the prosodic annotation scheme. The first pair represents a noun-verb compound; the second, a noun-propernoun compound; the third, a noun-noun compound; the fourth, a noun-verb-noun compound; and the fifth, a verb-noun compound.

Thai script	Phonemic transcription	English translation
1. (a) □□□□□□□□□□	/ k□□ŋ phèt mâak paj /	'The curry is too spicy.'
(b) □□□□□□□□□□	/ k□□ŋphèt mâak paj /	'There is too much curry.'
2. (a) □□□□□□□□□□□	/ phîi nŭu làp jùu /	'Nuu's sister is sleeping.'
(b) □□□□□□□□□□□	/ phîinŭu làp jùu /	'Sister Nuu is sleeping.'
3. (a) □□□□□□□□□□□□□□□	/ lûuk lăan maa jiâm b□□j /	'Our great grandchildren came to visit us quite often.'
(b) □□□□□□□□□□□□□□□□	/ lûuklăan maa jiâm b□□j /	'Our children and grandchildren came to visit us quite often.'
4. (a) □□□□□□□□□□□	/ khon khàp rót cháa mâak /	'People drive too slowly.'
(b) □□□□□□□□□□□	/ khonkhàprót cháa mâak /	'The chauffeur was too slow.'
5. (a) □□□□□□□□□□□	/ ph□ˆ□ khàat thun b□□j /	'Father often runs out of capital.'
(b) □□□□□□□□□□□	/ ph□ˆ□ khàatthun b□□j /	'Father often suffers business loss.'

References

Bailly, G. 1983. Integration of Rhythmic and Syntactic Constraints in a Model of Generation of French Prosody. *Speech Communication*, 8, 137-146.

Chomsky, N. and M. P. Schutzenberger. 1963. The Algebraic Theory of Context-free Languages. In P. Braffort and D. Hirschberg, eds., *Computer Programming and Formal Systems, Studies in Logic Series,*. 119-161. North-Holland, Amsterdam.

Gee, J. P. and F. Grosjean. 1983. Performance Structures: A Psycholinguistic and Linguistic Appraisal. *Cognitive Psychology*, 15, 411-458.

Luangthongkum, T. 1977. *Rhythm in Standard Thai*. Ph.D. thesis, University of Edinburgh.

Nespor, M. and I. Vogel. 1986. *Prosodic Phonology*. Dordrecht_Holland: Foris.

Potisuk, S. and M. P. Harper. 1996. CDG: An Alternative Formalism for Parsing Written and Spoken Thai. *Proceedings of the Fourth International Symposium on Languages and Linguistics*, pp. 1177-1196.

Price, P., M. Ostendorf, S. Shattuck-Hufnagel and C. Fong. 1991. The Use of Prosody in Syntactic Disambiguation. *Journal of Acoustical Society of America*, 90(6), 2956-2970.

Selkirk, E. O. 1984. *Phonology and Syntax: The Relation between Sound and Structure*. MIT Press.

Vongvipanond, P. E. 1993. Linguistic Problems in Computer Processing of the Thai Language. *Proceedings of the Symposium on Natural Language Processing in Thailand*, pp. 519-545.

Relation Extraction Using Convolution Tree Kernel
Expanded with Entity Features[*]

Longhua Qian, Guodong Zhou, Qiaomin Zhu, Peide Qian

School of Computer Science and Technology, Soochow University.
215006, Suzhou, China

{qianlonghua, gdzhou, qmzhu, pdqian}@suda.edu.cn

Abstract. This paper proposes a convolution tree kernel-based approach for relation extraction where the parse tree is expanded with entity features such as entity type, subtype, and mention level etc. Our study indicates that not only can our method effectively capture both syntactic structure and entity information of relation instances, but also can avoid the difficulty with tuning the parameters in composite kernels. We also demonstrate that predicate verb information can be used to further improve the performance, though its enhancement is limited. Evaluation on the ACE2004 benchmark corpus shows that our system slightly outperforms both the previous best-reported feature-based and kernel-based systems.

Keywords: Information Extraction; Kernel-based Relation Extraction; Support Vector Machines.

1. Introduction

Information extraction is an important research sub-field in natural language processing (NLP) which aims to identify relevant information from large amount of text documents in digital archives and the WWW. Information extraction subsumes three main tasks, including Entity Detection and Tracking (EDT), Relation Detection and Characterization (RDC), and Event Detection and Characterization (EDC).

This paper will focus on the ACE RDC task[1] and employ kernel method to extract semantic relationships between named entity pairs. Many feature-based approaches transform relation instances into feature vectors of high dimension, and compute the inner dot product between these feature vectors. Current research (Kambhatla 2004, Zhao et al 2005, Zhou et al. 2005, Wang et al. 2006) shows that it is very difficult to extract new effective features from relation examples. Kernel methods are non-parametric estimation techniques that computer a kernel function between data instances. By avoiding transforming data examples into feature vectors, kernel methods can implicitly explore much larger feature space than could be searched by a

---

[*] This research is supported by Project 60673041 under the National Natural Science Foundation of China and Project 2006AA01Z147 under the "863" National High-Tech Research and Development of China. We would also like to thank Dr. Alessando Moschitti for his great help in using his Tree Kernel Toolkits, including binary package and source codes.

[1] http://www.ldc.upenn.edu/Projects/ACE/.

feature-based approach. Thereafter, kernel methods especially on discrete structures (Haussler 1999) attract more and more attentions in relation extraction as well as other fields in NLP.

Prior work on kernel methods for relation extraction includes Zelenko et al. (2003), Culotta and Sorensen (2004), Bunescu and Mooney (2005). Due to strong constraints that matching nodes be at the same layer and in the identical path starting from the roots to the current nodes, their kernels achieve good precision but much lower recall on the ACE2003 corpus. Zhang et al. (2006) proposed a composite kernel that consists of two individual kernels: an entity kernel that allows for entity-related features and a convolution parse tree kernel that models syntactic information of relation examples. However, their method needs to manually tune parameters in composite kernels that are often difficult to determine.

This paper describes an expanded convolution parse tree kernel to incorporate entity information into syntactic structure of relation examples. Similar to Zhang et al. (2006), we employ a convolution parse tree kernel in order to model syntactic structures. Different from their method, we use the convolution parse tree kernel expanded with entity information other than a composite kernel. One of our motivations is to capture syntactic and semantic information in a single parse tree for further graceful refinement, the other is that we can avoid the difficulty with tuning parameters in composite kernels. Evaluation on the ACE2004 corpus shows that our method slightly outperforms the previous feature-base and kernel-based methods.

The rest of the paper is organized as follows. First, we present our expanded convolution tree kernel in Section 2. Then, Section 3 reports the experimental setting and results. Finally, we conclude our work with some general observations and indicate future work in Section 4.

2. Expanded Tree Kernel

In this section, we describe the expanded convolution parse tree kernel and demonstrate how entity information can be incorporated into the parse tree.

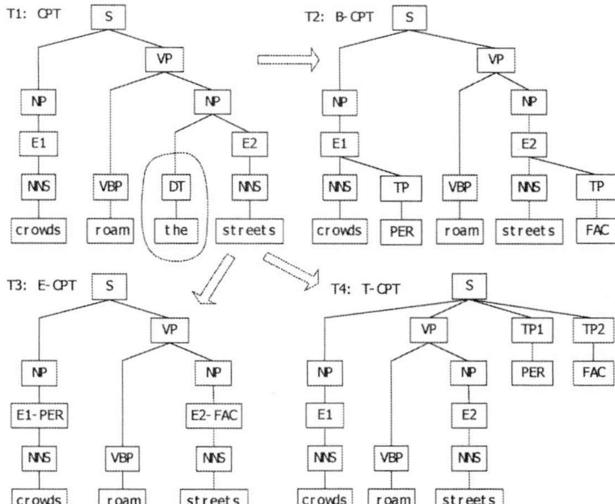

Figure 1: Different representations of a relation instance in the example sentence "in many cities, angry crowds roam the streets.", which is excerpted from the ACE2004 corpus, where a relation "PHSY.Located" holds between the first entity "crowds"(PER) and the second entity "streets" (FAC).

We employ the same convolution tree kernel used by Collins and Duffy (2001), Moschitti (2004) and Zhang et al. (2006). This convolution tree kernel counts the number of subtrees that have similar productions on every node between two parse trees. However, the kernel value will depend greatly on the size of the trees, so we should normalize the kernel.

From ACE definition on relation types and subtypes, we know that entity features impose a strong constraint on relation types. For example, PER-SOC relations describe the relationship between entities of type PER. Zhang et al. (2006) described five cases to extract the portion of parse tree for relation extraction. Their experiments show that PT (Path-enclosed Tree) achieves best performance among those cases, so we begin with PT and then incorporate entity features at different locations as depicted in Figure 1. The four cases is listed as follows:

(1) Compressed Path-enclosed Tree (CPT, T1 in Fig.1): Originated from PT in Zhang et al. (2006), we further make two kinds of compression. One is to prune out the children nodes right before the second entity under the same parent node of NP. The other is to compress the sub-structure like "X-->Y-->Z" into "X-->Z" in the parse trees.

(2) Bottom-attached CPT (B-CPT, T2 in Fig.1): the entity type information is attached to the bottom of the entity node, i.e., two more nodes whose tags are "TP" are added under the first and the second entity nodes respectively.

(3) Entity-attached CPT (E-CPT, T3 in Fig.1): the entity type name is combined with entity order name, e.g. "E1-PER" denotes the first entity whose type is "PER". This case is also explored by Zhang et al. (2006), and we include it here just for the purpose of comparison.

(4) Top-attached CPT (T-CPT, T4 in Fig.1): the entity type information is attached to the top node of the parse tree. In order to distinguish between two entities, we use tags "TP1" and "TP2" to represent the first entity type and the second entity type respectively.

From the above four cases, we want to evaluate whether and how the entity information will be useful for relation extraction and in what way we can embed the entity information (especially the location where we attach) in the parse tree in order to achieve the best performance.

3. Experiments

3.1. Experimental Corpus and Setting

We use the ACE RDC 2004 corpus as our experiment data. The ACE RDC 2004 data contains 451 documents and 5702 relation instances. It defines 7 entity types, 7 major relation types and 23 subtypes. The portion of training data we use contains 347 documents, 121K words and 4307 relations. Evaluation of kernel is done on the training data using 5-fold cross-validation. First, the corpus is parsed using Charniak's parser (Charniak, 2001). Then, we iterate over all pairs of entity mentions occurring in the same sentence to generate potential relation instances.

We choose SVM (Vapnik 1998) as the binary classifier, since SVM has achieved the state-of-the-art performances for many classification problems like text categorization (Joachims 1998). For efficiency, we apply the one-against-others approach to convert binary classifier to multi-class classifier. The final decision of a relation instance in the multi-class classification is determined by the classifier which has the maximal SVM output. In our implementation, we use the binary-class SVMLight (Joachims, 1998) and Tree Kernel Tools (Moschitti, 2004). For comparison with the composite kernels (Zhang et.al. 2006), our training parameter C (SVM) and λ (tree kernel) are set to 2.4 and 0.4 respectively.

3.2. Experimental Results

In this section, we present and analyze the experimental results with respect to different settings.
(1) Different instance representations
According to the above discussion, we select CPT with entity order information as our baseline to try to discover whether and how entity information will be effective to relation extraction. In order to reduce training time, we only add major type information into the parse tree. Table 1 compares the performance of seven major types for three different setups in the ACE2004 corpus using expanded convolution tree kernel. It shows that:

- Using convolution parse tree kernel only embedded with entity order information achieves the performance of 67.8%/52.3%/59.0 in precision/recall/F-measure. This indicates that convolution parse tree kernel is somewhat effective for relation extraction.
- Compared with CPT, other three setups B-CPT, E-CPT and T-CPT improve the F-measure by 8.5/10.1/10.5 units respectively due to the increase both in precision and recall. This shows that entity major type information incorporated into the parse tree of relation instances produces significant improvement for relation extraction. This further suggests that our parse tree kernel can effectively capture both the entity information and the structured syntactic information of relation examples.
- Among the three different instance representations except CPT, the T-CPT (highlighted in bold font) achieves slightly better performance of 2.0/0.4 units in F-measure than the other two representations B-CPT and E-CPT respectively. This may be due to the following reason. From the definition of the convolution parse tree kernel, we introduce a decay factor λ (set to 0.4 here) to make the kernel less dependent on the tree size. However, this factor also decreases the contribution of the entity information on the kernel when they are attached to the bottom of the entity.

Table 1: Performance of seven major types for four different kernel setups in the ACE2004 corpus using expanded convolution tree kernel.

	P	R	F
CPT	67.8	52.3	59.0
B-CPT	75.1	61.4	67.5
E-CPT	76.4	63.1	69.1
T-CPT	**76.0**	**64.0**	**69.5**

(2) Different entity features
In addition to entity type, there are many other entity features about an entity, e.g. subtype, mention level, entity class etc. Do they have different contributions to relation extraction? We will answer this question in the following.

Table 2: Contribution of different entity features over seven major types in the ACE2004 corpus using the above T-CPT kernel. The asterisk on the upper right of the feature means this entity feature can greatly improve the performance while the minus sign means the entity feature doesn't increase the performance and should be removed from the feature set in the next round.

	P	R	F
CPT	67.8	52.3	59.0
+major type*	76.0	64.0	69.5
+subtype*	77.6	64.9	70.7
+mention level*	**79.0**	**66.4**	**72.2**
+entity class$^{(-)}$	79.1	66.2	72.1
+GPE role$^{(-)}$	79.1	66.5	72.2
+head word$^{(-)}$	80.1	64.7	71.6
+LDC type$^{(-)}$	78.9	65.9	71.8
+predicate base	*79.2*	*67.4*	*72.8*

Table 2 reports the contribution of different entity features over seven major types in the ACE2004 corpus using the above T-CPT kernel. It indicates that our system achieves the best performance of 79.0%/66.4%/72.2 in precision/recall/F-measure when combining some of the entity features. In order to measure the contribution of different entity features we add them one by one in the decreasing order of their potential importance. It also shows:

- Entity type feature is very effective for relation extraction and it increases precision/recall/F-measure by 8.2%/11.7%/10.5 units respectively.
- Entity subtype feature improves the F-measure by 1.2 units. This further shows that gracefully defined entity type and subtype features in the ACE2004 corpus contribute to most of the performance improvement among all entity features.
- Mention level feature is also useful and increases the F-measure by 1.5 units while both entity class and GPE role feature are futile because they don't lead to any improvement in F-measure.
- Other two entity features (i.e. "head word", "LDC mention type"), however, both decrease the performance by 0.6/0.4 units in F-measure respectively. This suggests that both of these features can't differentiate relation types from each other and their incorporations into parse tree make relation extraction even more difficult.
- In the last experiment (highlighted in bold and italic font) we add the base form of the predicate verb nearest to the second entity mention. Although it only improves the F-measure by 0.6 units largely due to the increase in recall, it indicates that moving verbs from the bottom to the top of the parse tree is helpful to relation extraction. This also suggests that constructing a parse tree that contains all necessary features and is designed specifically for relation extraction is very promising.

(3) Different relation lexical condition

In ACE vocabulary, relation lexical condition indicates the syntactic structure where the entity pair relates to each other. There are five relation lexical conditions in the ACE2004 corpus, i.e. "Possessive", "Preposition", "PreMod", "Formulaic" and "Verbal". Table 3 separately measures the recall performance of different relation lexical condition on one of the testing sets in the ACE2004 corpus. It also indicates the number of testing instance, correctly classified instances and wrongly classified instances for each condition respectively.

Table 3: Recall of different lexical conditions on the testing data in the ACE2004 corpus

	#Testing Instances	#Correct Instances	#Error Instances	Recall
Possessive	158	135	23	85.4
Preposition	215	146	69	69.3
PreMod	250	199	51	79.6
Formulaic	71	55	16	77.5
Verbal	174	42	132	24.1

This table shows:
- The recall performance is best in the condition "Possessive". This may be largely due to consistency of syntactic structure for this condition in the ACE2004 corpus.
- It is somewhat surprising that our system performs worse than we expected in the condition "Formulaic", since we think that there should be several fixed patterns for this condition. The reason may be that there are many syntactic errors in the parse trees produced by Charniak's parser although this parser represents the-start-of-art in parsing.
- Finally our system achieves surprisingly lowest performance in the condition "Verbal" although they occur frequently in the testing data. This may be that the syntactic structure in this condition is diverse and it contains too much noise in this kind of parse tree. It also suggests that much more noise needs to be pruned out from the parse tree while the key relation structure should remain in this condition.

(4) Comparison with recent work

Table 4 compares our system with recent work on the ACE2004 corpus. It shows that our system slightly outperforms recently best-reported systems. Compared with the composite kernel (Zhang et al, 2006), our system further prunes the parse tree and incorporates entity features into the convolution parse tree kernel. It shows that our system achieves higher precision, lower recall and slightly better F-measure than their method. Compared with feature-based systems (Zhou et al, 2006 and Zhao et al, 2005) that incorporate many lexical, syntactic and semantic features, our system improves the F-measure by 1.8/2.5 units over relation types respectively. This suggests that kernel-based systems can promisingly outperform feature-based systems, although much work like performance enhancement and reduction of training speed still needs to be done to further improve the system.

Table 4: Comparison of our system with other best-reported systems in the ACE RDC 2004 corpus using 5-fold cross-validation (Note: * for feature-based)

	Relation Detection			RDC on Types		
	P	R	F	P	R	F
Ours: SVM (expansion kernel)	86.3	73.4	79.3	79.2	67.4	72.8
Zhang et al (2006): SVM (polynomial expansion)	-	-	-	76.1	68.4	72.1
Zhou et al (2005): SVM (polynomial kernel)*	89.0	66.6	76.2	82.8	62.1	71.0
Zhao et al (2005): SVM (composite polynomial)*	-	-	-	69.2	70.5	70.3

4. Conclusion and Future Work

In this paper, we have designed a convolution parse tree kernel expanded with entity features for relation extraction using Support Vector Machines. Evaluation on the ACE2004 corpus shows that the expanded convolution parse tree kernel achieves better performance on relation extraction than recent feature-based and kernel-based systems. This may result from the following reasons: First, syntactic structure information of relation examples is very useful and can be effectively captured by the convolution parse tree kernel, therefore the convolution parse tree alone achieves comparable performance on relation extraction. Second, the expanded convolution parse tree incorporated with entity features significantly improves performance. And the higher we put entity feature node in the parse tree, the better performance we can get. We also discover that entity type feature contributes to most of performances improvement while some other features such as "head word" or "GPE role" conversely decrease the performance. Last, compared with other recent systems, performance enhancement of our system is limited, for many parse errors still exist both in short-distance relations and long-distance relations even though the Charniak's parser we use in our system represents the-state-of-the-art in full parsing. This suggests that the parser needs to be further improved in order to provide more accurate syntactic structure information.

In the future work, we will try to construct a dynamic relation tree to reflect both the syntactic structure and semantic information more accurately. First, we will further prune out the noise from the parse tree according to linguistic knowledge especially for lexical condition "Verbal". Second, more weight will be assigned to discriminative features no matter where they are located (e.g. entity features, predicate verb and preposition etc) to reflect their contributions. Last, we will use semantic resources such as WordNet to compute semantic similarity between terminal words (e.g. noun for entity and verb for predicate respectively) in the parse tree.

References

Bunescu R. C. and R. J. Mooney. 2005. A Shortest Path Dependency Kernel for Relation Extraction. *Proceedings of HLT/EMNLP-2005,* pp. 724-731.

Charniak E. 2001. Intermediate-head Parsing for Language Models. *Proceedings of ACL-2001,* pp. 116-123.

Collins M. and N. Duffy. 2001. Convolution Kernels for Natural Language. *Proceedings of NIPS-14,* pp. 625-632.

Culotta A. and J. Sorensen. 2004. Dependency tree kernels for relation extraction. *Proceedings of ACL-2004,* pp. 423-429.

Haussler D. 1999. Convention kernels on discrete structure. *Technical Report UCS-CRL-99-10.*

Joachims T. 1998. Text categorization with support vector machines: learning with many relevant features. *Proceedings of Europe Conference on Machine Learning (ECML-1998),* pp. 137-142.

Kambhatla N. 2004. Combining lexical, syntactic and semantic features with Maximum Entropy models for extracting relations. *Proceedings of ACL-2004(poster),* pp. 178-181.

Moschitti A. 2004. A Study on Convolution Kernels for Shallow Semantic Parsing. *Proceedings of ACL-2004,* pp. 335-342.

Ting W., L. Yaoyong, B. Kalina, C. Hamish, and W. Ji. 2006. Automatic Extraction of Hierarchical Relations from Text. *Proceedings of the Third European Semantic Web Conference (ESWC 2006), Lecture Notes in Computer Science 4011, Springer.*

Vapnik V. 1998. *Statistic Learning Theory.* Chichester: John Wiley.

Zelenko D., C. Aone and A. Richardella. 2003. Kernel Methods for Relation Extraction. *Journal of Machine Learning Research,* 2(2003), 1083-1106.

Zhang M., J. Zhang, J. Su and G. D. Zhou. 2006. A Composite Kernel to Extract Relations between Entities with both Flat and Structured Features. *Proceedings of ACL-2006,* pp. 825–832.

Zhao S.B. and R. Grisman. 2005. Extracting relations with integrated information using kernel methods. *Proceedings of ACL-2005,* pp. 419-426.

Zhou G. D., J. Su, J. Zhang and M. Zhang. 2005. Exploring various knowledge in relation extraction. *Proceedings of ACL-2005,* pp. 427-434.

Summarization and Evaluation; Where are we today?! [*]

Mehrnoush Shamsfard[a], Amir Saffarian[a], Samaneh Ghodratnama[b]

[a] NLP Laboratory, Electrical and Computer Engineering Department,
Shahid Beheshti University, Velenjak, Tehran, Iran
m-shams@sbu.ac.ir
a_saffarian@std.sbu.ac.ir

[b] Department of Computer Science and Engineering,
Shiraz University, Molasadra, Shiraz, Iran
ghodratnama@cse.shirazu.ac.ir

Abstract. The rapid growth of the online information services causes the problem of information explosion. Automatic text summarization techniques are essential for dealing with this problem. There are different approaches to text summarization and different systems have used one or a combination of them. Considering the wide variety of summarization techniques there should be an evaluation mechanism to assess the process of summarization. The evaluation of automatic summarization is important and challenging, since in general it is difficult to agree on an ideal summary of a text. Currently evaluating summaries is a laborious task that could not be done simply by human so automatic evaluation techniques are appearing to help this matter. In this paper, we will take a look at summarization approaches and examine summarizers' general architecture. The importance of evaluation methods is discussed and the need to find better automatic systems to evaluate summaries is studied.

Keywords: Summarization, Evaluation, Recall, Precision, Pyramid, ROUGE

1. Introduction

Today, having access to information summaries is one of the important needs for humans which may affect their lives. These summaries generally are produced with the help of other humans. The question arises here is that in this era where we are encountering a huge volume of increasing data and information, with limited resources to decide on, may it be really possible to use humans as information summarizers? We believe not.

So, researchers have created methods to automatically do summarization task and extract the most important concepts of the information without any need to involve humans. Now a second question emerges. How could we know about the correctness and the completeness of the results generated in an automatic manner? The answer is hidden in evaluation techniques on which we are going to focus in this paper. Therefore besides the growth of summarization methods, evaluation techniques must improve and mature so as to provide acceptable scores for summaries according to some sort of evaluation metrics.

Evaluation approaches mostly evaluate created summaries based on (1) ideal (gold) summary, (2) use in an application and (3) original document. Techniques from the first category compare system generated summaries with a summary known as the best possible summary! This ideal summary currently is created by humans and it could be influenced by subjective effects from judges. Application driven techniques evaluate content of summary by analyzing the level of information that could be obtained from it for a specific task. In this approach the performance of the application is analyzed when using the original document and

---

its summary separately. On the other hand evaluation by original document is really ambiguous because specifying evaluation parameters and metrics is hard but it is more natural.

In this paper we focus on the first category of evaluation approaches; comparing with an ideal (gold) summary. Section 2 of this paper provides a brief explanation about the summarization methods and their high level architecture. Then in the following sections some recent methods for summary evaluation are introduced.

2. Document Summarization

Text summarization is the process of extracting the most important parts of information from source document(s) to produce a reduced version for a particular user or a particular task. According to Mani (2001) automatic summarization is an automated process in which a computer takes a piece of information, also called the source (i.e. an electronic document), selects the most important content in it, and presents that content to the user in a condensed form.

Automatic text summarization can be used in various areas of applications such as telecommunications industry, intelligent tutoring systems, text mining, and filters for web-based information retrieval and word processing tools. Researchers are also investigating the application of this technology to a variety of new and challenging problems, including Multilingual Summarization, Multimedia News Broadcast, Summarization of Online Medical Literature of a Patient, Audio Scanning Services for the Blind and Providing Captions for TV Programs.

2.1. High Level Architecture

As a general view for summarizer architecture, the input to the system could be one or more documents in different forms of text or multimedia. The process of summarization has three main phases:
1. Analyzing the input text or *Topic Identification*
2. Transforming it into a summary representation or *Interpretation*
3. Synthesizing an appropriate output form or *Generation*

Any summary can be characterized by (at least) three major classes of characteristics: (1) Input: characteristics of the source text(s), (2) Output: characteristics of the summary as a text (3) Purpose: characteristics of the summary usage which is discussed in more details in Hovy (2000).

The output may be an extract of the source, or an abstract. Extracts consist of portions of text extracted verbatim, but abstracts consist of novel phrasings which describe the content of the original document(s). In general, producing abstracts requires stages of topic fusion and text generation, but producing extracts requires only the stage of topic identification. Moreover, summarizers can usually produce either generic or user–focused summaries. A user-focused summary is the one in which specific information is selected in order to satisfy the requirements of a particular user group. As opposed to that, a generic summary is more suitable for the average reader. There are also two types of summaries depending on their function. There can be informative and indicative summaries. The purpose of the first type is to deliver as much information as possible to the user and can also serve as a substitute for the source. Indicative summaries on the other hand are only meant to help the user decide whether or not to read the source document.

2.2. Approaches

As defined by Mani (1999) there can be surface-level, corpus based, and discourse structure based and knowledge based approaches for single document summarization. All these approaches could successfully be applied to multi-document summarization.

The surface-level approach requires shallow understanding of the text and this usually involves analysis of the syntactic structure of sentences. It is used to extract salient information by taking into account some key features of a sentence. Corpus based approaches involve statistical analysis of large bodies of text (corpora) to find specific features about the documents in them.

Human abstractors create a mental discourse model of a document while reading it. Discourse-level approaches try to create similar model of the discourse structure of a document which can later be used for the generation of a summary. Knowledge based approaches are used for the creation of summarization systems which act in a specific domain (i.e. domain dependent approaches). Such systems usually produce high quality summaries but do not have the ability to adapt to different types of documents (domains).

Almost all of the summarizer systems in the world use a combination of approaches mentioned above. The final report of SUMMAC project by Mani (1998) listed some the systems in its time. For example, BT's ProSum used statistical techniques based on the co-occurrences of word stems, the length of sentences and their position in the original text to calculate the importance of a sentence in the context of the overall text in which it occurs. The most important sentences are then used to construct the summary. CIR created a thematic representation of a text that included nodes of thematically related terms simulating topics of the text. Related terms were identified using a thesaurus specially constructed for this task. CGI_CMU used a technique called "Maximal Marginal Relevance" (MMR) which produces summaries of very long documents by identifying key relevant, non-redundant information found within the document. This technique is also used for eliminating or clustering redundant information in multi-document summarization applications. Cornell SabIR used the document ranking and passage retrieval capabilities of the SMART IR engine to effectively identify relevant related passages in a document. GE identified the discourse macro structure for each document and selected the passages from each component that scored well using both content and contextual clues. Currently, we are working to create a more updated list of single- and multi-document summarizer systems and classifying them by the methods they use to create summaries.

3. Summary Evaluation

Text summarization is still an emerging field and serious questions remain concerning the appropriate methods and types of evaluation. There are a variety of possible bases for comparison of summarization system performance e.g., summary to source, machine to human generated, system to system.

The problem with matching a system summary against a best of breed summary is that it is really hard and maybe impossible to find an ideal summary. Indeed, the human summary may be supplied by the author of the article, by a judge asked to construct an abstract, or by a judge asked to extract sentences. There can be a large number of generic and user-focused abstracts that could summarize a given document, just as there can be many ways of describing something.

3.1. Categories of Methods

Methods for evaluating text summarization approaches can be broadly classified into two categories.
1. Intrinsic methods which are based on the comparison of the automatically produced summary with an ideal summary usually produced by human abstractors.
2. Extrinsic methods which are mostly based on tasks that use the output results of summarization systems.

From another point of view we can divide evaluation methods into manual and automatic ones. In manual techniques an individual or a group of individuals compare machine or human generated summaries (peers) to an ideal summary (model) or source text to find out about the extent of coverage of the main concepts between peer and model summaries. At the end an average of the scores given by group of judgments are used for the diversity of ideal summaries mentioned in the previous paragraph.

In the other hand, automatic methods, without any human interference, try to reduce subjective effects that may influence evaluation scores. Members of this family may have different levels of complexity according to the level of details they use for comparison. Those that use lexical similarities as their main approach are the simplest and those which use semantics to find the coverage of concepts are the most complex techniques here.

3.2. Evaluation Metrics

The comparison between summaries is best carried out by humans, but it can also be computed automatically. A variety of different measures can be used. Evaluation metrics can be grouped in at least three categories: (1) Sentence Recall measures, (2) Utility-based measures and (3) Content-Based measures (Mani, 2001-2).

There are many metrics to evaluate summaries but precision and recall measures are used extensively in ideal summary based evaluation of summarization systems. However, they are not appropriate for the summarization task due to their binary nature and the fact that there is no single correct summary. An example of how the binary precision and recall measures fail the task is as follows: suppose there are two sentences which are interchangeable in terms of producing a summary.

If five human subjects extract sentences to build a summary, two of subjects chose sentence 1, two of them chose sentence 2 and the 5th chose sentence 1 by chance. By majority method, sentence 1 will be an ideal sentence. In evaluation, if a summarization system chooses sentence 1, it wins, if it chooses sentence 2, it loses, although sentence 1 and 2 are interchangeable. This is obviously not a good measure (Jing, 1998).

A tested summary should agree with model not only in content but also in length, an aspect which is measured by Precision. Combining both informativeness and brevity is possible through F-Score, a measure often used in Information Retrieval:

$$F - Score = \frac{2*Precision*Recall}{Precision+Recall} \qquad (1)$$

There could be situations that a combinational metrics is used based on the several parameters. For example in Rigouste (2003) a recall metric is introduced which is using the unigram and bigram matching techniques mentioned by Lin and Hovy:

$$F - Score = \frac{1}{3}\frac{Overlap_{Unigrams}}{N} + \frac{21}{3}\frac{Overlap_{Bigrams}}{N} \qquad (2)$$

4. Pyramid, a Manual Evaluation Technique

The motivation behind pyramid method (Passonneau, 2003) is that most of the contents which appear in human summaries are conceptions from the source text, expressed by different sentences or words. The fact behind generating subjective summaries that avoids any two summaries to be unique is that information units in them could be prioritized based on their importance in people views. Pyramid method is introduced to abstract and prioritize content units in source text considering this human behavior.

Actually, a pyramid is made up of summary content units (SCU). There is no accurate definition of SCU because the granularity of information comprising it, is not clear enough. In this technique functional or semantic specifications of SCUs are not very important; however focus is on the way in which summaries are compared to find similar and non-similar SCUs. All

SCUs are weighted according to the frequency they appear in different summaries and after that each summary is scored based on the SCUs it is comprised of. More information about SCU and how to identify them could be found in DUC2005 SCU Annotation Guide[1].

Suppose the pyramid has n tiers, with tier T_n on top and T_1 on the bottom. The weight of SCUs in tier T_i will be i. Let $|T_i|$ denote the number of SCUs in tier T_i. Let D_i be the number of SCUs in the summary that appear in T_i. Other SCUs in a summary that do not appear in the pyramid are assigned weight zero. The total SCU weight D is computed as in equation 3 and the optimal content score for a summary with X SCUs is shown in equation 4.

$$D = \sum_{i=1}^{n} D_i \qquad (3)$$

$$Max = \left(\sum_{i=j+1}^{n} w_{T_i} + |T_i|\right) + w_{T_i} + \left(X - \sum_{i=j+1}^{n} |T_i|\right) \qquad (4)$$

$$where\ j = \max_i\left(\sum_{i=j+1}^{n} |T_i| \geq X\right)$$

With the help of Pyramid, score of a candidate summary (D) is computed with dividing the frequency of SCUs appeared in D by the value acquired by the best distribution of SCUs in an ideal summary (Max).

The strengths of pyramid scores are that they are reliable, predictive, and diagnostic. There are also two problems with Pyramid method. First, pyramid scores ignore interdependencies among content units, including ordering. Second, creating an initial pyramid is laborious so large-scale application of the method would require an automated or semi-automated approach. DUC conference data of year 2005 and 2006 are analyzed using Pyramid method and the results are available in Nenkova (2005) and Passonneau (2006).

There are two tasks involved in Pyramid evaluation: creating a pyramid by annotating model summaries, and evaluating a new summary (peer) against a pyramid. Ideally, an automated evaluation component would address both tasks. However, the task of creating a pyramid is far more complex than the task of scoring a new summary against existing (hand created) pyramid, and the automated scoring component is useful when doing a large amount of evaluation (of multiple summarizers, or different versions of the same summarizer). Pyramid creators have proposed a four step algorithm to score summaries according to the manually created pyramid. Steps are as follows (Harnly, 2005):

- **Enumerate** Enumerates all candidate contributors (contiguous phrases) in each sentence of the peer summary.
- **Match** For each candidate contributor, find the most similar SCU in the pyramid. In the process, the similarity between the candidate contributor and all pyramid SCUs is computed.
- **Select** From the set of candidate contributors, find a covering, and disjoint set of contributors that have maximum overall similarity with the pyramid.
- **Score** Calculate the pyramid score for the summary, using the chosen contributors and their SCU weights.

More details including the reliability and robustness of the Pyramid method could be found in Nenkova (2007).

5. ROUGE, an Automatic Summary Evaluation System

ROUGE stands for Recall-Oriented Understudy for Gisting Evaluation. It includes measures to automatically determine the quality of a summary by comparing it to other (ideal) summaries created by humans (Lin ,2004).

---

[1] http://www1.cs.columbia.edu/~ani/DUC2005/AnnotationGuide.htm

There are five metrics introduced in ROUGE that we will briefly explain. ROUGE-N is an n-gram recall between a candidate summary and a set of reference summaries. ROUGE-L, computes the ratio between the length of the two summaries' longest common sub-sequence (LCS) and the length of the reference summary. One advantage of using LCS is that it does not require consecutive matches but in-sequence matches that reflect sentence level word order as n-grams. The basic LCS also has a problem that it does not differentiate LCSs of different spatial relations within their embedding sequences. To improve the basic LCS method, another metric called ROUGE-W or weighted longest common sub-sequence that favors LCS with consecutive matches is introduced.

Skip-bigram co-occurrence statistics, ROUGE-S, measure the overlap ratio of skip-bigrams between a candidate summary and a set of reference summaries. Skip-bigram is any pair of words in their sentence order, allowing for arbitrary gaps. One potential problem for ROUGE-S is that it does not give any credit to a candidate sentence if the sentence does not have any word pair co-occurring with its references. To accommodate this, ROUGE-S is extended with the addition of unigram as counting unit. The extended version is called ROUGE-SU.

To assess the effectiveness of ROUGE measures, the correlation between ROUGE assigned summary scores and human assigned mean coverage scores is computed. The intuition is that a good evaluation measure should assign a good score to a good summary and a bad score to a bad summary. The ground truth is based on human assigned scores. The effectiveness of ROUGE measures are examined on 2001-2003 three years of DUC data and the result could be found in Lin (2004).

6. A Framework for Summary Evaluation Systems

Researchers have always been looking for a summary evaluation system that provides stable and reliable scores. Almost all current systems do their job by comparing peer summaries with some reference (human generated) ones but even without considering different styles of evaluation, comparison based on summary content does not have enough precision (subjective effects).

Experiences have shown that evaluation by sentence units is not good enough because sentences may have subparts with different importance. Even though comparison at the word level does not consider the effects of the context in which the words are used.

Basic Elements (BEs), as a new concept, was introduced by Hovy (2005) toward establishing a framework for automatic summary evaluation. They addressed the problem of unit size by automatically producing a series of increasingly larger units, starting at the single word level. Experimentally Basic Elements could be defined as:

1. The head of a major syntactic constituent (noun, verb, adjective or adverbial phrases), expressed as a single item, or
2. A relation between a head-BE and a single dependent, expressed as a triple (head | modifier | relation).

In order to implement Basic Elements as a method of evaluating summary content, four core questions must be addressed (Hovy, 2005):

- What or how large is a Basic Element? The answer to this is strongly conditioned by: How can BEs be created automatically?
- How important is each BE? What basic score should each BE have?
- When do two BEs match? What kinds of matches should be implemented, and how?
- How should an overall summary score be derived from the individual matched BEs' scores?

Different answers to each of these questions provide a different summary evaluation method. The Pyramid Method, takes approximately clause-length semantic units shared by the reference summaries as BEs; gives each unit a score equal to the number of reference summaries containing it; allows two units to match when they express all or most of the same semantic content, as judged by the assessors; and derives the overall score by summing the scores of each unit of the candidate summary and normalized by the overall score of an ideal summary of equal size.

In contrast, ROUGE uses various n-grams (for example, unigrams) as BEs; scores each unigram by a function that depends on the number of reference summaries containing that unigram; allows unigrams to match under various conditions (for example, exact match only, or root form match); and derives the overall summary score by some weighted combination function of unigram matches.

The BE Package is an overall framework in which various solutions to the four core questions are provided, and therefore serves as a generalization over the particular methods and as an environment to compare them. BE package contains four subsystems:

- **Breaker Units** which accepts a sentence as input and produces a list of BEs as output. Different BE Breakers produce different BEs.
- **Scoring Units** which could assign each BE some points for each reference summary it participates in.
- **Comparing and Matching Units** that use a range of increasingly sophisticated matching strategies like lexical identity, lemma identity, synonym identity to match phrases.
- **Combining Scores and Ranking Units** that add the point values of each BE in the summary to be evaluated and use some optimizations in the score integration task.

The major problem is developing powerful BE matching routines; if one can match minimal BEs (and paraphrases) accurately then building matchers for compound BEs should be an interesting but not an impossible difficult exercise. Similarly, determining optimal weighting functions for individual BEs and for their combination to maximize correlations with human judgments requires careful but not an impossible hard work, and resembles the work done by Lin (2004). The results for DUC[2] 2005 evaluation using basic elements could be found in Hovy (2005).

7. Conclusion

In this paper we have talked about document summarization and the new techniques recently used for their evaluation. It is clear that the current trend of summary evaluation approaches is toward automatic methods and this field of research is still immature mainly because:

1. Lack of accurate and clear definition for a summary which should be independent of the influences which come from summarizer (mainly humans).
2. The way humans try to evaluate summaries is not completely understood and clearly formulated.

Today, researchers are moving forward to find more important metrics in order to formulate the complete human judgment. They are accepting the subjective influences that affects summarizations as a fact and try to provide a basic framework based on these remarks that matches real world conditions. Pyramid as a tool could help us in evaluating summaries but the main problem was the effort needed to construct it. We reviewed some ideas about making this construction task automatic. Others suggested using machine translation techniques in the evaluation. Using paraphrases concerning subjective effects that appear in summaries is discussed in Zhou (2006).

---

[2] Document Understanding Conferences, http://duc.nist.gov/

References

Lin, C.-Y. 2004. Looking for a Few Good Metrics: *Automatic Summarization Evaluation - How Many Samples Are Enough?*, In Proceedings of NTCIR Workshop 4, Tokyo, Japan.

Harnly, A., A. Nenkova, R. Passonneau and O. Rambow. 2005. *Automation of Summary Evaluation by the Pyramid Method. Recent Advances in Natural Language Processing (RANLP-2005)*, Borovets, Bulgaria.

Hovy, E. and C.Y. Lin. 2000. *Automated Text Summarization and the SUMMARIST System ",
Information Sciences Institute of the University of Southern California*, 197-214.

Hovy, E., C.-Y. Lin, and L. Zhou. 2005. Evaluating DUC 2005 Using Basic Elements. Document Understanding Workshop, Vancouver, B.C., Canada.

Jing, H., R. Barzilay, K. McKeown and M. Elhadad. 1998. *Summarization evaluation methods experiments and analysis. In AAAI Intelligent Text Summarization Workshop (Stanford, CA, Mar. 1998)*, 60--68.

Mani, I., D. House and G. Klein. 1998. *The TIPSTER SUMMAC Text Summarization Evaluation. Technical Report MTR 98W0000138*, MITRE Corporation, Virgina.

Mani, I. and Mark T. Maybury eds., 1999. Advances in Automatic Text Summarization. The MIT Press.

Mani, I. 2001. Automatic Summarization. John Benjamins Publishing Co.

Mani, I. 2001. Summarization Evaluation: An Overview. *Second NTCIR Workshop on Research in Chinese & Japanese Text Retrieval and Text Summarization. National Institute of Informatics*, Tokyo, Japan

Nenkova, A., R. Passonneau, K. McKeown and S. Sigelma. 2005. Applying the Pyramid Method in DUC 2005. Document Understanding Workshop, Vancouver, B.C., Canada.

Nenkova, A., R. Passonneau and K. McKeown. 2007. The Pyramid Method: Incorporating Human Content Selection Variation in Summarization Evaluation. ACM Transactions on Speech and Language Processing, 4, 2 (May. 2007), 4. DOI= http://doi.acm.org/10.1145/1233912.1233913

Passonneau, Rebecca and Ani Nenkova. 2003. Evaluating content selection in human- or machine-generated summaries: The pyramid method. Technical Report CUCS025 -03, Columbia University.

Passonneau, R., K. McKeown, S. Sigelma and A. Goodkind. 2006, Applying the Pyramid Method in the 2006 Document Understanding Conference. Document Understanding Workshop, Brooklyn, New York USA.

Zhou, L., C.-Y . Lin, D. S. Munteanu and E. Hovy. 2006. ParaEval: Using Paraphrases to Evaluate Summaries Automatically. In Proceedings of the Main Conference on Human Language Technology Conference of the North American Chapter of the Association of Computational Linguistics (New York, New York, June 04 - 09, 2006). Human Language Technology Conference. Association for Computational Linguistics, Morristown, NJ, 447-454. DOI= http://dx.doi.org/10.3115/1220835.1220892

Rigouste L. 2003. *Evolution of a Text Summarization System in an Automatic Evaluation Framework. Master`s Thesis, Ottawa-Carleton Institute for Computer Science, School of Information Technology and Engineering*, University of Ottawa.

Refinement of Document Clustering by Using NMF[*]

Hiroyuki Shinnou and Minoru Sasaki

Department of Computer and Information Sciences, Ibaraki University,
4-12-1 Nakanarusawa, Hitachi, Ibaraki JAPAN 316-8511
{shinnou, msasaki}@mx.ibaraki.ac.jp

Abstract. In this paper, we use non-negative matrix factorization (NMF) to refine the document clustering results. NMF is a dimensional reduction method and effective for document clustering, because a term-document matrix is high-dimensional and sparse. The initial matrix of the NMF algorithm is regarded as a clustering result, therefore we can use NMF as a refinement method. First we perform min-max cut (Mcut), which is a powerful spectral clustering method, and then refine the result via NMF. Finally we should obtain an accurate clustering result. However, NMF often fails to improve the given clustering result. To overcome this problem, we use the Mcut object function to stop the iteration of NMF.

Keywords: document clustering, Non-negative Matrix Factorization, spectral clustering, initial matrix

1. Introduction

In this paper, we use non-negative matrix factorization (NMF) to improve the document clustering result generated by a powerful document clustering method. Using this strategy, we can obtain an accurate document clustering result.

Document clustering is a task that divides a given document data set into a number of groups according to document similarity. This is the basic intelligent procedure, and an important factor in text-mining systems, from Berry (2003). Relevant feedback in information retrieval (IR), where retrieved documents are clustered, is a specific application that is actively researched by Hearst *et al.* (1996), Leuski (2001), Zeng *et al.* (2001) and Kummamuru (2004).

NMF is a dimensional reduction method and an effective document clustering method, because a term-document matrix is high-dimensional and sparse, from Xu *et al.* (2003).

Let X to be a $m \times n$ term-document matrix, consisting of m rows (terms) and n columns (documents). If the number of clusters is k, NMF decomposes X to the matrices U and V^t as follows:

$$X = UV^t$$

where U is $m \times k$, V is $n \times k$ and V^t is the transposed matrix of V. The matrix U and V are non-negative. In NMF, each k dimensional column vector in V corresponds to a document. An actual clustering procedure is usually performed using these reduced vectors. However, NMF does not need such a clustering procedure. The reduced vector expresses its cluster by itself, because each column axis of V represents a topic of the cluster. Furthermore, the matrices V and U are

---

[*] This research was partially supported by the Ministry of Education, Science, Sports and Culture, Grant-in-Aid for Scientific Research on Priority Areas, "Japanese Corpus", 19011001, 2007.

obtained by a simple iteration, from Lee (2000), where the initial matrices U_0 and V_0 are updated. Therefore, we can regard NMF as a refinement method for a given clustering result, because the matrix V represents a clustering result.

In this paper, we use NMF to improve clustering results. Providing NMF with an accurate document clustering result, we can ensure a more accurate result, because NMF is effective for document clustering. However, NMF often fails to improve the initial clustering result. The main reason for this is that the object function of NMF does not properly represent the goodness of clustering. To overcome this problem, we use another object function. After each iteration of NMF, the current clustering result is evaluated by that object function.

We first need the initial clustering result. To obtain this, we perform min-max cut (Mcut) proposed by Ding *et al.* (2001), which is a spectral clustering method. Mcut is a very powerful clustering method, and we can obtain an accurate clustering result by improving the clustering result generated through Mcut,

In the experiment, we used 19 data set provided via the CLUTO website. Our method improved the clustering result generated by Mcut. In addition, the accuracy of the obtained clustering result was higher than those of NMF, CLUTO and Mcut.

2. Refinement using NMF

2.1. Features of NMF

NMF decomposes the $m \times n$ term-document matrix X to the $m \times k$ matrix U and the transposed matrix V^t of the $n \times k$ matrix V, from Xu *et al.* (2003), where k is the number of clusters:

$$X = UV^t.$$

NMF attempts to find the axes corresponding to the topic of the clusters, and represents the document vector and the term vector as a linear combination of the found axes.

NMF has following three features:

i. V and U are non-negative.

The element of V and U refers to the degree of relevance to the topic corresponding to the axis of its element. It is therefore natural to assign a non-negative value to the element. SVD can also reduce dimensions, but negative values appear unlike with NMF.

ii.   The matrix V represents the clustering result.

The dimensional reduction translates high-dimensional data to lower-dimensional data. Therefore, we usually must perform actual clustering for the reduced data. However, NMF does not require this, because the matrix V represents the clustering result. The i-th document d_i corresponds to the i-th row vector of V, that is, $d_i = (v_{i1}, v_{i2}, 4, v_{ij})$. The cluster number is obtained from $\arg\max_j v_{ij}$.

iii. V and U do not need to be an orthogonal matrix.

LSI constructs orthogonal space from document space. On the other hand, in NMF, the axis in the reduced space corresponds to a topic, therefore, these axes do not need to be orthogonal. As a result, NMF attempts to find the axis corresponding to the cluster that has documents containing identical words.

2.2. NMF algorithm

For the given term-document matrix X, we can obtain U and V by the following iteration, shown by Lee (2000).

$$u_{ij} \leftarrow u_{ij} \frac{(XV)_{ij}}{(UV^tV)_{ij}} \qquad \text{(Eq.1)}$$

$$v_{ij} \leftarrow v_{ij} \frac{(X^tU)_{ij}}{(VU^tU)_{ij}} \qquad \text{(Eq.2)}$$

Here, u_{ij}, v_{ij} and $(X)_{ij}$ are the i-th row and the j-th column element of U, V and a matrix X respectively.

After each iteration, U must be normalized as follows:

$$u_{ij} \leftarrow \frac{u_{ij}}{\sqrt{\sum_i u_{ij}^2}}$$

The iteration stops by the fixed maximum iteration number, or the distance J between X and UV^t:

$$J = \left\| X - UV^t \right\| \qquad \text{(Eq.3)}$$

Here, J is the decomposition error.

2.3. Clustering result and initial matrices

In general, the initial matrices U_0 and V_0 are constructed using random values. In this paper, we construct the U_0 and V_0 through a clustering result.

In particular, if the cluster number of the i-th data is clustered into the c-th cluster, the i-th row vector of V_0 is constructed as follows:

$$v_{ij} = \begin{cases} 1.0 & (j = c) \\ 0.1 & (j \neq c) \end{cases}$$

Here, U_0 is constructed via XV_0.

2.4. Problem of the object function of NMF

We can use NMF as a refinement method for a clustering result, because the initial matrix of NMF corresponds to a clustering result. However, NMF often fails to improve the given clustering result. This is because the object function of NMF, that is, Eq. 3, does not properly represent the goodness of clustering.

To confirm this problem, we performed NMF using the document data set ``tr45" which is a part of the data set used in Section 5. The initial matrix was constructed using the clustering result obtained by Mcut. Figure 1 shows the results of this experiment. LINE-1 and LINE-2 in Figure 1 show the change in J in each iteration and the change in the clustering accuracy, respectively. From Figure 1, we can confirm that a smaller J does not always mean a more accurate clustering.

To overcome this problem, we evaluated the current clustering result using another object function after each iteration of NMF.

Specifically, we used the object function of Mcut. We calculated the value of the object function after each iteration of NMF. If the best value was not improved for three consecutive iterations, we stopped NMF.

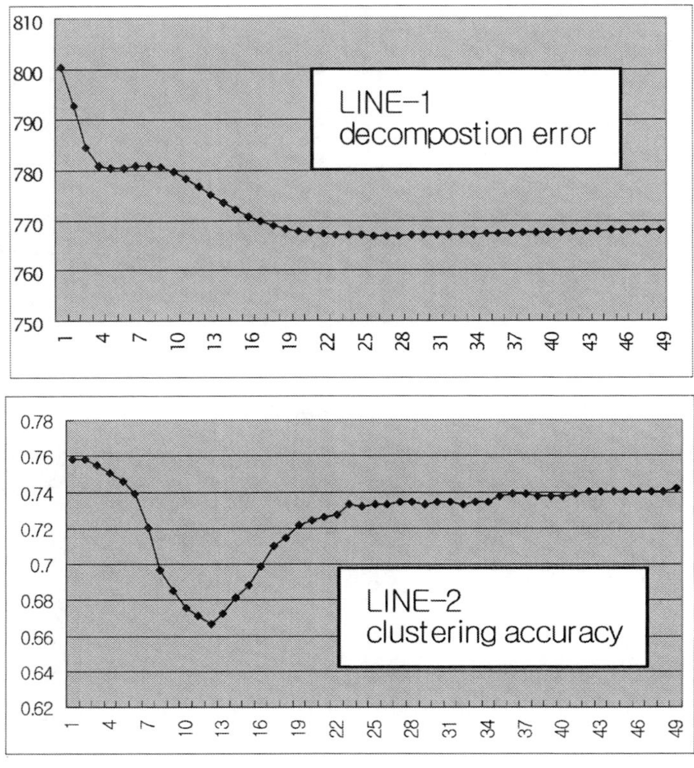

Figure 1: Decomposition error and clustering accuracy

3. Mcut

Next, we needed the initial clustering result. To obtain this, we used Mcut proposed by Ding *et al.* (2001) which is a type of spectral clustering.

In this spectral clustering method, the data set is represented as a graph. Each data point is represented as a vertex in the graph. If the similarity between data A and B is non-zero, the edge between A and B is drawn and the similarity is used as the weight of the edge. From this graph, clustering can be seen to correspond to the segmentation of the graph into a number of subgraphs by cutting the edges. The preferable cutting is such that the sum of the weights of the edges in the subgraph is large and the sum of weights of the cut edges is small. To find the ideal cut, the object function is used. The spectral clustering method finds the desirable cut by using the fact that an optimum solution of the object function corresponds to the solution of an eigenvalue problem. Different object functions are proposed. In this paper, we use the object function of Mcut.

First, we define the similarity *cut(A,B)* between the subgraph *A* and *B* as follows:

$$cut(A,B) = W(A,B).$$

The function *W(A,B)* is the sum of the weights of the edges between *A* and *B*. We define *W(A)* as *W(A,A)*.

The object function of Mcut is the following:

$$Mcut = \frac{cut(A,B)}{W(A)} + \frac{cut(A,B)}{W(B)} \qquad \text{(Eq.4)}$$

The clustering task is to find A and B to minimize the above equation.

Note that the spectral clustering method divides the data set into two groups. If the number of clusters is larger than two, the above procedure is iterated recursively.

The minimization problem of Eq.4 is equivalent to the problem of finding the n dimensional discrete vector y to minimize the following equation:

$$J_m = \frac{y^t(D-W)y}{y^tWy} \qquad \text{(Eq.5)}$$

where W is the similarity matrix of data, $D = diag(We)$ and $e = (1,1,4 \ ,1)^t$. Each element in the vector y is a or $-b$, where $a = \sqrt{\dfrac{d_B}{d_A d}}$, $b = \sqrt{\dfrac{d_A}{d_B d}}$, $d_X = \sum_{i \in X}(D)_{ii}$ and $d = d_A + d_B$. If the i-th element of the vector y is a (or $-b$), the i-th data element belongs to the cluster A (or B). We can solve Eq.5 by converting the discrete vector y to the continuous vector y. Finally, we can obtain an approximate solution to Eq.5 by solving the following eigenvalue problem:

$$(I - D^{-1/2}WD^{1/2})z = \lambda z \qquad \text{(Eq.6)}$$

We obtain the eigenvector z, that is, Fielder vector, corresponding to the second minimum eigenvalue by solving the eigenvalue problem represented by Eq.6. We can obtain the solution y to Eq.5 from $z = D^{1/2}y$. By the sign of the i-th value of y, we can judge whether the i-th data element belongs to cluster A or B.

Note that Eq.4 is the object function when the number of clusters is two. The object function used in NMF is the following general object function for k clusters $\{G_i\}_{i=1:k}$.

$$Mcut_K = \frac{cut(G_1,\overline{G_1})}{W(G_1)} + \frac{cut(G_2,\overline{G_2})}{W(G_2)} + 4 \ + \frac{cut(G_k,\overline{G_k})}{W(G_k)} \qquad \text{(Eq.7)}$$

where $\overline{G_k}$ is the complement of G_k. The smaller $Mcut_K$ is, the better it is.

4. Experiment

In the experiment, we used the data set provided via the CLUTO website
http://glaros.dtc.umn.edu/gkhome/cluto/cluto/download.
In total, 24 data sets are available. We used data sets that had less than 5,000 data elements. As a result, we used 19 data sets, shown in Table 1. In each data set, the document vector is not normalized. We normalize them by TF-IDF.

Table 1: Document data sets

Data	# of documents	# of terms	# of non-zero elements	# of classes
cacmcisi	4,663	41,681	83,181	2
cranmed	2,431	41,681	140,658	2
fbis	2,463	2,000	393,386	17
hitech	2,301	126,373	346,881	6
k1a	2,340	21,839	349,792	20
k1b	2,340	21,839	349,792	6
la1	3,204	31,472	484,024	6
la2	3,075	31,472	455,383	6

mm	2,521	126,373	490,062	2
re0	1,504	2,886	77,808	13
re1	1,657	3,758	87,328	25
reviews	4,069	126,373	781,635	5
tr11	414	6,429	116,613	9
tr12	313	5,804	85,640	8
tr23	204	5,832	78,609	6
tr31	927	10,128	248,903	7
tr41	878	7,454	171,509	10
tr45	690	8,261	193,605	10
wap	1,560	6,460	220,482	20

Table 2 shows the result. NMF-rfn in the table refers to our method. That is, we obtained the initial clustering results by Mcut and then improved it by performing NMF. The NMF-rfn column in Table 2 shows the ratio of values of Eq.7 obtained using our method to those obtained using Mcut. As shown in Table 2, the value of Eq.7 of our method is less than (or equal to) Mcut absolutely. This means that our method absolutely improves the clustering results considering Eq.7.

Table 2: Comparison of the object function value

Data	NMF-rfn
cacmcisi	1.0000
cranmed	1.0000
Fbis	0.9350
Hitech	0.9345
k1a	0.6340
k1b	0.9630
la1	1.0000
la2	0.9862
Mm	0.9979
re0	1.0000
re1	0.9974
reviews	0.6503
tr11	0.8971
tr12	1.0000
tr23	0.9806
tr31	0.9728
tr41	0.9409
tr45	0.8242
Wap	0.7679
Average	0.9201

Next, we checked the accuracy of our method. Table 3 and Figure 2 show the results. The column of NMF, CLUTO[1] and Mcut in Table 3 shows the accuracy of NMF, CLUTO and Mcut respectively. And the column of NMF-ref is the accuracy of our method.

Table 3: Accuracy of each method

Data	NMF	CLUTO	Mcut	NMF-rfn
cacmcisi	0.5788	0.6054	0.6858	0.6858
cranmed	0.5825	0.9975	0.9930	0.9930
fbis	0.4125	0.4921	0.5278	0.4941
hitech	0.4633	0.5228	0.3859	0.5059
k1a	0.4107	0.4799	0.4658	0.5684
k1b	0.6389	0.6081	0.5205	0.5342
la1	0.6798	0.7147	0.6879	0.6879
la2	0.5873	0.6582	0.7028	0.6924
mm	0.5470	0.5331	0.9583	0.9556
re0	0.3710	0.3198	0.3670	0.3670
re1	0.3826	0.4146	0.4490	0.4599
reviews	0.7196	0.6316	0.6776	0.6424
tr11	0.5556	0.6812	0.6546	0.7295
tr12	0.6422	0.6869	0.7764	0.7764
tr23	0.3971	0.4559	0.4363	0.4363
tr31	0.5696	0.5674	0.7228	0.6624
tr41	0.5239	0.6412	0.5661	0.6014
tr45	0.6347	0.5986	0.7580	0.7101
wap	0.4686	0.4487	0.4109	0.5096
Average	0.5350	0.5821	0.6182	0.6322

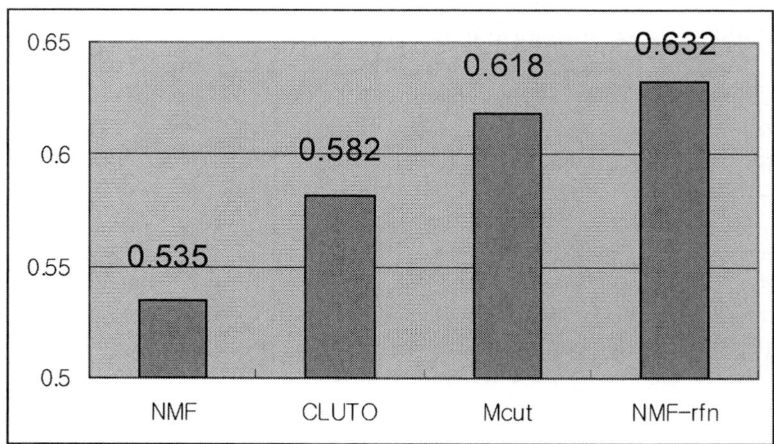

Figure 2: Average accuracy of each method

---

[1] CLUTO is a very powerful clustering tool. We can get from the following website. http://glaros.dtc.umn.edu/gkhome/views/cluto (version 2.1.2a)

Clustering accuracy is the most rigorous evaluation of the clustering result. However, accuracy is difficult to measure. First of all, all data must be labeled. Fortunately the data sets used satisfy this condition. Next, we must map each obtained cluster to the cluster label. This mapping is usually difficult. In this paper, we assigned the label to the cluster to assure the accuracy is high, by using dynamic programming. As a result, we obtain accurate clustering.

The measure of similarity and the clustering method of CLUTO must also be examined We can select these via the optional parameter of CLUTO. In our experiments, we conducted CLUTO without any optional parameters, that is, by using the default setting. In this case, CLUTO uses the cosine similarity measure and the k-way clustering method, which takes a top-down approach to divide data into two partitions and iterates this division until k partitions are obtained. In general, the k-way clustering method is more powerful than k-means for document clustering.

There were six data sets for which the accuracy was degraded by performing NMF after Mcut. But in seven data sets, the accuracy was improved by NMF. In the remaining six data sets, the accuracy was not changed. Figure 2 shows that the average accuracies of CLUTO, Mcut and NMF-rfn were 58.21%, 61.82% and 63.22% respectively. That is, our method showed the best performance.

5. Discussions

5.1. Search for the optimum solution

The object function value of the end clustering result is never degraded from the value in Mcut. However, as shown in Table 2, there are some data sets for which the clustering accuracy of NMF-rfn is worse than that of Mcut.

This is because the object function used does not refer to the goodness of clustering in a precise sense. All object functions suffer from the same problem. Especially, the object function J in Eq. 3 is not so good. In fact, we confirmed that the Mcut object function is better than J in Eq.3 for NMF from another experiment.

The clustering task has two parts: one is the object function, and the other is the search method for the optimum solution to the object function. Mcut-rfn uses Eq.7 as the object function and combines the search methods of Mcut and NMF as its search method.

Recent theoretical analysis shows the equivalence between spectral clustering and other clustering methods. For example, Dhillon *et al.* (2005) show that a search for an optimum solution via spectral clustering can be performed using the weighted kernel k-means. Additionally, Ding *et al.* (2005) show the equivalence between spectral clustering and NMF. By using these techniques, a search for an optimum solution may be constructed in a consistent manner, unlike with Mcut-rfn.

However, such a consistent manner cannot avoid falling into a local optimum solution. It is therefore helpful to add a mechanism to jump out from a local optimum solution. Our hybrid approach is an example of such a method.

The ``*local search*'' proposed by Dhillon *et al.* (2002) is relevant to our approach. This method first obtains a solution by k-means and then improves it by the ``*first variation*'' and iterates these two steps alternately. Mcut-rfn first obtains a solution by Mcut and then improves it by NMF, but it does not iterate them, because the input of Mcut does not need to be a clustering solution. Using the weighted kernel k-means, we can take the ``*ping-pong*'' strategy like the local search.

5.2. Initial matrices and accuracy of NMF

In NMF, clustering accuracy depends on the initial matrices. This is because the local optimum solution obtained by NMF varies according to the initial value. Therefore, deciding what initial matrices should be used is a difficult problem, from Wild *et al.* (2004).

Regarding the object function, initial accuracy must be improved. Thus, we took the approach to set the value that had a high accuracy as the initial value. However, even if NMF starts from initial values that have low accuracy, NMF can still obtain highly accurate results. For example, for the data set ``k1a'' and ``tr11'' in our experiments, CLUTO was better than Mcut. Using the result of CLUTO as the initial value, accuracy was not improved by NMF. On the other hand, in the case of Mcut, accuracy was improved by NMF, and the final accuracy was better than that of CLUTO.

Finally, clustering is an NP-hard combinatorial optimization problem after the object function is fixed. It is impossible to find the optimal initial value. Thus, the clustering algorithm must take an approach that improves the solution gradually. Under such a situation, our approach to set a feasible solution to the initial value is practical.

5.3. Future works for document clustering

The clustering task is a purely engineered problem once data is translated into vectors. To get more accurate clustering, we should actively use knowledge on data at the pre-translated stage. In the case of document clustering, we should remember that the data is a document. It may be important to ensure that meta-information such as the publication place, author, aim of clustering is incorporated into the clustering process or vector-translation process.

Clustering is unsupervised learning. The effective way to raise accuracy is therefore to assign supervised labels to data. Recently, semi-supervised clustering using user-interaction has been actively researched by Basu *et al.* (2002), Bilenko *et al.* (2004) and Xing *et al.* (2003). This semi-supervised clustering using meta-information shows promise.

6. Conclusion

In this paper, we have shown that NMF can be used to improve clustering result. For practical use, we used another object function, and we evaluated the current clustering result using that object function after each iteration of NMF. By performing Mcut to obtain the initial clustering result, we can obtain an accurate clustering result. In the experiment, we used 19 data set provided via the CLUTO website. Our method improved the clustering result obtained by Mcut. In addition, the accuracy of the obtained clustering result was higher than those of NMF, CLUTO and Mcut. In future, we will research semi-supervised clustering using meta-information.

References

Basu, S., A. Banerjee, and R. J. Mooney. 2002. Semi-supervised Clustering by Seeding. *Proceedings of ICML-2002*, pp.19-26.

Berry, M. W. 2003. *Survey of Text Mining: Clustering, Classification, and Retrieval*. Springer.

Bilenko, M., S. Basu and R. J. Mooney. 2004. Integrating Constraints and Metric Learning in Semi-Supervised Clustering. *Proceedings of ICML-2004*, pp.81-88.

Dhillon, I. S., Y. Guan and J. Kogan. 2002. Iterative Clustering of High Dimentional Text Data Augmented by Local Search. *The 2002 IEEE International Conference on Data Mining*, 131-138.

Dhillon, I. S., Y. Guan and B. Kulis. 2005. A Unified View of Kernel k-means, Spectral

Clustering and Graph Cuts. *The University of Texas at Austin, Department of Computer Sciences. Technical Report TR-04-25.*

Ding, C., X. He and H. D. Simon. 2005. On the Equivalence of Nonnegative Matrix Factorization and Spectral Clustering. *Proceedings of SDM 2005.*

Ding, C., X. He, H. Zha, M. Gu and H. Simon. 2001. Spectral Min-max Cut for Graph Partitioning and Data Clustering. *Lawrence Berkeley National Lab. Tech. report 47848.*

Hearst, M. A. and J. O. Pedersen. 1996. Reexamining the Cluster Hypothesis: Scatter/gather on Retrieval Results. *Proceedings of SIGIR-96*, pp.76-84.

Kummamuru, K., R. Lotlikar, S. Roy, K. Singal and R. Krishnapuram. 2004. A Hierarchical Monothetic Document Clustering Algorithm for Summarization and Browsing Search Results. *Proceedings of WWW-04*, pp.658-665.

Lee, D. D. and H. S. Seung. 2000. Algorithms for Non-negative Matrix Factorization. *Proceedings of NIPS-2000*, pp.556-562.

Leuski, A. 2001. Evaluating Document Clustering for Interactive Information Retrieval. *Proceedings of CIKM-01*, pp.33-40.

Wild, S., J. Curry and A. Dougherty. 2004. Improving Non-negative Matrix Factorizations through Structured Initialization. *Pattern Recognition*, Vol.37, No.11, 2217-2232.

Xing, E. P., A. Y. Ng, M. I. Jordan and S. Russell. 2003. Distance Metric Learning, with Application to Clustering with Side-information. *Advances in Neural Information Processing Systems* 15, 505-512.

Xu, Wei., X. Liu and Y. Gong. 2003. Document Clustering Based on Non-negative Matrix Factorization. *Proceedings of SIGIR-03*, pp.267-273.

Zeng, H.-J., Q.-C. He, Z. Chen, W.-Y. Ma and J. Ma. 2001. Learning to Cluster Web Search Results. *Proceedings of SIGIR-04*, pp.33-40

Constraints and Type Hierarchies for Korean Serial Verb Constructions
- An Analytic Study within the HPSG Framework -[*]

Sanghoun Song

Dept. of Linguistics, Korea Univ.
Anam-dong Seongbuk-Gu, Seoul, 136-701 Korea
yooseon21@korea.ac.kr

Abstract. This paper provides a fine-grained analysis of Korean serial verb constructions within the HPSG framework, and covers major descriptive characteristics of the phenomena. This paper discusses constraints on serial verb constructions in terms of four aspects; transitivity, argument structure, semantic properties, and complementizers. As a result, 17 constraints have been built, which support the type hierarchies for Korean serial verb constructions. This paper also presents a sample derivation on the basis of on the constraints and the type hierarchies.

Keywords: serial verb, SVC, KSVC, HPSG, constraint, type hierarchy

1. Introduction

Sohn (1999:380) offers a general explanation to Korean Serial Verb Constructions (henceforth KSVCs) as the following.

(1) Serial predicate constructions consist of two or more predicate (flanked by a complementizer) which denote sequential actions or states that denote a single coextensive or extended event.

From a cross-linguistic perspective, Serial Verb Constructions (hereafter SVCs) are well-known for productivity. Dixon (2006:338) claims that 'a SVC is a clearly recognizable, robust grammatical constructions type which carries a considerable functional and semantic load.' Since the same goes for Korean, SVCs frequently appear in Korean, too. For example, (2) are extracted from the *Sejong POS-tagged Corpora*,[1] which take *mek-* 'eat' as V2 within the frame of 'V1 + *e* + V2.'

(2) *nanwu-e mek-ta* 'divide and eat', *kkulhi-e mek-ta* 'boil and eat', *mandul-e mek-ta* 'make and eat', *cap-a mek-ta* 'catch and eat', *cip-e mek-ta* 'pick up and eat', *ssip-e mek-ta* 'chew and eat', *kwu-e mek-ta* 'broil and eat', *ppal-a mek-ta* 'suck and eat',…

---

[*] I would like to return thanks to Prof. Jae-Woong Choe, who helped this study forward. I also want to appreciate the comments of anonymous readers. Due to the comments, I could elaborate this paper. Of course, all errors are my responsibility.

[1] I extracted all data from these resources (morpheme-tagged corpora which cover ten million *eojeol*). According to inquiry into the corpora, 27% of verbs marked with 'vv' can be used as members in SVCs.

The purpose of this study is to provide an overall picture of KSVCs within the framework of the unification-based grammar[2], in particular, Head-driven Phrase Structure Grammar (HPSG)[3]. This paper makes a fine-grained analysis of constraints on KSVCs, and also proposes the type hierarchies for KSVCs within the HPSG framework.

2. Basic data

The expression form that this paper deals with is like (3), and examples that Sohn (1999:380) provides are given in (4).

(3) V1 + COMP[*e/a, ko, eta*] + V2
(4) a. *Cihwan.i-nun   ttek-ul   son-ulo   cip-e   mek-ess-e.*
    Cihwan-TOPIC   cake-ACC   hand-with   pick up-INF   eat-PST-INT
    'Cihwan (picked up and) ate the rice cake with his fingers.'
  b. *mulkoki-ka   kom-eykey   cap-hi-e   mek-hi-ess-ta.*
    fish-NOM   bear-by   catch-PAS-INF   eat-PAS-PST-DC
    'The fish was (caught and) eaten by the bear.'
  c. *Milan.i-nun   kapnag-ul   an   tul-ko   ka-ss-e.*
    Milan-TOPIC   bag-ACC   not   hold-and   go-PST-INT
    'Milan didn't take her bag with her.'
  d. *wuli-nun   tongkwul   sok-ul   tuli-eta   po-ass-ta.*
    we-TOPIC cave   inside-ACC   put in-TR   see-PST-DC
    'We looked into the cave.'

Though the KSVC is a productive operation as aforesaid, yet there are selectional restrictions between V1 and V2. The constraints on how to combine with are exemplified below.

(5) a. *mek-* 'eat', *masi-* 'drink', *cip-* 'pick up', *chayngki-* 'take care of, collect'
  b. **masi-e mek-ta, *mek-e masi-ta*
  c. *cip-e mek-ta, *mek-e cip-ta*
  d. *chayngki-e mek-ta* 'take meals', *mek-e chayngki-ta* 'profiteer'

Verbs in (5b) cannot combine with each other regardless of their ordering. (5c) shows that the verb which denotes a manner is followed by the other verb, and the reversed order cannot be accepted. Both orders in (5d) are possible, but they have different meanings respectively. This paper gives an account of these restrictions with the typed feature structure of HPSG.

While other researches generally have not regarded *-ko* and *-eta* as complementizers[4] (hereafter COMP) which is used to form KSVCs, Sohn (1999) says that *-ko* and *-eta* as well as *-e/a* are used for KSVCs. Accepting his idea, I suppose constructions such as (4c-d) to be a sort of KSVCs. To be sure, if *-ko* in (4c) is regarded as a COMP for SVCs, it should be differentiated from its homonym, *-ko* 'and,' which is used for coordination constructions.

---

[2] Sag and Wasow (1999:52) defines unification as below.
    Unification, then, is just a general method for allowing two compatible descriptions to amalgamate the information they contain into a single (usually larger) description.
The function of unification implies that HPSG can provide a more superior solution to SVCs, because SVCs basically stand for the process that two or more verbs are unified into one single unit.
[3] I find few studies have been done on KSVCs in HPSG. An overview of Korean grammar within the HPSG framework is given in Chang (1995) and Kim (2004), but they do not deal with KSVCs.
[4] This term may be rather controversial because KSVCs are not complex clauses in a general sense. I tentatively define the suffix that attach to V1 as COMP in this paper, which is similar to a COMP of Chang (1995:16) or a complementizer affix of Kim (2004:52).

(6) *Mia-ka   phathi-eyse mek-ko   masi-ess-ta.*
    Mia-NOM party-LOC   eat-and   drink-PST-DC
    'Mia ate and drank at the party.'

Despite a superficial resemblance, there is an obvious difference between *-ko* in (4c) and *-ko* in
(6). A tense marker such as *-ess* can attach to V1 *mek-* in (6), while it can not attach to V1 *tul-* in
(4c). I treat the construction like (4c) as KSVCs on the ground of this difference. In the case of *-
eta*, I think it is a variation of *-e/a*, which has been formed through a historical development.

 Aikhenvald (2006) suggests that SVC functions like a single predicate to represent 'One
Event.' Building upon her claim, I assume that two verbs combine with each other before
anything else to be a single predicate. I also consider V2 the head of SVCs, because tense or
aspect makers should attach to V2, which is similar to Chung (1995)'s structure.

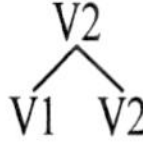

Figure 1: The structure of KSVCs (Chung 1995:70)

3. Constraints

In this section, I will inspect the constraints on KSVCs in terms of four aspects; transitivity,
argument structure, semantic properties, and COMPs. In order to make this study based on more
synthetic approach, I tried to collect relevant data in a systematic way from large corpora. To
tell in the concrete, I made practical application of the *Sejong POS-tagged Corpora*.
Implementing some programs which aim to extract the form 'X/vv + X/ec + X/vv' from the
corpora, I could obtain first data. After that, I excluded problematic forms from the list in
conformity to criteria for distinguishing between KSVCs and others. From now on, all analyses
to constraints are grounded upon these demonstrative data.

3.1. Transitivity

After investigating the data, I discover the forms that the transitivity of V1 is smaller than that
of V2 or equal to are more common. However, there are also the cases that the transitivity of V1
is bigger than that of V2. For instance, *cip-e ka-ta* 'pick up and go' is made up of transitive V1
cip- and intransitive V2 *ka-*. In this case, it is interesting that V2 is a deictic verb almost
invariably.[5] This analysis is also applicable to the constructions which take *-ko* as a COMP; for
example, *tul*[transitive]*-ko ka*[intransitive, DEIXIS +]*-ta* 'hold and go' in (4c). Meanwhile, I
also observe that 'V1[ditransitive] + V2[transitive]' constructions are not SVCs, because their
arguments cannot be unified.

3.2. Argument structure

From the data shown below, I conclude that grammatical cases are unified into the single
predicate which is composed of V1 and V2. And also (7) shows that oblique cases will not be
constraints on KSVCs. They are merely subsumed into the unified argument structure.

(7) a. *Mia-ka   hak.kyo-ey   kel-e   ka-ass-ta.*
       Mia-NOM   school-DIR   walk-INF   go-PST-DC
       'Mia went to school on foot.'
           ket(kel)- 'walk' (NOM/AGT)
           ka- 'go' (NOM/AGT, OBL/DIR)

---

[5] It is analogous to Hashimoto and Bond (2005:153)'s analysis of V-V Compounds in Japanese.
 *Another peculiarity involves the fact that the V2 is restricted to a monotrans verb that expresses
 a spatial motion, while the V1 is transitive and must not be a spatial motion verb.*

b. *Mia-ka   ppang-ul   hak.kyo-ey   cip-e   ka-ass-ta.*
   Mia-NOM   bread-ACC   school-DIR   pick up-INF   go-PST-DC
   'Mia picked up the bread and went to school.'
        cip- 'pick up' (NOM/AGT, ACC/THM)
        ka- 'go' (NOM/AGT, OBL/DIR)
c. *Mia-ka   sakwa-lul   khal-lo   kkakk-a   mek-ess-ta.*
   Mia-NOM   apple-ACC   knife-INST   pare-INF   eat-PST-DC
   'Mia pared an apple with a knife and ate it.'
        kkakk- 'pare' (NOM/AGT, ACC/THM, OBL/INST)
        mek- 'eat' (NOM/AGT, ACC/THM)
d. *Mia-ka   Cihwan.i-ekey chayk-ul   sa-a   cu-ess-ta.*
   Mia-NOM   Cihwan-DAT   book-ACC   buy-INF   give-PST-DC
   'Mia bought a book and gave it to Cihwan.'
        sa- 'buy' (NOM/AGT, ACC/THM)
        cu- 'give' (NOM/AGT, ACC/THM, OBL/DAT)

3.3. Semantic properties

Maunsuwan (2000) introduces FIRST and LAST features into the analysis of Thai SVCs, because a 'manner-of-motion' verb is followed by a 'deictic' verb in Thai.

(8) FIRST and LAST (Maunsuwan 2000:241)
    a. manner-of-motion verbs or verbs that entail motion are lexically marked as [FIRST +], meaning that a VP headed by a verb from this class must occur first in the SVC.
    b. verbs that take a deictic verb as complement are lexically marked as [LAST +], meaning that a VP headed by a verb from this class must occur last in the sequence of verb complexes.
    c. other non-deictic serial verbs are lexically marked as [FIRST boolean, LAST boolean] meaning that they are not constrained in their order of occurrence.

Although Maunsuwan adopts double-headed structure for SVCs, the above solution is similarly available for KSVCs. But, it is so difficult to classify all verbs into subclasses only by intuition. Instead, this paper defines the feature of a verb by inductive methods based on large corpora. Since I extracted verbs' frequency according to their distribution from the corpora previously, it does not fall into hard work.

(9)   a. [FIRST +, LAST −]: *cip-* 'pick up', *kkekki-* 'be broken', *khay-* 'dig', *cec-* 'stir', …
    b. [FIRST −, LAST +]: *masi-* 'drink', *kku-* 'extinguish', *sey-* 'count', *kkaywu-* 'wake up', …
    c. [FIRST boolean, LAST boolean]: <u>*ka-* 'go'</u>, <u>*ket(kel)-* 'walk'</u>, <u>*tani-* 'wander'</u>, *wus-* 'laugh', ,
      mek- 'eat', *chayngki-* 'take care of, collect', *ccic-* 'tear', *chac-* 'find', *tat-* 'close', …

The restriction on ordering between V1 and V2, mentioned in (5b-c), can be solved with these typed feature structures, which will be presented in (18). There is, however, a weak point in the collection (9). The underlined items in (9) belong to the so-called motion verbs, but (9) cannot give a solution to discriminate between acceptability and unacceptability in (10). Since motion verbs play a significant role in SVCs in any kind of languages, the grammar for SVCs should take motion verbs into consideration.

(10) a. *kel-e ka-ta, *ka-a ket-ta*
    b. *tani-e ka-ta, *ka-a tani-ta*
    c. *kel-e tani-ta, *tani-e ket-ta*
    d. **wus-e ka-ta, *ka-a wus-ta*

Lee (1977) classifies motion verbs into two subclasses; one denotes a 'manner-of-motion', the other denotes a 'spatial movement.' In (10), *ket(kel)-* 'walk' expresses a 'manner-of-motion,' *ka-* 'go' is a typical deictic verb, and *tani-* 'wander' belongs to both the former and the latter. In line with Lee's classification, I build up types for motion verbs as below.

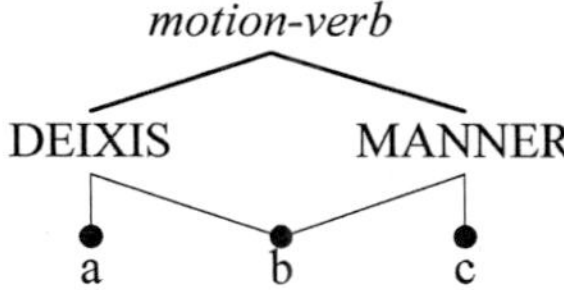

Figure 2: The types of motion verbs

(11) a. [DEIXIS +, MANNER –] : *ka-* 'go'
      b. [DEIXIS +, MANNER +] : *tani-* 'wander'
      c. [DEIXIS –, MANNER +] : *ket(kel)-* 'walk'

(11) offers a solution to the puzzle raised in (10a-c). On the other side, verbs which do not express motion, such as *wus-* 'laugh,' have the typed feature structure like [DEIXIS –, MANNER –]. This structure plays a role to block the ungrammatical construction such as (10d). With these types, I can seek an appropriate treatment for KSVCs which include motion verbs. The related constraints will be shown in (21) and (22).

3.4.COMPs

The constructions with *-e/a* are classified into six subclasses with reference to each composition. They are exemplified in (12)[6].

(12) a. intransitive + intransitive : *kel-e ka-ta* 'go on foot'
      b. transitive + intransitive : *cip-e ka-ta* 'pick up and go'
      c. ditransitive + intransitive : *ponay-e o-ta* 'send to me/us'
      d. transitive + transitive : *cip-e mek-ta* 'pick up and eat'
      e. intransitive + transitive : *ttwi-e nem-ta* 'jump over'
      f. transitive + ditransitive : *sa-a cu-ta* 'buy and give'

The construction with *-ko* has only one type such as 'transitive + intransitive' (e.g. *tul-ko ka-ta* 'hold and go'). In this case, it is clear that the intransitive V2 has a [DEIXIS +] feature.

In the case of the construction with *-eta,* although Sohn (1999) presents only one case whose V2 is *po-* 'look', there are various cases in my data. It is noticeable that the constructions with *-eta* select their verbs in restricted lexicon. In other words, *-eta* constructions have a tendency to become lexicalized.

(13) a. V1 in constructions with *-eta*: *kaci-* 'have', *nay-* 'put out', *nay-li-* 'be set down', *tuli-* 'put in', *pili-* 'borrow', *chi-* 'hit', …
      b. V2 in constructions with *-eta*: *peli-* 'discard', *po-* 'see', *po-i-* 'be seen', *ssu-* 'use', *phal* 'sell', …

There are two types in *-eta* constructions. One is 'transitive + transitive' (e.g. *tuli-eta po-ta* 'look inside'), the other is 'intransitive[PASSIVE +] + intransitive[PASSIVE +]' (e.g. *nay-li-eta po-i-ta*[7] 'be looked down').

3.5.Summary

Generalizing facts discussed so far, I sum up constraints on KSVCs as follows.

---

[6] (12) is partially adapted from Lee (1994).
[7] In this example, I come to the conclusion that *nay-li-* is transformed into passives after once becoming causatives (i.e. *na-*[root] → *nay-*[causative] → *nay-li-*[passive]).

(14) Constraints on KSVCs
      a. If the transitivity of V1 is bigger than that of V2, the V2 is an intransitive verb which
         has a [DEIXIS +] feature.
      b. Grammatical cases are unified into the argument structure of their mother-category,
         whereas oblique cases are subsumed.
      c. V1 has a [FIRST +] feature and V2 has a [LAST +] feature.
      d. If a SVC includes motion verbs, V1 has a [MANNER +] and V2 has a [DEIXIS +].
      e. In *-ko* constructions, V2 is an intransitive with a [DEIXIS +].
      f. In *-eta* constructions, the set of lexicon is rather restricted.

4. Type Hierarchies

Dixon (2006:342), from a typological standpoint, claims 'two basic varieties of SVC can be distinguished, asymmetrical and symmetrical.' Asymmetrical constructions consist of some limited lexicon (e.g. motion verbs) and tend to become grammaticalized, whereas symmetrical constructions where both members come from an open class tend to become lexicalized.

It is said that grammaticalization is the development from lexical expression to functional expression. The other way around, lexicalization refers to 'process whereby concepts are encoded in the words of a language (O'Grady et al. 2005:212).' In this context, it seems that a deictic verbs are under grammaticalization because the original meaning of *ka-* 'go' or *o-* 'come' is diluted in KSVCs. In contrast, *-e/a* constructions, the ordinary form of KSVCs, are inclined to become lexicalized. The obvious evidence is the so-called compound verb.

(15) a. *Mia-ka   pam-ul   kka-a   mek-ess-ta.*
        Mia-NOM chestnut-ACC   peel-INF   eat-PST-DC
        'Mia peeled a chestnut and ate it.'
      b. *Mia-ka   yaksok-ul   kka-a   mek-ess-ta.*
        Mia-NOMappointment-ACC peel-INF   eat-PST-DC
        'Mia forgot an appointment.'   (Oh 1997:26)

(15) shows that the expression such as *kka-a mek-ta* 'peel and eat, forget' is being lexicalized. *mek-e chayngki-ta* 'profiteer' in (5d), likewise, is the result of lexicalization, because it cannot convey senses of *mek-* 'eat' and *chayngki-* 'take care of, collect' wholly. In addition, *-eta* construction, as stated before, is another evidence for lexicalization of symmetrical KSVCs. If we remember members in *-eta* construction are both transitive or both intransitive[PASSIVE +], we can suggest the *-eta* construction shows a typical symmetry. In sum, we can divide KSVCs into two groups in accordance with compositionality.

(16) Compositionality of KSVCs
      a. Asymmetrical constructions: TRANSITIVITY(V1) > TRANSITIVITY(V2)
      b. Symmetrical constructions: TRANSITIVITY(V1) ≤ TRANSITIVITY(V2)

In this paper, I adapt above compositionality as a prominent branching node for type hierarchies. The reason why I consider compositionality as a major point of hierarchies is that the unification of argument structure mainly depends on compositionality. In asymmetrical constructions, the first complement of the mother-category is co-indexed with the first complement of V1. On the other hand, in symmetrical constructions, the complements of V2 are mainly transmitted to the complements of the mother-category. Another important criterion to decide its types is what COMP is made use of. The major types are sketched out below.

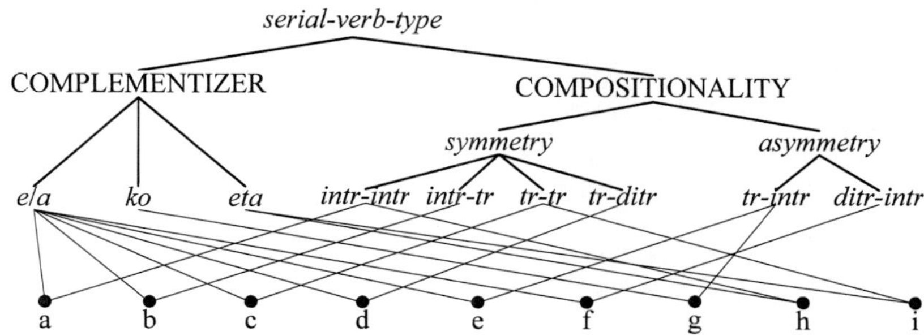

Figure 3: The major types of KSVCs

(17) a. *serial-ea-sym-intr-intr*: *kel-e ka-ta* 'go on foot'
b. *serial-ea-sym-intr-tr*: *ttwi-e nem-ta* 'jump over'
c. *serial-ea-sym-tr-tr*: *cip-e mek-ta* 'pick up and eat'
d. *serial-ea-sym-tr-ditr*: *sa-a cu-ta* 'buy and give'
e. *serial-ea-asym-tr-intr*: *cip-e ka-ta* 'hold and go'
f. *serial-ea-asym-ditr-intr*: *ponay-e o-ta* 'send to me/us'
g. *serial-ko*: *tul-ko ka-ta* 'hold and go'
h. *serial-eta-intr*: *nay-li-eta po-i-ta* 'be looked down '
i. *serial-eta-tr*: *tuly-eta po-ta* 'look inside'

Korean syntactic structure presented below is adapted from Kim(2004:76). I would like to locate *hd-serial-ex* as a subclass of *lex-ex*, because V1 and V2 combined with each other to build a new verbal expression at the stage of lexical category.

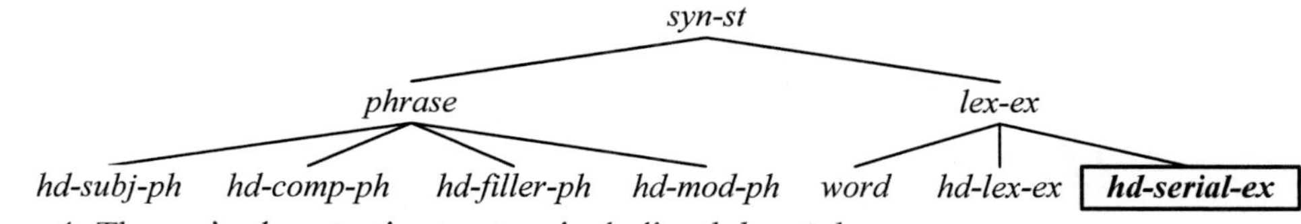

Figure 4: The revised syntactic structure including *hd-serial-ex*

hd-serial-ex shares some properties with *hd-lex-ex* from the points that two verbs combine with each other so as to be a single verb, and the V2 is the head. But, *hd-serial-ex* draws a clear difference with *hd-lex-ex* in respect of argument structure. In *hd-lex-ex* such as the auxiliary construction, V2 takes V1 as its complement (see Kim 2004:123), whereas both V1 and V2 in *hd-serial-ex* do not take each other as complement. The whole type hierarchies that I propose are shown below.

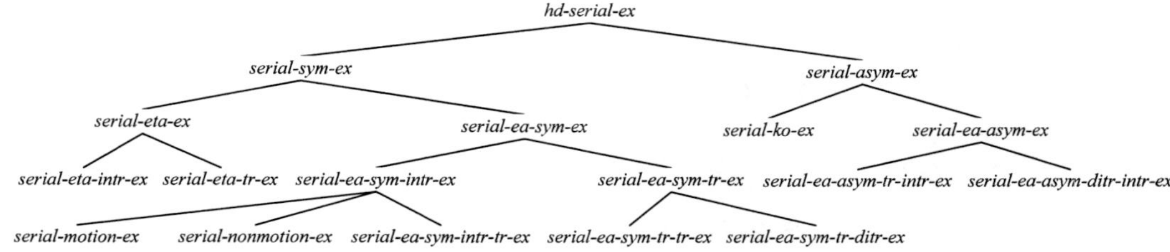

Figure 5: The whole hierarchies for *hd-serial-ex*

Constraints for each type are given as follows. In particular, (18), the top node of KSVCs, indicates that V1 and V2 share the subject, they have a [FIRST +] feature and V2 has a [LAST +] feature, and the head of SVCs is V2.

(18) *hd-serial-ex* ⇒

$$\begin{bmatrix} \text{VAL} \mid \text{SUBJ} \; ① \\ \text{ARGS} \left\langle \begin{bmatrix} \text{VAL} \mid \text{SUBJ} \; ① \\ \text{FIRST} + \end{bmatrix}, \mathbf{H} \begin{bmatrix} \text{VAL} \mid \text{SUBJ} \; ① \\ \text{LAST} + \end{bmatrix} \right\rangle \end{bmatrix}$$

(19) *serial-ea-sym-ex* ⇒

$$\begin{bmatrix} \text{ARGS} \left\langle [\text{VFORM } ea], [\;] \right\rangle \end{bmatrix}$$

(20) *serial-ea-sym-intr-ex* ⇒

$$\begin{bmatrix} \text{VAL} \mid \text{COMPS} \; ① \\ \text{ARGS} \left\langle [\;], [\text{VAL} \mid \text{COMPS} \; ①] \right\rangle \end{bmatrix}$$

(21) *serial-motion-ex* ⇒

$$\begin{bmatrix} \text{ARGS} \left\langle [\text{MOTION} \mid \text{MANNER} +], \begin{bmatrix} \text{MOTION} \mid \text{DEIXIS} + \\ \text{VAL} \mid \text{COMPS} \left\langle [\text{CASE} \mid \text{SCASE } scase] \right\rangle \end{bmatrix} \right\rangle \end{bmatrix}$$

(22) *serial-nonmotion-ex* ⇒

$$\begin{bmatrix} \text{ARGS} \left\langle [\text{MOTION} \mid \text{DEIXIS} -], [\text{MOTION} \mid \text{DEIXIS} -] \right\rangle \end{bmatrix}$$

(23) *serial-ea-sym-intr-tr-ex* ⇒

$$\begin{bmatrix} \text{ARGS} \left\langle [\text{VAL} \mid \text{COMPS} \langle \; \rangle], [\text{VAL} \mid \text{COMPS} \left\langle [\text{CASE} \mid \text{GCASE } acc], ... \right\rangle] \right\rangle \end{bmatrix}$$

(24) *serial-ea-sym-tr-ex* ⇒

$$\begin{bmatrix} \text{VAL.COMPS} \langle ①, ... \rangle \\ \text{ARGS} \left\langle [\text{VAL} \mid \text{COMPS} \langle ①, ... \rangle], [\text{VAL} \mid \text{COMPS} \left\langle ① [\text{CASE} \mid \text{GCASE } acc], ... \right\rangle] \right\rangle \end{bmatrix}$$

(25) *serial-ea-sym-tr-tr-ex* ⇒

$$\begin{bmatrix} \text{VAL} \mid \text{COMPS} \langle [\;], ① \rangle \\ \text{ARGS} \left\langle [\text{VAL} \mid \text{COMPS} \langle [\;], ① \rangle], [\text{VAL} \mid \text{COMPS} \langle [\;] \rangle] \right\rangle \end{bmatrix}$$

(26) *serial-ea-sym-tr-ditr-ex* ⇒

$$\begin{bmatrix} \text{VAL} \mid \text{COMPS} \langle [\;], ①, ② \rangle \\ \text{ARGS} \left\langle [\text{VAL} \mid \text{COMPS} \langle [\;], ② \rangle], [\text{VAL} \mid \text{COMPS} \langle [\;], ① \rangle] \right\rangle \end{bmatrix}$$

(27) *serial-eta-ex* ⇒

$$\begin{bmatrix} \text{VAL} \mid \text{COMPS} \; ① \\ \text{ARGS} \left\langle \begin{bmatrix} \text{VFORM } eta \\ \text{VAL} \mid \text{COMPS} \; ① \end{bmatrix}, [\text{VAL} \mid \text{COMPS} \; ①] \right\rangle \end{bmatrix}$$

(28) *serial-eta-intr-ex* ⇒

$$\begin{bmatrix} \text{ARGS} \left\langle [\text{PASS} +], [\text{PASS} +] \right\rangle \end{bmatrix}$$

(29) *serial-eta-tr-ex* ⇒

$$\begin{bmatrix} \text{ARGS} \left\langle [\;], [\text{VAL} \mid \text{COMPS} \left\langle [\text{CASE} \mid \text{GCASE } acc], ... \right\rangle] \right\rangle \end{bmatrix}$$

(30) *serial-asym-ex* ⇒

$$\begin{bmatrix} \text{VAL} \mid \text{COMPS} \langle ①, ... \rangle \\ \text{ARGS} \left\langle [\text{VAL} \mid \text{COMPS} \left\langle ① [\text{CASE} \mid \text{GCASE } acc], ... \right\rangle], [\text{MOTION} \mid \text{DEIXIS} +] \right\rangle \end{bmatrix}$$

(31) *serial-ea-asym-ex* ⇒

$$\begin{bmatrix} \text{ARGS} \left\langle [\text{VFORM } ea], [\;] \right\rangle \end{bmatrix}$$

(32) *serial-ea-asym-tr-intr-ex* ⇒

$$\begin{bmatrix} \text{VAL} \mid \text{COMPS} \langle [\;], ① \rangle \\ \text{ARGS} \left\langle [\text{VAL} \mid \text{COMPS} \langle [\;] \rangle], [\text{VAL} \mid \text{COMPS} \; ①] \right\rangle \end{bmatrix}$$

(33) *serial-ea-asym-ditr-intr-ex* $\Rightarrow$

$$\begin{bmatrix} \text{VAL} \mid \text{COMPS} \langle [\ ], ①, ② \rangle \\ \text{ARGS} \langle [\text{VAL} \mid \text{COMPS} \langle [\ ], ① \rangle], [\text{VAL} \mid \text{COMPS} ②] \rangle \end{bmatrix}$$

(34) *serial-ko-ex* $\Rightarrow$

$$\begin{bmatrix} \text{VAL} \mid \text{COMPS} \langle [\ ], ① \rangle \\ \text{ARGS} \left\langle \begin{bmatrix} \text{VFORM } ko \\ \text{VAL} \mid \text{COMPS} \langle [\ ] \rangle \end{bmatrix}, [\text{VAL} \mid \text{COMPS} ①] \right\rangle \end{bmatrix}$$

Finally, referring to Kim and Yang (2006), I suggest Head-Serial-Lex Rule as (35) for the semantic representation of KSVCs.

(35)

$$\begin{bmatrix} \text{LEX} + \\ \text{C-CONT} \mid \text{RELS} \left\langle \begin{bmatrix} serial\text{-}rel \\ \text{L-IND} ① \\ \text{R-IND} ② \end{bmatrix} \right\rangle \end{bmatrix} \rightarrow \begin{bmatrix} v\text{-}word \\ \text{LEX} + \\ \text{INDEX} ① \end{bmatrix}, \begin{bmatrix} v\text{-}word \\ \text{LEX} + \\ \text{INDEX} ② \end{bmatrix}$$

5. A sample derivation[8]

This section, instead of conclusion, provides the concrete syntactic structure with a sample sentence given in (7b). For convenience' sake, (7b) is re-written down.

(36) *Mia-ka   ppang-ul   hak.kyo-ey   cip-e   ka-ass-ta.*
    Mia-NOM   bread-ACC   school-LOC   pick up-INF   go-PST-DC
    'Mia picked up the bread and went to school.'
        cip- 'pick up' (NOM/AGT, ACC/THM)
        ka- 'go' (NOM/AGT, OBL/DIR)

Since *cip-e ka-ass-ta* in above sentence belongs to *serial-e-asym-tr-intr-ex*, I present the AVM which represents the SVC as (37). The final tree structure is also sketched out below.

(37)

$$\begin{bmatrix} serial\text{-}e\text{-}asym\text{-}tr\text{-}intr\text{-}ex \\ \text{PHON} \langle cip\text{-}e \ ka\text{-}ass\text{-}ta \rangle \\ \text{HEAD} ① \\ \text{VAL} \begin{bmatrix} \text{SUBJ} \langle \text{NP}_{[nom]} \rangle \\ \text{COMPS} \langle \text{NP}_{[acc]}, \text{NP}_{[dir]} \rangle \end{bmatrix} \\ \text{C-CONT} \mid \text{RELS} \left\langle \begin{bmatrix} serial\text{-}rel \\ \text{L-IND} ② \\ \text{R-IND} ③ \end{bmatrix} \right\rangle \\ \text{ARGS} \left\langle \begin{bmatrix} \text{PHON} \langle cip\text{-}e \rangle \\ \text{INDEX} ② \end{bmatrix}, ① \begin{bmatrix} \text{PHON} \langle ka\text{-}ass\text{-}ta \rangle \\ \text{INDEX} ③ \end{bmatrix} \right\rangle \end{bmatrix}$$

---

[8] I have tried to implement the type hierarchies for KSVCs into the *Linguistic Knowledge Building* system in order to check the computational feasibility of my proposals. All sample sentences in this paper have been tested in the *Linguistic Knowledge Building* system.

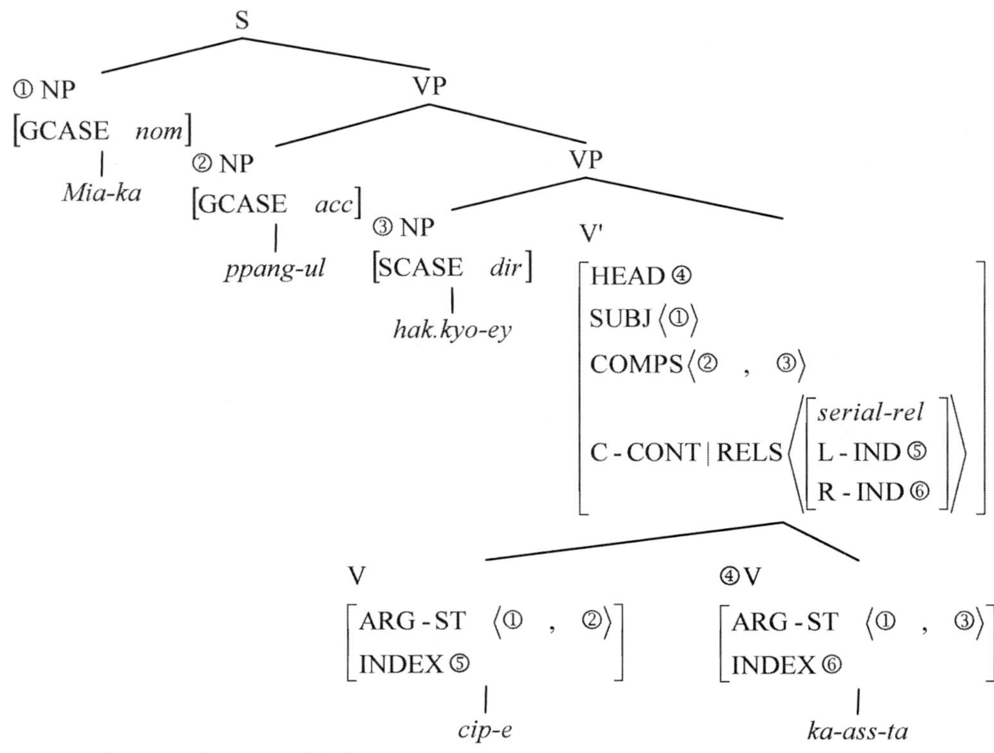

Figure 6: The tree diagram of (36)

References

Aikhenvald, A. Y. 2006. Serial Verb Constructions in Typological Perspective. In A. Y. Aikhenvald and R. M. W. Dixon, eds., *Serial Verb Constructions*, 1-68. Oxford University Press.

Chang, S. 1995. *Information-based Korean Grammar.* Seoul: Hanshin. Publishing Co.

Chung, T. 1995. Argument Structure Theory and Serial Verb. *Studies in Generative Grammar*, 5(1), 63-95.

Dixon, R. M. W. 2006. Serial Verb Constructions: Conspectus and Coda. In A. Y. Aikhenvald and R. M. W. Dixon, eds., *Serial Verb Constructions*, 338-350. Oxford University Press.

Hashimoto, C. and F. Bond. 2005. A Computational Treatment of V-V Compounds in Japanese. *Proceedings of the 12th International Conference on Head-Driven Phrase Structure Grammar*, 143-156.

Kim, J. 2004. *Korean Phrase Structure Grammar*. Seoul: Hankook Munhwasa.

Kim, J. and J. Yang. 2006. Coordination Structures in a Typed Feature Structure Grammar: Formalization and Implementation. In *Lecture Notes in Artificial Intelligence 4139*, 194-205. Springer-Verlag.

Lee, K. 1977. Semantic Analysis of Verb 「o-ta」「ka-ta」. *Mal*, 2, pp. 139-160.

Lee, S. 1994. Serial Verb Constructions in Korean. *Studies in Generative Grammar*, 4(2), 445-493.

Maunsuwan, N. 2000. Directional Serial Verb Constructions in Thai. *Proceedings of the 7th International Conference on Head-Driven Phrase Structure Grammar*, pp. 229-246.

O'Grady, W., M. Aronoff, J. Rees-Miller, and J. Archibald. 2005. *Contemporary Linguistics*. Bedford/St. Martin's.

Oh, M. 1997. *The Study of Korean Serial Verbs*. MA. thesis, Korea University.

Sag, I. A. and T. Wasow. 1999. *Syntactic Theory*. CSLI Publications.

Sohn, H. 1999. *The Korean Language*. Cambridge: Cambridge University Press.

From Tombstones to Corpora: TSML for Research on Language, Culture, Identity and Gender Differences[*]

Oliver Streiter[a], Leonhard Voltmer[b], Yoann Goudin[c]

[a]National University of Kaohsiung, Taiwan, ostreiter@nuk.edu.tw
[b]European Academy Bolzano/Bozen, Italy, lvoltmer@eurac.edu
[c]Ecole des Hautes Etudes en Sciences Sociales, France, goudin@yahoo.com.fr

Abstract. Tombstone inscriptions represent a linguistic genre which yields insights in culture and language. Creating corpora from tombstones is thus a complementary approach for the study of languages and cultures. For the annotation of tombstone corpora, we propose TSML, the Tombstone-Markup-Language, developed during the massive annotation of Taiwanese tombstones and a number of tombstones from China, Indonesia and Europe. We discuss our conceptual framework in the annotation of tombstones and derive successively and present preliminary research data to show how the usefulness of the annotations. Finally, we will encourage researchers to participate in the specification of TSML to obtain soon an annotation language for annotations across cultures and languages.

Keywords: Tombstones, corpora, XML, TSML, Tombstone-Markup-Language, Taiwan.

1. From Tombstones to Corpora

Tombstone inscriptions represent a linguistic genre which, due to the moment it represents, allows for profound insights in culture and language. When the trivia of life don't matter anymore and the cullets of life are swept together in a few strokes in marble, language is frequently the only agent and the only trace in a battle between conflicting identities, social relations, conceptual systems, mythologies and religions.

Plate 1 to 4: From left to right, a sinicized aborigine tomb, a Japanese-style Han tomb, a christianized Han tomb and a de-sinicized aborigine tomb.

Tombstones can be found worldwide. Their form and content follow ethnic and religious traditions, cf. Rath 1986, Frembgen 1998,The Hindu 2005). Notwithstanding global trends, tombstone preserve very local customs. Even on a small island like Taiwan, tombstones in the North and South, East and West are different, blending the flavors of ethnic or religious traditions with local craftsmanship (cf. Clark 1989/1992). In addition, traditions in contact borrow from each other and create particular forms as shown in Plates 1 to 4.

Research on tombstones thus backs the study of language and culture. Creating a corpus of tombstones, as opposed to other research designs used with to tombstones, requires most

---

investments, but is also the most rewarding strategy. First, a corpus can reveal facts, such as local, temporal, ethnic, religious, social or gender-related differences, that cannot be learned from individual tombstones. In addition, a corpus, when properly balanced, paves the way to innumerable investigations beyond the initial motivation for the construction of the corpus. Third, a corpus with digital recordings such as photos as integral part can be continuously annotated, opening new perspectives with each new annotation. Finally, corpora from different resources can be used in comparative studies.

Tombstone corpora cannot bridge the gap between the rapid extinction of cultures and languages (Wurm 1991) and the missing research activities in language documentation. Although one might hope that tombstones will still be recoverable after the death of a culture, factors like urbanization, industrialization, tourism and construction work or acid rain threaten the existence of these mute witnesses. Although after 100 years one might still find individual tombstones, any systematic comparison across regions, ethnicities or time periods would be difficult. Our study on Taiwanese tombstones confirms the precarious state, showing a massive loss of tombstones of the time before 1950.

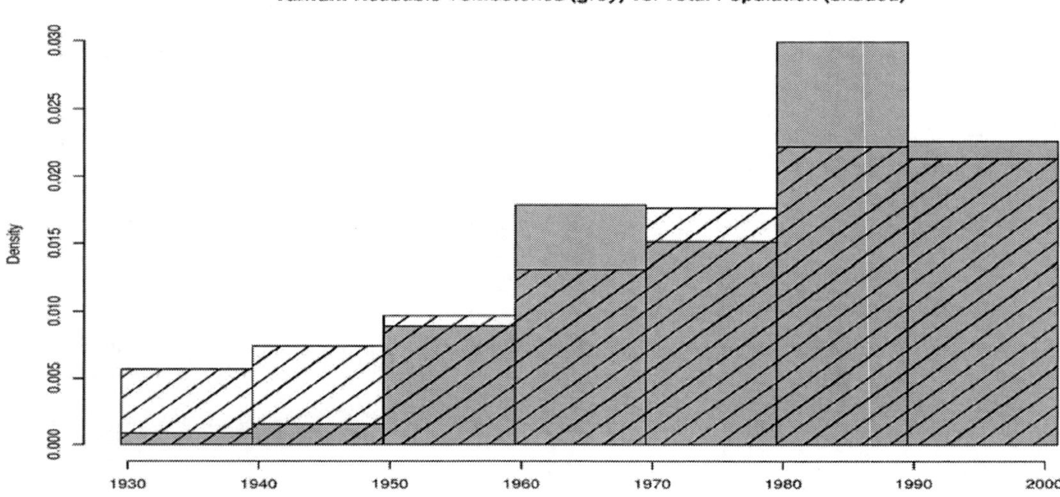

Figure 1: The density of tombstones compared to the density of the population in Taiwan through time. The lack of older tombstones cannot be explained through a smaller population in earlier times. Data are based on 3000 tombstones from 30 graveyards.

2. Annotating Tombstones

Different grass-root activities have sprung up, e.g. in the US and Australia, to preserve the cultural heritage of tombstones by photographing or transcribing them (e.g. http://www.rootsweb.com/~cemetery/). However, the nature of the transcriptions determines the use one can make of them, cf. Debartolo Carmack 2002. Unstructured transcriptions, for example, leave too much ambiguity for automatic analysis. The word 'Brown' might be a name or a color, 'Miller' a name or profession. 'Brown' thus should be annotated as 'name' and 'Miller' as 'profession'. To achieve this we use *textual segments* as 'date', 'location', 'epitaph' which describe the arrangement of the inscription. The knowledge of the *textual segments* allows for the determination of *reference systems, references* and *meanings. Reference systems* and *references,* as opposed to textual or editorial annotations, constitute a conceptual framework for corpus annotation which are important for cross-cultural and cross-linguistic comparisons.

XML (Bray et al. 2004) is, without question, the best supported annotation meta-language. To our knowledge, however, no XML language for tombstone corpora has been developed so far. EpiDoc for example, aims at the annotation of Epigraphs (Anderson et al 2007) and developed a rich scheme for the textual elements on the basis of TEI (Sperberg-McQueen & Burnard 2002).

However, EpiDOC yet does not provide an annotation framework beyond the text, such as the description of graves, graveyards or their ethnic and religious environments. In addition, EpiDoc stresses the individuality of the object, given   the function of the epitaphs as revelation of the individual personality (cf. Edgette 1989/1992).

A corpus, however, serves a different purpose. In a corpus the individual stone, as well as any other individual feature is meaningless. When annotating a corpus, we annotate only those features which, beyond the purposes of data management and data retrieval, enter a system of meaningful oppositions (cf. Fages 1968). In terms of statistics, a feature is not annotated as long as there is no conjecture of a correlation with another feature. TSML is thus basically designed , for the annotation of features of correlation, developed on the basis of our experience with the massive annotation of Taiwanese tombstones and some tombstones from other countries.

2.1.TSML, Basic Structure

Simplicity, uniformity and flexibility of TSML is achieved by using the <div> element in combination with a type-attribute as shown in Figure 2. We do not specify any constraints on the hierarchy of div-types as there are tombs without graveyards, tombs within tombs, graveyards without tombs, tombs in a church, tombstones without tombs and a tombstone-side, for example as photo, without the stone. Symbols, images, photos, maps can be at all levels, as well as texts which can be within the images, on the grave or on the tombstone.

```
tsml>
<div type='graveyard' north='55.34254' east='13.55456'religion='christianism'>
  <media mime_type='image/jpg' src='http://......'/>
  <div type='church' background_color='green' set_up='1954-10-05' />
  <div type='graveyard_section' ethnicity='ami people'>
   <div type='tomb' direction='180' background_color='red' orientation='downhill'
        set_up='1962-09-02'>
      <div type='tomb_side' side='inside' vertical='90' direction='270>
        <div type='image' description='fish'/>
      </div>
      <div type='tombstone'>
        <div type='version' set_up='1962-09-02' status='lost'/>
        <div type='version' set_up='2002-01-05'>
          <media mime_type='image/jpg' src='http://......'/>
          <div type='tombstone_side' background_color='white' foreground_color='black'
              writing_direction='t2br21' script='han-zi'>
          <div type='photo' floating='top' size='6cm' description='male'>
            <media mime_type='image/jpg' src='http://......'/>
          </div>
          <div type='symbol' floating='top' size='10'
              description='presbitarian cross'/>
          <div type='text' floating='top'>
           <div type='text' floating='right'>
            <div type='p'>text goes here</div>
           </div>
            <div type='text' floating='right' language='ami' script='katakana'>
            <div type='p'>text goes here</div>
```

Figure 2: The basic XML-structure of TSML based on *div*-elements and *type*-attributes, describing here an imaginary tomb. *Type*-attributes cascade from *div* to *div*.

Table 1: Values of the type-attribute of the div-element in TSML.

	Explanation
graveyard	Site where tombs are located.
graveyard_section	Graveyard sections may relate to different ethnicities or religions.
church, temple, ...	A building related to cults which contains a grave or is located in a graveyard.
tomb	A site containing the remains of one or more deceased.
tomb_side	An inner or outer wall of a tomb.
tombstone	The tombstone as 3-dimensional object.
tombstone_side	A 2-dimensional view on the tombstone.
tombstone_unit	Relatively independent units within a tombstone or a tombstone-side.
text, p, w, c, stroke	Containing mainly text.

image	Containing mainly an image
symbol	Containing mainly a non-figurative symbol
photo	Containing mainly a photo

For all div-elements, attributes are assumed to be inherited (to cascade) from the mother div-element to the daughter div-element in the absence of a more specific value. The information contained by some of these attributes cannot be seen on the tomb or tombstone directly and must be inferred or measured from other sources (GPS, compass, map, archives).

Table 2: Attributes of the div-element to be inherited from mother-div to daughter. Attributes marked '*' have been suggested in this or similar way in Debartolo Carmack 2002.

	Examples	Explanation
name*	Taipei Fude	Graveyards, graves may have official or unofficial names.
description		Free text input
location*	Taipei	Name of town, city, township where the entity is located.
caretaker*	Taipeishi	
caretaker address*		Caretakers might be contacted for additional information.
composition*	marble	Basic material: *marble, slate, granite, sandstone, limestone, metal, brick, concrete, ceramics.*
status*	abandoned	Useful to explain data loss, data endangerment. Values: *abandoned, maintained, overgrown, eroded, broken, lost.*
north	5,88789	Latitude as decimal WGS84 datum (cf. NIMA 97).
east	52,87465	Longitude as decimal WGS84 datum (cf. NIMA 97).
elevation	417	The elevation above mean see level in meter.
direction	90	Cardinal direction: *0=360=North, 90=East, 180=South, ...*
orientation	downhill	Non-compass directional system: *uphill, downhill, upcoast, downcoast, upstre am, downstream, landward, seaward, lakeward, mountainward, streetward, concentric.*
side	inside	*Inside, outside* with respect to the outer border of an object.
vertical	90	*90*=vertical, *0*=horizontal, wall and roof respectively.
set-up	2001-09-01	Time of construction/ building/ writing/ photographing.
floating	right	Relative position within the mother div-element, observer position opposite to the orientation, as in CSS absolute position (Bos et al. 2007). Alternative values: *right, left, top, bottom.*
display	block	Display according to CSS (Bos et al. 2007). Alternative values: *block, inline, list-item, superimposed, none.*
background- color	red	The color of the background, as in Çelik and Lilley 2003.
foreground-color	red, green, ...	The color of the foreground, as in Çelik and Lilley 2003.
religion	Buddhism, ...	The main religious orientation according to XNLRDF[1].
ethnicity	Hakka, Ami	The main ethnicity according to XNLRDF.
language	eng, deu	ISO 639-3 language codes, cf. XNLRDF.
writing-direction	t2bl2r, l2rt2b t2br2l, ..	Top-to-bottom left-to-right (Chinese), right-to-left top-to-bottom (English), top-to-bottom left-to-right (Mongolian), cf. XNLRDF.
script	Latin, Arabic	The set of characters or signs used according to XNLRDF.
nb_of_tombs	301	The number of tombs in this div.
nb_of_tombstones	417	The number of tombstones in this div.

2.2. Balanced Data

A corpus should be balanced (Biber et al. 1998). Although for a tombstone corpus, criteria of balancedness might be better to define than for a text corpus, e.g. collecting one photo per 1000 tombs, balancedness through sampling is impossible to achieve. Nobody knows all graveyards and how many tombs there are and those that we find may be inaccessible or decayed. In addition, naïve balancedness is not what we want. We want a tombstone corpus to have different

---

[1] XNLRDF, the Natural Language Research Description Framework, cf. Streiter et Stuflesser 2006.

granularities for different subset of the data. Graveyards of minorities are photographed and annotated exhaustively. In relatively uniform Han-communities of major cities samples are taken. Under uniform sampling conditions, no comparison inside smaller groups would be possible. We therefore introduce weights to achieve a numerical balancedness. A weight, stipulates how many items of the population are represented by one sampled item. Using the given, estimated or interpolated values or *inhabitants*$_{ly}$ and *life-expectancy*$_{ly}$ for a locality l and a year y, we estimate *population-of-tombs*$_{ly}\Box$*inhabitants*$_{ly}$/*life-expectancy*$_{ly}$. Then, *population-of-tombs*$_{ly}$/*sample-size*$_{ly}$ *yields* the weight for the graves of a location. The weight of these graveyards for larger geographic or administrative units can be derived by multiplying the weight of the smaller unit with the quotient of *population-of-tombs*$_{larger\ unit}$/*population-of -tombs*$_{smaller\ unit}$. Additional refinements in this calculus handle different locations sharing one graveyard and, graveyards associated with locations of different hierarchical levels. To sum up, although the details of this model can be refined this kind of **calculated balancedness based on census data** with the possibility to have different granularities in different sub-corpora is conceptually superior to the sampling for text corpora.

```
<div type=graveyard name='anping old street, both sides of the road'>
 <weights>
 <weight  year='2005'  loc='anping'  value='289'/>
 <weight  year='2005'  loc='tainan city'  value='3468'/>
 <weight  year='2005'  loc='tainan city + tainan county'  value='6936'/>
 <weight  year='2005'  loc='taiwan'  value='55488'>
 </weights>
```

Figure 3: The weights assigned in TSML to each tombstone of a graveyard: One sampled tombstone of the year 2005 in Anping represents 289 assumed tombstones in Anping of the same year and 3468 tombstones in Tainan City of the same year.

2.3. Lost Data

Like any historic document, tombstones or images may become unreadable. If something is totally unreadable, this has to be marked as unreadable as opposed to not yet annotated. If something is partially readable, say like the given name *Deb?rah,* where *?* stands for the unreadable, we almost for certain recognize the name, but we would falsify the data if we would write that we have read *Deborah*. It would equally be suboptimal to encode the entire name as unreadable, as this data loss cannot be made up by every corpus user, e.g. for a foreign language like Hebrew: דבו?ה. In TSML we thus keep track of what the interpretations of the decaying traces are. Interpretations can be complemented with probabilities.

 As readability, especially of Chinese characters or Egyptians hieroglyphs might vary below the level of a character at the level of a radical or stroke, we cannot rely on character indices as for the annotation of the American National Corpus (cf. Ide & Romary 2006). If, for example, we can read a vertical stroke in a position where we expect a Chinese number, we might interpret this as 一(1) or if an additional scratch we see is a vertical stroke, as 十(10). Such phenomena can be described by the use of the <analysis> and <interpretation> element in combination.

```
<v type='s'>He eats fish
<analysis type='3ps'>
<div type='w' include='yes'>He</div>
<div type='c' include='no'> </div>
<div type='verb_root' include='no'>eat</div>
<div type='infl_morph' include='yes'>s</div>
<div type='c'> </div>
<div type='w'>fish</div>
</analysis>
</div>
```

Figure 4 (left): An example of how an discontinuous structure is annotated with the help of the *analysis*-element. **Figure 5 (right)**: An example of how different interpretations are derived from different analyses.

The <analysis> element provides a syntagmatic analysis of the mother element while repeating its content. Those elements marked as *include='yes'* belong to the type analyzed (*<analysis type='xxx'*, here the markers of a 3rd person singular subject). The <interpretation> element list possible paradigmatic choices. Preferences in their selection are marked by *selected='yes'/'no'* or *probability='0.8'*.

```
<div type='p'>min guo 5
     <interpretation>
          <div type='c' language=" writing-direction=" probability=" selected='yes'>1
               <analysis type='c'>
                    <div type='stroke' include='yes' >--</div>
               </analysis>
          </div>
          <div type='c'   language=" writing_direction=" probability="
selected='no'>10
               <analysis type='c'>
                    <div type='stroke' include='yes'   display='superimpose'>-
-</div>
                    <div type='stroke' include='yes'
display='superimpose'>|</div>
               </analysis>
          </div>
     </interpretation>
</div>
```

Fig 2: This tombstone became unreadable in it's lower right part. Which characters can be seen and which can be guessed?

 At this level we describe single characters, as shown here for the hypothetical case that the first character of a date might be read as 1 or 7 and the second is completely unreadable.

2.4.Meaningful Data

 The content of the div-elements may have a *reference*. The name of a person and a photo may have the same reference. Sometimes tombstones are bilingual, containing in two languages the same references.

 The *references,* like times, persons and places are entities which across time lead an imagined or real existence independently from the grave or the tombstone and which are referred or alluded to in the tomb or tombstone. Relations among references are treated as references. Temporal references are obtained by translating the date we find in a specific calendar uniformly into the corresponding date of a calendar of reference. This calendar of reference might or might not be among the reference systems. In the same way we can map the names of a city onto a reference system of imagined or real cities, or personal names to a reference repository of persons. The interest in annotating references derives from the historical, geographical or sociological facts they reflect. Such facts might be apprehended through tombstones or they provide background information for the interpretation of other data on the tombstones. The references to time on the tombstone, for example, can be used to analyze historical developments in the form and content of tombstones.

 We identify *reference systems* with social mediators which shape experience and awareness for members of a culture. For a description of mediation as psychological process see, among others, Wertsch 1988. Thus, for some researchers looking at tombstones, neither the exact date (which we will call *reference)*, nor the exact wording (which we will call *meaning)* of a date might be interesting, but instead what kind of calendar is used. The calendar is a social construct which mediates psychological processes. Similarly, researchers might be interested in whether symbols taken from a Christian symbol repository or from a Jewish symbol repository instead of the symbol used (the *meaning*) or what the symbol means (the *reference).* The way that people are referred to, or the language and the writing system, all are additional, all too obvious reference systems that merit an analysis. We hypothesize that whichever reference system is used, it reflects the social and psychological reality of the community and the different reference systems (calendar, language, names etc) do not cooccur randomly.

In our research on Taiwanese tombstones, still another reference system, that of the local origin is of central importance. Many Taiwanese families actually have the possibility to chose between the *Tanghao,* a mythological place name in North China, a place name in South China from where the ancestors immigrated (Jiguan) or the place name in Taiwan where the family lived (Taiwan diming). The name might not be important for an analysis, the reference system of the origin however hints on identities communities maintain. In addition, we expect the reference system (tanghao/jiguan/taiwan diming) to cluster with other reference systems, such as the calendar (Japanese/Chinese/Republican/Gregorian).

http://140.127.211.213/img/tombo/xishu2007-06-13/dsc00785.jpg
http://140.127.211.213/img/tombo/3--2007-09-24/dsc07455.jpg
http://140.127.211.213/img/tombo/3--2007-09-24/dsc07457.jpg

Figure 3: Left to right. Three local reference systems, the Tanghao, the Jiguan (place name in China), the place name in Taiwan.

http://140.127.211.213/img/tombo/12--2007-07-11/dsc02679.jpg
http://140.127.211.213/img/tombo/13--2007-07-11/dsc02660.jpg
http://140.127.211.213/img/tombo/9--2007-07-09/dsc02162.jpg
http://140.127.211.213/img/tombo/10--2007-07-12/dsc03237.jpg

Figure 2: Left to right, top to bottom. Four calendars found on Taiwanese tombstones and their references: Japanese calendar, the traditional Chinese calendar, the Republican calendar and the Gregorian calendar.

Another, important category for analysis are *meanings. Meanings* derive from *reference types,* where *reference types* are intentional abstractions of references, for example, 'person', 'father', 'date', 'date of birth' etc as they can be apprehended from the DTD. Thus, while 'Bill, father of John' has a reference which represents this fact, 'X, father of Y' has a reference type, here that element in the DTD that describes 'father of'-relations. Reference types are annotated if we want to analyze and compare the different meaningful components of a tombstone (symbols, words, expressions, arrangement) across regions, cultures and languages. If we annotate these meaningful component with a reference type, for example, 'father of', we can access all meaningful expressions with the reference type in their context. Note, that this model requires all quasi-equivalent expressions, which in corpus-linguistic approaches might be simply defined by a synset, to be defined in relation to *references* within the XML This might be too strong a claim and imply that that one has to invoke the apparatus of the reference system during annotation, even if the reference system allows for one reference only. We can tweak this by making the *reference type* obligatory and the *reference system* optional as in *<div type='text' ref_type='location' ref_system='tanghao' ref_id='12' value='Longxi'>,* in *<div type='text' ref_type='honorific' value='xiankao'>* or in *<div type='image' ref_type='state of defunct' ref_system='Chinese symbols' ref_id='9' value='bat'>*

The relation between the *reference type, reference* and the *meaning* can be described as follows. The *meaning* of a component without a reference derives from its *reference type* ('honorific') and the difference between this component (*<div type='text' ref_type='honorific' value='xiankao'>*) and all others with the same *reference type.* If there is a reference, the *meaning* of a component derives from its *reference* ('9') and the difference between this component (*<div type='image' ref_type='state of defunct' ref_system='Chinese symbols' ref_id='9' value='bat'>*) and all others with the same *reference.*

In addition to linguistic expressions, symbols, colors or arrangements may have references and thus can be grouped into reference types. During the annotation process the color of a segment *<div color='green'>* might be elaborated into *<div type='color' value='green' ref_type='state of defunct' ref_type='...' ref_id='...'>*. Given the formulaic nature of tombstones, meanings and references are not necessarily transparent, even for members of that linguistic or cultural community, and thus have to be annotated.

3. Conclusion

Just more text.

And more text in second indented paragraph.

4. References

Biber, D., Conrad, S., Reppen, R. 1998. *Corpus Linguistics. Investigating Language Structure and Use.* Cambridge University Press.

Bos, B., Çelik, T., Hickson, I. & Lie, H.W. 2007. Cascading Style Sheets Level 2 Revision 1 (CSS 2.1) Specification. W3C Candidate Recommendation 19 July 2007. URL: http://www.w3.org/TR/CSS21/cover.html, accessed 24.9.07.

Bray, T., Paoli, J., Sperberg-McQueen, C.M., Maler E., Cowan, J., Yergeau, F. eds., 2004. *Extensible Markup Language (XML) 1.1*, W3C. URL: http://www.w3.org/TR/xml11, accessed 22.6.07.

CES, Corpus Encoding Standard, Part 5: Encoding Linguistic Annotations. 2000. URL: http://www.cs.vassar.edu/CES/CES1-5.html, accessed 22.6.07.

Çelik, T. & Lilley, C. 2003. CSS3 Color Module, W3C Candidate Recommendation 14 May 2003. URL: http://www.w3.org/TR/css3-color, accessed 24.9.07.

Clark, E.W. 1989/1992. The Bigham Carvers of the Carolina Piedmont: Stone Images of an Emerging Sense of American Identity. In: R.E. Meyer ed., *Cemeteries & Gravemarkers, Voices of American* Culture. Utah State University Press.

Debartolo Carmack, S. 2002. *Your Guide to Cementary Research*, Betterway Books.

Edgette, J.J. 1989/1992. The Epitaph as Personality Revelation. In: R.E. Meyer ed., *Cemeteries & Gravemarkers, Voices of American* Culture. Utah State University Press.

Elliott, T. ed., 2007. EpiDoc: Guidelines for Structured Markup of Epigraphic Texts in TEI. URL: http://www.stoa.org/epidoc/gl/5/, accessed 22.6.07.

Fages, J.B. 1968. *Comprendre le structuralisme.* Privat, Toulouse.

Frege, G. 1892. Sinn und Bedeutung. In: *Zeitschrift für Philosophie und philosophische Kritik*, NF 100, 1892, S. 25-50.

Frembgeni, J.W. 1989. Religious Folk Art as an Expression of Identity: Muslim Tombstones in the Gangar Mountains of Pakistan. In: *Muqarnas*, Vol. 15, pp. 200-210.

Good, J. & Hendryx-Parker, C. 2006. Modeling Contested Categorization in Linguistic Databases. In: *2006 EMELD Workshop on Digital Language Documentation, Tools and Standards, the State of the Art.* Michigan State University in East Lansing, Michigan, June 20-22.

Ide, N., Romary, L. 2006. Representing Linguistic Corpora and Their Annotations. Proceedings of the *Fifth Language Resources and Evaluation Conference (LREC)*, Genoa, Italy.

The Hindu. Buddhist Tombstone discovered at Chittayam, *The Hindu, online edition of India's National Newspaper* 8.7.2005, URL: http://www.hindu.com/2005/07/08/stories/2005070811950300.htm, accessed 23.6.07.

NIMA Technical Report TR8350.2, "Department of Defense World Geodetic System 1984, Its Definition and Relationships With Local Geodetic Systems", Third Edition, 4 July 1997. URL: http://earth-info.nga.mil/GandG/publications/tr8350.2/tr8350_2.html, accessed 24.9.07.

Rath, G. 1986. Hebrew Tombstone Inscriptions and Dates. In: *Chronicles (Newsletter of the Jewish*

Genealogical Society of Philadelphia), Vol. 5, No. 1 (Spring 1986), pages 1-4.

de Saussure, F. 1916/1995. *Cours de linguistique générale*, éd. Payot.

Sperberg-McQueen, C.M. & Burnard, L. eds., 2002 *Guidelines for Text Encoding and Interchange.* University of Oxford.

Statistical yearbook of the Republic of China, 2002.

Streiter, O. & Stuflesser, M. 2006. Design Features for the Collection and Distribution of Basic NLP-Resources for the World's Writing Systems. In: *Intl. Workshop Towards a Research Infrastructure for Language Resources*, LREC Workshop, Genova, Italy, 22 May 2006.

Wertsch, J.V. 1988. *Vygotsky and the Social Formation of Mind*. Harvard University Press.

Wurm, S. ed., 2001. *Atlas of the World's Languages in Danger of Disappearing*. Paris, UNESCO.

Exploring the Microscopic Textual Characteristics
of Japanese Prime Ministers' Diet Addresses
by Measuring the Quantity and Diversity of Nouns[*]

Takafumi Suzuki[1] and Kyo Kageura[2]

[1]Graduate School of Interdisciplinary Information Studies, University of Tokyo,
7-3-1 Hongo, Bunkyo-ku, Japan
qq16116@iii.u-tokyo.ac.jp
[2]Graduate School of Education, University of Tokyo,
7-3-1 Hongo, Bunkyo-ku, Japan
kyo@p.u-tokyo.ac.jp

Abstract. This study explores the textual characteristics, more precisely the quantity and diversity of nouns, of Japanese prime ministers' Diet addresses. In the field of stylistics, textual characteristics independent of the content have been examined with the aim on detecting the authors, genres, and chronological variations of texts. This study focuses instead on textual characteristics related to the content of texts, namely the quantity and diversity of nouns, because our aim is to analyze texts to better understand two political phenomena: (a) the difference between the two types of Diet addresses delivered by Japanese prime ministers, and (b) the perceived changes made to these addresses by two powerful prime ministers. It is a case study of the microscopic characterization of texts, which has become more and more important with the expansion in the scope of stylistics and the production of a wide variety of new types of texts following the advent of the Web.

Keywords: Japanese prime ministers' speeches, quantity and diversity of nouns, microscopic textual characteristics, Monte Carlo simulation

1. Introduction

In the field of stylistics, as computational approaches have been developed and many on-line corpora have been constructed, statistical textual characteristics have been systematically examined. These textual characteristics have traditionally been used for detecting the authors, registers, and chronological variations of texts. Recently, they have also been used for more practical applications such as spam filtering (Argamon, Whitelaw, Chase, Raj Hota, Garg, and Levitan, 2007). With this expansion in the scope of stylistics and the production of a wide variety of new types of texts especially with the growth of the Web (Aitchison and Lewis, 2003), the microscopic characterization of different types of texts has become more and more important.

Turning our eyes to the field of political science, the content of political speeches is regarded as   important for analyzing the policies, attitudes and thoughts of political actors (Axelrod, 1976). Among such speeches, prime ministers' Diet addresses are recognized as the most

---

[*] This study was supported by a Suntory Foundation Research Grant, 2007-2008. We would like to express our gratitude for this support. An earlier version of this study was presented at the 35th annual meeting of the Behaviormetric Society of Japan. We would like to thank the participants for their useful comments.

important material for understanding Japanese politics as they reflect Japanese governmental policies, and prime ministerial attitudes and thoughts (Watanabe, 1974; Kusano, 2005). As the role of the media and the performance of politicians increase in importance in contemporary politics (Kusano, 2006), the style of prime ministers' speeches, as well as their content, have attracted more attention (Ahrens, 2005; Azuma, 2006).

Against this background, this study explores the textual characteristics of Japanese prime ministers' Diet addresses, focusing on (a) the difference between the two types of Diet addresses and (b) the perceived changes made to these addresses by two powerful prime ministers, comparing the characteristics of their addresses with those of all prime ministers from 1945 to 2006. In order to clarify these points, we focus on the quantity and diversity of nouns, textual characteristics strongly related to the content of texts, instead of conventional content-independent stylistic characteristics, because the purpose of this study is to analyze these characteristics in order to better understand two political phenomena: the difference and changes in political content. From the point of view of computational linguistics, this study can be seen as a case study for exploring microscopic textual characteristics. The rest of this paper is organized as follows. In Section 2, we review previous work, and in Section 3, explain our two research questions in detail. In Section 4, we describe our data, and in Section 5, discuss the results. In Section 6, we make concluding remarks.

2. Previous work

In the field of stylistics, many textual characteristics have been examined (Grieve, 2007). Those which have been frequently measured are the length of sentences, the length of words and the relative frequency of different parts of speech (Kenny, 1982). Lexical richness measures including those we use in this study have been systematically examined by Tweedie and Baayen (1998). Textual characteristics have been examined for formalizing the mathematical characteristics of texts (e.g., Simpson, 1949; Yule, 1944), and also for authorship attribution (Hoover, 2003) and genre-based text classification (Cortina-Borja and Chappas, 2006). They have proved to be reliable measures for classification because they take the information of function words as well as   content words (Garcìa and Martìn, 2007). But for our purpose, the lexical diversity of specific parts of speech need to be examined, and there are few studies examining these characteristics.

Some studies in political science examine prime ministers' Diet speeches using quantitative methods, but most studies focus only on the frequencies of specific words (e.g., Watanabe, 1974). Though Azuma (2006) examined sentence lengths and other specific functional expressions in the speeches, and Reinem (2005) used comprehensive types of content words for her analysis, the lexical quantity and diversity of Diet speeches have not been examined fully.

3. Research questions
The two issues we address in this study are as follows:

3.1 The difference between the two types of Diet addresses
Japanese prime ministers deliver two types of Diet addresses: Shisei Hoshin Enzetsu (Speech to Express Policy: SEP) and Syoshin Hyomei Enzetsu (Speech to Express Belief: SEB).[1] The SEP is delivered at the ordinary Diet session in which the budget is compiled. The SEB, on the other hand, is delivered at extraordinary Diet sessions in which the budget is not a major issue. In the SEP, prime ministers deal with many political issues related to the budgets, while in the SEB they highlight the particular political goals they wish to achieve. But some studies insist that the two types of addresses need not be distinguished when analyzing their content because they are

---

[1]Both of these two types of addresses are normally translated as 'general policy speech' in English.

similar (Reinem, 2007). By examining the textual characteristics of the two types of Diet addresses, we will clarify this point. It will help us to determine which (or both) types of addresses should be analyzed when we wish to investigate the political content related to the budget or content related to political goals prime ministers would especially like to achieve.

3.2 The perceived changes made to these addresses by two prime ministers

Nakasone, one of the strongest and most powerful prime ministers in Japanese political history, is reported to have increased the length of his Diet addresses by developing his own philosophy and ideas in order to show the concentration of political power in the office of prime minister (Shinoda, 1994). Koizumi, another powerful and strong prime minister, is famous for having used more dramatic and entertaining style of speech (Kabashima and Steel, 2007). His speech style is thought to have been characterized by the repetition of specific topics (typically privatization of the postal system). He succeeded politically partly because he was able to attract people by his way of speaking (Otake, 2006). However, these perceptions about the distinctive styles of speech of these two powerful prime ministers have never been empirically examined. We do so by measuring the textual characteristics of their Diet addresses, thus providing empirical evidences for discussion of their political styles or media strategy as revealed through their speeches.

4. Data

The corpora we used in this study consists of 150 Diet addresses covering the 28 tenures in office of 27 Japanese prime ministers[2] from 1945 to 2006.[3] We downloaded the addresses from the on-line database *Sekai to Nihon (The World and Japan)*.[4] We applied morphological analysis to the addresses using ChaSen, a Japanese morphological analysis system (Matsumoto, Kitauchi, Yamashita, Hirano, Matsuda, Takaoka, and Asahara, 2003). We extracted nouns according to part-of-speech tags assigned by ChaSen. Table 1 shows the number of addresses, the number of tokens and the number of types of the SEP and the SEB after 1953.[5] Table 2 sets out the names, the initials, the date of assumption to office, the number of addresses, and the total and mean number of tokens for each prime minister.

Table 1: Basic data of the two types of Diet addresses

	Address	Token	Type
SEP	61	120005	6056
SEB	72	91635	5374

5. Lexical indices

The three lexical indices we used in this study for analyzing the difference between and the changes in the addresses were number of tokens, type-token ratio and Simpson's D (Simpson, 1949) of nouns. These simple measures reflect the quantity and the diversity of political content in the Diet addresses, and can explain the two questions we proposed in Section 3.

Number of tokens
The first index is the number of tokens, which we denote as N. It shows the number of items

---

[2] Yoshida was elected prime minister twice. We treat these as different tenures.
[3] The texts of the speeches are written down by secretaries in shorthand.
[4] http://www.ioc.u-tokyo.ac.jp/~worldjpn/index.html
[5] We used only the addresses from after 1953 in our analysis, as before that date the two types of addresses were not distinguished.

used in the sample. N of nouns reflects the quantity of political content mentioned in the addresses.

Type-token ratio
The second index is a type-token ratio formulated as follows:

$$TTR = \frac{V \; N}{N}$$

where $V(N)$ represents the number of types. It shows the diversity of items used in the sample. *TTR* of nouns reflects the diversity of political content per unit noun-tokens. A high *TTR* means that a variety of political content is mentioned, but the average amount of discussion devoted to each topic is limited. A low *TTR* indicates the opposite.

Table 2: Basic data of Japanese prime ministers and their addresses

Name	Initials	Date	Address	Tokens(total)	Tokens(mean)
HIGASHIKUNI Naruhiko	HN	8/1945	1	5779	5779.0
SHIDEHARA Kijuro	SK	10/1945	1	2981	2981.0
YOSHIDA Shigeru	YS1	5/1946	3	5426	1808.7
KATAYAMA Tetsu	KTe	5/1947	2	9072	4536.0
ASHIDA Hitoshi	AH	3/1948	1	3506	3506.0
YOSHIDA Shigeru	YS2	10/1948	16	26685	1667.8
HATOYAMA Ichiro	HI	12/1954	5	8318	1663.6
ISHIBASHI Tanzan	IT	12/1956	1	2665	2665.0
KISHI Nobusuke	KN	2/1957	9	18089	2009.9
IKEDA Hayato	IH	12/1960	11	35220	3201.8
SATO Eisaku	SE	11/1964	21	56731	2701.5
TANAKA Kakuei	TK	6/1972	4	15097	3774.3
MIKI Takeo	MiT	12/1974	5	18222	3644.4
FUKUDA Takeo	FT	12/1976	5	17030	3406.0
OHIRA Masayoshi	OM	12/1978	4	15629	3907.3
SUZUKI Zenko	SZ	6/1980	4	13878	3469.5
NAKASONE Yasuhiro	NY	11/1982	10	47422	4742.2
TAKESHITA Noboru	TN	11/1987	4	18448	4612.0
UNO Sosuke	US	6/1989	1	3669	3669.0
KAIFU Toshiki	KTo	8/1989	5	23541	4708.2
MIYAZAWA Kiichi	MK	11/1991	4	19110	4777.5
HOSOKAWA Morihiro	HM	8/1993	3	1460	4869.7
HATA Tsutomu	HT	4/1994	1	4185	4185.0
MURAYAMA Tomiichi	MuT	6/1994	4	20454	5113.5
HASHIMOTO Ryutaro	HR	1/1996	5	26809	5361.8
OBUCHI Keizo	OK	6/1998	5	20702	4140.4
MORI Yoshiro	MY	4/2000	4	20149	5037.3
KOIZUMI Junichiro	KJ	4/2001	11	46996	4272.4

Since the number of types and type-token ratio depend heavily on the number of tokens (Tweedie and Baayen, 1998), we adjusted it by Monte Carlo simulations when comparing: the two types of addresses; those before Nakasone, and including and after Nakasone;[6] and Koizumi's and every other prime minister's addresses. The process of simulation was as follows: we merged the addresses to make: the SEPs; the SEBs; those before Nakasone; those including

---

[6] Nakasone's change of Diet addresses are thought to continue after his resign, we compare the lexical indices before Nakasone, and including and after Nakasone.

and after Nakasone; and those of each prime minister. We then extracted 500 words to 6000 words incremented by 500 words by random sampling. Each extraction was made 1000 times and the mean and 95% confidence intervals were obtained.

Simpson's D
The third index is Simpson's D which is formulated as follows (Simpson, 1949):

$$D = \sum_{m=1}^{V(N)} V(m, N) \frac{m}{N} \frac{m-1}{N-1}$$

where $V(m, N)$ denotes the number of tokens occurring m times.[7] It represents the concentration or skewness of distribution of items used in the sample. The D of nouns reflects the repeat rates of different kinds of political content. D is an index of both relative concentration, which means that it represents inequality of items in the sample, and absolute concentration, which means that it represents the absolute number of items in the sample (Yoshikane, Kageura, and Tsuji, 2003). This kind of index suits our purposes because the number of times each kind of political content is repeated is important, as is inequality among different kinds of political content when we discuss repetition in political speech. A high D means that specific political content is repeated. A low D means that each political content is explained in a balanced way.

6. Results and discussion

In Figure 1, the solid line represents the smoothed value of N,[8] and the dotted lines represent the smoothed values of $V(N)$ and TTR. In Figure 2, the solid line represents the smoothed value of D. N and D in each address is plotted by P (the SEP) and B (the SEB) and the mean value of N and D for each prime minister is plotted by the prime ministers' initials (see Table 2) in Figure 1 and Figure 2 respectively.

6.1. The different characteristics of the two types of addresses

Table 3 describes the mean values, standard deviations (s.d.) and coefficient of variances (c.v.) of N, $V(N)$, TTR and D of the SEP and the SEB. The results indicate that the SEP has a significantly larger N than the SEB, and the two types of addresses are not distinguished by D.[9] In Figure 3, the solid line represents the mean value of TTR of the SEP, the dashed line represents the mean value of TTR of the SEB and dotted lines represent 95% confidence intervals of TTR of both types of addresses, incremented by 500 tokens constructed by Monte Carlo simulations. The solid line and the dashed line are almost identical in the figure and are not distinguished from each other within 95% confidence intervals. The results show that the two types of addresses are not distinguished by TTR. The finding that the SEP has a significantly larger N than the SEB means that the SEP has a greater amount of political content than the SEB.

Table 3: Comparison of the SEP and the SEB

		N	$V(N)$	$V(N)/N$	D
SEP	mean	1738.25*	684.39*	42.57*	41.85
	s.d.	784.83*	235.12**	8.13	10.07

---

[7] As D takes all the frequency spectrum into consideration, it is completely constant to the number of tokens.
[8] In this section, we use notations N, $V(N)$, TTR and D as representing those of nouns.
[9] We used the f-test and t-test. When the p-value of f-test is less than .05 (variances are not equal), we used the Welch method of the t-test.

	c.v.	0.45	0.34	0.19	0.24
SEB	mean	1261.41*	545.90*	46.56*	42.48
	s.d.	562.82*	178.21**	8.17	8.43
	c.v.	0.45	0.33	0.18	0.20

* significant (p < .01)
** significant (p < .05)

The different textual characteristics typically represent the different character of the two types of Diet addresses: the SEP has a greater amount of political content because it relates to the budget compilation and the SEB has more selective political content, namely the goals prime ministers would like to achieve. The finding that the SEP is not distinguished from the SEB regarding *TTR* or *D*, indicates that prime ministers refer to a similar diversity of political content and in a similarly balanced way in the two types of addresses. It means that even if a prime minister talks about the political goals which he would especially like to achieve in the SEB, he does not change the way he speaks at the level of diversity of nouns.

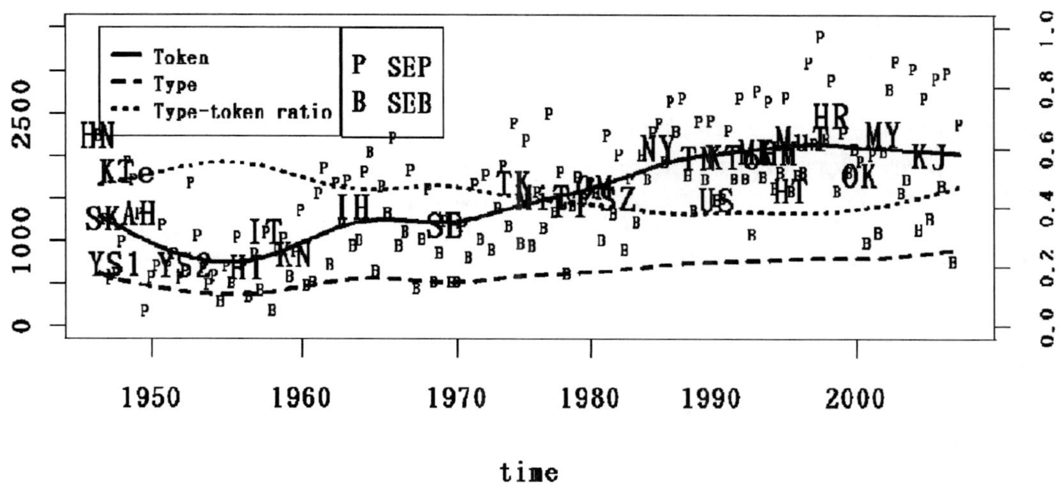

Figure 1: The *N* of an address is plotted by P (the SEP) and B (the SEB). The mean value of *N* for each prime minister is plotted by the prime minister's initial (see Table 2). The solid line represents the smoothed value of *N*, the dashed line represents the smoothed value of *V(N)*, and dotted line represents the smoothed values of *TTR*.

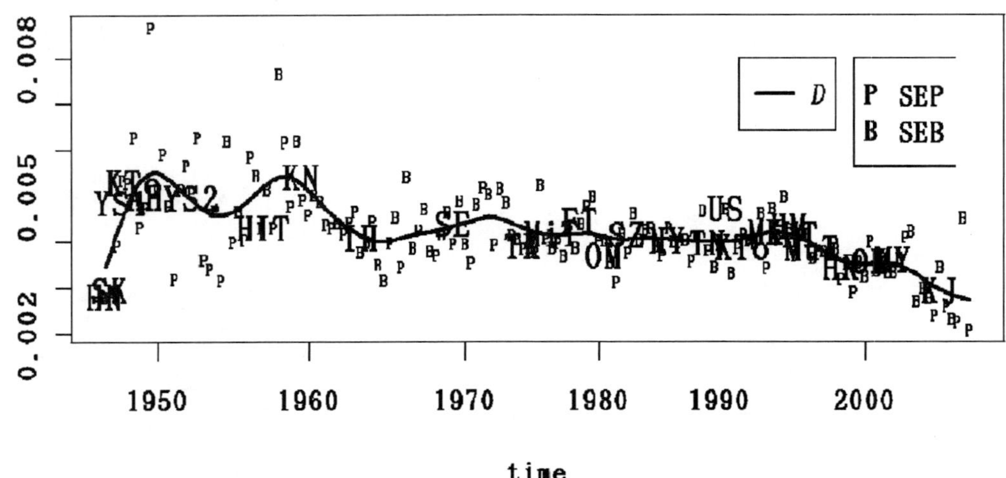

Figure 2: The *D* of an address is plotted by P (the SEP) and B (the SEB). The mean value of *D* for each prime minister is plotted by the prime minister's initial (see Table 2). The solid line represents the smoothed value of *D*.

6.2. The changes made to these addresses by two prime ministers

6.2.1. Before Nakasone, and including and after Nakasone

Table 4 describes the mean values, standard deviations (s.d.) and coefficients of variances (c.v.) of N, $V(N)$, TTR, and D before Nakasone, and including and after Nakasone. The results indicate that N is significantly larger including and after Nakasone than before him.[10] In Figure 4, the solid

---

[10] It also indicates that $V(N)$ and D are also significantly different between the addresses before Nakasone, and including and after Nakasone. These results must be caused by Koizumi (see Section 6.2.2 and also Figure 1 and 2).

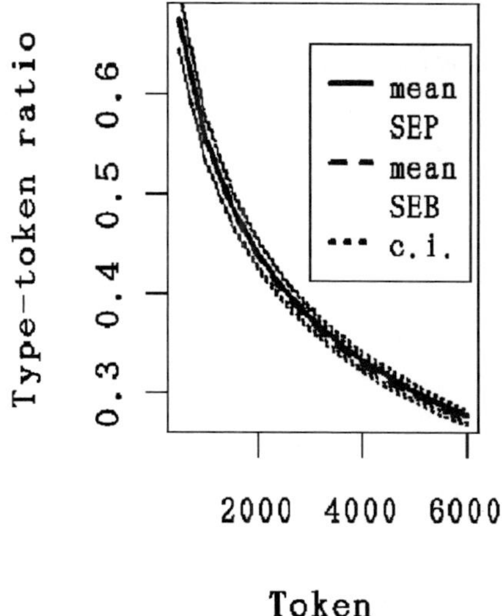

Figure 3: The *TTR* per 500, 1000, ... , 6000 tokens constructed by Monte Carlo simulations. The solid line and the dashed line represent the mean values of the SEP and the SEB respectively, and the dotted lines represent the upper and lower limits of the 95% Monte Carlo confidence intervals of the SEP and the SEB.

line represents the mean value of of *TTR* of the addresses before Nakasone, the dashed line represents those including and after Nakasone, and the dotted lines represent 95% confidence intervals of *TTR*, incremented by 500 tokens constructed by Monte Carlo simulations. Though the results show that the addresses before Nakasone, and including and after Nakasone start to be distinguished when N reaches 6000 tokens, they are rather similar to each other and the slight difference must be caused by Koizumi's special value as we discuss in Section 6.2.2. below.

The finding that N is significantly larger including and after Nakasone than before him corresponds to the argument that Nakasone increased the length of his addresses (Shinoda, 1994). This must have been driven by his intention to concentrate political power on himself. As opposed to that, the diversity of nouns does not change much before Nakasone, and including and after Nakasone. This means that he did not change the way he speaks in the addresses. He may be unconscious of how he speaks at the level of diversity of nouns, as opposed to his interest to the amount of political content in his speech.

6.2.2. Koizumi and others

Table 5 describes the mean values, standard deviations (s.d.) and coefficients of variances (c.v.) of N, $V(N)$, *TTR* and D for Koizumi and others. The results indicate that Koizumi's D is significantly lower than the others, though N did not show significant difference. In Figure 5, the solid line represents Koizumi's mean value of *TTR* and the dotted lines represent his 95% confidence intervals of *TTR*, incremented by 500 tokens constructed by Monte Carlo simulations. The dashed lines represent the mean values of *TTR* of the other prime ministers (more than 6000 tokens) incremented by 500 tokens constructed by Monte Carlo simulations. The results indicate that Koizumi's *TTR* is significantly higher than the others and the highest of all prime ministers.

Table 4: Comparison of the addresses before Nakasone, and including and after Nakasone

		N	*V(N)*	*V(N)/N*	*D*
Before NY	mean	1170.27*	513.55*	47.53*	45.20*
	s.d.	560.96	177.07	8.38*	9.51*
	c.v.	0.48	0.34	0.18	0.21
Including	mean	2071.00*	790.63*	39.45*	37.17*
and after NY	s.d.	613.80*	171.89	5.44*	6.41*
	c.v.	0.30	0.22	0.14	0.17

* significant (p < .01)
** significant (p < .05)

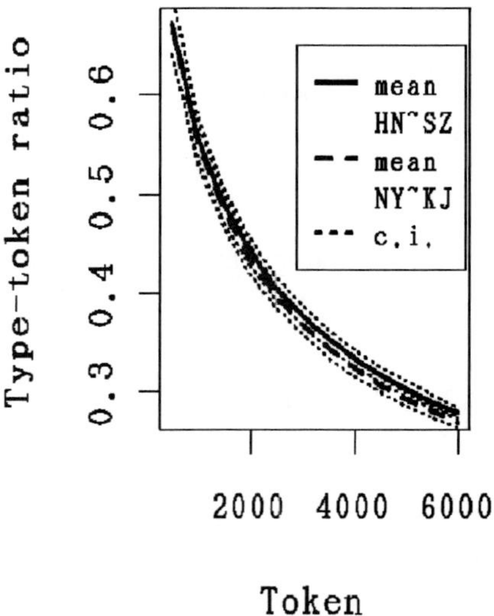

Figure 4: The *TTR* par 500, 1000, ... , 6000 tokens constructed by Monte Carlo simulations. The solid line represents the mean values of prime ministers before Nakasone. The dashed lines represent those including and after Nakasone. The dotted lines represent the upper and lower limits of the 95% Monte Carlo confidence intervals of prime ministers before Nakasone, and including and after Nakasone.

The results demonstrated that Koizumi, though he was not distinguished from the others by the number of tokens of nouns, used more diverse types of nouns and repeated those nouns less. This   shows that Koizumi in fact mentioned more diverse political content in a balanced way, despite the common perception that his speaking style was characterized by the repetition of specific political content many times. One possible reason for this may be that the common perception of his speaking style is based on speeches he made outside the Diet. He may have distinguished between Diet speeches and speeches outside the Diet and also distinguished how he speaks in them strategically.

Table 5: Comparison of the addresses of Koizumi and others

		N	*V(N)*	*V(N)/N*	*D*
Koizumi	mean	2016.64	863.64*	44.79	29.55*
	s.d.	812.30	266.79	6.02	7.97
	c.v.	0.40	0.31	0.13	0.26
Others	mean	1472.66	599.47*	44.43	43.17*
	s.d.	707.65	205.53	8.53	8.67
	c.v.	0.48	0.34	0.19	0.20

* significant (p < .01)
** significant (p < .05)

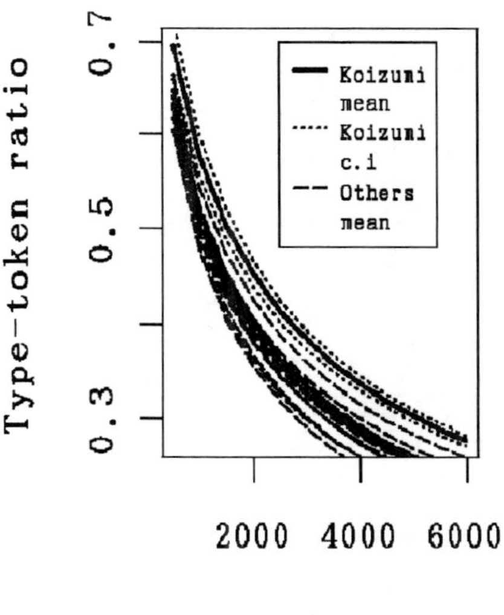

Figure 5: The *TTR* per 500, 1000, ... , 6000 tokens constructed by Monte Carlo simulations. The upmost solid line represents the mean value of Koizumi. The dotted lines represent the upper and lower limits of the 95% confidence intervals of Koizumi. The dashed lines represent the mean values of other prime ministers.

7. Conclusion

In this study, we explore the microscopic characteristics of Japanese prime ministers' Diet addresses by the quantity and diversity of nouns. Content-dependent textual characteristics tend to be avoided in stylistic text classification studies because they are not good indicators of genres or authors. By examining the quantity and diversity of nouns, we demonstrated these types of characteristics, instead of conventional stylistic ones, enable us to interpret textual characteristics for questions in political science; namely, clarifying the difference between the two types of Diet addresses and the changes made to them by the two prime ministers.

The distributional characteristics related to the content which this study tried to explore can be called the 'form of content' dimension of textual information. This implies that conventional content analysis studies, which mainly examine the frequency of specific words, and in which the meaning of each word is taken seriously into consideration, focus on the 'meaning of content' dimension of textual information, and as opposed to that, conventional stylistics mainly investigates the 'form of the styles' dimension of textual information; the distributional characteristics of content-independent features. The dimension that has yet to be clarified is the 'meaning of the styles' of textual information. Developing a kind of computational sociolinguistics, which could become a potentially important areas of stylistics (Argamon et al. 2007) would help to shed light on this dimension. We would like to explore this dimension in further studies.

References

Ahrens, K. 2005. People in the State of the Union: Viewing Social Change Through the Eyes of Presidents, *Proceedings of PACLIC19, The 19th Asia-Pacific Conference on Language, Information and Computation*, pp. 43-50.

Aitchison, J. and D. M. Lewis ed. 2003. *New Media Language*. London: Routledge.

Argamon, S., C. Whitelaw, P. Chase, S. Raj Hota, N. Garg and S. Levitan 2007. Stylistic text classification using functional lexical features, *Journal of the American Society for Information Science and Technology*, 58(6), 802-822.

Axelrod, R. ed. 1976. *Structure of Decision: the Cognitive Maps of Political Elites,* Princeton, New Jersey: Princeton University Press.

Azuma, S. 2006. *Rekidai Syusyo no Gengoryoku wo Shindan Suru*. Tokyo: Kenkyu-sya.

Cortina-Borja, M. and C. Chappas. 2006. A Stylometric Analysis of Newspapers, periodicals and newsscripts, *Journal of Quantitative Linguistics*, 13(23), 285-312.

Garcìa, A. M. and J. C. Martìn. 2007. Function words in authorship attribution studies, *Literary and Linguistic Computing*, 22(1), 49-66.

Grieve, J. 2007. Qualitative authorship attribution: an evaluation of techniques, *Literary and Linguistic Computing*, 22(3), 251-270.

Hoover, D. L. 2003. Another perspective on vocabulary richness, *Computers and the Humanities*, 37(2), 151-178.

Kabashima, I. and G. Steel. 2007. How Junichiro Koizumi seized the leadership of Japan's Liberal Democratic Party, *Japanese Journal of Political Science*, 8(1), 95-114.

Kenny, A. 1982. *The Computation of Style: an Introduction to Statistics for Students of Literature and Humanities*. Oxford: Pergamon Press.

Kusano, A. 2006. *Terebi wa Seiji wo Ugokasu ka*. Tokyo: NTT publishing.

Matsumoto, Y., A. Kitauchi, T. Yamashita, Y. Hirano, H. Matsuda, K. Takaoka and M. Asahara. 2003. *Japanese Morphological Analysis System ChaSen ver. 2.2.3* (chasen. naist. jp).

Otake, H. 2006. *Koizumi Junichiro Popurizumu no Kenkyu: sono Senryaku to Syuho*. Tokyo: Toyo Keizai Shinpo-sya.

Reinem, M. 2005. Japanese political thought as seen from prime ministers' speech: Koizumi's singularity, *Koukyo Seisaku Kenkyu*, 5, 179-198.

Reinem, M. 2007. Content analysis of Japanese prime ministers' policy speeches: the political thought of Murayama and Koizumi, *Ronsyu Gendai Bunka / Koukyo Seisaku*, 5, 165-201.

Shinoda, T. 1994. *Souridaijin no Kenryoku to Shido-ryoku: Yoshida Shigeru kara Murayama Tomiichi made*. Tokyo: Toyo Keizai Shinpo-sya.

Simpson, E. H. 1949. Measurement of Diversity, *Nature*, 163, 168.

Tweedie, F. J. and R. H. Baayen 1998. How Variable May a Constant be? Measures of Lexical

Richness in perspective, *Computers and the Humanities*, 32, 323-352.

Watanabe, A. 1974. Taigai ishiki ni okeru 'senzen' to 'sengo': syusyo gaisyo no gikai enzetsu no bunseki ni motozuku jakkan no kosatsu, in *Kindai Nihon no Taigai Taido*, ed. by S. Sato, and R. Dingman, pp. 225-274. Tokyo: University of   Tokyo Press.

Yoshikane, F., K. Kageura, and K. Tsuji. 2003. A method for the comparative analysis of concentration of author productivity, giving consideration to the effect of sample size dependency of statistical measures, *Journal of the American Society for Information Science and Technology*, 54(6), 521-528.

Yule, G. U. 1944. *The Statistical Study of Literary Vocabulary*. Cambridge: Cambridge University Press.

What L2 Learners' Processing Strategy Reveals about the Modal System in Japanese: A Cue-based Analytical Perspective[*]

Mizuho Tamaji and Kaoru Horie

Takamatsu University, Tohoku University
tamaji@takamatsu-u.ac.jp, khorie@mail.tains. tohoku.ac.jp.

Abstract. Japanese does not exhibit deontic-epistemic polysemy which is recognized among typologically different languages. Hence, in Japanese linguistics, it has been debated which of the two types of modality is more prototypical. This study brings Chinese learner's acquisition data of Japanese modality to bear on the question of which of the two types of modality is more prototypical, using the Competition Model (Bates and MacWhinney 1981). The Competition Model notion of 'cues' as processing strategy adopted by learners reveals the continuity/discontinuity between these two modality domains.

Keywords: prototype, the Competition Model, cues, processing strategy

1. Introduction

It is cross-linguistically not uncommon for a single modal marker to represent both deontic modality (the conditioning factors being external to the relevant individual) (Palmer 2001: 9) and epistemic modality (speakers' judgments about the factual status of the proposition) (ibid: 8), as in English *should*. This phenomenon is defined as polysemy (Traugott & Dasher 2002: 9). The deontic-epistemic polysemy is considered as a typologically prevalent tendency (Bybee et. al. 1994).

Unlike this cross-linguistic tendency, deontic modality and epistemic modality are generally encoded by two distinctive modal markers in Japanese.

This raises an intriguing question as to whether deontic is more prototypical than epistemic modality, or vice versa, or neither is. The aim of this study is to analogize the relationship between deontic modal markers and epistemic modal markers in Japanese based on the data of Chinese speakers' L2 acquisition.

2. Deontic-epistemic polysemy in cognitive linguistics and grammaticalization

---

[*] Thanks are due to two anonymous reviewers for their constructive criticism. The usual disclaimer applies. This study was supported in part by a grant from the Japan Society for the Promotion of Science (#19520349).

The phenomenon of polysemy between deontic and epistemic modalities is observable among typologically different languages, therefore this phenomenon is considered as a cross-linguistically prevalent tendency. There are two main approaches which propose to account for the deontic-epistemic polysemy prevalent across languages, i.e. (I) the **polysemic approach** and (II) the **monosemic approach**.

2.1. The polysemic approach

According to recent studies of cognitive linguistics (Sweetser 1990) and of grammaticalization (Bybee et al. 1994, Traugott and Dasher 2002), the deontic-epistemic modality results from the cognitive-diachronic process whereby epistemic modal meaning derives from deontic epistemic modal meaning rather than vice versa. For example, Sweetser (1990) explains this process as in (1).

(1) John *must* be at home right now.

The sentence (1) can be interpreted in two ways: (i) John is obliged to be at home (deontic usage of *must*) and (ii) the circumstance compels the speaker to judge that John is at home (epistemic usage of *must*). Deontic usage implies that the force-dynamics in a real world imposed by the speaker and/or other several actors compels the subject (or others) to perform a certain action. Epistemic usage suggests that cognitive force employed by a certain actor compels the speaker (or people in general) to reach the conclusion described in a sentence. There is parallelism in force dynamics between deontic and epistemic usages. Force dynamics in a socio-physical domain derives force dynamics in a cognitive domain. Therefore, it is considered that deontic usage derives epistemic usage and the former is more prototypical than the latter.

2.2. The monosemic approach

There is another approach to explain the relationship between deontic and epistemic modalities. This approach, referred to as the 'monosemic' approach, was advocated by Kratzer (1981). It proposes that each modal marker generally contains a common core meaning which covers several different interpretations. Papafragou (2000) developed Kratser's approach and proposed that the interpretation of modal meaning is context-dependent, by adopting the 'relevance theory' by Sperber and Wilson (1995).

The monosemic approach was proposed because there are some cases which cannot be explained by the 'polysemic' approach. While the polysemic approach regards a semantic change from deontic to epistemic modality as metaphoric mapping in force-dynamics from socio-physical domains to epistemic domains, the monosemic approach regards modal meanings as clear-cut, i.e. either deontic or epistemic. Contrary to the polysemic approach, the monosemic approach proposes that modal meaning is not determined by *a priori* but is determined by specific contexts.

3.   A cognitive account for the absence of deontic-epistemic polysemy in Japanese

As noted in Section 1, modal markers in Modern Japanese generally fail to exhibit the deontic-epistemic polysemy. For example, the deontic modal sense of *should* is encoded by a periphrastic modal marker *bekida*, while its epistemic modal sense is encoded by another periphrastic marker *hazuda*. This tendency is further exemplified by another set of modal markers *nakerebanaranai* and *nichigainai*. Both are translated into English *must*: the deontic modal sense of *must* corresponds to *nakerebanaranai*, while its epistemic modal sense corresponds to *nichigainai*.

The virtual non-existence of deontic-epistemic polysemy in Japanese suggests that the relationship between deontic modal markers and epistemic modal markers cannot be explained by the cross-linguistically observable unidirectional grammaticalization process of modal markers. Yamada (1990) thus maintains that both categories of modality originated independently and that neither of them is more prototypical than the other. This view accords with the monosemic approach in that both views consider that deontic modality and epistemic modality are distinctive cognitive domains.

The other approach maintains that epistemic modality derives deontic modality and, therefore, epistemic modality is more prototypical than deontic modality in Japanese, unlike the cross-linguistically prevalent reverse tendency (Kurotaki 2005). This approach is similar to the polysemic approach in that both approaches consider deontic and epistemic modal meanings to be continuous.

A most common method to examine the prototypicality of modal meaning in a language is to examine the process of diachronic grammaticalization in that language. Grammaticalization in the area of modality refers to the process of semantic change of modal markers: the prototypical meaning emerged earlier than the peripheral one. The evidence of diachronic grammaticalization, however, is not available to explain the prototypicality of Japanese modal markers, because the development of the modal markers in Modern Japanese is apparently independent of the modal markers in Classical Japanese (Onoe 2001). Therefore, we examine the relationship between deontic modal markers and epistemic modal markers using the data of second language acquisition as an alternative method.

4. Studies of Chinese learners' acquisition of Japanese modal markers

4.1. The parallelism between L2 acquisition and diachronic grammaticalization

Certain parallelism between grammaticalization and the order of acquisition of polyfunctional words has been recognized in functional-cognitive linguistics. That is, the emergence and the acquisition of core meaning have been known to precede those of peripheral one. Recently, this parallel relationship was extended to a research program that describes the typological characteristics of grammaticalization of a language based on the language acquisition order of polysemous words (e.g.Giacalone-Ramat 2003, Giacalone-Ramat and Crocco-Gales 1995).

Unlike L1 acquisition, the order of L2 learners' acquisition of polysemous words does not involve the creation of new patterns of grammaticalization like diachronic grammaticalization. Instead, it demonstrates various ways of approximating to a subsystem (Giacalone-Ramat 2003:

28). Therefore, L2 acquisition, especially the strategy utilized by adult learners, recapitulates the internal factors of the diachronic grammaticalization in the target language more overtly than L1 acquisition. Hence, we consider that the data of second language acquisition will be an appropriate method in order to analogize the relationship between deontic and epistemic modal markers in Japanese.

4.2. The target and the hypothesis

According to the parallelism between the order of acquisition of meaning and diachronic grammaticalization, learners acquire more prototypical modal markers earlier than non-prototypical ones. This suggests that the modal marker acquired earlier is more prototypical. The notion of the parallelism between the order and the degree of prototypicality is also applicable to the acquisition of Japanese modal markers, in which deontic modality and epistemic modality are encoded by two distinct modal markers.

In this study, we will deal with the case of Chinese learners' acquisition of two pairs of Japanese modal markers *bekida/hazuda* and *nakerebanaranai/nichigainai*. *Bekida* and *hazuda* correspond to a single modal marker *ying¹gai¹* in Chinese, whereas *nakerebanaranai* and *nichigainai* are correspond to a single modal marker *yao⁴* (the numbers indicate the intonation of Chinese: number 1 stands for flat tone, 2 for rising tone, 3 for falling-rising tone, and 4 for falling tone). Chinese is a language in which the deontic-epistemic polysemy is manifested, with the deontic meaning more prototypical than the epistemic meaning (Li 2003). The mapping patterns of deontic modal markers and epistemic modal markers and the degree of prototypicality are thus different between the two languages.

Our null hypotheses are that (i) learners acquire more prototypical modal markers earlier than non-prototypical ones, and that (ii) neither of deontic or epistemic meaning is more prototypical than the other if learners acquire them simultaneously. We define the survey of prototypicality based on the order of acquisition as the survey 1.

5.   Survey 1: the prototypicality of Japanese modal markers based on the second language acquisition

5.1. Methodology

The tasks in Survey 1 were given in the form of multiple choice questions. Chinese learners of Japanese were instructed to choose one appropriate modal marker out of four alternatives for a question. Two out of four choices given were *bekida* and *hazuda*, which competed with each other. There were 20 questions in total. The learners had to choose *bekida* as the correct answers for 10 questions and *hazuda* for another 10 questions.

(2) is an example of the task. Learners are instructed to read the sentence and to choose the appropriate modal marker among the four alternatives. As demonstrated by (c) and (d), two out of the four alternatives are *bekida* and *hazuda*, which compete with each other.

(2) *sake-wa*   *tomokaku*   *tabako-wa*   (   ).
      alcohol-TOP   if not   tobacco-TOP
      'You (   ) tobacco, if not alcohol.'

(a) *herasa nai monoda*   (b) *herasu wakeda*
      'do not naturally cut down on'   'no wonder cut down on'

(c)   *herasu hazuda*   (d)   *herasu bekida*
      'are supposed to cut down on'   'ought to cut down on'

In this experiment, Chinese learners were divided into 3 groups according to the results of a pretest (the grammar test of the second grade Japanese proficiency test), i.e. basic, intermediate, and advanced groups. Each group consisted of 20 examinees.

This task is developed based on the Competition Model (Bates and MacWhinney 1981). The Competition Model is a functionally oriented model for second language acquisition. The model is based on a functional theory of grammar wherein the relationship between the underlying meaning/intention and its expression in surface form is stated as directly as possible (Givón, 1979). Hence, this modal is suitable to analyze the process of the acquisition of grammatical features where the form-meaning correspondences in L1 and L2 are in competition.

The tasks consisted of 20 questions for a pair *bekida/hazuda* and 20 questions for a pair *nakerebanaranai/nichigainai*. Out of 20 questions for the former pair, 10 questions required deontic *bekida* and the remaining 10 required epistemic *hazuda*. Similarly, out of 20 questions for the latter pair, 10 questions required deontic *nakarebanaranai* and the remaining 10 questions required epistemic *nichigainai*.

An analysis was conducted of the learners' differential choice of modal markers for each block of 10 questions that required each modal marker as the correct answer from the viewpoints of L1 transfer and the development of interlanguage. Specifically we examined the learners' differential choice of correct modal markers, i.e. the choice between the correct modal marker (e.g. *hazuda*) and the competing modal marker (e.g. *bekida*) and other modal markers (e.g. *monoda*) using a statistical test.

5.2 The results of Survey 1 and the examination of the prototypicality between modal markers

The figures below indicate the relationship between the choice of modal markers and the proficiency levels of learners for questions requiring each modal marker as the correct answer.

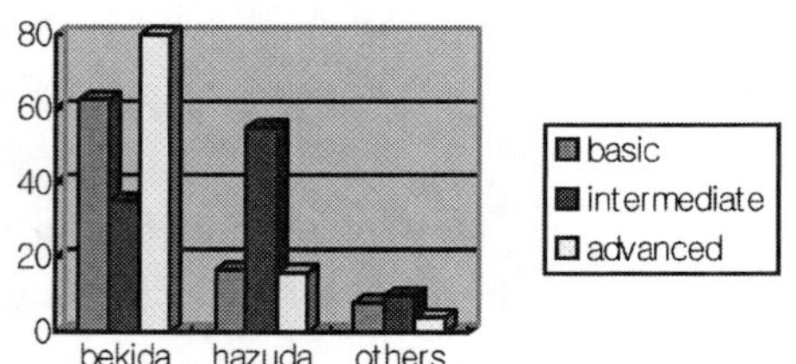

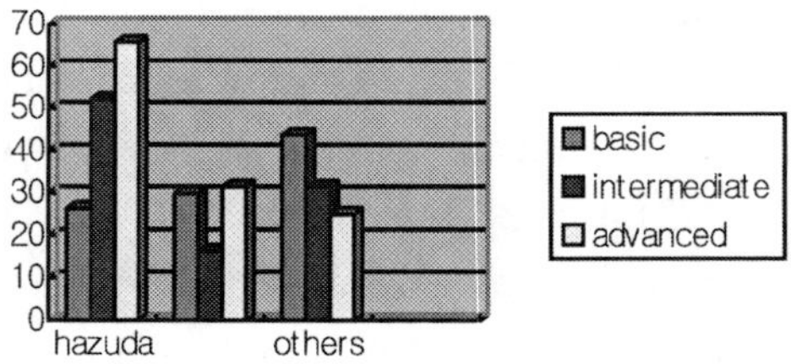

Figure 1. questions for *bekida*   Figure 2. questions for *hazuda*

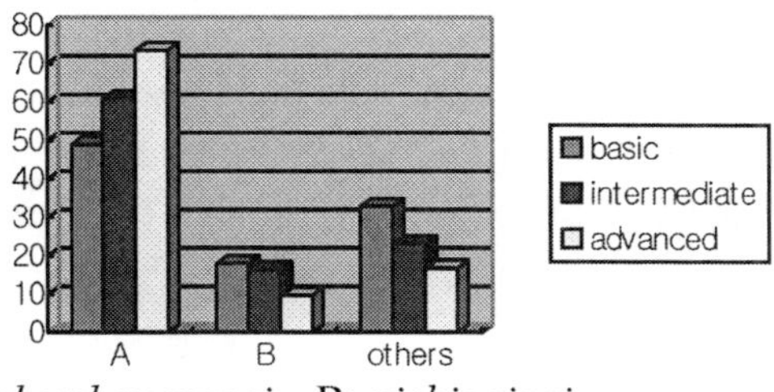

A: *nakerebanaranai*   B: *nichigainai*

Figure 3. questions for *nakerebanaranai*

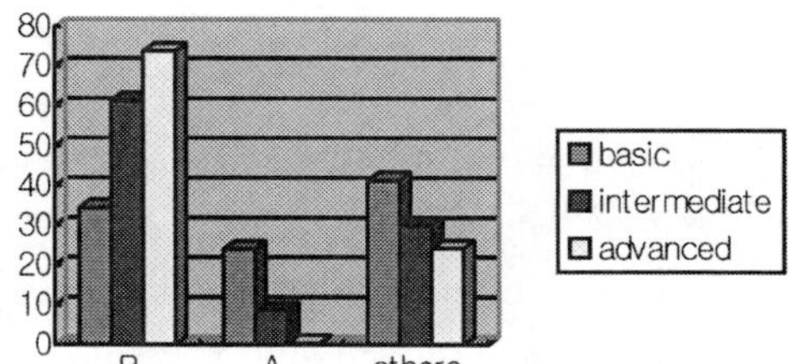

B: *nichigainai*   A: *nakrebanaranai*

Figure 4. questions for *nichigainai*

The results of Surevey 1 are summarized as follows: (i) intermediate learners who incorrectly selected epistemic *hazuda* instead of the correct deontic *bekida* outnumbered basic and advanced learners; (ii)the number of learners who incorrectly selected epistemic *hazuda* for the questions requiring it instead of deontic *bekida* steadly increased in proportion to their proficiency level. These results suggest that (iii) Chinese learners' acquisition of *bekida* and *hazuda* is influenced in its beginning stage by their native language where deontic modality is more prototypical than epistemic modality, as suggested by the high accuracy rate of the deontic *bekida* usage; (iv) it then shifts to an 'interlanguage' stage characterized by the intermediate learners' overgeneralization of epistemic *hazuda*; (v) and finally the advanced learners' performance shows closer resemblance to that of Japanese native speakers as characterized by the gradual increase in the accuracy rate of the correct epistemic *hazuda* usage.

Unlike the acquisition of *bekida/hazuda*, learners at all levels tended to respond correctly to the questions respectively requiring *nakerebanaranai* or *nichigainai* as the correct answer. Thus, the learners could recognize that *nakerebanaranai* and *nichigainai* have different functions from the beginning and they did not go through the stage of 'interlanguage' on the process of the acquisition of *nakerebanaranai* and *nichigainai*

The acquisition process of two sets of modal markers suggests: **(I) modal meanings of *nakerebanaranai* and *nichigainai* developed independently as maintained by Yamada (1990); but (II) the stage of 'interlanguage' indicates that *hazuda* is more prototypical than *bekida* as maintained by Kurotaki (2005).** The greater degree of prototypicality of *hazuda* suggests that the monosemic approach is applicable to explain the relationship between *bekida* and *hazuda*. We will confirm this finding based on the processing strategy that the learners utilized in the next section and we define this task as survey 2.

6.   Survey 2: the cue-based analysis

6.1. The parallelism between processing strategy and the notion of 'cue'

Similar to the parallelism between language acquisition and diachronic grammaticalization, there is arguably also a parallelism between the processing strategy adopted by adult L2 learners and the internal factors of diachronic grammaticalization. The notion of 'cue' employed in the Competition Model is a useful method to describe this parallelism.

The connector between the underlying meaning and its surface manifestation is defined as a 'cue'. This term includes all the information utilized by speakers and hearers to determine the relationship between form and meaning. Cues include case-marking particles, word order, inflectional morphology etc (MacWhinney 1987). This model focuses on the understanding of sentence processing, therefore cues normally refers to surface forms of the sentences that activate the underlying function utilized by listeners. Hence, the differences in surface forms between deontic and epistemic modal markers can be the cue for learners to differentiate both modalities.

6.2. The definition of cues for survey 2

Tables 1 and 2 represent a cluster of formal/grammatical features respectively characterizing deontic modality and epistemic modality in Japanese.

Table1. Cues for deontic *bekida* in Japanese

Grammatical Subject	Explicit or implicit, [+ volitional, +animate]
Predicate	Action verb
Negation	Negative form of the modal marker (*~suru beki dewa nai*)
Tense	Past form of the modal marker (*~suru beki datta*)
Voice	Active

Table 2. Cues for epistemic *hazuda* in Japanese

(Semantic) subject	The speaker
Thematic subject	Explicit or implicit, [+ or − animate]
Predicate	Verb, noun, adjective
Negation	Negative form of the modal marker (*~suru beki dewa nai*) Negative form of the embedded predicate (*~shi nai hazuda*)
Tense	Past form of the modal marker (*~suru beki datta*) Past form of the embedded predicate (*~shita hazuda*)
Voice	Active, passive, potential

From Tables 1 and 2, it is obvious that an epistemic modal marker *hazuda* has more variable surface formal manifestations than its deontic counterpart *bekida*. Some formal (or grammatical) features are specific to *hazuda* such as the possible occurrence of an inanimate subject, of noun and adjective in the predicate position, the availability of a negative, past, passive or potential form of the embedded predicate. Therefore, we can presume that learners are guided by these formal features to become sensitivized to the usage conditions/constraints on epistemic *hazuda*.

On the other hand, sentences with deontic *bekida* can have its animate subject present or absent and typically co-occur with a volitional action verb. These formal features might be employed by learners as possible cues to distinguish deontic *bekida* from epistemic *hazuda*.

However, there can be a sentence with epistemic *hazuda* whose surface structure is identical to that with deontic *bekida*. e.g. an epistemic sentence with the animate subject and the present action verb. This is exemplified by the example (3) below.

(3) *Furaipan   de sakana   wo yaku   toki wa,   bataa wo   yoku   tokasu (   )..*
 frying pan   by. fish   ACC fry   when TOP, butter ACC   well   melt should.
 'When you fry fish using frying pan, you should melt butter well.'

In fact, this sentence can receive either deontic or epistemic interpretation and both *bekida* and *hazuda* are available in the blacket.

Kail (1989) categorized the types of cues into two types, **local cues** and **global cues** according to the difference of the amount of effort in the sentence processing. Local cues refer to the cues requiring local processing. In the case of local cues, we can recognize particular usage based on one lexical word and it is not necessary to consider other lexical words. On the other hand, global cues require topological processing in which we need to consider other lexical words.

According to this definition, the cues exclusive to epistemic usage and the cues typical to deontic usage are local cues. In contrast, the cues for example (3) are global cues.

The subject (the person executing certain action) in (4) is implicit, but it is possible to interpret (3) as (a) a generic statement by the speaker (epistemic usage) and (b) a specific situation where the speaker requires a particular person to perform certain action (deontic usage). The difference between (a) and (b) corresponds to the view of the monosemic approach that maintains the difference of deontic and epistemic usages is contextual. This implies that the global cue is the core/common meaning between two usages as the monosemic approach stated.

Unlike the case of *bekida* and *hazuda*, there are no global cues between *nakerebanaranai* and *nichigainai*. For example, a sentence contains an animate subject and a present tense of action verb can be interpreted as both deontic and epistemic meanings. However, there is a difference in the surface forms when the verb prefix to *nakerebanarana*i and to *nichigainai*. The sentences (4) and (5) exemplify the difference.

(4) *Okureru toki wa renraku **shi** nakerebanaranai*
 Late. Time TOP contact do.must.
 (When you are late,) you must make a contact to us.

(5) *Okureru toki wa renraku **suru** nichigainai.*
 (When you are late,) you must make a contact to us.

When the present tense of an action verb *suru* ('do') is attached to a modal *nakerebanaranai*, it becomes inflected and changes to *shi* like (4). On the other hand, the same verb *suru* does not alter its form when it is attached to *nichigainai* like (5).

6.3. The result of Survey 2

The analysis of cues thus reveals that *bekida/hazuda* has a global cue and *nakerebanaranai/nichigainai* does not. According to Kail (1989), a local cue is easier to acquire than a global cue due to the amount of the effort in the processing. There is no global cue between *nakerebanaranai* and *nichigainai*, therefore learners could perceive two modal markers have different functions from the beginning of the acquisition. On the other hand, the existence of global cue between *bekida* and *hazuda* makes it difficult for learners to distinguish them.

The cue-based analysis of the acquisition of *bekida/hazuda* demonstrates that learners utilized different types of cues. Basic level Chinese learners of Japanese tend to choose deontic *bekida* not only in questions requiring it as the correct answer but also in questions requiring epistemic *hazuda*. This is a possible instance of transfer from the knowledge of L1 (where the deontic sense of *ying1gai1* is primary and prototypical) in processing an L2 sentence. Unlike basic learners, intermediate learners performed well for the questions requiring epistemic *hazuda*. These learners, however, tended to choose *hazuda* for the questions requiring deontic *bekida*. These findings imply that intermediate learners utilizes epistemic local cue. They attempted to utilize global cue rather than to utilize deontic local cue independently. Advanced learners can choose appropriate modal markers according to the contexts, which means that these learners can utilize all types of cues correctly. The strategy employed by intermediate learners and that by advanced learners indicate that the existence of continuity between *bekida* and *hazuda* and that the difference between them is determined by the contexts. This suggests that the monosemic approach is more appropriate in explaining the relationship between these two modal markers.

7. Conclusion

This study examined the prototype relationship between deontic modality and epistemic modality in Japanese based on Chinese learners' L2 acquisition data. Two pairs of periphrastic modal markers in Japanese *bekida/hazuda* and *nakerebanaranai/nichigainai*, which respectively correspond to single modal markers in Chinese, were objects of our inquiry. In both cases, the mapping correspondence of modal markers between Chinese and Japanese is 1:2. Nevertheless, the results of Chinese learners' acquisition of *bekida/hazuda* and *nakerebanaranai/nichigainai* were shown to be different. This result has the following implication for considering the relationship between deontic and epistemic modalities in Japanese. Though the two semantic categories are formally coded by different periphrastic modal markers, unlike their counterparts in languages like English and Chinese, there are cases where the two categories are in a pseudo-prototype relationship, i.e. epistemic modality being more prototypical than deontic modality, as exemplified by the pair *bekida/hazuda*. Conversely, there are also cases where the two categories are discontinuous, as in the pair *nakerebanaranai/nichigainai*.

References

Bates, E. and B. MacWhinney. 1981. Second Language Acquisition from a Functional Perspective: Pragmatic, Semantic & Perceptual Strategies. In H. Winitz, ed., *Annuals of Science Conference on Native and Foreign Language Acquisition,* pp. 198-219. New York: New York Academy of Sciences.

Bybee, J., R., Perkin,s and W. Pagliuca. 1994. *The Evolution of Grammar, Tense, Aspect and Modality in Languages of the World,* Chicago.: Chicago University Press.

Giacalone-Ramat, A. 2003. *Typology and Second Language Acquisition.* Berlin: Mouton de Gruyter.

Giacalone-Ramat, A.and G. Crocco-Gales. 1995. *From Pragmatics to Syntax: Modality in Second Language Acquisition.* Tubingen: Gunter Narr Verlag.

Givón, T. 1979. *On Understanding Grammar.* New York: Academic Press.

Kail, M. 1989. Cue Validity, Cue Cost, and Processing Types in Sentence Comprehension in French and Spanish. In: B. MacWhinney, and E. Bates, eds., *The Crosslinguistic Study of Sentence Processing,* 21-54. New York: Cambridge University Press.

Kratzer, A.A. 1981. Notional Category of Modality. In H. Eikmeyer and H. Rieser eds., *Words, Worlds and Contexts,* 38-74. Berlin: Walter de Gryuter.

Kurotaki, M. 2005. *Deontic kara Epistemic heno Huhensei to Soutaisei: Modaritii no Nichiei Taisho Kenkyu.* (Universality and relativity from Deontic to Epistemic: A Contrastive Study of Modality between Japanese and English). Tokyo: Kuroshioshuppann.

Li, R. 2003. *Modality in English and Chinese: a Typological Perspective.* Amsterdam: Lighting Source Incorporation.

MacWhinney, B. 1987. Applying the Competition Model to Bilingualism. *Applied Psycholinguistics,* 8, 315-327.

Onoe, K. 2001. *Bunpo to Imi* I. (Grammar and meaning I). Tokyo: Kurosio.

Palmer. F. R. 2001. *Mood and Modality.* 2nd ed. Cambridge: Cambridge University Press.

Papafragou, A. 2000. *Modality: Issues in the Semantic-Pragmatics Interface.* Amsterdam: Elsevier.

Slobin, D. 1994. Talking Perfectly. Discourse Origins of the Present Perfect. In W. Pagliuca, ed., *Perspectives on Grammaticalization,* pp. 119-133. Amsterdam: John Benjamins.

Sperber, D. and D. Wilson. 1995. *Relevance: Communication and Cognition.* Oxford: Blackwell.

Sweetser, E.E. 1990. *From Etymology to Pragmatics Metaphorical and Cultural Aspects of Semantic Structure.* Cambridge: Cambridge University Press.

Traugott, E.C. and R.B. Dasher. 2002. *Regularity in Semantic Change.* Cambridge: Cambridge University Press.

Yamada, S. 1990. *Modaritii.* (Modality). Tokyo: Dogakusha.

Movie Review Classification Based on a Multiple Classifier[*]

Kimitaka Tsutsumi[a], Kazutaka Shimada[a] and Tsutomu Endo[a]

[a]Department of Artificial Intelligence,
Kyushu Institute of Technology, Iizuka, Fukuoka 820-8502 Japan
{k_tsutsumi, shimada, endo}@pluto.ai.kyutech.ac.jp

Abstract. In this paper, we propose a method to classify movie review documents into positive or negative opinions. There are several approaches to classify documents. The previous studies, however, used only a single classifier for the classification task. We describe a multiple classifier for the review document classification task. The method consists of three classifiers based on SVMs, ME and score calculation. We apply two voting methods and SVMs to the integration process of single classifiers. The integrated methods improved the accuracy as compared with the three single classifiers. The experimental results show the effectiveness of our method.

Keywords: Sentiment analysis, p/n classification, Integration, Movie reviews, WWW.

1. Introduction

The World Wide Web contains a huge number of on-line documents that are easily accessible. Finding information relevant to user needs has become increasingly important. The most important information on the Web is usually contained in the text. We obtain a huge number of review documents that include user's opinions for products. For example, buying products, users usually survey the product reviews. Movie reviews are likewise one of the most important information for users who go to a movie. More precise and effective methods for evaluating the products are useful for users.

Many researchers have recently studied extraction of evaluative expressions and classification of opinions (Kobayashi et al., 2005; Osajima et al., 2005; Pang et al., 2002; Turney, 2002). Studies of opinion classification are generally classified into three groups: (1) classifying documents into the positive (p) or negative (n) opinions, (2) classifying sentences into the positive or negative opinions, and (3) classifying words into the positive or negative expressions. In this paper, we focus on the classification of movie review documents. Pang et al. (2002) have reported the effectiveness of applying machine learning techniques to the p/n classification. They compared three machine learning methods: Naive Bayes, Maximum Entropy and Support Vector Machines. In their experiment, SVMs produced the best performance. Osajima et al. (2005) have proposed a method for polarity classification of sentences in review documents. The method is based on a score calculation process of word polarity and outperformed SVMs in the sentence classification task.

The previous studies, however, used only a single classifier for the classification task. We (Tsutsumi 2006 et al.) have proposed a method consisting of two classifiers: SVMs and the scoring method by Osajima et al. (2005). The method identified the class (p/n) of a document on the basis of the distances that were measured from the hyperplane of each classifier. It obtained

---

the better accuracy as compared with the single classifiers. This method, however, contained a problem for the determination of the final output, namely positive or negative. We needed to normalize the classifier's outputs manually because the scale of the scoring method was different from that of SVMs.

To solve this problem, we apply the 3rd machine learning method (Maximum Entropy) into the method based on the scoring and SVMs. Figure 1 shows the outline of the proposed method. In this paper, we compare three processes for the method: naive voting, weighted voting and determination with SVMs.

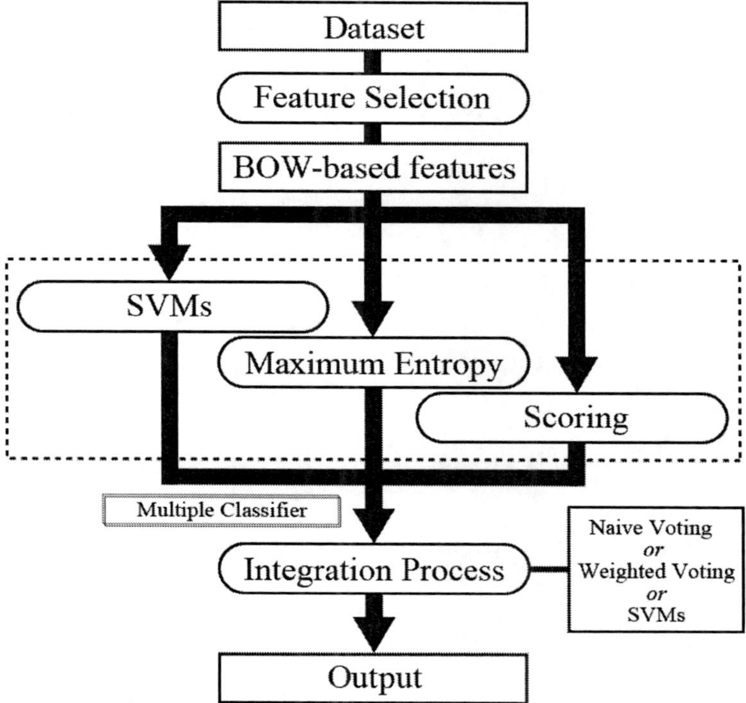

Figure. 1. The outline of our method.

2. Classifiers

In this section, we explain classifiers for a multiple classifier that will be proposed in this paper. The 1st and 2nd classifiers are SVMs and Maximum Entropy respectively. These classifiers have been used in related work by Pang et al. (2002). In their paper, they reported that SVMs produced the best performance. The 3rd classifier is based on polarity scores of words in documents. The method is an expansion of Osajima et al. (2005).

2.1.SVMs

SVMs are a machine learning algorithm that was introduced by Vapnik (1999). They have been applied to tasks such as face recognition and text classification. An SVM is a binary classifier that finds a maximal margin separating hyperplane between two classes. The hyperplane can be written as:

$$y_i = w \cdot x + b \quad (1)$$

where x is an arbitrary data point, i.e., feature vectors, w and b are decided by optimization, and $y_i \in \{+1, -1\}$. The instances that lie closest to the hyperplane are called support vectors. We use SVM^{light} package[1] for training and testing, with all parameters set to their default values (Joachims, 1999).

2.2. Maximum Entropy

Maximum entropy modeling (ME) is one of the best techniques for natural language processing (Berger et al., 1996). The principle of the ME is expressed as follows:

$$P_\Lambda(c \mid d) = \frac{1}{Z_\Lambda(d)} \exp\left(\sum_i \lambda_{i,c} f_{i,c}(d,c) \right) \quad (2)$$

$$Z_\Lambda(d) = \sum_{d,c} \exp\left(\sum_i \lambda_{i,c} f_{i,c}(d,c) \right) \quad (3)$$

where $Z_\Lambda(d)$ is a normalization function. $\Lambda = \{\lambda_1, \ldots, \lambda_n\}$ are parameters for the model. These parameters denote weights and significance of each feature. The parameter values are a set that maximizes the entropy concerning the classifier. $f_{i,c}(d,c)$ is a feature function that is defined as follows:

$$f_{i,c}(d,c') = \begin{cases} 1 & \text{if } exist(d,i) > 0 \text{ and } c' = c \\ 0 & \text{otherwise} \end{cases} \quad (4)$$

where $exist(d,i)$ is a indicator function. The value is 1 in the case that a feature i exists in a document d.

In this paper we use Amis, which is a parameter estimator for maximum entropy models[2]. We estimate parameters by using the generalized iterative scaling algorithm.

2.3. Scoring

Osajima et al. (2005) have proposed a method for polarity classification of sentences in review documents. The method is based on a score calculation process of word polarity. In this paper we apply some adjustments to the feature selection of the method.

First we explain score calculation of each word. The score of a word w_i is computed as follows:

$$Score_W(w_i) = \log\left(\frac{pos(w_i)+1}{\sum pos} \times \frac{\sum neg}{neg(w_i)+1} \right) \quad (5)$$

where $pos(w_i)$ and $neg(w_i)$ are the frequency of a word w_i in the positive opinions and the negative opinions respectively. $\sum pos$ and $\sum neg$ are the number of words in the positive and negative opinions respectively.

In the classification process, we compute the sum of scores of which words appear in a document d.

$$Score(d) = \sum_{ALLw_i \in d} Score_W(w_i) \quad (6)$$

---

[1] http:/svmlight.joachims.org
[2] http:/www-tsujii.is.s.u-tokyo.ac.jp/amis/index.html

where d denotes a document. The $Score_W(w_i)$ are given by Eq. 5. Finally, we evaluate the score as follows:

$$d = \begin{cases} Positive & Score(d) > 0 \\ Negative & Score(d) \le 0 \end{cases} \qquad (7)$$

As expansions, we apply two conditions to the feature selection of the classifier.
- Use of POS tags

  We use weighted scores for adjective words.
- Selection with χ^2-test

  We select features for the classifier by using the result of χ^2-test. We reject words that possess low reliability. We set 20% on the significant level for the experiment.

3. Integration of classifiers

We examined the outputs of three classifiers, i.e. an error analysis. As a result, we obtained knowledge that the misclassifications of each classifier are often different, that is exclusive misclassifications. In other words, a single classifier could classify a document correctly even though other single classifiers could not classify it correctly. This result shows the significance of integration of single classifiers.

In this section we explain three methods for combining the classifiers. In this paper we adopt two voting processes, naive voting and weighted voting, and integration with SVMs.

Naive voting As the final output, we use the majority vote from three classifiers, namely SVMs, ME and Scoring methods.

Weighted voting This method uses each distance from hyperplanes of each classifier as weights (confidence) of the outputs. This is based on a supposition that an output that is close to the hyperplane of a classifier contains low reliability. However ranges of each distance computed from each classifier are not equivalent. We normalize each distance as follows.
Scoring: The actual value of the output from the classifier
SVM: $dist(d) \times l$

ME: $(p(postive, d) - p(negative, d)) \times m$

where $dist(d)$ is the distance from the hyperplane. $p(postive, d)$ and $p(negative, d)$ are the probabilities of a document d as positive and negative opinions. l and m are constant numbers for the normalization. The values are computed beforehand from training data. In other words, the values are determined from the results obtained from training data by using each classifier constructed from it. l and m in this paper are based on the average of the distance from the hyperplane in the classification results.

SVMs We use SVMs again for the integration process of single classifiers. Here the features for SVMs are the three outputs of each single classifier, namely distances from hyperplanes. We do not normalize each output. First, we need to construct training data for SVMs in this integration process. In this paper we use the same training data for learning both the single classifier and the integration process. In other words, this SVM obtains a hyperplane for the integration from the training data that is used in the learning process of the single classifiers. Figure 2 shows the outline of the process.

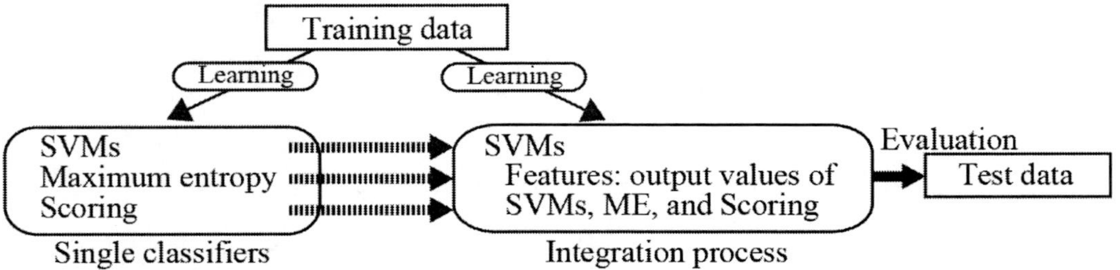

Figure. 2. The integration process with SVMs.

4. Experiment

In this section, we explain a dataset and basic feature selection for this experiment first. Then we evaluate our methods with the dataset and compare them with single classifiers.

4.1.Dataset and features for the classifiers

First we describe the data set for the experiment. We evaluated our method with movie review documents that were used in Pang et al. (2002). The dataset consists of 700 positive reviews and 700 negative reviews. We divided the data into three equal-sized folds in the same manner as the previous work (Pang et al., 2002). In other words, we tested our method with three-fold cross-validation.

We extracted basic features for classifiers in the same way the previous work did. The conditions of the previous work for the feature selection were as follows: (1) no stemming or stopword lists were used, (2) use of the negation tag, and (3) limitation of the frequency of words. For the 2nd condition, we added the tag "NOT_" to every word between a negation word ("not", "isn't", "didn't", etc.) and the first punctuation mark following the negation word[3]. For the 3rd condition, we used words appearing at least four times in our 1400-document corpus.

We constructed the feature space for each classifier on the basis of the basic features. For the scoring method, we used features extracted with the conditions described in Section 2.3 (use of POS tags and χ 2-test). For the tagging, we used the Brill's Tagger[4]. However, we used basic features for SVMs and ME[5].

4.2.Experimental results

First, we compared six methods in this experiment: single classifiers (SVMs, ME and Scoring) and the proposed method based on naive voting, weighted voting and SVMs. Table 1 shows the experimental result[6].

As a result, our methods, namely multiple classifiers, outperformed single classifiers. Even the naive voting produced higher accuracy than these methods. This result shows the effectiveness of our method consisting of some classifiers.

---

[3] For example, the sentence "It is not good" is converted to "It is not NOT_good". As a result, we can treat a polarity reversal correctly.

[4] http://www.cs.jhu.edu/ brill/

[5] The reason is that there was no significant difference between the methods with the conditions and without the conditions. The same tendency was reported in the previous work.

[6] Note that the results of SVM and ME in this paper differ from the accuracy described in Pang et al. (2002). These accuracies were based on our implementation. We think that the reason is that (1) negation words that we used might be not completely same as the previous work and (2) the tool and the iterative scaling method for ME also differed from the method of the previous work.

Table 1. The experimental result

The method		Accuracy
Single	SVM	82.2%
	ME	80.5%
	Scoring	83.4%
Multi	Naive Voting	85.8%
	Weighted Voting	86.4%
	SVM	87.1%

In this experiment, the integration method with SVMs produced the best performance. For the weighted voting, we used the values computed beforehand from training data: l and m. If we tuned up these values optimally, the accuracy was 87.5%. This result denotes that the weighting process was one of the most important processes in the multiple classifier. The weighting process in this paper was a very simple weighting method. It was based on the average of distance obtained from a tentative dataset.

One approach to improve the accuracy is refinements to the weighting for the voting process. Boosting is one of the most famous techniques in ensemble learning methods (Freund and Schapier, 1996). We applied the boosting algorithm to the integration process. In the method, SVMs, Scoring and ME are weak learners for the boosting. However the accuracy was lower than SVMs and the weighted voting method. To improve the accuracy, we need to add other machine learning methods as weak learners. Furthermore, we need to consider other ensemble learning methods, such as Bagging (Breiman, 1996) and Random Forests (Breiman, 2001).

In this paper we used BOWs for the feature set of the classifiers. Matsumoto et al. (2005) have argued the significance of syntactic relations between words, that is frequent word subsequences and dependency sub-trees. For their experiment with the same dataset, using dependency sub-trees led to the improvement of the accuracy: the accuracy was 87.3%. Bai et al. (2004) have proposed a new method based on a two-stage Bayesian algorithm that is able to capture the dependencies among words. The accuracy of this method was 87.5%. Although the feature set for our method was very simple and naive (BOWs), the accuracy was equivalent as compared with these methods that used relations between words. Furthermore, since our method can incorporate other single classifiers flexibly, applying them as single classifiers boosts up the accuracy rate of our method.

We also need to handle the confidence of each classifier's output appropriately. In this paper we regarded the confidence computed from the output of a classifier as a linear function. However, Platt (1999) has reported a method to convert the output of SVMs into probability by using the sigmoid function and showed the effectiveness as a probability function. We need to consider a method for converting the output to the best suited confidence.

Next we explain a coverage rate of the proposed method. Our method can not classify a document into positive or negative correctly if every single classifier for the multiple classifier classifies it incorrectly. In other words, our method contains the possibility that it can classify a document correctly if a single classifier identifies the class label (p/n) of a document correctly. Therefore the coverage of our method for this dataset is computed as follows:

$$Coverage = \frac{CorrectNum}{N}$$

where N is the number of documents in test data. *CorrectNum* is the number of documents that are classified correctly by at least one classifier. The result is shown in Table 2. The coverage with three classifiers was 94.9% although the best accuracy in this experiment was

87.1% (See Table 1). This result shows that our method, namely a multiple classifier, can improve the classification accuracy essentially.

Table 2. The Coverage

Combination	Coverage
SVM + Scoring	91.6%
ME + Scoring	91.8%
SVM + ME	92.2%
SVM+ME+Scoring	94.9%

5. Conclusion

In this paper, we proposed a method to classify movie review documents into positive or negative opinions. The method consisted of three classifiers based on SVMs, ME and score calculation. We compared two voting process, naive voting and weighted voting, and the integration with SVMs for the method. Our methods consisting of three classifiers outperformed single classifiers. Even the naive voting produced higher accuracy than these classifiers. In this experiment, SVMs in the integration process produced the best performance. If we tuned up the weights for the voting method optimally, it obtained the best accuracy. Our future work includes (1) evaluation with the ensemble learning methods, (2) addition of other single classifiers and (3) use of other feature sets, such as dependency trees, for classifiers

References

Bai, X., R. Padman, and E. Airoldi. 2004. Sentiment extraction from unstructured text using tabu search-enhanced markov blanket. *Proceedings of the International Workshop on Mining for and from the Semantic Web (MSW2004)*.

Berger, A. L., S. A. Della Pietra, and V. J. Della Pietra. 1996. A maximum entropy approach to natural language processing. 22(1):39–71.

Breiman, L. 1996. Bagging predictors. *Machine Learning*, 24:123–140.

Breiman, L. 2001. Random forests. *Machine Learning*, 45:5–23.

Freund, Y. and R. E. Schapier. 1996. Experiments with a new boosting algorithm. *Proceedings of ICML*, pages 148–156.

Joachims, T. 1999. Transductive inference for text classification using support vector machines. *Proceedings of the Sixteenth International Conference on Machine Learning*, pages 200–209.

Kobayashi, N., R. Iida, K. Inui, and Y. Matsumoto. 2005. Opinion extraction using a learning-based anaphora resolution technique. *Proceedings of the Second International Joint Conference on Natural Language Processing (IJCNLP- 05)*, pp. 175–180.

Matsumoto, S., H. Takamura, and M. Okumura. 2005. Sentiment classification using word subsequences and dependency sub-trees. *Proceedings of the 9th Pacific-Asia International Conference on Knowledge Discovery and Data Mining (PAKDD-05)*, pp. 301–310.

Osajima, I., K. Shimada, and T. Endo. 2005. Classification of evaluative sentences using sequential patterns. *Proceedings of the 11nd Annual Meeting of The Association for Natural Language Processing (in Japanese)*.

Pang, B., L. Lee, and S. Vaithyanathan. 2002. Thumbs up? sentiment classification using machine learning techniques. *Proceedings of the Conference on Empirical Methods in Natural Language Processing (EMNLP)*, pp.79–86.

Platt, J. 1999. Probabilistic outputs for support vector machines and comparison to regularized likelihood methods. In B. Schoelkopf D. Schuurmans A.J. Smola, P. Bartlett, editor,

Advances in Large Margin Classifiers, pp. 61–74. MIT Press.

Tsutsumi, K., K. Shimada, and T. Endo. 2006. Sentiment classification using reliability of multiple classification results (in Japanese). In *SIG-FPAI-A601*, pp. 27–32.

Turney, P. D. 2002. Thumbs up? or thumbs down? semantic orientation applied to unsupervised classification of reviews. *Proceedings of the 40th Annual Meeting of the Association for Computational Linguistics*, pp. 417–424.

Vapnik, V. N. 1999. *Statistical Learning Theory*. Wiley.

Korean-Chinese Person Name Translation for Cross Language Information Retrieval[*]

Yu-Chun Wang[ab], Yi-Hsun Lee[a], Chu-Cheng Lin[ac],
Richard Tzong-Han Tsai[d*], Wen-Lian Hsu[a]

[a]Institute of Information Science, Academia Sinica, Taiwan
[b]Department of Electrical Engineering, National Taiwan University, Taiwan
[c]Department of Computer Science and Information Engineering, National Taiwan University, Taiwan
[d]Department of Computer Science and Engineering, Yuan Ze University, Taiwan

{albyu, rog, as1986}@iis.sinica.edu.tw
thtsai@saturn.yzu.edu.tw
hsu@iis.sinica.edu.tw
[*]corresponding author

Abstract. Named entity translation plays an important role in many applications, such as information retrieval and machine translation. In this paper, we focus on translating person names, the most common type of name entity in Korean-Chinese cross language information retrieval (KCIR). Unlike other languages, Chinese uses characters (ideographs), which makes person name translation difficult because one syllable may map to several Chinese characters. We propose an effective hybrid person name translation method to improve the performance of KCIR. First, we use Wikipedia as a translation tool based on the inter-language links between the Korean edition and the Chinese or English editions. Second, we adopt the Naver people search engine to find the query name's Chinese or English translation. Third, we extract Korean-English transliteration pairs from Google snippets, and then search for the English-Chinese transliteration in the database of Taiwan's Central News Agency or in Google. The performance of KCIR using our method is over five times better than that of a dictionary-based system. The mean average precision is 0.3490 and the average recall is 0.7534. The method can deal with Chinese, Japanese, Korean, as well as non-CJK person name translation from Korean to Chinese. Hence, it substantially improves the performance of KCIR.

Keywords: Person Name Translation, Korean-Chinese Cross Language Information Retrieval

1. Introduction

Named entity (NE) translation plays an important role in machine translation, information retrieval, and question answering. It is a particularly challenging task because, although there are many online bilingual dictionaries, they usually lack domain specific words or NEs. Furthermore, new NEs are generated everyday, but the content of bilingual dictionaries cannot be updated frequently. Therefore, it is necessary to construct a named entity translation (NET) system.

Economic ties between China and Korea have become closer as China has opened its markets further, and demand for the latest news and information from China continues to grow rapidly in Korea. One key way to meet this demand is to retrieve information written in Chinese by

---

using Korean queries, referred to as Korean-Chinese cross-language information retrieval (KCIR). The main challenge involves translating NEs because they are usually the main concepts of queries. In Chen (1998), the authors romanized Chinese NEs and selected their English transliterations from English NEs extracted from the Web by comparing their phonetic similarities with Chinese NEs. Al-Onaizan and Knight (2002) transliterated an NE in Arabic into several candidates in English and ranked the candidates by comparing their occurrences in several English corpora. In the above works, the target languages are alphabetic; however, in K-C translation, the target language is Chinese, which uses an ideographic writing system. Korean-Chinese NET is much more difficult than NET considered in previous works because, in Chinese, one syllable may map to tens or hundreds of characters. For example, if an NE written in Korean comprises three syllables, there may be thousands of translation candidates in Chinese.

In this paper, we focus on translating person names, and propose an effective hybrid method to improve the performance of our Korean-Chinese cross-language information retrieval system

2. Difficulties in Korean-Chinese Person Name Translation for IR

In this section, we discuss the phenomena observed in the transliteration of person names in Korean and Chinese. We begin with a brief review of the relationship between the Korean and Chinese languages.

Korean is an Altaic language, while Chinese is a Sino-Tibetan language; hence, their phonology and grammar are quite different. Due to a long history of contact with Chinese, Koreans adopted Chinese characters and incorporated a lot of Chinese vocabulary into their language. Chinese characters used in Korean are called "Hanja", and Chinese loanwords used in Korean are called Sino-Korean words.

The pronunciation of Hanja in Korean is very different from modern Chinese, Mandarin, because it follows the pronunciation of Middle Chinese; thus, it has not undergone many of the sound changes evident in modern Chinese, Interestingly, Song (2005) mentioned that over 52 percent of the words in the modern Korean vocabulary are Sino-Korean

In 1443, Koreans invented their own alphabetic writing system called "Hangul". Each Hanja character has a corresponding Hangul character based on its Korean pronunciation. However, Hanja is only used in some limited domains now.

2.1.Korean Name Translation

Korean and Chinese name systems are very similar. Because of historical links, almost all Koreans have names that are exclusively Hanja (Han- "Chinese, "-ja "characters"). Therefore, the most straightforward way to translate a Korean name into Chinese is to adopt its Hanja equivalent. Take the Korean president's name "노무현" (No Mu-Hyeon) as an example. In this case, we can adopt the Hanja equivalent "盧武鉉" (Lu Wu-Xuan) directly. However, if a Korean's Hanja name is unknown, the name is translated character by character. Each Hangul character is basically translated into its corresponding Hanja character. For example, the name of the Korean actor "조인성" (Cho In-Seong) is usually translated as "趙仁成" because '조' is mapped to '趙', '인' is mapped to '仁', and '성' is mapped to '成'. However, that translation may not be the same as the actor's Hanja name. In addition, some Hangul characters do not have corresponding Chinese characters, so Chinese characters with similar pronunciations are used to translate the Hangul characters. Take the Korean actress "김하늘" (Kim Ha-Neul) for example. Her given name "하늘" ("ha-neul" meaning "sky") is a native Korean word that has no corresponding Hanja characters. We use "荷娜" (He-Na) or "哈嫩" (Ha-Nen), which have similar pronunciations to translate "하늘" (ha-neul). These examples show that there may be many Chinese translations for a Korean name. This phenomenon makes Korean-Chinese information retrieval more difficult because reporters usually use one or two common translations to write articles. However, we cannot guarantee that our translations are the most common ones.

2.2. Chinese Name Translation

To translate a Chinese person name written in Korean, we consider two ways that are used to translate a Chinese person name into spoken Korean. The first method uses Sino-Korean pronunciation. For example, consider the name "馬英九" (Ma Ying-Jiu, the ex-chairman of the Kuomintang (KMT), a Taiwanese political party); its Sino-Korean pronunciation is "마영구" (Ma Yeong-Gu). However, in recent years, Koreans have started to transliterate a Chinese person name based on its Mandarin pronunciation. Therefore, the name "馬英九" is transliterated to "마잉주" (Ma Ing-Ju). Translating Chinese person names by either method is a major challenge because one Hangul character corresponds to several Chinese characters that have the same pronunciation in Korean. This results in thousands of possible combinations of Chinese characters, making it very difficult to choose the right one. Therefore, we must develop different techniques to find the correct Chinese translation that is used in articles.

2.3. Japanese Name Translation

Chinese and Korean use different strategies to translate Japanese person names. Korean transliterates a Japanese person name into Hangul characters based on the name's pronunciation in Japanese, whereas, Chinese speakers use the name in Kanji directly. Take the Japanese ex-premier "小泉純一郎" (Koizumi Junichiro) for example. In Korean, his name is transliterated into "고이즈미 준이치로" (Ko-i-jeu-mi Jun-i-chi-ro). In contrast, the Kanji name "小泉純一郎" (Xiao quan chun yi lang) is used directly in Chinese. Therefore, it is very difficult to translate Japanese names written in Korean into Chinese based on phonetic information.

2.4. Non-CJK Name Translation

In both Korean and Chinese, transliteration methods are used to translate non-CJK person names. Korean uses the Hangul alphabet for transliteration. Because of the phonology of Korean, some phonemes are changed during translation because the language lacks such phonemes as described in Oh (2003) In contrast, Chinese transliterates each syllable in a name into Chinese characters with similar pronunciation. Although there are some conventions for selecting transliteration characters, there are still many possible alternatives. For instance, Greenspan has several Chinese transliterations, such as "葛林斯班" (Ge-lin-si-ban) and "葛林斯潘" (Ge-lin-si-pan). In summary, it is difficult to match a non-CJK person name transliterated from Korean with its Chinese transliteration due to the latter's variations. However, this task is the key to retrieving Chinese articles by using Korean queries.

3. Our Method

We now describe our Korean-Chinese person name/NE translation method for dealing with the problems described in Section 2. We either translate NE candidates from Korean into Chinese directly, or translate them into English first and then into Chinese.

3.1. Named Entity Selection

The first step is to identify which words in a query are NEs. In general, Korean queries are composed of several eojeols, each of which is composed of a noun followed by the noun's postposition, or a verb stem followed by the verb's ending. We remove the postposition or the ending to extract the key terms, and then select person name candidates from the key terms. Next, the maximum matching algorithm is applied to further segment each term into words in the Korean-Chinese bilingual dictionary[1]. If a segment's length is equal to one, the term is regarded as an NE candidate to be translated.

3.2. Using Wikipedia for Translation

Wikipedia is a multilingual online encyclopedia comprised of content written by volunteers all over the world. Unlike traditional encyclopedias, the number of articles in Wikipedia increases rapidly, and each article usually lists hyperlinks to other relevant content. Currently, Wikipedia is available in 252 languages. It is a highly consistent, human-made corpus.

Each article in Wikipedia has an inter-language link to other language editions, which we exploit to translate NEs. An NE candidate is first input to the Korean Wikipedia, and the title of the matched article's Chinese version is treated as the NE's translation in Chinese. However, if the article lacks a Chinese version, we use the English edition's version to acquire the NE's translation in English. The English translation is then transliterated into Chinese by the method described in Section 3.5.

3.3. Using the Naver People Search Engine for Translation

The Naver people search engine is a translation tool that maintains a database of famous people's basic profiles. If the person is from China, Japan, or Korea, the search engine returns his/her name in Chinese. For example, if we input the Japanese actor's name "사나다 히로유키" (Sanada Hiroyuki) to the Naver people search engine, it will return his Japanese name "真田広之" with Chinese characters. In such cases, we can adopt the retrieved name directly. However, for other nationalities, the Naver search engine returns person names in English, and we have to translate them into Chinese. The translation method is also described in Section 3.5.

3.4. Web-Based Korean-English Transliterations

Obviously, the above methods cannot cover all possible translations used in newspaper articles. Therefore, we propose a web-based transliteration method. First, each NE candidate, NEC, is input to Google to retrieve snippets of relevant documents in the first ten pages. Second, we use the following template to extract the NEC's English translation from the snippets.

$$NEC_K(e_1e_2e_3...e_n),$$

where NEC_K represents the NEC in Hangul characters and $e_i \in$ English alphabet. The string $e_1e_2e_3...e_n$ is regarded as the NEC's English translation. In Section 3.5, we describe the method used to further transliterate an NEC's English translation into Chinese.

3.5. Searching English-Chinese Transliteration in the CNA Database and Google

In this section, we discuss two methods that we use to transliterate English names generated by the above Korean-English translation methods into Chinese. The first obtains the Chinese translations of English names from Taiwan's Central News Agency (CNA) database[2], which stores all the transliterations used by CNA since 1954. The second method exploits the Web to extract other possible Chinese transliterations not available in the CNA database. The latter have a significant influence on IR's performance. The English name NECE is also input to Google and snippets are extracted from the first 10 returned pages. Then, we use the following template to extract the Chinese translation:

$$w_{boundary}c_1c_2c_3...c_m(NEC_E),$$

---

[1] http://cndic.daum.net
[2] http://client.cna.com.tw/name/

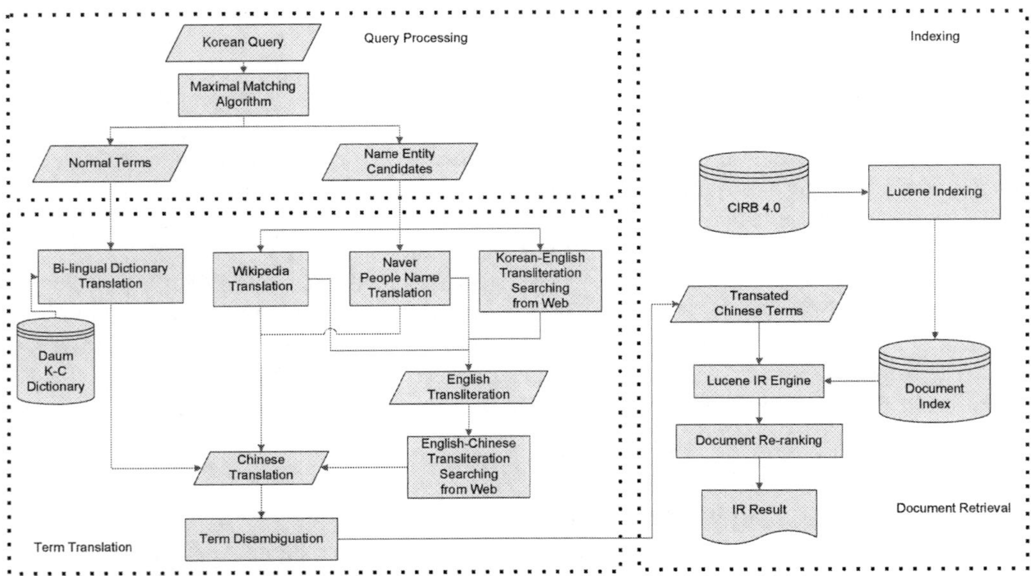

Figure 1: System Architecture of our CLIR system

where $w_{boundary}$ represents boundary words such as punctuation, titles, occupations, or nationalities; and $c_i \in$ Chinese characters. The string $c_1c_2c_3...c_m$ is regarded as the NEC_E's Chinese translation.

4. System Description

We construct a Korean-Chinese cross language information retrieval (KCIR) system to determine how our person name translation methods affect KCIR's performance. A Korean query is translated into Chinese and then used to retrieve Chinese documents, as shown in Figure 1. The following are the four stages of our KCIR system.

4.1. Query Processing

First, the postposition or verb ending in each eojeol is removed. Then, NE candidates are selected using the method described in Section 3.1.

4.2. Query Translation

Key terms not selected as NE candidates are sent to the online Daum Korean-Chinese dictionary to get their Chinese translations, while NE candidates are translated into Chinese by the methods described in Sections 3.2 - 3.5. The Daum Korean-Chinese dictionary is written in simplified Chinese, as are many pages in Chinese Wikipedia. We use the conversion tool provided by Microsoft .Net Framework to convert simplified Chinese characters into traditional Chinese characters.

4.3. Term Disambiguation

A Hangul word may have many meanings. For instance, the word "이상" has four meanings: "理想" (ideal), "以上" (above), "異常" (unusual), and "異狀" (indisposition) because these four Sino-Korean words are written as the same Hangul word. This phenomenon causes ambiguity during information retrieval. To solve the problem, we adopt the mutual information score (MI score) to evaluate the co-relation between a translation candidate tc_{ij} for a term qt_i and all translation candidates for all the other terms in Q; tc_{ij}'s MI score given Q is calculated as follows:

$$\text{MI score}(tc_{ij} \mid Q) = \sum_{x=1, x \neq i}^{|Q|} \sum_{y=1}^{Z(qt_x)} \frac{\Pr(tc_{ij}, tc_{xy})}{\Pr(tc_{ij}) \Pr(tc_{xy})},$$

where $Z(qt_x)$ is the number of translation candidates of the x-th query term qt_x; tc_{xy} is y-th translation candidate for qt_x; $\Pr(tc_{ij}, tc_{xy})$ is the probability that tc_{ij} and tc_{xy} co-occur in the same sentence; and $\Pr(tc_{ij})$ is the probability of tc_{ij}. Only the translation candidate with the highest score is used for retrieval.

4.4. Document Indexing and Retrieval Model

We use the Lucene information retrieval engine to index all documents and the bigram index based on Chinese characters. The Okapi BM25 function described in Robertson (1996) is used to score a retrieved document's relevance. The function is

$$\sum_{T \in Q} w \frac{(k_1 + 1) \, tf \, (k_3 + 1) \, qtf}{(K + tf)(k_3 + qtf)} + k_2 \cdot |Q| \cdot \frac{avdl - dl}{avdl + dl},$$

where Q is a query containing term T; w is the Robertson-Sparck Jones weight described in Robertson (1988); K is $k_1((1-b)+b \cdot dl/avdl)$; k_1, b, k_2, and k_3 are parameters whose values are set to 3, 1, 3, and 0.3 respectively; tf is the term frequency within a specific document, and qtf is the term frequency within the topic from which Q was derived; dl is the document length; and $avdl$ is the average document length.

In addition, we employ the following document re-ranking function described in (Yang et al., 2007):

$$\sqrt{\frac{\left(\sum_{i=1}^{K} df(t, d_i) \times f(i)\right) / K}{DF(t, C) / R}} \times \sqrt{|t|} \qquad df(t, d_i) = \begin{cases} 1 & t \notin d_i \\ 0 & t \in d_i \end{cases},$$

where d_i is the ith document; R is the total number of documents in the collection C; $DF(t,C)$ is the number of documents containing a term t in C; and $|t|$ is t's length, $f(i)=1/\text{sqrt}(i)$.

5. Evaluation and Analysis

To evaluate our KCIR system, we use the topic collection and document collection of the NTCIR-5 and NTCIR-6 CLIR tasks. The document collection is the Chinese Information Retrieval Benchmark (CIRB) 4.0, which contains news articles published in four Taiwanese newspapers from 2000 to 2001. The topics have four fields: title, description, narration, and concentrate words. We select 18 topics containing person names and use the title field as the input query because it is similar to the queries input to search engines. The nationalities of the person names in the 18 topics are shown in Table 1.

Table 1: Nationalities of Person Names

Nationality	Count
Chinese	2
Japanese	4
Korean	4
non-CJK	9

Table 2: Evaluation Results

Run	MAP		Recall	
	Rigid	Relax	Rigid	Relax
baseline	0.0491	0.0671	0.2765	0.2834
baseline + Wikipedia	0.1112	0.1443	0.4570	0.4578
baseline + person name translation	**0.2835**	**0.3490**	**0.7382**	**0.7534**
Google translation	0.1048	0.1312	0.4837	0.4893
Chinese monolingual	0.2698	0.3396	0.7708	0.7882

We construct five runs as follows:
- **Baseline**: using a Korean-Chinese dictionary-based translation.
- **Baseline + Wikipedia only**: the baseline system plus the Wikipedia translation.
- **Baseline + Person Name Translation Methods**: the baseline system plus our translation methods, namely, Wikipedia, the Naver people search engine, and web-based transliteration.
- **Google Translation**: using the Google translation tool.
- **Chinese monolingual**: using the Chinese versions of the 18 topics given by NTCIR directly.

We use the Mean Average Precision (MAP) and Recall in Saracevic (1988) to evaluate the performance of IR. NTCIR provides two kinds of relevance judgments: Rigid and Relax. A document is rigid-relevant if it is highly relevant to the topic; and relax-relevant if it is highly relevant or partially relevant to the topic.

The evaluation results demonstrate that our method improves KCIR substantially, as its performance is more than five times better than that of the baseline system. Interestingly, it is even better than Chinese monolingual IR. Wikipedia translation improves the performance, but not markedly because Wikipedia cannot cover some names. Google translation is not very satisfactory either, since many person names cannot be translated correctly. In the following, we analyze why our method can improve the overall performance and handle difficult cases. We also explain why the IR system with our person name translation method performs better than Chinese monolingual IR.

5.1. Effectiveness of Wikipedia

Wikipedia is a useful tool for translating famous person names. In our topics, names like "김대중" (Kim Dae-jung, South Korea's ex-president), "김정일" (Kim Jong-il, North Korea's leader), "주룽지" (Zhu Rong-ji, China's ex-premier), and "빈라덴" (Osama bin Laden) are all translated correctly by Wikipedia and improve the performance of IR. In addition to person names, Wikipedia is also very useful for translating other kinds of NEs.

5.2. Effectiveness of the Naver People Search Engine

We observe that names, especially Japanese and some non-CJK person names, can be successfully translated by the Naver people search engine; for example, "코엔" (William Cohen, the ex-Secretary of Defense of U.S.) and "이치로" (Ichiro Suzuki, a Japanese baseball player). Therefore, the Naver search engine is effective for KCIR.

5.3. Effectiveness of Web-based Korean-English Transliteration

Our web-based method can successfully translate most non-CJK names that cannot be found in Wikipedia or the Naver people search engine. For example, our template can extract the following non-CJK names from Google snippets successfully: "제니퍼 카프리아티" (Jennifer Capriati, the American tennis player), "데니스 티토" (Dennis Tito, the first space tourist), and "웬호 리" (Wen-ho Lee, the American scientist who stole nuclear secrets for China).

5.4.Effectiveness of Searching English-Chinese transliteration

All English names generated by the Naver people search or derived by Korean-English web-based transliteration can be successfully transliterated into Chinese by our English-Chinese transliteration method. Notably, our method can extract a larger number of possible Chinese transliterations. Take "Tito" for example: its six common Chinese transliterations: "迪托" (di-tuo), "蒂托" (di-tuo), "帝托" (di-tuo), "提托" (ti-tuo), "提多" (ti-duo), and "狄托" (di-tuo) can be extracted by our approach. This result is similar to that derived by query expansion. Under our method, the rigid MAP of this topic achieves 0.8361, which is much better than that of the same topic in the Chinese monolingual run (0.4459) because the Chinese topic has only one transliteration "帝托" (di-tuo).

5.5.Error Analysis

Person names that cannot be translated correctly can be divided into two categories. The first contains names not selected as NE candidates. The two Japanese person names "후지모리" (Alberto Fujimori, Peru's ex-president) and "모리" (Yoshiro Mori, the ex-premier of Japan) are in this category. In the name "후지모리" (Fujimori), the first two characters "후지" (hind legs) and the last two characters "모리" (profiting) are Sino-Korean words, so the name is regarded as a compound word, not an NE. The Japanese surname "모리" (Mori) is the same because it is also a Sino-Korean word.

The other category contains names with few relevant web pages, like the two non-CJK names "홀링스위스" (Holingswiss) and "안토니오 토디" (Antonio Toddy). We can only obtain a few relevant web documents from web sites related to NTCIR. This means that, except for NTCIR, these names do not appear in any of the web documents maintained by Google. They might be a error transliteration or very obscure.

6. Conclusion

In this paper, we describe the difficulties that arise in translating person names from Korean to Chinese for IR. We propose a hybrid method for Korean-Chinese person name translation that exploits Wikipedia, the Naver people search engine, and the Google search engine. To evaluate our method, we use the topic and document collection of the NTCIR CLIR task. Our method's performance on KCIR is over five times better than that of a dictionary-based translation system. Moreover, its average MAP score is 0.3490, which is even better than that of the Chinese monolingual IR system. The proposed method can deal with Chinese, Japanese, Korean, as well as non-CJK person name translation. Hence, it substantially improves the performance of KCIR.

References

Al-Onaizan, Y. and K. Knight. 2002. Translating Named Entities Using Monolingual and Bilingual Resources. *Proceedings of the 40th Annual Meeting of the Association of Computational Linguistics*, pp. 400-408.

Chen, H.-H., S.-J. Huang, Y.-W. Ding and S.-C. Tsai. 1998. Proper Name Translation in Cross-Language Information Retrieval. *Proceedings of 17th COLING and 36th ACL*, pp. 232-236.

Oh, M. 2003. English Fricatives in Loanword Adaption. *Explorations in Korean Language and Linguistics*, pp. 471-87.

Robertson, S.E. and K.S. Jones. 1988. Relevance Weighting of Search Terms. *Taylor Graham Series In Foundations Of Information Science*, 143-160.

Robertson, S.E., S. Walker, M. Beaulieu, M. Gatford and A. Payne. 1996. Okapi at TREC-4. *Proceedings of the Fourth Text Retrieval Conference*, pp. 73-97.

Saracevic, T., P. Kantor, A. Y. Chamis and D. Trivison. 1988. A Study of Information Seeking and Retrieving. *Journal of the American Society for Information Science*, 39(3),161-76.

Song, J. J. 2005. The Korean Language Structure, use and context. Oxon: Routledge.

Yang, L., D. Ji and M. Leong. 2007. Document reranking by term distribution and maximal marginal relevance for Chinese information retrieval. *Information Processing and Management*, 43(2), 315-26.

Research on a Model of Extracting Persons' Information Based on Statistic Method and Conceptual Knowledge[*]

XiangFeng Wei[a], Ning Jia[a,b], Quan Zhang[a], HanFen Zang[c]

[a]Institute of Acoustics, Chinese Academy of Sciences, China
[b]Graduate University of Chinese Academy of Sciences, China
[c]Captical University of Economics and Business, China
{wxf, zhq}@mail.ioa.ac.cn, gnin_aij@sina.com, zanghf@163.com

Abstract. In order to extract some important information of a person from text, an extracting model was proposed. The person's name is recognized based on the maximal entropy statistic model and the training corpus. The sentences surrounding the person's name are analyzed according to the conceptual knowledge base. The three main elements of events, domain, situation and background, are also extracted from the sentences to construct the structure of events about the person.

Keywords: Person's Name Recognition; Hierarchical Network of Concepts; Main Elements of Events; Semantic Parsing; Information Extraction

1. Introduction

In news reports, person is one of the most important elements. On the internet politicians, famous enterprisers, celebrities and hot persons are always the focus what people want to know. It would be very useful and valuable to compile and extract the information about a person with the assistance of using automatic information extraction technology. ACE (Automatic Content Extraction) program is organized by NIST (National Institute of Standards and Technology, U.S.A). It is aimed to develop automatic content extraction technology to support automatic processing of human language in text form, including the detection and recognition of entity, value, time, relation and event. In the description of events, ACE defined the allowable roles of an event, such as person, place, position, etc. Persou, which is studied by Liu and etc. (2006), is a web search engine for searching persons' information. It can distinguish automatically or semi-automatically the persons who own the same name, and produce their resume and activities. A fame evaluation system studied by Zan and etc. (2003) can calculate the correlative degree between the basic information such as name, specialty, affiliation, character words of a person and the information of a web page. If the count of the strong correlative web pages is greater than a threshold, the relative person will be a famous person. In above studies, they all adopted statistic method. The advantage of using statistic models is high efficient performance

[*] This work is supported by the National Basic Research Program of China (973 Program, the contract No. 2004CB318104) and the Fund for Excellence by the Director of the Institute of Acoustics, Chinese Academy of Sciences (the contract No. GS13SJJ04).

to process large-scale data, but the precision is restricted by training set and it is not suitable to process sparse individual data, although the data is very important to the user.

This paper proposed an model of information extraction based on statistic algorithm and conceptual semantic knowledge to extract persons' information from the text. The primary information of a person includes name, gender, age, nationality, department in organization, career, title, and so on. The name of a person was recognized by using maximal entropy statistic model. The text around the name was analyzed based on conceptual model. According to some associated key words about the primary information, the information was extracted from the context. If there are some events in the text, the main elements of events will be extracted based on the conceptual structures of a sentences and the conceptual knowledge base, which was stored in computer in advance.

2. The model of extracting persons' information

Figure 1 shows the whole process of extracting a person's name, his or her primary information and events about a person. In this process, recognizing persons' names is one of the key sub-processes. In order to recognize a person's name, there must be some tagged texts which indicate the right persons' names. In the tagged texts, the contexts around the names present some statistic characters. Therefore, recognizing a person's name was transformed into classifying a word belongs to a name or not. This paper focused on Chinese names. A Chinese name is composed of two parts. The first part is family name and the second is given name. Most family names are limited in about 100 Chinese characters. These characters are used to activate persons' names. The Chinese character (one or two) behind the family will be considered as candidates of a person's name. A classifier can divide all candidates into name or non-name according to the statistic model based on the tagged texts.

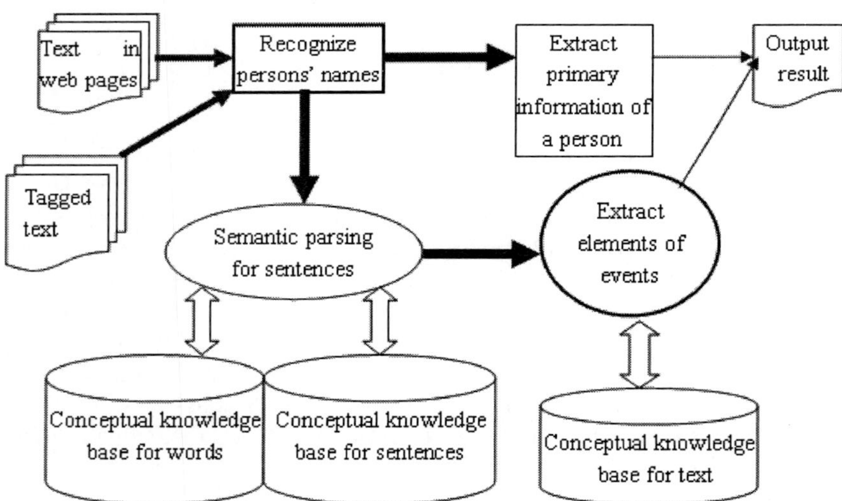

Figure 1: The model of extracting persons' information.

Once a person's name is recognized, the surrounding sentences will be analyzed to extract the primary information and the events about the person. To extract the primary information of a person, there are some activating words to point out the information. For example, 'he' pointed to a person's name indicates that the person's gender is male, and 'president' points out the person's title. To extract the information of events about the person, we must analyze the related sentences at first. All sentences are mapped into the conceptual structures, and the main elements of events are extracted from text based on conceptual knowledge bases. There are three kinds of conceptual knowledge bases for words, sentences, and text respectively, as showed in figure 1.

3. Recognition of Chinese names

The maximal entropy model is a well adaptive, flexible, and high-efficient statistic model. It can synthetically process all kinds of related and irrelated characters from data. The key point of the model is fitting the known data and equably distributing the unknown data. To apply the maximal entropy model, the restricted condition is described as an character function f(a,b) {0,1} with alternative value. For example, a function to judge whether a noun is name is described as formula (1).

$$f(a,b) = \begin{cases} 1 & (a=\mathrm{Pr}\,esident\,)\cap(b==Noun\,), \\ 0 & otherwise. \end{cases} \qquad (1)$$

For a character function, its expectation relative to the experiential probability is calculated as formula (2).

$$E_{\tilde{p}} f_i = \sum_{a,b} \tilde{p}(a,b) f_i(a,b). \qquad (2)$$

Its expectation relative to the model is calculated as formula (3).

$$E_p f_i = \sum_{a,b} \tilde{p}(b) p(a \mid b) f_i(a,b). \qquad (3)$$

In the training data set, the two expectation are assumed to be equal as formula (4).

$$E_p f_i = E_{\tilde{p}} f_i. \qquad (4)$$

If there is more than one restricted condition, a classifying problem will be changed into working out the optimized answer as formula (5).

$$P = \{p \mid E_p f_i = E_{\tilde{p}} f, i = 1,2,4\ ,k\},$$
$$p^* = \arg\max_{p \in P} H(p). \qquad (5)$$

The optimized answer is showed as formula (6) by using Lagrangian arithmetic.

$$p^*(a \mid b) = \frac{1}{\pi(b)} \exp\left(\sum_{i=1}^{k} \lambda_i f_i(a,b) \right),$$
$$\pi(b) = \sum_{a} \exp\left(\sum_{i=1}^{k} \lambda_i f_i(a,b) \right). \qquad (6)$$

λ_i is the parameter of the statistic model. It can be worked out by learning from the training data set. If λ_i is known, the probability distributing function can also be worked out.

The character function is very important for maximal entropy model. It is also an advantage of the maximal model because the flexible configuration of character functions can make full use of all kinds of information to improve the performance. To recognize Chinese names in text, a

Chinese character used as surname or given name, a word (contains one or two Chinese characters) used as given name, and Chinese characters used as non-name are all useful information to construct character functions in the maximal entropy model. When a Chinese character in surname character set does not act as a person's name, it often acts as a word by combining with the Chinese character before or behind it. So a word, which is composed of two or more Chinese characters but not act name, should appear frequently in the training text set. It is useful information to construct character functions. There are sixteen character functions in our maximal entropy model to recognize Chinese names.

The first step of recognizing a person's is selecting a rough name candidate set according to Chinese surname character set and the useful context. Secondly, non-name and name was divided by the maximal entropy model. The third, the probability of one Chinese Character as given name and two Chinese characters as given name are both calculated. If the maximal probability is greater than a threshold δ, the name candidate is considered as a person's name. The training set is the text in People's Daily (a newspaper of China), January 1-20, 1998. The rest text in the newspaper January, 1998 was selected as test set. There are total 1,932,693 Chinese characters and 8,670 person's names in the training set. In test set there are total 1,056,961 Chinese characters and 6909 person's names. With different δ in the maximal entropy model, there were different result data as in Table 1.

Table 1: The result of recognizing persons' names with different δ

	$\delta = 0.3$	$\delta = 0.4$	$\delta = 0.5$	$\delta = 0.6$
Accurate names	6392	6341	6241	5984
Inaccurate names	2903	1588	1492	765
Σ	9295	7929	7733	6749
Precision rate (%)	68.77	79.97	80.71	88.66
Recall rate (%)	92.52	91.78	90.33	86.61

In table 1, the item 'Σ' means the total number of the recognized persons' names by the system. The item 'Recall rate' in table 1 is the percent of accurate names in the actual persons' names (the total number is 6909), which were tagged by human being.

4. Parsing sentences with conceptual model

It is hypothesized that there is only one linguistic conceptual space in human brain, which can be mapped from more than 6,000 languages in the world. This linguistic conceptual space is divided into four layers: conceptual primitives, semantic categories of sentences (SCs), contextual elements and contexts, by Huang (2004). They can be mapped from words, sentences, sentence group and article respectively. In our practice, the linguistic conceptual space is based on a redesigned symbolic system for classifying concepts. Most concepts are distinguished by two kinds of concepts: concrete and abstract. Some concepts are between them. The concrete concepts are material, such as people and the objects in the nature. The abstract concepts are not visible and touchable. The abstract concepts are described from five properties: dynamic(v), static(g), attribute(u), value(z), result(r).

Action-Effect chain is the groundwork of the symbolic system of concepts. The most essential fundamental relationship between two concepts is action. The action brings on an effect, and the effect creates a new action, the new action brings on a new effect. It is a timeless repeating process. It is called Action-Effect chain, by Huang (1998). Based on the Action-Effect chain, a hierarchical symbolic network of primitive concepts is established. The symbols are associated each other through conceptual relations. Any word can be explained by the primitive concepts or their compounding. For example, the mapped conceptual symbol from the word '*think*' is 'v80', and the mapped conceptual symbol from the word '*idea*' is 'r80'. The close relation between the two words is uncovered by the common symbol '80', as their relation in the fixed phrase '*think an idea*'. So the conceptual relationship between two words can be expressed perspicuously by the symbols.

Starting with the Action-Effect chain, some primitive concepts are attached to the primitive SCs. The most essential fundamental SCs are action, process, transfer, effect, relation, state and judgment. They are the primitives of the semantic category of a sentence (SC). The compound SC is mixed by two primitive SCs. Under a conceptual semantic parsing model, all sentences can be mapped into the SCs. For example, the sentence '*They **have also continued**, in the practice of historical activities and by making comparisons, **to seek, reveal and develop** the truth that guides their advance.*' is a complex sentence with more verbs. The head meaning of the sentence lies on the verbs '***seek, reveal and develop***'. According to the head verbs, the sentence is mapped into the compound SC mixed by action SC and effect SC. A SC is constructed of the main semantic chunks whose number and properties are transcendental in the linguistic conceptual space. The main semantic chunks are divided into two kinds of semantic chunks. One is eigen semantic chunk (EK); the other is generalized object semantic chunk (GBK). EK is corresponded with the characteristic parts of a sentence, like the head verbs '***seek, reveal and develop***' in the example sentence. GBK are corresponded with the objects what the sentence describes, as the subject or object in a sentence, like '*they*' or '*the truth*' in the example sentence.

In order to get the right SC of a sentence, the approach of 'Hypothesis Testing' is adopted. When parsing a sentence, the parser firstly hypothesized the EK according to some special concepts. The second, the SC of a sentence is hypothesized according to the EK. The third, the parser tests the hypothesized SC and its structure according to the words in the sentence and the conceptual knowledge base in the computer. If all semantic chunks in the sentence are corresponded with the transcendental concepts in the conceptual knowledge base, the SC is confirmed. Otherwise, the SC is rejected.

5. Extracting the main elements of an event

After parsing the semantic conceptual structure of a sentence, it is possible to parse the semantic conceptual structure of text. Because text is made up of sentences, parsing the text must be constructed on the results of parsing sentences. Besides the name, the primary information of a person includes gender, age, title, career, etc. Sometimes they appear in the sentences near the person's name. For example, the male role is often surrounded with 'he', 'his', 'boy', 'man' and so on. After recognizing the person's name, the sentences (usually from 3 to 5 sentences) near the name were selected to find out the associated words like 'he'. Then the pattern or structure extracted from the sentences will be matched to the pattern which is abstracted from the training set according name and associated words. If the patterns are matched, the information attached the pattern will be extracted.

When extracting the main elements of an even, it is more difficult because the relationships between the main elements are not a simple co-occurrence model. For an event, the main elements include time, location, people, process, state etc. The main elements are distributed in the text. They can be well organized into a story by human brain. To extract the main elements of an event and their relationships in text by computer, we consider that the essential main elements of an event include: domain, situation, and background.

Domain is the most basic information of the context in sentence group. It describes any activity about human being. The categories of domain is classified according to the first kind of extended concept primitive and the second kind of extended concept primitive in the conceptual symbolic system. Domain also includes instinctive activities, disaster, and state. Situation is the dynamic description of an event. It indicates the semantic relationships between the participants of an event. Background describes the subjective and objective conditions of an event. Background is divided into two. One is the background of the event; the other is the background of the narrator. The background of the event mainly includes the source of text, language type, date, time, location etc. The background of the narrator mainly includes the age, nationality, standpoint etc.

In order to extract the main elements in text, it is necessary to cut the text into sentences and then analyze the semantic chunks of the sentences (details in section 4). Domain information is implicated in the conceptual concepts of some words. It is convenient to extract the domain information from the semantic chunks which is made up of words. If more than one semantic chunk contain domain information, which domain should be extracted? There is a principle to tackle this problem. Because the station and significance of semantic chunks in a sentence is different, domain information in different semantic chunks possesses different priority. The priority is revealed as the following: Eg>El>C>B or A[1]. Different domains also possess their own priorities. If there are more than one domain to be selected in different sentences, the highest priority domain will be selected. After affirming domain, a SC expression with domain can also be confirmed according to the conceptual knowledge base. Based on the SC expression with domain, the framework units of situation can be constructed. The framework unit of situation must be described as the following: EK name[EK conceptual symbol] | GBKm name[GBK conceptual symbol], the value of m is from 1 to 3. If the same EK or GBK appears in different sentences, the framework units of situation must be combined according to the sequence of appearance. In general, the background is extracted from the supplemental semantic chunks, such as time supplemental semantic chunks, space supplemental semantic chunks, and so on.

By processing the text sentence by sentence, all sentences are mapped into conceptual symbols and the structure of a semantic category. Domain, situation and background are extracted from the conceptual symbols and semantic chunks. To affirm the domain of text, there is also a 'Hypothesis Testing' algorithm. Hypothesizing the domain of text, and then the domain will be tested by the conceptual knowledge base for text. If the conceptual symbols of the sentences are matched to the knowledge base, the domain will be affirmed. Once domain is affirmed, it is easy to construct situation and background according conceptual knowledge base.

6. Conclusion

As an automatic or semi-automatic technology of information processing, information extraction especially web information extraction will be applied into wider fields in our lives. Information extraction is aimed to retrieve the entities and their relationships, the content of special templates and events in text by establishing pattern, domain knowledge, tagged corpus and statistic model. The accuracy of the recognition of named entities is beyond 70%, and the accuracy of the recognition of events seems stuck at 50%-60% (see URL: http://www.cs. cmu.edu/~ref/mlim/chapter3.html). In this paper, an approach of recognizing Chinese name based on the maximal entropy was proposed and the performance is at about 80% precision and 90% recall. In order to extract the primary information of a person and the events from text, the surrounding sentences near the person's name are analyzed into semantic conceptual structures based on a conceptual symbolic system and the conceptual knowledge base. With the 'Hypothesis Testing' algorithm, which is used in analyzing sentences and texts, the main elements of an event are extracted into a semantic framework, which contains domain, situation, and background. We have manually annotated a Chinese corpus, which contains about 350 thousand Chinese characters, for extracting name, gender, title, and events of a person. We are studying how to describe the information and the events in Web Ontology Language (OWL) and improve the performance of extracting persons' information with combining statistic training model and conceptual knowledge.

---

[1] Eg is a kind of EK, which lies on the top layer of a sentence. El is a kind of EK, which lies on the clause or phrase in a sentence. C, B and A are GBKs in a sentence, C means the Content, B means the oBject, and A means the Actor.

References

Huang ZengYang. 1998. *The Theory of Hierarchical Network of Concept*, Tsinghua University Press, Beijing, China, 6-9.

Huang ZengYang. 2004. *The Basic Theorem and Mathematic and Physical Expression in Lingual Concept Space*, Ocean Press, Beijing, China,. 9-10.

Liu Yue, HongBo Xu and XueQi Chen. 2006. The Progress of Researches on Web Mining and Search. *Proceedings of the Academic Conference for 25th Anniversary of Chinese Information Processing Society of China*, pp.18-33.

URL: *http://www.cs.cmu.edu/ ~ref/mlim/chapter3.html*

Zan HongYing, YuMei Su, Bin Sun and ShiWen Yu. 2003. The WebPages Relevance Research Based on the Shallow Parsing. *Proceedings of the 2003 National Joint Symposium on Computational Linguistics of China*, pp. 501-506.

Text Categorization for Authorship based on the Features of Lingual Conceptual Expression[*]

Quan Zhang[a], Yun-liang Zhang[a,b], and Yi Yuan[a]

[a] The Institute of Acoustics, CAS, Beijing 100080, P. R. China
[b] Institute of Scientific & Technical Information of China, Beijing 100038, P. R. China

{zhq, yuan}@mail.ioa.ac.cn

Abstract. The text categorization is an important field for the automatic text information processing. Moreover, the authorship identification of a text can be treated as a special text categorization. This paper adopts the conceptual primitives' expression based on the Hierarchical Network of Concepts (HNC) theory, which can describe the words meaning in hierarchical symbols, in order to avoid the sparse data shortcoming that is aroused by the natural language surface features in text categorization. The KNN algorithm is used as computing classification element. Then, the experiment has been done on the Chinese text authorship identification. The experiment result gives out that the processing mode that is put forward in this paper achieves high correct rate, so it is feasible for the text authorship identification.

Keywords: Lingual Conceptual Space, Hierarchical Network of Concepts (HNC) theory, Text Categorization, KNN Algorithm, Authorship of a text.

1. Introduction

Along with the progress of social information industry, especially with the Internet development, more and more documents exist in the electronic form. It provides convenience for information automatic processing. The text categorization is the basic work for the automatic processing, and it is the foundation for the information retrieval, information mining, and question-answer system too.

In some applications, it is need to identify the text authorship. The identification need use the documents written by the author as reference. Since the literary style of an author is relatively steady in some time, if we can mine the style character of the author then the identification is realized. Of course, the more documents which are gathered, the better result which is achieved. In many cases, the text authorship identification is treated as text categorization as the researchers can accomplish the work according the text categorization way. In this way, the frequency of glossary, punctuation, n-Gram string, syntax feature, average sentence length, the length of paragraph, and so on, are be used as the features to identify the author of a text

---

[*] The paper is supported by the National Fundamental Research Project (973 Project) (Grant No. 2004CB318104) and The Knowledge Innovation Engineering Project of The Institute of Acoustics, CAS (Grant No. 0654091431).

[Burrows J. F. 1987, Baayen R. H. 1996, David I Holmes 1997, Yuta Tsuboi 2002]. The texts are often literature, and sometimes they are internet text, such as E-mail [Olivier de Vel 2001].

Presently, there are a few research works in the Chinese text authorship identification, and many of them orient to the linguistic research for the concrete literature. Sun and Jin [Yi-jian Jin, Xiao-ming Sun, and Shao-ping Ma, 2003] use the vector space model (VSM) which takes the syntax structural words as feature to identify the text authorship, they achieved good result in novel author identification. The best precision of pattern matching, KNN algorithm and SVM algorithm are 89.51%, 91.54%, and 93.58% separately. Ma and Chang study the E-mail authorship identification successively [Jian-bin Ma 2004, Shu-hui Chang 2005]. In addition, Wu introduces the HowNet knowledge base; he performs the text authorship identification according to the evaluation method of glossary semantic similarity. His best marco-average F-measure is 86.23% that is achieved in 202 People Daily texts written by 5 reporters [Xiao-chun Wu 2006].

In text categorization, one important aspect is text expression. The text is mainly expressed as discrete glossary. As to Chinese, it is also expressed as Chinese character, phrase, term, n-gram string, etc. When the discrete unites are obtained, they can be used in feature vector constructing.

These features that come from natural language directly can represent the topic of the text and the writing style of the author in some aspects. However, these features also arouse the spare data and too large feature space in the computing, because there are more than ten thousand basic words in natural language, and the total of words even come to million, the dimension of the corresponding vector space is huge. In order to perform the computing, it is necessary to reduce the dimension.

Huang put forwards the linguistic conceptual space according his Hierarchical Network of Concepts (HNC, in short) theory [Zengyang Huang 1998, 2004]. The HNC conceptual primitives of the linguistic conceptual space and its word knowledge expression can be used to reduce the dimension. In fact, the structure of HNC conceptual primitives is a tree list, which the nodes are semantic primitives. The word meaning is expressed with the primitives, and it can accomplish the computing of correlation in the glossary, finding the thesaurus, and reducing the dimension.

Therefore, we explore the Chinese text authorship identification with the KNN classifier that adopts the HNC conceptual primitives as the features carrier. We explain the HNC conceptual primitives and the semantic expression in the following firstly.

2. The HNC conceptual primitives and the semantic expression

The network of primitives provides a necessary semantic description system in HNC, which expresses the semantic with formalization and conceptualization. The basic unite of the primitives network is conceptual tree, the node in the tree is the element for semantic expression, the relation between trees and the nodes in one tree provides the relevancy of the primitives. There are 456 trees, which are defined in HNC.

Fig. 1 is an example for the conceptual tree. This branch provides the definition and reference for its dominative category. It defines part concepts of the professional activities in detail. The letter and the string, such as a, a1, a119, are the concept identifier for the node, and the content in the brackets is the comment for the conceptual node. All these are merely abstract definition, not for the concrete instance. When expressing the concrete instance, we need to combine more concepts according its meaning. For example, the "U.S.A. Government" can be expressed in "a119+fpj2*304", the meaning of the "a119" can be found in the Fig. 1, and the "fpj2*304" refers in particular to the United Stats.

The goal of the HNC conceptual primitives is to take out and generalize the commonness of the things, and identify them with a well-defined string.

The network just describes the meaning of the words. As to the denotative function of a word, the HNC introduces five elements for the abstract concepts: v (verb), g (noun), u (attribute), z (value), and r (effect); two elements for the concrete concepts: w (matter) and p (people); and one element between the abstract and concrete concept: x (quality). These elements are called "classification of concept". They are also primitives, and need to combine to express a word denotative function.

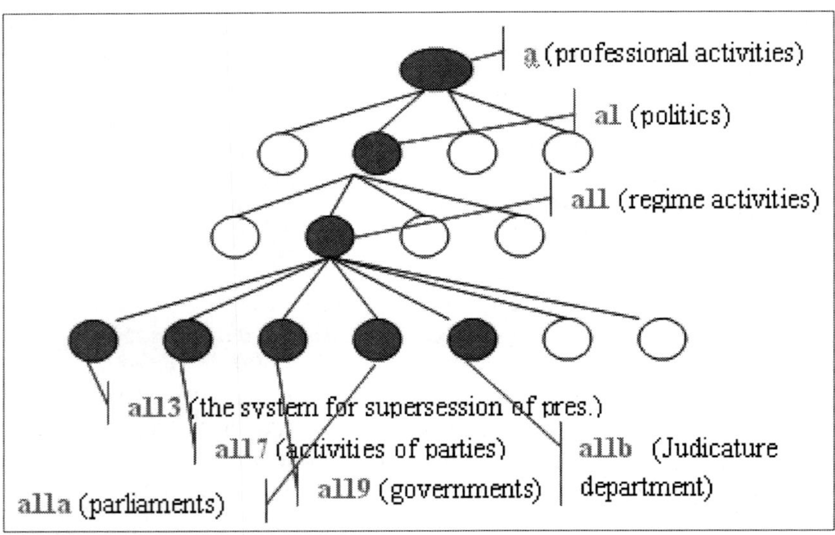

Figure 1: A branch of the conceptual tree.

Table 1: Chinese word in HNC primitives expression.

Word	Classification	Conceptual meaing
哀愁 Sad and worry	v,g	v7132+v7200e72
巡警 Cop	p	pa41+va11
诱发 Arouse	v	((va71,v9441)#(v900;v80))

We will adopt the classification of concept as categorization feature. The basic condition of the categorization feature is that the concepts which belong to one classification must not be too few, and the distinguish ability between the classifications is enough. Then we use the 12 kinds classification as feature.

Table 2: The 12 kinds classification for the feature.

No.	Name	The symbol of the classification of concept
1	Abstract noun	g/r/ xr / gr
2	Concrete noun	p/w
3	Entity	f
4	Verb	v/vv
5	Attribute and quality	u/ug/gu/x/ jx/px /gx / rx
6	Adverb	uu/uv

7	Quantifier	zz/zzv
8	Time	j1
9	Space	j2
10	Syntax structural words	l0-l5/l8
11	conjunction	l6-l7/l9-lb
12	Idiom	f1-fb

3. The algorithm and evaluation [Yun-liang Zhang 2006]

The effect of the KNN（K-Nearest Neighbor, KNN）algorithm is better in all of the VSM algorithm, and it is easy to implement, and its adaptability is robust. The basic idea of this algorithm is that the K texts in the training set which are the nearest to the input text are gotten, and then determine the input text type according the K texts.

The Formula 1 shows how to compute the similarity between the texts, where the a_{ik} indicates the k dimension value of the feature vector d_i

$$\text{sim}(\vec{d_i}, \vec{d_j}) = \frac{\sum_{k=1}^{n} a_{ik} \times a_{jk}}{\sqrt{(\sum_{k=1}^{n} a_{ik}^2)(\sum_{k=1}^{n} a_{jk}^2)}} \tag{1}$$

The a_{ik} can be calculated as Formula 2.

$$a_{ij} = \frac{\log(TF_{ij}+1.0)*\log(N/DF_i)}{\sqrt{\sum_k [\log(TF_{kj}+1.0)*\log(N/DF_k)]^2}} \tag{2}$$

Where the TF_{ij} is the frequency of the feature i occurred in the document j，N is the total of texts in the text set, DF_i is the document frequency of the feature i.

Then, the Formula 3 shows how to calculate the probability that represents the input text to belong to which type in the text set.

$$p(\vec{x}, C_j) = \sum_{\vec{d_i} \in KNN} sim(\vec{d_x}, \vec{d_i}) p(\vec{d_i}, C_j) \tag{3}$$

Where $p(\vec{d_i}, C_j)$ is categorization function, i.e. if $\vec{d_i}$ belongs to C_j，then the value is 1, less the value is 0.

We categorize the input text to the type with the largest probability.

We evaluate the categorization result with MAFM（Micro-Average F-Measure）[Yun-liang Zhang 2006].

4. The experiment and result

The texts in this paper are novels that are download form Internet. There are 25 authors' novels; the detail is shown in Table 3. We sample 20 texts for each author as testing text, and divide into two set equally, one for train and the other for testing.

Table 3: The experiment texts

Author	Ba Jin(巴金)	Ding Ling (丁玲)	Jin Yong (金庸)	Lao She (老舍)	Liang Yun-sheng (梁羽生)	Lu Xun (鲁迅)	Lu Yao (路遥)
Amount	148	58	1618	415	730	32	280
Author	Ma Feng (马烽)	Mao Dun (茅盾)	Qian Zhong-shu（钱钟书）	Qiong Yao (琼瑶)	Qu Bo (曲波)	Shen Cong-wen (沈从文)	Cao Xun-qin (曹雪芹)
Amount	54	19	75	950	32	72	80
Author	Wang Shuo (王朔)	Wang Xiao-bo 王小波	Yang Muo (杨沫)	Ye Sheng-tao (叶圣陶)	Yu Hua (余华)	Zhang Ailing (张爱玲)	Zhang Henshui (张恨水)
Amount	175	76	74	30	105	59	425
Author	Zhao Shu-li (赵树理)	Zhou Li-bo (周立波)	Zhou Mei-sen (周梅森)	Luo Guang-bin (罗广斌)		Amount	
Amount	56	51	336	30		5916	

Table 4: The result of Abstract noun feature

K	1	2	3	4	5	6	7	8	9	10	11
MAFM	0.871	0.871	0.863	0.88	0.871	0.88	0.896	0.888	**0.9**	0.896	0.892
K	12	13	14	15	16	17	18	19	20	21	22
MAFM	0.892	0.884	0.884	0.888	0.888	0.888	0.884	0.884	0.888	0.888	0.884

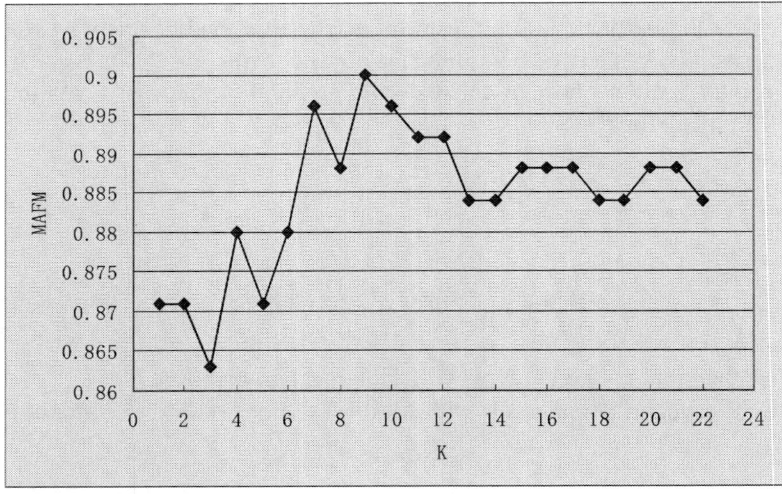

Figure 2: The result of Abstract noun feature

Table 5: The result of Concrete noun feature

K	1	2	3	4	5	6	7	8	9	10	11
MAFM	0.606	0.606	0.586	**0.618**	0.59	0.586	0.574	0.538	0.546	0.554	0.558
K	12	13	14	15	16	17	18	19	20	21	22
MAFM	0.554	0.554	0.55	0.526	0.518	0.518	0.522	0.506	0.514	0.506	0.502

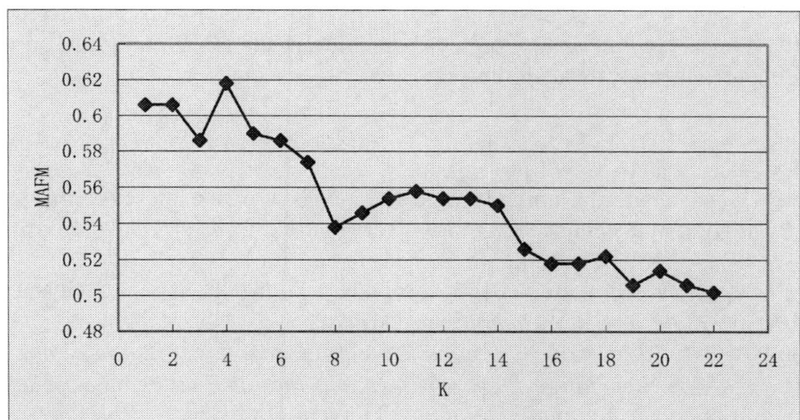

Figure 3: The result of Concrete noun feature

Table 6: The results of 12 kinds features

The Classification of the concepts	MAFMmax	The best K
Abstract noun	0.9	9
Verb	0.88	6
Adverb	0.819	4
Attribute and quality	0.731	10 or 11 or 14 or 15
Entity	0.655	8
Syntax structural words	0.655	4
Concrete noun	0.618	4
Time	0.582	10
Quantifier	0.546	27
conjunction	0.534	14 or 15
Space	0.526	4 or 7
Idiom	0.502	8

5. Discussion

We adopt the simple KNN algorithm as the computing tool, and the HNC conceptual primitives as the features carrier that can express the word meaning, then we contracture a mode to identify the text authorship. The experiment result indicates that this mode can work well, and achieves high correct rate. It means that the HNC conceptual primitives are suitable to express the text feature in text authorship identification.

   Meanwhile, comparing with the natural language words as text feature, there are also some advantages when take the HNC conceptual primitives to express the text feature:

   1.   As the HNC conceptual primitives give the words meaning in concept, so some words with different form can be expressed in same symbol when they have the same meaning, such as the "distress" and "sad" they have the same symbol in HNC conceptual primitives. Then, they can be treated as same one.

2. The conceptual primitives are hierarchical symbols; they are suitable to compute the correlation. It is easy to reduce the dimension by merging the low frequency concept into a high frequency concept, according the correlation among concepts.

3. The HNC conceptual primitives are a kind of artificial semantic symbol, their meaning is well defined, and the natural language words always have ambiguous meaning. It is hard to get the clear meaning, and the HNC conceptual primitives provide the convenience: we can obtain the word meaning in the HNC conceptual primitives form after sentence analysis according the HNC processing.

References

Baayen R. H., H. van Halteren, and Tweedie F J. 1996. Outside the cave of shadows: using syntactic annotation to enhance authorship attribution. *Literary and Linguistic Computing*, 11(3):121-131.

Burrows J. F.. 1987. Word patterns and story shapes: the statistical analysis of narrative style.*Literary and Linguistic Computing, 2:61-70.*

David I Holmes. 1997. Stylometry:its origins, development and aspirations. *Joint international conference of the association for computers and the humanities and the association for literary and linguistic computing.* Norway: University of Bergen, 98-103.

Jian-bin Ma. 2004. The Study on the Authorship Mining for Chinese E-mail documents based on SVM, *Master's Dissertation*, Hebei Agriculture University.

Olivier de Vel, A. Anderson, M. Corney, and G. Mohay. 2001. Mining E-mail Content for Author Identification Forensics. *SIGMOD:Special Section on Data Mining for Intrusion Detection and Threat Analysis*, 55-64.

Shu-hui Chang. 2005. The Study on the Authorship Identification for Chinese E-mail documents Based on the Literary Style, *Master's Dissertation,* Hebei Agriculture University.

Xiao-chun Wu, Xuan-jing Huang, and Li-de Wu. 2006. Authorship Identification Based on Semantic Analysis. *Journal of Chinese Information Processing*, 20(6):61-68.

Yi-jian Jin, Xiao-ming Sun, and Shao-ping Ma. 2003. Stylistics based Writer Identify on Internet. *Journal of Guangxi Normal University (Natuarl Science Edition)*, 21(3):62-66.

Yun-liang Zhang, and Quan Zhang. 2006. A Text Classifier Based on Sentence Category VSM. *Proceedings of the 20th Pacific Asia Conference on Language, Information and Computation*, 244~249. Wuhan.

Yuta Tsuboi. 2002. Authorship Identification for Heterogeneous Documents. *Master's Thesis*, Nara Institute of Science and Technology.

Zengyang Huang. 1998. *The Hierarchical Network of Concepts theory.* Tsinghua University Press, Beijing .

Zengyang Huang. 2004. *The Fundamental theorem and mathematic physics expression of the language concept space.* Ocean Press, Beijing.

Distal Demonstrative *Hitlo* in Taiwanese Southern Min[*]

Yi-jing Zhao

National Taiwan Normal University, Linguistic Program,
Taipei, Taiwan
jyjing7@yahoo.com.tw

Abstract. This article investigates the use of distal demonstrative *Hitlo* in Taiwanese Southern Min (TSM) from a discourse-pragmatic perspective. The analysis is based on a 5-hour corpus of spoken data, including daily conversations, radio interviews, TV drama series, and some random examples. A total of 172 tokens of *Hitlos* are identified in the data. They can be divided into six categories according to their functions: firstly, exophoric usage, those *Hitlos* which refer to an object non-linguistically which can be identified in the immediate situation; secondly, endophoric usage, those which refer to an element textually; thirdly, referent introducing function, those which can be used to introduce a new but identifiable referent into the conversation (the referent usually has topical importance); fourthly, hedging expression, those which serve as a marker of imprecision; fifthly, a condition introducing marker, those which function as an indicator of the coming of a conditional sentence; finally, pause fillers, those which help speakers to manage speech turn or indicate the mental states   In addition, an interactive function which *Hitlo* is found to serve will be discussed. Moreover, a grammaticalizational process involving semantic bleaching which Hitlo is probably undergoing is revealed in general. Finally, a filled demonstrative principle, stating that it may be a universal phenomenon to use demonstratives as filled pause will be proposed.

Key words: Deixis; Pause Filler; Demonstrative; Grammaticalization; Taiwanese Southern Min

1. Introduction

Deixis refers to certain elements in language whose interpretations rely highly on the situation within which an utterance takes place. Deictic terms refer frequently to personal, temporal or locational information of an immediate situation. It includes personal pronouns (e.g. *I, you*), demonstratives (e.g. *this, that*), and certain adverbs that indicate time (e.g. *tomorrow*) and place (e.g. *here, there*). The investigation of deictic terms has been one of the most prevalent topics in linguistic inquiry. In Mandarin Chinese, for instance, the complexity of demonstratives has been examined by scholars like Huang (1999) and Liu (2003). Through exploring the versatility of Chinese demonstratives in natural occurring conversations, Huang argues that

---

[*] I am grateful for the crucial comments from the anonymous reviewers, which help sharpen and clarify several main points in this paper. Special thanks go to Professor Miao-Hsia Chang and Professor Hsueh-O Lin for the critical comments and suggestions. Also, I thank my grandfather, Zhu-Mu Zhao, my parents, Su-Ying Chen and Shan-Long Zhao, my brother, Shi-Jie Zhao and my sister Ya-Ling Zhao for the encouragements on all occasions.

distal deixis *nage* is being grammaticalized as a definite article in Mandarin Chinese. Latter, Liu investigates the complexity of proximal deixis and it is emphasized that *zheyang(zi)* has been grammaticalized from a demonstrative to a discourse boundary marker in natural conversations.

Demonstratives in Taiwanese, however, have not been fully investigated. Specifically, previous studies relating to Taiwanese demonstratives frequently restrict their analyses to syntactic patterns or semantic diversities. Very few of them can take a discourse-pragmatic perspective to explore versatile usages of Taiwanese demonstratives in natural conversations. Li (1999) and Chang (2002) are among the few scholars who can take a discourse-pragmatic approach to examine demonstratives in Taiwanese. Li stresses an interactive function of *He* and *Che* in Taiwanese and a grammaticalization development of *He* and *Che* are also revealed in the study. Chang takes a parallel approach as Li. She classifies *Anne* in Taiwanese into six categories in accordance with its functions and syntactic patterns and some grammaticalization effects are observed in the study. However, a detailed study of *hitlo* 'that' in Taiwanese has not yet been conducted and it performs functions which are not found in the aforementioned deictic elements. *Hitlo*, a distal demonstrative, is frequently used in Taiwanese Southern Min. The purpose of this paper, hence, is to analyze the use of distal deixis *hitlo* in Taiwanese spoken discourse from a discourse-pragmatic perspective. The focus will be on various functions which *hitlo* can serve in spoken discourse. In particular, the study will show that *hitlo* seems to serve an interactive function in Taiwanese Southern Min. Moreover, the present study will reveal a grammaticalization process which *hitlo* is probably undergoing in Taiwanese spoken discourse.

The data for this study consist of 27 stretches of talk drawn from audio recordings of daily conversations, telephone conversations, radio interviews, TV drama series and random examples. A total of 172 tokens of *hitlo* are identified in the data bank. The data are transcribed into intonation units (IU) and the transcription notations proposed by Du Bois et al. (1993) are followed.

Following this section, section 2 will provide a review of previous relevant works on which the analysis and discussion are based. Section 3 discusses versatile functions of *hitlo* in Taiwanese. Section 4 reveals the grammaticalization process of *hitlo*. Section 5 is the conclusion.

2. Review of literature

This section is divided into two parts. First, previous works related to demonstratives. Due to a lack of direct studies on *hitlo*, works on demonstratives will be discussed instead. Also, the grammaticalizational phenomenon will be reviewed in general. The latter will serve as the theoretical background knowledge of the present study.

2.1. Demonstratives in previous studies

Traditional analyses for demonstratives are usually restricted to identify their meanings and distributions at sentential level. Chao (1968) classified uses of demonstratives into referential and non-referential usages. Cheng (1989) also investigated various functions of deixis. He found that distal deixis in Taiwanese can function as a proform of a predicate. This specific use of distal deixis, according to Cheng, is to "substitute for adjectives which the speaker is unwilling to explicitly state (1)."

(1) 你 抵即 的　態度 實在 有　一點　傷過 彼lo　啦
　　you just ASSC attitude really have a.little too　that　PR
　　'Your attitude is really too that.'

This proform usage is similar to the hedging expression of *hitlo* which will be discussed in detail in section 3. Compared to Chao (1968), much more functions of demonstratives are scrutinized in Cheng's study. However, both studies focus on sentence level and examples used in both analyses are not extracted from spoken discourse. Their analyses, hence, may not be enough to provide a persuasive and satisfying overview of multiple functions that demonstratives can fulfill.

Not until recently have versatile functions of demonstratives been investigated at discourse level (Biq 1990; Tao 1994, 1999; Huang 1999; Lee 1999; Chang 2002).   Biq (1990) studies the use of *na(me)* in Chinese. She tries to argue that as a discourse connector, *na(me)* is used to mark a connection of units of talks and thus establish the relevance of the following talks to the prior. Tao (1994, 1999) emphasizes the intricacy of demonstrative discourse usages in Chinese in order to argue against the restricted view of demonstrative usages proposed in traditional studies. Huang (1999) identifies eight discourse functions of Chinese demonstratives; a more significant finding is that the distal demonstrative *nage* may undergo a grammaticalizational effect and may evolve into a definite article in spoken Chinese. Compared to Biq, Tao and Huang, who investigate Chinese demonstratives, Li and Chang explore the versatile discourse functions of demonstratives in Taiwanese. Li (1999) takes a pragmatic-discoursal approach to study Taiwanese proximal deixis *che* and distal deixis *he*. In her study, Li holds that the meaning contrast between *che* and *he* does not depend primarily on the spatial distinction, but on an interactive aspect, *che* signaling speaker's own involvement, while *he* being a mark of addressee's involvement.   Chang (2002) adopts the same approach to examine multiple functions of Taiwanese proximal deixis *anne* and classifies its usages into six categories based on its discourse functions and syntactic patterns. Furthermore, both Li and Chang have argued that a grammaticalizational effect concerning semantic shift is demonstrated in the use of Taiwanese proximal deixis. In contrast to the traditional analyses, all of these studies base their arguments on spoken data beyond sentence level, making their analyses more convincing. However, their studies still do not illustrate overall functions that demonstratives can fulfill in Taiwanese, for example, filled pause and hedge expression (These usages will be discussed in section 3 in detail); more specifically speaking, studies relating to Taiwanese demonstratives are still insufficient. The investigation of *hitlo* in the present study, hence, aims to supplement the limitations of previous studies.

2.2. Theoretical assumption

The theoretical assumption of this study is that the semantic and pragmatic change of a lexical item is a dynamic and unidirectional process which follows a path from deictic through textual to communicative functions (Traugott 1982, 1989, 1990, 1991). Traugott in 1989 revised this path to the following three tendencies:
1.   Semantic-pragmatic Tendency I:
Meanings based in the external described situation → meanings based in the internal (evaluative/ perceptual/ cognitive) situation
2.   Semantic-pragmatic Tendency II:
Meanings based in the described external or internal situation → meanings based in the textual situation
3.   Semantic-pragmatic Tendency III:
Meanings tend to become increasingly situated in the speaker's subjective belief-state/attitude toward the situation

Note that all three tendencies proposed by Traugott suggest that the directionality of grammaticalization is from concrete to abstract. The shift of *while* in English from a noun or adverb meaning of 'period, time' through a conjunction meaning 'at the time' to a marker denoting adversative or concessive meaning is an obvious example of this kind of grammaticalization path.

3. Discussion

3.1. Exophoric use and endophoric use

A demonstrative may refer to an entity located in an immediate situation within which the speech event takes place. When used to refer to an object in an extralinguistic situation, demonstratives often accompany gestures or eye contact. In addition to its exophoric usage, distal deixis *hitlo* is also used to refer to a referent in previous discourse. The two common usages are not the focus of this paper, so examples will not be provided.

3.2. Referent-introducing function

According to Huang (1999), the distal deixis *nage* in Chinese can introduce a new but familiar and identifiable referent into the discourse. In addition, the referent being introduced usually has topical significance. Distal deixis *hitlo* is found to fulfill the same function in Taiwanese. The following extract is an illustration of the referent-introducing function served by *hitlo*:

(4) (Speaker F and M is talking about what kinds of dishes people should eat in
   January 1st according to the lunar calendar.)
F1:(0)你 你　正月　初一,
    you you　January first
    ...有　吃 什麼　菜　bo.
    have eat　what dish PR
F1: 'What kind of dish do you eat on January first?'
M1:..eN,
   FP
→　..阮 正月　初一 是　吃 彼 lo,
    we January first be　eat　hitlo
    ..<L2 什錦菜 L2>.
    Chowchow
M1: 'We usually eat chowchow on January first.'
F2:...喔.
   RT
    ..宛若 有　吃　<L2 什錦菜 L2> 喔.
    also　have eat　　chowchow　RT
F2: 'You also eat chowchow.'
M2:(0)heN 阿.
    yes　PR
    ..十四　項.
    fourteen　CL
    ..裏底 是 十四　項.
    inside be　fourteen CL
M2: 'Yes. There are fourteen ingredients.'
F3:..有影　喔.
   really PR
F3: 'Really.'
M3:(0)heN.
    RT
M3: 'Yes.'
F4:...喔=.
   RT
   ...按呢 復 卡　厲害.

     anne still more great
F4: 'This is better than us.'
M4:..heN.
        RT
     M4: 'Yes.'

In (4), Speaker F and M is talking about a kind of dish which people used to eat in January 1st.
In (M1), the dish, chowchow, is introduced by *hitlo* into the discourse and is instantly accepted
by F. Then, they go on to talk about this dish for a total of 13 intonation units.

Notice that the occurrence of *hitlo* in (4) can be omitted without affecting the addressee'
understanding of the intended meaning by the speaker. This forces us to consider that why
speaker M selects to add the seemingly redundant distal deixis here. A closer observation on
the context seems to suggest we should adopt a different perspective to view the choice of *hitlo*
by the speaker. If a need to ensure interpersonal involvement is taken into account, the question
is probably not that difficult to answer. Cheshire (1996) defines 'involvement' as "an
assumption that spoken discourse is a collaborative production, with speakers and addressees
working together to produce meaning as the discourse unfolds." Viewing *hitlo* from this
perspective, then, the occurrence of *hitlo* in (4) can be explained more easily and thoroughly.

Now, let's reconsider example (4). In (4), speaker F asks what kind of dish speaker M usually
eats in January 1st. Speaker M in M1 answers with a common dish which people usually eat in
January 1st. Obviously, speaker M assumes that speaker F must know this dish for it is a
culturally related concept and a kind of shared understanding. The use of *hitlo* overtly
manifests the speaker's intention to invite the addressee to concentrate on their shared
knowledge with an aim to achieving a common understanding. The use of *hitlo* here, thus,
indicates an interpersonal involvement. Cheshire (1996) and Li (1999) are among the few
researchers that recognize the interactive function of demonstratives.

3.3.Hedging expression

Hedging expressions are elements in language "which makes messages indeterminate, that is,
convey inexactitude, or in one way or another mitigates or reduces the strength of the assertions
that speakers or writers make" (Mauranen 2004). These expressions fall into two main types:
vagueness indicators and mitigators. Vagueness indicators are elements indicating fuzziness,
imprecision, approximation and so on (2004: 179). Though Cheng (1989) senses this function
which *hitlo* can perform, he did not explain it in detail and discuss it in discourse level. The
following example aims to supplement the deficiency.

(5)(Speaker E, an English teacher, is talking with the other three speakers about English
education.)

E:按呢 就　勿會—
 anne TOH not
就　有夠　a la.\
TOH enough PR PR
..<L2 那%L2>--
      that
你　若講　欲　<L2 再　學得　更　深 L2>,_
you if say want   more learn even in-depth
參像講—
for example
<L2 外面 L2>就　是　講　我　質馬　在—
  outside TOH be say I   now   at

...<L2^比喻 L2> e　彼　寡　　彼 lo hoN,\
　similitude　NM　that some　hitlo　PT
...<L2 幼兒 L2> e　　彼　寡　　<L2 英文 L2> e=--
　children　ASSC　that　some　　English　ASSC
hoN,\
PR
彼　類　彼　寡　彼._
That kind that some that
...<L2 何嘉仁 L2> la　hoN,_
　　Hess　　　PR　PR
啊　足濟 e　　la.\
PR　many ASSC PR
替　伊　廣告　　沒　要緊　la,_
for　it　advertise　no　matter　PR
E: 'This is enough. If you want to learn more, there are many ways, for
example, English cram schools for children or something like that. Hess or
something. There are many cram schools outside. It does not matter to
advertise for it (Hess).'

In this excerpt, speaker E is talking about English cram schools for children. However, she does
not want to specify these cram schools for she is afraid that her audience will think she is
advertising for these cram schools. To avoid being regarded as advertising in a public place,
speaker E uses many vague category markers such as 彼寡 'some' and 彼類 'that kind',
together with 彼 lo 'that', to indicate that an unspecified category is being talked about. These
vague expressions together convey the meaning that it is not important to know each instance in
this category for it is not the focus of the present conversation. The use of *hitlo* helps the
addressee interpreting utterances of the speaker more easily, and directs the addressees'
attention on the vague category. *Hitlo*, hence, expresses the speaker's intention to get her
addressees into the conversation.

3.4. Condition introducing marker

Some *hitlos* in the data occur in the context that the speaker wants to express a condition. These
hitlos seem to designate an upcoming conditional sentence.

(6) (A is talking about fruits.)
A: (0) 其實　　hoN,
　Actually　PR
你　講　柳柳丁　hoN,
you　say　oranges　PR
　→　..柳丁　若　彼 lo hoN,
　Oranges　if　hitlo　PR
..差不多　過年　　　　了　後　盡量　　勿會 吃.
　Almost　Chinese.New.Year　Asp　after　had.better　not　eat
因爲　伊　彼　大部份　攏　洗　藥仔　攏　起來 擱.
Because　they　that　most　all　wash　medicine　all　up　preserve
　　A: 'Actually, if it is almost the time after the Chinese New Year, you'd
　　　better not to eat oranges because most oranges at the time are preserved
　　　by some medicine.'

In this excerpt, speaker A is trying to tell his hearer that if it is about the time after the Chinese New Year, the hearer had better not to eat the oranges. Because most oranges during the time are preserved by medicines, eating these oranges may be harmful to heath. Hence, the hearer had better not to eat oranges after Chinese New Year. *Hitlo* in the fourth intonation unit occurs in the context of a condition. The occurrence of *hitlo* here, thus, seems to indicate that a conditional sentence will follow. Note again that *hitlo* here has a signaling function. The speaker uses *hitlo* to alert the hearer that a conditional sentence is coming while constructing the emerging utterance. The use of *hitlo* here, thus, is still interactive in nature. It facilitates hearer's understanding of the planes of discourse context. Again, an addressee-involvement is achieved by the use of *hitlo*.

3.5.Pause filler

The use of demonstratives as filled pauses (FPs) has been sensed by many linguists. Huang (1999) explicitly specifies that demonstratives can be used as a filled pause and he provides a more detailed description of this function. However, he did not notice the interactive function these demonstratives serve. Later in Zhao et al. (2005), they claim that "besides reduced vowel FPs, Mandarin intensively employs demonstratives as FPs." This study, however, is a preliminary one and the focus of the study seems to be on the acoustic features and distributional patterns of Filled pauses. In order to have a complete understanding on the pause filler function of demonstratives, a more detailed observation is required. The present study shows that *hitlo* also serves as a pause filler in Taiwanese. Moreover, *hitlos* serving as pause fillers can be further grouped into three different functions: first, floor maintaining; second, planning difficulty and third, boundary of discourse topics. These functions have been widely discussed in the literature, so examples will not be given in the study.

4. Discourse functions of *Hitlo* in relation to its grammaticalization

In section 3, several functions which demonstrative *hitlo* performs in the planes of discourse are illustrated. The discussion reveals that these functions of *hitlo* cannot be explained in terms of a pure deictic word. In fact, a close observation of the versatile functions seems to suggest that *hitlo* is probably undergoing a grammaticalizational process including semantic bleaching from its fundamental deictic usage to a discourse marker. In this section, thus, a possible grammaticalization process of *hitlo* will be explored in general.

An examination of the functions of *hitlo* shows that the grammaticalizational process proceeds from extralinguistic through textual to interactive. The basic deictic meaning of *hitlo* is to refer to a referent situated in the immediate utterance context, that is, an extralinguistic function. Latter, the deictic usage is extended to indicate what has been or is going to be mentioned in the co-text, that is, an exophoric usage, referent-introducing function and hedging expression. The extension of deictic meaning to textual reference seems to suggest the existence of a metaphorical shift from the domain of non-linguistic real world situation to the domain of discourse universe. Latter, the use of *hitlo* extends to a metalinguistic function. It serves a signaling function as to foretell the hearer the coming of a conditional sentence. Finally, it further extends to a discourse marker, connecting two units of discourse. The process seems to correspond to the three stages of grammaticalizational tendencies proposed by Traugott. The grammaticalization process of *hitlo* seems to go from Tendency I through Tendency II to Tendency III.

In addition, a careful scrutiny of the transformation in its syntactic distribution or semantic content also supports the idea that *hitlo* is undergoing a grammaticalizational effect. Syntactically, *hitlo* seems to descend from an intra-sentential position through a clause boundary further to a discourse boundary. Among its referential usages, that is, exophoric usage, endophoric usage, and hedging expression, *hitlo* does participate in the syntactic structure of the sentence. Omitting it seems to result in some kind of ungrammaticality.

However, when it functions as a condition introducing marker or pause filler, its significance in syntactic structure seems to reduce dramatically. The omission of *hitlo* under these two circumstances will not affect the grammaticality of the sentences. Semantically, *hitlo* seems to proceeds from a lexical element through a text-building signal to a semantic void discourse marker. Again, when functioning referentially, *hitlo* does contribute its semantic content to the proposition of the sentence. However, when serving non-referential condition introducing or pause filler function, its semantic content seems to reduce at most to a vacant discourse marker. The syntactic distribution of *hitlo* progresses from central to peripheral, corresponding to its semantic change proceeding from concrete to abstract. The multi-functions of *hitlo* in Taiwanese Southern Min, hence, may be the evidence that it is undergoing a grammaticalizational effect.

Moreover, we want to further propose a filled demonstrative principle, which states that it seems to be a universal phenomenon to use the demonstrative as a pause filler. In the literature, demonstratives in English, Chinese, Japanese, and Taiwanese are all found to serve as a pause filler. We want to relate this phenomenon with the interactional function which hitlo serves in Taiwanese. Because demonstratives can signal an interpersonal involvement, it is favored by the speaker to use demonstratives as filled pause. It illustrates that discourse is a cooperative process which the interlocutors always try to coordinate with each other even during an utterance gap.

Furthermore, this principle may also suggest that these demonstratives are experiencing a grammaticalization effect. This, in turn, may suggest that grammaticalization phenomenon is probably a universal process which occurs cross-linguistically.

5. Conclusion

This study has investigated the discourse functions of *hitlo* in spoken Taiwanese and also discussed the interactive function in relation to these functions based on authentic conversations. The findings can be summarized in the following.

First, as recognized in the previous studies, distal demonstrative *hitlo* is also found to refer to an element either textually or extralinguistically. However, the deictic usage is not enough to account for the complexity of *hitlo* in discourse level. A close observation reveals that it is also used to signal the coming of a new but identifiable referent in the conversation.

On the other hand, *hitlo* serves as a hedging expression, conveying imprecision of assertions, and signaling uncertainty or vagueness of statements.

In addition, *hitlo* is found to occur in the context that when the speaker is about to utter a conditional sentence. It seems to foretell the coming of a conditional sentence to the hearer.

Finally, in spoken Taiwanese, *hitlo* also functions as a pause filler. *Hitlos* occurring in this category can fulfill three different functions: to keep speech turn, to signal the planning difficulty or to indicate the boundary of discourse topics.

Specifically, an interactive function in relation to the use of *hitlo* in spoken Taiwanese is witnessed. In spoken discourse, *hitlo* can be used to indicate an addressee involvement.

Furthermore, these coexisting versatile functions seem to exhibit that *hitlo* in Taiwanese Southern Min is undergoing a process of grammaticalization. It seems to progress from a lexical element to a semantically vacant discourse marker.

In conclusion, the distal deixis *hitlo* in spoken Taiwanese is not merely a deictic term. *Hitlo* can fulfill several functions; deictic expression is just one of its diverse usages. The different functions of *hitlo*, hence, can only be interpreted by different planes of discourse contexts. The study shows that the dynamic nature of discourse context gives rise to the emergence of new discourse functions of a linguistic unit and forces it to become a highly grammaticalized discourse element. This, in turn, proves the dynamic nature of grammar and language. It reveals that language and grammar are not static systems but shaped by interlocutors in the process of language use.

References

Arnold, Jennifer E., Maria Fagnano, and Michael K. Tanenhaus. 2003. Disfluencies signal theee, um, new information. *Journal of Psycholinguistic Research,* 32, 25-37.

Bortfeld, Heather, Silvia D. Leon, Jonathan E. Bloom, Michael F. Schober, and Susan E. Brennan. 2001. Disfluency rates in conversation: effects of age, relationship, topic, role, and gender. *Language and Speech*, 44, 123-147

Cheng, Robert ed., co-translated by Hsun-hui Chang, Shu-fen Fujitani, and Lianying Wu. 1989. *Mandarin Function Words and Their Taiwanese Equivalents.* Taipei: The Crane Publishing Co.

Cheshire, J. 1996. That jacksprat: an interactional perspective on English *that. Journal of Pragmatics*, 25, 369-393

Chang, Miao-Hsia. 2002. Discourse functions of *Anne* in Taiwanese Southern Min. *Concentric: Studies in English Literature and Linguistics*, 28(2), 85-115

Crystal, David. 1980. *A Dictionary of Linguistics and Phonetics.* City, UK: Blackwell Publishing Co. Ltd.

Dong Zhong-si, Shu-xian Cheng, and Ping-sheng Zhang eds., 2001. *Taiwan Minnanyu Cidian.* Taipei: Wu-nan Culture Enterprise.

Goto Masataka, Katunobu Itou, and Satoru Hayamizu. 2002. Speech completion: on-demand completion assistance using filled pauses for speech input interfaces. *In Proceedings of the 7th International Conference on Spoken Language Processing (ICSLP-2002)*, 1489-1492. September 2002.

Huang, Shuanfan-fan. 1999. The emergence of a grammatical category *definite article* in spoken Chinese. *Journal of Pragmatics,* 31, 77-94.

Kubler, Cornelius. 1988. Code switching between Taiwanese and Mandarin in Taiwan. *The Structure of Taiwanese: A Modern Synthesis*, ed. by Cheng, Robert L., and Shuanfan Huang, 263-284. Taipei: The Crane Publishing Co.

Li, Ing Cherry. 1999. *Utterance-Final Particles in Taiwanese: A Discourse-Pragmatic Analysis.* Taipei: The Crane Publishing Co.

Lee, Yu-hsin. 1999. *Discourse functions of He and Che in Taiwanese.* National Taiwan Normal University MA thesis.

Liu, Fang-chun Fanny. 2003. *Zheyang(zi) in Taiwan Mandarin: discourse functions and grammaticalization.* National Taiwan Normal University MA thesis.

Mauranen, Anna. 2004. "They're a little bit different"... : observations on hedges in academic talk. *Discourse Patterns in Spoken and Written Corpora*, ed. by Aijmer, Karin, and Anna-Brita Stenström, 173-197. Philadelphia: John Benjamins Pub. Co.

O'Connell, Daniel C., and Sabine Kowal. 2004. The history of research on the filled pause as evidence of the written language bias in linguistics (Linell, 1982). *Journal of Psycholinguistic Research*, 33, 459-474.

Rose, Ralph. 1998. *The communicative value of filled pauses in spontaneous speech.* University of Birmingham MA thesis.

Wasow, Thomas. 1997. Remarks on grammatical weight. *Language Variation and Change*, 9, 81-105. Cambridge: Cambridge University Press.

Wilkins, David P. 1993. Interjections as deictics. *Journal of Pragmatics*, 18, 119-158.

Zhao, Yuan, and Dan Jurafsky. 2005. A preliminary study of Mandarin filled pauses. *In Proceedings of Diss'05, Disfluency in Spontaneous Speech Workshop*, 10-12, September 2005, Aix-en-Provence, France.

Children's Acquisition of Demonstrative Pronouns
in Mandarin Chinese[*]

Yi-jing Zhao

National Taiwan Normal University, Linguistic Program,
Taipei, Taiwan
jyjing7@yahoo.com.tw

Abstract. This paper investigates children's comprehension and production of demonstrative pronouns (DPs), 'zhege' (this) and 'nage' (that), in Mandarin Chinese. Subjects are children of ages three, four, five and six. Based on the results of the present experiment, children's developmental stages and the corresponding age grading are provided. Also, the present study incorporates a physical clue into the experiment. The result suggests that in the acquisition of deixis children rely highly on physical context to work out the meaning distinction. In addition, Piaget's egocentrism hypothesis and H. Clark's marking hypothesis are examined in the study. The result seems to support the egocentrism hypothesis. Subjects under the age of six do fail to shift the deictic center when they and the experimenter have a different perspective. As for the marking hypothesis, the study seems to challenge the hypothesis. The result shows that children actually performed better on the marked term 'zhege' than the unmarked member 'nage'.

Keywords: deixis; demonstrative; pronoun; egocentrism; language acquisition.

1.   Introduction

Languages are primarily designed for face-to-face communication in daily life and thus can not be separated from context of utterance (Lyons 1977a). All natural languages, hence, have 'gear' to relate the utterance with its context. Deixis is perhaps the most useful gear in reflecting the relationship between language and context. Deictic terms can link the utterance with specific person, time, place, or speech event. They include personal pronouns (e.g. *I, you*), demonstratives (e.g. *this, that*), and some adverbs indicating place (e.g. *here, there*) and time (e.g. *tomorrow*) (Levinson 1983). In the field of language acquisition inquiry, these deictic words are found to emerge early and frequently in children's language. According to literature, early in their very first word stage children can use deictic terms with the form 'ah', 'eh', or 'da' (Lindner 1898, Leopold 1949) and by the age of two and a half, deictic words like 'here', 'there', 'this' and 'that' appear in children's language (Grant 1915; Nice 1915; De Villiers and De Villiers 1974; Rodrigo 2004).

---

[*] I am grateful for the crucial comments from the anonymous reviewers, which help sharpen and clarify several main points in this paper. Special thanks go to Professor Chun-Yin Chen for the critical comments and suggestions. Also, I thank my grandfather, Zhu-Mu Zhao, my parents, Su-Ying Chen and Shan-Long Zhao, my brother, Shi-Jie Zhao and my sister Ya-Ling Zhao for the encouragements on all occasions.

One thing worth mentioning is that these deictic terms usually appear along with all kinds of physical expressions. In actual language use, speakers make use of a variety of nonlinguistic clues such as eye gaze and gestures while producing the deictic words. Previous studies also prove that from about age one onwards children can and do utilize the non-linguistic clues of the speaker to identify what is the intended joint attention (Leung and Pheingold 1981; Tomasello, Call, and Gluckman 1997; Moore and Dunham 1995). If this is the case, we should expect that these physical cues should play an important role in children's acquisition of certain deictic terms. This expectation will be examined in the present study.

Children's acquisition of demonstratives in Mandarin Chinese, however, has not been investigated in literature so far as I know. Previous studies relating to children's acquisition of demonstratives usually limit their analyses to western languages (e.g. English or Turkish) and to an adjective-like function (e.g. Make 'this' chicken hop). Also, age-grading of participants in previous studies is usually not broadly-based. To understand children's acquisition of demonstratives and of different functions of demonstratives, more studies are required. The purpose of this study, hence, is to investigate children's acquisition of proximal demonstrative 'zhege' (this) and distal demonstrative 'nage' (that) in Mandarin Chinese. The focus will be on the pronominal function which the two words are found to serve in Chinese. Four age groups ranging from three to six years old are involved in the study. Five research questions will be addressed in the present study: (1) How do children work out the meaning of DPs? (2) Can H. Clark's (1973) marking hypothesis be applied to children's acquisition of DPs? (3) What are the developmental stages and the corresponding age grading of performance? (4) Does Piaget's (1926) egocentrism hypothesis do exist? (5) Is there any age effect in children's comprehension and production of these DPs?

Following this section, section 2 will provide some basic properties of demonstratives in Mandarin Chinese. Section 3 offers an issue review of relevant theories and works on which the analysis and discussion are based. Section 4 is the methodology. Section 5 is a combination of results and general discussion. Section 6 concludes the finding and reveals some limitations.

2.   Properties of Chinese demonstrative pronouns

This section illustrates some basic properties of demonstrative pronouns (DPs) 'zhege' (this) and 'nage' (that) in Mandarin Chinese. In literature, a spatial distinction is often used to differentiate between 'zhege' and 'nage' in Mandarin Chinese. Generally speaking, 'zhege' is defined as a proximal DP whose major function is to indicate a referent near the speaker while 'nage' is a distal one used to refer to an object far away from the speaker:

(1)   wo yao chi zhe-ge
I want eat this-CL
        'I want to eat this.'

(2)   wo yao chi na-ge
I want eat that-CL
        'I want to eat that.'

This spatial distinction has been recognized in works such as Chao (1968) and Cheng (1989). Chao glosses 'zhege' and 'nage' as demonstrative-measure compounds used to refer to an object either proximal ('zhege') or distal ('nage') to the speaker. Cheng makes similar remarks on the two DPs.

In general, to master demonstrative pronouns 'zhege' and 'nage' in Mandarin Chinese, children at least have to learn two things: (1) the speaker is the deictic center and (2) the proximity distinction is a major contrast between the pair.

3. Literature review

3.1. Piaget's egocentrism hypothesis (1926)

The egocentrism hypothesis is first proposed by Piaget. According to Piaget (1926, 1928, 1929, 1956, 1958), children think in an ego-centric way up to the age of 7. That is, young children believe that they themselves are the center of the universe, and that all the others think in the same way like them. Thus, they fail to adopt points of view other than their own. The mastery of deictic terms, however, requires children to incorporate interlocutors' viewpoint into consideration. That is to say, they have to know that the speaker is the deictic center. If children do think in an ego-centric way, they may have difficulty in shifting the deictic center. This hypothesis has been received a wide range of discussion in the literature. Some studies prove that egocentrism do exist in children's minds. Webb and Abrahamson (1975) examine children's comprehension of some deictic pairs and the result shows that children perform better when their perspective is the same as the experimenter, suggesting that egocentrism may be a central factor in the experiment. Clark and Sengul (1977) argue that in acquiring deictic contrasts, children tend to choose themselves as the deictic center. Other studies, on the other hand, provide evidence to challenge the egocentric view. In De Villiers and De Villiers' (1974) study, they conclude that at the age of 3 or 4 years old, children are capable of adopting speaker as a point of reference in the comprehension and production of certain deictic terms. These studies show that the notion of egocentrism is still a controversial one and more researches are required to provide additional tests for the validity of the hypothesis.

3.2. H. Clark's marking hypothesis (1973)

The marking hypothesis is established in H. Clark's (1973) study which states that an unmarked member of a pair will be acquired before a marked one. For spatial demonstratives, 'that' is often identified as the unmarked term of the pair 'this' and 'that' (Kuroda 1968; H. Clark 1973). The prediction that 'that' will be learned earlier than 'this' then follows. This hypothesis is still under examination. Donaldson and Wales (1970) study children's acquisition of certain relation terms. Their results support the marking hypothesis in which the positive terms of word pairs are learned first by subjects. A similar result is obtained in De Villiers & de Villers's (1974) study. Generally speaking, subjects in their study did better on distal terms than on proximal ones. Opposite results, however, are demonstrated in the following researches. As shown in Webb and Abrahamson's (1975) experiments, children actually perform better on the word 'this' than 'that'. Kuczaj & Maratsos (1975) argue that children demonstrate no difference in their comprehension of 'front' and 'back'. Tanz (1980) also obtains an opposite result in observing children's acquisition of 'far' and 'close'. She illustrates that the marked member, 'close', appears to be acquired earlier than 'far'. The controversy over this issue suggests that more researches are needed to examine the legitimacy of this hypothesis.

3.3. Children's acquisition of demonstratives in previous studies

Children's acquisition of demonstratives is a prevalent topic in linguistic inquiry. To gain a complete understanding of children's acquisition of demonstratives, scholars conduct various kinds of experiments. These experiments do help readers to grasp a general concept on this issue. Webb and Abrahamson (1975), for example, investigate children's use of 'this' and 'that', and propose that children first learn the proximity distinction between the two words and then lean that the speaker is the point of reference. Latter, Clark and Sengul (1977) argue that in acquiring deictic contrasts, children go through three phases: from 'No Contrast' through 'Partial Contrast' to 'Full Contrast'. Recently, Kuntay et al. (2006) explore children's acquisition of Turkish demonstrative system which necessarily encodes both proximity distinction and the addressee's visual attention (present or absent on the referent), and reveal that the ability to take the hearer's visual attention into consideration during conversation is not obtained even by the age of six. The aforementioned studies, however, suffer from some limitations. These studies are all about western languages (e.g. English and Turkish) and their major concern is the adjective like usage of demonstratives (e.g. Pick up 'this' candy). Moreover, the age range of subjects participated in these researches is not broadly-based. To get a full understanding of children's acquisition of versatile usages of demonstratives, more studies are required. The investigation of children's acquisition of demonstrative pronouns in Mandarin Chinese, hence, aims to supplement the limitations of previous studies.

4. Method

4.1. Subjects

The participants were eight nursery school children in Taipei city. The choice of the participants was based on previous studies. It is generally held that deictic words like *this* and *that* are usually present by the age of two and a half (Grant 1915; Nice 1915; Rodrigo 2004) and not until the age of six or seven can children demonstrate adult-like competence in their use of demonstratives (Clark and Sengul 1977; Kuntay 2006). To examine children's developmental stages and age differences in their use of DPs, eight children aged between three and six were chosen. They were divided into four age groups, each containing two children (n=2): Group 1 three-year-olds, Group 2 four-year-olds, Group 3 five-year-olds, and Group 4 six-year-olds. All the participants were monolingual Mandarin Chinese speakers and all were individually tested in a quiet classroom at their schools.

4.2. Comprehension task

4.2.1. Stimuli

The stimuli included twelve sentences: four with the word 'zhege', four with the word 'nage', and four fillers. The testing order of these sentences was randomized in the task.

4.2.2. Materials

Two identical small cartons, one with candies inside and the other with cookies, and 12 puppets were used to test children's comprehension of DPs. The 12 puppets were animals familiar to children, for instance, monkey, bear, and koala.

4.2.3. Procedure

The task was composed of two trials, one with the experimenter sitting beside the child in front of a desk (the same perspective trial), and the other with the experimenter sitting at the opposite side of the desk (the different perspective trial). On the desk, there were two identical cartons, one with candies and the other with cookies; the candy carton was placed nearer the child's side of the desk, and the other nearer the opposite side of the desk. Each trial required children to make a two-alternative, forced-choice decision between candy and cookie. The child first received six testing sentences (randomized order) in the same perspective trial, two of 'zhege' (one with a non-linguistic cue and the other without), two of 'nage' (with or without a non-linguistic cue) and two fillers, and then s/he received the same six sentences in the different perspective trial. To start the experiment, the experimenter first explained to the child that they were to play a role-play game in which the child had to pick up either candy or cookie to testing sentences like '我要買這個' (I want to buy this) or '我要買那個' (I want to buy that) (see Table 1). Notice that if the testing sentence is the one with a non-linguistic cue, the experimenter will give a clear eye gaze at the correct object; if it is the one without a non-linguistic cue, the experimenter will look directly at the child, avoiding any gestural clues or eye-gazing. As shown in Figure 1, to start the task, the experimenter first sat at position 1 (the same perspective trial) and then after the same perspective trial, the experimenter moved to position 2 to begin the different perspective trial. Note that the two cartons were placed at points equidistant from the child, about an arm's reach, to avoid any possible bias. Children's responses will be recorded by an assistant to the experimenter. Each child was recorded by a digital recorder during the task, respectively.

Table 1: Testing sentences used in the comprehension task.

			Test Sentence	Correct Object	Object chosen
Same perspective trial	With non-linguistic cue	這個	我要買這個 (with eye gaze)	Candy	
		那個	我要買那個 (with eye gaze)	Cookie	
	Without non-linguistic cue	這個	我要買這個 (without eye gaze)	Candy	
		那個	我要買那個 (without eye gaze)	Cookie	
	Filler		我要買糖果		
			我要買餅乾		
Different perspective trial	With non-linguistic cue	這個	我要買這個 (with eye gaze)	Cookie	
		那個	我要買那個 (with eye gaze)	Candy	
	Without non-linguistic cue	這個	我要買這個 (without eye gaze)	Cookie	
		那個	我要買那個 (without eye gaze)	Candy	
	Filler		我要買糖果		
			我要買餅乾		

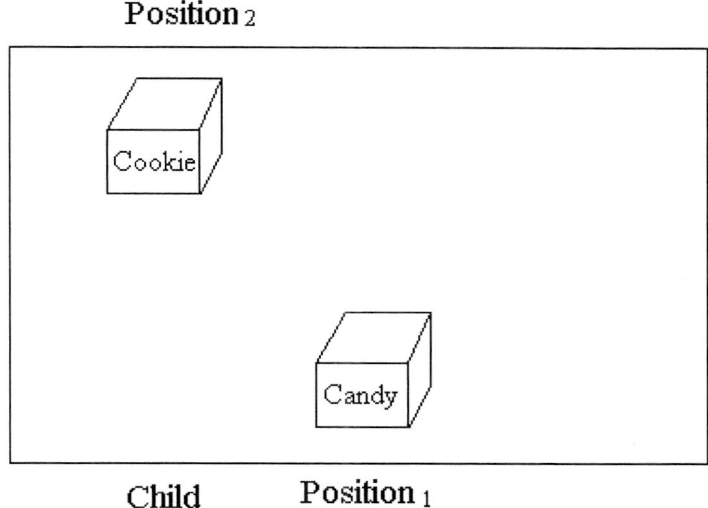

Figure 1: Situation used in the comprehension task.

5.   Results and discussion

This section provides detailed results and general discussion of the experiment in the order of the research questions. Note that one subject in Group 2 was dropped in the experiment because she seems to always choose her preferred snack but not the one required by the experimenter, causing the inconsistency of the result.

Mean scores of correct responses with and without eye gaze for each age group were shown in Table 2 and 3, respectively. As can be seen, the existence of a non-linguistic cue does assist children in comprehending these DPs. Compare Table 2 and 3, children achieved a higher score for instructions with a clear eye gaze than for instructions without any physical clues. Table 3 illustrates that without any physical clue children did slightly on 'zhege' than 'nage', and on same than different perspective trial in general. However, with the aid of a clear eye gaze, as shown in Table 2, children did almost equally well in same and different perspective trials, and in 'zhege' and 'nage' across the four age groups. Actually the effect of this non-linguistic clue was not apparent on Group 4, and on 'zhege' in same perspective trial compared with Table 3; however, if the scores of 'nage', of 'zhege' in different perspective trial, and of the other three younger groups were considered, the effect of this physical clue was significant.

The high scores in instructions with eye gaze seem to suggest that children depend highly on physical clues to figure out the meanings of deictic terms. This argumentation is not unfamiliar in the linguistic field. Clark (1973) and Donaldson and McGarrigle (1974), though not examining DPs, also argue that children's beginning assumption toward word meanings depend highly on context. At first, children may not know the precise meanings of these deictic terms and make use of all kinds of non-linguistic clues such as eye gaze and gestures to determine the intended focus of the speaker. Latter, they gradually grasp the impression that 'zhege' is used specifically under the context that when the speaker wants to refer to a near object while 'nage' is used to refer to a far object. In other words, physical expressions may play a central role in assisting children to work out meanings of certain deictic terms.

To answer our second research question, let's consider Table 3 again. The scores in Table 3 reveal that children's performance was slightly better on the proximal term than the distal one especially in same perspective trial. Compare this result with the scores of production task in Table 4. The results seem to correspond to each other. As illustrates in Table 4, children did significantly perform better on 'zhege' than 'nage'.

Both results, hence, seem to challenge H. Clark's marking hypothesis. H. Clark (1973) argued that children should acquire the positive, unmarked member of a word pair first. However, in the present study children actually performed better on 'zhege' than 'nage'. In fact, this hypothesis has been challenged by results of some empirical studies and some alternative explanations have been provided in the literature (Kuczaj and Maratsos, 1975; Clark and Sengul, 1977; Tanz, 1980). In Kuczaj and Maratsos's (1975) study, they propose that the order of acquiring members of a pair of demonstratives may correlate with the degree of shifting of reference of the members, that is, the more shifting, the harder to learn. For 'this' and 'that', they suggest that 'that' shifts reference more than 'this'; this may also account for the better performance on 'zhege' than 'nage' in this study.

Due to a limitation of subject numbers, the overall results for the task were not significant enough to let us judge children's developmental stages. For that, the children were divided into subgroups based on their individual response patterns in instructions without eye gaze. The representation and classification of response patterns and the grouping of children patterned after Clark and Sengul' (1977) study with some modification. Following their study, each child's pattern was represented as a quadruple of ones and zeros. Take the pattern 1001 of Group 1 as an example, the first two digits, 1 and 0, encode the child's reply to 'zhege' and 'nage' in same perspective trial correspondingly. The next two digits, 0 and 1, encode his/her response to 'zhege' and 'nage' in different perspective trial. The pattern 1001, thus, shows that the child was correct on 'zhege' in same perspective trial while on 'nage' in different perspective trial. Based on individual response patterns, Clark and Sengul divided children into three subgroups, No contrast, Partial contrast, and Full contrast, corresponding to their developmental stages.

As shown in Table 5, participants in this study can be assigned to different stages, too. Three subjects were at the No contrast stage. They are all in the younger groups, Group 1 and 2. These subjects seem to consider the two words as pure deictic terms without any meaning contrast. Three subjects were at the Partial contrast stage. Two of them are from Group 3 and one from Group 4. They seem to have a rough idea that the two terms have a distance contrast and hence can differentiate them under some circumstances but not all. The final subject was at the Full contrast stage, having a full control over the two words. The result suggests that in acquiring Chinese DPs, children also go through three successive developmental stages like western children, from No contrast through Partial contrast to Full contrast.

Although the developmental stages were proposed in Clark and Sengul's (1977) study, the corresponding age grading was not clearly provided in their study. The result of this study seems to suggest that children under or equal to the age of four are still in the No contrast stage; from five to six years old, they may pass into the Partial contrast stage and until the age of six or seven they may have gained a full control over these DPs. These successive stages also indicate that the acquisition of deictic meanings is a gradual process.

As for Piaget's egocentrism hypothesis, the result of this study seems to support the hypothesis. Consider children's response patterns shown in Table 5 again.

According to Clark and Sengul (1977), children with the patter 1001, 0110 and 1100 are child-centered while 1011 and 1111 are speak-centered. Based on their assumption, Group 1, 2 and 3 in the present study are all child-centered and Group 4 is speaker-centered. Thus, under the age of six children may still not know that the use of these DPs requires a constant shifting of reference point. The result, hence, suggests that egocentrism do exist in young children's minds (Webb and Abrahamsom, 1975; Clark and Sengul, 1977) and they seem to apply this bias to language learning, too.

As for the age effect, there was no clear evidence shown in the overall comprehension scores. Though Group 4 did perform better than the other three younger groups in instructions without eye gaze, the effect was not clear in the other three groups. However, if the scores of production task (see Table 4) were considered, a patent age effect was revealed. Though the performance of 'zhege' did not reveal any considerable difference across age groups, the scores of 'nage' did suggest a clear age effect. Children's ability in producing 'nage' seems to increase with age. The performance of Group 1 and 2 were the worst; Group 3 did slightly better and Group 4 gained a full control over the production of the two terms. Also, note that children at the No contrast stage were younger than those at the Partial and Full contrast stages; children at the Partial contrast stage were slightly younger than the one at the Full contrast stage (see Table 5). The subjects in the present study, hence, showed a steady improvement with age. Thus, age does improve children's learning capacity. It is an important factor in learning deictic terms (De Villiers and De Villiers, 1974; Webb and Abrahamson, 1975; Clark and Sengul, 1977).

Table 2: Mean scores of correct responses for instructions with eye gaze in each age group

Age group (n=2)	Same Perspective		Different Perspective	
	zhege	nage	Zhege	Nage
1	1	1	1	1
2	1	1	1	1
3	0.5	1	0.5	1
4	1	1	1	1

Table 3: Mean scores of correct responses for instructions without eye gaze in each age group

Age group (n=2)	Same Perspective		Different Perspective	
	zhege	nage	zhege	nage
1	1	0	0	1
2	0	1	1	0
3	1	1	0	0
4	1	0.5	1	1

Table 4. Mean scores of correct production in each age group

Age group (n=2)	zhege	Nage
1	1	0
2	1	0
3	0.75	0.5
4	1	1

Table 5: The grouping of children according to their response patterns in instructions without eye gaze

	Age Group (n=2)		Response Patterns	
No Contrast	1	A	1001	Child-centered
		B		
	2	D	0110	
Partial Contrast	3	E	1100	
		F		
		G	1011	Speaker-centered
Full Contrast	4	H	1111	

(cf. Clark and Sengul, 1977)

6.   Conclusion and limitation

If we compare the present study with the previous works related to demonstrates, some tendencies can be generalized. First, the course of language acquisition is obviously a gradual progression. As proved by many western children, Chinese children also do not learn to use demonstratives all of a sudden. Their control over the use of DPs improves steadily with the increasing of age. The other point is that since the present study reveals that apparently Chinese speaking children do think in an egocentric way just like English speaking children illustrated in earlier works, it seems to be reasonable to argue that egocentrism is probably a universal phenomenon existing in young children's minds and affecting children's language acquisition.

Except for the aforementioned seemingly universal tendencies, some deviation can also be found. Piaget states that egocentrism probably requires at least seven years eliminating. However, the present study illustrates that some children as young as the age of six have already knew how to adopt other people's point of view to comprehend the Chinese DPs. The erasing of the bias in learning languages, hence, may not take such a long time. Six or seven years may be enough for some children at least for some Chinese children to eliminate the bias.

Due to a limitation of time and strength, the total subject numbers are relatively small. The results, thus, may not be reliable enough. Also, still some other common functions which demonstratives can serve such as an anaphoric usage are not investigated in this paper. As a result, further researches are required to gain a comprehensive understanding over children's acquisition of demonstratives.

References

Bates, E.. 1976. *Language and Context: the Acquisition of Pragmatics*. New York: Academic Press.

Clark, Eve V.. 1973. What's in a word? On the child's Acquisition of Semantics in his first language. *Cognitive Development and the Acquisition of Language*, ed. T. E. Moore. New York: Academic Press.

---- 2003. *First Language Acquisition*. Cambridge: Cambridge University Press.

Clark, Eve V. and C. J. Sengul. 1977. Strategies in the Acquisition of Deixis. *Journal of Child Language,* 5, 457-75.

Clark, H.. 1973. Space, Time, Semantics and the Child. *Cognitive Development and the Acquisition of Language*, ed. T. E. Moore. New York: Academic Press.

De Villiers, Peter A. and Jill G. De Villiers. 1974. On this, that, and the other: nonegocentrism in very young children. *Journal of Experimental Child Psychology,* 18, 438-47.

Donaldson, M. and R. Wales. 1970. On the acquisition of some relational terms. *Cognition and the Development of Language*, ed. J. R. Hayes. New York: Wiley.

Donaldson, M. and McGarrigle, J.. 1974. Some clues to the nature of semantic development. *Journal of Child Language,* 1, 185-94

Fillmore, C.. 1997. *Lectures on Deixis*. Stanford, CA: Center for the Study of Language and Information.

Franco, F. and G. Butterworth. 1996. Pointing and social awareness: declaring and requesting in the second year. *Journal of Child Language,* 23, 307-36

Kuczaj II, Stan A. and Michael P. Maratsos. 1975. On the acquisition of *front, back,* and *side*. *Child Development,* 46, 202-10.

Kuntay, Aylin C., Asli Ozyurek, and Max Planck. 2006. Learning to use demonstratives in conversation: what do language specific strategies in Turkish reveal?. *Journal of Child Language,* 33, 303-20.

Laurendeau, M. and A. Pinard. 1970. *The Development of the Concept of Space in the Child*. New York: International Universities Press.

Nice, M. M.. 1915. The development of a child's vocabulary in relation to environment. *Pedagogical Seminary,* 22, 35-64

Piaget, Jean. 1926. *The Language and Thought of the Child*. London: Routledge and Kegan Paul.

----. 1928. *Judgment and Reasoning in the Child*. London: Routledge and Kegan Paul.

----. 1929. *The Child's Concept of the World*.

Piaget, Jean and Inhelder, B.. 1956. *The Child's Conception of Space*. New York: Norton.

Inhelder, Barbel and Jean Piaget. 1958. *The Growth of Logical Thinking from Childhood to Adolescence*. Basic Books, Inc., Publishers.

Rodrigo, Maria Jose, Angela Gonzalez, Manuel de Vega, Mercedes Muneton-Ayala, and Guacimara Rodriguez. 2004. From gestural to verbal deixis: a longitudinal study with Spanish infants and toddlers. *First Language,* 24, 071-90.

Slobin, D. I.. 1973. Cognitive prerequisites for the development of grammar. *Studies of Child Language Development*, ed. C. A. Ferguson and D. I. Slobin, 175-208. New York: Holt, Rinehart and Winston.

Tanz, C.. 1980. *Studies in the Acquisition of Deictic terms*. Cambridge: Cambridge University Press.

Tomasello, <u>Michael</u> and <u>Katharina</u> Haberl. 2003. Understanding attention: 12- and 18-month-olds know what is new for other persons. *Developmental Psychology,* 39, 906-12.

Webb, Pamela A. and Adele A. Abrahamson. 1975. Stages of egocentrism in children's use of '*this*' and '*that*': a different point of view. *Journal of Child Language,* 3, 349-67.

Ambiguity of Reflexives and Case Extension[*]

Richard Zuber

CNRS, Paris, France
Richard.Zuber@linguist.jussieu.fr

Abstract. It is suggested that the difference between co-referential and bound reflexive pronouns found in many languages can be accounted for by using the notion of the case extension of a type <1> quantifier. Given this proposal the co-referential pronouns get their meaning when the corresponding NP takes nominal case extension first. Bound reflexives are reflexivisers in the sense that they are not case extensions of quantifiers although they also transform binary relations into sets. Examples from Japanese and from Polish are discussed.

Keywords: Co-referential and bound reflexives, case extension of a quantifier.

1. Introduction

One of well-known distinctions concerning reflexives, and more generally anaphors, is the distinction, introduced in Reinhart (1983), between co-referential and bound reflexives (or anaphors). In English the distinction between co-referential and bound reflexive can be illustrated by the possible ambiguity of the sentence in (1):

(1) Only Leo washed himself.

This sentence can mean, at least theoretically, either (2a), the co-referential reading of reflexive, or (2b), the bound reflexive:

(2a) Only Leo washed Leo.
(2b) Leo is the only person who washed himself.

Obviously (2a) and (2b) are not equivalent: if nobody in addition to Leo washed himself and Leo was washed, in addition to Leo himself, by someone else then (2a) is false and (2b) is true; and if nobody, except Leo himself, washed Leo and some other person, in addition to Leo, washed him/herself that (2a) is true and (2b) is false.

This distinction is related to the distinction between sloppy and strict readings of some pronouns (Dahl 1973) and is illustrated in (3)-(5); the possible interpretation of these sentences is given in the corresponding (b) and (c) sentences:

(3a) Only Leo loves his wife
(3b) Leo is the only person such that that person loves his own wife
(3c) Leo is the only person such that that person loves Leo's wife
(4a) Leo loves his wife and so does Bill
(4b) Leo loves his (own) wife and Bill loves Leo's wife

---

[*] Thanks to Yasunari Harada for the help with the Japanese data and to Robert Freidin for help with English.

(4c) Leo loves his (own) wife and Bill loves his own wife
(5a) Leo considers himself competent, and so does Lea
(5b) Leo considers himself competent and Lea considers Leo competent, too
(5c) Leo considers himself competent and Lea considers herself competent too

In (a) sentences we have a bound variable reading of the reflexive or possessive pronoun and thus the sloppy identity between the corresponding NPs (those related by the anaphor). In (b) sentences we have the strict identity and co-referential readings of pronouns.

Notice that the ambiguity does not always arise. In (6) we have only sloppy reading:

(6) Leo criticized himself and so did Bill

This sentence cannot mean that Bill criticized Leo.

In English the distinction between the bound variable reading and the co-referential reading of pronouns is not formally or lexically marked. In many other languages this distinction is more overt and thus it is easier to illustrate it since in those languages different reflexive pronouns can express the corresponding readings. For instance in Polish there are two (at least) reflexive pronouns, the clitic *sie* and the full pronoun *siebie* (Lubowicz 1999). As it will be suggested *siebie* corresponds to co-referential reflexive and *sie* - the anaphoric reflexive. The situation in Polish is, however, more complex since not all transitive verbs can take both reflexive as complements. For instance verbs of "saying" like *criticise* or *blame* or some "psychological" verbs, like *hate* (in Polish) can take only *siebie* as possible direct object complement.

Of course the indicated difference between co-referential and bound reflexive pronouns occurs in many other languages and it has been often studied, in particular in Germanic (Scandinavian, cf. Hellan 1888) and, as indicated above, in some Slavic languages. Various attempts have been made to explain the difference, basically in the framework of binding theory, that is a syntactic theory. In addition the difference can be easily represented in the lambda calculus for instance. In this paper I will analyse the difference between co-referential and bound reflexives from the (formal) semantic point of view. For that purpose I will use some tools from the generalized quantifier theory, and, in particular the notion of the semantic case theory (SCT) and of the case extension of a quantifier, as introduced by Keenan (1987, 1988, 2007).

2. Formal preliminaries

SCT is an extension of the generalized quantifiers theory which allows us to treat semantically NPs (which denote   type $<1>$ quantifiers) when they take non-subject position in the sentence. Subject NPs are functions from sets (denotations of VPs) to sets of sets and thus they denote sets of sets. To interpret NPs on non-subject position one extends the domain of type $<1>$ quantifiers: they are treated as reducers of arity of their arguments, that is as functions which when applied to n-ary relations give (n-1)-ary relations. Thus when they apply to binary relations (denotations of transitive VPs) they give sets (considered as unary relations) as result (and sets are denotations of intransitive VPs). This extension of the domain of type $<1>$ quantifiers allows us to make precise the notion of a case extension, and in particular the accusative extension of a given type $<1>$ quantifier. This is possible because in such a case extension the result of an application of the quantifiers is obtained by taking into account specifically the seconds members of the pairs composing a given binary relation. More formally Q_{acc} the accusative extension of Q, is defined in (i) and Q_{nom} the nominative extension of Q is defined in (ii):

$$Q_{acc}(R)=\{x: Q(xR)=1\} \quad (i)$$
$$Q_{nom}(R)=\{x: Q(Rx)=1\} \quad (ii)$$

where Q is a type $<1>$ quantifier, R- a binary relation and $xR=\{y: xRy\}$, and $Rx=\{y: yRx\}$.

The application of a type $<1>$ quantifier to a binary relation results in a (one-place) predicate. The application of the nominal case extension gives of course also a predicate but this predicate corresponds, roughly, to the passive predicate in which the subject NP is the agent.

In addition to quantifiers applying to relations (considered as functions from binary relations to sets) there are other functions from relations to sets: the function REFL, denoted by the standard reflexive pronoun, is one of them. It is defined as follows: for any binary relation R, REFL(R)={x: xRx}.

Given the above definitions the sentence NP^1 NP^2 TVP has two logical forms, (iii) and (iv):

$$Q^1 \, (Q^2_{acc}(R)) \, \text{(iii)}$$
$$Q^2(Q^1_{nom}(R)) \, \text{(iv)}$$

Logical sentences (iii) and (iv) need not be equivalent: the difference between them often corresponds to the difference between subject wide scope and object wide scope readings of a given transitive sentence with two nominal arguments. When, however, NP^1 or NP^2 is a proper name (iii) and (iv) are (provably) equivalent (cf. Zimmermann 1992).

It might be interesting to illustrate the difference in meaning due to the differences in the case extension of a given quantifier and in particular the result of the application of the nominal case extension to a given relation. Consider the sentence in (7):

(7) Every student knows the same languages

Informally (7) means that there are languages such that both Leo and Lea know them. In other words (7) should be interpreted with the object NP (its appropriate extension) taking wide scope over the subject NP. This fact can be represented precisely with the help of the notion of the case extension. Thus the basic meaning (which should be completed by some existential presuppositions) of (7) is given in (8):

(8) (NO TWO LANGUAGES) (SOME AND NOT EVERY STUDENT)$_{nom}$ KNOW

What (7) basically means is that there are no (two) languages which are known by some but not by all students and not that for every student there are two languages such that he/she knows them. Thus in this representation the use of the nominative case extension is essential.

3. Analysis

In this paper I want to apply the SCT basically to some reflexive pronouns in Japanese and discuss some of these applications in the context of similar pronouns in Polish. It is generally admitted that Japanese has a very rich system of reflexive pronouns and a powerful machinery which is used during the process of reflexivisation. It is thus interesting to compare it, at least partially, with similar mechanisms in other languages.

Most studies of reflexives in Japanese concern their syntactic properties (see Aikawa 2003 for a review). It has been pointed out in Richards (1997), following an unpublished work of Aikawa, that Japanese pronouns *kare-jishin* and *jibun-jishin* are unambiguously interpreted, respectively, as the co-referential and bound reflexive. So in this talk I investigate, using the SCT, the semantic differences and similarities between Japanese pronouns *jibun-jishin* and *kare-jishin* (and its plural version *karera-jishin*) on the one hand and how this difference is possibly related to the difference between Polish reflexive pronouns *sie* and *siebie* on the other hand. All these pronouns, in Japanese and in Polish, roughly correspond to the English reflexive pronoun *self*.

I am concerned with the following problems: sentences (9a) and (9b) are equivalent and both mean (9c). This is not the case for sentences in (10): (10a) has purely reflexive meaning and says that Taro criticized himself and Jiro criticized himself whereas (10b) has a mixed reflexive-reciprocal reading and entails that Taro criticised himself and Jiro and Jiro criticized himself and Taro:

(9a) Taroo-ga jibun-jishin o hihanshita.
(9b) Taroo-ga kare-jishin o hihanshita.
(9c) Taro criticised himself.
(10a) Taroo to Jiroo ga jibun-jishin o hihanshita.
(10b) Taroo to Jiroo ga karera-jishin o hihanshita.

So clearly the above examples exhibit the difference we are looking for.

Observe in addition that sentence (11a) means what (12a) means and (11b) means what (12b) means and thus (11a) and (11b) are different in meaning. For instance (11a) is true if Taro was in, addition blamed by Jiro whereas (11b) is false in such situation (cf. Hiraga and Nissenbaum 2006):

(11a) Taroo dake-ga jibun-jishin o semeta
(11b) Taroo dake-ga kare-jishin o semeta.
(12a) Only Taro blamed himself.
(12b) Only Taro blamed Taro

The above data show that the difference between *kare-jishin* and *jibun-jishin* is clearly related to the difference between the bound anaphora and co-referential anaphora. These facts cannot be easily explained if we just assume that although both pronouns require a local c-comanding antecedent, *kare-jishin* should be interpreted as a co-referential reflexive and *jibun-jishin* as a bound reflexive (Richards 1997). We need in addition a semantic characterisation of various possible antecedents.

Now my proposal is as follows: *jibun-jishin* in Japanese (and *sie}* in Polish) always denote REFL (roughly, they are "reflexivisers", that is specific functions from binary relations to sets which are not extensions of quantifiers). Concerning *kare-jishin* and *siebie* they indicate that their antecedent should be interpreted by nominal case extension. Thus, to take only the case of Japanese, sentences of the form (v):

NP KARE(RA)-JISHIN TVP (v)

have as their semantic representation given in (vi):

$$Q \, (Q_{nom}(R)) \text{ (vi)}$$

where NP denotes Q and TVP denotes the relation R In other words to get the meaning of sentences with JIBUN-JISHIN apply first the function REFL to the (denotation of) the transitive TVP and then apply the (denotation of) the subject (which is also the antecedent NP) to the result of the first operation. In the case of sentences with KARE(RA)-JISHIN apply the nominal extension (of the denotation) of antecedent of KARE(RA)-JISHIN to the TVP and then apply the (denotation of) the antecedent NP (without any case extension) to the result of the first operation.

It can be checked that given this interpretation of reflexives we account for the problems mentioned above.

This is not enough, however. We need some additional tests showing in particular that antecedents *of kare-jishin* and *siebie* are related to nominal case extensions and *jibun-jishin}* and *sie* are not. Two types of such tests will be proposed.

First, one observes that questions like *Whom did/does NP V* (as in *Whom does Bill wash/hate* must be preferably answered by co-referential pronouns. This is the case in Polish, and even if less clear, also in Japanese: the question *Kogo myje Bill* (Whom is washing Bill) cannot be answered by the reflexive pronoun *sie*.

In the second test I propose to use constructions with conjunctions in which non-standard constituents occur or constructions with a conjunction of a pronoun with a full NP. In (13) we have a sentence with a non-standard constituent:

(13) Leo hates Sue and Bill himself

One observes that in the corresponding sentences in Japanese and in Polish preferably co-referential pronouns should be used at the place of *himself*. Thus in Polish (14a) is grammatical and the corresponding sentence (14b) with the pronoun *sie* is not:

(14a) Leo nienawidzi Sue a Bill siebie
(14b) *Leo nienawidzi Sue a Bill sie

The following examples illustrate the constraint on possible conjunctions. The English sentence (15a) must be translated in Polish by (15b) , where the pronoun *siebie* occurs and cannot be translated by (15c) which is not acceptable:

(15a) Leo is washing Sue and himself
(15b) Leo myje Sue i siebie
(15c) *Leo myje Sue i sie

The fact that *jibun-jishin* and *sie* are not related to case extensions is just the formal consequence of the definition of the function REFL (cf. Keenan 2007). Keenan shows that the function REFL, even if it is denoted by a kind of a NP, cannot be a case extension (neither nominal not accusative) of any type <1> quantifier.

Finally we observe that reflexive pronouns occurring in sentences with plural subjects sometimes get reciprocal interpretation. Such an interpretation is not possible, however, with co-referential reflexive pronouns. The Polish sentence (16b) (with the pronoun *siebie)* corresponding to English (16a) cannot mean (17a) whereas in the sentence (17b), where the pronoun *sie* occurs the pronoun can get the reciprocal meaning:

(16a) Leo and Lea are washing themselves
(16b) Leo i Lea myja siebie
(17a) Leo and Lea are washing each other
(17b) Leo i Lea myja sie

Notice, in passing, that the English sentence (16a) cannot get the reciprocal interpretation either.

4. Conclusions

I have proposed to use the notion of the nominal case extension to describe the meaning of reflexive pronouns corresponding, in some languages, to co-referential anaphora. Such anaphors are usually opposed to bound variable anaphors. My proposal has been illustrated by some examples from Japanese and Polish, which have been used to show some interesting differences between reflexives in Japanese and in Polish. In particular some arguments have been given to show that the Japanese pronoun *kare-jishin* and Polish pronoun *siebie* correspond to the co-referential anaphors and as such are not reflexivisers. Their meaning is obtained by replacing them by their antecedent taken in the nominal case extension. Similarly with the Polish pronoun *siebie* which also has to be taken in the co-referential interpretation.

The proposal made here explains some specific behaviour of certain reflexive pronouns, in particular the fact that co-referential anaphors cannot get reciprocal interpretations. It also shows how possible scope differences can be explained by the machinery of the case extension.

Concerning possible differences it has been observed that Polish bound-variable pronoun *sie* must be basically used with active transitive verbs and not with psychological verbs or verbs of saying. This fact is to be related to the observation that complex sentences with VP anaphors which often give rise to the ambiguity between bound and co-referential readings have only one reading, the bound variable reading, in sentences containing the psychological verbs of verbs of saying (cf. example (6) above).

From the theoretical point of view the proposal dispenses with the use of often cumbersome indices whose theoretical status is not very clear, as far as I can tell. Of course the proposal applies also to specific reflexives in other languages and, in particular, as I hope, to some other types of anaphora (to *same/different* anaphors, as indicated above and to reciprocals).

Notice finally that the proposal made here has some other applications. Concerning Japanese it explains for instance the "asymmetric" ambiguity of the negations of (5). Similarly the proposal applies to sentences in (8) since by fixing one NP (Jiroo}) one can consider that *hanasu* (to talk (about)) denotes a binary relation. It also explains the sloppy vs strict readings to which reflexives give rise (cf. the difference between (9a) and (9b)):

(8a) Taroo-ga Jiroo ni jibun-jishin nituite hanashita
(Taro talked to Jiro about him(self))
(8b) Taroo-ga Jiroo ni kare-jishin nituite hanashita
(9a) Taroo-ga kare-jisin-o   semeta, (soshite) Jiroo-mo semeta.
(Taro criticized himself (then) Jiro also criticized)
(9b) Taroo-ga jibun-jisin-o semeta, (soshite) Jiroo-mo semeta.

For many speakers in (9b) we have only a sloppy reading whereas in (9a) both a strict and a sloppy readings are possible.

Of course many things remain to be done concerning the meaning of pronouns and their typology (cf. Kiparsky 2002).

References

Aikawa, T. 2003. Reflexives. In Tsujimura, N. ed. *Handbook of Japanese Linguistics,* 154-190, Blackwell Publishing.

Dahl, O. 1973. On so-called 'Sloppy Identity' *Synthese* 26:1, 81-112

Hellan, L. 1988. *Reflexives in Norwegian and the theory of grammar.* Dordrecht: Forris

Hiraga, M. and J. Nissenbaum, 2006. Sloppy readings of a 'referential pronoun' in Japanese. *Proceedings of the 7th Tokyo Conference on Psycholinguistics,* 121-144

Keenan, E. L. 1987 Semantic Case Theory, in Groenendijk, J. and M. Stokhof, eds. *Proceedings of the Sixth Amsterdam Colloquium*

Keenan, E. L. 1988 On Semantics and the Binding Theory, In Hawkins, J. ed. *Explaining Language Universals*, Blackwell, 105-144

Keenan, E. L. 2007 On the denotations of anaphors. *Research on Language and Computation* 5:.5-17

Kiparsky, P. 2002 Disjoint reference and the typology of pronouns. In Kaufmann, I. and Stiebels, B. eds. *More than Words, Studia Grammatiuca* 53, 179-226

Lubowicz, A. 1999. Two Views of Polish Reflexives, in Bird, S. *et al.* eds. WCCFL 18 Proceedings, Cascadilla Press, 337-350.

Reinhart, T. 1983. *Anaphora and semantic interpretation,* London: Crom Helm

Richards, N. 1997 Competition and disjoint reference, Linguistic Inquiry 28. 178-187

Zimmermann, T. E 1993. Scopless Quantifiers and Operators, Journal of Philosophical Logic 22: 545-561